Photo courtesy of International Business Machines Corporation

Personal computers and other electronic equipment affect the sending and receiving of business messages. Changing methods and media, however, increase rather than decrease the importance of human communications through written and spoken word.

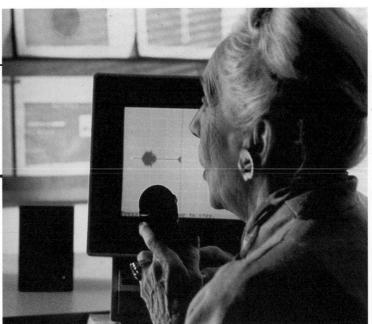

Using the new IBM Personal System/2® SpeechViewer™ vocalization tool, individuals who are speech- or hearing-impaired can learn to communicate more effectively.

Photo courtesy of International Business Machines Corporation

Successful Communication for Business and the Professions

Successful Communication for Business and the Professions

FIFTH EDITION

Malra Treece
Memphis State University

ALLYN AND BACON
Boston   London   Toronto   Sydney   Tokyo   Singapore

Photo Credits:

p. 10: © Frank Siteman MCMLXXXIII; p. 21: Mark Antman, The Image Works; p. 24: Lorraine Rorke, The Image Works; p. 27: Laimute E. Druskis, Taurus Photos; p. 35: Ken Karp, Omni-Photo Communications; p. 123: H. Armstrong Roberts; p. 141: H. Armstrong Roberts; p. 204: Richard Younker, Click/Chicago; p. 238: Ken Karp, Omni-Photo Communications; p. 276: H. Armstrong Roberts; p. 278: Ann Hagen Griffiths, Omni-Photo Communications; p. 281: H. Armstrong Roberts; p. 313: Eric Kroll, Taurus Photos; p. 330: Alan Carey, The Image Works; p. 388: H. Armstrong Roberts; p. 394: Frank Siteman, The Picture Cube; p. 398: H. Armstrong Roberts; p. 405: Richard Younker, Click/Chicago; p. 414: H. Armstrong Roberts; p. 417: P. Damien, Click/Chicago; p. 418: Jerry Howard, Positive Images; p. 427: Laimute E. Druskis, Taurus Photos; p. 437: H. Armstrong Roberts

Copyright © 1991, 1989, 1986, 1983, 1978 by Allyn and Bacon
A Division of Simon & Schuster, Inc.
160 Gould Street
Needham Heights, Massachusetts 02194

Previous editions of this book were published under the titles
Communication for Business and the Professions and *Successful Business Communication.*

Series Editor: *Jack Peters*
Senior Editorial Assistant: *Carol Alper*
Cover Administrator: *Linda Dickinson*
Manufacturing Buyer: *Megan Cochran*

Library of Congress Cataloging-in-Publication Data

Treece, Malra.
    Successful communication for business and the professions / Malra
 Treece. — 5th ed.
        p.   cm.
    Rev. ed. of: Communication for business and the professions.
    Includes bibliographical references and index.
    ISBN 0-205-12345-7
    1. Business communication.   2. Business writing.   3. Communication
in management.   I. Treece, Malra. Communication for business and
the professions.   II. Title.
HF5718.T73   1991   90-38446
658.4′5—dc20   CIP

*HF
5718
.T73
1991*

Printed in the United States of America

10 9 8 7 6 5 4 3 2 1   94 93 92 91 90

Brief Contents

Contents

Preface

This book is based on the premise that all elements of communication are inter-related. Principles of effective writing also apply to effective speech. Nonverbal communication enters into both oral and written messages.

Changing technology continues to affect media and methods of communication. Nevertheless, human behavior and the use of language continue to be the most important tools for achieving harmonious human relationships and effective organizational management.

Approach

The study of communication for business and the professions is interdisciplinary. Thus this book contains instruction in aspects of speech, journalism, language, research sources and methods, individual and organizational behavior, general business management, office management, personnel management, marketing, persuasion, and ethics. Emphasis throughout is upon effective writing and speaking.

Although professional in content and organization, all chapters are planned for easy and interesting reading. Readability and interest are considered important from three major standpoints:

to enable readers to enjoy the book,

to illustrate techniques of readable and interesting writing, and

to exemplify by the textbook itself one of the most important attributes of human communication: consideration for the receiver of the message.

Successful communicators are much more than skilled technicians; they must have an understanding of the process of communication, of the effect of varying perceptions and emotions upon the reception of meaning. In addition, they are knowledgeable in the subject matter about which they communicate, and their messages are sincere. Sincerity, perhaps the most essential element of all communication, is stressed throughout the book.

Organization and Contents of the Book

Part I, Chapters 1 and 2, "An Overview of Business Communication," prepares the student for the remaining portions of the textbook and the course. Chapter 1 includes a summary of the principles of communication, discussion of communication within and from organizations, and a summary of concepts and characteristics of effective writing and speech. Chapter 2 provides an overview of communication technology as it affects written and oral messages.

Part II, Chapters 3, 4, and 5, "Principles of Effective Communication," presents additional theory as applied to business and professional writing and speech. Topics include the wise choice of words, correctness, conciseness, completeness, readability, techniques of emphasis, and building goodwill.

Part III, Chapters 6 through 10, "Principles of Effective Communication Applied to Letters and Memorandums," contains examples and exercises that apply the principles covered in Part II.

Part IV, Chapters 11 and 12, "Communicating about Employment," deals with the subject of obtaining career employment, including preliminary research before looking for a job, application letters and resumes, interviews, follow-up letters, and other messages about employment.

Part V, Chapters 13 throught 16, "Communicating throught Reports," discusses business research and the preparation of formal and informal reports.

Part VI, Chapters 17, 18, and 19, "Oral, Nonverbal, and Intercultural Communication," includes instruction about public speaking, listening, interpersonal communication, nonverbal communication, and intercultural communication.

Appendices A, B, C, D, and E include discussion and examples of effective and efficient dictation (Appendix A); the appearance and format of business letters (Appendix B); documentation and the appearance of reports (Appendix C); a brief guide to English usage (Appendix D); and legal and ethical considerations that affect business communication (Appendix E).

New to the Fifth Edition

Successful Communication for Business and the Professions, Fifth Edition, has been revised and rearranged to strengthen the overall approach and to provide new and varied examples and problems. Portions of the text have been condensed in order to provide a concise, but still complete, discussion.

The important and ever-changing areas of technology and intercultural communication have been expanded from previous editions, not only in chapter coverage but by integration into other chapters through discussion, illustrations, and related questions and problems. As in previous editions, opportunity is provided throughout for application of communication principles to both writing and speaking, but more of these applications now concern intercultural communication and communication technology.

Chapter 3, "Choosing Appropriate and Effective Words," is new to the Fifth Edition. Although word choice had previously been discussed and applied throughout all chapters, as it continues to be, Chapter 3 gives added emphasis to the importance of words.

Writing principles, including word choice, have been strengthened through out the Fifth Edition. In addition to Chapter 2 and an exercise at the end of each chapter that reviews both chapter content and correct usage ("Test Yourself: Correct Usage"), a series of short inserts entitled "Check Your Writing" is carried through all chapters. An additional teaching aid is a computer disk, "TUTOR," that is provided for all teachers adopting the book. This disk may be freely copied for student use. Appendix D, as in previous editions, serves as a brief guide to language usage.

The section on reports now consists of four chapters and Appendix D.

Legal and ethical considerations are now included in Appendix E. This placement encourages earlier and more frequent discussion of this most important topic than if it were included in a chapter. In addition to Appendix E, ethical questions in relation to other topics and assignments are included throughout the book.

The five appendices contain material that is as important, if not more so, than the content of preceding chapters. The contents of these appendices can be easily used in their present position with any or all of the preceding chapters, or instructors may prefer to assign the appendices as they do chapters.

Illustrations and cases have been updated and new ones have been added. Similar changes have been made in the comprehensive *Teacher's Handbook,* including the addition of new questions and the revision or omission of others. As in previous editions, pages are arranged in a format ready for photocopying for immediate use in the classroom. In addition to the hundreds of ready-to-use questions in the Handbook, a test bank is available on a computer disk.

A group of approximately one hundred professionally made transparencies accompanies the Fifth Edition. These transparencies are complimentary to all teachers using the textbook.

Acknowledgments

Utmost gratitude is expressed to the many persons, including teachers and hundreds of students at Memphis State University, who contributed their ideas and words of encouragement during the preparation of this book and previous editions. Most important of all are the words of suggestions from teachers all over the United States and Canada who have used the book: You told me you liked it, but you also told me how to make it better. You will always have my deepest appreciation. I wish I could thank each of you personally.

Special appreciation goes to the following firms and individuals for the use of their material:

L. L. Bean

Greentrees Civic Association and O. Norris Avey, Jr.

National League of American Pen Women and Wanda Rider

The New York Life Insurance Company

The New Yorker Magazine

Outward Bound

The Prudential Insurance Company of America

The Royal Bank of Canada

3M Company

Union Planters National Bank, Memphis, and Bruce Mitchen

Waterford Crystal

Xerox

Tim Adams, Charmaine Hill, Vivian A. Douglas, and Rebecca Langham Nash, students, Memphis State University

Vanessa Dean Arnold, University of Mississippi

Ruth C. Batchelor, Associate Professor Emeritus, New York University

Mona J. Casady, Southwest Missouri State University

Ann Denton, Memphis State University

Karen English, Memphis State University

Barbara Forte, artist

Ed Goodin, University of Nevada, Las Vegas

Larry Hartman, Brigham Young University

Retha H. Kilpatrick, Western Carolina University

Terry Mendenhall, Pittsburg State University, Pittsburg, Kansas

Glynna E. Morse, Memphis State University

John Munoa

J. William Murphy

Binford Peeples, Memphis State University

Lydel Sims, Columnist

Jean W. Vining

Thanks also to John D. Peters and Rowena Dores, Allyn and Bacon; Elydia Davis, Director, Superscript Associates; Lynda Griffiths, copy editor; and Judy Baird, assistant, Memphis.

Further appreciation goes to members of the Association for Business Communication, who for many years have made valuable contributions to the field of business communication. My colleagues in this worthy organization have provided information, ideas, and inspiration that are reflected in *Successful Communication for Business and the Professions*, Fifth Edition.

Successful Communication for Business and the Professions

CHAPTER **1**

An Introduction to Your Study of Business Communication

Welcome to your study of business communication. No other ability will be more valuable to you than the ability to relate effectively and harmoniously with other people through communication.

The Importance of Communication to Your Career and Personal Life

Communication is an integral part of daily life. Unless you are a hermit or spend long hours working alone in an occupation that does not include speaking, writing, reading, or listening, communication with others makes up the major part of your life, both in actual time spent and importance. Even when you are completely alone, you are communicating with yourself and, in a way, with other persons. Your memory and reasoning power are sorting out, organizing, and accepting or rejecting previous bits of conversations, lectures, movies, or written materials. As long as your mind is alive, it will send messages to be received by other minds, and you will receive messages from everyone and everything around you.

Your success in a career, whatever your occupation, position, or organization, will depend greatly on your ability to communicate, perhaps more so than on any other knowledge or skill, including highly specialized ones. You will spend far more time communicating than assuming all other responsibilities of your job. As you are promoted to higher levels, communication will become even more important.

In addition to the vocational and professional benefits derived from excellent written and oral communications, your personal and social life is vitally affected, for better or worse, by your relationships with other people. These relationships are built by communication.

Definitions of Communication

The word *communication* comes from the Latin word *communis*, meaning "common." Thus, for successful communication we are trying to meet on common ground, at least momentarily, with the receivers of our messages. We are trying to establish a *commonness* or a sharing of information, attitudes, ideas, and understanding.

Dictionary definitions of communication include such phrases as *to impart information or knowledge, to make known, to impart or to transmit,* and *to give or interchange thoughts, feelings, information, or the like by writing, speaking.* Other definitions are limited to stimulus-response situations in which messages are deliberately transmitted in order to invoke a response, as when asking a question and expecting an answer, when giving instructions that are expected to be followed, when telling a story to make other persons laugh or cry, or when writing advertising copy to stimulate people to buy.

A simplified definition of communication is a transfer of meaning. Another definition is that communication is a "process by which one mind influences another mind."

A broader definition of communication includes situations in which there is no intention of transmitting messages, as in much of nonverbal communication, such as an unplanned facial expression, body movement, or a blush.

We also communicate unintentionally by our choice of words that carry meanings other than or in addition to those stated. Such messages are known as *metacommunications.* For example, the compliment "I've never seen you look

Question: Here I am, about to finish my education and I still don't know how to spell all the words I need to use. What is the matter with me?

Answer: Is that all you have to worry about? Most likely your teachers and textbook writers are not sure of the exact spelling and meaning of a number of words. If they are, why do they keep dictionaries on their desks or bookshelves?

Nevertheless, we are all responsible for correctness in written work, including spelling. Thus we use dictionaries and word processing software to guide us. When you are not absolutely sure about the spelling of a word, look it up.

Although spelling guides are available, you will waste much time if you must stop to confirm the correct spelling of a large proportion of the words you use. Such a procedure slows your creative processes. A rough draft may speed the writing process; complete your message, then check for spelling errors and revise.

Even worse, poor spellers often limit their use of words—a process that most definitely impedes their ability to communicate. In addition, many errors are left for their readers to find.

A good way to improve your spelling is to review commonly misspelled words. (See Appendix D.) Although the words that many other writers misspell are not necessarily the ones that confuse you, it is a good idea to double-check.

---

so lovely" could imply that the listener's usual appearance should be greatly improved.

Communication occurs not only between humans but also from machines (particularly computers) to humans and from humans to machines, although perhaps it could be argued that machines are activated only by human thought. Once machines have been set into motion, they can communicate with one another. Animals communicate with one another and with humans, and humans communicate with animals.

Communication can be classified according to the number of persons to whom it is addressed. *Intrapersonal* communication is within the mind of the individual. *Interpersonal* communication is one-to-one contact, as in conversation between two persons (although other persons may be present and also interacting). Interpersonal communication can also occur from writer to reader, as in letters. *Group communication* includes large or small groups, in which all persons retain their own identity, as in a classroom, office organization, or club. *Mass communication* is sent to very large groups of people, especially by radio, television, or newspapers; each person as an individual has little opportunity for identification or feedback.

As you will learn later in the course, however, all communication should be approached as if it were on a one-to-one basis. For example, an effective advertisement sells one person at a time; that is, the wording sounds as if the readers or hearers were being individually addressed. (This is called the *you-approach.*)

Communication Brief

We take language for granted, yet it is one of the most complex things we do. Language allows us to convey our emotions, to share ideas, to create fresh forms of expressions, and to communicate our most intimate thoughts. Without language the very notion of human civilization would be unthinkable. It is not only vivid confirmation of the mind within us; the need to communicate with other humans through language seems as fundamental as the existence of the mind itself.

Grammatical competence means the ability to understand concepts like subject, noun phrase, and verb phrase, without which . . . you cannot formulate the rules of human language. . . . And without grammatical competence, there is no understanding of syntax, the relationship of words to one another in a sentence.

Richard Restak, *The Mind* (New York: Bantam Books, 1988), 197, 201.

Communication is either *verbal* or *nonverbal*. *Verbal* means "with words"; *nonverbal* means "without words." The five processes of *verbal* communication are *speaking, writing, reading, listening,* and *thinking*. (In the thinking process—which is often in exact words—the sender and the receiver of the message are the same individual.)

Nonverbal communication consists of all methods of communication other than the sending and receiving of words or other verbal symbols. The various methods of nonverbal communication are discussed in Chapter 16 and elsewhere throughout the book as they apply to various kinds of verbal messages.

How We Communicate

We communicate by sending meaningful messages. The message transmitted, even though it is meaningful when it leaves the mind of the sender, is often less so when it reaches the mind of the receiver. The process of communication consists of four elements: (1) the sender, (2) the message, (3) the medium, or channel, and (4) the receiver.

Noise often, if not always, hinders the process of communication and prevents or alters the reception of the intended message. *Noise* is any distraction that interferes with the exact transmission of the intended message; it can occur in the encoding, sending, or receiving process, or in all of these.

Feedback is the return message from the receiver of the original message.

Various models of the communication process have been devised during the past forty or so years. C. E. Shannon constructed one of the first. Although his model was planned to apply to mathematical or mechanical communication problems, it also basically applies to all forms of communication. The model was first published in the Bell System Technical Journal and later included in *The Mathematical Theory of Communication,* co-authored with Warren Weaver.[1] It is now known as the Shannon-Weaver model. The general assumption is that the message must move from the source to its destination through a channel, but that its reception may be blocked or altered by noise.

[1]Claud Shannon and Warren Weaver, *The Mathematical Theory of Communication* (Urbana: University of Illinois Press, 1949), 7.

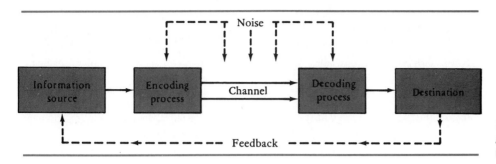

FIGURE 1–1
A communication model

A modified version of the Shannon-Weaver communication model is shown in Figure 1–1. The Shannon-Weaver model does not include feedback—an essential element of communication, especially of human communication. Perhaps the reason it was omitted is that feedback is actually another act of communication, with the role of the original sender of the message reversed to that of the receiver of the return message.

Verbal encoding processes are speaking and writing; other encoding processes are touching, smiling, gesturing, or, as when transmitting music, playing the piano. Verbal decoding processes are the receiving processes of reading and listening. Other decoding processes include seeing, tasting, smelling, and touching.

The most important idea illustrated by both these models is that communication is incomplete until it is received and that ideally the message is received in exactly the same form as that intended by the sender. Realistically, however, we must be satisfied with an inexact reproduction. But the received message must be reasonably similar to the transmitted one or communication cannot occur.

The minds of the sender and the receiver vitally affect the content and delivery of the message. Because the perception of the sender is different from that of the receiver, the message in the mind of the receiver is almost certain to be different from that intended by the sender of the message. In addition, various changes in even the most simple message—written, oral, or nonverbal—can occur between the encoding and decoding stages, resulting in inexactness.

Why We Communicate

Three often-stated purposes of communication are *to inform* (or *to inquire*), *to persuade,* and *to entertain.* These three purposes are often accomplished in one communication. The intellect does not function separately from the emotions, and the imparting of seemingly routine information is influenced by the emotions of the sender and the receiver of the message—hence persuasion enters into the process. Entertainment often acts to change opinions and to give information. Communication planned mainly to be persuasive can also inform and entertain, as illustrated by some television commercials.

All intentional communication is persuasive in the sense that the sender wishes the receiver to understand the message and to accept or be influenced

Communication Brief

Sometimes we talk simply for the sake of hearing ourselves talk; that is, for the same reason that we play golf or dance. The activity gives us a pleasant sense of being alive. Children prattling, adults singing in the bathtub, are alike enjoying the sound of their voices. Sometimes large groups make noises together, as in group singing, group recitation, or group chanting, for similar presymbolic reasons. In all this, the significance of the words used is almost completely irrelevant. We may, for example, chant the most lugubrious words about a desire to be carried back to a childhood home in old Virginny, when in actuality we have never been there and haven't the slightest intention of going.

S. I. Hayakawa, *Language in Thought and Action* (New York: Harcourt, Brace & World, 1949), 71.

by the message. David Berlo states: "In short, we communicate to influence—to affect with intent."[2]

In simple terms, successful communication has occurred when

1. The message is understood.
2. The message accomplishes its purpose.
3. The sender and the receiver of the message maintain favorable relationships.

These three attributes of successful communication apply to *intentional* messages. For example, a memorandum addressed to employees must be understood in approximately the same way as the writer intended; it must result in the expected outcomes, such as a change in procedure; and it must build or maintain goodwill. An advertisement must present the product or service in a way that the listener or reader will understand; it must sell the product; and it must build or maintain goodwill.

Much communication is *unintentional*, however. Often our tone of voice, facial expression, or body motions convey messages entirely different from our spoken words. In addition, much conversation is casual, with no definite purpose of being informative, persuasive, or entertaining. We communicate simply because we must. We have a normal, demanding urge to smile when we are happy, to laugh when we are amused, to shout when we are angry, to weep when we are sad. We want to express our emotions and opinions and to have them received, understood, and accepted by other persons. This urge is one reason, perhaps the most important one, that some people write poetry or novels, compose music, paint, or communicate through photography. It is why we want to talk with those we love, as well as to converse with strangers we meet on the bus or in a waiting room.

To inform, to persuade, to entertain, or a combination of these purposes—these broad categories describe much casual communication, but not all. The remark, "Isn't it a lovely day?" does not actually present unknown information about the weather. It does impart information about the speaker. It tells the listener: "I accept you, at least to a limited extent. You and I share together this lovely day." At least this is the usual message sent to psychologi-

---

[2]David Berlo, *The Process of Communication* (New York: Holt, Rinehart and Winston, 1960), 12.

cally mature, secure individuals. Like all other messages, though, even this simple one can become distorted by the time it reaches the mind of the receiver, as will be illustrated in the following section.

Why the Message Goes Astray

Suppose that the person who makes the often heard comment, "Isn't it a lovely day?" is the president of a company and the listener is a new employee. The listener may attach far more significance to the casual, routine remark than the speaker intended. "Ah, he's noticing me already; soon he'll ask me to lunch." Or, if the employee has a weak self-concept or a suspicious nature, or if he has not been having a good day, he may feel that the president is testing him to determine whether he can converse with important persons. As a result, his stammering reply indicates that he is not able to converse with anyone.

A young woman may think, on hearing the words from a man, that he is making a pass. If she is not interested, her reply may sound curt; and the weather commentator will think that somehow he has offended her—or that she does not approve of him.

An unhappy person has not noticed the lovely day. He agrees that it is nice, since that is the expected answer, but he is not really convinced because his own world is less than fair.

An unfavorable reception can occur because of many reasons: because the listener does not like the speaker's appearance, voice, foreign or regional accent, or the magazine he is holding in his hand; because the speaker resembles someone that the listener dislikes; because he distrusts all strangers who speak to him.

Some persons will not even hear the remark because of being engrossed in their own thoughts. Some will not hear because the speaker mumbles. Some will not hear because an automobile horn or other sound drowns out the speaker's words.

A listener may not agree (although she may not say so) because she has already made up her mind that she doesn't like the climate of the particular city, so there can be no such thing as a lovely day.

If a speaker and a listener meet each day and the speaker usually comments on the foulness of the weather, he will be expected to do so again, and the listener may actually believe that he said, "Isn't it a rotten day?" We often receive the meaning that we expect to receive. If a listener has no understanding of the English language, she will not understand the meaning of the words in the remark; but a pleasant look on the face of the speaker may make her nod and smile. She has not understood the code system of the language, but rather the nonverbal symbols.

If so many things can go wrong in the reception of the simple comment, "Isn't it a lovely day?" is it any surprise that an intended message does not always reach the mind of the reader or listener, or, if it does, that it does not achieve its intended purpose? Even less surprising, written messages are often unread, misunderstood, and unaccepted; sales messages do not always sell; newspaper stories do not convey to all readers the same understanding of the printed word; instructions are not always understood or followed.

These varying reactions to a simple comment about the weather show how the preconceived opinions, attitudes, and beliefs of the receiver affect the message. The receiver's emotions also affect understanding and acceptance. The mind of the sender of the message also affects the process of communication as the message is prepared (encoded) and as the thought is transmitted.

The intended message is often drastically changed by the time it is sent from one mind to another and interpreted according to the receiver's knowledge, perception, and emotions (that is, *decoded*). Outside sources such as car horns and other noises prevent the passage of an idea from one mind to another. A poor television picture or sound interferes with whatever bits of information, entertainment, or persuasion are being presented.

The word *noise* is used to mean any interference with the reception of the intended message. Noise occurs in both sending and receiving: the speaker mumbles or the receiver does not listen. In written communication, noise (distraction) occurs because of poor writing, unusual letter styles, poor typewriting, incorrect spelling, or an inappropriate letterhead.

A speaker may inject noise into a presentation by confusing gestures, an unpleasant voice, unusual choice of clothing, or visible lack of confidence. Even conditions that are usually considered desirable can create noise. For example, a student stated that his French teacher was so beautiful and charming that he couldn't concentrate on learning French. (Could this have been a rationalization?)

To summarize, less than perfect communication occurs because of weakness on the part of the sender or the receiver of the message, or of both, and also because of influences exerted along the way.

Feedback

Feedback occurs after a communication is received and is an indication to the sender of acceptance and understanding, or the lack of it. Most persons will pleasantly agree that it is a lovely day. Others will ignore the comment and turn away, not wanting to get involved in a conversation or a possible friendship. The foreigner may smile and nod pleasantly; although he does not understand the words, he has understood by nonverbal means.

One person will state emphatically that it is a miserable day, for no weather is like that in San Diego and he has already made up his mind that he wants to return. Another person will say that the day would be all right if she didn't have this horrible cold. (Personal problems have interfered with the perception of reality.) Some persons will suddenly realize that it is a lovely day; they hadn't thought of the weather until it was mentioned.

Feedback is received by letter writers when they learn that their letters have accomplished their purpose or that they have not. It is obtained by a speaker when listeners react, if only by going to sleep. The effectiveness of sales campaigns is measured by the number and amount of sales. The basketball coach receives feedback from the results of the team's performance. The teacher receives feedback, positive or negative, through students' examination scores, their comments, the expressions on their faces, and many other reactions.

The results of communication are obtainable only through feedback, which in turn exerts influence over future messages. In successful communication there is an interdependence between the original source and the receiver, with the receiver becoming the source of a subsequent message.

Communication within and from the Organization

Successful communication is vital to the functioning of any organization. It cannot be considered a separate part of organizational management. It permeates every experience and decision and is an almost continuous activity. Clerical jobs, supervisory work, sales, and advertising are made up almost altogether of communication activities. Accountants communicate with figures, graphic presentations, and oral and written words. All personnel in any occupation, with the possible exception of production workers and manual laborers, communicate with other people throughout most of their working day.

Just as communication is an almost continuous process in the personal life of the individual, it is the most vital and continuous force within any organization. Effective communication in a business organization involves, in addition to human processes, the efficient management of mechanical tools of communication—computers, typewriters, telephones, dictating and duplicating machines, specialized audio and video players and recorders, and all the other technical equipment of the modern electronic office.

If you are an employee skillful in communicating, you have a definite advantage over co-workers who do not possess this skill. Your reporting to management may be the key to your success and job satisfaction. Everything that you can do while you are in college to increase your communication ability will have a most practical value when you begin work in a business organization—or when you begin any career.

Communication within the Organization

In almost all business organizations, and in almost all departments, oral communication is more important—as far as actual time spent—than is written communication. As the cost of written communication continues to increase, even more emphasis is expected to be given to the many forms of oral communication, although they can also be expensive. The public address system, intracompany telephone systems, closed-circuit television, radio communication systems, voice store-and-forward systems, voice mail, and many other arrangements are used in business organizations to facilitate oral communication.

Much reporting is done orally, and in some instances the same report may be presented in both oral and written forms. Meetings and conferences are often used throughout the business organization and in professional organizations. Many of the presentations at meetings and conferences could be classified as oral reports.

Employee councils and forums, interviews, routine face-to-face communication, casual conversation in the halls or in the coffee room—all these forms of oral communication affect employee performance, morale, and the smooth, efficient, profitable functioning of the employing company.

Written communication within an organization is most likely to be in the form of a note or memorandum, whether prepared and sent by traditional

Many of the communications within and from organizations consist of spoken words, either face-to-face or by telephone. Basic communication principles apply to both written and oral messages.

methods or through the use of computers. Messages sent from computer to computer, now often used to replace typewritten memorandums, are referred to as *electronic mail* (see Chapter 2). Memorandums are by far the most widely used type of typewritten communication between members of an organization.

In addition to memorandums, many prepared forms are used for communication within the organization, as well as for external communication. These standardized presentations of information must be used to decrease costs, if for no other reason. In addition, clarity is more likely to be achieved if the same kinds of information are presented in the same way on the same form.

The informal communication network in an organization is known as the *grapevine*. It may carry far more information than formal networks, and the message moves faster. Much of this "information," however, consists of gossip, rumors, and half-truths. Managers recognize the existence of the grapevine, and some try to use it in order to advance the overall effectiveness of company policies and procedures—to spread information that they wish to circulate. They determine the leaders of the grapevine and communicate to them the material that is to be sent through the company via the grapevine. This use of the grapevine has obvious dangers, however, not only because the message is likely to be garbled into many versions (usually incorrect ones), but because the procedure may give the appearance of favoritism.

The best way to eliminate or decrease undesirable effects of the grapevine is for management to maintain an open policy of communication so that employees feel that they are being kept informed—and even better, that they have a part in making decisions that affect their company and themselves. Complete information cannot be released to all employees at all times; some must be kept secret until a public announcement is made, for various reasons.

But all personnel should be made to feel that they are trusted employees and that management and the overall organization can be trusted. Without this atmosphere of confidence, the most highly structured and carefully supervised communication networks within an organization are far less effective, as well as less conducive to pleasant employee-management relationships, than they would be otherwise.

Communication from the Organization

External communication takes many of the same forms and has some of the same purposes as internal communication. The organization must build and maintain goodwill with customers and with the public, as it must with employees. Customers and the public receive directions and instructions about the use of the company's products or services. The organization receives and sends information from customers, stockholders, the public, and government agencies in order to plan and to proceed with manufacturing, selling, and promotional activities.

Customer or potential customer communication includes retail and wholesale selling by personal contact, telephone conversations, written messages, and various kinds of advertising and public relations releases. Other purposes of customer communication are instructions about credit, collection messages, and the adjustment of claims and complaints. A major part of external communication efforts is directed toward building and maintaining goodwill.

The telephone is becoming even more widely used because of rapidly increasing costs of business correspondence, although word processing centers and equipment are reducing some of these costs by decreasing labor expense.

The business letter is the most widely used form of external written communication to individuals. The kinds of letters most frequently written are listed below according to purpose.

- inquiry and request letters
- general administrative letters
- replies to requests and inquiries
- "executive" correspondence, including goodwill messages
- miscellaneous letters, including informational and customer service
- goodwill messages

Other types of letters, not written so frequently, include:

- letters about employment
- claim and adjustment
- credit and collection
- sales and sales promotion

The kinds of letters and other forms of communication depend upon the kind of organization or department. For example, credit departments naturally deal mostly with credit letters, but these letters are also written in small business firms with no official credit department.

It would be impracticable, if not impossible, to approach each type of letter as a differing unit, for in addition to the most commonly written types listed here, there are many others. All of the varying kinds of letters and other written messages are much more similar in content and approach than they are dissimilar.

In some of the chapters that follow, you will find illustrations and discussions of the most frequently written letters, and you will have practice in composing them. But most important in your study is a mastery of the communication principles and techniques that apply to all speaking and writing, whatever the particular purpose and format, and the acquiring of an understanding of business methods, policies, and procedures as they relate to communication.

Determining a Code of Ethics for Business Communication

A sound and workable system of communication is based on openness and honesty. The old-fashioned virtues of dependability, sincerity, and loyalty build a lasting foundation for business organizations, governments, and individuals. Without trust and confidence, there can be no real communication. Honest and ethical business practices are essential for an enduring and successful business enterprise.

A Sincere Approach

No thinking, ethical person disputes the premise that communication should be sincere, honest, and truthful. Without sincerity, all the techniques of skillful writing or speech become only cleverness, a quality far less desirable than wisdom or genuine goodwill. This entire book is based on the assumption that you and the organization you represent are worthy of the goodwill of the customers and of the general public and that goods and services are truthfully presented and not unreasonably priced.

Being honest and sincere does not require bluntness and curtness. Certain basic principles of effective communication—diplomacy, the you-attitude, the positive approach, and persuasion—are viewed with skepticism by some persons, who think that all these principles should be disregarded in order to avoid hypocrisy. This attitude causes their writing and speech to become unnecessarily direct, blunt, and harsh. Although honest, this attitude actually is discourteous to the receiver of the message and disloyal to the employing company of the writer.

The *you-attitude*—a long-used term in business communication that is discussed further in Chapter 3—is near in meaning to empathy, or looking at a situation from the viewpoint of the reader or listener. The you-attitude should not be interpreted as a manipulation of readers or listeners, as a way of ingratiating ourselves into their favor so that we can sell our goods or convince them to do as we wish. Even if this is the attitude of the communicator, it is difficult to

Truth is resilient and can be stretched pretty far. Lies—even little ones—should be avoided like the plague—not only for moral reasons, but because, unless you are a master of the game (in which case, I don't want anything to do with you), they are almost always going to come back to haunt you.

Betty White, *Betty White in Person* (New York: Doubleday, 1987), 23.

simulate a concern that we do not feel. A reader or listener does not need to be completely alert to realize that the wording sounds "fishy" or that the writer or speaker is trying for a "snow job." A message that provokes these reactions is worse than one that is harshly direct, but there is no reason for either of these two extremes.

Business communicators, although using the you-approach, must continue to be concerned with the needs of their own company. You naturally are more interested in your own welfare than in that of some person to whom you are writing a letter, likely a person you have never met. The recognition of these realities, however, does not preclude genuine concern for others or the desire to serve, to play fair, and to understand the reader's point of view.

Good intentions are not enough. Though filled with genuine goodwill, the writer or speaker may not be able to make this feeling apparent in letters and other communications. The desire to serve, although an essential element, does not guarantee proficiency in written or spoken business communication. In order to achieve all the desirable qualities of communication, the writer or speaker must acquire the skills that are presented throughout the remainder of this book.

Conviction, Not Persuasion or Manipulation

Persuasion is considered to be the approach most likely to make the reader act or think in the way that the writer wishes. The word *persuade* connotes urging, coaxing, or "bending the will." *Convince* does not have this implication, but denotes understanding.

In sales writing, buyers are not *persuaded* to buy because the writer wants them to do so. They are *convinced* that the product will fill their needs or desires. This conviction is not necessarily based on common sense; for example, no one actually *needs* beautiful paintings, an expensive stereo set, or handmade boots. These things, however, may be worth far more to the buyer than their cost; if so, they are a bargain regardless of the price.

Products and services are sold because buyers believe that it will be to their advantage to buy, not because the seller by eloquent persuasion or hard-sell tactics caused them to buy. The skillful salesperson has, nevertheless, been able to convince the buyer that the product is more valuable than the price. Ideally, this conviction is accomplished by truthfully and completely presenting the features of the product or service and showing how these features will meet the buyer's needs.

Although the term *persuasive writing* is used in this book, as in other books, to describe sales messages and other material in which the writer asks the reader to take certain actions, the term should not be interpreted as *manipulation* or *coaxing. Convincing* readers that the desired action will be for their own benefit is the key to successful persuasive writing. All effective business writing or speech is persuasive if it convinces the reader to take a certain course of action or even to believe in the company from which the message comes. (Chapter 10 deals in more detail with persuasive writing.)

Truth, But Also Diplomacy

To be ethical in business communication does not necessarily mean that every message must contain a detailed listing of the complete truth. Each message, however, should contain nothing but the truth. To be diplomatic and tactful, as well as to emphasize the positive aspects of a situation, sometimes we communicate best by what we refrain from saying.

We are not completely truthful with our friends, family, husband, or wife. To be completely, absolutely, and harshly truthful is, as we have all witnessed, devastating to the ego. Persons who take pride in plain speaking describe themselves as "not beating around a bush" or "calling a spade a spade." (Sometimes a spade should be described as an instrument used in digging, and *not* called a spade. The spade referred to by overly frank individuals is at times *exactly* an instrument for digging—into another person's pride and dignity.)

The use of general words instead of overly specific ones can soften an unpleasant message. Unpleasant details that are not necessary for the reception of the intended message are often best omitted. For example, only a sadistic personnel manager would spell out the unwelcome news that a person was not hired because he scored lower than anyone else had ever scored on a company aptitude test.

In sales writing, you need not include the information that the product you are selling can be bought at a lower price from a competing organization. If your company operates as it should, it is giving something for this extra cost—perhaps a guarantee, free delivery, or a convenient location. Or perhaps the competing company is selling the item at a discount for one of many possible reasons. Stress the real benefits that the customer receives from buying the product from your organization. To stress these benefits instead of price is not being untruthful, and to do otherwise would be disloyal to your employer. In business communication, as in other situations, it is only sensible to put your best foot forward and to make sure that the foot is covered by a well-polished shoe.

Summary

Your success in business, whatever your specialization or employing organization, will depend to a great extent on your ability to communicate, perhaps more so than on any other ability. You will spend much more time communicating than in any other aspects of your job.

A simplified definition of communication is "the transfer of meaning from the sender to the receiver." Communication involves thinking, reading, listening, speaking, and writing, as well as various nonverbal methods.

Although meaningful in the mind of the sender (or information source), the message transmitted is often less meaningful by the time it reaches its destination. The message is not exact or complete until it is understood and accepted in the mind of the receiver.

Noise is any distraction that interferes with the exact transmission of the intended message; it can occur in the encoding, sending, or decoding processes. Feedback is the return message to the sender of the original message.

A sound and workable system of communication is based on openness and honesty. Without trust and confidence, there can be no real communication. Ethical communication practices are essential for an enduring and successful business enterprise.

The attributes of successful writing and speech do not occur separately but are parts of the whole. Communication cannot be completely successful if it is weak in any area, regardless of how strong it is in other areas.

Test Yourself: Chapter Review

1. Explain how the Latin word *communis* relates to communication.

2. Verbal messages that carry meanings other than those stated are known as

   _____.

3. Communication within the mind of an individual (thinking) is also described as

   _____.

4. Communication with one or a few persons is known as _____ communication.

5. Communication through such media as television, radio, and newspapers is described as _____ communication.

6–7. Distinguish between *verbal* and *nonverbal* communication.

8–12. What are five processes of verbal communication?

13–15. What are three purposes of communication?

16. Any distraction that interferes with the exact transmission of the intended message is called

   _____.

17. The return message from the receiver of the message to the sender is called

   _____.

18–20. What are three tests of successful communication?

21. The informal communication network within an organization is referred to as

   _____.

Test Yourself: Correct Usage

(Related to material in Chapter 1 and principles of correct usage.) Insert all necessary punctuation, including quotation marks, hyphens, and apostrophes, and remove punctuation that has been inserted incorrectly. Choose correct word from each pair or group. Make any other necessary changes.

1. Communication involves all our senses our experiences our emotions and our intelligence.

2. Before a message is sent it must be encoded that is it must be put into words.

3. Before a message is finally received it must be decoded the word decoded means interpreted.

4. The process of communication consists of four elements sender message channel and receiver.

5. Verbal encoding processes are speaking and writing other encoding processes are touching smiling and gesturing.

6. Decoding processes in addition to reading and listening include tasting smelling and touching.

7. Connotative meanings are based on these factors experiences attitudes beliefs and emotions.

8. Success in a career is (affected, effected) favorably or unfavorably by communication ability.

9. Communication you (receive, recieve) from others in response to your own messages is called *feedback*.

10. The you-attitude, which is similar to empathy must be (sincerly, sincerely) felt and expressed.

11. A letter of (congradulations, congratulations), like all other letters must be written with the reader in mind.

12. The five processes of verbal communication are these speaking writing reading listening and thinking.

13. Much of a (companys, company's, companies, companies') communication efforts are directed toward building goodwill.

14. When we talk about the you-approach, persuasion, and building goodwill we do not mean that we should be untruthful or manipulate our (readers', readers).

15. We can be truthful and at the same time diplomatic to do otherwise even for the sake of persuasion is unethical.

Questions and Problems

1. Step to the front of the classroom. Introduce yourself to your instructor and to your classmates. Tell them about your major field of study and your career goals. Describe your present employment, if any, especially as it relates to written or oral communication. Tell them anything else about yourself that you wish, provided you keep your remarks to no more than the time limit set by your instructor.

2. This assignment is an alternative for the previous one. Form into groups of two. Meet with someone with whom you are not already acquainted, preferably someone you have never seen before entering this class. Spend 5 to 10 minutes (or the time limit set by your instructor) in becoming acquainted with your classmate.

3. Introduce your friend (Problem 2) to your instructor and to your classmates, much as you would introduce a speaker at a conference or at another speaking engagement. Tell the class something about this person, perhaps some of the information described in Problem 1.

4. "Comments and Bits of Information" assignment. The purpose of this assignment is to direct your thoughts to the wide field of communication and to give you an opportunity to present a bit of information to the class. To find this comment or bit of any information, look in any printed source. (Do not use your textbook). Try to find recent sources, and, as much as possible, make the comment understandable to other students who, like you, are probably beginning their first course in business communication.

   Your comment or bit of information should be about communication. For example, you might say something like this: "Time is a factor in nonverbal communication, and not all persons view tardiness in the way we do in the United States. In many countries, time is treated much more casually than it is here." Give your source for your particular bit of information; you may use the exact words of the author, but if you do so, include a statement to that effect. For example, you might obtain your comment simply by glancing at a newspaper and noting that postage rates are expected to rise. Be prepared to present orally to the class in the time allowed by your instructor.

5. Prepare your "Comments and Bits of Information" assignment (Problem 4) in written form according to the directions of your instructor. If you are asked to use memorandum format, refer to Chapter 6. Give a complete bibliographical reference for your published source, including author, title, publication, and date. Refer to Appendix C.

6. If you are now employed, describe your communication activities in relation to the discussion in this chapter. Examples of topics to be discussed or questions to be answered are these:

   a. Do you spend more time in written communication or in oral communication?

b. What kinds of written messages do you prepare?

c. By which methods (telephone, conversation, group discussion, or public speaking) do you communicate orally? What are the purposes of these forms of oral communication?

d. Do you feel that management personnel of your organization keep you adequately informed of decisions and policies?

e. If you should become president of your employing organization, what would you do to improve communication within and from the organization?

7. Consider how you spent your day. When, how, why, and to whom have you communicated? Has this communication been particularly effective or ineffective? What forms of feedback did you receive? How well have you received the communication of others, and what kind of message did you send in return? What kinds of noise have existed in your communication efforts?

8. Using an example from your experience, write a short description of an instance of miscommunication.

9. In the library, look in the *Business Periodicals Index* or in the ABI/Inform computer database under "Communication in Management" to find two articles that have been published within the past two years. Try to find articles related to your field of specialization; for example, if you are majoring in personnel management, find articles about communication in the field of personnel management. Give the complete bibliographical references to these articles, as explained in Appendix C.

10. Write a one-page summary of one or both of these articles. Be prepared to present this summary, or these summaries, orally to the class.

Henry's Morning

11. To illustrate the forms of communication, as well as the omnipresence of communication during our waking hours, consider the early part of a day in the life of a business student, Henry Commons, who works part-time in an accounting office.

His first message of the day, apart from his dreams, is the sound of the clock radio. Although the voice from the radio is intoning the news of the day, it is also telling him that it is time to get up. This message is an unpleasant one, although it is the one that Henry intended when he set the clock the night before. Henry groans, a sound that communicates to his wife that he really isn't ready and willing to begin his day. He groans again at a news item and communicates to his wife, without speaking, that he is unhappy with the state of the world. He goes back to sleep.

His wife nudges him with her elbow—a signal that expresses, without a word being spoken, that if he doesn't get up this minute he will be late for the scheduled examination and then perhaps late at his office, and that if he is late again he may not receive the promised raise, and that if he doesn't get the raise they can't trade in the old car or even have it repaired, and that she has to arise, too, even though she is tired, and that if he hadn't watched the late show the night before he wouldn't be so sleepy, and . . . her second nudge with her elbow signifies stronger language.

Several other forms of communication occur as Henry eats breakfast, kisses his wife, dresses, and drives to class. He has short bits of conversation with his wife while he glances hurriedly at the newspaper and at his class notes. From the notes he is in effect again receiving communication from his professor, as the notes bring to mind the details of the professor's lectures. He drinks his coffee and notices that it is too strong. He wisely refrains from mentioning this to his wife. The cat rubs against his legs; he strokes her and she purrs. Then the cat goes to the door and meows, saying that she wants to go into the backyard. Henry opens the door.

As he drives to work, a red light communicates to him that he should stop. A singer's voice comes to him from the car radio. So does the voice of an announcer, who asks him to buy a particular kind of soap. The hunched, hurrying figures of pedestrians indicate that it is a cold morning.

As he enters the classroom, he is vaguely disturbed that the chairs have been rearranged and that another student is sitting in his customary place in the room by the back window.

The professor enters the room and distributes copies of the examination. At the top of page 1, the words *name* and *section* appear. Students immediately write their names and the section number on the blanks indicated.

The teacher stands silently before the roomful of students. Instead of his usual attire, a conservative business suit, he wears crumpled corduroy slacks, a baggy sweater, and worn, casual boots. He does not explain his change of dress, but Henry surmises that he is leaving the campus immediately after class.

As Henry writes the answers to the examination questions, he tries to express to the reader of the paper his ideas and some of the information that he has obtained during the semester. His ability in written communication will vitally affect his success, although the course is not described as being a course in communication.

The professor seems hurried and asks twice if everyone is nearly finished, although he assures the class that there is still plenty of time. He says that he wishes them well in the completion of the examination. A student raises her hand; he does not seem to see. He looks at his watch.

The examination has not been neatly typewritten and reproduced. Several words are so dim that they are almost impossible to read, and parts of sentences have been omitted. These weaknesses evoke responses of hesitation, confusion, misunderstanding, and irritation, although the students say nothing. Henry notes mentally that he must be more careful in his own written communications that he sends from his office, and that he will insist that the part-time secretary who types his letters and memorandums improve the appearance of the messages he signs.

When the bell rings, signifying the end of the period, Henry has not completed the last discussion question. He folds the paper, places it on the teacher's desk, and hurries from the room without meeting the teacher's eyes. In the hall he meets a friend; he slaps him on the back in a gesture of affection. He meets another professor, smiles, and says good morning. He stops to read a notice on a bulletin board. He hears the next bell, which indicates that it is ten-thirty. He carries his coat on his arm in response to the overheated building. He smells the newly waxed floors of the building and the perfume of a girl who rides with him on the elevator. In the student lounge he puts 50 cents into the coffee machine, which responds to his instructions to deliver black coffee; he had punched the wrong button, for he wanted coffee with cream.

Then it is time for Henry to go to work. When he reaches his office, the receptionist smiles, says good morning, and comments that it is miserable outside today. Henry agrees, although he had found the cold air invigorating. The receptionist goes back to reading the newspaper.

Two memorandums are on Henry's desk. He reads them, makes a note on one, puts it in the "out" basket, and crumples the other and throws it at the wastebasket. He sits at his small desk, in the uncomfortable chair, in the dark corner of the room.

The employer comes into the room. He does not smile or say good morning but asks immediately about a report that Henry completed the day before. Henry hands him the report and begins to explain some of the details that are important for the proper interpretation of the report. His employer nods impatiently, frowns, and walks back into his office. Henry wonders whether he should have been more emphatic about the importance of what he had tried to say. He sighs and begins work on another report that he plans to revise.

Refer to the experiences of Henry Commons in answering the following questions.

a. What were the forms of written messages?

b. Oral messages?

c. Nonverbal communication?

d. Communication from humans to machines?

e. Communication from machines to humans?

f. Which messages were received through touch?

g. Smell?

h. Taste?

i. Other forms of sensory perception?

j. Which attempts at communication were successful?

k. Unsuccessful?

l. What types of noise occurred?

m. In which instances was the sending or the receiving of the message, or both, especially affected by personal relationships?

n. What forms of feedback occurred?

CHAPTER 2

Changing Methods and Media of Communication

This chapter provides an overview of the ways in which technology affects the sending and receiving of oral and written business messages. Change has been rapid during the past few years, especially since computers have become smaller, easier to use, more sophisticated, and less expensive. As this change is expected to continue and to accelerate, we as communicators must be aware of these trends and developments and use them to our advantage.

Unchanging Principles of Communication in Relation to Ever-Changing Technology

Regardless of changing methods and media, the principles of human communication are constant and universal. "The more things change, the more they stay the same" is an adage that applies to effective communication of all kinds. This book and your course in business communication are built around principles that apply everywhere, regardless of how written or oral messages are prepared, sent, and received. These basic principles apply to casual conversation in the halls and to panel discussions heard by thousands of people via public television or teleconferencing. They apply to written messages sent from one computer to another, or transmitted by satellite, as well as to notes hastily written with pencils on memo pads, and to telephone calls.

"Nothing endures but change" is a quotation of the Greek philosopher Heraclitus, written about 500 B.C. Your workplace, whatever your position or area of specialization, is likely to be different from that of similar workers twenty years ago. You will see many other changes throughout your career, some of which now seem to be impossible. You cannot prepare yourself completely for these changes during your college years, for you will find it necessary to keep on learning, as experienced workers are now doing and will continue to do.

A foundation of basic knowledge and skills, including a study of human behavior (as much as it can be studied) and an expert use of language, will enable you to adapt to ever-changing conditions and responsibilities. Most important of all, you should expect change, welcome it when it is beneficial, and exert the necessary effort to meet new challenges with confidence in your ability to succeed.

Business messages, however they are encoded, transmitted, and decoded, involve the five processes of verbal communication: speaking, writing, listening, reading, and thinking. These skills will not decrease in importance with changing technology; they will become even more important. So will harmonious personal relationships, which are built through communication.

Business messages at one time were written with a quill pen and, in earlier times, carved on bark or chipped on stone tablets. Now they can be printed and transmitted by computers or beamed into outer space by satellites. Facsimiles of

---

Communication Brief

The computer industry in Silicon Valley is a textbook illustration of the way in which the language coined in California is quickly adopted throughout the English-speaking world. The heartland of America's electronics industry is a super-rich suburb immediately north of San Jose, half an hour's drive south of San Francisco. It is the home of more than 3000 companies, including famous information-technology names like Apple and Hewlett-Packard. . . . The streets have names like Semiconductor Drive. The valley is the home of the video game, the VDU, the word processor, the silicon chip, and, for the English language, it is a rich jargon factory. Words like *interface, software, input, on-line,* and *data-processing* are already in the dictionary. *High-tech, computer hacker, to access, diskette,* and *modem* will be added to subsequent editions.

Robert McCrum, William Cran, and Robert MacNeil, *The Story of English* (New York: Viking Penguin, 1986), 37.

anything written, typed, drawn, or photographed can be sent thousands of miles in a few seconds. Word processing equipment can communicate directly with typesetting equipment. Each year the various kinds of equipment used to process information become more comprehensive and amazing; nevertheless, language remains the most useful tool of communication, as it has always been. Automated, sophisticated machines cannot be designed or operated without the use of communication between humans and, especially, the application of human thought.

Rapid Development of Communication Technology

The economy of the United States and other developed countries is now predominantly that of the production, processing, and distribution of information. Our nation has progressed from being a manufacturing society to an information society, as in previous years it changed from an agricultural society to an industrial one. It is no exaggeration to say that business *is* communication.

For young people, a world without computers is difficult to imagine; yet the computer was not invented until after World War II, and microcomputers did not become available until the 1970s. Now computers are used extensively

Travel agent using computer to make flight reservations. (Do you think she should straighten up her "executive work station"?)

in various ways to facilitate communication. Microcomputers with word processing software are rapidly replacing typewriters.

Although communication itself began even before the development of language—and business communication began when our most remote ancestors first transacted business of any kind—much of the equipment now considered commonplace in offices all over the world has been in use less than a century, and some of the most important equipment less than a decade. Even after various kinds of equipment were invented, they often remained in crude form for a number of years.

After personal computers were developed, their acceptance was delayed because of the lack of software. (*Software* means a disk or disks that contain instructions to make computers accomplish what the user wants them to do. For example, in order to use a personal computer as a word processor, you must have word processing software.)

Within a few years after the invention of personal computers, literally thousands of software packages were marketed on a wide scale for almost every conceivable business purpose, as were computer games, instructional material, and software for home use. In addition, programmers designed individual packages for particular companies or specialized purposes.

Now the problem is not the lack of software systems, but the overwhelming number from which to choose. Even if you were interested only in word processing packages, you would find that the great number on the market makes selection time-consuming and perhaps inexact.

The following brief chronology summarizes the approximate dates of inventions and developments that have changed the way people communicate with one another—in business and in their personal lives—through written and spoken words.

First typewriters

Working typewriter, 1857

Commercial typewriter (developed by Christopher Sholes), 1867

Electric typewriter (Thomas Edison), 1872

Successful electric typewriter, 1935

IBM Selectric, 1961

Self-correcting electric typewriters, decade of the 1970s

Electronic typewriters with word processing capabilities (limited), decade of the 1980s. (Much improvement has recently occurred.)

First voice-recording and voice-transmission equipment

Telephone (Alexander Graham Bell), 1876

Drum recording device (Thomas Edison), 1877

Radio, 1902

Reel-to-reel recorders, late 1930s

Interoffice communication system (intercom), 1936

Cassette recorders, late 1960s

First computers

General-purpose electronic computer, ENIAC, 1946

First computer used in government, UNIVAC I, 1951

IBM's first successful computer, 650 RAMAC, 1956

IBM System/360, 1964

First personal computer, the Apple II, 1977

IBM Personal Computer, 1981

First word processing equipment

IBM MT/ST (Magnetic Tape/Selectric Typewriter), 1964

Wang WP 55, 1976

Word processing software for personal computers, soon after introduction of personal computers

First xerographic photocopier

Xerox 914, 1959

Responsibilities of management personnel and other employees have changed because of new equipment and methods. Larry Hartman, former manager of software documentation, Zenith Data Systems, describes changing responsibilities in this way:

> Business managers do create their own reports and letters on terminals at their desks.
>
> Dictation skills are essential in established word processing communication systems.
>
> Letters, memos, reports, and instructions are created at the desk and are stored and transmitted electronically anywhere within a network system at night.
>
> Editing, formatting, proofreading, and correcting messages on microcomputers, word processors, or other electronic terminals are accepted fundamental skills in today's business.
>
> Electronic data base management, storage and retrieval systems exist and are established in small as well as large businesses.
>
> Basic quantitative skills assist decision making and problem solving and assist with statistical applications, graphic displays, and charting.
>
> Teleconferencing, videoconferencing, and computerconferencing permit immediate access and instant feedback for business decision makers. These systems exist and are available for hire in hotels with national and international chains.[1]

These preceding statements were published in 1983. Many other changes and improvements have occurred since 1983, particularly in electronic mail, voice mail, and facsimile transmission.

Discussion of several of the preceding terms, as they apply to communica-

---

[1]Larry D. Hartman, "What a Future!" in *Information Systems and Business Communication,* ed. Raymond W. Beswick and Alfred W. Williams (Urbana, Ill.: American Business Communication Association, 1983), iii.

Public affairs writer watching videos.

tion in business, follows in the remainder of this chapter. Such a discussion, however, can at best be a limited overview because of space limitations and rapidly changing methods and equipment. You will find new developments in communication technology reported in daily newspapers, in *The Wall Street Journal,* in special trade magazines, and in various other publications.

Using Word Processing Equipment and Systems

Many business people, including executives, now prepare their own memorandums and letters by using a computer terminal or, more likely, a personal computer equipped with a word processing package. This trend is expected to increase. Many of these messages are sent from computer to computer without appearing in printed (hard copy) format. Such transmission is one kind of electronic mail, as discussed later in this chapter.

The greatest portion of the cost of a written communication, regardless of how it is prepared, is the cost of labor. Labor costs continue to be the most important factor even with word processing systems, although such systems, when used wisely, reduce overall costs.

Word Processing Centers and Dictation Systems

Word processing centers use automated typewriting equipment and a planned procedure to increase the production of written material and to decrease cost.

Communication Brief

Just a few years ago, most business writing was tedious work. To start, you usually wrote the first draft of a document in longhand. Then, if you were lucky, someone else would type it for you or enter it into a word processing system. If your document required visual aids, you drew rough drafts by hand, and you frequently drew the final drafts too. As you moved up the organization chart, of course, you got more clerical help for your typing and drawing. But you still did a lot of proofing as you reviewed the several drafts of a typical business document.

Today, thanks to computers, you don't need clerical help for your writing. Personal computers (PCs), in particular, have changed the way many people in business write. Starting at a cost of about $1,500, a modern PC can help you double your writing productivity. It can also help you make dramatic improvements in the effectiveness of your writing.

Mike Murach, *Write Better with a PC* (Fresno, CA: Mike Murach & Associates, Inc., 1989), 3.

The productivity of secretaries can be increased when each secretary performs specialized tasks.

Word processing equipment resembles a standard electric typewriter. In addition to ordinary typewriting, however, operators can make corrections, shift words and paragraphs from one part of a manuscript to another, and freely add or delete. Another important advantage is the storing of material on disks to be used or revised later.

Typewritten material can appear on a screen or be printed on a typewritten page. When the copy on the screen or on the page is exactly as desired, the operator enters it into a memory, or storage unit. To reproduce the material, the operator activates a printing code key. The machine itself or a separate printer types the material exactly as keyboarded at a speed much faster than that of the most expert human typist, perfectly accurate with the exception of any errors that may have remained before the copy was put into memory. The copy can be printed in various formats or linked with other information/ communication devices to form an integrated, automated electronic network. (This description of word processing applies also to the use of word processing software with a personal computer.)

Word processing presents an alternative to the general-purpose secretary by allowing for a division of work. In a word processing center, typewriting duties are taken over by a keyboard specialist who is called a *typist-transcriber, a correspondence secretary,* or *a word processing operator.* The secretary's other duties are assumed by an assistant in an administrative support center, or secretaries remain in their original offices but assume the role of administrative secretaries or administrative assistants.

The word processing center is a separate office staffed by keyboard specialists, a supervisor or supervisors, and perhaps other support personnel, such as proofreaders. Letters and other written materials are produced for many "word originators" throughout the organization.

Dictation may be given over the telephone to recording machines in the word processing center. Dictation is also done through the use of individual desktop or portable voice-writing machines, with the tape or disk sent to the word processing center for transcription. In some organizations, handwritten materials are supplied to keyboard specialists in the word processing center,

No one ever set out to make you uncomfortable with computers. You probably decided that on your own. You may have based your conclusion on well-intentioned articles and books that tried to explain to you how computers work. The fact is, you don't have to know how they work. I don't know how my camera works, but I can take pictures. I don't know what a carburetor does, but I find my car not only useful, but fun. It sure beats getting around on a mule.

If you're still writing with pencil and paper, you're riding a mule. Even ordinary electric typewriters are on their way out. Word processors are replacing them. In another five years, it will be as difficult to find an electric typewriter in a major corporate office as it is to find a manual one now. Besides, sitting there hunched over the yellow pad feels too much like doing homework to be anything like comfortable, much less fun. Can business writing be fun? Sure.

Patricia King, *Mind to Disk to Paper* (New York: Franklin Watts, 1984), xviii.

much as material is given to private secretaries. Word processing systems, however, are planned for receiving material through dictation. If less efficient methods of word origination are used, the cost effectiveness of word processing centers is decreased.

Word processing centers may serve an entire company. "Minicenters" are provided for departments or divisions of an organization.

A recent development in dictation systems is equipment that converts the voice into digital pulses to be stored on a fixed disk. Unlike older tape systems, digital equipment allows the user to revise material in much the same way as written material is revised during word processing.

Although a speaker using a tape recorder can back up and revise previously dictated material, the original material is erased. Digital equipment allows a new space to open on the disk so that new material can be added without deleting the original dictation. Digital dictation systems are now more efficient and less expensive than when they were introduced in the early 1980s.

The principles of effective dictation described in Appendix A apply to origination of messages to be transcribed in word processing centers, as well as messages dictated to a secretary, either personally or by using a desktop or portable recorder. In organizations using word processing, efficient dictation practices are even more important than they are in other organizations. Because originators of written messages may never meet the secretaries who transcribe their words, it is even more important that dictation be clear, with all necessary instructions.

Some organizations use external word processing services; these are private businesses that provide word processing services to other businesses, usually those that are too small for extensive word processing equipment of their own.

An important advantage of word processing systems is that the equipment can be tied to data processing equipment and various copying and printing processes, including typesetting equipment. Another important advantage, which has been apparent since the first automatic typewriter was invented a number of years ago, is that copies of typewritten work can be made automatically, resulting not in "copies" as such, but in actual typewritten pages. In addition, the material can be stored on disks for future use.

Not all organizations are large enough to require or afford a centralized word processing center. In smaller companies a separate word processing unit, known as *stand-alone equipment,* may be used. Word processing can also be done at personal computers at each secretary's desk or at the desk of the originator of the message. In addition, electronic typewriters can now serve as word processors, although their functions and storage capacity are more limited than those of a personal computer.

Word Processing with Personal Computers

Word processing is one of the many functions of a microcomputer, or of a terminal tied to a mainframe computer. Literally thousands of software packages for word processing are on the market.

A microcomputer or a computer terminal is often provided for individual employees at what is described as an *executive work station.* Some combination software packages include word processing, data processing, graphic capabilities, and spreadsheets. Graphs and other illustrations can be constructed at the computer, then entered into a report. The manuscript pages can be searched for misspelled words. Software packages can even determine reading levels and evaluate sentence construction.

With the increasing use of microcomputers, which can be linked together in various ways, the ability to type, or to "keyboard," is becoming increasingly important, even for executives. Although people in management positions should not be expected to spend time keyboarding long manuscripts, skillful use of a computer key-

Word processing with a microcomputer and printer.

*Improve
Your Writing*

Question: Is it true that word processing packages and other computer software will now take care of proofreading? If so, why do some errors remain even in printed material?

Answer: Although a computer equipped with the appropriate software can find many proofreading errors, you as a writer must continue to find many for yourself.

Most word processing packages include a system that checks every keyboarded word against a "dictionary" stored in the software. Such a check alerts you to many errors, but not to all. Even the smartest computer cannot know what you meant to write. For example, *affect* and *effect* are often confused. Because both are correct words, the computer does not indicate either as incorrect. (Some packages, however, ask you whether your choice of these words and similar ones are what you actually mean.)

If you write *now* instead of *not*, only a human proofreader can find the error. This error could be serious. For example, if you state that you are not interested in a job for which you have interviewed, the reader may not continue far enough to determine that you actually meant that you are now interested.

Spelling or grammar checkers cannot find omitted words, doubled words, omitted lines, and numerous other inconsistencies. Although their help is invaluable, the writer must do additional proofreading.

---

board for short messages requires less time than calling a secretary or sending material to a word processing center.

Although much computer work can be accomplished with only a few keyboard strokes, typewriting proficiency greatly facilitates word processing. Apart from word processing, typewriting or keyboarding is a valuable personal skill. Some people have not learned to type because they do not want to become typists or secretaries. Such an attitude is similar to refusing to learn to drive an automobile because one does not wish to be a taxicab driver.

Using a word processor for personal or business messages saves time and results in more professional work. Word processing also decreases frustration because it decreases repetitive work, particularly retyping. Advantages of word processing to you as a writer are summarized below.

Ease of Revision and Correction A major advantage of word processing, however it is used, is that letters, words, lines, sentences, paragraphs, or entire documents can be instantly deleted, added, moved, corrected, or revised. Material is entered and displayed on a screen (monitor) through keyboarding, much as material is typewritten. Revisions can be made at any point in the composing process or after the first draft is completed. (The term *document* is a bit of computer jargon, now considered standard usage, to describe anything that you have designated as a document.)

Instant revision results in better overall results, whatever you are writing. As writers and teachers have long advocated, revision is almost always desirable in order to produce professional-quality work. A truism is "The only good writing is rewriting."

Rewriting using a typewriter is extremely time-consuming. Few writers wish to retype an entire page in order to replace an almost right word with an exact one or to divide material into shorter, more readable paragraphs if the page is at least acceptable as it is. Such changes can be made in a few seconds using a word processor.

Word processors have even more important benefits to error-prone typists (almost everyone) and poor spellers. Typographical errors, if noticed, can be immediately corrected. In addition, a spelling checker, available with most word processing software, recognizes errors in the spelling of words in its "dictionary."

Proofreading is still necessary, however, because some errors escape detection by the spelling checker. For example, the words *some* and *same* are both correct words; only the writer can determine which one is desired. The computer cannot detect omitted words or passages, repeated words, or numerous other errors.

Some software packages evaluate other aspects of composition, including sentence length, repetition of words, readability level, number of verbs in the passive voice, and number of sentences that begin with *There* and *It*. No computer or formula, however, can accurately and completely evaluate writing of any kind. Although such programs can be an aid to even experienced writers, they cannot replace personal evaluation and revision.

Improved Appearance of Material Letter-quality printers, properly used, prepare written material in a perfectly arranged printed copy.

Storage and Retrieval of Materials A major advantage of word processing is the storage of material on floppy or hard disks. This storage saves filing space, makes documents easier to find, and, most important, quickly provides exact copies months or years after the documents are prepared.

Wide Choice of Word Processing Software As when making any important decision, you will benefit from extensive research before buying a word processing package. Your choice will depend upon the kind of material you write. For example, some packages prepare bottom-of-page footnotes and include subscripts and superscripts. If you do not need these features, some other package may be less expensive or more specifically planned for your needs. Other packages include such features as "mail merge," which is used to place names and addresses on duplicate copies of letters or other messages. Although this feature is invaluable to organizations that mail a great number of individually addressed form letters, it is of little use to the average student.

You may be able to try various software packages before you buy them; many stores provide this opportunity. Make sure that the package you select includes a well-written instruction book. Tutorial disks are available with some packages or may be purchased separately. A few of the many word processing packages are Word Perfect, Displaywrite, Wordstar, Multimate, and PFS Write.

Learning word processing, using even the most simple system, requires time. The ease of composition and printing, however, will soon convince you that the time and effort spent in the learning process have been rewarded.

Desktop Publishing[2]

Desktop publishing is a term that commonly describes professional quality publishing using a personal computer or microcomputer. Desktop publishing software such as Aldus' PageMaker or Xerox's Ventura integrates text and graphics to produce high-quality print publications using laser printers. Desktop publishing allows the use of boxes, borders, illustrations, clip-art, multicolumns, various size type fonts, and other features associated with professional printing. Common applications of desktop publishing for businesses, clubs, nonprofit groups, and educational units include newsletters, brochures, flyers, pamphlets, posters, and sales messages.

The options in desktop publishing software packages vary from over $1,000 to under $100, depending on the range and complexity of features offered in the desktop publishing software package. High-end desktop publishing has the ability to use any image, including scanned photographs, graphs, and drawn artwork. Many packages offer a clip-art library of professionally drawn illustrations and symbols. Image control options include the ability to change the brightness, the contrast, and the size of images used in desktop publishing. The more complex desktop publishing software has the ability to import text from popular word processing, spreadsheet, and database software packages. Although the laser printer provides high-quality printing, dot matrix printers can be used for less professional output or for draft copy.

Many software producers are adding desktop publishing to word processing packages. For example, Word Perfect 5.0 allows for a variety of typefaces, type sizes, and type sizes along with graphic elements of boxes and rulings. In addition, Word Perfect 5.0 can import graphics from other software applications such as Lotus 1-2-3 and Harvard Graphics. Charts, figures, and graphic aids similar to those in Chapter 15 can be added to word processing text. As software producers add more visual capabilities to word processing software packages, the distinction between desktop publishing and word processing becomes less.

Style and Grammar Checkers

Style and grammar checkers such as Grammatik and RightWriter can analyze data generated on most common word processing software for incomplete sentences, cliché phrases, active-passive voice, sentence length, readability index, subject-verb agreement, repeated word usage, and spell checking. The style and grammar analysis will appear in the form of comments or as a summary in a copy of the word processing text. The writer can then make editing changes or leave the text in its original form. Style and grammar checkers will catch many of the common writing errors, but writers must still use judgment in the subjective qualities of what is considered "good writing."

Electronic Mail (E-Mail)

The term *electronic mail* is used in more than one way. In its broadest sense, it includes any kind of message sent electronically, as its name implies. Thus it

[2]This section was written by Glynna Morse and is used here by permission.

includes the teletypewriter, telephone, facsimile transmission, and other methods and equipment discussed in this chapter. A more specific use, however, refers only to messages sent from computer to computer by linked networks (used for internal mail), telephone lines, or satellite. This specific usage, also described as electronic message systems and E-mail, applies in this discussion.

Electronic mail is sent from one computer screen to another. The receiver of the message may be next door or thousands of miles away. Messages are composed on a computer screen, as in word processing, and sent to the "mailbox" of the receiver until he or she can conveniently pick them up. The sender can be signaled when a message has been retrieved.

The receiver of the message reads the message after it is printed on a computer screen. It can then be printed out as "hard copy," although a hard copy is often unnecessary. Messages can be stored and filed electronically by user-chosen guide words, much as other computer files are stored on disks.

People in widely separated time zones can send messages back and forth without the inconveniences caused by the time differences. Electronic mail eliminates the frustration and expense of "telephone tag." It allows the receiver of the message to respond at a convenient time instead of answering the telephone when it rings. Electronic mail provides for the "broadcast" of messages to many mailboxes, either in the same office or to distant locations. Thus, instead of the more usual photocopied memorandums, business people receive computer messages.

E-mail is used both internally (within the same organization) and externally (to receivers outside the organization). Ordinarily external messages are carried by telephone lines; this method requires a computer, modem, and a communication software package. The receiver of the message, as well as the sender, must have a computer and be on the same E-mail system. Computer messages are often sent after ordinary business hours in order to be billed at lower long-distance rates.

Entire manuscripts can be sent from computers to publishing houses. Newspaper reporters send in stories in this way, even from foreign countries, transmitting messages via satellite.

Some advantages of electronic mail are the following:

- Transmission of messages is almost instantaneous.
- Messages are often more personal and informal. (This characteristic can be a disadvantage as well as an advantage.)
- Compared to telephone calls, the problem of "telephone tag" is reduced or eliminated.
- The time necessary for meetings is reduced.
- Electronic mail can replace many memorandums and routine letters.
- Electronic mail can be sent at any time, day or night, thus decreasing costs and problems brought about by differences in time zones.
- Messages can be sent to many receivers simultaneously.

Some disadvantages of electronic mail are the following:

- Cost. (Depending upon company needs, systems *can* be cost effective.)

- Because E-mail messages are prepared more quickly than most letters and memorandums, senders are more likely to make errors in facts and approach, in addition to errors in logic, grammar, and spelling.
- Incompatibility of electronic mail systems prevents the sending and receiving of messages between these systems.
- E-mail messages may be taken less seriously than traditional business letters.
- The sender of the message has no assurance that the intended receiver will check his or her mailbox or respond to the message.
- The space available on an E-mail screen is less than that of a single-spaced typewritten page. Multiple screens are likely to be more annoying than a long typewritten letter or memorandum would be.

How will you as a business writer or speaker be affected by electronic mail? Perhaps the effect on your communication responsibilities and success will be less than you think.

Certainly the system should make the sending and receiving of messages more prompt, efficient, and reliable. Nevertheless, the basic principles of business communication remain the same. You must still know your subject, convey accurate and complete information, express your thoughts in exact words, convince the receiver to accept your ideas or follow your instructions, and strengthen harmonious working relationships. The overall ability to communicate is as important when using electronic mail as when using regular mail, conversing with your business associates, or making a speech. Learning to use the necessary equipment and software is a minor consideration compared to your ability to interact effectively with other people and to use language effectively. (You can make friends or enemies using electronic mail just as you do when you use regular mail.)

Voice Mail

Voice mail is also referred to as *Voice Store-and-Forward (VSF)* and *phone mail;* a newer term is *voice processing.*

Telephone answering devices are the simplest and least expensive form of voice mail, although voice mail systems have many additional features. A major difference is that with voice mail systems, which include store-and-forward and routing, the user *plans* to leave a voice message, not to talk directly with a person by telephone. Thus, voice messages are like letters in that they evoke no immediate response.

Like written messages sent by electronic mail, voice messages are placed in "mailboxes." The same message can be "broadcast" to numerous mailboxes simultaneously. Recipients control when the messages are taken, picking them up at their convenience. This feature, however, can result in delayed responses, as with electronic mail or business letters sent by regular mail.

Voice mail can conveniently replace short, rather routine letters, such as requests, replies to requests, notices, or announcements. They are useful in replacing telephone calls for which an immediate response is not needed.

Another feature of voice mail is that it provides information to inquirers

A voice store-and-forward system (VSF) frees executives from writing. This executive can call up information on the computer while conducting a telephone conversation, dictating material to be transcribed, or originating a voice message that will be forwarded and stored in someone's voice mailbox. (Photo courtesy of Wang Laboratories, Inc.)

who do not use a computer, but only a touch-tone telephone. For example, banks provide information about account balances and whether or not particular checks have cleared. This information is provided by a computer, although the inquirer has the option of being transferred to a customer service representative.

Many of the advantages and disadvantages that apply to written messages sent by electronic mail also apply to voice mail. When wisely planned and used, however, advantages far outweigh disadvantages.

Users who transmit messages by voice mail must be especially careful to plan their communications so that they are complete, clear, and concise. They must be sure that their words are clearly enunciated and free of tones, words, or accents that would be confusing to people from other countries or various regions of the United States and Canada.

In 1986, approximately 2,000 voice mail systems were sold; in 1989, approximately 22,000 systems were sold. The voice mail industry is growing at an annual rate of 40 to 50 percent and is expected to pass the $1 billion mark in 1990.

Facsimile Transmission

Facsimile (FAX) transmission provides an advantage not available through any other form of electronic communication—the transmission to other FAX machines, anywhere in the world, of exact copies of written material, drawings, photographs, maps, charts, or other pictorial material. This transmission is completed in only a few seconds, being sent over regular telephone lines or by satellite.

Facsimile machines provide the fastest-growing form of business communications in the United States. Although the first facsimile machines were invented more than a century ago, only in recent years have they been so economical and of such good quality that they are practical for even small businesses.

Facsimile transmission is widely used in international communication, supplementing or replacing Telex transmission, an older method of transmission.

Modern facsimile machines were perfected by the Japanese. Because the Japanese alphabet contains 4,000 characters, facsimile transmission is especially useful in order to decrease the number of typewritten copies.

Facsimile equipment can be linked with personal computers and E-mail systems. Certain software packages allow users to create a document at a personal computer and automatically fax it to various locations. This material can be sent immediately or delayed to another time, day or night, in consideration of different purposes or time zones.

The various systems of electronic communication are merging, according to Paul D. Thomas:

> The merging of fax into E-mail is part of a broader trend. Only a few years ago, computer-based E-mail, telex, voice mail, local area networking and facsimile were considered distinct and thus incompatible. . . . PCs, telex machines, phones, and fax units are becoming nothing more than different types of messaging terminals.[3]

Teleconferencing and Videoconferencing

Teleconferencing is electronic communication between three or more people at two or more locations. In its simplest form, it is the telephone conference call that has been available for many years. With speakerphones in each office, the number of participants can be greatly increased. When using two-way calls, all participants can speak with all other participants. In one-way conference calls, oral messages (for example, statements from a company president) are delivered simultaneously to many locations.

Videoconferencing (also referred to as *teleconferencing*) includes televised pictures of the participants, either as still shots or in full action, like regular television. Videoconferencing can be either one-way or two-way, with several variations of each. A frequently used method, particularly appropriate for large groups, is video presentation of the speaker or speakers, with opportunity for telephone feedback from audiences at widely scattered locations. College courses are taught by this method.

Because of increasing travel costs, some organizations hold meetings by videoconferencing, either nationwide or in limited geographical areas. An advantage, besides economy, is that more employees are able to participate. A disadvantage is that teleconferencing at its best cannot take the place of face-to-face interaction. As people, we like and need to talk with people—even to reach out and touch them. This fact is not likely to change, regardless of innovations in technological transmission.

Other Specialized Office Equipment and Processes

The automated electronic office consists of information and communication devices linked together, many of which can be accessed from individual computer

[3]Paul D. Thomas, "Merging Fax into Corporate Networks," *The Office,* February 1989, 15.

*An "open office"—
a large office with
cubicles.*

terminals. Word processing centers, which have now been in use for a number of years, are usually considered part of the secretarial function. With personal computers or "intelligent" terminals and the appropriate software, executives or managers have their own system of sending and receiving information, often being able to bypass the secretary and communicate directly with other managers or whoever is to receive the intended messages. (Intelligent terminals, unlike "dumb" ones, have processing functions of their own; dumb ones are merely a link with the mainframe computer.)

Special Telephone Services

Besides numerous uses of telephone lines mentioned earlier, there are other special services, including leased lines, also called *tie-lines*, reserved for the exclusive use of a particular organization. For example, a corporation might use tie-lines to connect plants or branch offices in various cities.

Wide Area Telecommunication Service (WATS) is a telephone service that provides long-distance calling within a designated area for a flat fee instead of billing for individual calls. WATS provides for the origination of calls. An 800-service allows the reception of calls for a set fee, paid by the organization that accepts the calls.

Direct Distant Dialing, which is more economical than other methods of placing a call, is available almost everywhere in the United States for both voice and data. Message Telephone Services (MTS) and similar plans provide direct dialing, from push-button telephones only, at reduced rates.

International Direct Distant Dialing makes possible immediate telephone conversations with people in many foreign countries.

Executive Work Stations

Managers or other employees at executive work stations can receive information without going to data processing specialists in a general system.

An integrated information system may include terminals that provide both data processing and word processing, including text editing. A writer at a terminal can compose letters, memorandums, reports, or any other material in perfect typewritten form. If material is to be printed, it can be sent electronically to photocomposer equipment, which will prepare the material in camera-ready form.

Intelligent terminals can be used to create or recall written work, process it, store and retrieve it, and transmit it to a nearby office or over great distances. The writer can also dictate communications at the terminal for typists to prepare and send by conventional methods. Graphs, designs, flow charts, and similar work can be prepared through the use of the terminal.

Optical Character Readers

Optical character readers, also referred to as *optical scanners* or *OCR scanners*, recognize and interpret typewritten characters. Some of the newer scanners can read material prepared on regular typewriters; older scanners can read only a special typeface.

OCR scanners can be used to read written material into computers or word processors. Major advantages of using OCR scanners as an input medium are reduced input time and increased accuracy. Each page of a manuscript can be shown on a display terminal so that a typist can make desired changes. The corrected page is then printed or stored for future processing.

A recent development is a hand-held optical character reader described as Handscan. Thus, a page of typewitten text can be placed on a disk without keyboarding.

The Teletypewriter

The teletypewriter is a typewriter with a telephone dial located on the keyboard. Messages are keyboarded on the teletypewriter, transmitted over telephone lines, and printed automatically as hard copy at the receiving terminal. Telex and TWX are the two teletypewriter networks owned by Western Union. Some large organizations have their own teletypewriter networks for communication between distant offices.

Teletypewriters combine the advantages of a letter with those of a telephone call. They provide a written copy, yet permit typewritten conversations between people at distant locations. The use of teletypewriters is relatively inexpensive.

Telegrams sent by Western Union are transmitted by teletypewriters to receiving stations. Telegrams are usually telephoned by the sender to a Western Union office. An advantage of using telegrams is that tapes of telegrams are kept by Western Union; if necessary, these tapes can serve as proof of the contents of a message.

Mailgrams

Mailgrams, although more expensive than regular letters, provide several advantages. Mailgrams are sent by Western Union, using their computerized communications networks, to a teletypewriter located at a post office near the address of the receiver of the message. The teletypewriter prints the message, which is then put into an envelope and delivered by regular postal carriers.

Mailgrams imply a sense of importance and urgency. Sometimes they are used in the last stage of a credit collection series. They can be helpful in sales campaigns. Reply forms, to be returned by regular mail, can be attached.

Reprographics

The term *reprographics* refers to the making of duplicate copies. The term includes photocopiers and duplicators. Some reprographic equipment, when linked into the information system, can produce copies directly from electronic data.

Some new photocopiers can send information directly to a computer or transmit documents to another copier via telephone lines. Future models are expected to receive and print material directly from a computer.

Copiers can print on both sides of the paper, collate, and staple. Some copiers copy in color.

Photocopiers have almost replaced the use of carbon paper, although carbon paper is often more economical. Desktop copiers may soon be widely used to provide immediate access and prevent waiting.

Micrographics

Micrographics is the process of photographing documents in order to produce miniature transparencies, which are microforms such as microfilm or microfiche. These microforms require magnification in order to be read. Pages can be reduced as much as one-fiftieth of their original size. Files recorded on microforms require up to 94 percent less storage space than does ordinary paper stored in file cabinets.

Computer-stored records can be reproduced directly into microfilm. This process eliminates the need for a hard copy.

How You as a Communicator Will Be Affected by Changing Methods and Equipment

Technological changes affect us all. Although computers and related equipment provide opportunities for release from repetitive work so that our time can be spent more creatively, rapid changes are frustrating and frightening to many people. Resisting change of any kind is only human. When technological developments threaten employment status, prestige, and feelings of self-worth, as some people believe computers do, people are understandably reluctant to give up older methods and equipment. They believe that computers are bringing about a nonhuman and nonhumane society that is too impersonal and mechanistic. In addition, people see the many errors caused by computers, or at least those attributed to computers, and they prefer traditional human errors.

Communication is becoming faster, easier, and more direct. Mailed letters, as they are now used, are likely to decrease. More messages will be spoken and sent by voice mail or other methods of telecommunications, without being transferred to paper. A completely "paperless office," however, is likely to be rare or nonexistent.

Improved software will provide more help to the writer or other user of word processing equipment.

Sometime, no doubt, typewriters will be developed that will produce typewritten copy directly from spoken dictation. Such typewriters are now in existence, but their vocabularies are limited. Because of varying accents and tones of voice, usually these typewriters must be programmed for each dictator; this is an extremely expensive process. In addition, the finished transcript is only about 95 percent accurate.

Effective oral communication, always important, is becoming even more important. None of these changes in methods and equipment, however, mean that effective writing will decrease in value; the opposite is true. Whether words are written on paper, printed on a display screen, or transmitted from computer to computer has little bearing on the choice of words and their arrangement in a convincing message.

Summary

Changing technology affects the sending and receiving of business messages. These changing methods and media do not affect the importance of human communication through written and spoken words.

Word processing is a method that uses automated typewriting equipment to increase the production of written material and to decrease costs. It presents an alternative to the general-purpose secretary by allowing for a division of work. Systems are planned for receiving material from dictation. Word processing equipment can be tied to computers and other communicating equipment. Personal computers are widely used for word processing.

The automated electronic office consists of information and communication devices linked together, many of which can be accessed from individual computer terminals. Equipment in electronic offices includes, in addition to computer terminals, optical character readers, reprographic and micrographic equipment, and various other sending, receiving, and processing devices.

Electronic mail, voice mail, and facsimile transmission are three rapidly growing methods of business communications. All provide almost immediate delivery. Facsimile equipment (FAX) transmits exact copies of drawings, photographs, and other illustrations in addition to typewritten work. FAX is replacing or supplementing Telex in communication between countries.

A major purpose of technological changes in the sending and receiving of communications is cost control. Another is speed and accuracy of transmission.

1. Our nation is no longer predominantly a manufacturing society, but an _____ society.

2. In which decade were microcomputers first used?

3. What is meant by the term *paperless office?*

4–6. Name three advantages of using word processing instead of older methods of preparing written communications.

7. The workplace of an employee using a microcomputer or a computer terminal is referred to as an _____.

8–9. Some combination software packages include word processing, _____, and _____.

10. Scanners that can be used to read written material into computers are called

_____.

11. What is meant by the term *reprographics?*

12. What is meant by the term *micrographics?*

13. Briefly describe the purposes and uses of a teletypewriter.

14. Exact copies of documents are sent by _____ transmission.

15–17. What are three advantages of electronic mail?

18–19. Name one advantage and one disadvantage of teleconferencing.

20. What is an advantage of voice mail?

21. What do you believe is a disadvantage of voice mail?

(Related to material in Chapter 2 and principles of correct usage.) Insert necessary punctuation, including quotation marks, hyphens, and apostrophes, and remove punctuation that has been inserted incorrectly. Choose correct word from each pair or group. Make any other necessary changes.

1. Because the rise of two career marriages makes many professional people reluctant to move (companys, company's, companies, companies') are trying harder to link offices electronically.

2. Nothing endures but change is a quotation from Heraclitus an ancient philosopher who lived about 500 B.C.

3. Modern technology continues to change the media and methods of transmitting oral and written messages students must be aware of these changes.

4. Facsimiles of anything written typed drawn or photographed can be transmitted in a few seconds.

5. Automated sophisticated machines cannot be designed or operated without the use of communication between humans especially the application of human thought.

6. Successful business writers and speakers must have meaningful messages to send forth that is they must know what they are talking about.

7. The term "paperless office refers to an office where everything is recorded by electronic means not on paper.

8. Some people beleive that they recieve unnecessary messages through electronic mail. And voice mail.

9. (Principles, principals) of effective communication remain the same (regardless, irregardles) of the method of transmission.

10. Wise planning and use (affect, effect) the overall cost of word processing systems.

Problems

1–2. Repeat Problems 4 and 5, Chapter 1, except that your comment or bit of information should come from recently published sources that relate to topics discussed in Chapter 2. Perhaps the source that you used for the assignments in Chapter 1 was also on the subject of technological developments that affect communication in organizations. If so, find another; sources are plentiful. *The Business Periodicals Index, The Wall Street Journal Index,* and the more general guide to articles, *Readers' Guide to Periodical Literature,* all include lists of articles that pertain to this general topic.

3. Write a one- or two-page summary of an article on a topic related to this chapter. You can find this article through the indexes mentioned above or from other sources. Give the complete bibliographical reference to your published source, as illustrated in Appendix C.

4. If you are employed or have been employed, write a letter telling your instructor of your experiences, if any, with computers or any of the equipment mentioned in Chapter 2. Limit your letter to one typewritten page. If you have no experience in using computers or any of the other equipment mentioned in Chapter 2, convey this information to your instructor, limiting your letter to one typewritten page. (See Appendix B for letter format.)

5. Be prepared to present orally in class the information included in the answer to Problem 4.

CHAPTER 3

Choosing Appropriate and Effective Words

Have you ever thought of the many ways in which words affect our lives?

Do you believe that words have definite, exact meanings, which are given in dictionaries, and that you will become an effective writer and speaker—and achieve harmonious relationships with others—if you can only learn these dictionary definitions?

Do you feel that when you know these definitions, you will be able to handle communication problems logically and sensibly—that is, with the application of common sense?

The answers to these questions, with the exception of the first, would be "not necessarily" or "it depends." Many words have emotional effects, and they are far from exact. Our relationships with other people, which are built almost entirely on verbal and nonverbal messages, depend on all our past experiences and our maturity.

The Importance of Words

Our world is filled with words. Unless we shut ourselves off from them, they come to us constantly—from television and radio, from newspapers and magazines, from the pulpit, from professors and other lecturers. Sometimes it seems that we are bombarded with words, but we in turn add to the total profusion. An overload of information is one of the reasons we sometimes have difficulty in listening to words we truly wish and need to hear.

People have long been aware of the importance of words in our lives, as shown by many maxims and proverbial sayings. For example, from the Book of Proverbs, "A word fitly spoken is like apples of gold in pictures of silver"; from Don Quixote, "An honest man's word is as good as his bond." Mark Twain said, "There is as much difference between the right word and the nearly right word as there is between lightning and the lightning bug." And the common sayings, "I could have bitten off my tongue" and "I really put my foot in my mouth" exemplify our concern with the use and misuse of language.

Words, particularly when arranged into slogans, influence not only our personal and business life but also the history of nations and of the world. Consider the ways that the following words have affected the thought and actions of the American people and the course of American history: "Give me liberty or give me death" (Patrick Henry); "We have nothing to fear but fear itself" (Franklin D. Roosevelt); "We shall overcome" (song and slogan of Civil Rights movement); "Ask not what your country can do for you, but what you can do for your country" (John F. Kennedy).

Presidential campaigns have been won or lost because of slogans. Advertising campaigns, tasteful or otherwise, make extensive use of catch phrases. Some become so well known that they can be considered part of the language, at least temporarily. Remember "Where's the beef?" and "I can't believe I ate the whole thing"?

Communication Brief

By any standard, English is a remarkable language. It is, to begin with, the native tongue of some 300,000,000 people—the largest speech community in the world except for Mandarin Chinese. Even more remarkable is its geographic spread, in which it is second to none: its speakers range from Point Barrow, Alaska, to the Falkland Islands near Cape Horn; from the Shetland Islands north of Scotland to Capetown at the southern tip of Africa; from Hong Kong to Australia's island state of Tasmania. It is the predominant language in two of the six inhabited continents (North America and Australia), and possesses a large block of speakers in a third (Europe) and a sizable one in a fourth (Africa).

English is also by far the most important "second language" in the world. It is spoken by tens of millions of educated Europeans and Japanese, is the most widely studied foreign tongue in both the U.S.S.R. and China, and serves as an "official" language in more than a dozen other countries whose populations total more than a billion.

Robert Claiborne, *Our Marvelous Native Tongue* (New York: Times Books, 1983), 3.

Question: When I look up words in a dictionary, I find that the same word can be more than one part of speech. Is there one simple rule to go by? Does knowing the parts of speech really make any difference?

Answer: Yes, recognizing the parts of speech, as they are used in particular sentences, is an aid to constructing and punctuating effective sentences.

No, there is no one simple rule. Have you found such a rule for anything else? Knowing the eight parts of speech will not make you a good writer. Knowing the names of oceans, rivers, and lakes will not enable you to swim. Recognizing the parts of speech will not make you creative, interesting, or knowledgeable about your subject matter.

Learning the parts of speech will not completely change your life, but the knowledge is practical and useful. If you were a mechanic, you would perhaps want to know the difference between an engine and a back bumper. An engine is what makes your car go. A verb is what makes your sentence go.

Words are the tools—as well as the building material—of your writing. It is possible, however, that you now write well even if you have forgotten the parts of speech. You may have developed writing ability and clear thinking through wide reading. Even if this is the case, your writing can become more exact and concise because of your knowledge of words and how they behave in sentences.

The eight parts of speech are noun, verb, pronoun, adjective, adverb, conjunction, preposition, and interjection. Their roles in particular sentences depends on how they are used.

The maxim "Sticks and stones can break my bones, but words can never harm me" is far from being accurate. In some cases, words can harm more than sticks and stones: they can lead to frowns, misunderstandings, anger, and the use of sticks and stones, to say nothing of the far more devastating weapons of modern warfare.

Simple, Direct, and Natural Words

Work for a simple, direct, and natural writing style. A letter or memorandum should sound like informal conversation with your reader.

Short words, provided that they best express the desired meaning, should be preferred to long words. Short words do not, however, always best promote readability. An unusual short word that the reader is not likely to understand is not as desirable as a more familiar longer word. Also, when we are writing to people who are specialists in our own field, the longer, more specialized word is preferable to a shorter one that is used mistakenly to make the written material simple and more readable.

Short words, appropriately chosen, not only increase readability but also

Communication Brief

Writing works best when it fits the sounds and rhythms of speaking and listening. Perhaps that is why when we reject one expression for another as we write, we often say: "Oh, the first one didn't sound right."

Write as you speak—when you are speaking very well—because you will then write more clearly and humanly. And people will understand you better.

Arn Tibbetts, *Practical Business Writing* (Boston: Little, Brown & Co., 1987), 135.

help to form a vivid and forceful writing style. Compare the effectiveness of these words.

Instead of	Why not use
approbation	approval
approximately	about
ameliorate	improve
incorporate	include
interrogate	ask
promulgate	publish
peruse	read
utilize	use
engrossment	attention
expectancy	hope
utilizable	useful
salience	importance

Choose words carefully, even when you are trying, as you should, to simplify. Few words have exact synonyms, long or short. Find the word most likely to express your exact meaning to the mind of the reader—but remember that this word is most often a short, familiar one.

Denotative and Connotative Meanings

Words have special characteristics of their own, aside from their dictionary, or denotative, meanings. They have connotative meanings: either general connotative meanings to most persons who see or hear the word, or special connotative meanings to particular individuals because of their specific experiences with the word.

The *denotative meaning* is the relation between a word and its referent, the thing to which the word refers. For example, you could point to your automobile instead of saying *automobile* or to your house instead of saying *house.* As you say or write the word *house,* for example, the word stands for the object.

The *connotative meaning* is the suggestion a word acquires through association; it includes qualitative judgment. Connotative meanings are based on experiences, attitudes, beliefs, and emotions. Denotative meanings are informative, while connotative meanings have affective results.

We cannot rely only on denotative (or "dictionary") meanings. Complete dictionaries, however, give various illustrations of words in the context of how they are used and often give some indication of their connotative meaning.

Although no word is completely specific, regardless of usage and definition, denotative meanings are considered more concrete and tangible than connotative meanings, which are based on experiences, attitudes, beliefs, and emotions. To many minds, the word *home* brings pleasant memories of family, fireside, laughter, good food, friends, comfort, and security. The word *house* has a more neutral meaning. If you sell real estate, do you refer to a piece of property as a residence, a building, a house, or a home?

If your prospective buyer doesn't like the property, he or she may think of it as a shack, a dump, or a hovel. If one perceives the place as particularly desirable, the neutral *house* may become a *mansion* or a *dreamhouse*. A *cottage by the sea* may be thought of as a *dream come true;* a cottage that must accommodate a large family on a year-around basis will be purchased only because the owner cannot afford a more spacious domicile.

Regardless of the words with which it is described, a house is most likely to sell quickly if it is painted a soft yellow, according to real estate experts. Colors as well as words have emotional effects.

Words that usually have unpleasant connotations beyond their actual denotative meanings are *criticize, you claim,* and *cheap*. Although the word *criticize* means to evaluate either positively or negatively, the word almost always connotes an unfavorable evaluation.

We cannot know and control individual connotations based on the experience of the individual reader or listener. Although *criticize, cheap,* and similar words and phrases are likely to convey similar emotions to most people, other words have various connotative meanings to individuals based on their particular experiences.

For example, if a person has had an automobile accident on Perkins Road, the words alone will elicit unpleasant memories and feelings. (He or she may not want the house you are selling on Perkins Road, even if it is painted yellow.) If a young man is in love with a girl named Linda, another girl with the same name will seem more attractive than one named Anna Lou. If a person has been spurred and bitten by a rooster, the word *rooster* arouses in her or his mind a vivid picture, not of an industrious early bird awaking the world, but of a foul fowl that she or he never wants to see or hear of again.

Although a comprehensive and reliable dictionary remains an essential tool for all of us, learning the true nature of words consists of far more than memorizing definitions. Because words have various denotative as well as connotative meanings, humorous misuse sometimes occurs in the translation of passages from one language to another. As an example, the *body* of an automobile was once translated to *corpse.*

Aside from their emotional effect, words have their own particular shades of meaning. *Although words are described as synonyms for other words, there are few real synonyms.* Words are often similar in meaning to other words; but, because of their particular connotations or the context in which they are ordinarily used, they cannot be substituted for their near-synonyms without some slight change in meaning.

A word is said to have a weak connotation if it has no strong or significant overtones; such a word is also described as being neutral, although in fact no word is completely neutral to all readers and listeners. As mentioned, a *house* has more of a neutral tone than does *home*, which has favorable and pleasant implications. The word *student* is more neutral than *scholar* or *bookworm*.

Words connote high and low status. Garbage collectors are becoming "sanitation engineers"; janitors are called "maintenance engineers," "building engineers," or "managers." Salespersons are referred to as "representatives," "special representatives," or "registered representatives." Secretaries want to be referred to as "executive secretaries" or "administrative assistants." In our status-conscious society, perhaps titles are important. The mere change of title can be a morale booster and an asset to a person moving to another department or organization.

In department stores, the "complaint department" became the "adjustment department" and then the "customer service department." A credit card is now often called a "courtesy card."

Words pertaining to liquor are avoided by some individuals, corporations, and government agencies. Funds for cocktail parties are referred to as *entertainment* or *public relations*. The State Department has drawn money for liquor from a *representation fund*.

Consider the implications of the following words:

- scheme—plan—program of action
- proposition—proposal—presentation
- gamble—speculation—calculated risk
- scrawny—skinny—slim—slender
- stupid—retarded—exceptional
- stupid—unsound—unadvised
- favoritism—leaning—undetachment

You could make long lists of similar words. Do you recognize that words have differing and definite personalities of their own?

Changing Meanings of Words

The English language, like all other living languages, is constantly changing. Could you expect it *not* to do so? It must change to meet our needs. The change is neither good nor bad, but inevitable.

New words are added and others become obsolete. Many words and phrases are borrowed from other languages, as they always have been. Technology adds to the vocabulary of general usage the words that were first used as specialized terminology, jargon, or slang of a particular field or occupation.

"New" words are not necessarily ones that have never been used before. They may be old ones used in a new way. For example, the term *hardware* is used in connection with computers to describe the equipment and machinery with which data are processed. *Software* refers to instructions and programs stored on computer disks.

Some slang finds its way into dictionaries and becomes acceptable even for standard or formal usage. Much slang, though, fades away and is forgotten, such as "It's the berries" and "the cat's pajamas" of the twenties. Other slang remains for centuries; *bones* was the slang term for dice in Chaucer's day and it remains somewhat in use today. Although dice are no longer made of bones, but of plastic, this fact probably has little to do with the decrease in the use of the term. Words remain in general use long after the original reason for being has disappeared.

Shakespeare used "beat it" to mean "go away." The word *dough*, meaning money, has been in use for more than one hundred years.

Examples of words now in standard usage that were once considered slang are *mob; phone* for *telephone; phony; blizzard; movie;* and *type* for *typewrite.* (An earlier use of the word *typewriter* was to describe the person who used the machine as a typewriter, not as a typist.)

Slang, like more formal language, often uses contradictory terms to express the same idea. A person who grew up in the thirties or forties perhaps still uses the phrase "not so hot" to mean something that is not at all "cool."

Many thousands of words have changed since the time of Chaucer. Spelling has also changed, as well as what is considered correct usage. At one time, "you was" was correct; now only "you were" is acceptable. Words change in shades of meaning, as well as completely reversing themselves. At one time, *silly* meant *holy; fond* meant *foolish; tree* meant *beam;* and *beam* meant *tree.* The *charity* of the King James Bible now means *love.*

Examples of other words that have changed in meaning are *naughty*, which meant *poor,* or one who had naught. *Intoxicated* meant *poisoned*—and now *poisoned* is slang (or the actuality) for *intoxicated.* A *comrade* was originally one who shared a room, and a *companion* was one who shared food. In the early 1990s, however, we have yet to coin an acceptable description for half of a living-together couple or for their relationship.

The English language, like all others, has always been in a process of change. Compared to previous centuries, written material today includes shorter sentences and wording that is more direct, natural, informal, and conversational. All these changes make a great deal of sense. As in conversation itself, however, writing is either stimulating, mediocre, or banal, according to the particular participants.

Formal and Informal Language

Language in the United States is often less formal than it was one hundred years ago, in both writing and speaking. Although much writing and speech in professional and business situations cannot be described as formal, neither is it extremely informal. As in all communication situations, you must consider the environment, the message, and the audience. When in doubt, use a touch of formality—provided you do not misinterpret the word *formal* as it pertains to communication. All writing and speech should be natural, simple, and correct. Regardless of the formality of the situation, long words and sentences are less desirable than well-chosen, understandable, and emphatic ones.

Some communication situations are more formal than others. Your letter to a member of Congress or the president of your company will differ in format and wording from a note that you scribble on the back of an envelope to be left on a friend's door or automobile.

You behave and speak more formally at a wedding or a funeral than you do at a neighborhood party. You don't ordinarily wear to church the attire in which you wash your car or take your dog to the vet. (*Vet* is an example of an informal word that is not stored in your word processor's memory.)

Some people outside the United States believe that we are too informal, sometimes to the point of being disrespectful. They do not like our free and early use of given names, particularly in business offices and with older people. Many Americans consider such use to be appropriately personal and friendly, both in writing and speaking, and the use of "Mr.," "Ms.," or "Mrs." to be overly formal. A touch of formality, however, at least toward new acquaintances, is a better approach than familiarity that could be offensive.

The use of slang should always be avoided in formal writing, although it can sometimes be used effectively in casual conversation. (As with many other words, *formal* and *casual* are relative. How formal is formal and how casual is casual?)

The informal style may occasionally make use of some kinds of slang. Slang, however, should be used with the utmost discretion, for several reasons. First, slang is often not nationwide, so it may not be understood by the reader. Second, even the mildest slang offends some persons; or, if it doesn't offend, it is in questionable taste and unbusinesslike. Third, slang becomes quickly dated, and what seems fresh and new to the writer may have already been discarded by the reader. Fourth, the use of unusual or startling words or phrases may be distracting and thus delay the reception of the message.

Regardless of how the writing is described or how formal the situation, the writing should not sound unnatural, stilted, or pretentious. A scholarly essay will be more formal than a routine memorandum, but both the essay and the memorandum should be interesting, natural, and easy to read. Both should use correct English, and both should be arranged and worded with the reader in mind.

Strictly formal writing will not include contractions, any expression that could be considered slang, or any abbreviated sentences or sentence fragments. It is likely to be written in the impersonal tone, with no first- or second-person pronouns. The informal style will most likely use the personal tone. It may include contractions and casual conversational phrases or modes of expression.

However the writing is described or however formal the situation, the writing should not be unnatural, stilted, or pretentious. Both formal and informal writing should be grammatically correct, and both should be arranged and worded with the reader in mind.

Your choice of writing style—light or serious, informal or formal—must be influenced by your relationship with the reader and the subject matter of your message. A light, humorous tone, no matter how clever, is inappropriate in some situations. On the other hand, business and professional communications are often concerned with subjects of less than immortal impact—although they are desirable or necessary for whatever purpose they are planned to accomplish.

Some words are designated in dictionaries as *informal*. Other designations are *colloquial*, which, according to *Random House Dictionary*, means "characteristic or appropriate to ordinary conversation rather than formal speech or writ-

Question: Is it acceptable practice to begin a sentence with *and* or *but*? Is it correct to end a sentence with a preposition? *Improve Your Writing*

Answer: Yes, provided that such use does not result in an awkward construction and accomplishes the desired emphasis.

Warnings against these two constructions are often given because amateur writers may use them inappropriately and perhaps too frequently. Also keep in mind that the first word of a sentence receives more emphasis than words within the sentence. Do not use *and* or *but* to begin a sentence if you should use some other word to emphasize another idea.

H. W. Fowler (a recognized authority on English usage) makes this statement about *and*, additionally referring to the same statement in regard to *but*.

That it is a solecism to begin a sentence with *and* is a faintly lingering superstition. The *OED* [*Oxford English Dictionary*] gives examples ranging from the 10th to the 19th chapter; the Bible is full of them.

H. W. Fowler, *A Dictionary of Modern Language Usage,* 2nd ed., revised by Sir Ernest Gowers (Oxford: Oxford University Press, 1965), 29.

Similar advice applies to a preposition at the end of a sentence. Some prepositions at the end of sentences are not misplaced, but unnecessary; for example, "Where is it at?" In other sentences a preposition should definitely not be placed at the end because to do so results in an awkward, amateurish construction or does not achieve the desired emphasis.

A well-known anecdote about Winston Churchill relates his opinion. A proofreader checked a speech that Churchill had written and moved a preposition that Churchill had placed at the end of a sentence. Churchill wrote this note: "This is the kind of nonsense up with which I will not put."

ing." (The word *colloquial* is sometimes thought to mean *regional*—that is, pertaining to speech in particular regions of the country. Although regional speech is a form of colloquial language, not all colloquial usage is regional.)

To repeat and reemphasize, formal words (or at least those that are not definitely informal) are not unnecessarily long. They should not sound pompous or pretentious, nor should they be chosen mainly to impress or to display an extensive vocabulary. Well-chosen words, regardless of the formality of the occasion, are almost always short, familiar, natural words.

Words and phrases inappropriate for most business writing are shown below, with synonyms or near-synonyms that are more appropriate.

Too informal	More appropriate
(Slang, colloquial, or regional expressions; trite words or phrases)	
hassle	struggle, difficulty
bread, dough, green stuff	money
mix-up, foul-up, snafu	confusion, chaos

Too informal	More appropriate
(Slang, colloquial, or regional expressions; trite words or phrases)	
kiddies	children
hubby	husband
kibitz	confer, consult
tip, two cents' worth	advice
sweet talk, soft soap	exaggeration, flattery
hang in there, stick it out	persevere
steer clear of, not touch with a ten-foot pole	avoid, evade, circumvent
hankering, pining	yearning
wild about	enthusiastic

Personal and Impersonal Writing Styles

The *impersonal writing style* is more formal than the personal writing style. *It is ordinarily used when a report or other written material is considered formal in format and wording.* Written material can convey formality even with the use of first- and second-person pronouns. *Formal writing style and impersonal tone are not synonymous, although they are often used together in the same report.*

The *impersonal writing style* is also referred to as the *third-person objective writing style.* It includes no *I*'s, *we*'s, *you*'s, or other first- or second-person pronouns.

Most writing for business and the professions is in the personal tone. (The use of *I* and *we* is excessive, even when using the personal tone, if it gives an appearance of expressing the *I-attitude,* not the *you-attitude*.) *Almost all letters and memorandums and many reports are written in the personal tone.*

An advantage of the impersonal tone is that this style of writing seems more objective and nonbiased because the writer is not speaking of himself or herself. The choice of writing style does not affect real objectivity; nevertheless, because it appears to do so, many persons prefer the impersonal tone. Another more important advantage is that by using no first- or second-person pronouns more emphasis is given to the facts and analyses being presented, which is where the emphasis should be.

Many traditionally minded readers of reports or other business writing, with the exception of letters or memorandums, will judge writing in the impersonal tone to be more professional, more objective, more scientific, and more carefully prepared than one written in the personal tone. If you are likely to encounter this reaction, you are decreasing the likelihood of the acceptance of your ideas by using the personal tone. The use of *I*'s, *we*'s and other first- and second-person pronouns may be a form of noise, distracting the reader's mind from whatever it is that you are trying to say.

Examples of passages in the personal and the impersonal writing styles are as follows:

Personal

I recommend that our department adopt a flexible time schedule.

Impersonal

The Marketing Department should adopt a flexible time schedule.

Personal

You will notice that prices of some items have decreased about 5 percent.

Personal (implied *you*)

Notice that prices of some items have decreased about 5 percent.

Impersonal

Prices on some items have decreased about 5 percent.

Personal

Please telephone me when I can help.

Impersonal

Employees should telephone their supervisors when they need help.

Do not use the impersonal style unnecessarily. The personal tone is more friendly, natural, and direct. Some kinds of material, however, such as news releases and many reports, should be written in the impersonal style with absolutely no *I*'s, *we*'s, *you*'s, or other first- or second-person pronouns.

The Language of Business

There really is no "language of business," except for some specialized terms that exist in particular organizations, industries, offices, or occupations. The business jargon that some writers use is made up of unnecessary, trite, and wordy phrases. Some of these phrases are as follows:

- enclosed herewith
- enclosed herewith please find
- we beg to call your kind attention to
- kindly be advised
- in reply to your recent favor we wish to state
- thanking you for your kind attention
- the same being at hand I wish to state

Yes, these cumbersome phrases are still used in many letters and memorandums, but, fortunately, their use is decreasing. Business people seem to be more likely to include such unnatural wording than other writers.

The wordy phrases and trite business jargon cited in the following list should almost always be omitted or simplified. Phrases marked with an asterisk can safely be put into a "never" category for use in business writing. All should ordinarily be avoided because they are slow, wordy, and old-fashioned.

- it has come to my attention

- in the amount of (for)
- to the total amount of (for)
- for the amount of (for)
- amounting to (for)
- totaling the sum of (for)
- be assured, rest assured
- *be advised, *be informed, *consider yourself informed, *this is to inform you, *this is for your information
- herewith, herein, attached herewith, attached hereto, enclosed herewith, *enclosed please find
- *beg to state, wish to state, regret to state
- *reference to same, *compliance with same, *consideration of same
- *we beg to call your attention to the fact that
- *thank you in advance, *thanking you for your time, *thanking you for your consideration
- *we wish to remain, yours truly
- as of this date, as of this writing, as of the present time
- be kind enough
- due to the fact that, in view of the fact that
- *thank you kindly, *kindly, *we kindly thank you for
- at an early date
- along this line
- *we beg to remain
- pursuant to your request
- *the undersigned (except in legal papers)
- pending receipt of
- for the purpose of, for the reason that, due to the fact that (for, to, because)
- in spite of the fact that (because)
- evident and apparent
- your esteemed favor
- please do not hesitate . . .

Closely related to the wordy and trite phrases listed above are *fad* words or phrases, which soon become trite and meaningless because of overuse. Some of these overused words and phrases are as follows:

- at this point in time
- the bottom line
- cost effective
- effectuated
- hopefully (although not actually incorrect, it is becoming as frequent as "you know")
- to optimize

- to prioritize
- viable
- ballpark figure
- back to square one
- eyeball to eyeball
- interface (used to describe human communication)

Positive and Pleasant Words Versus Negative and Unpleasant Words

Positive and pleasant words are more effective than negative, unpleasant ones, as discussed in the preceding section "Denotative and Connotative Meanings" and in detail in Chapter 5, "Building Goodwill through Communication." Although some written and spoken communication must convey unfavorable information and such information must be made clear, even unfavorable messages can be expressed in positive words or in neutral, objective words.

Avoid extremely negative words such as *fail, reject, criticize,* and similar words. Express your meaning from the reader's or listener's point of view. Emphasize the positive aspects of a situation, not the negative.

Objective Words Versus Biased, Judgmental Words

Judgmental words, especially derogatory ones, should be used with caution, if at all. Objectivity is stressed in the discussion of research and report writing, but it is also important in all business writing.

Some of the many words that should ordinarily be omitted because of their negative connotations are as follows:

unfair	bribery
insane	discrimination
unheard of	high-pressure tactics
lazy	exorbitant
incompetent	senile
unbelievable	suspicious
the worst ever	gullible
calamity	unbelievable

At times unpleasant or negative descriptions must be given, as when evaluating employees. When such information is necessary, state specific facts, not your own negative opinions. Examples include the following:

Instead of

Joe Brown is irresponsible. He does not come to work half the time and is always late.

Write or say

Joe Brown has been absent for no stated reason seventeen days during the past year. He has been at least thirty minutes late eleven times.

Although judgmental words that express pleasant and positive ideas can and should be used more freely than those that express negative or accusing thoughts, even these nonobjective words should be used with discretion. Although so-called emotional wording is often used in sales messages and elsewhere, such usage is not as convincing as positive, concrete, and specific description of favorable attributes or circumstances.

Instead of

This marvelous Ivory soap is wonderful because it is pure.

And instead of

Ivory soap is amazingly pure.

And instead of

You will be astonished at the purity level of Ivory soap.

Prefer

Ivory soap is 99 and 44/100ths percent pure.

Instead of

Our superb president has provided incredible advantages for all of us.

Prefer

President Clifft has increased our profit-sharing income by 20 percent, provided an organized system of recognition and promotion, and encouraged employee participation in decision making.

Be especially careful to avoid nonobjective judgmental words, either positive or negative, in reports or other informational material.

Specific, Concrete Words Versus Vague, General Words

Ordinarily you should use concrete, specific words rather than general, nonspecific words. (For the sake of diplomacy, however, sometimes general, nonspecific words are preferable, as described further in Chapter 5.)

Instead of	Prefer
a leading newspaper	*The New York Times*
soon	next Thursday, January 9 (within ten days)
heavy paper	24-pound weight paper
computers	IBM personal computers

Instead of	Prefer
a good return	10.23 percent interest rate, compounded quarterly
a good beginning compensation	$19,000 annual beginning salary
contact	telephone (write) (arrange a meeting)
well educated	earned a master's degree in English
a well-known company	Federal Express
a high test score	a comprehensive score of 96.8 on the Graduate Record Examination
a long table	a 10-foot long conference table
a short speech	seven minutes
a long speech	fifty-nine minutes

For a number of obvious reasons, you cannot or should not be completely specific in all writing or speech. At times you should express your ideas in general terms to achieve diplomacy or an appropriate psychological approach. At times you may not know exact details; for example, you may not be sure that a conference table is exactly ten feet long. In other instances your reader or listener may not expect or want complete descriptions. If you work in an office equipped only with IBM personal computers, you need not describe them as such over and over.

Use specific, concrete, exact wording when it is possible and appropriate. Your writing and speech will be more clear, interesting, exact, and forceful.

Communication Brief

I got a polite, written reprimand the other day from the folks who invented the stuff you pour into your cat's litter box.

In a story, I used the words "Kitty Litter" generically, without capitalizing them or mentioning that Kitty Litter is a brand name. To tell the truth, I didn't know Kitty Litter was a brand name. Well, the people whose job it is to scour all the newspapers and periodicals in America for lower-cased Kitty Litters caught me.

Newspaper people run into this kind of thing every now and then. For instance, you can't use "Kleenex" if you mean just any old tissue. Instead of "STYROFOAM" (capitalize the whole thing), the trademark watchdogs suggest you say "a light polystyrene plastic foam." Right.

"We could lose our trademark if we didn't routinely protest its misuse," said Deborah Kayden, when I called to ask about the fuss over "Kitty Litter."

As a young reporter, I spent a month's salary on a Nikon camera, but my mother brought me back to earth. I proudly strutted through the house, trying to look nonchalant about the gleaming black hardware dangling from my shoulder. "Go snap a picture of my Thanksgiving table with your new Brownie," she said.

Any cleanser is "Bon Ami" to Mother, no matter if the label says "Comet" or "Dutch." All luggage is "Samsonite." To a lot of folks, all refrigerators are "Frigidaires."

Which would bother me a lot more if I owned "Whirlpool" or "Norge" or "General Electric" than if I owned "Frigidaire," but then there's no figuring corporate law.

Rheta Grimsley Johnson, *America's Faces* (Memphis: St. Luke's Press, 1987), 327–328.

Nondiscriminatory Language

Speech or writing can be inconsiderate and undiplomatic when words considered sexist by the reader or listener are used. Although the speaker or writer may be absolutely fair and nondiscriminatory in thought and actions, discriminatory language can build distrust and decrease acceptance and understanding.

Avoid Masculine Pronouns Except When Referring Specifically to Males

The English language has no singular pronoun to represent both sexes. Because of this lack, for centuries masculine pronouns (*he, him, his, himself*) were used with the understanding that they represented either gender.

Although masculine pronouns are still used by both men and women as generic words to indicate either gender, you are wise to avoid such use. It is offensive to many people. Sexist language can destroy goodwill.

In the past, masculine pronouns were used in such sentences as

Obsolete language and equipment; discriminatory his

> An engineer must know how to use his slide rule.

At the time the word *his* was more logical than it is today, but it is still likely to occur in such sentences as

Updated equipment; discriminatory his

> An engineer must know how to use his computer.

The idea that only men can be engineers is now as outdated as the slide rule. All occupations are open to women, but language is slow to reflect this change.

Neither masculine nor feminine pronouns should be used to describe a person whose sex is unknown. For example, do not refer to a secretary or a nurse as *she* unless you are referring to a particular woman who is a secretary or nurse. To do so is to imply that only women are secretaries or nurses or, worse, that only women should be secretaries or nurses.

In the sentences about the engineer used above, *his* is unnecessary in reference to either the slide rule or the computer. The simple article *a* is sufficient, whether or not the engineer actually owns the slide rule or the computer. Substituting *a* or *the* or reconstructing the sentence in some other way to avoid using pronouns is one of the most appropriate and convenient ways of avoiding *he, his, or him.*

Another method of attaining nondiscriminatory writing is to use plural nouns. For example, instead of

Avoid

> An accountant can update his knowledge by attending seminars

change the sentence to

Prefer

> Accountants can update their knowledge . . .

Another method of avoiding generic use of masculine or feminine pronouns is to repeat the noun, although this method should be used with discretion in order to avoid repetition. Also avoid frequent use of *he or she*, although the term may be used when there is no other way to avoid sexist wording and to make your meaning clear. Overuse of *he or she* is distracting and results in awkward writing.

Sometimes the passive voice can be used to avoid pronouns, although this method should also be used sparingly because the active voice is often more direct, concise, and forceful. For example, instead of writing

> Each employee should sign and return his approved vacation request form   } *Avoid*

say

> Approved vacation request forms should be signed and returned.   } *Prefer*

In this particular illustration, the sentence with the verb in the passive voice is shorter than the previous one. Apart from the elimination of *his*, the second sentence is preferable because emphasis is upon *approved vacation request forms*, where the emphasis should ordinarily be placed. If the writer wants to emphasize *each employee* and leave the sentence in the first arrangement, *the* can be used to replace *his*.

This sentence also could be expressed with a plural noun, as

> All employees should sign and return their approved vacation request forms.   } *Prefer*

Still another method of avoiding masculine pronouns is to use *you*, as discussed in preceding portions of this chapter. In the preceding example, if you are writing *to* the employees instead of *about* them, use *you* because it is more direct, friendly, and interesting, in addition to being a method of avoiding *his*. To make the preceding sentence more tactful and diplomatic, omit *should* and word the sentence in this way:

> Please sign and return your approved vacation request form.   } *Best of all*

Avoid Other Forms of Discriminatory Language

In addition to masculine pronouns used to designate either sex, several other kinds of words are viewed as sexist. Do not use such terms as *woman attorney, male nurse, woman doctor,* or *poetess*. Use *attorney, nurse, doctor,* and *poet*.

Do not say *girl* or *my girl* when referring to an assistant who is a woman. Instead, call her your assistant or, preferably, refer to her by name.

Do not use the term *businessman* unless you are referring to a particular man. Prefer *executive, business manager, businessperson,* or some other descriptive and accurate term. A *businesswoman* may be described by this term, but prefer *executive, business manager, vice-president,* or another word that accurately and fairly describes her position.

Instead of *salesman*, when the sex is unknown, use *sales representative* or *salesperson*.

Instead of *foreman,* use *supervisor*.

Question: When should words and phrases be abbreviated and when should they be spelled out in full?

Answer: When writing letters, memorandums, and reports, ordinarily you should not abbreviate except for a few well-known exceptions.

Exceptions include two-letter state abbreviations in addresses (for example, *MO* for Missouri and *NY* for New York); courtesy titles and other designations customarily abbreviated, such as *Mr., Mrs., Dr., Jr., Sr., Ph.D.,* and *M.D.;* abbreviations that are a part of a company name, such as *Inc., Co., Ltd.;* and expressions of time, such as *a.m., p.m., CST, MST, A.D.,* and *B.C.*

The courtesy title *Miss* is not followed by a period, although *Ms.* is followed by a period. *Miss* is a word in itself, thus it needs no period. *Ms.* is an abbreviation, but no one has yet decided what it is an abbreviation of. (Please do not expect customary and expected conventions to be completely logical. Even so, we are usually wiser to go along with expected usage. To do otherwise creates distraction, at least momentarily, diverting the reader's attention from the meaning of our words to such things as the use or omission of periods.)

Abbreviations are frequently used in technical writing, tables, and statistical material.

An acronym, a form of abbreviation, is derived from the initial letters of the complete form; for example, OPEC for Organization of Petroleum Exporting Countries. In report writing, indicate the meaning of an acronym the first time it is used; for example, ''OPEC (Organization of Petroleum Exporting Countries) is responsible. . . .'' The acronym may be used alone after it is once identified.

The word *chairman* is still used by many men and women, and some women prefer the term, saying that it is the name of a position, not a sexist term. Many others don't like it. Unless you are sure that the woman to whom you are referring chooses to be addressed as *chairman,* use some other word, such as *chairperson, chairwoman, presiding officer, coordinator,* or *department head.* In all instances, follow known preferences. If, for example, the head of a college department refers to herself as chairman of the department and shows her title on letters in this way, you are being discourteous if you address her as *Chairperson* or *Chairwoman.*

From the same standpoint, address women as *Ms., Mrs.,* or *Miss* according to their known preferences. If you do not know preferences, use *Ms.,* which is used more and more to refer to all women. (In examples of letters in this book, the use of a title other than *Ms.* is based on the assumption that the writer of the letter knew that the woman to whom the letter was addressed prefers *Mrs.* or *Miss.*) Women have the right to use the title they prefer, just as they have the right to spell or pronounce their names any way they wish. Writers are being discourteous when they do not accede to these wishes, whatever their opinions about sexist language. (See Appendix B for examples of how women may show their titles following their names.)

Frequently Confused or Misused Words

accept, except

- *Accept* means "to receive with approval."
- *Except* means "excluding."
  - All the employees *except* Mr. Jones *accepted* the small gifts.

adapt, adept, adopt

- *Adapt* means "to make suitable or fit," as for a particular use, purpose, or situation.
- *Adept* means "highly skilled, well trained, thoroughly proficient."
- *Adopt* means "to take by free choice into a close relationship, previously not existing."
  - With a few minor changes we can *adapt* this room for use as a study.
  - Because of his many years of experience, Bill is quite *adept* at newspaper writing.
  - The young couple has plans to *adopt* a child within the next year.

advice, advise

- *Advice* is a noun that means a "view, opinion, judgment."
- *Advise* is a verb that means "to give an opinion, inform, consider."
  - His *advice* was to think first, then respond with an answer.
  - The captain will *advise* the tourists of the risk involved as they board his vessel.

affect, effect

- *Affect* is a verb meaning "to influence."
- *Effect,* used as a verb, means "to bring about." *Effect* is also a noun meaning "result."
  - The weather *affects* our moods.
  - Do you think we could *effect* a change in working hours?
  - What will be the *effect* of the change?

all together, altogether

- *All together* means "in one group."
- *Altogether* means "entirely."
  - The committee members were *all together* when the vote was taken.
  - The committee members were *altogether* in agreement.

already, all ready

- *Already* means "previously."
- *All ready* means "entirely ready."
  - The secretary had *already* opened the office.
  - She had the conference room *all ready* for the meeting.

appraise, apprise

- *Appraise* means "to estimate value."
- *Apprise* means "to inform" or "to advise."

capital, capitol

- *Capital* means the city or town that is the official seat of government.
- *Capitol* is the building that contains the governmental offices. (Often not capitalized when referring to state capitol buildings.)

cite, sight, site

- *Cite* means "to quote."
- *Sight* means "something seen."
- *Site* means "position or location."

complement, compliment

- *Complement* means "to complete."
- *Compliment* means "to praise."

continual, continuous

- A *continual* action implies that the action is often occurring, but is not *continuous,* which means "uninterrupted."

council, counsel

- *Council* is a noun meaning "a group of persons delegated to give advice."
- *Counsel* used as a noun means "advice"; used as a verb, counsel means "to give advice."

credible, creditable

- *Credible* means "believable."
- *Creditable* means "worthy of credit."

flaunt, flout

- *Flaunt* means "to parade" or "to display boldly."
- *Flout* means "to treat with scorn."

formally, formerly

- *Formally* means "in a formal manner."
- *Formerly* means "previously."

its, it's

- *Its* is a possessive pronoun.
- *It's* is the contraction of "it is" or "it has."
  - The horse lost *its* saddle.
  - *It's* difficult to study before breakfast.

lose, loose

- *Lose* is a verb, the opposite of "find."
- *Loose* is an adjective, the opposite of "tight."

moral, morale

- *Moral* pertains to right conduct.
- *Morale* means a mental condition with respect to cheerfulness, confidence, and zeal.

passed, past

- *Passed* is the past tense of pass, as "The two ships *passed* in the night."
- *Past* means "gone by or elapsed in time," as "in *past* times," or "in the *past*."

personal, personnel

- *Personal* means "individual" or "private," as in "my *personal* opinion."
- *Personnel* means "the persons employed in an organization."

precede, proceed

- *Precede* means "to come before."
- *Proceed* means "to go ahead" or "to continue."

principal, principle

- *Principal* means "the most important." It is also "the amount of a loan."
- *Principle* means "a rule or basic truth."

quiet, quite

- *Quiet* means "not noisy."
- *Quite* means "entirely."
  - This room is not *quite quiet.*

sometime, some time

- *Sometime* is a point in time, as "The work will be completed *sometime* soon."
- *Some time* means "an amount of time," as "This method has not been in effect for *some time.*"

stationary, stationery

- *Stationary* means "not moving."
- *Stationery* is writing paper.

who's, whose

- *Who's* means "who is."
- *Whose* means "of or belonging to a person or persons as possessor or possessors."
  - *Who's* going to travel by train?
  - *Whose* little black puppy is this?

your, you're

- *Your* means "of or belonging to you or yourself."
- *You're* is the contraction for "you are."
  - *Your* talent in musical performance is superb.
  - *You're* not to pass another vehicle in this lane.

Summary

Words and slogans influence our professional and business lives and also the history of nations and of the world.

Words have both denotative and connotative meanings. The denotation is the "dictionary" meaning. The connotation is the special meaning of the word based on the individual's experiences and perception. Aside from the emotional effect, words have their own particular shades of meaning. Few words have true synonyms.

Language is constantly changing.

A simple, direct, and natural writing style is desirable for all kinds of material. Short words, provided that they express the desired meaning, should be preferred to longer ones.

The formality of writing and speaking differs depending on the subject, the occasion, the audience, and the content of the message. Most business writing is neither extremely formal nor extremely informal, but semiformal. The impersonal writing style includes no first- and second-person pronouns, which include *I, me, my, us,* and *you* (or implied you). The personal writing style may include these pronouns. Business writing should not include stereotyped phrases or business jargon.

Positive and pleasant words are preferable to negative and unpleasant ones, although clarity must never be sacrificed for diplomacy. Objective words are preferable to biased, judgmental ones.

Nondiscriminatory language does not include words and phrases that are often considered sexist. Masculine pronouns should be used only when referring specifically to males.

Test Yourself: Chapter Review

1. The meaning of a word as it is listed in a dictionary is described as its _____ meaning.

2. A word meaning that includes judgment and may differ from individual to individual is described as its _____ meaning.

3. A writing style that includes the words *I* and *you* is said to be written in the _____ tone.

4–5. A writing style that includes no first- or second-person pronouns is said to be written in the _____ tone or the _____ writing style.

6. What is meant by objective words?

7–9. Name three of the many reasons that language changes.

10–11. What is a disadvantage and a possible advantage of using slang?

12–13. Name two methods of avoiding the use of the word *he* when referring to either a man or a woman.

14. A verb meaning to influence is spelled _____.

15. A verb meaning to bring about is spelled _____.

Test Yourself: Correct Usage

(Related to material in Chapter 3 and principles of correct usage.) Insert necessary punctuation, including quotation marks, hyphens, and apostrophes, and remove punctuation that has been inserted incorrectly. Choose correct word from each pair or group. Make any other necessary changes.

1. Shall we (procede, proceed) with our discussion about words?
2. How do words (affect, effect) our everyday behavior?
3. Words have emotional (effects, affects).
4. A negative phrase that should ordinarily be omitted is "you claim
5. Connotative meanings are based on individual experiences attitudes beliefs and emotions.
6. Words are described as being synonyms for other words but there are few real synonyms.
7. The English language is constantly changing all other languages also change.
8. Well chosen words are likely to be short words.
9. Do you think that language changes by (one percent, 1 percent, 1%, one %) a year?
10. Old words develop new uses other words become obsolete.

Questions and Problems

1. Draw up a list of words of high and low status, such as sanitation engineer versus garbage collector; administrators versus clerks; maintenance engineer versus janitor.
2. Look in a dictionary of quotations. Find two quotations about words. Present these in a memorandum addressed to your instructor and/or be prepared to read these quotations to the class.
3. Find a word or phrase with a more favorable connotation for each of the following expressions. For some of the words you can think of at least two or more favorable expressions—one or more somewhat neutral and one or more so favorable that it would be considered a euphemism. For example, "scheme" can be replaced by "plan"; even more favorable is "program of action." Another example is "bogus," "artificial," and "simulated."

    In some instances you will change the meaning slightly. As stated in this chapter, there are few real synonyms. For example, as you try to find another word for "bribe," you could use "subsidy" or "gratuity." Although these words are not exactly synonymous, if used in the proper context their meaning would be clear—and unstated.

chore	the old woman
deal	poverty
cheap	racket
affair	blemish
liar	rule with an iron hand
messed up	blunder
under arrest	You're dead wrong!
stubborn	long-winded
bookworm	informer
smart aleck	ridiculous

4. "Invent" your own word and introduce it into the English language. (Look in an unabridged dictionary to make sure that it does not already exist!) Use it many times during the next few days. Do other persons begin to use it? Could they now "define" your word? Be prepared to describe to the class the introduction, promotion, and success of this new word.
5. Describe a paper clip so that a person who has never seen one will be able to draw it.
6. Write specific, detailed instructions on how to operate some business machine or equipment with which you are familiar. Be complete and concise.
7. What is your opinion as to the use of the word "he"

as a generic word to represent either a man or a woman? If you do not approve, how do you suggest that writing be adapted to avoid the use of "he," "his," or "him"?

8. Analyze three or four business letters. Do they include any of the phrases listed under the topic "Business Language" in this chapter?

9. Using an example from your own experience, write or orally describe an example of miscommunication because of varying interpretations of words.

10. From your travels to different sections of the United States or Canada, give examples of regional words or phrases. Have you witnessed instances when these expressions resulted in miscommunication?

11. What certain words have particularly pleasant or unpleasant connotations to you because of your experiences?

12. Can you think of words, in addition to those mentioned in the chapter, that have been replaced by higher-status words?

13. Ask a few people of retirement age whether they remember examples of slang that were in vogue when they were teenagers. Determine what has happened to these expressions. Have they become almost forgotten or have they become standard language? As your teacher directs, give an oral or written report to the class.

14. Which words in the following sentences would you change or omit because of their connotative meanings?

a. The new vice-president is the child of the founder of this company.

b. We have your letter in which you claim your check was mailed three weeks ago.

c. He was allowed to be president of his fraternity.

d. I can't say that I blame you. On the other hand . . . .

e. Yes, you got a good buy. But I always feel uncomfortable in cheap clothes.

f. I'm not as frugal as you are.

g. You are the only person who has mentioned this problem, if it is a problem.

CHAPTER 4

Achieving Correctness, Conciseness, Completeness, Readability, and the Desired Emphasis

A concise *message is no longer than it needs to be in order to achieve its purpose.* Readability, *as the word implies, means that a written message is easy to read, that it is immediately clear. When written material is planned to achieve the desired* emphasis, *it is likely to be readable as well as arranged in an order that achieves the most desirable psychological approach.*

Readability and emphasis are influenced by word choice; by sentence length and paragraph length; by the length of the entire message; by the use or omission of subheads, listings, and other aspects of format; by careful organization, planning, and wording to achieve unit and coherence; and by the way the material is arranged on the sheet.

The shortest message is not necessarily the most clear. If details or explanations necessary for understanding are omitted or vaguely implied in order to keep the communication short, the message will not be understood, and further communication will be required. Material that is not complete cannot be clear or readable. All messages should be correct in content and in language usage.

Accuracy and Knowledge: The Vital Ingredients

No matter how skillfully we write or speak, this attempt at communication is not effective unless it is based on a sound knowledge of what we are writing about. It has been said that "You can't write writing." Neither can we "communicate communication." We communicate facts, ideas, and opinions. If we are employed in a business organization, we are paid to communicate facts, ideas, and opinions about business subjects—through face-to-face and telephone conversations; written memos, letters, and reports; and formal and informal presentations at meetings and conferences.

You will need to find out all you can about your job, your company, and your particular duties and responsibilities. You will need this knowledge and understanding in order to succeed in all functions of your employment.

As you communicate orally, at meetings and conferences or informally with colleagues, your certainty of the correctness of what you are saying will give you confidence and thus improve your communication techniques. Some people, however, even though they possess reliable information and a thorough knowledge of the subject, do not effectively express their thoughts to others. You can learn to communicate—although it is not always easy—if you have something to say. If you don't have anything to say, why bother?

Mark Twain, in one of his cynical moments, did not agree that success is built on real knowledge or ability. He said. "All you need in this life is ignorance and confidence, and then success is sure."

Don't bet on it, Mark Twain.

Every one of us can think back to mistakes we have made because we did not have certain necessary information, or because we were misinformed, or because we remembered details incorrectly. These errors will continue to occur, regardless of our effort, but at least we can minimize them with sufficient thought and effort.

Because data are reproduced by computers and by other forms of mass reproduction, one error can become thousands of errors. A bit of incorrect information on a letter sent to one individual is bad enough, but a form letter sent to thousands of people greatly multiplies whatever difficulties will be encountered because of the error.

A message can be inaccurate because it is incomplete—and perhaps it is incomplete because the writer or speaker is overly concerned with being brief. A message can have the same effect as being inaccurate if it is misunderstood; that is, the facts may be correct but presented in such a way that the receiver of the message

---

Communication Brief

Standard English is defined by scholars as the "prestige dialect" of our language. A Mark Twain or a Will Rogers can achieve humorous effects by deliberate and pointed use of nonstandard idioms. But the radio and television news is always delivered in a formal, generalized Standard English with little or no distinctive regional flavor. Business letters, legal arguments, scientific descriptions, magazine articles, and ceremonial speeches are also written in Standard English. Mastery of this prestige dialect is a key to success in most of the most prestigious activities of the world.

Success with Words (Pleasantville, N.Y.: The Reader's Digest Association, 1983), v.

misinterprets them. A message can be inaccurate—actually or in effect—if the chosen words do not mean the same to the receiver as to the sender of the message.

Messages are likely to be incorrect if the communicator is not adept in the use of the language with which he or she attempts to communicate. Although grammatical errors do not often result in misunderstanding, they are likely to weaken the reader's confidence in the writer's overall competence. At times, also, the wrong word can alter the intended meaning. Misplaced commas or the omission of needed commas can reverse the intended meaning. Notice the difference in meaning in the following sentences:

> All sales representatives who have exceeded their quotas will receive a 10 percent bonus.
>
> All sales representatives, who have exceeded their quotas, will receive a 10 percent bonus.
>
> The old publications which originally sold for $2 or less are to be destroyed.
>
> The old publications, which originally sold for $2 or less, are to be destroyed.

A misplaced apostrophe can also cause misinterpretation. Like the comma and other marks of punctuation, the apostrophe is sometimes used to convey meaning, not merely to make the meaning expressed by words more readily understood. In the following sentence

> The customers' orders were promptly filled

the meaning is not the same as in the sentence

> The customer's orders were promptly filled.

The first sentence indicates that there are at least two customers; the second sentence indicates that there is only one customer.

The misuse of words similar in meaning or spelling can also cause misreading and misrepresentation. Usually the words *affect* and *effect*, although often confused, do not change the intended meaning. They can do so, however, as in these sentences:

> Will the increase in total sales affect the expected salary increase?
>
> Will the increase in total sales effect the expected salary increase?

Although these words are similar in spelling and pronunciation, the questions differ in meaning: the first question asks whether the increase will influence (have an effect on) the expected salary increase; the second question asks whether the increase in sales will bring about a salary increase.

Notice the difference in the two sentences that follow:

> We are now expecting to make a change in personnel before the first of the year.

We are not expecting to make a change in personnel before the first of the year.

All these "errors" perhaps resulted from haste or the lack of attention. Similar or worse ones occur because the communicator does not have accurate knowledge to communicate. Acquiring this knowledge and judgment takes constant effort; by the time you have learned one method of procedure or one set of instructions, new ones will be put into effect, and then more and more.

The overall amount of information available in all fields is increasing at an alarming rate; what you learn in school will be at least partially obsolete in a few years. To be a leader (or even a good follower) you must be aware of change, accept it, and use it to your advantage and to that of your employing company.

Conciseness and Completeness

Conciseness is not a synonym for brevity. *Brevity*, like *short, informal,* and other descriptive words, is relative.

Conciseness is always a desirable quality of business communication; brevity is not necessarily desirable. When working for conciseness, remember that the purpose of the message is not merely the imparting of information but also the building and maintaining of goodwill. To build or maintain goodwill—or from the human standpoint of being friendly and courteous—the writer or speaker may be required to include additional words, paragraphs, or pages. A *please* and a *thank you* take little time and space. Even if they did, they would be well worth the effort.

A letter or other message that says *no* or relates unpleasant news usually should be longer than one that says *yes* or relates good news. Suppose, for example, you are refusing a request. You could convey the necessary information in this way:

> Dear Mrs. Baker:
>   No.
>   Sincerely,

This letter, although brief, lacks many of the necessary aspects of an effective letter. Although it relates all the necessary information, the message requires some explanation and a goodwill paragraph or two, unless the writer wishes to be particularly emphatic, likely at the expense of future pleasant

Communication Brief

Most people seem to think that simplicity and brevity are the same thing, or at least that they must always be together like Siamese twins. That's a superstition; plain talk can be slow and roundabout, and short, condensed sentences are often hard to read. The truth is that there are lots of different kinds of brevity; some make it easier and some harder.

Rudolf Flesch, *The Art of Plain Talk* (New York: Harper and Brothers, 1946), 120.

Vigorous writing is concise. A sentence should contain no unnecessary words, a paragraph no unnecessary sentences, for the same reason that a drawing should have no unnecessary lines and a machine no unnecessary parts.

William Strunk, Jr., and E. B. White, *The Elements of Style,* 3d ed. (New York: Macmillan, 1979), xiv.

Communication Brief

relationships. (The one-word sentence that makes up the total message dramatically illustrates a method of emphasis: using short, simple sentences standing alone.)

Some writers omit necessary details and explanations because of an over-concern with brevity. The shortest letter is not economical if it necessitates another letter or a telephone call to clear up what should have been clearly stated in the original letter.

Your reader or listener does not want needless and irrelevant details or explanations, but you must include sufficient facts and explanations, as well as courtesy.

Conservative, Businesslike Standards of Correctness

Correct writing and speaking, from the standpoint of grammatical correctness and the accuracy of information, is not necessarily effective communication, nor is it necessarily easily understood, interesting, or diplomatic. Correctness is only one of the many components of effective communication. Most business communication, however, cannot be completely effective if it is not basically correct, grammatically as well as in the information it reports.

Some people seem to have the idea that an exact and "correct" use of the English language is somehow unimportant—that they should be concerned about more important matters. This attitude is in some cases a "sour-grapes" approach by those who lack confidence in their knowledge of the language. To say that we need not be concerned with how we express our thoughts is the same as saying that we are willing to neglect a major aspect of general education and literacy, regardless of our occupation.

We send or receive messages through the use of language almost every waking moment. Why should we not give a great deal of effort to sending and receiving these messages exactly and convincingly?

We will continue to use language, for we must; therefore we should exert continued effort in order to use it effectively. Even though you perhaps will not be a professional writer or speaker, you will, and do, use the language in your profession, as well as in your personal life. In this sense it is a professional knowledge and skill, not only desirable but essential, in the perfection of whatever kind of work you do or will do.

Aside from its professional and social benefits, your growth in the use of the language will be a source of personal pride and accomplishment—and perhaps this is the most worthwhile motive.

Further discussion of effective and correct English usage is given in Appendix D. Two areas of frequent errors are given in the following section of this chapter.

Frequently Occurring Grammatical Errors

Subject-Verb Disagreement

This commonly occurring error is particularly troublesome when dictating. Because words or phrases often come between the subject and the verb, the wrong form of the verb is dictated unthinkingly. Using the wrong form of the verb—as in "the boys is" or "the girl are"—is a serious error, a real error, according to all authorities and handbooks, and to almost everyone who will read your message. In simple constructions like the examples in the preceding sentence, the mistake is not likely to occur. In slightly more complicated sentences, it often does occur, as in:

> The logic of good communicators seems to be . . .

Because the plural word *communicators* immediately precedes the verb, *seem* may creep into the sentence, although in a sentence no more involved than this one there is little reason for the wrong verb form, even when dictating. As more words intervene and the subject "gets lost," the wrong verb seems to be the appropriate one. One principle of good writing, however, is that it be simple and direct; *another guide is that the subject and verb be close together in a sentence.* Sentences constructed in this way are likely to include the correct form of the verb.

In the sentence below, the verb is singular to agree with the subject *box:*

> The box, together with the baskets, was sent to the shipping room.

The word *baskets* is not part of the subject, but because *baskets* immediately precedes the verb, it seems natural to use *were.* In the following sentence, *were* is the correct verb:

> The box and the baskets were sent to the shipping room.

Compare the above sentences with the following:

> Neither the box nor the basket was sent to the shipping room.
> Neither the box nor the baskets were sent to the shipping room.

The following guideline applies to sentences like the immediately preceding ones: When one subject is singular and the other is plural, the verb agrees with the subject closer to the verb.

The Wrong Case of the Pronoun

Using the wrong case of the pronoun is an error that seems to occur more in speech than in writing. It is especially common in sentences in which *I* is used incorrectly (instead of *me*) as the object of a verb or preposition. Few persons, whatever their position or educational background, say something like this:

Me and Jim are friends.

However, many persons say or write, inaccurately:

Jim and he are good friends of Mary and I.

In the preceding sentence, "Mary and *me*" should be used because the pronoun is the object of the preposition *of*. The *I* is just as incorrect as the *me* in "me and Jim," but for some reason the *I* seems to many persons to be more "cultured," more "elegant," more correct.

Remember these cases of pronouns:

Subjective:	I	you	he	she	it	we	they	who	whoever
Possessive:	my	your	his	her	its	our	their	whose	whosever
Objective:	me	you	him	her	it	us	them	whom	whomever

A pronoun in the subjective case is used

- as the subject of a main or a subordinate clause;
- as a predicate nominative (as in "it is I," although "it is me" is more frequently heard in conversation); and
- as a word that is in apposition with another word in the subjective case, as "only three persons intended—Jim, Jeannie, and I." (*I*, as well as *Jim* and *Jeannie,* is in apposition with *persons,* which is the subject of the sentence.)

A pronoun in the objective case is used when it is the object of a verb or a preposition or when it is used as an indirect object.

A pronoun modifying a gerund (a verb form used as a noun) is in the possessive case, as in:

We will appreciate your writing us immediately.

Some persons approach the *who* and *whom* distinction as they do the *I* and *me* usages, seemingly with the idea that if one *whom* (or *I*) is good, a great number is better. *Whom* used incorrectly for *who* is no worse, from a grammatical standpoint, than using *who* in place of *whom*; but to most of us, somehow it sounds worse—as if the speaker has made an effort to be proper, but failed.

Notice the reasons for the choice of words in the following sentences:

- Who is to be the new president? (subject)
- Who do you think will be the new president? (still the subject of the sentence, not the object of *think*)
- John Jackson, who is our new president, will be at the meeting. (*Who* is the subject of the subordinate clause. A more concise way to word this sentence is to omit *who is* so that *our new president* is used in apposition with *John Jackson.*)
- *For Whom the Bell Tolls.* (*Whom* is the object of the preposition *for*.)

Sentence Construction

A knowledge of sentence structure is essential to exact use of punctuation and, more important, to the most effective presentation of your thoughts.

As a general guide, use only complete sentences, although at times sentence fragments are effective in sales and advertising writing and in other informal material. Only complete sentences should be used in formal writing, which includes many reports. Because you do not know the individual preferences of your readers, you are safer *always* to write in complete sentences.

Kinds of Sentences

A commonly accepted definition of a complete sentence is that it has at least one subject and one predicate and that it can stand alone as a complete thought. Sentences are classified as *simple, complex, compound*, and *compound-complex.* These terms are confusing to some readers, including college students. For example, a simple sentence is not necessarily direct, short, and uncomplicated; and a complex sentence is often short and easy to read, even though it contains at least two clauses. Remember the distinction between a clause and a phrase: *a clause, but not a phrase, contains a subject and a predicate.*

To review your knowledge of sentence construction, examine the five sentences in the immediately preceding paragraph. Classify each sentence, noting the number and kind of clauses in each before you read the following paragraph.

Here are the answers to the classification of sentence construction:

- Sentence 1. *Complex sentence:* one main (independent) clause and two dependent (subordinate) clauses. The subject of the main clause is *definition;* the predicate is *is.* Each of the two dependent clauses begins with *that.*
- Sentence 2. *Simple sentence: Sentences are classified . . .*
- Sentence 3. *Simple sentence: These terms are confusing . . .*
- Sentence 4. *Compound-complex:* Subject and predicate, first main clause: *simple sentence is . . . ;* subject and predicate, second main clause: *complex sentence is . . . ;* subject and predicate, dependent clause: *it contains.*
- Sentence 5. *Compound.* First main clause: subject, you (understood); predicate: *remember;* second main clause: *clause . . . contains.*

If you were able to classify each sentence quickly and surely, you should have little trouble with sentence recognition and construction or with the rules of punctuation. If you were unsure, you will benefit from further study. A complete English handbook used with Appendix D will be of more value than Appendix D alone. Because of limited space, this textbook, which must include many other elements of communication, cannot explain language usage in full detail.

Further illustrations of types of sentences are given below.

Simple sentences
- I have returned.—Douglas MacArthur
- Understanding is joyous.—Carl Sagan (*Understanding* is used here as a noun and the subject of the sentence.)

- Towering genius disdains a beaten path.—Abraham Lincoln
- England and America are two countries separated by the same language.—George Bernard Shaw
- The fog comes on little cat feet.—Carl Sandburg
- Play it again, Sam. (The subject is the understood *you*.) (title of film; also adaptation of line from another film, *Casablanca*)
- I hate quotations.—Ralph Waldo Emerson

Complex sentences

- When people are least sure, they are often the most dogmatic.—John Kenneth Galbraith (introductory dependent clause)
- In spite of everything I still believe that people are really good at heart.—Ann Frank (Dependent clause begins with *that*.)
- He who enters a university walks on hallowed ground.—James B. Conant (Here the dependent clause, beginning with *who*, separates the subject and verb of the main clause: *he* and *walks*.)
- The future offers very little hope for those who expect that our new mechanical slaves will offer us a world in which we may rest from thinking.—Norbert Wiener (This sentence contains one independent clause and three dependent clauses. What are they?)

Compound sentences

- Wit has truth in it; wisecracking is simply calisthenics with words.—Dorothy Parker
- Life was meant to be lived, and curiosity must be kept alive.—Eleanor Roosevelt
- All animals are equal, but some animals are more equal than others.—George Orwell
- Talk low, talk slow, and don't say too much.—John Wayne (three independent clauses)

Compound-complex sentences

- Read over your compositions, and wherever you meet with a passage which you think is particularly fine, strike it out.—Samuel Johnson (*You* is the understood subject of both independent clauses; *read* and *strike* are the verbs. In the dependent clauses, *you meet, which is,* and *you think* are the subjects and verbs.)
- We can secure other people's approval if we do right and try hard; but our own is worth a hundred of it, and no way has been found of securing that.—Mark Twain (Three main clauses and one dependent clause, beginning with *if we do.*)
- And so, my fellow Americans, ask not what your country can do for you; ask what you can do for your country.—John F. Kennedy (two independent clauses and two dependent clauses)

Basic Errors in Sentence Construction

Most conspicuous weaknesses in sentence construction are the following:

1. Sentence fragment (although these can at times be used effectively)
2. The comma fault, also called a comma blunder, a comma splice, and a baby comma
3. A fused sentence, also called a run-on sentence
4. Nonparallel sentences or sentences of mixed construction
5. Sentences with dangling or misplaced modifiers

*Improve
Your Writing*

Questions: Must I understand sentence structure—simple and compound sentences and all the rest—to punctuate according to the rules? What are the most serious errors in the use of punctuation?

Answers: Yes, you must understand sentence structure in order to punctuate according to the rules. One of the most serious errors in punctuation is described as the *comma splice* or *comma fault*. Because it results in grade-school, amateurish writing, it is sometimes referred to as the *baby comma*.

The comma splice (or fault) occurs when two main clauses of a compound sentence are joined by a comma only, not by a comma and a coordinating conjunction or by a semicolon. An example is given below:

> The public library rents, but does not sell, videocassettes, they are interesting and also inexpensive.

The preceding sentence would be improved somewhat by replacing the comma after *videocassettes* with a semicolon or by inserting *and* after the presently used comma. Even with either of these changes the sentence would remain weak, although correct according to the rules of punctuation. The following modification is a *simple* sentence:

> The public library rents, but does not sell, interesting and inexpensive video-cassettes.

The following sentence is *complex.*

> Although the public library does not sell the interesting videocassettes available there, it provides an economical rental plan.

The immediately preceding sentence illustrates the rule that an introductory dependent clause should be followed by a comma.

A sentence fragment, the comma fault, and the fused sentence can also be considered as errors in punctuation. These weak constructions occur because the writer is not sure of what constitutes a sentence. The lack of necessary and wisely chosen punctuation results in these sentence weaknesses.

A sentence fragment is incomplete in itself; it is usually a phrase or a dependent clause, as in the following examples:

> This information is presented here. Because it is necessary to the understanding of the following pages.

Improve by eliminating the period:

> This information is presented here because it is necessary to the understanding of the following pages.

The *comma fault* occurs when two sentences that are definitely separate have been joined together with a comma. They should be punctuated as two separate sentences, joined with a conjunction, or joined with a semicolon. The method of connection depends, to a certain extent, on the desired meaning and emphasis. If the ideas are not related enough so that they belong in the same sentence, express them in separate sentences. Avoid using a great many semicolons as they can result in a choppy effect, just as a great number of short, simple sentences can. When one idea is more important than another, use a complex sentence.

Notice the following example of a comma fault:

> English is the principal language of international business, it is taught in schools throughout the world. (Improve by starting a new sentence with *it* or by using a semicolon before *it*.)

This sentence could also be revised in the following way, although the meaning and emphasis would be slightly changed. For example:

> English, the principal language of international business, is taught in schools throughout the world.

In short and closely related sentences, commas may at times be effectively used to join the clauses of compound sentences, as:

> I came, I saw, I conquered.
> Don't hurry, don't worry.

This construction, however, should be used with discretion and extreme caution, especially by the inexperienced writer. (See the discussion of the use of the semicolon under "Punctuation as an Aid to Readability" in Appendix D.)

A *fused sentence* occurs when two sentences are "run-on" with no punctuation at all. The sentences should be separated by a period, a semicolon, or a comma and a conjunction.

Nonparallel sentences occur when parallel ideas are not expressed in parallel form. An orderly arrangement is necessary for the immediate recognition of relationships of ideas.

The following sentences are not parallel because of the unnecessary shifts from active to passive voice.

> Jane wrote the music, and the lyrics were written by Mary Hicks.
> The play was well written, and the director did a capable job.

Improved versions of these sentences are:

> Jane wrote the music, and Mary Hicks wrote the lyrics.
> The play was well written and capably directed.

The following sentence is nonparallel because similar ideas are expressed in differing ways by the infinitive and by the gerund:

> Taking the elevator is not so healthful as to climb the stairs. (Improve by changing *to climb* to *climbing*.)

The following sentence is nonparallel because a relative clause and an infinitive phrase are used to express similar ideas:

> We want a personnel manager who can motivate all workers and to recruit experienced sales representatives.

An improved version of this sentence is:

> We want a personnel manager who can motivate workers and who can recruit experienced sales representatives.

A more concise version is:

> We want a personnel manager who can motivate workers and recruit experienced sales representatives.

The following phrases are not parallel because two gerunds and one infinitive are used in a sentence in which similar expressions should have the same form:

> Buying supplies, keeping the books, and to answer the telephone . . .

An improved version is:

> Buying supplies, keeping the books, and answering the telephone . . .

The following sentence beginning is not parallel because two phrases are used with a clause:

> Government of the people, by the people, and that is for the people . . .

The following sentences are nonparallel because of a misplaced correlative. (Correlatives are pairs of joining words, such as *either, or; neither, nor; both, and; not only, but also.*)

> Either to make a living or a life is not an easy task, if it is done well.
> Not only must we be concerned with the initial cost but also with the upkeep.

These sentences can be improved in this way:

> To make either a living or a life is not an easy task, if it is done well.
> We must be concerned not only with the initial cost but also with the upkeep.

Dangling or misplaced modifiers may consist of adjectives or adverbs; phrases, including participial, infinitive, or prepositional; and clauses. Any modifier is misplaced if it does not exactly and logically qualify (restrict, limit, describe) the word or words that it is intended to qualify.

A modifier is said to dangle when it has no reasonable or logical words to modify, as in this sentence:

> Working without a coffee break, the telephone calls were completed before noon.

As this sentence is constructed, the participle *working* seems to modify *telephone calls*, when obviously it cannot. The modifier here could also be described as all the words that come before the main part of the sentence, "working without a coffee break." The sentence should be improved in this way:

Working without a coffee break, I completed the telephone calls before noon.

Dangling participles sometimes occur because the writer is too much concerned with avoiding the word *I*. *I* and *we* should be used when they are natural and necessary to the sentence, except for the few kinds of business writing that use only the impersonal tone.

Here are more examples of dangling modifiers:

Being dark and winding, she could barely see the road.
Completely renovated two years ago, I was most impressed by the old building.

Avoid using a great many participial openings, even if they do not "dangle." Usually the sentence is more direct and forceful when it opens with the subject-verb combination.

Misplaced modifiers may be in sentence positions other than the beginning, as in the following sentence:

The woman riding the motorcycle in a red jogging suit is my grandmother. (misplaced prepositional phrase)
In the downtown section, with sirens screaming, we saw the fire truck skid to a stop. (misplaced prepositional phrase)

The word *only* is easily misplaced. *Rarely, merely, hardly, just, even,* and other words are also often not in the best location to refer to the exact word or group of words that they modify. As a general rule, put closely related words together.

The following sentence contains a misplaced *only,* although this particular construction is often used in conversing and sometimes in writing.

He only received a few dollars for his poem.

In formal writing, and preferably on all occasions, the following construction should be used:

He received only a few dollars for his poem.

Notice how the meaning changes, according to the placement of *only,* in the following sentences:

- Only MacArthur said that he would return.
- MacArthur only said that he would return.
- MacArthur said only that he would return.
- MacArthur said that only he would return.
- MacArthur said that he only would return.
- MacArthur said that he would only return.

*Improve
Your Writing*

Question: What is gobbledygook?

Answer: Gobbledygook is long-winded, multisyllable, complex, pretentious, pompous, ambiguous writing or speech that contains euphemisms, technical words, Latin words and phrases, and a concoction of other words and lengthy phrases that are almost impossible to understand and probably don't mean anything, anyway. (The previous sentence comes close to being gobbledygook.)

Government officials in high positions are likely to write gobbledygook, or at least they have the reputation of doing so. Politicians sometimes speak gobbledygook, perhaps in order to sound scholarly and to prevent their being understood.

Pennsylvania Dutch settlers used the word *gobbledygook* to describe mixed-together leftovers. In 1952, Texas Senator Maury Maverick applied the term to language.

Gobbledygook is also described as *jargon*, although jargon has an additional meaning: the use or overuse of terms peculiar to a particular group, occupation, or field of interest. We speak of business jargon, particularly as it applies to business writing in such phrases as "Enclosed please find" and "We have your letter of recent date." These phrases are jargon, but they are not considered gobbledygook. Both gobbledygook and jargon violate the principle of direct, simple writing. (Technical terms are useful when people in a specialized field communicate with readers in the same field.)

The following gobbledygook could have been written by a sociologist:

Socially oriented individuals tend to congregate in gregariously homogeneous groupings. (Birds of a feather flock together.)

In the next to the last sentence, the meaning is unclear because *only* could modify either *he* or *would return.*

Regardless of the formality of the writing, the expression is more exact if the modifier is in the best possible location in relationship to the rest of the words in the sentence. As another example, insert the word *only* in the seven possible positions in the following sentence in order to express six different meanings:

He told her he loved her.

Readable Sentences

Sentences should not be the same length. In order to avoid monotonous reading, both short and fairly long sentences should be used. Most important, sentences should be of the length that best conveys a wise choice of ideas and information so closely related that they belong together in the same sentence.

Average sentence length should not usually exceed twenty words, although a skillful writer can use longer sentences and achieve a readable style. A series of short, simple sentences, similar to a first-grade reader, is monotonous, juvenile, and unbusinesslike. A thorough and automatic knowledge of sentence construction is essential to the expert business writer, not only from the standpoint of readability but also from the standpoints of emphasis and correctness.

The length of sentence chosen for a particular idea depends on the idea to be expressed. Experienced writers do not consciously think of sentence construction as the material is written or dictated. They often change sentence structure as they revise, particularly to cut sentence length. All writers should check their work to make sure that only complete sentences are used and that there is a variety of sentence construction.

In most business writing, simple sentences should outnumber complex sentences and compound sentences. In almost all writing, compound sentences should be the fewest of the three. Complex sentences are useful for subordinating or emphasizing ideas.

Construction and Length of Paragraphs

Short paragraphs are useful in achieving readability in all kinds of writing. A paragraph of many lines is hard to read and discouraging to the reader. At times, paragraphs in a letter, memorandum, or report must be broken arbitrarily to increase readability, especially if the overall work is short.

Some business writers believe that a paragraph must have more than one sentence. Overall, paragraphs tend to be shorter in letters and memorandums than in some other types of writing. In business letters, often the first and last paragraphs consist of only one sentence. Any paragraph may be only one sentence in length if that is all that seems to fit into the particular paragraph, but one-sentence paragraphs should not be overused.

A short, one-sentence paragraph can be used for attention, interest, and emphasis, especially if the sentence is the first one in the communication. A one-sentence paragraph can also be used as a transition from one section of material to another.

Although no exact rule can be given about maximum paragraph length, you should regard with suspicion any typewritten paragraph more than seven or eight lines long, especially in short messages. Paragraphs should average fewer lines than this when they make up letters, memorandums, and short reports.

In general, remember that paragraphing calls for a good eye as well as a logical mind. Enormous blocks of print look formidable to a reader. Therefore, breaking long paragraphs in two, even if it is not necessary to do so for sense, meaning, or logical development, is often a visual help.

William Strunk, Jr., and E. B. White, *The Elements of Style*, 3d ed. (New York: Macmillan, 1979), 17.

Communication Brief

*Improve
Your Writing*

Question: Are one-sentence paragraphs permissible? Has this usage changed?

Answer: One-sentence paragraphs have always been permissible. At times they are not only permissible, but desirable.

One-sentence paragraphs should not be used to excess, however. They are emphatic; this emphasis is one reason for using them with discretion. Numerous one-sentence paragraphs in a letter or memorandum tend to emphasize a number of things—which in reality may be emphasizing nothing at all.

One-sentence opening and closing paragraphs can be especially effective. They can be used in any position, provided the content of the paragraph deserves emphasis. One-sentence paragraphs can also serve as transitional devices. They are useful not only in letters and memorandums, but in articles, essays, and reports, provided they are widely used.

The advice that a paragraph should be about only one topic is still a good one. But paragraphs in short business messages (and in other kinds of writing) cannot contain all necessary information about a topic; the letter or memorandum itself is ordinarily about only one topic.

Paragraphs in letters and memorandums are of necessity shorter than those in some journal articles; the entire communication is shorter, often no more than one page.

Short paragraphs, if wisely used, aid readability. Long paragraphs discourage the reader and cause confusion. *Almost all business writing is read hurriedly.* The writer should do everything possible to make messages immediately clear.

Readability Formulas

Several formulas, or indexes, have been developed, supposedly to measure readability. Two of these are the Flesch Reading Ease Formula and the Gunning Fog Index. The readability score obtained with a formula is expressed in terms of the general educational level of the reader, which may have little relationship to the actual grade completed in school. If, for example, the readability score is 17, this indicates that the material could be read by someone who has completed college. A score of 16 means that a person completing the sixteenth year of schooling, a college senior, could read the material.

Most effective writing of all kinds, however, has a lower readability score than 16 or 17, even if the material is planned for graduate students. Material may have a readability score lower than high school level and still be suitable for adults.

An important point to remember is that *formulas cannot measure the quality of writing, only its complexity, and that to a limited extent.* An expert writer can use long words and sentences and make the work more interesting and readable than a writer with less ability, although the expert's work has a higher readability score.

The formulas make no distinction between exact, well-chosen words and vague, confusing words, or between familiar words and rare ones. They measure only word length. They do not distinguish sentences that are constructed wisely in order to express ideas exactly. Excellent writing cannot be measured by any formula, but an average reader can usually recognize its quality and understand its meaning.

These cautions about using readability formulas are not given to disparage their worth, for their admittedly limited purposes are valid ones. *The formulas can be dangerous, however, if they are misused.* An appropriate readability score should not be accepted without question as an indication that the writing needs no improvement. Writing that has a score higher than the expected "norms" should not be automatically classified as lacking in readability, although it should be reexamined.

The Gunning Fog Index is as follows:

1. Select a sample of writing of at least 100 words. Divide the total number of words by the number of sentences. This is the average sentence length. [Using several samples will result in a more reliable source. The independent clauses of a compound sentence are counted as separate sentences.]

2. Count the number of words of three syllables or more. Don't count proper names, combinations of short, easy words, such as bookkeeper or teenager; or verb forms made into three syllables by adding *ed* or *es*. This figure is the number of "hard" words in the passage. Divide this figure by the total number of words to find the percentage of "hard" words.

3. Add the average sentence length to the percentage of hard words and multiply by .4. The figure obtained through these calculations is the Gunning Fog Index, or readability score, expressed in grade-reading level.[1]

Let's find the readability score for the following paragraph from *The Mature Mind,* written in 1949 by H. A. Overstreet. This book is much more readable than many other books on psychological subjects, but the 12.2 score is higher than an ideal score for short, nontechnical business communications. The example paragraph is well written. Another passage with a similar score might be much less understandable, according to the skill in sentence construction and word choice. (Overstreet does not mention television because in the year in which this paragraph was written, television was in its infancy.)

> Newspapers, *radio,* movies, and *advertising*—these might be called the "big four" of *communication.* These are the four great money-making *enterprises* of mind-making. It would be pleasant to report that they make for the fine *maturity* of human *character.* But the report must be otherwise. In spite of what each has *contributed* to our growth, each has, through its own *formula,* found it *profitable* to keep us from full *psychological maturing.* Or, to put the best *possible* face upon the matter, each has found in us some *immaturity* that waited to be tapped. Engaged in the tapping process, each of these *powerful* forces has been too busy to think about the long-range *consequences* of its *formula.*[2]

The paragraph contains 120 words and 7 sentences. The words of three or more syllables (those not excluded by the formula) total 16. (These words are

---

[1]Robert Gunning, *The Technique of Clear Writing* (New York: McGraw-Hill, 1968), 39.
[2]H. A. Overstreet, *The Mature Mind* (New York: W. W. Norton, 1949), 225–226.

shown in italics.) *Newspapers* and *otherwise* are excluded because they are combinations of short, easy words, like *bookkeeper,* mentioned in the formula.

The readability score of 12.2 was determined in this way:

1. 120 (total words) divided by 7 (sentences) = 17.1 (average sentence length).
2. 16 (number of difficult words) divided by 120 (total words) = 13.3 (percentage of difficult words).
3. Add 17.1 to 13.3 = 30.4.
4. Multiply 30.4 by .4 = 12.16 or 12.2 (readability score).

This reading-level score means that the material could be easily read by someone in the twelfth grade, or approximately so. This is similar to the reading level of such magazines as *Atlantic Monthly* and *Harper's,* although articles by different authors vary in difficulty. Other popular magazines, such as *Reader's Digest,* are written at a level below this twelfth-grade score. To obtain an accurate average score of writing of considerable length, we should use far more material than the paragraph measured here.

Using Format to Increase Readability

A letter, memorandum, report, or other communication should be arranged attractively, leaving plenty of white space. *A minimum of one inch in the side, top, and bottom margins should be left on all work.* For short and average-length letters, wider margins are better, as explained in Appendix B.

Subheads are essential to readability if the written message is long, and *long* usually should be considered to apply to any communication of more than one page. Subheads can also be used in material of one page or less. They aid readability in several ways.

Subheads force the writer to organize the material in meaningful units. If the subhead does not include a reference to the information under it, and only to that information, it is not a well-chosen one. Poor subheads are worse than none at all.

Lists and tabulations make ideas stand out and present ideas in a logical order. The arrangement of each statement, question, or idea on a separate line (as illustrated in the following list), with a line space between each line, makes each item easier to understand than if all were crowded together into a paragraph.

To illustrate the use of a listing, as well as to summarize, the following information is repeated.

Readable formats should include:

1. Plenty of white space
2. An overall attractive appearance
3. Subheads
4. Lists and tabulations

Basic Principles of Emphasis

When you apply the principles of emphasis, you are also increasing readability and achieving a desirable psychological approach. These and other qualities of excellent communication are interrelated.

Emphatic Positions

Position is one of the most important means of achieving emphasis. The beginning position in any kind of writing is the most emphatic one, provided the writer has used this location advantageously. In most communications, the beginning position should be used to present the most important idea. The arrangement is referred to as the *direct arrangement*.

The first paragraph is the most emphatic section of a memorandum, a letter, or any other short written message. In a long report, the first paragraph is still an emphatic one, but because of the comparative length, the first section, often titled the *Introduction,* becomes especially important because of its position, as well as for other reasons. The first sentence in a paragraph is ordinarily the most emphatic one. The use of a topic sentence as the first sentence therefore increases readability and emphasizes the principal meaning intended for that paragraph.

The first word of a sentence, along with the last one, is in an emphatic position, except for such sentence beginnings as *a, an,* and *the,* which are used as introductory words so that the emphasis shifts to the immediately following words. The emphatic first position of the sentence is one reason that it is best not to start several sentences on the same page with *I;* the *I* becomes overemphasized and does not convey the desired impression of the you-attitude.

The closing word, sentence, paragraph, or section of a written message is also emphatic, next in importance to the opening word, sentence, paragraph, or section. The last word of a sentence is second in emphasis to the first word of a sentence. Thus, to de-emphasize an idea or statement, do not place it in the opening or closing position of the written work.

This principle applies throughout business writing: *the idea to be de-emphasized should be somewhere within the body of the letter, not in the opening or the closing paragraph.* An idea can be subordinated within a sentence as well.

Emphatic Sentence and Paragraph Construction

The most emphatic way to present an idea is in a paragraph consisting of only one short, simple sentence. Because the most emphatic position is the first position, you achieve the greatest emphasis by letting this short, one-sentence paragraph be the first paragraph of your message. The short, simple sentence is emphatic because it stands alone, with no distracting or cluttering words or phrases to detract from the meaning.

Suppose that in a sales letter the price is stated in this way:

```
The cost is $15.98.
```

If this sentence stands alone as a paragraph, you are probably giving too much emphasis to the cost, for ordinarily the price of an article should be subordinated

Communication Brief

Use vivid verbs. Avoid the passive voice. Avoid the cliche. Be specific. Be precise. Be elegant. Omit needless words.

Stephen King, "Imagery and the Third Eye," in *The Writer's Handbook* (Boston: The Writer, 1983), 77.

and stated in connection with the benefits the purchase will bring. An exception is a sales letter in which an unusually low price is a favorable selling point. In such a letter you should emphasize the price.

In a complex sentence, place the idea to be emphasized in the main clause and the subordinated idea in the dependent clause. A phrase can also contain an idea to be de-emphasized. The cost is presented in a prepositional phrase in the following sentence:

You will receive for only $15.98 many hours of listening pleasure.

In addition to the use of the word *only*, the price is de-emphasized by placing it in a phrase and by placing it within the sentence, not at the beginning or the end.

Word Choice to Emphasize or to Subordinate

Specific, concrete language is more emphatic, as well as more descriptive and readable, than vague, abstract wording. Try to emphasize positive, pleasant ideas and to de-emphasize unpleasant ones, as discussed in Chapters 3 and 5. At times the general word, not the specific, is more diplomatic, although less emphatic and forceful.

An abstract word describes ideas or concepts that cannot be easily visualized. Examples of abstract words are *conception, democracy, abstractness, charity*. Examples of concrete words are *blackbird, plaid, crunch, dawn, rain, saxophone, automobile*—particular objects that can be seen, heard, felt, touched, smelled. These words are more vivid than abstract ones. Specific words are more emphatic than general words. An example of a general word is *music*; a more specific term is *piano solo*; still more descriptive is *Chopin's "Polonaise in A-Flat" played by Arthur Rubinstein*.

Fresh, natural words are more emphatic than stale, stereotyped expressions. Avoid trite phrases such as "spring is just around the corner" and "last but not least." These trite expressions also violate the principles of conciseness.

Attention to One Idea

Additional time in oral messages, and additional space in written messages, can be a method of emphasis. Giving more time or space to one idea emphasizes it over the remaining parts of the message. Ordinarily the writer does not think, "Well, I will give this more space because it is important," but instead writes the message in detail, which necessarily requires more space.

Use repetition with discretion in order to emphasize. Repetition is often used for sales writing or advertising, especially radio and television commercials, but not always to the best advantage.

The main idea of a message often requires more space in order to be conveyed completely and clearly, which is the reason that using more space is said to be a method of emphasis. You are, however, violating another principle of effective writing if you make the writing longer than necessary to convey the intended message.

Mechanical Means of Emphasis

Mechanical means are such methods as underlining; the use of all capitals, dashes, and special or unusual means of letter arrangement or indenting; and lists and tabulations. Different colors of ink, especially red, are often used in sales messages. Setting off lines with plenty of white space calls attention to these lines. Mechanical means of emphasis are similar to those used for readability, except that at times the methods used for emphasis are more unusual and extreme.

Subheads emphasize, as well as help to display, the organization of material. A postscript can be used to emphasize an important idea, but this postscript should not be used for something that should have gone into the letter itself.

When overused, mechanical means of emphasis lose any emphatic value that they might otherwise possess. Many points emphasized means that nothing is emphasized. In addition, some persons object to a message filled with underlining, all capitals, or portions typed in red, feeling that such an approach is unbusinesslike, emotional, or scatterbrained. The overuse of dashes contributes to a scatterbrained appearance of a written message.

Summarizing for Emphasis

Summarizing is useful for emphasizing important points, especially in longer works. In some reports or books, each section or chapter is summarized and then the entire work is summarized, perhaps through a synopsis attached to the report itself. Summarizing, like the other means of emphasizing, also contributes to readability.

A listing of points, such as those below, makes the items stand out and implies that they are important. They are easy to read and quickly understood.

Emphasis is achieved by:

1. Position
2. Sentence and paragraph construction
3. Word choice
4. Space
5. Mechanical means of emphasis
6. Summarizing

Revising for Professional Quality

The following letter is an extreme example of a message that violates principles of effective writing. (Only the body of the letter is given; all complete letters should contain the opening and closing lines discussed and illustrated in Appendix B.)

Dear Ms. Henson:

We are in receipt of your letter of recent date and in reply wish to state that we shall endeavor to submit to your claim and to send cheaper merchandise than that you previously and heretofore ordered us to send.

Attached please find a new invoice of this cheaper merchandise that you claim should sell better in your neighborhood. (Have you considered changing locations?) We expect payment immediately.

Thanking you in advance for your esteemed favor,

Sincerely,

Comments This letter is not concise because of the many old-fashioned, trite phrases. It also lacks tact and makes no effort to build goodwill.

These words and phrases should be omitted entirely:

In the first paragraph, everything is unnecessary before *we shall endeavor*. *Heretofore* is redundant, legal jargon, and imprecise. *Attached please find* is trite business jargon, as is *Thanking you in advance*. *For your esteemed favor*, always unnecessary and overly humble, has been considered old-fashioned for at least fifty years.

Words with unpleasant connotations are *cheaper* and *endeavor* in the particular way it is used in the sentence. *Claim* is a word that is often accusing, especially in *you claim*, which implies disbelief. In this letter, however, the first *claim* is inexact; the writer had made a request. *To submit to* is not only inexact but also inappropriate.

The suggestion that the store be moved to another location is sarcastic.

Although this letter includes unnecessary words and phrases, it is also incomplete; for example, the writer states that an invoice is attached but does not mention the merchandise or how it was or will be shipped.

Suggested revision

Dear Ms. Henson:

The economical men's clothing you requested is on its way to you. It was sent this morning by Parcel Express. We are glad to make this exchange.

Your letter came in time for us to stop your original order. The attached invoice applies to the revised list. By paying the full amount within ten days, you will receive a 2 percent discount, more than enough to cover the shipping costs. (Use the enclosed postage-paid envelope.)

You are wise to consider the special needs of your customers. Other budget-priced clothing, both men's and women's, is illustrated in the spring catalog that will soon be sent to you.

Thank you for your order. We are sure that your customers will like your choice of merchandise.

Sincerely,

1. Write simply. Don't try to impress your readers with an extensive vocabulary of five-syllable words, but also don't give the impression of oversimplification or "writing down." Prefer short words to longer words provided they are the exact ones to express your intended meaning. Consider the connotative meanings of words as well as dictionary definitions.

2. Express your thoughts exactly. To do so you must have an extensive vocabulary. Be specific. Do not state vague generalities.

3. Write clearly, concisely, coherently, and correctly. Give all necessary information diplomatically and convincingly. Provide answers to *Who? What? Where? Why? When? How?*

4. Write objectively. Base your interpretations and decisions on facts, not on your personal desires or unsupported beliefs. Although at times you must state what you believe about a situation, or what the data seem to indicate, make sure that the reader understands that this statement is an opinion; give concrete details to support your opinions. On the other hand, avoid an appearance of hedging and timidity. Nobody expects you to have positive and definite answers to everything. If you pretend to do so, nobody will believe you.

5. Use the pronoun *I* as necessary for desired tone and meaning, but avoid using an unnecessary number. Avoid numerous paragraphs and sentences that open with *I*. Some material, such as formal reports, is often written in the "impersonal" tone, or the "third-person objective" writing style.

6. Write in an interesting and vivid style. Keep sentences fairly short, but vary sentence length and construction. Avoid using many sentences that begin with slow expletive openings, such as *there are* and *it is*.

7. Use the active voice to emphasize the actor, the passive voice to emphasize the receiver of the action. Do not use the passive voice when the active voice will more exactly express your idea in vivid terms, as it often will. An exception is the use of the passive voice in order to be tactful and diplomatic.

8. Use strong language and sentence construction. Unnecessary adverbs and adjectives weaken writing. Decrease or eliminate weak modifiers, such as *very, rather, somewhat, little, pretty*. Do not use linking verbs unnecessarily; prefer more active, specific ones.

9. Use short paragraphs, especially beginning and ending ones. One-sentence paragraphs are acceptable and often desirable in business letters and memorandums.

10. Emphasize what you wish to emphasize. Methods of emphasis include position, word choice, sentence structure, and various mechanical means of emphasis, such as underlining. The first and last positions of a letter or memorandum are the most emphatic, as is a beginning topic sentence of a paragraph.

11. Organize! Ordinarily the best method of organization for short communications is the "direct" order, in which the most important part of the message is placed at the beginning. An exception is a message containing bad news or, at times, unexpected information.

12. Omit trite business jargon. If you insert phrases such as "enclosed please find" and "as per your request" because you have seen them in other business letters, *don't*. Write naturally, informally, and conversationally.

Test Yourself: Chapter Review

1–2. Distinguish between the terms *brief* and *concise*.

3–4. If a writer is overly concerned with brevity, the message may lack _____ or _____.

5–10. Name six methods of achieving the desired emphasis.

11–14. Simple, complex, compound, and compound-complex sentences are mentioned in this chapter. Compose an example of each type of sentence.

15. Explain how an expert knowledge of sentence construction is an aid to writing and revising.

16. According to your textbook, average sentence length for simple letters and memorandums should ordinarily not exceed _____ words.

17. Why are one-sentence paragraphs sometimes effective?

18. What is the name of the readability formula discussed in Chapter 4?

19–20. Name two weaknesses of readability formulas.

21–23. Name three rules for editing.

24. What is meant by a comma fault?

Test Yourself: Correct Usage

(Related to material in Chapter 4 and principles of correct usage.) Insert necessary punctuation, including quotation marks, hyphens, and apostrophes, and remove punctuation that has been inserted incorrectly. Choose correct word from each pair or group. Make any other necessary changes.

1. A letter or memorandum should be no longer than necessary to accomplish (its, it's) purposes but one of these purposes is to build or maintain goodwill.

2. If the writer is overly concerned with brevity the letter or memorandum may lack courtesy or completeness.

3. One purpose of your letter or memorandum is to convince the reader to (accept, except) your instructions or ideas.

4. The successful business writer is (adept, adopt, adapt) in the use of language and (altogether, all together) sure of company policies and (procedures, proceedures).

5. Business jargon (affects, effects) a letter in several undesirable ways.

6. One (effect, affect) of business jargon is to make a letter seem old-fashioned.

7. Another result of business jargon is to make a letter less concise. Than it would be otherwise.

8. The teacher gave this (advice, advise) to her students ''Write in your own words omitting trite stereotyped phrases.

9. Enclosed please find is a trite business phrase that should be omitted.

10. Another phrase that should be omitted is Thank you in advance.

11. Short paragraphs increase readability especially short first and last paragraphs of letters and memorandums.

12. The student (cited, sited) William Faulkner when the teacher (recommended, reccommended) short sentences.

13. A table or chart (emphasize, emphasizes) specific data.

14. The arrangement of charts and tables (affect, affects) comprehension.

15. The first paragraph as well as the last paragraph of letters and memorandums (is, are) emphatic.

1. Improve the following sentences from business messages.

   a. As an outstanding businessman, I request your opinion of the new tax regulations.

   b. The letter, as well as the two reports, were sent to you this morning.

   c. He was asked to remove the clutter, repair the fence, and that he must build a sidewalk.

   d. Taking claims and to analyze them is part of the job's responsibilities.

   e. We hope to receive the check within a week.

   f. We are in receipt of your order of a recent date and in reply wish to state that we thank you for same and for your check in payment that was attached thereto, which was in the amount of $42.50.

   g. That is the typewriter that makes the most noise of all those in the room.

   h. Graduates who are the ones with the highest grade point average will be the first ones who will be interviewed.

   i. During the passed year this principal has been in effect.

   j. The reasoning of all our salesmen and supervisors indicate that this product should be discontinued.

   k. Neither the teacher nor the students was concerned about the noise in the hall.

   l. The employer, who we went to Dallas to see, was most courteous to my wife and I.

   m. The secretaries and myself have long been concerned about this matter.

   n. Is it true that Jerry is the one whom is to be considered?

   o. Tennis racquets we carry come in two different types. The beginner and the professional with different prices for each type.

   p. Coming in two different types, I can send you either racquet you prefer.

   q. We only sell the two types. Not one for the intermediate player.

   r. This letter is in reply to your letter of November 6. In reply to this letter I wish to advise that in reference to your question about the Anderson account, it has now been partially paid $200 of the $350 has been collected.

   s. The question you asked is not a question that can be easily answered; your question raises another question.

   t. Do not hesitate to telephone me if you have questions about the policy enclosed herein and attached hereto.

   u. This policy not only must be read and understood it must be signed and returned.

   v. The arrival of the merchandise at this time is unfortunate, can it be returned?

   w. Meeting at noon, the constitution was completely rewritten by four o'clock by the Board of Directors.

   x. The manager is involved in the search for an answer.

   y. The last game of the season was played in by Bill.

   z. These three bills are the ones which are past due.

   aa. The workers in the department have worked here for three years.

   bb. The committee which is to make the decision will decide upon the cheapest of the alternatives.

   cc. The project was terminated as a result of not being able to bring it to fruition within the annual guidelines.

   dd. Working for efficiency, the new reconciliation procedure is considered to be more efficient than the old procedure by the controller.

   ee. The aforementioned data was taken under advisement and it was ascertained by management that procedures should be implemented immediately to rectify the situation.

2. Write instructions for using an electrical appliance, such as a tape recorder, clock-radio, or microwave oven in step-by-step, easily understood language. Speak to the reader directly instead of writing vaguely about the product.

3. Summarize a lecture from another business course in which you are enrolled. If you are taking no other business courses, summarize a lecture from any other course.

4. Discuss these statements:

   a. A short word can be less readable than a long one.

   b. Readability formulas can be misleading if used in the wrong way.

c. Specific words are more emphatic and forceful than general, abstract ones, but at times the more general word is the better choice.

d. The writer may find it easier to write a long letter, memorandum, or report than to write a short one.

e. The use of business jargon can possibly save time, but it may also waste time. In any event, the writer should work for fresh, original expressions.

f. We can never be "completely complete," as it is impossible to say everything about anything. Thus, all communication is a form of abstracting, choosing exactly what to communicate and what to omit.

CHAPTER 5

Building Goodwill through Communication

We find it easy to express goodwill when we actually feel it. If we have pleasant, positive attitudes toward ourselves, other people, and the company for which we work, this outlook will be reflected in our writing or other communication. If we do not have desirable attitudes, our writing and speech, if not blunt and unpleasant, may sound strained and forced. As much as possible, we should put ourselves into the place of our reader or listener. Although we may not agree with the other's viewpoint, we should try to understand it.

Although many of our letters will be to persons we have never met, we know that these persons are likely to be much like ourselves. They respond to fair and courteous treatment. They want to be treated as intelligent adults. They want their ideas and opinions to be taken seriously. They appreciate sincere praise, but they do not enjoy being scolded, bossed, or preached to. They realize that other persons make mistakes, and they are usually willing to overlook honest mistakes. They expect and deserve an apology when one is due, but they do not like excessive apologizing or undue humility.

A Sincere You-Attitude

The *you-attitude* (or the *you-approach*) looks at a situation from the viewpoint of the reader or the listener. The *you-attitude* is sincere. The opposite concept is the *I-attitude* (or *I-approach*).

A letter written entirely in the you-attitude includes a positive rather than negative approach, a cheerful rather than pessimistic outlook, and a pleasant rather than unpleasant tone. Organization of material and the actual physical appearance of business writing make up part of the you-attitude, for to mail a messy, carelessly typewritten letter is as discourteous as is going to a party in dirty clothes.

A writer can be filled with goodwill and yet not be able to make this feeling apparent in letters and other communications. The desire to serve does not guarantee proficiency in written or oral business communication, although it is an essential element. To achieve all the desirable qualities of communication and the total you-attitude, a writer must acquire certain techniques and skills.

Direct Your Communication toward the Reader

A type of wording that *violates* the you-approach appears in sentences such as these:

All I-approach (NOT you-approach) because of emphasis on writer or company

> Our company is pleased to announce the opening of our new store.
>
> We are very happy that the Smith Sporting Goods Company is now expanding.
>
> I am very happy to have your order.
>
> The Smith Sporting Goods Company is very happy to have your order.
>
> We at Smith Sporting Goods Company thank you for your order.

Each of these sentences, when read alone, seems only to show pride in the employing company, a worthy attitude but not enough. Letters may be built around the theme that a company is opening a new store or moving to a new neighborhood, but if the reader does not interpret these company changes in the light of personal benefits, the letter has not been written in the complete you-attitude.

When announcing expansion or other company changes, the writer should show how these changes will benefit the reader in convenience or economy. The sentence *We are now located in your neighborhood* is not nearly as effective as *You are now only five minutes away from the store that can fill all your sporting goods needs.*

The sentence

Emphatic opening word is we.

> We are shipping your goods today

could not be described as negative, for it tells what is ordinarily considered good news. It is even more effective, though, if written this way:

Emphatic opening word is your.

> Your goods will be shipped today.

Question: Is it true that paragraphs should always begin with some word other than *I* or *we*?

Answer: No. Such advice is too restrictive, although you should avoid starting numerous paragraphs with *I* or *we.*

Improve Your Writing

Paragraphs beginning with *I* and *we*, if used to excess, result in the appearance of the I-approach, not the you-approach. The opening word in a paragraph is particularly emphatic; ordinarily *I* and *we* do not deserve this much emphasis. Although you are wise not to begin a great number of paragraphs with *I* or *we*, to avoid such openings completely may result in clumsy, unnatural, nonconversational sentences.

The word *you* can be effectively used to open paragraphs, but even this approach can become monotonous if it is overused. All writing should be simple, direct, and natural. Working too hard to emphasize *you* and to subordinate *I* may result in writing that seems insincere.

When you find three paragraphs in sequence beginning with *I*, that's too many. If your letter contains five paragraphs and three of these paragraphs begin with *I* or *we*, revise.

Or, even better because of additional information,

> You should receive your complete order within a week. It was shipped today by United Parcel, as you requested.

You opening; also includes specific, positive information

Even more effective is a specific, descriptive word rather than *goods* or *order.* For example:

> Your beautiful suit is on its way to you [to be followed by specific, positive details].

You opening, plus resale

This sentence, in addition to being more exact as to the type of merchandise, implies that the suit was a wise purchase by describing it as beautiful. Such words and phrases can easily be overused, however; if so, they detract from the goodwill-building aspects of the message because they sound insincere.

The sentence that describes a suit as "beautiful" illustrates the sales approach known as *resale*; it emphasizes the value of a purchase already made. Resale can also be used to "resell" the company or other organization. It must be used with caution, particularly in bad-news messages such as refused adjustments. If used subtly and with discretion, resale passages are a form of the positive approach, discussed later in this chapter.

Resale is not exactly the same as *sales promotion*, a broader term. Sales promotion includes resale (along with various other kinds of sales messages). The announcement of a forthcoming sale is sales promotion, but not resale. A sales clerk's remark, "You made an excellent choice," is an example of resale.

In an attempt to avoid the use of *I* or *we*, some business writers continually use the organization name, as in a sentence like this:

> The Farmers National Bank thanks you for opening a checking account with us.

NOT you-approach because of emphasis on writer's bank

Communication Brief

Conventional formulas for "I" and "you" abound in many languages. English is the only language that capitalizes "I" in writing, whereas many languages capitalize "you," and this has been interpreted, rightly or wrongly, as a sign of an exaggerated ego on the part of English speakers. A few languages, including Siamese and Hungarian (the latter only in flowery speech), use "slave" for "I."

Mario Pei, *The Story of Language,* rev. ed. (New York: Lippincott, 1965), 84.

Avoid unnecessary use of a company name. In the first place, the company name is given in the letterhead. In the second place, unnecessary use of the company name is really the I-attitude. Even though the word *I* is not used, emphasis is away from the reader and back to the company from which the letter comes. Another disadvantage is that the letter sounds stuffy and formal instead of personal, natural, and friendly. The reader knows that the letter comes not from the company (companies can't speak or write letters), but from someone at the company. *I* and *we* should be used when to do otherwise seems stiff and unnatural.

Some writers routinely use *we* instead of *I,* even though they obviously mean *I.* Such usage is unnatural and unnecessary. If you are talking about yourself as an individual company representative—as is possible or desirable even though the you-attitude is used throughout—then the word to use is *I,* not *we.* If you are speaking of a group of employees or the company as an organization of individuals, *we* is appropriate.

Do not use *you* when you mean *I* or people in general. Such use is not only confusing and nonspecific but also may be interpreted as negative toward the reader or listener. For example, the sentence

Weak because of you *used to mean people in general; also negative approach*

> You can't hope to save money in these inflationary times

should not be worded in this way if the *you* does not refer to the reader or listener, but rather to the writer or speaker or to people in general. If you mean *I,* say so. If you mean that most people find saving money difficult, put your thoughts into these specific words. It is quite possible that your reader or listener *is* saving money.

Also avoid the greatly overused *you know.* Someday a listener will reply: "No, I *don't* know. Please say what you mean."

Almost all letters and memorandums, as well as many reports, are written in what is described as the "personal tone," in which first-person pronouns (*I, we, us, me,* and other pronouns that refer to the writer or speaker) are used when they seem desirable or necessary. The *personal writing tone* also uses second-person pronouns (*you* or other pronouns that refer to the reader or listener).

The "impersonal tone" also described as the "third-person writing style," includes no *I's, we's, you's,* or other first- or second-person pronouns. The impersonal tone is appropriate for many reports, most news stories, and other kinds of written material. A good communicator writes well in both the personal and the impersonal tone and chooses the most appropriate style for the particular material, situation, and readership.

Because as a writer you want to involve the readers, using the word *you*, as well as *I, me,* and other first-person pronouns, sets a tone that seems more directly related to the reader, provided that you do not use these words inappropriately or to excess. Remember that a letter or memorandum filled with *I's*, *we's*, and other words that refer to the writer is *not* likely to be written with the reader uppermost in mind. *Be especially careful not to begin all or most paragraphs with I.* The *I's* (instead of the *you's*) are given undue emphasis by their emphatic position at the beginning of a sentence.

True Consideration Consists of More Than the Choice of Pronouns

The sentence

> We are glad to receive your contract for our services

Wording suggests I-approach, NOT you-approach

may connote that the company is selfishly grasping for business. Although the reader realizes that the company must make a profit, this frank reminder is less than diplomatic.

The you-attitude may be contrasted with both the I-attitude and the neutral attitude. The I-attitude is conveyed by the use of the first-person pronoun, as in this sentence:

> We are happy to announce that we have increased the size of our store building.

Emphasis on we; *NOT you-approach*

Expressed with the use of the word *you*, the sentence would read like this:

> Now you will find a wider choice of merchandise in the greatly enlarged building.

Reader benefit

A third way of expressing this same idea does not actually bring the reader into the picture, as the preceding sentence does. This objective and neutral writing reads something like this:

> The enlarged store building has allowed for a much greater variety of merchandise.

A neutral approach, neither I *nor* you

Some readers will interpret this last sentence to mean that they now have a wider choice and that the company has increased its services to them. This meaning, however, is not as direct and personal as the one that makes use of the word *you*. Both the first and the second illustrations are written in the personal tone. The third is in the impersonal tone, which refers to neither the writer nor the reader.

The cost of a product is subordinated by the use of the neutral approach.

You are more diplomatic when you say:

Neutral wording, more diplomatic than use of you

> This product sells for $22

than when you say:

The word you *causes this sentence to be* less *diplomatic than the neutrally worded preceding sentence*

> This will cost you $22.

Even worse is:

Dictatorial; use of word you *detracts from true you-approach*

> You must pay $22 for this product.

The words *I, we, us, our,* and other first-person pronouns do not in themselves convey the I-attitude instead of the you-attitude, for the major consideration is *what* is said, not how it is expressed. On the other hand, an abundance of *I's* and other first-person pronouns gives an impression of disregard for the reader, an impression that is likely to be correct; otherwise, numerous references to the writer would not occur.

The word *you* may make a real difference in the reception of a message, even though the reader has no idea of the you-attitude and does not consciously note that the letter is written with more *I's* than *you's.*

As shown in the examples below, sentences written in the first person can sometimes be more pleasant and positive than those written in the second person.

True you-attitude although we is used

> We are sorry that we cannot grant a further extension of time on the loan.

Dictatorial; not you-attitude

> You must pay the full amount of your loan immediately.

Notice the wording of the following letter, which definitely does not convey the you-attitude:

Emphasis on writer, NOT reader; egotistical

> As newly elected membership director of the Junior Chamber of Commerce, I am in charge of recruiting new members. I would like very much for you to join. I am working for a record-making membership this year.

Accusing, negative

> I do not know why you are not a member, anyway; most of the other young business owners in this town are, you know.

Demanding

> Fill out the enclosed application blank and return with your check.

First Paragraph Notice the definite I-attitude in the emphatic first sentence. Throughout the paragraph, writer benefits are stressed, not those of the reader.

Second Paragraph Most undiplomatic. Even if readers had been planning to join, this letter is enough to keep them away forever.

Third Paragraph Dictatorial. Discourteous. No reader benefit.

An improved version of this letter could begin with a paragraph like this:

> You are wanted—and needed—by the Whitehaven Jaycees.

Emphatic you *opening*

The middle paragraphs could be devoted to describing the advantages of joining the Junior Chamber of Commerce, especially from the standpoint of how the organization helps the community. This letter is essentially a sales letter, as the reader is to be sold on the idea of joining the organization. A sales message should ordinarily be longer than the first version of this letter. In order to convince the reader to act, it must present sufficient evidence and motivation. An improved closing section could be:

> So that you can begin now to enjoy the benefits of membership and to contribute to the welfare of your community, fill out the enclosed membership application and send it in with your check. It will be a small investment that you will remember with pride.

Diplomatically stated request for action

> Our next meeting is Monday, September 8, at 7:30 p.m. at the Quality Inn. We are looking forward to seeing you.

Additional information in goodwill close

In summary, the you-attitude expresses a genuine consideration for the reader. Although the word *you* may at times appear to be more considerate than an *I*, the actual content of the message is more important than the choice of words. If the word *I* is used to a great extent, however, it is quite likely that the emphasis is on the writer, not the reader.

In the following example, each paragraph that makes up a letter is first given in an *incorrect, ineffective,* or *inappropriate* way. This version is followed by comments and a suggested revision.

Paragraph 1

> We are happy to inform you that our business has increased to the extent that we, Nationwide Airlines, are now serving Denver with air flights to two cities in Mexico, and we would like to have you take advantage of this added service. We believe that we, Nationwide Airlines, have the best airline in the country, and we are eager to add more cities. Hope to see you soon.

Poor opening paragraph; I-approach; trite, abbreviated sentence

Comments The preceding paragraph is extremely I-oriented, not you-oriented. In addition, it is too long for an opening paragraph. The writer should have been more specific; which two cities in Mexico? The phrase *to inform you* is wordy, unnecessary, and overly formal.

Although the words *we* and *Nationwide Airlines* appear far more often than the word *you*, thus decreasing emphasis on the reader, the actual use of these words alone is less important than the content of the message, which stresses throughout benefits to the airline, not to the reader.

The last abbreviated sentence seems to be a feeble attempt to avoid the use of the word *we* and to express goodwill. The words *I* or *we* should NOT be omitted in sentences such as this one, which is awkward and not grammatically correct because of the omitted subject.

Revised Paragraph 1

Improved opening paragraph

> Would you like to spend next weekend in Mexico City or Guadalajara? On our newly scheduled flights, you can leave Denver after a leisurely breakfast and arrive at either of these exciting Mexican cities in time for an early dinner.

Comments The potential vacationer or business traveler is more interested in the exact cities and the time of arrival than in the fact that Nationwide Airlines is prospering, that it is the finest airline company in the country, or that the writer hopes to see the reader soon.

A letter of this kind would require more than the two paragraphs illustrated in this extremely poor letter; at least three or four paragraphs that convincingly describe the cities or the pleasant flights should be included in order to persuade the reader to make reservations. Even if these paragraphs had been included, however, the following ending paragraph would be less than effective.

Paragraph 2 (closing paragraph)

Poor closing paragraph

> We are expecting many passengers on our new flights, so hurry to make your reservation. If you don't make it early, you may be left out. We do not offer discount rates, however.

Revised Paragraph 2

Improved closing paragraph

> To start planning your trip to Mexico City or Guadalajara, telephone 303-000-0000. Our helpful reservation agents are waiting to answer all your questions and arrange your flight.

A Positive, Pleasant, and Diplomatic Approach

A *positive approach* and the *you-attitude* are two of the most important elements of effective communication. In effect, we cannot fully achieve one without the other.

The positive approach includes several applications. One is the pleasant approach, which stresses the pleasant and not the unpleasant elements of a situation. Another is stating what can be done instead of what cannot be done. Another is eliminating as much as possible the actual grammatical negatives, such as *no, cannot, will not,* and *can't,* as well as other negative words and phrases, including *criticize, reject, fail, turn down, must, force,* and similar expressions. Another application of the positive approach is to avoid a *doubtful tone,* as discussed later.

Emphasize the Positive and Subordinate the Negative

An example of the use of the negative approach in an advertisement is given in the first example; the positive approach in the second.

Negative because of implication

> This line of cookware will not become scratched, and food will not stick to it. It won't be ruined in your dishwasher.

By telling what the cookware does *not* do, the first example suggests to some readers that it may do all these things. Although the second example is not guaranteed to inspire absolute confidence in all readers, it is more likely to do so than the negatively worded statement.

> Because this sturdy Teflon-coated cookware is highly resistant to heat and pressure, it is completely safe in your dishwasher. It will still be shining and beautiful after many years of non-stick cooking.

More positive

Saying that something *is not undesirable* is not nearly as effective or positive as stating that it *is desirable.* Even better is to give specific and definite information as to why it is desirable, in the terms of how it will benefit the reader or listener. The description of the cookware would be more convincing than the sentence given above if it included evidence of why the cookware will remain beautiful. Such evidence might include a descriptive statement of the material or the method of manufacture.

The sentence

> You will never regret using our bank

Implies possible regret

is not as positive as saying

> You will benefit from our many banking services.

States positive idea

Instead of saying

> The interest rate on your credit card is not exorbitant

Implies overcharging

say something like this:

> The balance of your account can be carried forward from month to month at an interest rate of 11 percent, up to an agreed-upon credit limit.

More positive and specific

Emphasize the benefits readers or listeners will gain from the product, not difficulties or misfortunes they will avoid. An unpleasant thought tends to make people turn away from the subject and think of something else. Notice the following examples of the negative and positive approach:

Negative	Positive
The cafe will close at 11:30 P.M.	The cafe will remain open until 11:30 P.M.
We cannot ship your sofa until July 1.	Your sofa will be shipped on July 1.

Notice the first example given above. Let us see how we can make the sentence even more negative or more positive. If we should write:

> We close the cafe every night at 11:30 so that we can go home

we are using not only the negative approach but also the I-attitude, instead of the you-attitude, because the emphasis is on the store and its employees rather than on the customer. Few writers would use such an extreme sentence, although emphasis on the negative and on *I* rather than *you* is far too common.

The first example of the more positive sentence can be made even better from the standpoint of the positive approach and you-attitude. Suppose we write:

> The cafe will remain open until 11:30 P.M. for the convenience of our customers.

This sentence tells how long the store will be open, not when it will close. It also brings in the you-attitude, provided the letter is being written to a customer.

This sentence can be improved still further. Suppose we write it this way:

> To extend the enjoyment of your dinner, the cafe will remain open until 11:30 P.M.

Do you see why this sentence better conveys the you-attitude than the preceding one? Here the actual use of the word *your* makes the difference, for the writing more directly aims at an individual. To this individual, the word *your* is more direct, more personal, and more friendly than the general and collective words *our customers.*

The word *you* is usually preferred over the term *our customers*, even though the message will be printed or duplicated in some form and distributed to thousands of customers. Although the same letter is being sent to many persons, each customer reading the message is an individual. Individuals think of themselves alone, not necessarily in relation to thousands of other customers.

Other examples of the positive versus the negative approach include the following:

Negative	Positive
After just one week of our weight-loss program you won't feel fat and miserable.	After only one week of "Aerobics for Fitness" your clothes will be looser and you will feel strong and trim.
Red Cross will not be conducting classes any time in September.	The date of the next Red Cross class is October 6. We invite you to enroll.
I will not be able to attend the dinner on Friday, March 3, but I will be present for the luncheon.	On Friday, March 3, I can attend only the luncheon.
If you do not donate the use of your pool for lifeguard training, we will be unable to train the guards you need.	The American Red Cross requests the use of your pool from March 3 through March 6 for lifeguard training. Our comprehensive and intensive course will provide you with capable personnel for the summer season.
Every resident will have to leave the dormitory over the Christmas holidays, from December 22 through January 13.	All dormitory residents will live elsewhere during the Christmas holidays, from December 22 through January 13. We wish you all a happy holiday season.

Negative	Positive
We cannot give you your paycheck until Friday after next.	You will receive your paycheck on Friday, February 27.
Your messy laundry won't be half bad after you use Brilliant detergent.	Your clothes will be fresh and bright after you wash them with Brilliant.
You will not be allowed to take vacation between January 1 and June 1.	Please schedule your vacation, at any time you choose, between June 2 and December 31.
You must pay your bill by the tenth of each month to receive a discount of 2 percent.	By paying your monthly invoice by the tenth, you will earn a 2 percent discount.

Avoid a Doubtful Tone

Success oriented describes another function of the positive approach. *Success-oriented passages imply acceptance or favorable action on the part of the reader.* This concept is also referred to as *success consciousness*. The opposite approach is called the *doubtful tone.* Words to avoid are *if, hope,* and *trust,* as well as any other words or phrases that suggest doubt.

Notice the doubtful tone in these sentence beginnings:

If you want to follow these instructions . . .

If my qualifications meet your requirements . . .

If you want to order this book . . .

We hope this meets your approval . . .

We trust this is a satisfactory arrangement . . .

I know that this is less than you expected, but . . .

I know you will be disappointed in us, but . . .

We hope that this unfortunate occurrence will not adversely affect our business relationship, for . . .

All these expressions imply that the reader will not agree to the suggested opinions or actions or will not continue to hold the writer in esteem. More persuasive wordings are these:

You will find these instructions helpful, for . . .

May I come for an interview to discuss my qualifications in detail?

Just sign the enclosed card and *Effective Reports* will soon be on its way to you.

We think you will like this change of procedure because . . .

Diplomatic and effective

Perhaps the other doubtfully worded sentences shown above could be omitted entirely. No matter what the situation, a statement such as:

We hope that this unfortunate occurrence will not adversely affect our business relationship

Extremely negative

is probably more harmful than the occurrence itself.

Sometimes the positive, diplomatic approach is achieved by what we refrain from stating. For example, you do not need to include the following statement in order to obtain the necessary information:

Includes negative word failed; accusing

> In your recent order, you failed to include your size.

A better wording is:

Asks for action without placing blame

> The sweaters come in these sizes: Small (34–36), Medium (38–40), and Large (42–44). Please check your size on the enclosed card.

This improved version omits the very negative and accusing word *failed* and moves directly to the requested action.

The following statement is another example of a fact that is often best left unexpressed:

Stresses a weakness

> Unfortunately, I have no business experience.

This statement from an application letter stresses a supposed weakness. You are not misrepresenting your experience by omitting such references. If no experience is described in your letter or data sheet, the reader should suppose that you have none. Stress strong points, not weaknesses, as:

Stresses positive factors

> My courses in business administration at Indiana State University have given me an understanding of the fundamentals of management and supervision.

To achieve the positive, pleasant, diplomatic tone, we should make use of the techniques of emphasis and subordination. An old song urges us to "accentuate the positive and eliminate the negative," or to stress the pleasant and subordinate the unpleasant. We stress or subordinate by position and arrangement, by sentence construction, and by word choice.

Use Specific Words to Express Pleasant and Neutral Ideas

Concrete, specific words should be used to express pleasant or neutral ideas, but more general, abstract terms should be chosen to express unpleasant ideas. For example:

Overly specific

> I'm sorry you have pneumonia and dermatitis

although specific and more accurate than

Improved

> I'm sorry you are ill

is certainly less diplomatic. Another extreme example is:

Far too specific

> We have learned of the unfortunate circumstances of your accident, illness, and losses in the stock market.

In a situation like this, choose to be less than specific and use some generalized word like *problems*. Although *problems* in most cases is a negative word, here, in comparison with the exact words, it is positively cheerful. Most likely, mention of the unfortunate circumstances should be omitted altogether.

Express pleasant and neutral ideas or statements in specific, forceful words. For example:

> Congratulations on being elected president of your senior class!
>
> I am interested in typewriting paper with 25-percent cotton content, 20-pound weight.

Specific, in order to emphasize and give necessary information

For most of your writing, choose specific, concrete words. They are more vivid, direct, and exact. At times, however, choose more general, abstract words in order to express ideas diplomatically.

Another principle of forceful, descriptive, concise writing—*prefer the active voice*—is reversed at times for the sake of tact and diplomacy. The following section is provided to refresh your understanding of active and passive verbs.

Choose the Active or the Passive Voice

A verb is the strongest and the most vivid part of speech. Verbs are stronger in the active voice—more direct, forceful, and concise—than in the passive voice. A good writer chooses the active voice unless there is a specific reason to use the passive voice. Only transitive verbs (those that have or imply an object) can be expressed in both active and passive voices.

The following sentences illustrate the difference between active and passive verbs:

- *Active:* The decorator rearranged the office furniture.
- *Passive:* The office funiture was rearranged by the decorator.

Of the two sentences, the first, with the verb in the active voice, is more direct, forceful, and concise. At times, however, the person who acts is irrelevant or unknown. In such cases, the best sentence construction is as follows:

- *Passive:* The office furniture has been rearranged.

More illustrations of the active-passive dimension are shown below:

- *Active:* We should include more colors in our line of denim slacks.
- *Passive:* More colors should be included in our line of denim slacks.

As the immediately preceding sentence illustrates, the passive voice emphasizes *more colors* by placement in the emphatic first position of the sentence. Perhaps this is the desired emphasis. In the following sentences, however, the active voice is more concise and direct.

- *Active:* Ruth asked many questions.
- *Passive:* Many questions were asked by Ruth.

- *Active:* The committee approved two changes in the constitution.
- *Passive:* Two changes in the constitution were approved by the committee.

The following sentences do not include verbs in the passive voice, but the construction results in the same slow, weak effect.

- It is desirable to include more colors in our line of denim slacks.
- There should be increased production of our denim slacks.

The words *there* and *it* are function words or "structural fillers" that replace true subjects. They are usually referred to as *expletives*. Weaker than specific subjects, they may be used with discretion. *There* and *it* sentence beginnings, provided they are not overused, may be at times the most natural and understandable expressions.

The passive voice is in no way incorrect; neither are sentences beginning with there *or* it. They are discussed here because many writers use the passive voice and *it* and *there* as subjects unnecessarily, especially when writing in the impersonal tone. Most sentences can be and should be written with "real" subjects and active verbs.

With the active or passive voice, as with word choice and sentence construction, the most important consideration is to express your meaning exactly.

Although we should usually prefer the active verb, at times the passive construction may be more conducive to goodwill. The following sentence is expressed with the verb in the active voice, but it is not diplomatic:

Accusing

> You failed to water the plants.

Expressed in the *passive* voice, the sentence reads:

Neutral

> The plants have not been watered.

Notice that in the first example *you* is the subject and *failed* is the verb. In the second sentence, *plants,* the subject, receives the action. Because the idea to be expressed is essentially negative, the passive construction is less accusing; emphasis is away from *you* and toward *the plants.* The word *failed* adds to the overall accusatory tone.

Rewording of such sentences, however, does not necessarily require the passive construction, as shown by this remedy:

Neutral

> The plants seem dry.

In this example, too, emphasis is away from *you* and on the plants.

This discussion of the positive approach does not mean that you will never use the words *no, not,* or *cannot.* Sometimes such words are necessary for your exact meaning, as in the sentence immediately preceding this one. It is better to use a somewhat negative statement than to run the risk of being misunderstood. Inoffensive writing can include such words as *cannot* and *no,* provided it is courteous and considerate. Even the word *must* may be necessary in urgent situations, although it should ordinarily be avoided.

Clearness should not be sacrificed for the sake of diplomacy, but good writing should be both clear and diplomatic. It can be, although at times there must be a direct order or an unmistakable refusal. For example, instead of *stop,* suppose that the roadside sign is worded, *pause, please, if you have time.*

The following letters illustrate the extreme lack of a positive approach because of the choice of words.

Weak letter because of negative approach

You did not submit your report on time. Jack, we cannot hope to complete the project if you are unable to discharge your responsibilities.   } *Accusing*

Otherwise, meeting our deadline will be impossible. We will not regret doing so, for the project is important.   } *Negative*

If you want to send in the report within a few days, let me know.   } *Negative because of doubtful tone*

Comments This extreme example illustrates various words, phrases, and sentence constructions that result in a negative approach. Seldom would a single letter contain so many negative expressions.

Another important principle is that clarity, importance, and urgency must not be forgotten when working for the positive approach or the you-attitude. For example, in the letter shown above, the reader must understand that the report has to be submitted immediately if the project is to be completed on time.

Suggested revision

Jack, we can complete the project on time only if your report is received in this office within five days.

Everything else is going well. We can meet the scheduled date soon after your report is received. We both realize the importance of this work, and we will both be rewarded for its prompt completion.

Please telephone and let me know when the report will arrive.

In summary, the positive approach is pleasant and diplomatic. It emphasizes what can be done, not what cannot be done; the pleasant, not the unpleasant. It emphasizes the benefits to be gained, not the unpleasant things that could occur, or even those that will not occur. It eliminates words or phrases that are likely to make negative impressions, no matter how the words or phrases are used (words such as *fail, reject,* and *criticize*).

Using the Direct and Indirect Arrangements to Achieve a Diplomatic Approach

The difference between direct and indirect arrangements of business communications is this: The direct (or the deductive) arrangement begins with the main gist of the message and uses the remaining space to expand on the central message by giving details, examples, or pertinent information. The indirect (or the inductive) builds up to the gist of the message. These arrangements can be used in written works of all lengths. *The direct presentation is usually preferable unless there is a definite reason for using the indirect.*

*Improve
Your Writing*

Question: Isn't an indirect arrangement of letters and memorandums beating around the bush? (I know that "beating around the bush" is a cliche, but cliches save a lot of time and space.)

Answer: A message arranged in an indirect order definitely should not appear to beat around the bush. If it does, it is poorly written. You are right that cliches are useful; they save time, space, and thought. (They may also waste time and space.) In addition, sometimes the meaning of even well-known cliches is not clear. What do we actually do when we beat around the bush, and what kind of bush is it?

Communications that appear to misrepresent, equivocate, evade, sidestep, hedge, prevaricate, or pussyfoot are worse than bluntly direct ones. Well-written messages, however, can be diplomatically arranged in an indirect order and also be clear, convincing, and truthful.

In conversation we ordinarily prepare our listeners for bad or unexpected news. We may say, "There's something I need to talk with you about, Bill. Do you have time for a soft drink?" Most of us would not call to Bill, as he walks down the hall, that his job is being eliminated.

All general principles have exceptions. Some bad news is so serious that opening with anything other than "I'm sorry" would be heartless. Such extremely bad news, however, should ordinarily be expressed orally, not in a letter or memorandum.

The direct arrangement is advantageous in that it is easier to read. The reader immediately knows what the message is about. The emphatic beginning of the message is used as it should be, to emphasize something important. The direct arrangement, however, has a psychological disadvantage in some instances. The reader may not be prepared for the most important part of the message if it is disappointing or something that the reader is not likely to believe or accept.

In such a situation, the indirect arrangement should be used in order to prepare the reader to accept or to believe the conclusions of the letter or report. For example, if reasons are given first or if information is included to show how the final conclusions and recommendations were reached, the reader is more likely to accept these conclusions and recommendations. In addition, some explanation of a situation is often necessary to make the important part of the message clear, even though the reader is willing to accept the message.

The direct order increases readability. News stories and news releases are usually written in the direct order; the main facts of the story are given in the first paragraph, facts of lesser importance are given in the second, and so on. This plan is used in news releases so that any necessary cutting can be done from the bottom. Even when the news article or release appears in its complete and original form, this arrangement of ideas, from the most important to the least, increases reader interest and understanding. Business letters, like newspapers, are often read hurriedly, so any arrangement that will increase quick and easy understanding should be used.

Not all material can be written in the direct order, even when there is no psychological aspect to consider, for to do so would decrease, not increase, reader understanding. The reader must have an idea of the subject to be discussed before understanding the conclusions. There may be need for introductory paragraphs or sections to help the reader comprehend the most important facts.

Choosing and Planning an Appropriate Order of Arrangement

The direct arrangement is usually the wisest choice for all letters and memorandums unless there is a definite reason for using the indirect or, occasionally, the chronological. The indirect prepares the reader, through reasoning or other explanatory or introductory material, to accept an unpleasant or surprising conclusion or statement. To determine the best arrangement of ideas, consider the nature of the message and the person or persons who will read the communication. Then decide on the reader's probable reaction to the message.

Some communications contain both good news and bad news. Unless the bad news far outweighs the good news, communications can be treated basically as good-news messages. To any message, readers will react in one of the following ways:

1. The reader will be pleased.
2. The reader will be displeased.
3. The reader will be neither pleased nor displeased but will have at least some degree of interest.
4. The reader will have little initial interest.

After considering these reader reactions (sometimes you will guess incorrectly), consider the following kinds of arrangement, classified according to the sequence of ideas, purpose, and probable reader reaction.

1. Good-news messages, to be arranged in the direct order.
2. Bad-news messages, to be arranged in the indirect order.
3. Neutral or informational messages in which the reader has some initial interest, to be arranged in the direct order.
4. Persuasive messages in which the reader is assumed to have little initial interest (sales messages, persuasive requests), to be arranged in a modification of the indirect arrangement, which is the "sales" arrangement of attention, interest, conviction, and action. The most important difference between this plan and the usual indirect arrangement is the wording of the first paragraph or two of the letter.

The neutral and good-news letters and memorandums discussed in Chapters 6, 7, and 8 fall into categories 1 and 3 in the list above. Those discussed in Chapter 9, bad-news messages, fall into category 2. Persuasive messages, as discussed in Chapter 10, apply to categories 3 and 4, most often to category 4.

The suggestions given below are usually advisable:

1. In good-news messages, include the good news near the beginning of the communication, usually in the first paragraph and often in the first sentence. If the message contains both good news and bad news, ordinarily the good news should be given first, although never give the appearance of trying to mislead. (If the bad news outweighs the good news, or if you are not sure how the news will be interpreted, treat the message as a bad-news letter.) In a neutral, routine request or other message, begin with the request or the gist of the information to be conveyed unless introductory statements or explanations are needed for clarity.

2. In bad-news messages, ordinarily do not begin with the bad news. Start with some pleasant aspect of the situation or develop a neutral, relevant, diplomatic paragraph.

3. In messages that request action from the reader, end with an *action close* in which you:
   a. State the requested action. Do not assume that the action is implied and will be understood; state it directly, and, if appropriate, in terms of benefits the reader will receive from taking the requested action.
   b. Make action easy. Do not ask the reader to write a letter but to check an enclosed card. If you ask for a telephone call, include your telephone number. If you ask the reader to come to your store, include the store address and the hours it is open.
   c. When appropriate, motivate prompt action. If there can be no real benefit to the reader, state, without being demanding or dictatorial, the time you will need the information and the reason for the deadline.

Further discussion and examples of openings and closings of direct, indirect, and persuasive messages are in Chapters 6–10.

Summary

The you-attitude, also called the you-approach, is a sincere concern for the reader or listener. It includes the desire to serve, to play fair, and to understand the reader's or listener's point of view. True consideration consists of far more than the choice of pronouns; that is, the use of *you* instead of *I* or *we*. Nevertheless, an abundance of *I's* and *we's*, with few *you's*, is likely to indicate that the message is more concerned with the interests of the sender than with those of the receiver.

The positive approach stresses the pleasant elements of a situation. It emphasizes what can be done, not what cannot be done. The positive approach eliminates as much as possible grammatical negatives, such as *no* and *cannot*, as well as other negative words and phrases, such as *fail, reject, turn down, criticize,* and *neglect.*

Messages can be arranged in the direct and the indirect order. The direct arrangement is preferable unless there is a definite reason for using the indirect. Direct arrangements open with the most important part of the message. Indirect arrangements do not open with the most important portion of the message. Good-news and neutral messages should ordinarily be arranged in the direct order. Bad-news messages, as well as others that need introductory material, should be arranged in the indirect order.

The passive voice is one of several techniques that can make writing or speech more diplomatic.

Test Yourself: Chapter Review

1–2. Looking at the situation from the viewpoint of the reader or listener is known as the _____ or the _____.

3–4. A self-centered approach is known as the _____ or the _____.

5. The term that re-emphasizes the value of a purchase already made is _____.

6. Written materials that include such words as *I* and *you* are described as being written in the _____ tone.

7–8. Written materials that include no first-person or second-person pronouns are said to be written in the _____ or the _____ writing style.

9–12. What are four applications of the positive approach?

13. A concept that is the opposite of *success oriented* is described as the _____.

14. A letter or memorandum that begins with the most important item of information is said to be arranged in the _____ order.

15–18. Name four categories for expected reader response.

Test Yourself: Correct Usage

(Related to material in Chapter 5 and principles of correct usage.) Insert necessary punctuation, including quotation marks, hyphens, and apostrophes, and remove punctuation that has been inserted incorrectly. Choose correct word from each pair or group. Make any other necessary changes.

1. The concept referred to as the you-approach has long been used in business writing textbooks but some people still do not understand (its, it's) meaning.

2. The you-approach a concept long taught in business communication classes is still not understood by some people.

3. Although the you-approach has been taught for many years some people still do not understand the concept.

4. Some writers seem to feel that in order to convey a you-approach they must no longer consider themselves this is a mistaken idea.

5. The you-approach and the positive approach are interrelated and often used together but the two techniques are not identical.

6. Sally Johnson the presidents secretary composes letters using a personal computer.

7. A secretary often writes letters using (her, a) typewriter.

8. (Its, It's) fortunate that personal computers are becoming less expensive.

9. A well known adage is expressed in these words You can't judge a book by (its, it's) cover.

10. Some words should be avoided completely or almost completely because of their negative connotations.

11. Specific words although ordinarily the better choice because they are more definite and emphatic are not the most diplomatic choice for expressing unpleasant information or ideas.

12. A direct arrangement is the better choice for most letters and memorandums but an indirect arrangement is more persuasive when conveying negative information.

13. At one time the word "he" was used routinely to refer to either sex this usage was taught in classes in English composition.

14. Although some women and men will not be offended by masculine pronouns used to refer to either sex the careful writer avoids such use.

Problems

1. Improve the following passages from business letters in their use of the you-attitude, diplomacy, and the positive approach. Assume any necessary and reasonable details.

   a. The Scott Appliance Company is pleased to announce the opening of our new store, to which all our customers are invited. *(From opening paragraph of letter to customers.)*

   b. It's against company policy, so we must reject your request for sample packages for your customers. You must realize that if we give away our merchandise you will have to pay more for what you buy. *(From manufacturer's letter to retailer.)*

   c. This letterhead paper is not the thin, flimsy kind that always comes out looking cheap.

   d. This scarf won't keep out the wind and the rain, but it's pretty.

   e. You waited two days past the end of the discount period to pay your bill, so you are not entitled to the discount, which you took anyway. You know our terms quite well, 2/10, net 30.

   f. Do not fail to finish the project by the end of this week.

   g. I have not had any experience except for helping my father in his real estate business.

   h. We cannot complete your patio while the temperature is below freezing.

   i. We are flattered that you want to open a credit account with us. *(From a credit refusal letter.)*

   j. I am surprised that you say that our merchandise has not given good service, but if you will bring it in, we will consider making some kind of adjustment.

   k. Your memo indicated that you are ignorant of policies in our credit department.

   l. I was sorry to hear that you have been fired.

   m. If you are interested in our offer, let us know.

   n. We trust that you will continue buying from us.

   o. You have neglected to reply to my letter of August 11.

   p. It will be impossible to open an account for you without copies of your financial statements.

   q. If you can manage to pay your account within ten days, we will allow you a 10 percent discount.

   r. We cannot finish your report until after my August vacation.

   s. It's against our policy, so we must reject your suggestions for the improvement of our products. Our engineers have already considered everything that people think are new ideas.

   t. This packaging material is not the kind that gets holes in it at the slightest touch.

   u. Your research is completely unscientific, and your writing style is at the third-grade level.

   v. If you are interested in this plan, you might let me know sometime.

   w. The applicant is not shy or timid, and he doesn't seem to be stupid.

   x. I am pleased to announce that our company, the Success Planners, is expanding and will begin classes for executives in organizations all over town, including yours, beginning on August 1.

   y. I am sorry to take up so much of your valuable time, but I really need this information. *(From letter sent with questionnaire.)*

   z. The instructions are plainly stated, as you can see for yourself by turning to page 5.

2. Collect several business letters. Compare these letters with all elements of effective communication studied

so far; also compare their style and appearance with the standards shown in Appendix B. Consider the features of business letters listed below and make any additional comments.

a. Appearance, including the choice of letter style and an attractive placement on the sheet. (See Appendix B.)

b. Order of presentation—direct or indirect? Is the order used for this particular letter the most appropriate one for the subject matter presented?

c. Appropriate, concise, and effective beginning and ending.

d. The you-attitude.

e. A positive approach.

f. Fairly short sentences and paragraphs. Notice especially the length of the first and last paragraphs.

g. Mechanical means of emphasis, if any.

h. Natural, conversational wording, with no trite business jargon or stereotype phrasing.

3. As your instructor directs, analyze or rewrite the following sentences. Each violates the you-attitude or a positive approach. (When writing or rewriting, make reasonable assumptions and add necessary details.)

a. We hope that our mistake will not adversely affect our business relationship. *(last paragraph)*

b. This letter is for the purpose of advising you that your order is being shipped and that credit is being extended, as you requested. *(first paragraph)*

c. In reference to your letter of October 21, we are advising you that your order is being sent to you on credit. Please make sure that you pay within thirty days. *(first paragraph)*

d. I am pleased to announce that we have increased our inventory by the addition of a large line of household appliances. *(first paragraph)*

e. We are sorry that we must reject your request. *(last paragraph)*

4. To improve the goodwill approach, rewrite the following sentences in the passive voice. (Use any other techniques to increase diplomacy.)

a. You delivered the package to the wrong office.

b. All your past employers told me something different about you.

c. You knew the instructions that I distributed to all personnel.

5. For each of the following sentences, all of which violate either the you-attitude or positive approach, or both, state specifically how the wording needs to be improved, including words that should be omitted because of their negative connotation. Rewrite each.

a. Since you have failed to complete the loan application properly, your loan request is denied.

b. As editor of the magazine I am forced to reject the article you submitted for publication.

c. If you do not follow the enclosed instructions, you will not be able to assemble the doll house.

d. In your recent letter you neglected to tell me the date and time of the proposed meeting.

e. I am pleased to inform you that we here at the bank have approved your request for an automobile loan.

f. As chairman of the fund-raising committee, I would like to request that you make a donation.

g. You cannot continue to use your credit card in our store.

h. I am looking forward to giving a sneak preview of my terrific new paintings.

i. I hope you won't be dissatisfied with the new procedure.

j. I hope you like this cheaper upholstery material.

k. We cannot guarantee your motorcycle if it is not serviced by an authorized dealer.

l. Failure to complete the enclosed form will result in shipping delays.

m. National Bank wants to lend you money because we are trying to increase our loan portfolio to be more competitive with area banks.

n. We can no longer mail a collection report twice a month because of the excessive personnel time that is required.

6. Rewrite the memorandum on next page.

To: All Personnel
From: Jane Jones, Your New Boss
Subject: Getting the Job Done
Date: January 21, 19--

Let me introduce myself. I am Jane Jones, the new owner of this company. I inherited the whole thing from my uncle, whom you knew well. He ran a tight ship. I mean to do likewise.

If you have any complaints of any kind, bring them directly to me, I will take care of all of them.

Don't think because I'm young I don't know anything about the business. My father had a similar business, and he taught me everything he knew, which was considerable. In addition, I have a degree in management from Kansas State and an MBA from Yale.

As you may or may not know, this company has suffered severe losses during the past two years. This trend must stop immediately. After I have been here a few weeks, I will tell you exactly what to do. In the meantime, I don't want to hear any pessimistic talk. Just do your job.

CHAPTER **6**

Writing Informational and Instructional Memorandums

This chapter applies the principles discussed in preceding chapters to the preparation of memorandums, emphasizing those that are routine and informational. Good news, bad news, and persuasive messages, discussed in detail in Chapters 8, 9, and 10, are also often written as memorandums, as are many reports. Reports in memorandum format are discussed and illustrated in Chapter 17 with the discussion of short, informal reports.

For the most part, letters and memorandums should be approached in a similar way. The techniques of goodwill building, a you-attitude and positive approach, conciseness, readability, and the proper use of emphasis apply to all kinds of written material, as do other qualities discussed in preceding chapters. The direct and indirect arrangements, as presented in Chapter 5, are as appropriate for memorandums as they are for letters.

The plural form of the word memorandum *is either* memorandums *or* memoranda. Memorandums *is used in this book to conform to the most widely used choice.*

The Frequency and Importance of Memorandums

The memorandum is by far the most widely used type of written communication between members of an organization, and at times it is also sent to readers outside the organization. The memorandum format serves as a medium for various kinds of messages.

No doubt some of the many thousands of memorandums written daily are unnecessary, as are many letters and reports. On the other hand, too little internal communication results in inefficiency and poor morale. Employees want and need information and instructions in order to carry out their duties and to understand organizational strategy and purpose. They want to know what is going on and why. Informed employees who believe that they are valued and trusted by management personnel are likely to be cooperative and to devote their efforts to organizational goals.

Because memorandums are so frequently used, they are not always given the attention they deserve. They should not be considered unimportant merely because of this routine use.

Your ability to write clear, convincing, and persuasive memorandums will be important to your career. Certainly poor memorandums will do nothing to increase the respect of your supervisors and peers.

The number of memorandums prepared in the traditional manner, dictated to a secretary or to a recorder and transcribed in typewritten form, is decreasing because of technological developments, as discussed in Chapter 2. As a beginning worker or manager, you are more likely than formerly to create your own memorandums (as well as letters and reports) at a computer or computer terminal at your desk. In addition, these memorandums or other written messages may be stored and transmitted elsewhere by various forms of electronic mail. The growing use of voice mail also decreases the need for typewritten memorandums.

The Format and Arrangement of Memorandums

Memorandums are usually typewritten on forms printed with these headings: DATE:, TO:, FROM:, and SUBJECT:. Although the printed headings are not always or necessarily in the exact order mentioned here and illustrated in Figures 6–1, 6–2, and 6–3, TO: usually precedes FROM: as a matter of courtesy.

Figure 6–1 is a memorandum about memorandums; material that would ordinarily be discussed in textbook fashion is shown in the memorandum itself. You are not likely to have occasion to write messages on this particular subject matter, but this example illustrates an easy-to-read format while presenting information that you will need as you prepare memorandums on other subjects.

Subheadings are helpful in all types of written messages, even long letters, to show organization and the flow of ideas. You probably will ordinarily need fewer subheadings than the number used in the memorandum illustrated in Figure 6–1.

Not all memorandums need the headings shown in Figure 6–1. An example of a shorter memorandum, without headings, is shown in Figure 6–2.

Most organizations provide printed memorandum forms with the conventional headings, DATE:, TO:, FROM:, and SUBJECT:, as mentioned earlier. If

TO: All Office Employees
FROM: Estella Sanchez, Office Manager
DATE: January 30, 19--
SUBJECT: Your Memorandums

Estella

The following suggestions should help you plan and prepare your writing to other employees in this organization.

SPACING

Memorandums may be single or double spaced. If they are single spaced, leave a double space between paragraphs, as you should do when single spacing any material.

PARAGRAPHS

Paragraphs may be blocked or indented, as in letters. The blocked style saves time and, to many readers, presents a more modern appearance. Paragraphs in memorandums, as in letters, should be fairly short. Long, unbroken paragraphs are hard to read.

MARGINS

The long line length (6 inches, which is 60 spaces pica, 70 elite) is ordinarily used in all memorandums, even short ones. Always leave at least one-inch margins, top, bottom, and sides, on all pages.

SIDE HEADINGS

Although side headings as shown here are not the only type that can be used in the memorandum, this all-capital side heading is easy to see and, if properly worded, immediately tells the reader something of the content of the following section.

FIGURE 6–1
A memorandum

you type memorandums on plain paper, it is not essential to include these headings. By arrangement you can show that your headings *are* the date, addressee, subject, and sender. A simplified memorandum arrangement is shown in Figure 6–3. This illustration is adapted from one recommended by Dr. Mona J. Casady, a professor at Southwest Missouri State University, and is used here by permission.

The memorandum in Figure 6–4 illustrates a message arranged in the direct order, as explained in Chapter 5. The "good news" is given in the subject line and in the first paragraph. The memorandum in Figure 6–5 is arranged in the indirect order, explained in Chapter 5. Notice the contrasting arrangements of these two memorandums; they are planned to illustrate the two most important methods of arrangement of any kind of written material. (Two other meth-

Your Memorandums   2   January 30, 19--

SECOND-PAGE IDENTIFICATION

The second page of a memorandum should be identified by
subject, page number, and date. Besides the identification shown
in the illustration above, the identification may be shown in this
order: subject, date, and page number.

SIGNATURE

No signature is required on most memorandums, although they
may be signed. They should be signed if the contents are of
special importance or if the writer wants the reader to know that
he or she personally wrote or dictated the message. A signature
adds a friendly, personal touch.

A complimentary close should not be used on a memorandum.

The signature may consist only of the writer's initials, placed at
the end of the memorandum or by the writer's typewritten name
at the top. The complete signature may also be placed in one of
these two positions.

TITLES

The writer should show his or her title or position unless the
readers are already sure of it, as in Estella Sanchez, Office Manager.
A woman does not usually show a Miss, Mrs., or Ms. before her
name in a memorandum, although it is not considered incorrect
to do so. A man never shows Mr. before his name in a
memorandum or elsewhere. Often a courtesy title should appear
before the name of the addressee, particularly if the addressee is
in a position of higher authority than the writer. Although there
is no rule to this effect, the writer is slightly discourteous to do
otherwise.

NEATNESS

As in all written communications, an attractive appearance is
psychologically conducive to the acceptance of ideas. In addition,
neatness is a matter of common courtesy.

FIGURE 6–1
(continued)

DATE: November 19, 19--

  TO: All correspondence secretaries

FROM: Judith Cox, Supervisor   *Judy*

SUBJECT: ARRANGEMENT OF MEMORANDUMS

Please single space all memorandums. Remember to double space between paragraphs, as illustrated in this memorandum to you.

} *The direct request*

Although memorandums can be correctly double spaced or single spaced, many of those you are typewriting would, if single spaced, fit on one page, instead of the two pages you are using. Although an extra sheet of paper may seem a small economy, numerous two-page memorandums require a great deal of paper. In addition, each extra page increases copying, filing, and handling costs.

} *Explanation*

Your work looks great! Thank you.

} *Goodwill*

FIGURE 6–2
An interoffice memo-randum with no sub-headings

---

9 September 19--

Cassandra DeCrow

VACATION TIME CHANGED

Yes, Cassandra, you are welcome to change your vacation period to January 4-18. Actually, this change is better for us, too. The early part of January is usually a slack time that can easily be covered by temporary help if necessary

} *Good news, with explanation*

You are always thoughtful of your associates as well as of our company's goals. Thank you for being such a fine employee!

} *Goodwill*

Mary

Mary Ruprecht

ds

FIGURE 6–3
A modified memoran-dum arrangement

The good news

Explanation

Goodwill

Explanation and reader benefit

Action close

FIGURE 6–4
Memorandum that conveys good news, arranged in the direct order

TRANSCONTINENTAL MOVING COMPANY

DATE: September 9, 19--

TO: All Employees

FROM: Samuel Powell, Personnel Manager

SUBJECT: INCREASE IN TAKE-HOME PAY

On October 1 your take-home pay will be increased.

This increase is due to a 9.09 percent decrease in your insurance premiums. For example, if your present monthly premium is $30, your next paycheck will be increased by $2.73. If your present premium is $40, your take-home pay will be $3.64 more.

Although this amount, which varies according to your present coverage, is relatively small, in these days of ever-increasing costs you are to be especially commended for your efforts that have made this saving possible.

If your excellent health and safety record continues, perhaps our insurance company (Countrywide) will lower premiums still further. If so, all decreases in premiums will be passed on to you as increases in take-home pay.

Should you have questions, please telephone me at 5423.

ods of arrangement, less frequently used, are the chronological and the persuasive, or "sales letter" arrangement.)

The subject line in Figure 6–4 is more specific than the subject line in Figure 6–5. Although in most kinds of writing specific wording is preferred, the subject line of Figure 6–5 is of necessity less descriptive than the one that conveys good news; for example, we definitely would *not* want to use "Decrease in Take-Home Pay." Although we have no intention whatsoever to mislead (a fact that would be discovered after the first paragraph in any event), the announcement of "bad news" displayed in the subject line would reveal the information that we are preparing the reader to receive by giving positive data first.

The first paragraph in Figure 6–5 is described as a *buffer*. The *decision*, the fact that premiums are to be increased, is given within the fourth sentence of the third paragraph.

Chapters 8 and 9 apply the direct and indirect order of arrangement to business letters. Look ahead to the opening pages of these chapters as you prepare memorandums, as basic principles of letters and memorandums are the same. You may wish, in addition, to review Chapter 5.

TRANSCONTINENTAL MOVING COMPANY

DATE: September 9, 19--

TO: All Employees

FROM: Samuel Powell, Personnel Manager

SUBJECT: HEALTH AND HOSPITALIZATION INSURANCE

As you may be aware, comprehensive health and hospitalization insurance benefits are provided to all of you through Countrywide Insurance Company, as they have been for many years.

Your policy covers more than 90 percent of all hospital and physicians' charges, with 100 percent coverage for major medical bills over $1,000. This is one of the most comprehensive plans provided for any organization in the nation.

Buffer paragraphs

Transcontinental plans to continue this coverage in the most economical way possible and will continue to provide half the cost of your insurance premiums. For every dollar that you pay, your company also pays one dollar. But medical costs have risen rapidly during the past twelve months. In order to meet these costs, Countrywide has been forced to increase monthly premiums by 22.2 percent effective October 1. Your payroll check on that date will reflect this adjustment.

The bad news combined with reader benefit

The amount paid by your company will also increase by 22.2 percent. Your comprehensive benefits remain the same.

Reader benefit

I hope you will remain so healthy that you will have no occasion to use the insurance that you buy. If you ever do so, you are well protected.

Goodwill

Should you have questions, telephone me at 4523.

Action close

FIGURE 6–5
Memorandum arranged in the indirect order because it contains bad news

Memorandums are often sent to more than one person, with the names of all receivers listed at the top or the bottom of the sheet. Knowing the distribution of the message is helpful to each reader.

Sometimes the memorandum is passed from one reader to another, with each checking his or her name after reading the memorandum before passing it to the next person on the list. This method of distribution, although somewhat less expensive than individual copies, is weak because having all readers receive the message at the same time may be crucial to its overall purpose. In addition, some readers tend to leave the memorandum on their desks for days before it is passed along. Individual copies are well worth the small additional expense.

COUNTRYWIDE INSURANCE COMPANY

SAN FRANCISCO BRANCH

INTEROFFICE MEMORANDUM

DATE: September 9, 19--

TO: Members of Committee IV: Brown, Gray, Roe, Dominguez, and Blair

FROM: Andrew Williamson, Chairman   *Andy*

SUBJECT: SEPTEMBER MEETING

The September meeting will be held in the conference room adjoining my office on Wednesday, September 17, at 2:30 p.m.

The attached agenda includes items retained from our last meeting, two that some of you suggested we consider, and an entirely new one, about a possible communication seminar, that I have added. Please let me know if you have items to add to the agenda.

Attachment
ms

FIGURE 6–6
Short memorandum
sent to five readers

A short memorandum sent to five readers is illustrated in Figure 6–6. The list of names could also have been shown at the bottom of the page. If the list had been longer, the bottom-of-page placement would have been the better choice.

Suggestions for Writing Memorandums

Your memorandums should build and maintain favorable relationships with your readers, as with all people with whom you communicate. These favorable human relationships cannot continue indefinitely, however, if your words are not sincere. On the other hand, even the best intentions cannot be made clear without using the techniques of effective writing.

Question: What is meant by "slow writing"?

Answer: Slow writing is not forceful or concise. It contains unnecessary words, phrases, sentences, or paragraphs. It is likely to contain numerous sentences starting with *there* or *it*. It may be filled with verbs in the passive voice. It does not seem to flow or move.

Unnecessary repetition results in slow writing.

Sentence structure affects the movement of thought; often a clause can be reduced to a phrase and a phrase to a word. Then perhaps the word can be omitted with no change in meaning or decrease in courtesy.

Vivid, active verbs are faster than vague, general ones. Specific nouns that can be visualized are faster (and more clear) than general, abstract ones.

Poorly organized material is slow because the reader must spend additional time in determining the writer's ideas and following the flow of thought. Poorly organized material, in addition to being slow, is extremely annoying to a reader.

Many first paragraphs are so slow that they are completely unnecessary; for example:

"We have received your recent letter." (If you hadn't received it, would you be answering it?)

"This memorandum is being written for the purpose of telling you . . ." (Just go on and say whatever you meant to say. In case you have bad news, use a subtle opening, but choose not to use a sentence that is slow as well as completely meaningless.)

Writing can move *too* swiftly, however, especially when ideas to be expressed are complicated, surprising, or unpleasant. In addition, a series of short, choppy sentences, although clear, can be annoying and appear to be the work of an amateur.

Achieving Readability and the Desired Emphasis

Memorandums, like most other written messages used in business offices, are almost certain to be read hurriedly. The writer should do everything possible to make sure that the reader can comprehend every message with the least possible effort. As this goal is attained, however, the writer must keep in mind all other principles of effective writing, including building harmonious human relationships.

In order to make memorandums and other messages easy to read, be extremely careful that your flow of thought is logical from the beginning of the message until the end. If there is no reason to use the indirect order of arrangement, such as presenting unfavorable news or a conclusion that needs explanation before the reader is ready to accept it, *prefer the direct order for all memorandums. Giving the gist of the message in the beginning paragraph and in the subject line provides the reader with an early understanding of the situation.*

Another feature of organization is to request any desired action near the end of the memorandum—unless it can logically be placed at the beginning. According to the principles of emphasis, beginnings and endings of messages receive the most attention and are best remembered.

Listings and subheadings provide emphasis to points within the memorandum. And, as with other kinds of writing, the same techniques that achieve the desired emphasis also aid readability.

One major weakness of many memorandums—large blocks of type—can be corrected by the simple procedure of shortening paragraphs. Long paragraphs are more difficult to read and are less emphatic. First and last paragraphs, in particular, should be short.

If used with discretion, mechanical means of emphasis, such as underlining and all capitals, are recommended. A subject line in all capitals is more emphatic than one in small letters. Avoid the use of numerous examples of such methods of emphasis, however, including many exclamation marks. When you try to emphasize many items of information, you are in effect emphasizing nothing.

Achieving the You-Attitude and the Positive Approach

The you-attitude and the positive approach are as effective and as necessary in memorandums as they are in letters or in oral communication. Some business people seem to have the attitude that memorandums are factual only, that they should be as brief and to the point as possible. Although you and your reader have no time for unnecessary words, you should take enough time and space to ensure that your readers understand and accept your messages. If you give instructions or directives, your readers have the right to know the rationale on which these instructions or directives are based.

As in most business writing (with the exception of some formal reports), speak directly to your reader in your memorandums. Some writers, when writing to their co-workers or to people they supervise, write vaguely to "all employees" or "employees" or "personnel." Although memorandums often go to a group of people, not to one individual alone, your memorandum will be read by *one person at a time.* By means of your written memorandum you interact *individually* with each reader.

Each person reading your words is responding positively or negatively. It is to your advantage when each reader understands your memorandum and responds in a pleasant, positive way. As much as possible, address your readers, regardless of the number, as *you.* Write *to* people, not *about* them.

Using Memorandums as an Effective Management Tool

Memorandums are used for the obvious purposes of transmitting information and requesting action, as well as to build goodwill. Moreover, memorandums are necessary for a written record of communications and are ordinarily filed in order to document past actions and decisions.

Reports of the decisions of committees and other groups, in addition to more formal minutes of meetings, may be recorded or reported in memorandum

*Communication
Brief*

Looking at David Selznick's memos today, they are all that business-writing teachers tell students memos should be. They are well organized. They are concise in statement of ideas. They are easy to read. They are deftly persuasive in arguing Selznick's views. They are phrased in ways to keep the reader's good will—no small matter in Hollywood, where people have long been known for giant egos and giant insecurities. Behind all this, their tone throughout shows Selznick's enthusiasm for his films and his urgent concern that they have high quality in all areas.

William Stephenson, "David Selznick and the Business Writing of Hollywood," in *Proceedings, 51st ABC International Convention* (Los Angeles: Association for Business Communication, 1986), 213–214.

format. Copies of memorandums on various subjects are sent to supervisors to explain actions taken in a department; for example, personnel policies. Memorandums may become supporting documents for reports or policy statements of many kinds.

Discreet managers recognize that some material of an extremely sensitive nature should not be put into written form; for example, matters involving such things as employee misconduct (unless such misconduct can be proved) or some legal matters that must be kept confidential. Even though you eventually need written documentation for almost any important action, be careful and cautious before putting some kinds of information into memorandums that will be read by a great number of people, or even by a few people other than those directly concerned. For the sake of the privacy of those concerned and for your own protection, do not include such information in routine memorandums. This

Perhaps that memo wasn't worded very well.

outlook does not contradict previous references to the importance of openness and keeping employees informed; in fact, such discretion is necessary to the equitable and ethical operation of any organization.

In addition, some matters are of such importance or sensitivity that they should be discussed *orally* with the person or persons involved, not stated in a more impersonal memorandum. For example, if an employee is to be dismissed, the person who must handle the unpleasant task of informing the individual should at the very least do so in a personal interview, although a written statement may be necessary later.

Memorandums should not be written unnecessarily. If no written record is necessary and the message to be conveyed is a simple one, oral communication will often suffice. Oral communication has many advantages, as well as disadvantages, over written communication. Regardless of the quality of your memorandums, you can never be completely sure that your reader or readers have understood your message or that they have accepted it. Oral communication provides instant feedback.

As with all other forms of communication, memorandums reflect a great deal about communicators and their relationships with readers. Writing skills are essential, but clever writing is far from enough. Memorandums must be based on knowledge and sound judgment about the situation being discussed and on consideration for the reader.

Summary

Most of the principles for writing effective memorandums are the same as those for writing effective letters. Writers of communications of any kind must be concerned with goodwill, conciseness, readability, the proper use of emphasis, clarity, and correctness.

The memorandum is by far the most widely used type of written communication between members of an organization; it serves as a medium for messages of all kinds.

Memorandums are usually typewritten on printed forms with the headings TO:, FROM:, SUBJECT:, and DATE:, although the order of these four headings may vary.

In writing memorandums, be especially careful to make your work easily readable. Subheadings, listings, and short paragraphs are elements of format that aid readability.

Ordinarily in a memorandum you speak directly to your reader, regardless of the number of readers of any particular message.

Memorandums, like all other communications, should not be used unnecessarily. Often oral communication can replace memorandums. In addition, some material of a sensitive nature should not be conveyed by memorandum.

1–4. Name four purposes that memorandums accomplish.

5–8. Name four ways of increasing readability through the use of format.

9. Illustrate an appropriate heading for the second page of a memorandum.

10. Discuss the advantages and disadvantages of using memorandums to convey information throughout an organization.

(Related to material in Chapter 6 and principles of correct usage.) Insert necessary punctuation, including quotation marks, hyphens, and apostrophes, and remove punctuation that has been inserted incorrectly. Choose correct word from each pair or group. Make any other necessary changes.

1. The (principles, principals) of effective letters and memorandums are (similar, similiar).

2. The you-approach is as important in memorandums as in letters perhaps even more so.

3. Increasing readability in many memorandums (is, are) accomplished simply by shortening paragraphs.

4. Some people say that they (receive, recieve) too many memorandums.

5. Although subject lines may be used or omitted in letters they are expected in all memorandums.

6. The secretary asked "Was the invitation meant for my husband and (I, me)

7. Make sure that you correctly spell the name of the person (who, whom) you address.

8. When you write a memorandum to members of a committee make sure you know the names of those (who, whom) are expected to attend.

9. The ability to write clear memorandums will (affect, effect) your credibility in an organization.

10. In memorandums one sentence paragraphs are acceptable and often desirable.

11. The secretary asked, "(Who, Whom) shall I say called.

12. When some action is desired from the reader the requested action should be specifically stated near the end of the memorandum.

13. As when writing letters, numerous paragraphs should not start with "I" or "we." (Hint: dangling modifier)

14. A long memorandum was sent to Mr. Harris, Ms. Brown, and (I, me).

15. Slow openings, such as "I have your memorandum of July 7," should be avoided. In memorandums as well as in letters.

Cases

1. Rewrite the following memorandum. Type in single-spaced form.

> TO: All sales people
> FROM: J. X. Taylor, Sales Manager
> SUBJECT: Negligence in Turning in Weekly Reports
> DATE: January 13, 19--
>
> All weekly sales reports must be received in this office not later than 2:00 p.m. on Wednesday of the week following the week that they cover. You have all been far too careless in submitting the reports on time. Toney and Smith have twice been almost a week late. Don't blame it on your secretaries. Your delay is putting everybody behind here in this office. You may not believe it, but it is actually slowing down the preparation of your paychecks. Maybe you don't need your check, but other people do. Don't forget!

2. Revise and condense the following memorandum, which is definitely not concise. Type in single-spaced form.

> TO: All Factory and Office Employees
> FROM: J. B. Winchester, Personnel Manager
> SUBJECT: HOLIDAY VACATION
> DATE: December 8, 19--
>
> It has come to my attention that many of you have been asking about a vacation during the holiday season. This memorandum is in answer to these questions that you have been asking.
>
> As a matter of fact, you will be happy and glad that according to our company policy established only this year, which may be true for only this year, there will be a holiday break during the Christmas season of eight days, including weekends, when everything is closed for all of the employees in the factory as well as all of those in the offices. These eight days begin at the end of the regular working day on December 23, which is, as you know, at 4:00 p.m., and extends to January 2 to the regular opening hour of 8:00 a.m.
>
> As I said, we will all be on vacation then. And the best part of it is that the regular pay will continue, for all the time of the vacation, except of course for the weekends, when you aren't paid anyway, unless you count what you earn during the week as being spread over the weekends. And you still get your regular vacation.

> Your company is grateful and appreciative of your work during the preceding and past year. As a kind of thank-you and bonus, we are making this time off available. Have a happy holiday season. Don't hesitate to call me if you have any questions.

3. Assume that you are the owner of a business organization located near the college campus. Write a memo to your employees telling them of the availability of a course in business communication in which you are presently enrolled. Assume that the company will pay all expenses and that the employees will be excused from work. Give all necessary details. You hope that all who receive the memorandum will attend during this semester or the following one, when the course will be offered at the same place and time. Ask for their choice of semester. You do not want them all away from the office during the same period of time.

4. Write a memorandum to your instructor informing him or her of the classes in which you are now enrolled, in addition to your course in business communication. Add to this memorandum any other information that could be helpful to your instructor, or any other information that your instructor requests.

5. Write a memorandum to your supervisor, Ms. Julia Long. She has requested that you give her your first and second choice for the two weeks' vacation you have for the coming summer. Your first choice is the first two weeks in July. Your second choice is the last two full weeks in June. (Check your calendar for exact dates.)

6. You are the administrative assistant to the office manager of Countrywide Insurance Company. Remodeling of offices is scheduled to begin on Monday of next week. This remodeling will require rearrangement of desks and other furniture, sharing of offices, other changes, and some inconvenience, as work proceeds from one floor of offices to the next. The entire remodeling process is scheduled to last three or four months.

   All loose paper and files need to be secured inside the desks before furniture can be removed. All books on shelves and personal items must be packed and labeled. Packing material will be available in your secretary's office tomorrow. Several of the offices look as if they have never been straightened. Some employees have said that they are too busy to do housekeeping chores. You believe that this packing will require quite a bit of time, but some people are likely to find things they thought lost forever.

   You fear that there could be problems in sharing offices, even temporarily, because of some personality conflicts.

   Assume that all details, such as the remodeling time schedule (tentative) and temporary office assignments, are on a separate sheet attached to your written message. Although you need not actually prepare it, refer to this schedule.

   Individuals who want to pick the colors of the walls of their remodeled offices should pick the color from the seven choices available; these colors are illustrated in a folder in your secretary's office. (Her name is Mrs. Helen Brown.) If they have not made their choice by Friday of next week, their offices will be scheduled to be painted an off-white, really a kind of soft cream.

   Write a memorandum to the group of employees on the third floor, which is to be remodeled first. Choose an appropriate arrangement and approach. Should you mention the messy condition of some offices?

7. Write memorandums to one or more of your classmates. Give specific, complete, and detailed instructions for one or more of the following procedures.
   a. How to change the ribbon on your typewriter
   b. How to change a tire on your automobile
   c. How to put film into your camera
   d. How to tie a shoe
   e. How to operate a can opener, blender, tape recorder, or other appliance
   f. How to draw a paper clip
   g. How to calculate the number of rolls of wallpaper needed to paper a room
   h. How to make a peanut butter and jelly sandwich
   i. How to check out a book in your school library
   j. How to check out a book in your public library
   k. How to use the computer terminals (or card catalog) in your library in order to locate books on a given subject
   l. How to drive from your college or university to your home

8. Collect at least two memorandums. Evaluate according to the evaluation sheet at the end of this chapter.

9. You are the public relations manager for a large company that does much television advertising. Some of your commercials are humorous, others are public service announcements, and others illustrate principles of effective advertising.

   Recently you have received a number of requests for copies of certain commercials from students, teachers, neighborhood organizations, and other companies. A meeting was held this morning to determine how to handle these requests.

   It was decided that the public relations value of fulfilling these requests outweighs the cost to buy the video tape and reproduce the commercials. The only legal problem is that tapes furnished to someone else must not be run on a commercial television station; to do so would violate a contractual agreement between the company and the actors in the commercial. To avoid this legal problem, a specific procedure must be followed.

   The employee who receives a telephone call or a personal visit from the individual requesting the tape is to ask specifically how the tape is to be used and to make careful notes of the reply. This information is to be passed on to you. If the request is made in a letter, it should be sent to you immediately.

   People who request the tape are to be told that you (the public relations director) will get in touch with them in a few days. The person who answers the telephone is to say neither yes nor no.

   Write a memorandum to all employees outlining the procedure to be followed.

10. Write a memorandum to your instructor explaining why you chose your major field of study.

11. Write a memorandum to your classmates giving exact and complete instructions on how to find the reference room of your school library. Do not assume any prior knowledge of the library; some of your readers may have recently transferred from some other school.

12. Write a memorandum to your instructor describing the methods by which you plan to seek career employment when you near graduation.

13. Write a memorandum addressed to newcomers in your organization (or college). Give them the names and addresses of all public libraries, including branches. Include hours of operation.

14. Write another memorandum to newcomers. Describe the procedure for obtaining a library card from the public library.

15. Write a memorandum to your classmates; describe the products, in addition to books, that are available in your public library.

16. **Building Goodwill, Morale, and Productivity through Communication.** Assume that you are the owner of a business organization. (You may choose the kind, size, and location.) You have inherited this business from your uncle. For many years the organization has been profitable, but during the past two years it has suffered severe losses, possibly because of economic conditions. Employee turnover is high.

   You feel confident of your ability to handle the technical and managerial responsibilities. You know, however, that you must have the cooperation of your employees.

   Write a memo to all employees; try to use introduction of yourself to build goodwill.

17. You are the director of human resources, Countrywide Insurance Company. The president has approved an Education Assistance Program for employees who want to take continuing education or correspondence courses, or courses toward a college degree. The courses or college program must be work-related.

   Employees must have worked full time for Countrywide for at least six months before enrolling in the Education Assistance Program. They must attend classes regularly and, if grades are awarded for the course or courses in which they are enrolled, earn at least a "C" for each course for which they will be reimbursed.

   At the end of the semester or course, the employee must submit proof of attendance and grade(s) earned, and must agree to work for the company for six months from the date the tuition reimbursement check is issued. If the employee resigns or is terminated before the end of the six months, the employee must repay the tuition to the company. No more than two courses, including correspondence courses, may be taken during each term or semester.

   Write a memorandum to employees informing them of the new Education Assistance Program. Encourage them to participate.

18. You are the president of Good Foods, a national food company. The production foreman has just rushed in to tell you that a random check of the fruits preserved in glass jars revealed small pieces of glass in the syrup. He surmised that the rim of the jar was broken by the sealing equipment as the top was pressed on. He didn't know how long this had been happening or which products were involved.

   You know that you must take immediate action. You decide that to preserve the company's reputation you must immediately halt production and notify the stores and the public of the problem. You want all jars removed from the shelves and you wish customers to return unopened jars for a refund.

   You must inform the officers, board of directors,

and line employees, and make a statement to the press. With your electronic mail system, you will contact all your distributors, in addition to telephoning. They will then contact the retail stores. A teleconference must be arranged for all regional managers, and finally, production must be temporarily stopped.

Write the memo to the line employees explaining the production halt. Then write your electronic mail communication. Outline the points to be covered in the teleconference and write your press release. Is there anything else you should do?

Write Your Own Assignments and Solutions

19. Write your OWN assignments, with solutions, for one or more of the kinds of memorandums described in this chapter.

This assignment provides practice in describing a situation and giving instructions as well as in writing memorandums. Your problem assignments (cases) may be on any subject, preferably about situations you have encountered in your work. Give all the information another student would need to write a memorandum as a solution to your problem, including names and addresses and enough details to enable the writer to make appropriate decisions.

Similar assignments are given in Chapters 8, 9, and 10.

Evaluation Sheet: Memorandums

	Yes	No	Not Sure
1. Is the subject line appropriately worded?	___	___	___
2. If not on a printed form, does the "To" line precede the "From" line?	___	___	___
3. Is the date shown in full, *not* abbreviated?	___	___	___
4. If sent to an individual, is the name of the receiver shown with a courtesy title?	___	___	___
5. Is the official title, such as "Manager," shown with the name of the writer?	___	___	___
6. Are paragraphs short? (Even a very short memorandum should be divided into at least two paragraphs.)	___	___	___
7. Is a penwritten signature (or initials) included with the writer's name or at the end of the memo?	___	___	___
8. If this is a good-news or a neutral message, does the first paragraph present the most important part of the message?	___	___	___
9. If some action is requested of the reader, does the memo end with a specific action close?	___	___	___
10. Are listings or other uses of format used to increase readability?	___	___	___
11. Is the memorandum sincere?	___	___	___
12. Is the memorandum tactful?	___	___	___
13. Is the you-attitude used throughout?	___	___	___
14. Is the positive approach used throughout?	___	___	___
15. Is the memorandum correct in facts?	___	___	___
16. Is the memorandum absolutely correct in format, grammar, spelling, and sentence structure?	___	___	___

CHAPTER 7

Writing Special Goodwill
Letters and Preparing Form Messages

This chapter considers special goodwill letters *and* form messages *of all kinds, including goodwill letters.*

These two kinds of written communication seem at first thought to be unrelated; for example, many goodwill letters definitely should be individually written, and form messages are used for many purposes other than merely expressing goodwill. Nevertheless, these two broad classifications of written communication have certain similarities. Form messages, for efficiency and economy, should be prepared for often-occurring situations that necessitate special goodwill letters. In addition, all form letters, along with fulfilling other purposes, should build goodwill.

The letter of welcome (Figure 7–6) shown later in this chapter is an example of a message that is likely to be both a form letter and a goodwill letter. Although the letter should be individualized with the readers' names and addresses (Mr. and Mrs. Bell) and prepared on word processing equipment for the best possible appearance, the paragraphs in the body of the letter could be written and stored on a computer disk, thus serving as the content of numerous similar letters. Further emphasis on the particular readers occurs in the third paragraph with mention of their new neighborhood and the location of the closest branch of Midwest Bank. These minor changes that individualize each letter can be made far easier than using an individually written or dictated letter for each newcomer to the city.

Because of their personal nature and the necessity for a completely individual approach, other goodwill letters illustrated in this chapter cannot be prepared as form letters.

Special Goodwill Letters

Goodwill building is an important purpose of all business writing, but most letters, memorandums, and other written materials have additional purposes. For example, a sales letter, which is planned to sell a product or service, must first build the buyer's confidence in the product or service and in the seller. A collection letter, to be successful, must collect and also retain the customer's goodwill. A memorandum to an employee, besides accomplishing its purpose of presenting information, ideas, or instructions, should promote pleasant working relationships.

Special goodwill letters or memorandums are those with the single purpose of building goodwill. They express appreciation, congratulations, sympathy, welcome, and good wishes.

The you-attitude and the positive approach, essential qualities of all business writing, are particularly important in special goodwill messages. *These messages must be sincere.* If they are written only to maximize profits, they are *not* sincere. These messages should also be conversational, natural, and an expression of your own thoughts. Adapting the wording of a model letter is not an acceptable way of expressing sincere goodwill. Such letters will almost always sound forced, unnatural, and impersonal.

Promptness in sending goodwill messages is most important. They should be sent as soon after the event as possible. On learning of the occasion for congratulations, sympathy, good wishes, or appreciation, immediately write and mail a letter.

Conciseness is desirable in special goodwill messages. Usually there is not a great deal to say. Say it in a pleasant, natural manner and stop. Do not be wordy or effusive. The following are examples of some occasions for special goodwill messages.

To customers and business associates, letters expressing appreciation for:

- Record of prompt payment of bills
- Special orders
- Long, continued patronage
- Special services
- Patience in trying situations

Communication Brief

Although he's not a company, our favorite illustration of closeness to the customer is car salesman Joe Girard. He sold more new cars and trucks, each year, for eleven years running, than any other human being. In fact, in a typical year, Joe sold twice as many units as whoever was in second place. In explaining his secret of success, Joe said: "I send out over thirteen thousand cards every month."

Why start with Joe? Because his magic is the magic of IBM and many of the rest of excellent companies. It is simply service, overpowering service, especially after-sales service.

Thomas J. Peters and Robert H. Waterman, Jr., *In Search of Excellence* (New York: Harper & Row, 1982), 157–158.

To Get Recognition, Give It Away. One way of thinking about the rewards employees receive is in terms of a triad: promotion, remuneration, and recognition. Of the three forms of reward, the first two are relatively unresponsive in the day-to-day operation of an organization. Promotions and wage hikes seldom come oftener than six months apart. On a daily basis, recognition is the reward most noticed and sought after. In the American Management Association survey to which I allude earlier, 40 percent of the respondents indicated that recognition for what they did was their most important reward.

Richard Tanner Pascale, ''Zen and the Art of Management,'' in *Harvard Business Review on Human Relations* (New York: Harper & Row, 1979), 132.

Communication Brief

To customers, business associates, friends, and fellow employees, letters expressing congratulations for:

- Promotions
- Special accomplishments
- Professional appointment or honors

Letters expressing greetings:

- At Christmas and on other holidays
- For birthdays
- For anniversaries
- For other special occasions

Other occasions:

- Condolences
- Get-well messages
- Best wishes of any kind
- Letters welcoming a person to the community or to the company

Because goodwill messages are personal and are applied to many and varying situations, there can be no suggested formula or plan of presentation. Each must be written individually. These messages may be either typewritten or handwritten. Although handwritten notes are more informal and personal, a typewritten letter is to be preferred to a hard-to-read or unattractive handwritten one. Ordinarily, if using the firm's letterhead, you should typewrite the letter. If you use your own personalized stationery, either typewrite or handwrite the letter.

The letters in Figures 7–1 through 7–6 are examples of special goodwill letters. *Remember, though, that no model letters are to be copied or slightly adapted to meet some particular circumstances. Be yourself. Your letters will necessarily be different, depending on the purpose and the relationship between you and your reader.*

As you look over the letter examples in this chapter or elsewhere, and as you write your own letters, keep in mind the following guidelines:

1. Letters should be placed attractively on the page. Appendix B gives instructions for letter arrangement and placement.

October 18, 19—

Dear Karen, John, George, and Matthew,

Our family shares your sorrow. You have our deepest sympathy.

Your mother's courage throughout her long illness will always be an inspiration to us. Her wonderful sense of humor prevailed until the end.

All of you are to be commended for the way you cared for her, even with your many other responsibilities. She was proud of you.

Love,
Martha

FIGURE 7–1
Example of a letter of condolence (often handwritten, without the company letter-head that is included on business stationery)

CENTRAL COLLEGE

Toronto

Management Department

January 22, 19—

Ms. Gloria Thomas
Director of Personnel Operations
Regional Medical Center
Toronto, ON M4L 2N4
Canada

Dear Gloria:

Congratulations! I have just learned of your present position from the "Executive Snapshot" column of the Toronto Business Journal.

I remember you well from several management classes here at Central College during the early seventies. You were a good student. I believed then that you would have a successful career; my predictions came true.

Best wishes for your continued success.

Sincerely,

Robert Jackson

Robert Jackson
Professor

FIGURE 7–2
Example of a letter of congratulations

2. Abbreviations should be used sparingly in all writing. Months and words of the return address or inside address (such as *Street* or *Road*) should be spelled out, with the exception of the two-letter state abbreviation. (These abbreviations for states and Canadian provinces are listed in Appendix B.)

3. One-sentence paragraphs are acceptable and often desirable in letters and memorandums. One-sentence paragraphs, especially opening ones, are useful for expressing the desired emphasis and for increasing readability.

4. Although the words *I* and *we* should be used as necessary and natural, avoid an excessive number. Avoid beginning several paragraphs with *I* or *we*.

HOLIDAY TRAVELS

On the Square
Oxford, Mississippi 38677

January 12, 19—

Mr. and Mrs. Daniel Robinson
Route 3, Box 511
Cleveland, MS 38732

Dear Mr. and Mrs. Robinson:

Congratulations! Fifty years is indeed a significant milestone. Your anniversary party sounds wonderful.

Having all your children together for your party will be another joy, I know. Your seven children and twelve grandchildren have scattered to far places.

In case you are wondering how I knew about the party, I will explain that I read about it in the Cleveland newspaper. Although I have worked with you on your travel plans for twenty years or so, I don't think I ever told you that Cleveland is also my home town. I left there more than 35 years ago, before you moved to Cleveland, but I still feel it is home.

I have enjoyed helping you with your several trips over the years. The most recent one was to Spain in 1988—right? Perhaps you are now ready for a trip around the world—stopping off to see your children and grandchildren.

May your special day be happy, as well as all the days to come.

Sincerely,

Elizabeth Barton

Elizabeth Barton
Travel Agent

FIGURE 7–3
A letter of congratulations, plus soft-sell sales promotion

2572 Cherry Roadway   *The Smart Shoppe*   Seattle, Washington 98008

July 5, 19--

Ms. Kyong Kim
The Clarke Company
2345 Hudson Avenue
Napa, CA 94558

Dear Ms. Kim:

Thank you for your help in making our Fourth of July sales campaign an outstanding success.

Your coaching of salespeople and the posters and brochures you displayed increased our total sales. Several customers commented on your window arrangements, which were attractive, creative, and colorful.

All of us here at the store enjoyed working with you. We look forward to continued business relationships that will be pleasant and profitable for both your firm and ours.

Sincerely,

Ann Harding

Ann Harding
Owner

FIGURE 7–4
Example of a letter expressing appreciation (Written to a wholesaler or manufacturer's representative, this letter is arranged in the semiblock style, a style that is now used less frequently than in former years. See Appendix B.)

Using Form Messages for Economical and Effective Communications

All the principles of effective communication previously discussed apply to form messages. As with letters or memorandums written for one reader, the writer must consider clarity, conciseness, and all the other attributes of effective written communication. The content and appearance of form letters are even more important than those of messages written to one reader because they are received by many readers, thus multiplying positive or negative effects.

3015 West Bankhead Drive
Denton, TX 76201
December 30, 19--

Mrs. Ruth Crocker
815 Silver Street
Calhoun City, MS 38246

Dear Mrs. Crocker:

Thank you for your efforts in my behalf when I was a student in
your English class in 1958–1959 at Bruce High School.

In spite of my opposition at the time, you did a tremendous job.
After all these years I express gratitude for your effort and dedication.

Because of your excellent instruction, I was able, after thirty years,
to make an "A" in a college English composition class at Southern
Methodist University. This good grammar background also enabled
me to do secretarial work for twenty-three years with no difficulty
with spelling, grammar, or punctuation. Your efforts toward
improving my knowledge of English usage helped me complete
successfully the CPS examination, thereby becoming a Certified
Professional Secretary.

Your students through the years are very fortunate to have had a
teacher of your stature. I appreciate your effort.

Sincerely,

Becky

Rebecca Langham Nash

FIGURE 7–5
A letter of appreciation arranged in the modified block style (See Appendix B.)

Necessity for Form Messages

Because of cost and time considerations, form messages are not only helpful but are also absolutely essential. Form messages, if used wisely, decrease the overall cost of business communications, accomplish their intended purposes, and build and maintain goodwill.

Form messages have advantages other than economy. For example, they provide a method of prompt response and are sometimes used merely to state that a more detailed individual reply will be mailed later. In other situations, such as early-stage collection periods, the impersonality of obvious form letters is an advantage, not a disadvantage, because debtors do not feel that they are being approached individually.

Midwest Bank
Hickory Hill Branch
3840 Hickory Hill
Cleveland, OH 44117

February 8, 19--

Mr. and Mrs. David Bell
2736 Murray Lane
Cleveland, OH 44117

Dear Mr. and Mrs. Bell:

Welcome to Cleveland! We are happy that you will enjoy your new home.

Selecting the right bank is one of the numerous decisions to be made in the process of relocating. Midwest Bank has been serving residents of Cleveland and the surrounding area for the past thirty-five years, and we would like to offer you the benefit of that experience.

For your convenience, branches are located throughout the city. Our Hickory Hill facility is located at 3840 Hickory Hill, just three blocks from your home.

Each branch offers a full range of banking services, including investment counseling. In addition, after-hours and weekend withdrawal and depository capabilities are provided. All deposits are FDIC insured.

The enclosed brochure lists our locations and describes each of the services available to you. Also enclosed is a map of Cleveland that may assist you in becoming more familiar with our city.

We would appreciate the opportunity to meet your banking needs.

Sincerely,

MIDWEST BANK

Vivian A. Douglas

Vivian A. Douglas
Director, Public Relations

Enclosures (2)

FIGURE 7–6
Letter of welcome to newcomers. This letter is also a sales promotion letter.

Kinds of Form Messages

The term *form message,* in its broadest sense, includes all written messages except those planned for one or a few readers. (Copies of letters sent to individuals other than the addressee are not ordinarily described as form letters.) Form messages may be prepared for most of the letters and memorandums previously discussed. For example, form messages are used for the following purposes, along with many others.

*Improve
Your Writing*

Question: I'm confused about the use of apostrophes. Has usage changed? Can we omit them completely?

Answer: The exact and most appropriate use of apostrophes has not changed. Your confusion may have resulted from reading various signs and mailboxes, which seem to include an apostrophe, if at all, anywhere the painter or printer found convenient. No, apostrophes cannot be omitted completely if writing is to convey its intended meaning.

Rules that apply to the use of the apostrophe are given in English handbooks and in Appendix D. Although they are too lengthy to be repeated here, check your use of the apostrophe in the often-used words, *company* and *companies.*

The plural of company is companies, with NO apostrophe.

CORRECT:	Two new companies have been established in our town during the past year.
INCORRECT:	Two new companys have been established in our town during the past year.
INCORRECT:	Two new company's have been established in our town during the past year.

The singular possessive of company is company's.

CORRECT:	One company's profits have increased.
INCORRECT:	One companys profits have increased.

The plural possessive of company is companies'.

CORRECT:	Both of the companies' profits have increased.
INCORRECT:	Both of the companies profits have increased.
INCORRECT:	Both of the company's profits have increased.
INCORRECT:	Both of the companys profits have increased.

- Some kinds of special goodwill letters; for example, letters of welcome to newcomers
- Order letters (or order blanks)
- Letters of inquiry
- Responses to inquiries
- Sales letters and other sales material
- Other letters about products or merchandise
- Letters to accompany orders
- Letters of acknowledgment of various kinds
- Collection letters
- Other letters about credit

- Memorandums of various kinds
- Various kinds of fill-in forms, for use by either the sender or the receiver of the message, or both
- Reports that retain the same format but change in reported information
- Letters or memorandums that contain space for a reply, either as fill-in blanks or with a written reply

Besides the kinds of messages ordinarily described as "form letters," thousands of forms are used in organizations; for example, expense reimbursement requests, employee evaluation forms, and many, many more. Because of the multitude of formats and arrangements, including combinations of letters or memorandums and fill-in forms, the distinction between *form letters* and *forms* is indistinct.

For the purpose of discussion, however, form messages are divided into the following broad categories:

- complete form
- fill-in form
- guide form
- paragraph form

Complete Form Messages Letters, memorandums, reports, or other material identical in content and format are described as complete form messages. Problems and examples in previous chapters illustrate complete form messages; for

A "paperless office" not yet fully achieved. Do you suppose that all these pieces of paper are absolutely essential?

example, memorandums to be distributed to all employees, letters to be sent to television viewers, and sales material planned for mass distribution. As these form messages are written, however, the fact that they are to be mass produced and distributed is irrelevant. Each message, whether to be read by one individual or many, should address the reader directly; the content and approach should be the same.

Personalized inside addresses and salutations are not used in complete form letters, and memorandums are not personalized with each reader's name. If a salutation or other address is used, it is some general term like "Dear Customer" or "To Our Stockholders." Many complete forms are mailed with other material; for example, sales letters that accompany brochures or letters included with shipped merchandise.

For economy, complete letter forms are usually printed. Even when word processing equipment is available, vast numbers of copies must be prepared in some other way. Photocopying is another method of reproduction of a limited number of copies. Whichever method is used, the final product should be attractive and, if it is in letter format, should resemble an individually typewritten letter.

Fill-In Forms As the name indicates, fill-in forms include spaces for filling in information on previously prepared letters, memorandums, or other material. Fill-in forms may be printed in quantity, and, as needed, blanks are filled in with a pen or typewriter.

Fill-in form messages may be stored on a disk for use on word processors. The operator calls up the letter, inserts the necessary information, including date, name, and address, and prints the revised copy, which is indistinguishable from an individually typewritten letter.

Figure 7–7 is an example of a short collection message, which would be reproduced on letterhead stationery and used in the early stage of a collection cycle.

Although you might use Figure 7–7 for the first letter in a collection series, more likely you would choose a printed *complete form*. Individualized letters are especially appropriate in middle-stage and late-stage collection messages.

When using the procedure illustrated by Figure 7–7, you should prepare another letter for customers who have *not* been prompt with previous payments.

In addition, fill-in form messages are prepared to be filled in for individual readers according to the particular situation. Figure 7–8 shows such a fill-in form.

Guide Form Letters Letters or other messages may be prepared in advance to use in writing similar messages. They differ from complete form messages in that they are not meant to be used exactly as they are, but only as a guide. Guide form letters are often placed in correspondence manuals, and they may be stored on disks for use with word processors.

Guide Form Paragraphs Guide form paragraphs are like guide form letters except, as the term indicates, they consist only of paragraphs that are combined in various ways to make up complete letters or other communications. Such paragraphs, written in advance for recurring situations, have been used in busi-

_____)
_____)
_____)
_____)   Space for date, inside address,
_____)   salutation
_____)
_____)
_____)
)

    Your check for last month's purchases, totaling _____ ,
has not yet been received by our credit office.

    Your prompt payments in previous months are appreciated. We
believe that the present delay is only an oversight.

    Telephone me at 555-0000 if you have questions.

Sincerely,

Ann Henderson

Ann Henderson
Credit Manager

rt

FIGURE 7–7
Example of a fill-in
form letter

We cannot process your check for the following reason:

_____ The check is unsigned.

_____ The check is postdated. Checks should be dated as of the
       day they are signed.

_____ The amounts shown in figures and in words are different,
       or both are incorrect. The correct amount is
       _____ .

_____ Other:_____

Please send a correctly completed check in the enclosed envelope.

FIGURE 7–8
A fill-in form to be
completed for each sit-
uation

nesses for many years. Often they are placed in correspondence manuals, or they may be stored on disks for use with word processors.

Each paragraph is marked with a number, a letter of the alphabet, or both. The originator of a letter or other message may tell the transcriber: "Use Paragraphs 2B, 3E, 5N, and 1A." Or the originator may dictate a new beginning paragraph, give the transcriber instructions to use certain form paragraphs, and dictate a closing paragraph. Using paragraphs in various ways saves time in composing, but an elaborate system of paragraphs could result in even more time being spent in preparing correspondence than would be necessary for individually dictated letters.

Dangers of Using Form Messages

Although form messages are necessary for economical communications, use them with discretion. Because form messages are so easy to use, they are sometimes misused.

All the criteria by which individually dictated letters are judged must be applied to form letters. If they can be judged outstanding by these criteria, considering the particular situation and the individual reader, then they are ready for use.

Other Time-Saving Methods of Communication

You may save a great deal of time by omitting unnecessary communications, a fact that seems obvious but also seems to be overlooked. Telephone calls or personal conversations can accomplish the purpose of the communications in less time, depending on the situation and the necessity for written records. Postal cards and short-note replies are time-saving methods of written communication.

Postal Cards Postal cards or picture postcards, like full-sized letters, can be preprinted as complete form messages or as fill-in forms. They can be used to replace regular typewritten letters, although, like form messages, they should be used with careful judgment. Do not use cards for any message that could be considered the least bit confidential. Moreover, some readers will be offended by what they consider to be a cheap method of reply.

Short-Note Replies A prompt and economical method of communication consists of only a short handwritten note on the margin of a letter or memorandum to which you are responding. You would then photocopy the original letter or memorandum, including your added handwritten note, for a file copy. The original letter or memorandum is returned to the person who wrote it.

Like postcards and form messages, short-note replies should be used only in certain circumstances. Such methods of communication are extremely informal, can convey only limited information, and may be resented by the reader.

Summary

Special goodwill letters or memorandums are business messages planned for the single purpose of building goodwill. Some goodwill messages are written not for business purposes but for expressing our feelings to other persons, including persons we have known through business relationships.

Goodwill messages express appreciation, congratulations, sympathy, welcome, and good wishes. They must be sincere. They should be written promptly or at the appropriate time.

The four major categories of form messages are complete forms, fill-in forms, guide form letters, and guide form paragraphs. These categories may also be combined; for example, a complete form, as it is used in the originating company, may contain a fill-in form for the respondent.

Other time-saving methods of written communication include the use of postcards and of short-note replies, which are handwritten notes added to the original communication.

Test Yourself: Chapter Review

1. Discuss the appearance of some goodwill letters as compared with the usual business letter.

2–3. What is an advantage of using form letters? What is a possible disadvantage?

4–7. What are four basic categories of form letters?

8–11. Briefly describe each of the four categories of form letters.

12. Why does the term *form letter* sometimes convey a negative connotation?

Test Yourself: Correct Usage

(Related to material in Chapter 7; letter styles and arrangement, discussed in Appendix B; and principles of correct usage.) Insert necessary punctuation, including quotation marks, hyphens, and apostrophes, and remove punctuation that has been inserted incorrectly. Choose correct word from each pair or group. Make any other necessary changes.

1. A letter of welcome was written by the director of the Chamber of Commerce to my partner and (I, me).

2. We (received, recieved) the letter one week after we moved to the city, on (June 9, June 9th), 1987.

3. A letter of welcome, along with congratulatory notes and letters of appreciation (are, is) used by many organizations to keep in touch with their customers and friends.

4. Form messages if used wisely save time and money.

5. Letterhead (stationary, stationery) should be used for many form letters.

6. One of the (four, 4) kinds of form messages is described as a fill-in form.

7. The (complimentary, complementary) close, ("Yours truly," "Yours truely") is considered by some people to be old-fashioned.

8. The word ("Sincerly," "Sincerely") is a widely used complimentary close.

9. Some writers when placing the date on letters misspell the word ("February," "Feburary") they should learn to spell the name of a month that will occur once a year for the remainder of their lives.

10. Leave at least (3, three) line spaces for a signature on a letter.

11. Postcards like full sized letters can be printed as complete form messages or as fill-in forms.

12. The name of the addressee should be shown this way in the inside address: (Ms. Wendy Ritger, Wendy Ritger).

13. The salutation of a letter should be shown in this way: (Dear Wendy Ritger, Wendy Ritger, Dear Ms. Ritger).

14. Prefer to address a letter to an individual at an organization using his or her name instead of addressing the letter to the company.

15. When (adressing, addressing) a letter make absolutely sure that you spell the (readers, reader's) name correctly.

Cases

1. Analyze two or more business letters of any kind, except mass-distributed sales letters. Do these letters effectively build goodwill? Why or why not? Report your opinion about these letters according to the directions of your instructor.

2. Find examples of special goodwill letters as described in this chapter. Analyze these letters from the standpoint of what you have learned about building goodwill.

3. Look through a newspaper for notices or news items indicating that the persons involved have merited letters of appreciation or congratulations. Write one or more letters.

4. Write a letter of appreciation to a person toward whom you feel real gratitude—for anything.

5. Write a letter expressing holiday greetings to employees you supervise.

6. Write a letter of congratulations to a friend or acquaintance for a recent honor or accomplishment.

7. Write a letter to salespeople extending Easter greetings and appreciation for extra effort and longer hours during the pre-Easter sale.

8. Write a letter of welcome to newcomers to your city. Assume that you are the public relations director of a local chain of grocery stores.

9. Write a letter to your mayor or to another city official expressing support for his or her position on some question pertaining to city government.

10. Write a letter to a state representative or senator, or to the governor of your state, expressing agreement with his or her position on some question pertaining to state government.

11. Write a letter to your representative or senator in Washington, D.C., expressing agreement with his or her position on some question pertaining to national government or support for a sponsored bill.

12. Write a letter thanking a former employer, teacher, or business associate who recommended you for a job you recently obtained.

13. Assume that fifteen years from now you learn that a student who sits next to you in this class has just been elected to Congress, representing your district. Write a letter expressing your congratulations and support. (Spell the person's name correctly.)

14. Write a letter to one or more of your high school or elementary teachers. Thank the teacher for your school year and state how the instruction has benefited you.

15. You are the credit manager of Goldsmith's Department Store, Midland, Texas. For more than thirty-one years Mr. and Mrs. Hector Aquadro have been good customers. Their monthly bills have always been paid within a few days after receipt. Write a letter of appreciation. Their address is 12416 Hideway Cove, Midland, TX 79702.

16. You are the public relations director of a manufacturer that sponsors a popular afternoon soap opera. (Naturally, you do not refer to the program as a soap opera.) During the past week, the hero and the heroine were married in an elaborate, hour-long ceremony and party. Letters are pouring in from viewers, thanking your company for sponsoring such a "lovely, lovely wedding of the dear, dear people." Other writers state that they happened to tune in by accident and that they never saw such a silly, sentimental program in their whole lifetime; they do not intend to buy your products again if they can remember to refrain from doing so. Write form letters to be sent to each group of viewers.

17. Write a letter to the sponsor of a radio or television program that you particularly enjoy.

18. Write a letter to the television or radio station (or network) that broadcasts a program that you particularly enjoy. Express your gratitude.

19. Write a letter to the television or radio station (or network) that broadcasts a program that you would like very much if certain changes were made. Carefully state your suggested changes, with reasons, in your letter.

20. Write a letter of appreciation to the manufacturer of a product that you use and like.

21. Bring to class, for discussion and evaluation, responses to the letters for Cases 17, 18, 19, and 20.

22. As assistant to the director of admissions, your college or university, write a letter of welcome to incoming freshmen. Think back to the time when you entered college. What did you need and want to know? Write a one-page letter.

23. You are a mathematics professor in your thirty-first year at Central College. Five years ago Merrill Berlson came to Central College as the new director of Physical Plant and Planning. Since that time he has made many improvements in landscaping. Flowers are everywhere, and permanent plantings of native shrubs and trees have added much beauty to the campus, which was previously rather barren. Even within a limited budget, Mr. Berlson has done an outstanding job. Express your appreciation in a letter to Mr. Berlson.

24. Modify Problem 23 to fit a person at your own college or university who, in your opinion, deserves appreciation for a job well done. Write the letter and mail it. (As your instructor directs, keep a copy for use in your class.)

25. Look in a newspaper for the "Letters to the Editor" section. Bring these letters to class for discussion and evaluation.

26. Write a letter to be published in the "Letters to the Editor" section of your local newspaper. These letters, for example, could support some action of the City Council or a neighborhood group; they could also describe positive aspects of your school or university.

27. Bring to class examples of actual form letters. Evaluate each letter according to all the criteria of effective communication of any kind.

28. You are a systems engineer employed by Valley Equipment Company in San Francisco. Last month you were responsible for replacing the computer terminal equipment in Sacramento and training the personnel to use the new equipment. You encountered many unforeseen problems that caused the conversion and training to take three days rather than the one day scheduled.

The conversion process was very disruptive to normal warehouse operation. Workers in the warehouse were required to work overtime as a result of the problems. Although frustrated, they were understanding and cooperative.

Write a letter of appreciation to the warehouse manager, Chong Shin, Valley Equipment Company, 200 Valley, Sacramento, CA 74325. Also write a letter of appreciation to all workers for the warehouse manager to distribute. (You do not remember all their names.)

29. You are the director of development for Central College and are about to begin the fall Greater Toronto Campaign. In this campaign, major corporations throughout the city are solicited to contribute funds to the college. Several letters will be written in conjunction with the campaign.

a. The president of the college will write a letter to all companies being solicited as an introduction for the volunteer who will soon be calling on them.

b. The fund drive chairman will write all volunteers thanking them for joining the campaign.

c. As a two-week follow-up, the fund drive chairman will write all volunteers requesting that all solicitations be made prior to Thanksgiving.

d. At the end of the campaign, the fund drive chairman will thank all volunteers for their help throughout the campaign. Write all these letters. (Use assumed names and addresses.)

30. Find a poem or short story that you particularly like in a recently published periodical or book. Write a note of appreciation to the author, in care of the magazine or publisher. Include comments about why you like the writer's work.

31. Write to a columnist you read regularly, addressed in care of the magazine or newspaper in which the column appears. Refer to a particular column; agree or disagree with the writer's opinions. State your ideas tactfully, but specifically.

32. **Letter to Retiring Sales Representative.** Write a letter of best wishes and appreciation to Mr. Herbert F. Gatlin, 71 Perkins, Philadelphia, PA 19102. Mr. Gatlin is retiring after thirty-seven years with Quality Office Products as a sales representative. He is now seventy-four years old. He has many loyal customers and friends throughout his territory. He has been cooperative and helpful throughout his career, especially in training new employees. He now plans to spend more time with his hobby, photography, and to build it into a second career. He also plans to spend more time with his wife and grandchildren.

33. You are the office manager for a local finance company. Prepare a form letter to be sent to preferred customers offering to lend them money. Let them know that they have been chosen for their excellent credit rating. State that they can have an existing account and still borrow additional money. All they have to do is call.

Evaluation
Sheet:
Goodwill Letters
and
Memorandums

	Yes	No	Not Sure
1. Is the message completely sincere?	___	___	___
2. Is the message sent promptly?	___	___	___
3. Does the message OMIT			
▪ obvious flattery?	___	___	___
▪ gushiness?	___	___	___
▪ excess words?	___	___	___
▪ unnecessary, undesirable repetition?	___	___	___
▪ negative or "sad" words (as in condolences)?	___	___	___
▪ envy (as in letters of congratulations)?	___	___	___
4. If sales promotion is used at all, are you absolutely SURE that it is appropriate for this particular message and circumstance?	___	___	___
5. Does your metacommunication (implied messages) agree with your written words?	___	___	___
6. Is the letter or memorandum written entirely in the you-approach, without condescension or undue humility?	___	___	___
7. Is the letter correct in every way?	___	___	___
8. If you received this letter or memo, would you feel better than you did before you received it?	___	___	___
9. Is the message absolutely correct in format, grammar, spelling, and sentence structure?	___	___	___

CHAPTER 8

Writing about the Routine
and the Favorable

Requirements and considerations for favorable good-news messages and for routine, neutral, or merely informational messages were discussed briefly in relation to material in Chapters 3 through 7. This chapter provides further discussion of the content of such communications, with examples of some of the variations of routine and favorable letters.

Planning Routine and Favorable Messages

Because the first position of any communication is an emphatic one, use this position advantageously by opening with a statement that tells the good news or sums up the main idea. When you write inquiries or requests, your inquiry itself can often be the opening sentence of the letter.

A subject line is especially useful and appropriate in good-news letters, routine and neutral letters, and in direct inquiries and requests. A well-chosen subject line tells the reader at the beginning what the message is about. It saves explanations or references that would otherwise come in the first paragraph, allowing the first paragraph to be used to move the discussion more quickly into the remainder of the message. Subject lines are also an aid to rapid filing.

On letters, a subject line is ordinarily placed a double space *below* the salutation, as illustrated in Figures 8–2 and 8–7. If no salutation and complimentary close are used, the subject line is placed two or three lines below the inside address. (A subject line is used in all memorandums.)

When you request or impart bits of information, arrange and word questions or statements so that they are easy to read and understand. Lists and tabulations, or statements standing alone as paragraphs, make material much easier to read than if presented in long paragraphs. Subheads, underlining, numbering, and other arrangements in format increase readability (see Chapter 4).

Letters that present favorable or neutral information are ordinarily conducive to pleasant human relationships, but they can result in an opposite effect. They are less than pleasant and positive if written in a grudging tone. Sometimes they seem to imply that although the writer is doing what the reader requested, the action is inconvenient or unnecessary, or that the reader is not justified in making the request. These approaches can harm pleasant relationships or customer goodwill more than a diplomatic, reasonable refusal letter.

Ordinarily, favorable letters or memorandums are shorter than unfavorable ones because there is less need for reasons and explanations and for convincing the reader that the action taken is a reasonable one. But *even favorable messages can be so short that they seem curt and convey less than complete and necessary information.*

In routine and favorable messages, as in all communication, *we must be concerned with goodwill,* whatever the other purpose or purposes of the messages and whether they are directed to people outside or within the organization. In addition, we must be concerned with all other elements of effective communica-

---

Communication Brief

German letters then are more formal; there are several graduations of familiarity, and it is important to know at which level a relationship is. Most people resent it if the writer is too familiar and informal. They feel as if the writer invades their personal space. American business people have to be particularly careful when writing to a German audience.

Iris Ingrid Varner, "Comparison of American and German Business Communication," in *Business Communication—What's New? (Proceedings of the 1984 American Business Communication Association International Convention),* 20.

tion, including readability, conciseness, completeness, a positive approach, and correctness.

Good-news messages arranged in the direct order were discussed in "Choosing and Planning an Appropriate Order of Arrangement," in Chapter 5. Further details about letters ordinarily best arranged in a direct order are given below. Notice that the items listed do *not* indicate individual paragraphs. Although opening and closing sections often consist of only one paragraph, middle sections are usually longer.

Good-news letters

1. Good news or other pleasant ideas. May open with goodwill, followed by good news.
2. Details, information, instructions, or other necessary material.
3. Closing thought—a pleasant goodwill close or, if some action is requested of the reader, an appropriate, diplomatic action close. Closing section may include resale or sales promotion.

Neutral letters

1. The most important idea or bit of information, or a brief summary of the entire message; can also open with short expression of goodwill, followed by gist of message.
2. Details, information, instructions, or other needed material.
3. Closing thought—a pleasant goodwill close, or if some action is requested of the reader, an appropriate, diplomatic action close. May include resale or sales promotion.

Direct requests or inquiries

1. The request or inquiry, or, if appropriate, an expression of goodwill, followed by the request or inquiry. Request or inquiry can also be stated in subject line.
2. Details, information, instruction, or other needed material.
3. A specific, but diplomatic, action close.

The *action close* should specify the desired action, preferably in terms of reader interest and benefit. Make the action easy and motivate prompt action, if appropriate, or give a date with reasonable explanations of when the action should be taken. The action close, although specific, should not be demanding or dictatorial in tone.

Beginnings and Endings in the Direct Arrangement

Beginnings

We should make sure that the important first paragraph of business messages is planned to include material that we want to emphasize, not that which is better subordinated. We are especially concerned with the first sentence of the first paragraph and with the first word of the first sentence. Often the first sentence of a business message should make up the entire first paragraph. This short sentence, stand-ing alone at the beginning of a letter, occupies perhaps the most emphatic position possible.

In a good-news letter, the good news ordinarily belongs in the first para-graph.

Here are some examples of opening sentences from good-news letters:

The enclosed check for $520 is in payment for your excellent article on gardening.

The educational materials you requested are being mailed today.

Congratulations! You won a blue ribbon for your photograph, "Wagon Wheel."

Your credit account has been approved, and your first shipment of Happy Day shoes is on its way to you.

The enclosed salary check is larger than last month's because of a $22 decrease in health insurance.

It is especially important that the first paragraph be short. Nothing is more discouraging to the reader than a long block of type at the beginning of a letter or memorandum. Additional sentences take away from the emphasis that a short paragraph would otherwise express.

Avoid slow, wordy, unnecessary beginnings such as

Unnecessary; also not you-approach

> We have received your letter of October 1.
>
> We are writing this letter to advise you . . .

This phrasing is unnecessary—just go on and say whatever is to be said. *Advise* used in this way is probably misused; this word means *to give advice;* it should not be used in any other way.

Slow

> Referring to your letter of October 1 . . .

A slow, weak, participial beginning.

Slow; also dangling modifier

> Replying to your letter of October 1, you will find . . .

Another slow, weak, participial beginning. *Replying* is a dangling participle be-cause it does not modify *you,* although it appears to do so because of the sen-tence construction. (See Appendix D.)

> This letter is in reply to your letter of October 1.

Slow.

> Acknowledging receipt of yours of recent date . . .

Terrible!

Avoid letter or memorandum beginnings that stress the *I-approach* instead of the *you-approach,* as in the following sentences:

Our company has been operating in Miami since 1905.

We are pleased to announce the introduction of our new advertising campaign.

As chairman of the fund-raising committee of United Way, I am writing you . . .

The Smith-Wright Company is pleased to announce . . .

We at the Smith-Wright Company . . .

In replies to requests for information, the first paragraph may give part of the requested information:

John J. Harris, about whom you inquired in your letter of November 30, was employed in our marketing department as a research assistant from 1971 to 1974.

Yes, 700 copies of *Cultural Literacy* can be shipped immediately.

Our dress material #2112 is 100 percent cotton. It is definitely appropriate for the shirts you plan to manufacture.

If the information requested is lengthy and complicated, it should be arranged in an orderly, easy-to-understand presentation, perhaps through a tabulation or list. For such a letter, your first paragraph could read:

We are happy to send you the information you requested.

Although this paragraph opens with a *we,* it is acceptable because it is written with a courteous, service-oriented attitude. *Do not feel that you must eliminate "I" openings entirely. To do so results in unnatural writing, sometimes stiff and seemingly insincere.*

Inquiries may begin with a specific question, as:

Do you have the book *The Status Seekers,* by Vance Packard?

Will you please send me information about your dress material #2112, especially as to its fabric content?

Purpose is stated immediately

Goodwill messages often open with a greeting, as:

Congratulations!

Best wishes for a happy voyage.

Thank you for . . .

Happy Columbus Day!

Endings

Many letters and memorandums should end with an *action close. Messages written to obtain some action from the reader*—to buy a product, come into a store, pay a bill, supply the requested information, or follow the suggested instructions—*should end with a definite statement of this desired action.*

The reader should know how, when, why, and where this action is to take place. The writer should make this action as easy to accomplish as possible for the reader. For example, do not request a letter in reply, but rather a check mark on a card that you have enclosed. If you ask readers to come into your store, they should be given the location and the hours the store is open. If you ask them to telephone you, include your number and business hours.

The action close should be definitely worded, but it should not appear to be demanding or dictatorial. It should include, when appropriate, some motivation for prompt action. Certain sales letters state that a special discount or bonus will apply to orders received before a deadline. The only motivation appropriate for some messages is a reasonable explanation of the necessity for prompt action.

Try to give a valid reason for setting a deadline, preferably one of some benefit to the reader. Most of us tend to procrastinate if we do not have stated times for a task to be completed or for a letter to be answered.

A doubtful tone, or a tone reflecting a lack of success consciousness, should not appear in letter endings, although it often does. Examples of *weak, doubtful* phrasing are:

Weak ending; negative

> If you want to look at this set of books, just call our representative . . .

An improved statement is:

> To examine this valuable set of books in your own home, just call . . .

The following expressions

Doubtful tone

> If this plan meets your approval . . .
>
> We hope that you won't disapprove of this suggested plan . . .

are better stated in this way:

> I believe you will find this plan to be helpful to both departments.

Some letters and memorandums are not written for the purpose of obtaining immediate action. Examples are letters that give information only and that ask for no further contact, and memorandums telling of changes in methods or procedures.

You are considerate and courteous when you keep channels open for further communication if it is desirable or necessary. You may ask the reader to telephone you or write again for further help or instructions. Such statements should not be used routinely, however, for they may have the negative effect of

Communication Brief

Ninety-nine out of a hundred business letters start with an acknowledgment of the addressee's last letter. Have you ever asked yourself why? The only plausible answer I found is that it's always been done that way. It's an old, old custom.

Of course, people who have the souls of file clerks always say this stock opening is needed for filing purposes. But that's no argument: there's always room for a reference somewhere in a corner of the letter; and quite often it doesn't make a bit of difference to anybody who wrote what on what date.

Rudolf Flesch, *The Art of Readable Writing* (New York: Harper & Brothers, 1949), 46–47.

suggesting trouble or misunderstanding. They may also encourage unnecessary continuing correspondence.

The simple statement

    We are glad to be of service

can be an appropriate ending. Sales promotion material can be used not only to promote sales but also to provide a pleasant letter ending. For example:

    We have just received a shipment of new spring raincoats. They are
    especially colorful and attractive this year and are priced lower than last
    year's models. Come in early so that you will have a wide choice of
    styles and colors.

In long letters, the final paragraph or paragraphs can serve as a summary.

Orders, Inquiries, and Direct Requests

Orders, inquiries, and direct requests are considered routine because they are often necessary and because they are not likely to result in reader displeasure or resistance.

Order Letters

Although orders for merchandise or services are often placed by methods other than by writing a letter, the order letter still has a place both in business communication and in your personal business transactions. Order letters are simple to plan and arrange, but many are less than effective because they omit necessary information or ordinary courtesy.

Another common weakness is that information about the merchandise ordered is presented in a way that is hard to read and understand immediately, or in a way that can be easily misunderstood. Necessary information includes the quantity; price; catalog number, if any; and such descriptions as color, size, and model number. In addition, information must be included—if it is not already clear from previous transactions—about the plan of payment and shipping instructions.

The order letter is a direct request, and certainly one that the seller of the

Question: I'm still confused about the use of the apostrophe. How is it most often misused?

Answer: One of the most frequent ways in which an apostrophe is misused results from the confusion of *its* and *it's*. Another inconsistency is the various ways in which an apostrophe is used with singular and plural names.

The possessive form of *it* is *its*, with no apostrophe. *It's* means *it is*, and absolutely nothing else.

Another error, although much less frequent, is the incorrect use of an apostrophe in *theirs*, in which no apostrophe is used.

Another construction in which a needed apostrophe is commonly omitted is illustrated by these phrases: *two weeks' vacation, one year's experience.* (No apostrophe is needed in the following phrases: *two weeks of vacation, one year of experience.*)

Apostrophes are often omitted or used inconsistently in family names, particularly on mailboxes. Consider the name Johnson.

If only one person lives in the house, his or her mailbox may be labeled *Johnson* (or Ann Johnson or Bill Johnson). If two or more people named Johnson live in the house, *The Johnsons* adequately identifies the place, but does not show possession. (We can assume that Johnson or The Johnsons have possession, at least temporarily.)

If Bill Johnson wants to show that the house is his alone, the term *Johnson's* will so indicate. If Bill and Ann share the house and mailbox, the possessive designation should be *The Johnsons'.* If Betty and Joe Box share a house and mailbox, the sign should read *The Boxes* (a simple plural) or *The Boxes'* (plural possessive).

No wonder your neighbors are mixed up. But let it go. Harmonious relationships are more important than the exact use of the apostrophe, at least on someone else's mailbox.

---

merchandise or service will not resist, provided the merchandise is available and the buyer can be expected to pay.

The example letter in Figure 8–1 is an order sent to Ireland by a shop owner. If such merchandise had been ordered from a source in the United States, the order might have been placed some other way than by letter, perhaps by telephone.

Direct Inquiries

Inquiries are, in effect, requests for information. Some inquiries are about products or services being considered for purchase. Replies to these letters are referred to as *solicited sales messages.* Other requests for information are of various kinds, including information about people being considered for employment or as credit customers.

When giving information about an applicant for employment (as well as

2572 Cherry Roadway   *The Smart Shoppe*   Seattle, Washington 98008

June 2, 19--

Shannon Mail Order
Shannon Free Airport
Ireland

Please send the following items by Fastmail.

6	#GB34126	Aran Tam O'Shanter	$ 9.40 +	$ 3.50
6	#GB22330	Hand-crocheted vest (medium)	56.50 +	6.40
6	#GB22330	Hand-crocheted vest (large)	56.50 +	6.40
2	#GB86665	Mohair Cape	296.40 +	14.80

Notice that I have listed Fastmail charges by each item, as shown in your catalog, although you have noted that you pay half of the mailing charges when the order is more than $150. Will you make further discounts because I have ordered more than one of each item and because my order is far more than $150?

In addition, can you offer special prices because I am buying these items to be resold? If so, I may be able to continue making purchases for my shop, which specializes in items from all over the world.

Please charge my gold American Express card (00000) for the lowest amount, including shipping charges, for which you can send the merchandise listed above. I understand that U.S. duty, if levied, will be collected upon delivery.

Ann Bowling
Ann Bowling
Owner

Arranged in "functional" style with no salutation or complimentary close

Begins with most important information, the desired merchandise

Request for discount with reasons

Action close

No complimentary close

FIGURE 8–1
Order letter

for a credit applicant, as discussed later in the chapter), your reply may be of extreme importance to the applicant and to the inquiring organization. You have several important considerations. *You must be fair to both the applicant and the inquirer. In addition, you must abide by civil rights and all other applicable laws. You must be aware of possible legal problems that may arise, even if your reply is completely factual. Be extremely careful about negative information, but do not give a positive recommendation that you know is not justified. Give only verifiable facts and let the inquirer make a decision based on these facts. State that the provided information is confidential.*

Some companies provide only the title and dates of employment.

Requests for Adjustments or Refunds

Requests for adjustments, refunds, replacement of merchandise, modification of terms, or similar requests concerning merchandise or service should be considered as routine. They should be arranged in the direct order, unless something about the situation indicates otherwise. Approaching the request directly indicates that you feel that there will be no hesitation in settling the matter.

These communications, like all others, should be pleasant, positive, and confident. Anger, sarcasm, or a demanding tone will be self-defeating.

The usual and most desirable outlook of company personnel, when receiving requests for adjustments, should not be one of annoyance, but one of interest in finding out what happened and whether or not the customer is indeed entitled to an adjustment or refund.

They know that even the best products will at times be less than perfect; that accidents and errors occur; that people can make mistakes. The customer also realizes these things, and the request letter should be approached in an attitude that reflects this outlook.

The next letter, Figure 8–2, is a follow-up to that shown in Figure 8–1.

Other Direct Requests

An invitation is a direct request, since it asks for the reader's presence at some function. It is also a good-news message if it can be assumed that the reader is pleased to receive the invitation.

The letter in Figure 8–3 requires no specific and definite action close because employees are not requested to make reservations. This letter has no inside address because it was photocopied and distributed to all employees. Individual typewritten letters would have been far more expensive and would add little to the goodwill approach.

Acknowledgments

A letter of acknowledgment is not necessary for every order. In many instances, especially with a regular customer, filling the order exactly as instructed and shipping it immediately is acknowledgment enough, although a goodwill sentence or two or a *thank you* is appropriate on the invoice.

New customers should be sent a letter of acknowledgment and welcome with the first order. If credit is being granted, the terms should be exactly stated.

Sometimes an order cannot be shipped because the buyer has given incomplete information. Such replies, along with others that are not completely favorable, are discussed in Chapter 9.

Figure 8–4 is a simple acknowledgment of merchandise ordered from a company that sells specialty items by direct mail and through their catalogs. This letter is a printed form letter, as it must be if cost is to be considered. Customers realize that money spent for individually typewritten letters must be added to the price that they pay for merchandise. A courteous tone and attractive appearance, even though a letter is obviously printed, builds goodwill and further sales for the company.

The letter was mailed separately to new customers, although it could have

2572 Cherry Roadway   *The Smart Shoppe*   Seattle, Washington 98008

July 12, 19--

Mr. Michael O'Daniel
Sales Manager
Shannon Mail Order
Shannon Free Airport
Ireland

Dear Mr. O'Daniel:

REQUEST FOR ADJUSTMENT IN MAILING CHARGES   *The request*

Thank you for the prompt shipment of my order of June 2.   *Goodwill*
Everything is beautiful.

I also appreciate your discount because I purchased the
merchandise for resale in The Smart Shoppe, although, frankly, I
had expected a larger discount, similar to wholesale prices here   *Explanation*
in the United States. Nevertheless, I shall keep all the items
because I want Ireland to be represented in our international
collection.

Please notice, however, that I was charged full mailing costs, not
half of this amount, which is advertised in your catalog as being
applicable to any order of $150 or more. This overpayment of   *Explanation*
mailing costs is almost as much as the discount you allowed
because of my quantity purchase for resale.

Will you please send me a check for one-half the mailing costs,
an amount which is calculated on the attached copy of your   *Action close*
invoice?

Sincerely,

Ann Bowling

Ann Bowling
Owner

FIGURE 8–2
Request for adjustment

Public Relations Department/3M

3M Center
St. Paul, Minnesota 55144
612/733 1110

September 17, 19--

Dear Employees:

The invitation (request)

You and your family are cordially invited to attend the Open House at our manufacturing laboratories and administrative and research headquarters on Sunday, September 30, from 1:30 to 4:30 p.m.

Explanation and instructions

Each family attending the Open House will receive a gift box containing several of the products we make, particularly those that are especially useful in the home. Please bring this letter with you so that you can obtain your gift.

Refreshments will be served in the cafeteria, and there will be drawings for valuable attendance prizes. All employees and their family members attending the Open House are eligible to win.

The enclosed information sheet contains your numbered ticket for the attendance prizes. Fill it out and drop it in the drawing box when you arrive. Additional tickets may be picked up at the door.

Goodwill and action close

We look forward to seeing you and your family. Please take this opportunity to meet other employees and their families.

Sincerely,

Cindy M. Olson

Cindy M. Olson
Public Relations

rn

FIGURE 8–3
An invitation. This letter does not contain an inside address because it was not individually addressed and mailed.

HOLIDAY HOUSE
798 Lake Nora South
Indianapolis, IN 46240

August 13, 19--

Dear Customer:

Thank you for your order. It is being shipped today by parcel post, as you directed.

Courtesy and good news

Welcome to the group of discerning buyers who are our customers. Some have been with us for many years, and perhaps you will be, too.

Goodwill

Look through the new fall catalog that is enclosed. You will find many things that you can buy nowhere else in the world. On the other items that can be purchased elsewhere, you will find no lower prices.

You will be delighted with almost everything you purchase. We are sure of this because of the experience of our many other customers. But if you want to send something back, we'll be glad to take it with no questions asked.

Sales promotion

If you prefer, use your VISA, MasterCard, or American Express account. Just show your card number and the expiration date on the enclosed order blank.

Action close

Sincerely,

Martha

Martha L'Orange, Owner

FIGURE 8–4
An acknowledgment. For reasons of economy, such a message is often printed. The date is added by hand or sometimes omitted. (Preferably, all letters and memorandums of any kind include a date.)

been included with the merchandise. A similar letter is included with the packaged items in subsequent orders.

Favorable or Routine Replies and Announcements

When the news is good, this information is the best way to open a letter or memorandum planned to convey the good news. The opposite approach applies when bad news must be conveyed, as discussed in Chapter 9, although under no circumstances should a writer misrepresent, even momentarily.

The letter shown in Figure 8–5 opens with two words that summarize exactly what the reader wants to know—"You won!"

Newburg Fabrics
Newburg, South Carolina 29207

October 25, 19--

Ms. Sally Jones
Sales Representative
Western Region
Newburg Fabrics
7070 Smith Grove Road
Anaheim, CA 72043

Dear Sally:

The good news

You won!

Good news, continued

You were the top sales representative in the Western Region. You are to be commended for the dedication and hard work that earned you this top place—and a cruise through the Canary Islands, along with your spouse or other family member.

Explanation

The second-place winner in the Western Region, Victor Sims of Salt Lake City, has also been awarded a cruise, along with the first- and second-place sales leaders of the other regions. Saundra (my wife) and I will also go along. I'm sure we will all have a wonderful time.

Explanation

Winners will be announced at the annual sales meeting next week. Start making plans. You will receive more details at the meeting.

Sincerely,

Robert Shaw

Robert Shaw
Sales Manager

FIGURE 8–5
A good-news letter

Approved Adjustments

An adjustment letter is usually written in response to a claim or complaint. Prompt, cheerful adjustments, made by letter, in person, or by telephone, do much to increase customer goodwill. Adjustments are also approved for employees. Building or maintaining company loyalty is as important as building and maintaining favorable relationships with customers and the general public.

Each claim should be investigated before an adjustment is granted. In fairness to all other customers, or to all other employees, unjustified claims should not be granted. The customer is not always right. When you are not sure what should be done, in general, it is best to give the claimant the benefit of the doubt. (Refused adjustments are discussed in Chapter 9.)

One purpose of granting adjustments is to maintain goodwill. Another purpose, even more important, is to resolve legitimate complaints. Even when an adjustment is granted, however, a letter will not build or maintain goodwill if it is written in an inconsiderate, hurried, or grudging tone. Your reader may have been inconvenienced by an error made by your organization. You as a company representative must do everything possible to restore faith in your organization and to assure your customer, or your employee, that you are happy to make things right.

Avoid words and phrases like *grant, we will allow, we want to keep you satisfied,* and *we are willing to*. Such wording sounds condescending and grudging. The person who receives a favorable adjustment should know that you are happy to make it. You should not imply that the adjustment was made merely to satisfy a customer or to avoid controversy.

As in other good-news messages, the information that the reader's request is being approved should come first in the letter, followed by necessary details, explanations, and a goodwill close. At times, however, when the error is serious and an apology is warranted, the apology should come first in the letter—a reversal of what is ordinarily considered a positive arrangement. In most situations an apology, if necessary, can come after the good news, along with necessary explanations. Do not be overly apologetic.

Do not refer to the error in the emphatic closing paragraph. End with a goodwill paragraph. If appropriate, include resale or sales promotion.

Figure 8–6 is an adjustment letter; candy boxes were not filled.

Establishing the Credit Relationship

Effective letters about credit applicants and credit procedures greatly decrease the number of necessary collection letters. Letters about credit include inquiries and replies about credit applicants; credit approval letters that include a specific statement of terms, due dates, interest rates, and other necessary details; and letters refusing credit.

Inquiries about Credit Applicants

A request for information about a credit applicant is similar to an inquiry about an applicant for employment; both are similar to most other routine requests. Many credit inquiries are made by telephone. When written messages are used, often form messages with fill-in blanks are chosen for convenience, economy, and prompt response.

Replies to Requests for Credit Information

Many replies to requests for credit information consist only of filling out the form messages mentioned earlier. Regardless of whether the information is presented through fill-ins or check marks on a printed form, in a letter, or by

• roscoe's candy shop •   890 Minert Road   San Leandro, CA 94577

December 26, 19--

Ms. Vicki Wu
Office Manager
Schroder Music Company
2027 Parker Street
Berkeley, CA 94704

Dear Ms. Wu:

The good news

The candy you requested is on its way and will arrive in time for your secretaries to enjoy it on New Year's Eve. All thirteen boxes have a decorative "Happy New Year" cover.

Explanation, sales promotion, goodwill

Because your satisfaction is of real concern to us, we have made arrangements today to have all the packing equipment thoroughly inspected. We want to know why the boxes you received were not filled with our luscious and delightful candy. If this equipment needs replacing, it will be done—long before you order candy next Christmas.

Roscoe's wraps and delivers candy for all occasions. (Have you thought of giving each employee a box of candy on his or her birthday?)

Happy Holidays!

Roscoe

Roscoe

FIGURE 8–6
Approved adjustment

telephone, the considerations already mentioned about applicants for employment apply to credit applicants. Be sure that all information is factual. Confine your remarks only to the requested information. State that your communication is to be considered confidential. Give only data that apply to your own organization; do not report on any investigations that you have made on the applicant. A person who is refused credit has a legal right to know why an application was denied; be prepared to substantiate any facts you report.

Be particularly careful about providing negative information. Determine the policy in your own company. Some organizations simply refuse to answer or ask the inquirer to consult a credit bureau.

A letter providing information about a credit applicant is shown in Figure 8–7.

Xerox Corporation
P.O. Box 1600
Stamford, Connecticut 06904
203 329-8700

July 15, 19--

Mrs. Nina Goldberg
Credit Manager
Orchard Equipment Company
1329 Lettie Hill Street
Pittsburgh, PA 15216

Dear Mrs. Goldberg:

Subject: Confidential Credit Information about

Quality Office Products, Philadelphia

Quality Office Products has had an active account with Xerox for the past five years. They currently have charges due within thirty days with no overdue balance.

The most important information

Their record of payment is excellent. Our terms are 2/10, net 30. Quality Office Products takes advantage of the discount on a regular basis.

Their credit limit of $20,000 has been sufficient for their needs. If their needs should increase, we would gladly increase their credit limit.

Further details

We regard Quality Office Products as a profitable account.

A conclusion

Sincerely,

Elmer Freyder

Elmer Freyder
Assistant Credit Manager

FIGURE 8–7
Letter providing credit information

Credit Approvals

Credit approvals, like other messages that convey positive information, ordinarily should open with the news that the credit relationship has been established. So that the debtor will be completely sure of the time when payments are due, how payments are to be made, and credit terms, you should include specific statements about these regulations in the credit approval letter. In addi-

August 13, 19--

Ms. Frances Zorsybski
ABC Sales and Service
420 Greenwood Avenue
Wyncote, PA 19095

Dear Ms. Zorsybski:

Approval {

Because of your excellent credit rating, we are happy to provide all your office supply needs on our regular credit terms.

Statement of terms {

The full account balance is due not later than thirty days from the date of your monthly statement. You will receive a 2 percent discount if the full amount is paid within ten days.

Other information {

Use your credit freely. Charge up to $700 a month. When you need to make larger purchases, telephone or come in and talk with me. Perhaps you will want to take advantage of our extended credit terms.

Sales promotion {

We look forward to a long pleasant business relationship. Mary Ann Flowers, our sales representative, will drop by within a few days and bring you a complete catalog of our office equipment and supplies.

Sincerely,

Margaret Rose

Margaret Rose
Credit Manager

ah

——— **Quality Office Products** ———

4646 Poplar Avenue   Philadelphia, PA 19043   215 243-5123

FIGURE 8–8
Credit approval letter

tion, the customer must be informed in writing, although not necessarily within the letter itself, of the annual interest rate.

In the credit approval letter to Mrs. Zorsybski (Figure 8–8) the *excellent credit rating* mentioned should be just that or the words should be omitted.

A credit approval letter is an appropriate message in which to use sales promotion sentences and paragraphs, as well as other goodwill-building passages.

Newburg Fabrics

DATE: January 5, 19--

TO: All Employees

FROM: Laura Maxwell, General Manager

SUBJECT: ADDITIONAL WEEK OF VACATION

All of you will receive an additional week of paid
vacation during the coming year.

You have earned this vacation time because of your
talent and hard work that made the past year our best
ever. This extra week is in addition to the cash bonus
you received at Christmas.

As for now, consider this additional week as the policy
for this year only. We don't yet know about future years,
but the outlook is favorable.

I know you will work to make the coming year as
successful as last year.

FIGURE 8–9
Good news memorandum

Other Messages Arranged in the Direct Order

The direct order is preferable for all letters and memorandums for which there is no evident reason for using the indirect or the persuasive arrangement. The direct order is more concise and it increases readability.

In letters and memorandums of all kinds and in many longer reports, you must consider the expected reaction of the reader. Arrange your message accordingly, as outlined in the first section of this chapter. The various types of letters, such as "acknowledgments" and "approved adjustments," are shown separately in this chapter to facilitate discussion and an orderly presentation. *Nevertheless, these letters should not be considered as types, with a special arrangement or formula for each.* All neutral or good-news messages of any kind, whether they are letters or memorandums, are basically the same as all other direct messages. Conversely, each letter or memorandum is different from all others, depending on circumstances, necessary information, and the relationship between the writer and reader. Each individual letter or memorandum that you write should be approached from the standpoint of your own judgment, not copied from an example in this book or any other.

A good-news memorandum is shown in Figure 8–9.

Summary

Favorable, routine, and neutral letters should ordinarily be arranged in the direct order, as should letters planned primarily to convey information. Because the first position in any communication is an emphatic one, it is the best place to tell the good news or to sum up the main idea.

A subject line is particularly useful and appropriate in letters arranged in the direct order. An action close should be used near the end of direct letters when an action of some kind is requested of the reader. Questions and terms of information within a letter should be arranged to aid immediate understanding.

Suggestions for direct-approach letters are these:

1. Use a positive, pleasant tone.
2. Avoid a slow opening, such as *We have received your letter*. Instead, immediately give the good news or state the request.
3. Avoid a dictatorial or demanding action close.
4. Avoid a doubtful, overly humble tone, as *We hope this meets your approval*.
5. Include complete information.
6. State the request or other opening sentence in simple, direct, and specific words.
7. Avoid trite phrasing, such as *please be advised*, *attached hereto*, and *enclosed please find*.
8. Consider the use of specifically worded subject lines.
9. Use a specifically stated action close. Ordinarily, give a date when action should be completed.
10. Use a goodwill close if no action is requested. This close may include resale or sales promotion.

Test Yourself: Chapter Review

1–3. Name three advantages of a subject line.

4–6. What is the three-step sequence recommended for good-news messages?

7–9. What is the three-step sequence recommended for neutral messages?

10–12. What is the three-step sequence recommended for a direct request or inquiry?

13–14. Give two examples of "slow" letter openings.

15–17. What are three characteristics of an action close?

Choose the correct phrase or sentence from each pair or group.

18. (From first paragraph of a good-news letter)
    a. You will receive a $750 bonus with your regular July check.
    b. We have received your letter asking about your bonus.

19. (Subject line for request for information about prospective employee)
    a. Request for Information
    b. Request for Information about Michael B. Scott

20. (Subject line of a letter supplying information about a prospective employee who is to be highly recommended)

   a. An Answer to Your Request

   b. Recommendation of Michael B. Scott

21. (Subject line of a letter that includes some unfavorable information about a prospective employee)

   a. Information about Michael B. Scott

   b. Unfavorable Information about Michael B. Scott

22. (First sentence, letter described in Question 20)

   a. The following information applies to Michael B. Scott.

   b. Michael B. Scott, in my opinion, is an excellent choice for your position as assistant credit manager.

23. (First sentence, letter described in Question 21)

   a. Michael B. Scott is probably not the best choice for your position as assistant credit manager.

   b. I am glad to supply the information you requested about Michael B. Scott.

24. (From a good-news letter)

   a. Enclosed please find the brochures you requested on October 9.

   b. Here are the brochures you requested on October 9.

   c. We have your letter of October 9 in which you request brochures.

25. (First sentence, request for return of questionnaire)

   a. As Chairman of the Department of Marketing, I am writing you in order to obtain certain information.

   b. Because you were a marketing major, your information and suggestions will be valuable to us as we plan changes in the marketing curriculum.

26. (First sentence)

   a. Referring to your letter of January 9, you will find enclosed a copy of my resume.

   b. The enclosed resume describes my qualifications for Plough's management training program.

27. (Ending, letter requesting information)

   a. Thank you for your time. Please return the questionnaire by January 20 in the enclosed stamped envelope.

   b. Will you please return the questionnaire by January 20, when we plan to tabulate the data. A stamped envelope is enclosed.

Test Yourself: Correct Usage

(Related to material in Chapter 8 and the principles of correct usage.) Insert needed punctuation and remove punctuation that has been inserted incorrectly. Choose correct word from listed pairs. Make any other necessary changes.

1. An action close should specify how when why and where the requested action is to occur.

2. The action close should be (definitely, definately) worded but it should not be dictatorial.

3. A well chosen subject line is useful in routine and favorable letters and other written messages.

4. Writing is the hardest way of earning a living. With the possible exception of wrestling alligators. [Olin Miller]

5. If people cannot write well they cannot think well, if they cannot think well others will do their thinking for them. [George Orwell]

6. Although the apostrophe has only three basic uses it is frequently omitted or used incorrectly.

7. Apostrophes are used to form possessives to form a few plurals and to indicate omissions.

8. A letter or memorandum in a direct arrangement (state, states) the most important news near the beginning usually in the first paragraph.

9. Short paragraphs especially first ones are desirable in letters and memorandums.

10. (Its, It's) true that a well written paragraph regardless of (its, it's) length is easier to read than an incoherent one.

Cases

Order Letters

1. You want to order six dozen shirts of a new style that you have seen in a direct mail advertisement sent to you by Campus Wear Company, 3140 Kellwood, La Puento, CA 86703. The shirts are offered in three sizes (small, medium, and large) and in two colors (yellow and blue). You need one dozen shirts of each size in each color. Order the shirts (Style No. 2293a) and charge them to your account. You work for Evans and Company, 201 West 7th Street, Norwood, NM 87421. The price of the shirts is $146.60 a dozen, and your firm normally buys on terms of 3/15, n/30.

2. Examine the classified advertising section of *USA Today, Sunset, Yankee, Southern Living,* or another general-interest periodical. Find an advertisement for something you wish to order. Write the order letter. You will send a check or charge to your credit card, with specific name and number of the card, plus the date it expires. Refer to the advertisement you are answering; give name of periodical, date, and page number. Attach a copy of the advertisement to your letter.

3. You are a fan of Emily Dickinson. From *Reader's Guide to Periodical Literature* you learn that *Yankee Magazine* published an article entitled "Is It Really You, Emily Dickinson?" in the November 1983 issue. Your library does not subscribe to *Yankee.* Write to the magazine (Dublin, NH 03444) and ask to buy the back issue of November 1983. Tell them that you will send a check if they will let you know the amount. If they have no back issues, ask for a photocopy of the article.

4. You have established a nursery, Gardens of Eden, in your home city specializing in rare plants that are not available elsewhere in local nurseries or stores. Gardeners who want such plants must order them from catalogs, provided they can find a source, or grow plants from seeds, often a disappointing task for home gardeners.

    You decide to order the seeds, grow the plants, and sell them at a profit, even though the seeds themselves are expensive.

    Order the following seeds from Park Seeds, Cokesbury Road, Greenwood, SC 29647-0001. They pay shipping.

    Gerbera Rainbow, 16 packages (two each of the eight colors listed) with 50 seeds in each package, $11.95 a package.

    Caltha, Marsh Marigold (wildflowers), 10 packages with 25 seeds in each package, $2.95 a package.

    Abelmoschus (oriental red), 20 packages, 25 seeds in each package, $1.75 a package.

    You wish to pay by MasterCard. Have the seeds sent to your home address.

Direct Inquiries

5. Write the manufacturer of some item in which you are interested, such as a camera or skin diving equipment. Think of all the qualities of the item that are important to you, of all the information you will need before you make this rather important decision. Request this information. Ask for the names of local dealers.

6. Write to a competitor of the manufacturer you addressed in Case 5. Ask for the same information.

7. You are an administrative assistant at Countrywide Life Insurance, 420 Madison Avenue, New York, NY 10577. You have interviewed Sally Ann Benson for a responsible secretarial position. She has recently graduated from Ingram Community College, Ingram, Texas, with a major in English and a minor in office administration. She gave as a reference one of her former teachers, Dr. Rosemary Randall, Associate Professor of Office Administration, Ingram Community College, Ingram, Texas 78025.

    You are especially interested in a secretary who can handle correspondence on her own without having each letter dictated to her, who is good with figures, and who is capable of supervising other office workers. You would like a person who is likely to remain with Countrywide for some time as it is expensive to find, hire, and train new people. You wonder whether Ms. Benson will remain in New York or perhaps became homesick and return to her home and family in Texas. You also want to know something of her scholarship ability and accomplishments. Write to Dr. Randall requesting the information you need.

Requests for Adjustments (Claims)

8. Are you now using a product that has been less than satisfactory? Do you feel that you are honestly entitled to a refund or an adjustment? If so, write the required letter to the retailer or manufacturer, as appropriate.

9. You have recently opened a new grocery store. You have chosen Sealfresh Foods to supply ice cream to your store. The chocolate-chip ice cream in your last delivery had no chocolate chips in it. Your customers

who bought this ice cream have complained and demanded their money back. Write to Sealfresh.

10. You receive the rare plant seeds ordered in Case 4. Because the seeds are so expensive, you count the seeds in each packet. One of the packages supposedly containing Caltha, Marsh Marigold is completely empty. Ask for a replacement package.

11. You received the replacement package of Caltha, Marsh Marigold. You plant all the seeds. The Marsh Marigolds develop into beautiful plants, which you sell for $4.98 each. A customer, Mrs. Harris, was delighted with the plants and bought twenty of them, which she planted by a small lake on her estate. The plants are an ideal choice for damp, shady spots.

In late autumn, however, Mrs. Harris telephoned you to say that the plants had not bloomed. You tell her that the blooms are small. She says she knows that, but she can tell whether or not they bloomed, and they didn't. You offer to refund her money, but she says that the plants themselves are attractive and that perhaps they will bloom the following summer.

The next autumn she comes by to tell you that again the plants did not bloom. You tell her that you will furnish replacement plants in the spring, free of charge. She says fine, that she will keep the others, even if they never bloom, and add the twenty others.

Now you are to write to Park Seeds. You ask them to reimburse you for the price of the plants (20 at $4.95 each).

Other Direct Requests

12. As chairperson of the committee to arrange a retirement dinner for Mrs. Margaret Lee, write a letter to all other employees of your organization. Tell them that Mrs. Lee is retiring on December 31, after thirty years of employment with your organization. Your committee has planned a dinner party to be held at the Knickerbocker Inn, 1917 East Hudson Road, at 7:30 P.M. on Saturday, December 11. (It is now November 17.) Cost for each person is $17.50, which includes the price of the dinner (menu is not yet chosen), wine, and a $2.50 contribution toward a gift for Mrs. Lee (also not yet chosen).

Mrs. Lee recently donated $5,000 to be applied to the cost of recreational facilities, including a jogging path, to be made available for use by all employees.

Employees are urged to bring their spouses or friends as guests. The cost for each additional person is $15. Reservations, with checks, must be received by November 27. Tell your readers where and how to make their reservations.

13. It is now December 10. Your city is covered with eighteen inches of snow. Write to employees who have made reservations (Case 12). Tell them that because of the snow you will cancel plans for the banquet. You ask their permission to hold their checks and reservations for a dinner to be scheduled later. (You could not buy a gift because of the snowstorm.) (Employees have fax machines or home computers to receive electronic mail.)

Favorable or Routine Replies or Announcements

14. Write a letter to the people who made reservations for the retirement dinner for Mrs. Lee (Cases 12 and 13). Tell them that the dinner has been rescheduled for Tuesday, December 22, at the Knickerbocker Inn at 7:00 P.M. (It is now December 15.)

15. You have been asked to serve on the Traffic Appeals Committee of your college or university. Write Mr. Kim Lee, Assistant Dean of Students, accepting the appointment.

16. Assume that you are employed by the Chargecard Company. Write a letter enclosing an application blank for a Chargecard. This card has been requested by telephone by Mr. Samuel Fenner, 211 Blackstone Avenue, Nevada, IA 50201. (This is not a credit approval; credit will be investigated after he fills in and returns the application blank.)

17. You are now Dr. Rosemary Randall (Case 7). Write to the administrative assistant of Countrywide Life Insurance. You know Sally Ann well. She has a grade-point average of 3.78 based on a 4-point scale. As could be expected with this scholastic record, she is good with both words and figures. She also seems to get along well with other people. During her last two years on campus, she was an officer of the Student Government Association.

You are not sure that she will remain with the insurance company, but you do believe that she will stay in New York. She really wants to work for a publishing company and edit and write. You believe, though, that the insurance company will get more than its money's worth from her, no matter how short her stay, because of her exceptional mind and her excellent secretarial skills. Should you mention her editorial and writing ambitions? You want to be fair to both Sally Ann and the insurance company.

18. You work in a personnel department. Write one letter to *all* employees in your company based on the information listed below. Make any reasonable assumptions.

   a. All employees are to receive a Christmas bonus, although this does not apply to those who have worked for less than six months.

b. The amount of the bonus is two weeks' base pay. The company does not allow overtime, commissions, or any kind of extra pay to be counted when figuring the amount of the Christmas bonus.

c. The bonus will be added to the check of December 11.

d. Some employees have been working extra hard because of the end-of-year rush.

e. All employees will receive a food basket containing a turkey or ham, fruitcake, and other food and gift items.

This letter is to be prepared on word processing equipment, with individual names and addresses added.

For the purpose of this assignment, show the inside address and the employee's name in the usual way. (Letters prepared by this method cannot be distinguished from individually typewritten letters.) Use this inside address:

Mr. James T. Holloway
1967 Luzon Cove
Oklahoma City, OK 73077

19. You are the director of public relations. Write a letter to Professor Chin Chu, Marketing Department, California State University, School of Business, Fresno, CA 93740. He has requested the tape of one of your commercials, "It's a Sin to Tell a Lie," which deals with advertising methods and, naturally, emphasizes that your organization always tells the truth about their advertised products.

You are happy to furnish the tape, but it must not be shown on commercial television stations because of the legal considerations discussed in Case 9, Chapter 6. Be pleasant and positive but emphatic. Should you use an enclosure of some kind?

20. You are an executive assistant in the president's office of your college. Write a memorandum or letter to all permanent, full-time employees. Those employees under thirty-five are eligible for a company-paid physical examination every two years. Those age thirty-five and over are eligible for a physical examination every year. These examinations are recommended but not compulsory

Examinations will be done by the college physician (Dr. Greer) or by a physician approved in advance by Dr. Greer. One doctor that Dr. Greer has approved (because of the great number of physical examinations to be performed) is Dr. Elaine V. Dowling, 20 South Dudly Street, your city, state, and zip code.

This examination is an important fringe benefit to employees.

Personnel are considered permanent if they have been employed continuously for one year. They are eligible for the examination on the anniversary date of their employment but may take it within two months thereafter. For example, employees whose anniversary date is July 1 may take the examination any time during July or August. Tell employees to make appointments with the examining physician early.

21. You are a division manager and have been given the responsibility of overseeing the building of your new plant, which will open this coming Friday, November 23, at 10:00 A.M. Your main office, as well as the new building, is located in a medium-sized town in a farming area. This expansion will be a big boost for the city and should create about 280 new jobs. Besides being very functional, the plant itself will be extremely modern and beautiful.

The president of the company has suggested you write a letter to the local newspaper to request additional publicity. Even though your company is in good standing with the community, you will want to stress the natural beauty of the building in its wooded surroundings. Write a letter to one of the newspapers inviting reporters to come and help celebrate the grand opening. (Assume a name and address for the newspaper.)

The address of your new plant is 1000 Hilton Drive. Refreshments will be served, and you plan on having as many people as possible there to show community support.

22. You are in charge of mail orders at Benson's Groves, Inc., an Orlando, Florida, company that ships tree-ripened fruit throughout the world. On May 5 you received an order for a bushel of oranges to be sent to Raleigh, North Carolina. The customer sent a check with the order and asked you to enclose a card saying, "Happy Mother's Day, Love, Sue."

The customer apparently relied on an old price list, as the cost of the fruit ordered is now $2.50 more than the customer's remittance. If the fruit is shipped on May 6, it will arrive in time for Mother's Day. If you wait for the customer to send the balance due, the order will be delayed at least a week. Write a letter to the customer to handle this situation. Her name and address are Susan F. Allison, 420 Bay Tree, Farmington, MA 02213.

23. You are the manager of a beautiful historic inn, Woodfield Inn, in Flat Rock, North Carolina. You receive a note from Ruth Ryder, 312 East Liberty, Rapid City, SD 57701. She and her husband, John Ryder, were recent guests. She is enthusiastic in her praise for the inn—"its spacious rooms, its lovely view, the long upstairs porch, the flowers, the food, everything." She states, however, that she must have left her white cotton jacket that goes with a sundress. She asks you to find and mail the jacket. Write a letter

saying that you have found the jacket. It is being mailed separately.

24. Because of wise management and a great deal of luck, the organization you founded the year you graduated from college is now a successful multinational corporation. You wish to make major contributions to charitable or public service organizations in your hometown. Choose such an organization in your community. Write a letter to the director, informing the director of your first annual contribution of $10,000. The check will be presented to the organization sometime during the coming Christmas season, at a time and place of the director's choice.

25. You are the manager of a newly opened resort hotel, the Jamaican Happy Inn, part of an international chain. You are proud of the inn and want to continue the long tradition of friendly, courteous, and honest service established by the founder of the first Happy Inn.

Jamaica's climate is ideal for winter vacationers. Your air-conditioned hotel, located on the beach, provides comfortable surroundings all year round, but many U.S. visitors prefer to come in winter to escape the cold weather of their home states.

The rates of your inn are higher in winter months than in the summer, spring, and fall. You have one set of rates for November, December, January, February, and March; another for April, May, and October; and still another for June, July, August, and September.

It is now April 15. A retired couple from New Jersey spent seven nights at Happy Inn, from April 2 through April 9. A recently employed cashier charged them the March rate, although they were eligible for the lower April rate. The couple paid their bill without protest; you do not know whether they knew they were paying the higher winter rate.

Refund the overpayment of $350. (For some reason the cashier charged the correct amount of tax.)

In your letter, do not place the blame on the cashier. You want your customers to believe in all Happy Inns. You know that mistakes will happen occasionally, even at a Happy Inn.

The cashier, along with all other employees, is now enrolled in a daily two-hour class, which they take on company time.

Address the letter to Mr. and Mrs. Herbert Moses, 362 Dodd Lane, Princeton, NJ 08540.

Approved Adjustments

26. You are customer service director of Park Seeds. Write a letter to the owner of Gardens of Eden approving the adjustment requested in Case 11.

27. You own a townhouse complex. By mistake you refunded a security deposit of $150 to a tenant who had made a deposit of $200. (You raised the deposit recently but thought that tenant had moved in when the lower deposit was in effect.) The tenant left the townhouse in perfect condition. Write a letter, enclosing a check for $50, to Ms. Annabella McVey, 1299 Diana Street, your city and zip code.

Credit Inquiries

28. You are office manager of a government agency. One of your most capable secretaries has been denied credit at a retail store in a national chain. The secretary is young, single, and rather nonassertive. She has performed outstanding work during her three years of employment under your supervision. As a close friend of her family, you are sure that she has had no credit difficulties of any kind. She has successfully paid out two loans, one for an automobile and one for cash from the Federal Credit Union of your city. Federal law prohibits discrimination in the extension of credit for reasons of sex and/or marital status.

You decide to write to the credit manager of the local store where her credit was denied. If necessary, you will write later to the national headquarters of the company. (Should you mention this fact?) Her name is Miss Maxine Peterson, 612 West Florida Avenue, your city and zip code. (Maxine uses the title *Miss*, not *Ms.*, in the signature block of her own letters. You refer to her in the same way.) The credit manager of the local store is Virginia Harper, Hensen's Department Store, 911 Murray Canyon Drive, your city and zip code.

29. You are Irene Abel, D.D.S. A patient has applied for a six-month payment plan for extensive dental work that you have not yet begun. Although you ordinarily ask patients to finance such work through their banks, this patient, John Charlton, does not wish to do so, saying that he refuses to pay their outrageous interest rate.

If you were firmly established in your practice, you would tell him to go through the bank or to find some other dentist. You would like to do his work, which you have estimated to cost $4,500. He has agreed to this price and, in addition, to a 6 percent interest rate. Because the loan on your new equipment is not yet paid, you need the case.

As references, he lists the local Teachers Credit Union, located at 1326 Luther Lane, St. Louis, MO 63122, and First National Bank, Southeast Branch, 117 East Bodley, St. Louis, MO 63111. He is a professor at George Washington University. Write to one or both of the listed references. (Do you think that you should confirm his employment?)

Credit Approvals

30. As Irene Abel, D.D.S. (Case 29), write to Professor Charlton (13447 Waterford, Florissant, MO 63033) to tell him that you can begin his dental work immediately. Payments are to be made at the beginning of each month. Each payment is to be one-sixth of the total amount (state the exact amount), plus interest of one-half of 1 percent on the unpaid balance.

31. You are J. A. Harris, branch manager of First Missouri Bank. Robert Anderson, owner of Computer World of St. Louis, has applied for a $5,000.00 unsecured line of credit for his business. The company as well as the owner have no previous credit experience with your bank.

    Computer World of St. Louis has been in business for 16 years and has an excellent reputation in the community. The credit bureau report on the owner, the Better Business Bureau report on the company, and two of the three suppliers contacted checked out very favorably. One of the suppliers showed the company was 30 days past due twice during four years of credit experience. This supplier indicated that Computer World of St. Louis was currently up to date on their account.

    Write a credit approval letter to the owner of Computer World of St. Louis approving the $5,000.00 line of credit. The terms are at an interest rate of prime plus 2 percent with a payment of $150.00 due the first of each month. When the balance is under $150.00 the monthly payment will be the same as the balance. There is no initial fee charge to open this account. Should you make any mention of the one supplier's rating? Should you offer your bank's other services?

The address of Computer World of St. Louis is 2230 Lindbergh Avenue, St. Louis, MO 63042.

Write Your Own Assignments and Solutions

32. Write your OWN assignments, with solutions, for one or more of the kinds of letters (or memorandums, if appropriate) described in this chapter.

    order letters

    direct inquiries

    requests for adjustments or refunds

    other direct requests

    acknowledgments

    favorable or routine replies and announcements

    approved adjustments

    OR

    other letters or memorandums to be arranged in the direct order

    This assignment provides practice in describing a situation and giving instructions as well as in writing letters and memorandums. Your problem assignments may be on any subject, preferably about situations likely to occur in a business office. Give all the information another student would need to write a communication as a solution to your problem, including names and addresses and enough details to enable the writer to make appropriate decisions. (By using this assignment, you can write messages useful in your own organization, perhaps actual ones.)

    A similar assignment is given at the end of Chapters 6, 9, and 10.

	Yes	No	Not Sure
1. Is the request specifically stated in the first paragraph or in the subject line?	⎯⎯	⎯⎯	⎯⎯
2. Does the request *OMIT* slow openings?	⎯⎯	⎯⎯	⎯⎯
3. Does the request *OMIT* trite business jargon?	⎯⎯	⎯⎯	⎯⎯
4. Is the request courteous?	⎯⎯	⎯⎯	⎯⎯
5. Does the request exemplify the you-approach, not the I-approach?	⎯⎯	⎯⎯	⎯⎯
6. Is gratitude expressed without using such phrases as "Thank you in advance"?	⎯⎯	⎯⎯	⎯⎯
7. Does the request exemplify the positive, not the negative, approach?	⎯⎯	⎯⎯	⎯⎯
8. Does the request provide all necessary information?	⎯⎯	⎯⎯	⎯⎯
9. Are all paragraphs relatively short?	⎯⎯	⎯⎯	⎯⎯
10. Does the request end with an appropriate action close?	⎯⎯	⎯⎯	⎯⎯
11. Does the request *OMIT* all doubtful phrases?	⎯⎯	⎯⎯	⎯⎯
12. Overall, is the message easy to read?	⎯⎯	⎯⎯	⎯⎯
13. Is the message sincere?	⎯⎯	⎯⎯	⎯⎯
14. Is the letter or memorandum absolutely correct in format, grammar, spelling, and sentence structure?	⎯⎯	⎯⎯	⎯⎯

Evaluation
Sheet:
Direct Requests
(Letters or
Memorandums)

Evaluation Sheet: Good-News and Routine Letters and Memorandums

	Yes	No	Not Sure
1. Is the good news or the gist of the message given in the first paragraph or very near the beginning of the letter?	___	___	___
2. Does the message *OMIT* slow openings such as "We have received your letter" and "This letter is in reply to your request"?	___	___	___
3. Does the message *OMIT* trite business jargon such as "Please find enclosed" and "As per your request"?	___	___	___
4. Have you used a subject line? (Although a subject line is not required, it is especially appropriate for good-news and routine letters.)	___	___	___
5. Is the message courteous?	___	___	___
6. Does the letter exemplify the you-approach, not the I-approach?	___	___	___
7. Does the message exemplify the positive, not the negative, approach?	___	___	___
8. Does the message provide all necessary information?	___	___	___
9. Are all paragraphs relatively short?	___	___	___
10. Does the message end appropriately, either with a diplomatic action close or a goodwill statement?	___	___	___
11. Does the message *OMIT* all doubtful phrases, such as "If this is not what you expected" or similar ones?	___	___	___
12. Overall, is the message easy to read?	___	___	___
13. Is the message sincere?	___	___	___
14. Is the letter or memorandum absolutely correct in format, grammar, spelling, and sentence structure?	___	___	___

CHAPTER 9

Writing about the Unpleasant and the Uncertain

The kinds of letters and memorandums discussed in this chapter should ordinarily be arranged in the indirect order, mentioned in Chapter 5. Communications that convey unpleasant or uncertain news fall into two categories, defined by expected reader reaction:

- *Messages with which the reader will be displeased or will have little initial interest.*
- *Messages for which reader reaction cannot be predicted.*

The indirect order alone does not guarantee a pleasant, diplomatic, and convincing tone. It does not ensure, by any means, that your ideas and suggestions will be accepted. In addition, good writers can arrange bad-news messages in the direct order and, because of word choice and other factors, compose pleasant and convincing messages. Even these skillful writers, however, could often improve their work by using the recommended indirect order of arrangement for the kinds of communications discussed here.

The better choice for disappointing messages is usually the indirect order. *Such messages should be wisely planned and skillfully worded.*

Planning Disappointing or Unfavorable Messages

A sincere you-attitude, desirable in all communication, is even more essential for diplomatic bad-news messages. Even when the request must be refused, you can apply the you-attitude by looking at the situation from the other person's point of view and by presenting your message from that standpoint.

Open with some pleasant part of the situation if you can find one. If not, open with a neutral statement or agree with the reader about something.

A suggested outline for unpleasant messages is shown below:

1. *Buffer.* Usually one paragraph but can be two. Tells what the letter is about but does not state the obvious. Says neither yes nor no. Pleasant and relevant. Leads naturally to the following paragraphs.

2. *Explanation and analysis of situation.* Reasons for refusal or other decision. May be one or several paragraphs.

3. *Decision, stated diplomatically or (preferably) clearly implied.* If indicated, an alternative or counterproposal. Decision presented, if possible, in terms of reader benefit. Do not repeat decision.

4. *A friendly, positive close: a related idea that takes the emphasis away from the refusal or bad news.* If appropriate, low-pressure sales promotion, resale, or action close based on the counterproposal.

The Buffer

The buffer paragraph is planned to get in step with the reader. Dangers to avoid are implying that the answer will be *yes,* stating or implying that the answer is to be *no,* beginning too far away from the subject, and seeming to be evasive.

Ordinarily, do not apologize, either in the buffer section or elsewhere, for refusing a request; to do so weakens your explanation of why the request cannot be granted. *Although at all times we should apologize when an apology is due,* a refusal letter usually requires not an apology but courtesy and, for the sake of goodwill, justification.

Consider these ideas for openings for a disappointing communication:

1. Some pleasant aspect of the situation.

2. Agreement or understanding. If you agree with some point of the reader's letter to you, say so. Show an understanding of the reader's needs or problems.

3. Appreciation. Say *thank you* for information, a check, application, or whatever applies, but make sure that the expression of appreciation makes sense and is sincere. Do not use such phrases as *we were happy to receive your request* if the request is to be denied. (Why are you happy—because you have an opportunity to refuse?)

4. Assurance. Show that careful consideration and investigation occurred before the decision was made.

5. Cooperation. Show a sincere desire to be as reasonable and helpful as possible.

6. Sympathy. Express sympathy in serious situations and in all other instances if the expression is sincere.

Communication Brief

Note: The following portion of an actual letter was composed in 1987 by a writer in Tokyo, Japan, to an acquisitions librarian in the United States. The names of the writer and the receiver have been omitted. As discussed in Chapter 18, Japanese writers traditionally open letters with a reference to the season, whether the message is "good news" or "bad news."

It is getting more like spring here. I hope you are doing well. In what season are you now? The spring in Japan is known for cherry blossoms. But nowadays cherry blossoms in Washington, D.C. are rather known. Are you getting along well?

In this time, thank you very much the order "The Divine Renewal of ISE SHRINE, the 60th Shikinen Sengu." I am sorry from the heart that the "VIDEOCASSETTE" has to be late.

7. Resale. Use only if appropriate, and use this approach subtly and wisely to avoid an I-attitude.

8. Sales promotion. Use only if appropriate and, as with resale, with discretion. (As explained earlier, *resale* techniques reemphasize the value of goods or services already purchased. *Sales promotion* refers to encouraging future purchases or to building goodwill for a sales organization.)

Although openings of bad-news letters and memorandums are less direct than openings of good-news or routine messages, they should not consist of slow, unnecessary wordings such as *we have received your letter, this letter is in reply to your request, we have your request,* or *we are writing this letter in response to your request.*

A thank-you opening (Number 3 in the preceding list) can be used as a buffer if there is any reason for appreciating the letter. If so, *thank you for your letter* is better than the slow openings mentioned in the preceding paragraph. Remember, though, that *thank you for your letter* is so widely used that it has become rather stale, although sincere appreciation will never become trite.

Although an expression of regret can easily violate the principle of the positive approach, it can at times be used appropriately. Suppose that a man has written to you asking that you repair without charge his eleven-year-old heating system, although your guarantee expired eight years ago. You should *not* open the letter by saying that you are sorry that you cannot repair the equipment without charge, for you would be stating the refusal too early in the letter. In addition, a statement like this one implies that you feel you really should comply with his wishes, but you are not going to do so. You can, however, empathize with the customer to the extent that you can say sincerely, *I'm sorry that your heating system is not working properly.*

Let's look at some opening paragraphs that would be definitely worse:

```
We will not repair your heating system without charge because your
guarantee expired eight years ago.
```

This opening gives the answer too soon and is also tactless.

```
We are sorry that we cannot repair your heating system.
```

Although this is more diplomatic than *we will not*, it is still undesirable, as discussed above.

> We will be happy to repair your heating system.

Although you don't say so, the reader will think that the services will be free. A misleading statement is worse than a blunt refusal.

> Thank you for your letter . . .

What do you have to thank him for? Nothing, except for the knowledge that your heating systems can break down after eleven years, as you might have guessed. Or you could thank him for the possibility of the amount to be collected for repair, a favor he hasn't meant to grant.

A more satisfactory opening is:

> We will be glad to send a service representative to help you determine the cause of your heating problems.

Another refusal letter could open in this way:

> Your suggestions for the improvement of our product are greatly appreciated.

A request for photographs used in advertisements could be answered in this way, provided that the request is to be refused:

> Thank you for your compliments on our advertising.

or

> We are glad you like our advertising program.

The following paragraphs can be devoted to reasons why the photographs cannot be released, plus a goodwill closing paragraph.

Details and Reasons for the Unfavorable Decision

In correspondence about difficult situations, use a positive, helpful approach and give convincing reasons. In some instances you will be unable or unwise to give exact, specific reasons because of the need for confidentiality or because the explanation would be long and involved. Do not appear evasive, but emphasize that the request has been carefully and sincerely considered.

Do not use such phrases as:

1. *It's against company policy.* This is a blanket excuse that is usually meaningless to the reader, as well as somewhat insulting and arbitrary. (The reader may think, "Well, why don't they change the policy?") To the reader, you *are* the company, or at least you express the procedures and the outlook of the company.

In addition, do not blame someone else in your company, or do not imply that you would comply except for "company policy." If you think that company policies should be changed, suggest these changes after you have been employed long enough to understand the procedures and to make sure that you are right. But until they are changed, follow them without criticism. To do otherwise is disloyal.

2. *We cannot afford to.* A statement like this reflects the I-attitude, not the you-attitude.

3. *We must reject* (or *turn down, refuse, disappoint you,* or other negative terms). Also avoid, as much as possible, the use of grammatical negatives, such as *no* and *cannot.* In addition, avoid negative words to refer to the problem, such as *failure, defective, inferior,* and *trouble.*

4. *You surely understand, please understand,* or other dictatorial or condescending terms.

5. *We were surprised at your request.* This suggests that the customer is unreasonable. So is the implication that because all other customers are satisfied with the product he or she must just be a complainer.

6. *You claim, you state,* or other phrases suggesting disbelief.

7. *This is the best we can do.* This phrasing implies that what you are doing is very little indeed.

Perhaps you feel that all the *don'ts* given above leave little for you to include in details and reasons. As in all communication situations, however, your sincere and accurate reasoning, stated diplomatically and in terms of the reader's interest, is your best guide to an acceptable psychological approach.

The Decision

The reader must understand your decision. This is of first importance. An implied decision, however, can be completely clear, as you will notice in some of the following examples.

If the decision can be clearly implied, do not use an *I cannot* expression. For example, if you say *we sell only to retailers,* you do *not* need to add the statement, *therefore, we cannot sell to you, an individual consumer.*

If there is a possibility that the decision will be misunderstood, state it plainly and clearly, even if you must use a *cannot* or similar expression. But state the decision after most of the explanatory material has been given. Although we wish to subordinate the unpleasant, it is more important that the reader understands what we are saying.

Remembering the principles of emphasis, use the reverse procedures to subordinate the refusal or the other unpleasant news. You make use of a principle of subordination when you move the statement or implication of the decision away from the opening section of the letter, as well as when you refrain from mentioning the unpleasant news in the emphatic position of the last paragraph. Also remember that exact, vivid, and specific words emphasize, while more general words are softer in expressing unwelcome news.

Because a one-sentence paragraph is emphatic, do not express the bad news in a short sentence standing alone.

If you cannot include with the expression of the unfavorable news some positive aspect of the situation, *offer a counterproposal.* For instance, if you cannot grant credit, offer a special discount for cash or suggest a layaway plan. *A counterproposal can do much to soften a refusal.*

Resale techniques can be used, when appropriate, in the decision section and the remaining sections of the letter to reemphasize the value of a previous purchase or decision. Use resale with care and discretion, however, because such an approach may be interpreted as sarcasm or as a greedy push for sales or the acceptance of the writer's ideas.

A Courteous, Positive Ending

Do not refer to the unfavorable news in the closing paragraph, one of the most emphatic positions in a message.

You may need an action close. Perhaps you have suggested an alternative and have asked the reader to make some kind of decision. Such an action will be similar to those used in other kinds of messages, including sales letters. As in all communication, avoid a demanding or "hard-sell" tone. Do not use an action close unnecessarily. In some situations, you do not want to correspond any further. You hope that the reader will drop the whole matter, but you must still be concerned with maintaining goodwill.

Resale or sales promotion material can be effectively used in the closing section of a disappointing message, but make sure that such material is appropriate and diplomatic for the particular situation.

Don't close with a suggestion of further trouble, as in

    If you have any more trouble, . . .

Also, don't express doubt that the decision will be accepted, as in

    We hope this meets your approval . . . or We hope you will not be
    disappointed . . . or We hope you will not be angry.

Even worse, don't imply that you fear you will lose a customer or friend, as in

    We hope you will keep on doing business with us . . . or We hope we
    will remain on good terms.

Do not offer future help if it will give an appearance of insincerity. For example, if you have been able to do absolutely nothing for the reader, don't end with

    If we can help further . . . or Call on us again if . . .

The closing paragraph, like the opening one, is particularly emphatic. Use this paragraph to advantage or at the very least as a pleasant close to a disappointing message. Avoid ending all messages too abruptly, and particularly avoid abrupt endings in disappointing messages.

Refusing Requests

Requests are made for many purposes. Some seem completely unwarranted, presumptuous, and absolutely ridiculous to the person receiving the request. In most instances, though, the request seems valid and reasonable to the person making it.

You should assume that people who make requests are sincere and plan the reply from this standpoint. Even if they have in mind "getting something for nothing," a courteous reply will perhaps make them sorry that they tried to hoodwink such a helpful, cooperative organization that had the good sense to refuse their outrageous requests.

The example in Figure 9–1 is a refusal to serve as a sponsor. Nowhere in the letter is there a direct refusal such as *I cannot* or *I must refuse.* (Don't ever use the word *refuse,* even when that's what you are doing.) The writer for L. L. Bean has taken time to explain, diplomatically, why the company "does not utilize endorsements." The writer of the letter shown in Figure 9–2 also refuses by implication and offers a counterproposal, the offer to speak at another time.

Figure 9–3 is a bad-news memorandum. Memorandums, as much as letters, must be diplomatic and build goodwill.

A letter to an applicant who was not chosen for employment is shown in Figure 9–4. Such letters are often written because applicants so greatly outnumber openings in most organizations. Although even the best qualified applicants have received or will receive notification that they were not chosen, each refusal is a disappointment. Even though they know that they cannot be the absolutely best choice for all positions, each occurrence is a blow to the ego, often lessening self-confidence, at least temporarily.

When it is your turn to write such letters, remember how you felt when you received similar ones—as you are likely to do if you have not already done so.

Writing Unfavorable Messages about a Product or Service

An organization is not always able to provide the merchandise or service that a customer requests. A product may be discontinued, temporarily out of stock, in short supply and reserved for regular customers, or sold to retailers only and not to individuals. Or perhaps the merchandise cannot be shipped because the prospective buyer sent incomplete information. Replies in these situations must be planned with special consideration in order to avoid an implication or accusation.

Whatever the reason for a refused or delayed shipment, the letter of explanation is basically a bad-news message and should be arranged in the sequence of ideas used for other refusals. Avoid such expressions as *you did not state the color* or, even worse, *you failed to state the color.*

Refusing Claims and Adjustments

According to the outlook of most business establishments, some requests for adjustments must be refused or some compromise must be made.

L.L.Bean
FREEPORT, MAINE 04033
Outdoor Sporting Specialties
TEL. (207) 865-4761

August 14, 19--

Ms. Joan Doe
1435 Eleonore Street
Somewhere, WV 70115

Dear Ms. Doe:

Buffer

Thank you for supplying such a clear view of your objectives and your plans. Because of our performance and dependability, we are frequently asked to support trips, expeditions, and competitors.

Explanation, leading to implied decision

We appreciate your offer to advertise our equipment, but "L. L." long ago learned the value of word-of-mouth advertising. He believed that by doing the job right, customers spread the good word more effectively than any other medium. Experience bears out his contention.

Explanation and convincing resale

In addition, we believe in rigorous product testing. Our product managers, our executives, our employees, and many outdoor professionals are involved in testing products before they are offered for sale. We listen to our customers and we monitor returned merchandise. On top of all that we have a well-staffed quality assurance department with a testing lab.

Goodwill and implied decision

So you see we take all our customers very seriously. We do not single out one or several for special treatment through sponsorships.

We wish you the very best on your Appalachian Trail Hike.

Sincerely,

D. Kilton Andrew, Jr.
Representative for Public Affairs

DKA:ma

FIGURE 9–1
Example of a refusal letter (Courtesy of L. L. Bean, Inc.)

1172 Broad Avenue   Apt. 713
Springfield, MO 65808
April 1, 19--

Miss Ellen Glass
233 Missouri Street
Thayer, MO 64111

Dear Ellen:

    Thank you for asking me to speak to the senior class about a career in television. I am honored that you asked.   *Buffer that expresses appreciation*

    As you probably know, I am a college student in addition to being a newscaster on KWTO-TV. The week of final semester examinations is the same week that you suggested I speak. In addition to the time spent in the examinations themselves, I will need many hours for study.   *Explanation and decision*

    Can another date be arranged, either earlier or later? Any time during the morning would be convenient for me, as I am now assigned to the six o'clock news. I sincerely want to come.   *Counterproposal*

    Please telephone me at 000-000-0000 after ten at night.   *Action close*

Sincerely,

Ashley Scott

Ashley Scott

FIGURE 9–2
Refused request, with counterproposal

As a refusal or compromise is explained, the writer must be concerned with maintaining goodwill, as in all communications. Outstanding letters of adjustment can do more to keep customers and build sales—at least concerning the particular customers receiving the letters—than expensive advertising campaigns and extensive sales promotion procedures.

Some companies seem to take the position that the customer is always right, regardless of the particular occurrence. Although some large organizations that follow this policy seem to prosper (no doubt the absolute and unconditional guarantee of satisfaction builds public confidence), to accede to all requests for refunds or adjustments, regardless of merit, forces customers who do not make unreasonable demands to subsidize those who do.

In your writing or oral communication about adjustments, you will of necessity follow the set and expected procedures of the organization. If the choice is yours, fairness to all customers seems to indicate that you should determine each adjustment situation on its individual merit.

In adjustment letters, whether they are granted or refused, you should

CENTRAL COLLEGE

TO: Ronnie Caruthers, Registration Coordinator

FROM: Harold Evans, Administrative Vice President

SUBJECT: Seminar, Association of American Colleges and
Universities

DATE: September 12, 19--

Buffer

Ronnie, seminars like the one you requested have
been extremely beneficial to Central College in terms
of new and innovative means of improving
organization, planning, and job performance. We have
been happy to recommend seminars of the type you
requested.

The decision

Recent controls on spending and budget cuts have
made it necessary for me to review carefully your
request to attend the seminar on registration and
planning, to be held in Boston in April. In order to
meet the revised budget guidelines for our department,
such trips must be deferred until next year at the
earliest.

Because of the benefits you would gain from this
seminar and in turn pass on to Central College, I
regret the necessity of having to make this decision.

A forward look

Please keep me informed about seminars, workshops,
and conferences scheduled for the next fiscal year,
which begins July 1. As soon as budget restraints are
eased, consideration will be given to continuing our
participation.

FIGURE 9–3
**Bad-news memo-
randum**

subordinate references to the weaknesses of the product or service. Remember
to use specific words to emphasize, general ones to subordinate.

For example, you are being too specific in this sentence: *You say that your
washing machine runs over every time you use it and floods your kitchen floor.* This
sentence is bad from at least three standpoints. First, the *you say* indicates
disbelief. Second, you are wasting both reader and writer time by repeating
what the writer told you. Third, you are recalling much too vividly the cause
of customer dissatisfaction.

October 16, 19--

Mr. Jay Richard Palmer
1129 Piping Rock Drive
Fort Lauderdale, FL 33316

Dear Mr. Palmer:

Thank you for the time you spent with us during your recent interviews. I hope that you enjoyed your few days in Philadelphia.

Goodwill buffer

We have carefully considered your application for the position of advertising director. As you know, this is a new position that is crucial to our success in a highly competitive market. You are extremely well qualified, as were a number of other finalists. Our extensive interviews indicated that you have very high potential indeed.

Explanation

Your resume is being filed with the hope that we will soon have another position that will more nearly fit your particular background and abilities. Another candidate, the one chosen, has extensive experience in another company similar to Quality Office Products.

Implied decision

Best wishes for your continued success.

Goodwill

Sincerely,

David Rose

David Rose
Sales Manager

es

—— **Quality Office Products** ——

4646 Poplar Avenue   Philadelphia, PA 19043   215 243-5123

FIGURE 9–4
Bad-news letter to employment applicant

This situation is not one that lends itself to a positive description, regardless of the skill of the writer. (Have you ever mopped a flooded kitchen floor?) Here, though, the words *problem* or *trouble,* although negative in themselves in most instances, are preferable to these exact, descriptive words. An even better approach is to make your answer clear without using negative words of any kind.

Use resale, when appropriate, to reemphasize the value of goods or ser-

TRANSCONTINENTAL MOVING COMPANY
P. O. Box 10000
Coral Gables, FL 33134

January 29, 19--

Ms. Roberta Koleas
% Excel Company
314 West 17th Street
Costa Mesa, CA 92627

Dear Ms. Koleas:

We are sorry that your many plants were damaged in your move to your new home in California. Nothing adds life and vitality to a home quite as much as green plants.

The most sturdy plants, however, are not able to stand a cross-country move in a closed van. Even if our drivers had the knowledge and time to water and tend them daily, the plants would suffer from either heat or cold.

Because your plants must have even more care than your finest furniture, we have always asked owners to move their plants in their automobiles—or to pass them on to friends they leave behind. When people move to California, as you did, they must leave their plants behind because state laws prohibit bringing uninspected plants into California. We would never knowingly break this law.

Your plants are not shown on the contents list; in addition, the contract specifically excludes plants, animals, and other property. Any agreement between you and the driver must not be in violation of the written contract.

The enclosed $60 check is a reimbursement for your broken flowerpots, which are covered by our insurance. We feel sure you will soon have California plants that you prize just as much as you did your previous ones.

The enclosed booklet contains tips on traveling with plants. If you should move again to a state that admits plants, perhaps these suggestions will be helpful. So will Transcontinental.

Sincerely,

W. B. Canestrari

W. B. Canestrari
Customer Service Representative

Enclosure

FIGURE 9–5
Refused request for reimbursement

Question: I am never sure where within a sentence to place words like *only*. Which of the following sentences is correct?

Improve Your Writing

> I only saw him two weeks ago.
> OR:
> I saw him only two weeks ago.

Answer: The second example is the better choice. *Only* is an adverb that modifies *two weeks*.

Only and similar words are often used inexactly, especially in conversation. Usually the intended meaning is clear, but not always.

For example, if you state that they only graduated a month ago, you are literally saying that graduation is of little importance or that graduation was their only activity a month ago. Instead, say that they graduated only a month ago.

"He is only doing his job" does not mean the same as "He is doing only his job" (no one else's job) or "Only he is doing his job" (no one else is working).

Other words that are often misplaced are *merely, scarcely, nearly,* and *almost.* Entire phrases and clauses can also be misplaced. Ordinarily, modifiers should be placed adjacent to or very near the word or words they modify.

---

vice, but use discretion. Telling the customer that it is a fine washing machine when the customer is mopping the floor is not exactly convincing. Neither is the fact that the machine was bought at a reduced price.

The letter shown in Figure 9–5 is in reply to a customer's claim for reimbursement for lost plants. The customer had made a special "deal" with the driver of the van that transported her furniture from Florida to California, paying him $100 to water her plants, which she placed in the van, although her moving contract specifically excluded plants, animals, and certain other property.

All twenty-seven plants died, and, because the containers could not be packed like other breakable objects, six large flower pots were broken.

The letter to the customer is not critical of the driver, although he was reprimanded for his actions. Adverse remarks about any employee weaken confidence in the organization as a whole, although in this instance the customer was not blameless.

Nothing would be gained by pointing out more specifically the unethical actions of either the driver or the customer, although you most certainly do not want a recurrence of a circumstance that resulted in your organization breaking a California law, which prohibits bringing uninspected plants into the state.

Some writers would have perhaps opened the letter with the one bit of good news, that the flower pots were insured and that the customer was receiving a check for $60. Because the customer had claimed $620 for the plants, however, the news that she was to receive only $60 is far from good.

Another refused adjustment is shown in Figure 9–6.

May 7, 19--

Mrs. R. W. Feller
Route 2, Box 506
Kenbridge, VA 23944

Dear Mrs. Feller:

Buffer

We are glad you enjoyed our annual spring sale last week. As the city's largest retail sports merchandiser, we take pride in offering you quality as well as the lowest prices in town.

Reasons and decision

Reasonable prices and frequent sales are a major reason you shop with us, we feel sure. At all sales, we invite you to try on the merchandise and thoroughly inspect it before you take it home. These low prices are possible because we accept returns only for regularly priced merchandise.

Sales promotion

The first week of May we will have on display a new line of clothes—the Doris May Playwear. Come in to see us. When you buy $25 worth of merchandise, you are eligible for a 10 percent discount.

Sincerely,

Mary Vaughn

Mary Vaughn
Customer Service Representative

FIGURE 9–6
Refusal of adjustment

Refusing Credit

Credit refusals present all the problems inherent in any refusal or bad-news message, plus other ticklish aspects of dealing with the reader's ego and reputation, both of which must be involved when credit is not allowed. In addition, the writer must make sure to abide by all legal stipulations. Some writers give no reasons at all unless readers respond with questions. Then they are given the company's source of information.

The letter in Figure 9–7 is to a college student who had provided no credit information.

Mention of a sale for cash, if it is subtly worded to convey a you-attitude, softens the refusal in that it indicates to the applicant that he or she continues to be a valued customer. In addition, employees in all departments of organizations that sell merchandise or service must promote sales, even though they are not classified as sales representatives.

Regardless of choice of wording, however, the customer will not be pleased. A curt letter, though, would accomplish nothing except to alienate the applicant.

HOLIDAY TRAVEL

On the Square
Oxford, Mississippi 38677

January 14, 19--

Ms. Becky Sue Bird
Box 2400
University, MS 38677

Dear Ms. Bird:

A Holiday Touraway card can indeed make trips convenient and enjoyable.

> Buffer

When reviewing your application, we noticed that credit references were omitted, in addition to the amount of your income. Your application is being returned to you so that you may complete this section.

> Tactful explanation

Once you have provided favorable credit information, which is required of all applicants, we will be happy to review your application again. Until such time, we will serve you on a cash basis, doing everything possible to make your trips convenient, economical, and enjoyable.

> The decision

May we help you plan your Caribbean cruise during your spring break? The enclosed brochures describe several different ships and ports of call.

> Goodwill and sales promotion

Sincerely,

Ann Harbison

Ann Harbison
Travel Agent

Enclosures: brochures

FIGURE 9–7
A credit refusal

Writing Other Messages Arranged in an Indirect Order

Various other messages, particularly those that convey bad news, are best arranged in an indirect order. The direct and indirect arrangements are as useful and appropriate for memorandums as they are for letters. The same consideration—expected reader reaction—is your guide to the choice of arrangement.

Summary

Letters and memorandums that convey unpleasant information should ordinarily be arranged in the indirect order, which consists of (1) a buffer; (2) explanation and analysis; (3) an implied or diplomatically worded decision; (4) a counterproposal, if appropriate; and (5) a friendly, positive close. A sincere you-attitude, desirable in all communication, is absolutely essential for diplomatic and convincing bad-news messages.

An implied decision is more diplomatic than a specifically worded one. When using an implied decision, you must make sure that your reader will have no reason to misunderstand.

General classifications of bad-news messages include refused requests, unfavorable messages about a product or service, refused adjustments, and credit refusals.

Test Yourself: Chapter Review

1. What is meant by a *buffer* as the term is used in planning the arrangement of a letter or other written material?

2–4. Following a buffer, name three major portions of a disappointing or unfavorable business letter. (These parts of a letter are not necessarily one paragraph each; neither are they completely discrete, or separate, from other parts, which flow together to form logical thought.)

5–10. Give six suggestions for the content of the buffer paragraph or paragraphs.

11–15. Give five examples of sentences or phrases that are often included in bad-news messages but should be avoided.

Which is the best choice in each group of sentences of bad-news letters arranged in the indirect order?

16. (from last paragraph)
    a. Best wishes for a happy holiday season.
    b. Again, we are sorry that we cannot do as you asked.
    c. We apologize for any inconvenience.

17. (from last paragraph of a letter to an unsuccessful applicant)
    a. No doubt you can find work elsewhere.
    b. We apologize for taking so much of your time.
    c. We believe that you will be successful in your chosen career.

18. (from third paragraph of a letter wishing to return sale merchandise)
    a. We do not accept returns on sale merchandise.
    b. Our low prices are possible because we accept returns only on regularly priced merchandise.
    c. No, we are sorry, but you cannot return the merchandise.

19. (from first paragraph of an answer to a request for use of copyrighted material)
    a. We are sorry that we cannot allow you to use the material you requested.
    b. Your writing project sounds interesting and worthwhile.
    c. Per your request of October 1, our material cannot be released.

20. In Question 19, which statement makes up part of a buffer?

a.

b.

c.

21. In Question 19, which statement contains an example of stereotyped business jargon?

a.

b.

c.

Test Yourself: Correct Usage

(Related to material in Chapter 9 and principles of correct usage.) Insert necessary punctuation, including quotation marks, hyphens, and apostrophes, and remove punctuation that has been inserted incorrectly. Choose correct word or sentence from each pair or group. Make any other necessary changes.

1. One or two paragraphs ordinarily (make, makes) up a buffer.

2. The buffer should let the reader know what the letter is about, it won't if it is completely unrelated.

3. A subject line if used in a letter or memorandum that contains bad news is less specific than the subject line in a good news letter or memorandum.

4. Although a subject line is expected in all memorandums it is not required in most letter styles, in some letters a subject line should be omitted.

5. Resale and sales promotion can be effective when used with discretion but they can sometimes result in an I-approach.

6. Sometimes congradulations should be expressed in a refusal letter. Provided the words are sincere.

7. Words can have a favorable or unfavorable (affect, effect) on the acceptance of a refusal.

8. We can never be sure how our words will (affect, effect) a particular reader.

9. Although an indirect order of arrangement is (recommended, reccommended, recomended, reccommended) for most bad news messages we must continue to use judgment and discretion at times this arrangement may not be the best possible choice.

10. Because a one-sentence paragraph is emphatic do not express the bad news in a sentence standing alone.

Cases

Refused Requests and Other Bad-News Messages

1. You are the industrial relations manager for Good Foods, Incorporated, based in Louisville. As part of Good Foods' comprehensive benefits package, employees who have worked full time for at least one year are eligible for educational reimbursement if they are pursuing a college degree in their spare time. A waiver for an employee who has worked less than one year can be obtained with a favorable recommendation from his or her immediate supervisor and a favorable one from you. You normally agree with supervisors' recommendations because they are more familiar with applicants' work.

   Bill Johnson, a supervisor at the Atlanta facility, has submitted a request for educational reimbursement while pursuing an MBA degree at Georgia Tech. Bob Nelson, Bill's immediate supervisor, has given an unfavorable recommendation, citing Bill's four months' experience with the company and his rather weak performance. This situation is further complicated by the fact that Bill's fellow supervisor in Atlanta, Jim Smith, has recently been granted a waiver for educational reimbursement.

   Classes begin in three weeks. Write to Bill, refusing his request for a waiver (Production Department, Good Foods, Incorporated, 6880 Peachtree, Atlanta, GA 30366).

2. You are the director of administration for Legend Cor-

poration, a company that owns and operates five Happy Inns franchises in four cities in the United States. You have interviewed candidates for an opening as a high-level administrative assistant in Legend's home office in Denver. After a long search you have found a highly qualified, experienced woman for the position, and she has accepted your offer. Your new task is to write letters of rejection to the many other applicants.

Because your company is growing rapidly, you know that you will have similar openings within a year or two. Some of the candidates that you must refuse are very well qualified; some definitely are not, for various reasons. Write two different letters, one to be sent to the applicants whom you would like to interview in the future and one to be sent to the applicants whom you do not wish to encourage.

Letters to both groups should be tactful and diplomatic. Although they will differ slightly in content, they should not differ in tone and courtesy.

3. You are vice-president of Newburg Fabrics in charge of the Western Region. One of the people you supervise is Joe Reeves, sales manager of the Western Region, a position he has held for 18 years. He has been with the company for 23 years. His goal is to become national sales manager.

A few years ago, Robert Shaw joined Newburg Fabrics. He had just completed his marketing degree from San Francisco State University. This was his first job. Because Reeves was the regional sales manager, he trained Shaw for the job, and it did not take Shaw long to learn.

In a short period of time Shaw began sharing his new and innovative ideas. Due to his effective marketing strategies and knowledge of present market trends, the company earned handsome profits. In addition, from the beginning the president of the company seemed to like Shaw, as did the president's daughter, who is now married to Shaw. After three years with the company, at age 25, Shaw was promoted to national sales manager.

The president asked you to talk with Reeves before the announcement was made public. Reeves was angry and bitterly disappointed. He said that he would remain with the company only on one condition, that he be transferred to the Southern Region, with headquarters in Charlotte, North Carolina. He wants to be sales manager of the Eastern Region instead of the Western Region. His parents live in Charlotte. (He is recently divorced.) You do not believe the president will want to move the sales manager of the Eastern Region, but you tell Joe you will talk with the president.

As you expected, the president does not want to disrupt the sales manager of the Eastern Region, although she has been there for less than one year. Write to Joe and tell him the news. Try to convince him to remain in his present position with the assurance that you will do everything you can to move him to Charlotte if the position should become vacant. Urge him to at least take the two months' vacation that he has coming in order to think it over.

4. Each year your company participates in a community fund drive, making contributions based on percentage of sales. This year sales have fallen considerably. The vice-president of your company has received a letter regarding the corporate donation and asking that the company's contribution be increased by 10 percent. The vice-president decides that there will be a decrease in this year's contribution. The public relations manager believes that this decision could prove to be detrimental to a retail firm doing business with the general public.

The two discuss the situation and decide to match last year's contribution instead of either increasing or decreasing the amount. Write a letter to the director of the Loyalty Fund from the vice-president explaining that your company cannot increase the contribution by 10 percent as requested. You will contribute the same amount as last year. How can you explain reasons without presenting a negative image of your company? The vice-president's name is Barbara Barnes. The director's name is Lawrence Cole, 2369 Goodwyn, your city and zip code.

5. You are the manager of a large record store (also selling compact disks and cassettes) in a shopping mall. You supervise twenty employees who have varying musical tastes. Many promotional albums, disks, and cassettes are sent to your store from music companies for in-store promotional play. There have been some disagreements among the employees about what kind of music to play in the store.

With this many people working together, you will have some people who prefer heavy metal music, some classical, some country, some easy listening. One wants only Elvis's music, and one would play Willie Nelson's records all day long. Everyone cannot be pleased at the same time. However, the music played in the store is not for the enjoyment of the employees but for the sale and promotion of the music.

Write a memo to all the employees about this situation. What will you say? (You cannot talk with them in a meeting because they work different hours; at no time are all employees in the store together.)

6. You are manager of the local Quality Office Products store. For many years you have been supplying novelty items to customers and other individuals and

groups. Marketing representatives take these items with them on visits to their customers' offices or have the items mailed. These advertising novelties consist of such things as pencils, note pads, paperweights, ashtrays, rain hats, and sewing kits. They have been successfully distributed by the Marketing Department and have become rather well known throughout the city. The company now receives requests from individuals and groups for these free items. They are especially popular for "goody bags" to be given to attendees at conventions.

Over the years the cost of the items has increased. Because the company's profits have fallen considerably, your accountant has advised you to cut expenses wherever possible.

Part A. Write a memorandum to be sent to all sales representatives telling them that only note pads will be distributed once the present supply of other advertising items is depleted. (Note pads can be made from short lengths of your own paper and printed with your company name and advertising message. You will make a special effort to see that these pads are unusually convenient and attractive.) You have on hand what would ordinarily be a three-month supply of assorted items. Ask customers to use this remaining supply with discretion. They are not to supply large numbers of anything except the note pads to organizations for "goody bags" or to individuals other than customers. Be sure not to stress negative aspects, including the decline in profits.

Part B. You receive a request from the local president of the alumni chapter of a sorority (Phi Gamma Nu) that is holding its national convention in your city. Ms. Ellen Glass asks for "300 items of everything that you have." Write a letter offering to supply note pads only. Her address is 1278 Macon, your city and zip code.

7. Every year the National Cotton Council selects and promotes a young woman to be the cotton industry's goodwill ambassador. This young woman, the Maid of Cotton, travels around the world promoting United States cotton through media appearances, public speaking appearances, and fashion shows.

Approximately 250 women apply for this position annually from all over the United States. Only fifteen are chosen as finalists to compete in the selection of the Maid of Cotton. Draft a rejection letter to go to the approximately 235 women not chosen as finalists. Suggest that they try again next year. Return the photographs that accompanied their applications. Assume that you are writing the letter for the signature of Anna Wilkens, Director of the National Cotton Council.

8. One of the requirements for entering the Maid of Cotton contest is that a young woman must be at least 5 feet, 5 inches tall. During the past several years the Cotton Council has received many letters from people asking why the height requirement is such. Some of the letters are very blunt in saying that the Cotton Council discriminates against short women.

Write a letter to have on hand to reply to similar letters you might receive in the future, although you hope your publicity on the subject will decrease the number of letters. The reasoning of your reply is as follows: The Maid of Cotton must model cotton clothing. Most models are taller than 5 feet, 5 inches, and, according to fashion designers, they should be in order to display the clothing to best advantage. In addition, a Maid of Cotton shorter than the specified height would require alterations in the garments she models. Alterations for her lengthy tour would be expensive and time-consuming.

9. Assume that you are Ally Madit. You and your husband, Fin, have finally moved into your beautiful new home in Delray Beach, Florida. It took you many years of hard work and frugal living to be able to purchase your dream home and decorate it just the way you want it, but your dreams have finally come true.

After you have lived in the house for only two weeks, you receive a letter from Maude, Fin's sister. (See letter on page 196.)

Write a letter to Maude declining the invitation that she has issued to herself. You feel that you and Fin will be able to pay for Maude and her family to spend a week in a nearby Holiday Inn, which has kennels for dogs, particularly if you decide not to go to Europe next year, as you had hoped. In addition, Fin has a friend who owns an employment agency in Seattle; you believe that he can find employment for Clay somewhere in the Northwest.

Remember—Maude is Fin's only sister.

(Problem written by Charmaine Hill and used by permission)

Dear Fin and Ally,

Time does fly, doesn't it? It seems like just yesterday when we last visited you, instead of being over two years ago, when you lived in your old house. (I'm glad you finally got out of that thing.)

That was the time our boys dismantled your backyard brick barbecue pit. You didn't use it that much, anyway. Oh, well, boys will be boys.

I do apologize for the cat. I do hope that Prissy didn't suffer any long-term effects from being shaved with Fin's imported razor by little Laura and Reggie. After all, the cat didn't receive too many cuts. I'm sure that it must have been so much cooler for the cat that summer without all that hair on her body.

I just know that you will be thrilled to learn that I truly think that our little Butch will be a fine carpenter some day. Right now he is busy taking the furniture apart and putting it back together again. He's not that good yet, but he's improving.

Randy is doing fine, too. He is practicing his trumpet every hour of the night and day. His teacher said that after a couple more years of practice he should be good at it.

It has been so long since we last visited you, and we enjoyed that visit so much. Because you just bought your new house, we are coming down there the first of next month to congratulate you in person. (I can't *believe* you have five bedrooms! The children will still be crowded together, but not nearly so much as they are here.)

Isn't that marvelous? Clay's out of work again, so it won't be any problem for us. We can stay as long as we like.

Well, I've got to run. The furniture store is delivering my new kitchen table.

Love, Maude

P.S. Greta—you remember, our Great Dane—had six puppies last week. But they will be old enough to travel by the first of the month.

---

10. *Part A.* You are a division director of a major corporation. The Board of Directors has decided to close your Indianapolis plant, which employs 450 people, and move the operation to a new plant in Bowling Green, Kentucky. This move will result in considerable long-term savings to the company and greatly increase future profits.

The Board has agreed to relocate Indianapolis employees who wish to move. The company will pay all moving expenses plus a $2,500 bonus to employees who relocate. Employees not wishing to move will receive four months' salary as severance pay. The company will also offer early retirement to employees over 50 (as of July 1 of the current year) with twenty or more years of service (also as of July 1 of the current year). Assistance will be given to employees seeking new employment.

Bowling Green has a population of about 50,000. The cost of living is fairly low, compared to Indianapolis. Outdoor recreation is abundant, and the schools are excellent.

Write a letter to be sent to each employee. Tell them about the closing and the available options. Stress that the company hopes all employees will go to Bowling Green.

Part B. In addition to writing the letter, discuss other methods of informing employees of this important decision. Should the employees have been told in some other way? If so, how? Explain your answer.

11. You are a recent graduate of Central College, having completed a two-year program. You are the only member of the class of business graduates now unemployed. You are now at the University of Toronto.

    Graduates have been asked to sponsor installation of central air conditioning in the business building. This installation is needed because of numerous hot days and nights (even in Lake City) and because classes are now held throughout the summer. Because your class is small, each share to be paid is quite large. If 100 percent participation is obtained, a local corporation will match the pledges, which are tax deductible.

    Pledges are due one month from today. You wonder why your classmates seem so eager to contribute. They must have far more money than you do. You realize that approximately $250 is not a magnanimous sum, but you are on a meager budget. You pay for your books and other necessities from your income as part-time student helper. You cannot afford to make a contribution of any amount.

    You have been subtly informed by two classmates that by not making a pledge you could keep your class from having 100 percent participation, resulting in cancellation of the whole project.

    Your savings have been depleted, you have outstanding loans, and your rent is a week overdue. Write to Harry Shaw, who is in charge of the fund-raising campaign. His address is 6001 Don Mills Road, Don Mills, Ontario, M3B 2X7 Canada. What will you say?

12. You are a librarian at Central College. You have received a telephone call from a former student who now lives in Maryland. You promise to write her after you have had time to investigate her statement that her transfer to the University of Maryland is being prevented by a hold that you have erroneously placed on her transcript.

    Your investigation reveals that while she was a student at Central College she checked out eight books that were returned through an outdoor book depository, more than two months late. They were watersoaked and mildewed. She did not reply to the two bills mailed to her for the replacement of the books. The amount of the bill was $132.

    On the telephone she explained that she had given the books to her father before the due date and that he had assured her they were properly returned. She thinks the books must have been damaged by rain blowing into the outside book depository.

    The library assistant who took the books from the outside depository tells you that he found no other water-damaged books in the large number that were in the depository. You know of no other instances of water blowing into the depository, and maintenance personnel reassure you that the container is designed to keep out wind, rain, and snow. It is emptied each weekday morning.

    Write to the former student. The $132 must be paid before you will authorize the Records Office to release her transcript. The procedure has been described in the official student handbook for many years. The student's name is Louisa Whitehead, 1416 Bellona Avenue, Lutherville, MD 21093.

13. James Watson, a currently enrolled student at Central College, has applied for a loan from the college. As director of financial aid, you are to refuse the request because the income of his parents (he lives at home) is more than adequate to pay his expenses. In fact, you consider the income extremely high because it is so much more than yours. James Watson has superior grades, but loans from Central College are based on need. (Perhaps there are other loans and scholarships available; but if he is smart enough to make all A's, shouldn't he be able to find out about the loans for himself?) What will you say? His address is 413 Bay Street, Toronto, M5H 2A8 Canada.

Unfavorable Messages about a Service or Product

14. You are the sales manager of Quality Office Products. One of your established accounts, Witt Manufacturing Company, has written you with a request for a sizable discount on their purchases.

    Witt Manufacturing is located thirty miles out of town. Your free delivery is limited by policy to within the city limits, but to keep the account you have been giving them free delivery and quantity discounts on their orders. The vice-president of Witt has been visiting their local plant for the last week, overseeing all operations. He told Mrs. Mary Johnson, the secretary in charge of ordering office supplies, that in California at the company headquarters Witt employees receive a 20 percent discount on all office supplies. It is now her job to secure this discount. The answer you must give is no.

    You did not know that Quality Office Products (your store is one in a national chain) was allowing discounts in California. Anyway, you make the policies in your store (or at least the general manager does), and you know you cannot afford a 20 percent discount plus free delivery. You will increase the quantity discounts to 5 percent on orders of $300 or more. You have now added another 5 percent discount for cash. Write to Mrs. Johnson, 310 Main, Hamlet, PA 19095, to inform her of your decision.

15. As a representative for Agricultural Systems, Incorporated, you sell an accounting service to farmers. You have just received a letter from Bill Larson, Route 3,

Tupelo, MS 38801. He has just signed a two-year contract. At the time of signing the contract, he paid the usual $200 fee to begin the system. You spent almost three days in going over his records and in setting up the system. The monthly fees have not yet started. Mr. Larson has changed his mind and does not want the service. He requests that the $200 be refunded and that the signed contract be voided. Write a letter voiding the contract, but do not refund the $200.

16. You are a general paving contractor. You receive a claim letter from Dr. Fred Crain, 9 High Plains Road, Branford, CT 06405. Dr. Crain states that the driveway has cracked after two years of use. When the driveway was paved, he refused the proper foundation of gravel and sand because of the cost. The lack of a good foundation was pointed out to him before the concrete was poured. Refuse the claim for a new driveway.

17. You are a financial officer of Northwest Housing Sales. Your company is selling a large block of townhouses. As part of the application, prospective buyers make a $1,000 deposit. They are told at the time they make application that the money will be placed in an escrow account at a local bank. This information is also on the customer's copy of the application. No mention is made that the checks will not be cashed.

    For an escrow account, the bank deposits the checks in an account that is closely monitored by the bank and company officials. The money is not available for use by Northwest Housing Sales. If the contract closes, the amount in the escrow account is applied toward the purchase. If the sale is not closed, the money is refunded to the person making the application, subject to certain guidelines set out in the application contract.

    Mr. and Mrs. Leon K. Smith have made application to buy a townhouse. He gave a check for $1,000. He had enough money to cover the check but did not think it would be cashed before the contract was closed. He then wrote seven more checks, which the bank returned because of insufficient funds. The Smiths were charged $84 for these returned checks.

    Mr. Smith has written you demanding that you reimburse him for the $84 service charges. Reply to his letter. His address is 235 West 16th Avenue, Spokane, WA 99203. You are not refunding the $84.

18. You own a local pool-building company that installs swimming pools for both residential and commercial customers. Last summer you installed a pool for Mr. Ed Williams at his home on Pinehurst Avenue (your city and zip code). The pool was of the vinyl type, which is constructed by building a rigid wall and then stretching a vinyl liner over the wall. The pool is guar-

anteed by your firm for a period of one year for any defects in materials or workmanship. The guarantee went into effect for Mr. Williams on August 1 of last year.

It is now June. In February Mr. Williams accidentally dropped a large oak log into the pool as he was moving firewood. The log split the liner from top to bottom. (You have examined the pool and talked with Mr. Williams about the accident.)

Mr. Williams has written you a letter requesting that the liner be replaced under the terms of the guarantee, although you have already told him in person and over the telephone that the guarantee doesn't cover accidents, only defects in materials and workmanship and durability under usual wear and tear. Write to Mr. Williams telling him that you cannot replace the liner free of charge, but that you will sell another one to him at your cost, plus installation.

19. You are customer service director of Park Seeds. You must reply to the request for adjustment (Chapter 8, Case 11) from the owner of Gardens of Eden, who sold twenty plants (Caltha, Marsh Marigold wildflowers) to a customer after having grown them from seeds purchased from Park Seeds. The amount of the requested reimbursement is $99 for twenty plants at $4.95 each.

    You will not grant the adjustment. These particular plants bloom the third year from seed. This statement is included in all your catalogs with the description of the seeds.

20. You are director of customer relations at Newburg Fabrics. You have just received a letter from Anderson Long, purchasing agent for Leisure Togs, requesting an adjustment on a batch of fabric No. 1183-088, which is 100 percent cotton dyed a dark navy blue. Leisure Togs used this cloth as trim on white sweatshirts. The adjustment request states that the blue dye migrated onto the white jersey cloth, resulting in inventory losses of $24,500. An accompanying shirt shows that the navy has indeed spread to the white jersey.

    This particular shade is not guaranteed to be colorfast. Newburg Fabrics specifically states that fact on the shipping invoices. The warning states that this particular shade is not to be sewn on any light-color fabric. In addition, your sales representative told the Leisure Togs representative that the material is not colorfast.

    Leisure Togs disregarded all warnings. You will not grant the allowance. Nevertheless, Leisure Togs is a major customer; goodwill is very important. Write Anderson Long at Leisure Togs, 3440 Park Avenue, New York, NY 02211.

21. You are the manager of New Product Development

for XALANT Tools, a company that manufactures industrial tools as well as products for the home market. If an employee in any department of the company has an idea for a new product, he or she submits a suggestion. If the product goes into production, the company awards the employee a $10,000 bonus.

In May of last year, Jerry Simmons, a mechanical engineer, submitted a suggestion for a new product called the Smart Gardener that was unlike anything on the market. The suggestion caused great excitement in the New Product Department. You were certain that the product would be a success. Jerry was called in several times to clarify some of the design aspects. Although it was never promised, you knew that Jerry assumed that the product was going into production and that he would receive a $10,000 bonus.

Yesterday you received word that because of financial difficulties no new products were to be developed until further notice. From past experience you know that this time could be anywhere from eighteen months to two years. You and your team have been moved to existing product line enhancement for this period.

It is your responsibility to tell Jerry Simmons this bad news. Although work was begun on his product and you believe it has definite potential, the suggestion guidelines plainly state that no bonus payments will be made until the time that the suggested product reaches production. Ordinarily you would discuss this matter in person, but he is away on vacation and you will be away when he returns. Write a memorandum.

Credit Refusals

22. You are a veterinarian in South City. Write to the owners of your patients. Tell them that after July 1 (it is now May 21) you will no longer carry charge accounts, as you have been doing ever since you came to South City. Now you will ask for cash at the time of each visit or accept Visa or MasterCard cards in payment. Customers will receive a 5 percent discount by paying cash. Write a letter to be included with the statement to be sent out June 1.

23. You are the consumer credit manager for a large Texas bank. (Give it a name.) One of your jobs is to approve applications for individual credit cards. You are young, bright, and ambitious. Important people in the community believe you have an excellent future with the bank and will perhaps be its president someday.

You have received an application from Jeff Blankenship, a college senior at Southern Methodist University in Dallas. He has a long history of poor banking practices, including two delinquent loans and several

returned checks. He is now unemployed and is considered an unacceptable risk to the bank.

Just as you are preparing to write a rejection letter, Robert Blankenship, the president of your bank, mentions that his son Jeff, who is a senior at Southern Methodist, will soon be home for the summer and is preparing for a trip to Europe. You had not known until now that Robert Blankenship has a son. Mr. Blankenship says that Jeff is eager for his own credit card.

Due to the credit policies established by the bank, you cannot issue a card to Jeff. Write to him; do not grant the credit card, but do all you can to stay in the good graces of top management.

His address is 2315 College Drive, Dallas, TX 75501.

24. You are vice-president of First Federal Savings and Loan. Mr. and Mrs. John Wilson have applied for a loan of $75,000 to buy a house.

The Wilsons have recently moved to St. Louis from Sacramento. While living in Sacramento, they were both employed as school teachers. Mrs. Wilson is now unemployed. She wants to stay home and take care of their five children. Mr. Wilson has been self-employed for three months as a building contractor. He stated that he has been working steadily. Their assets consist of household furnishings, a $50,000 life insurance policy, an automobile for which they owe $6,000, a paid-for truck, and an $11,000 savings account, $5,000 of which will be applied to the house, in addition to closing costs. They have an excellent credit rating.

The house at 3020 Estes has an appraised value of $85,000; it is offered for sale at $80,000. You have a policy of not granting credit to self-employed individuals until they have been in business for at least one year.

You regret that you must refuse the loan. Write to the Wilsons. The address is 5127 Blanding, St. Louis, MO 67894.

25. Your best friend wants to borrow $100. He has owed you $400 for a year. Refuse his request.

Write Your Own Assignments and Solutions

26. Write your OWN assignments, with solutions, for one or more of the kinds of letters (or memorandums, if appropriate) described in this chapter:

   refused requests or other bad-news messages

   unfavorable messages about a service or product

   credit refusals

   OR

   other letters or memorandums to be arranged in an indirect order

This assignment provides practice in describing a situation and giving instructions as well as in writing letters and memorandums. Your problem assignments may be on any subject, preferably about situations likely to occur in a business office. Give all the information another student would need to write a communication as a solution to your problem, includ-

ing names and addresses and enough details to enable the writer to make appropriate decisions. (By using this assignment, you can write messages useful in your own organizations, perhaps actual ones.)

A similar assignment is given at the end of Chapters 6, 8, and 10.

Evaluation Sheet: Bad-News Messages

	Yes	No	Not Sure
1. Does the letter or memorandum open with a buffer?			
2. Does the buffer make clear what the message is about?			
3. Does the buffer say neither yes nor no?			
4. Does the buffer build goodwill?			
5. Does the buffer lead naturally to the next paragraph?			
6. Is the refusal preceded by you-oriented and convincing details and explanations?			
7. Is the decision implied (preferably) or diplomatically stated?			
8. Does the letter or memorandum include a counterproposal? (Not necessary in all messages.)			
9. Does the letter or memorandum end with an action close, if appropriate, or with a goodwill close that takes the emphasis away from the refusal?			
10. Is the letter or memorandum courteous?			
11. Does the letter or memorandum exemplify the you-approach?			
12. Does the letter or memorandum exemplify the positive approach?			
13. Does the letter or memorandum omit all doubtful phrases or unnecessary apologies?			
14. Overall, is the message easy to read?			
15. Is the entire message sincere?			
16. Is the message completely correct in format, grammar, spelling, and sentence structure?			

CHAPTER 10

Writing Persuasive Messages

*All effective communication is persuasive if the term is construed in the broadest sense.
In this chapter we consider the kinds of communication that are usually described as
persuasive: sales messages, persuasive requests, and collection letters.*

Selling by Mail

A successful sales approach consists of a rather specialized application of the basic principles that pertain to all communication, particularly the principles of the you-attitude and the positive approach. Even more important is the ability to establish belief and trust.

Buying by mail has certain advantages, one of which is convenience. A disadvantage is that even with the most vivid verbal description and colorful photographs, the imagined product or service sometimes differs drastically from the actual one. This difference is caused by varying perceptions in the minds of the writer and the reader.

The sales approach, whether used with selling by mail or with any other method, should not be thought of as the "old hard sell," which was never a credible or creditable technique. Sales are made because potential customers are convinced that the purchase will meet their needs and will be more valuable than the cost, as well as more valuable than competing products. To build this conviction, *the seller presents the potential purchase in terms of what it will do for the buyer.* In addition, the customer must believe that the organization or organizations that manufacture and sell the product, as well as the salespeople, are sincere and trustworthy.

If you do not honestly believe that your product or service is valuable and worthwhile, you probably will not be able to make a convincing sales presentation. Customers are not easily fooled.

Mailing Lists

Effective selling by mail is a highly specialized and individualized approach. If you use an appropriate and up-to-date mailing list, your sales material will go only to those persons likely to be in the market for what you are selling.

The preparation or purchase of a suitable mailing list is expensive, but not so expensive as using a poor one. When mailings are sent to people who cannot use or who are most unlikely to want the particular product or service, these wasted mailings add greatly to the cost of the sales campaign.

Under the best of circumstances, some letters will be sent to readers who are certain not to be prospects, but these mailings should be kept to the minimum that can be achieved. Mailing lists become quickly outdated because so many people move each year. For this and for other reasons, no mailing list will be completely accurate even if it is frequently revised.

The use of inappropriate mailing lists is one of the reasons that direct-mail advertising is not always highly regarded. If you are a college student wondering how to pay for your next pair of shoes, you will not be interested in a retirement annuity and you cannot buy an expensive vacation home. A person who has completed a Ph.D. in English is not in the market for a book that will help the reader "speak like a college graduate." A president of a bank is not likely to be interested in a correspondence course in welding.

Mailing lists can be purchased from organizations that specialize in this service. As a general rule, the more difficult the list is to prepare, the more it costs. Thousands of different lists are available. A directory of companies that make, sell, and rent mailing lists is published by the U.S. Department of Commerce.

If a product or service is not so specialized that you need a particular mailing list, probably it should be sold by means other than direct-mail advertising, at least on a national basis. Nonspecialized products (in the sense that many persons could use them) can be profitably sold by mail in limited areas.

A Central Selling Point

A good product, even an outstanding one, must be sold. Potential customers do not beat a path to the door of a person who builds a better mousetrap if they do not know about it. Customers must be convinced.

In the selling process, even with the best mailing list, the message will go to some people who don't happen to need a mousetrap or who cannot afford to buy one. If the mousetrap maker is to prosper, the sales message must go to buyers who both need and can afford the product. These persons must be convinced that the product will meet their needs and that it is better than competing ones from the buyer's particular standpoint.

A mousetrap ordinarily will not meet their needs because it is beautiful or because it is made of the finest steel or wood (or whatever mousetraps are made of) but because it will catch mice—and more particularly, because it will catch the specific mouse that is now plaguing the potential buyer. (Although some people may be looking for a conversation piece for the coffee table, these buyers will no doubt be limited in number.)

The moral of this story is that the product or service must be presented in terms of the readers' most probable interest. To determine this interest, *we must know what the product will do and what the buyer is most likely to want.* This important principle of selling, regardless of the method, is a further application of the you-approach.

So how is the builder of the better mousetrap to choose a central theme, based on a central selling point, that will best market the merchandise? The first step is to analyze the product.

Analyzing the Product or Service

Is it true that the mousetrap is really better? If so, why? Is it better from all standpoints, or does it need improvements in certain areas? What are its best features in relation to the customers' expected needs? What are other desirable features? Of all possible selling points, which two are the most likely to be effective? Which particular point is likely to be most effective for the largest group of buyers?

To answer these questions, we must study the particular product or service, and its competition, in every detail. In such an analysis, we may find that even though the product is better overall than all the rest, some competing items have certain features that excel in comparison. For example, a competitor's mousetrap is painted a bright lemon yellow while ours is painted a dull gray (to match the mouse).

Or perhaps another product lasts longer but is not as effective. In this instance, we should not base our sales approach on color, or on our three-year guarantee if the competing model includes a five-year guarantee. These themes would not be the most effective, anyway, based on the customers' probable

An exhibitor points out features of machinery to a potential customer at a trade show. Do you think that the listener is enthusiastic and convinced?

needs. To determine these needs, we must analyze as much as possible the potential buyers.

Analyzing the Potential Buyer

The central selling point should be a feature in which the product excels, provided it is also a feature that is likely to make the customer want to buy. This is the real key to choosing a central selling point. What is it about a particular product that is most likely to make a particular person want to buy?

The central selling point is chosen to give unity and emphasis to the sales message. We can never be sure that we have chosen the best possible approach or that we have chosen the feature most likely to appeal to the particular reader or group of readers. For example, the prospective buyer who wants a mousetrap to serve as a paperholder on an office desk will not be interested in the fact that the product will also catch mice. If a person keeps mice as pets, a letter built around what seems to be a logical selling point will appear ruthless and offensive. If we were attempting to sell through conversation, we could determine individual interests and adjust our presentation accordingly. When, however, we write letters to a large group of readers, we must make an educated guess (an inference) and choose the approach that seems to be best fitted to the largest group.

How can you study the prospective buyer? Scientifically and objectively, there is no way, in spite of the many specialized books and journal articles about sales psychology. You can find many lists of psychological drives, differing somewhat from book to book. Even without books, we know that we are all interested, at least to a certain extent, in self-preservation, food, bodily comfort, sex, financial security, recognition, affection, pleasure, adventure, and the opportunity to grow and learn. We are also interested in communicating with other individuals so that we do not feel isolated and alone. Can you think of

Question: Are most mass-produced sales letters examples of correct writing and overall effective communication?

Answer: Because nationally distributed sales messages are written by professionals, they are usually examples of clear, correct, and convincing writing.

Good sales letters are well designed, using "white space" and other techniques of format. They include short paragraphs, a reader-approach, and vivid, specific descriptions of products and services.

However, not *all* sales letters, nationally distributed or otherwise, are examples of excellent communication. Some violate the most important principle of all—sincerity. Some statements are gushy, unbelievable, or downright silly.

Some sales letters include exaggerated words and phrases, which are also vague and meaningless; for example:

sensational	perfectly astounding
terrific	amazing
revolutionary	tremendous
the greatest	stupendous
the finest in the world	

Present a product, service, idea, or yourself in specific ways. If you actually believe that your product is stupendous (or all the other adjectives), prove it with specific, vivid, positive, reader-oriented words.

---

anything you have willingly purchased that did not help you meet one or more of these drives?

We should make use of such information as we have about our potential customers, such as age group, educational background, national origin, occupation, and hobbies. The more we know about our readers or listeners the more likely we are to be able to adapt our message to their particular interests. A carpenter is more likely to buy a hammer than is a kindergarten teacher, or such is a logical assumption, but the kindergarten teacher might be a more likely customer because the carpenter probably already has a hammer.

A teenager is perhaps more likely to be interested in the styling of a sports car, rather than in the economy, but this is not necessarily the case. His schoolteacher mother, who looks like the typical little old lady in tennis shoes, may be unconcerned with gas mileage and very much interested in the appearance of the car. This little old lady also may be about to purchase a $100,000 certificate of deposit while a well-dressed businesswoman is wondering how to buy her lunch.

Putting persons into categories—or stereotyping—is a dangerous practice. Each person is different from every other person. An individual approach, however, is impossible to obtain in sales campaigns in which the same message must be sent to many people because such an approach would be prohibitive both in time and expense.

Instead, we must generalize, and all generalizations are likely to be less than exact. For this reason, the central selling point is not likely to be the most appropriate one for all readers, provided that the contemplated purchase has more than one desirable factor.

Some writers of sales messages do not use a central selling point but try to stress equally all major factors of the product or service. Overall, however, a presentation is likely to be less effective if many points are equally stressed, an approach that in effect emphasizes nothing.

Presenting the Central Selling Point

As a general rule, sales letters are longer than other kinds of business letters. Many sales letters consist of four or more complete pages, plus enclosed leaflets and brochures. Longer sales letters, as well as the complete sales package, are most effective if they are based on a central selling point. In addition to the central selling point, sales letters also present other features of a product or service.

The message would probably be prepared as a form letter, perhaps by the use of a computer that would insert the name and address of each person, as well as the current date. This type of duplication is too expensive for letters that are sent out by the thousands, but this service being presented would not be sold to a great number of persons, at least in the present stage of development of the business enterprise. The letter could also be individually typewritten or prepared by other means of attractive duplication, such as good-quality photocopy or the offset process. If the individual's name is inserted in each letter, the typewriter ribbon should match the print.

The central selling point is ordinarily the outstanding feature of the product or service offered, chosen in relationship to the needs and desires of potential customers. In some instances, however, the central selling point may be price, or "affordability." In sales letters that are *not* built around price, it is subordinated; if price is the central theme, it is discussed throughout the message like any other central selling point. Price as a central theme must be chosen with caution, however, because readers can always decide to save even more money by not making a purchase at all.

Both product analysis and market analysis are essential, as discussed earlier. For example, can you imagine selling Waterford crystal, one of the most expensive brands available, using affordability as the central theme? Do you find any mention of price in the advertisement shown in Figure 10–1? The copy

Communication Brief	The corporate officers at IBM still make sales calls with great regularity. In New York one of us recently ran into a senior financial officer who makes customer calls and insists that all his people do so as well: "How's someone going to design a receivables policy if he doesn't know the customer?" Chairman John Open underscores the point: "You have to remember who pays the bills. No matter what the primary discipline—finance, manufacturing—you have to know and experience the excitement of sales. That's where you really see things happen."
	Thomas J. Peters and Robert H. Waterman, Jr., *In Search of Excellence* (New York: Harper & Row, 1982), 161.

Waterford pours forth memories. It conjures up fantasies, evokes
poetic imagery, provokes the creative spirit, celebrates life's
mysteries. It is never too early nor too late to assume the title:
Waterford Collector. Some begin at birth, others as nonagenarians.
To the collector, a piece of Waterford crystal is more than a
drinking vessel, more than a vase, a decanter, a lamp, a chandelier,
more than a family heirloom, more than an objet d'art; it is an
incentive to lose weight, to win forgiveness, a way to attract a lover,
to distract a patient, to symbolize hope, to crystallize a dream, to bid
adieu, to hail the seasons, to raise spirits, to diminish melancholy,
to mark events, to start traditions, to end a day; it is a noble rite of
passage. Born of the breath of man, Waterford is life's child.

—H. Pesin, from "The Collected Thoughts of Waterford Collectors"
Get this 160-page book ($3.50) at your Waterford Gallery

FIGURE 10–1
**An advertisement for
Waterford crystal** (Used
with permission of Water-
ford Crystal. Agency: Pesin,
Sydney, & Bernard Adver-
tising.)

was accompanied by a simple, close-up photograph of the most expensive pattern of Waterford crystal, with the petals of an exotic flower spilling over the
top. Another goblet, filled with wine, is in the background. Do the words in
the advertising copy shown in Figure 10–1 make you want to buy Waterford
crystal? If so, can you determine why the words are so effective? No central
theme is put into specific words. Can you put the central theme of the advertisement about Waterford crystal into specific words—or do you prefer to leave it
in the poetry in which it is written?

A letter from *The New Yorker* (used by permission) is shown in Figure 10–2.

Special Characteristics of Sales Letters and Other Sales Material

Some of the special characteristics of sales letters are these:

1. An overall informal tone. You have learned that most business messages are rather informal, but that the degree of formality differs according to
the purpose of the communication and according to the reader or readers. Sales
messages tend to be more informal than other kinds of letters. As in other
communication situations, you should plan the degree of formality to best fit
the purpose and readership, both of which will be influenced by the product
or service you are selling.

2. Special emphasis on descriptive, vivid, forceful words and phrases.

3. Special emphasis on the you-approach by describing the reader enjoying or benefiting from the purchase, perhaps by explaining how the reader can
solve problems or increase his or her pleasure by purchasing the item or service.

In the discussion of sales writing in this chapter and in the following

THE
NEW YORKER

AN INVITATION TO SUBSCRIBE. JUST 49.9¢ A COPY.

Dear Reader:

If you have days when almost everything goes wrong . . .

> . . . when the headlines are scary . . . when the stock market
> is down . . . when the bureaucrats have done it again . . .
> when rain is predicted for the weekend . . . when they've had
> the audacity to serve you a bread pudding that contains only
> two raisins . . .

. . . there's a magazine that can cheer you.

The New Yorker.

Its colorfully drawn covers can gladden your heart. Its cartoons
can put a smile back in the day. Its observations and comments
can help you regain your perspective. Its stories, articles, and
reviews can help restore your faith in your fellow-man.

> On one occasion or another, The New Yorker may have
> brightened your grandparents' lives. It has surely perked up
> your parents'. And now that your own time to be cossetted is
> at hand here's some happy news, first, for your wallet.

> When you return the enclosed subscription form promptly,
> you'll get a full year of The New Yorker for only 49.9¢ an
> issue. Not the $1.50 you'd pay at the newsstand or the
> regular subscription price of 62¢ a copy. As we said, just
> 49.9¢.

The New Yorker was created in the nineteen-twenties as a
journalistic and literary magazine. Its aim is to keep readers in
touch with the main social, cultural, and political currents of our
times, and this it seeks to do with probity, style, and wit.

Past contributors have included some of the most celebrated
writers and artists of this century. Storytellers like John Cheever,

FIGURE 10–2
Sales letter

Shirley Jackson, and John O'Hara. Critics like Edmund Wilson,
Clifton Fadiman, and A. J. Liebling. Cartoonists like Peter Arno,
Mary Petty, and James Thurber.

> Journalists like Janet Flanner, John Hersey, and E. B. White.
> Poets as diverse as Marianne Moore and Odgen Nash.
> Humorists such as Robert Benchley, S. J. Perelman, and
> Dorothy Parker, a resolute city dweller who once dismissed
> all bucolic phenomena as fresh air and trees with the
> statement "I am at two with nature."

Today's contributors are no less distinguished, and their range of
interests is astonishing. In one recent issue alone, you might
have had the start of a fascinating probe of the geology of the
Rockies . . . a communique from Mott Street, the main drag of
New York City's Chinatown, where the shrimp dumplings make
doing jury duty nearby not a civic duty but a civic delirium . . .

> . . . news of a Peruvian writer who has replaced Gabriel
> Garcia Marquez as the South American novelist for gringos to
> catch up on . . . brief encounters with (1) the man who's
> behind the Montrose Pet Hotel, a new inn so exclusive it
> doesn't accept people, and (2) the woman who's behind the
> Critter Car, a pet-sensitive chauffeuring service . . .

> . . . a report on an important new study on ballet and
> Tchaikovsky, along with the lamentable tidings that
> bookstores no longer seem to stock what has been called
> "the greatest act of historical witness of our century,"
> Solzenitsyn's "The Gulag Archipelago" . . .

> . . . anecdotes from an aficionado who uncannily remembers
> virtually all the whos, whats, whens, wheres, and whys of
> early jazz . . . a report on a new show of conceptual art that
> includes one room entirely devoted to charts and graphs
> recording how the artist has spent each moment of her life
> for the last fifteen years . . .

> . . . plus one poem . . . two short stories . . . reviews of a new
> play, three movies, and six concerts . . . all interspersed with
> twenty cartoons, one of whose captions reads, "Have you seen
> my castanets?"

(over, please)

FIGURE 10–2
(continued)

How much will you give to have a look at the drawing that this caption accompanies? To revel in The New Yorker regularly? To keep up with The Talk of the Town? To know better the world's movers and shakers through the magnifying glass of the magazine's Profiles?

To keep in closer touch, through the magazine's listings, with New York theatre, dance, night life, art, music, sports, movies, special events? To be stimulated, edified, moved, nourished, delighted?

You say you'll offer 40.3¢ a week? $21 for a full year? It's a deal. Just complete the order form, then mail it in the envelope enclosed. No postage needed. Thank you. Welcome to The New Yorker. High time!

Cordially yours,

Frank Mustacato
Circulation Director

FM:am

THE
NEW YORKER
25 West 43rd Street New York, New York 10036

FIGURE 10–2
(continued)

questions and problems, we shall refer to this particular application of the you-approach as *psychological description*. Psychological description pictures the product or service being sold in terms of reader benefit.

4. More use of the mechanical means of emphasis, such as all capitals, underlining, dashes, special arrangements, and color. The letter in Figure 10–2 does not use these devices to the extent that they are often used in sales letters.

Now let's look at the suggested arrangement of ideas in a sales letter.

Attention, Interest, Desire, Action

The arrangement of sales letters in terms of attention, interest, desire, and action has long been used in the discussion, planning, and writing of sales messages.

Other terms used to describe this pattern are *attention, interest, conviction,*

Communication
Brief

Weasel words. He [Carroll Carroll] defined a weasel word as "a description given by advertising people to that key word in a piece of copy that takes the responsibility out of the most exaggerated claim." As an example, he noted the dishwasher detergent that "leaves glasses virtually spotless." If you think that means without spots, you are wrong. It means practically without spots or with some spots. So, in point of fact, what the ad says is that your glasses will not be completely clean if you use this particular detergent. Another example is the remedy for "simple nervous tension." How do you define "simple"?

"Four out of five dentists surveyed recommend Blah-and-Blah for their patients who chew gum." Surveyed by whom? Perhaps by the manufacturer's 6-year-old daughter gathering material for Show and Tell? How many doctors were surveyed? All five witch doctors in Upper and Lower Slobovia? What was the form of their recommendation? Did they say "Oh, well, if you must chew gum, we suppose that Blah-and-Blah is the least harmful"? This simply is not using the language to convey truth. It is flimflam.

William Morris and Mary Morris, *Harper Dictionary of Contemporary Usage* (New York: Harper and Row, 1985), 617.

and *action; attention, interest, desire, conviction,* and *action;* and *attention, conviction,* and *action.* All these patterns are basically the same. In the first part of the letter, we must gain the reader's attention. In the middle section of the letter, we present convincing evidence. In the last part of the letter, we ask for action, as we have used the action close in other types of messages.

A description of a sales letter planned in this arrangement was included in a book by Harrison McJohnston, *Business Correspondence,* published in 1919:

1. Will the very first part of the letter get favorable attention and cause the reader to want to read on? (This usually means a direct, concrete, and convincing appeal to one or more of the reader's personal desires, and a forecast of the possible satisfaction of the desire as a result of reading the letter.)

2. Will the reader's interest increase as he reads? (Do you keep him in the letter? Could you add or subtract anything and thereby increase his interest?) Remember, you must make him read, and read with keen interest, or your effort is likely to be wasted. Lead him to a climax of thought and feeling which causes him to be willing to do as you wish.

3. Will the reader believe all the statements you make? Is it all the truth from his point of view? Do you give him facts, and not your own arbitrary opinions or conclusions? Do you avoid telling him what he already knows (as well or even better than you)? Especially, do you avoid telling him what he ought to know, so that he might get the impression that you think he does not know? Do you supplement his knowledge of facts so that he will be likely to conclude for himself that he ought to do as you want him to?

4. Do you cause him to get a vivid impression of the resulting good to him of doing as you want him to?

5. Will your closing sentences be likely to cause him to *act* upon his willingness to do as you want him to? Does he get a *definite* suggestion of just how he may do as you want him to? Have you avoided the hackneyed "do-it-now" close?

6. Is your expression effective? Is it all clear to him? Does it *all* sound natural

and sincere to him? Is it free from hackneyed phraseology and lifeless expressions? Is it direct and simple and definite, and free from waste of words and unnecessary statements? Does it attract the eye?[1]

All the suggestions presented by Harrison McJohnston in 1919 are as applicable today as they were at the time. Isn't it ironic that the *do-it-now* close (or *act today!* or *don't wait!* close), which had already become hackneyed in 1919, is still used in the last quarter of the century? (McJohnston had never heard of *nondiscriminatory writing,* discussed in Chapter 3.)

Obtaining Favorable Attention

The attention section of a solicited sales letter differs somewhat from that of an unsolicited one. In responses to inquiries, you already have the reader's attention, provided you have replied promptly.

In solicited letters you need only to open with favorable information about the prospective purchase, expressed in terms of the reader's interest. In unsolicited messages, you work harder to gain and keep attention and interest, in order to keep the letter from being thrown into the wastebasket. (A solicited sales letter is shown in Figure 10–3.)

The attention section of unsolicited messages may consist of a question, a startling statement, mention of an outstanding feature of the product, a proverb, a news announcement, a gadget or gimmick, or other similar approaches. Whatever you use to attract attention, it must make sense and tie in with the following paragraphs. Preferably the message begins with a reference to the chosen theme or leads directly to that theme. It should be reader centered.

The following sentence, used alone as an opening paragraph of a letter planned to sell a barbecue grill, begins with a quotation.

> Harry Truman once said, "If you can't stand the heat, you should get out of the kitchen."

This opening paragraph ties in with the central theme of the letter, that the reader will avoid heating the house with the range or oven by cooking outside and will enjoy meal preparation and dining on the patio. Here, as you no doubt recognize, Truman's analogy was reversed to its original and literal meaning.

The opening paragraph of a letter from a manufacturer to a dealer stresses features of the product in terms of reader benefit.

> When you show a customer a Gardener, a grass collector that sweeps and combs a lawn in one operation, you have obtained a quick sale, a satisfied customer, and a $40.81 profit.

[1]Harrison McJohnston, *Business Correspondence* (New York: Alexander Hamilton Institute, 1918, 1919), 207–208.

Outward Bound

**Pacific Crest
Outward Bound School**
1010 S.W. Bancroft St.
Portland, Oregon 97201
Telephone 503-243-1993

September 28, 1988

Mr. John A. Delves III
<u>Backpacker</u> Magazine
One Park Avenue
New York, NY 10016

Dear John:

You are right--your readers will be interested in Joshua Tree desert backpacking. I'm delighted you are considering such an article for <u>Backpacker</u>.

Attention

This area provides a perfect respite from winter . . . 68° weather, blue skies, dramatic granite rock formations, and a wide variety of flowering desert plants. Backpackers often hear the call of coyotes at night, and during the day they see wildlife which has also headed south for the winter. Wild donkeys, bighorn sheep, mule deer, and dozens of bird species are common in Joshua Tree.

Interest

You may be interested in sending a writer on one of two courses:

NS-104, October 19-22, four days--current enrollment--three men and three women from New Jersey, Colorado, California, and Missouri
NS-106, October 28-November 3, seven days--current enrollment--four men and one woman from Mississippi, Hawaii, California and New York.

*Desire
or
Conviction*

The four-day course is full of high-impact teamwork exercises. The seven-day course allows more time for enjoyment of the environment and for more extensive travel.

. . . over please

FIGURE 10–3
A sales letter in response to a request for information (Courtesy of Pacific Crest Outward Bound School.)

*Desire
or
Conviction*

Action

FIGURE 10–3
(continued)

Enrollment for both courses will increase up to the course date with a maximum of twelve people per group. Each group of students has two instructors. A chief instructor will be in charge of the course if there is more than one group of students in the field.

Courses include rock climbing and rappelling as well as backpacking. Our instructors also spend time on route finding and map and compass reading so that students will feel comfortable in an environment without trails.

We will have color backpacking and rock climbing slides shot in October, and they will be available for your story. I do hope Joshua Tree fits into your plans for <u>Backpacker</u>. Please give me a call to work out the details.

Cordially,

Darlene Gore

Darlene Gore
Marketing Director

page 2

From a letter to sell an expensive mantel clock:

Your time is precious, especially when it's kept by a clock as magnificent as this "thing of beauty which is a joy forever." Crafted of the finest quality Central American mahogany and hand-painted with traditional Chinese scenes, this masterpiece is worthy of becoming a family heirloom, to be passed on to your grandchildren, and theirs.

From a long advertisement from a men's store, accenting quality and traditional, timeless design:

THE KIND OF SPORTSWEAR WE SELL LOOKS BETTER THE OLDER IT LOOKS. ISN'T THAT A DUMB WAY TO RUN A BUSINESS?

The advertisement carried through with the theme that quality and classic design retain their appearance, even when old. The next sentence, after the opening above (which was typed at the top of the advertisement in capital letters) was this:

There are a few things we'd like you to know about our sportswear right from the start: it fades, it tends to wrinkle, and it isn't overly stylish.

From a letter from a publisher of textbooks to high school teachers:

> Have you ever heard the expression "It's books" to mean that school is now in session—that recess or another free period is over and that it's time to get down to serious business?

The next paragraph explained that "it's books" is an old-fashioned term once widely used, which expressed the early concern, appreciation, and awe with which students and teachers viewed the few books that were then available. The central theme of the message was that, to improve education and our society, books must be reliable, interesting, challenging, and appropriate, and that such books just happen to be the exact kind that the publisher is selling.

From a letter to sell a burglar alarm system to people who have just purchased citizens band radios to be installed in automobiles:

> Protect your new investment!

Watch for these weaknesses in opening paragraphs of sales letters:

1. A too-long first paragraph. Although opening paragraphs should be short in all business letters, overly long ones are particularly bad in sales letters, in which you must gain and hold attention.
2. Questions with obvious answers, such as *would you like to increase profits?*
3. Obvious statements, such as *to make a profit, you have to move merchandise.*
4. A writer-centered opening, such as *we are proud to announce the opening of our new store.*
5. Slow openings, such as *we have received your inquiry about our products, we are writing to give you the information you requested.*
6. Openings used only for a surprise or startling effect without regard for relevance or a tie-in with following paragraphs.
7. Obvious flattery, such as *a person with your social position, Mrs. Jones—*
8. Openings that mention a negative aspect of the product or service. These are especially likely to occur when replying to inquiries. The potential customer's questions need not be answered in the order they were asked.
9. A reference to the cost of the purchase unless price is to be used as the central selling point.

Presenting Convincing Evidence in Terms of Reader Interest

We must give specific, objective details about the product or service we are attempting to sell. In addition, we must present these details in terms of the reader's interest. (This approach is the *psychological description* mentioned earlier.) Instead of saying simply that a swimming pool is surrounded by a twelve-foot-wide redwood sundeck, reword the statement so that the buyer is described using the sundeck. The statement that it is a twelve-foot-wide redwood sundeck is good, as far as it goes, and much better than saying that the pool is surrounded by a wide sundeck. (How wide is wide?) But it is even better if you describe the sundeck in specific terms and also imagine the reader enjoying it, as in:

> The redwood sundeck (12 feet wide!) that surrounds the pool gives you plenty of room for cookouts and parties for many happy summers to come.

In addition to presenting sales material in emotional terms, give solid, tangible evidence, presented in terms of reader interest. For example:

> Look closely and you'll see seams sewn straight and strong, buttons attached to stay, and plenty of reinforcement where it's needed. Small details, perhaps, but important.
>
> The result of all this? Our sportswear won't suddenly fall out of fashion, fall out of your favor, or fall apart. So instead of replacing it every year, you can buy a little more.

A weakness of many sales letters is a lack of attention to conviction by hurrying through from the attention section to the action close. In the middle paragraphs of the letter, give enough time and space to build conviction. You will not convince with vague generalities, such as saying that the product is fine, beautiful, strong, or "absolutely the finest in the world." Give reasons, details, and specifications to convince the reader that the product is absolutely the finest in the world.

Do not speak in generalities. If it's sturdy, why and how? If it's roomy, how big is it? If it's dependable, how do you know? If it's economical to operate, how many miles to a gallon? How do you know that it gets that many miles to a gallon? How do you know that the tests were reliable?

As you describe the product or service, you will often find that you have a great many features to list or describe in addition to your central selling feature. Items are easier to read if they are set up in a listing instead of crowded together in paragraph form. For example, the format below

> In sales letters, use
>
> 1. Listings
> 2. Plenty of white space
> 3. Capitals, underlining, special arrangements
> 4. Any other form of mechanical emphasis, as long as it is not used to excess

is easier to read than if presented in this way:

> In sales letters, use listings, plenty of white space, capitals, underlining, special arrangements, and any other form of mechanical emphasis, as long as it is not used in excess.

The cost of an item should be subordinated unless it is used as a major selling factor. If it is not a good price, or only somewhat lower than competing products, it should not be used as a major selling factor.

Remember the principles of emphasis presented in Chapter 4. To subordinate the price, reverse the principles of emphasis. Present the price only after convincing evidence to justify it. But do not leave it for the last paragraph, which is one of the most emphatic ones, unless you wish to emphasize the price.

Do not present the price in a sentence standing alone as a paragraph, one of the methods of emphasis. You achieve more subordination by presenting the price in a minor clause or phrase than by putting it in the more emphatic main clause. You subordinate when you show how the reader will benefit by the purchase, with an emphasis on these benefits, not on the price.

Notice the methods of subordination in this paragraph from a cleaning service using the name "Suzy and Her Menfolks":

> Your free week, which Suzy and Her Menfolks by their efforts will make possible, is priced at only $48, including all costs of equipment and cleaning materials.

Although the $48 is presented in the main clause of the sentence, it is tucked into the middle of the sentence and not placed in the emphatic opening or closing position, both of which state definite and positive reader benefits. The *only* and *including all costs of equipment and cleaning materials* suggest that the service is a good buy. The remaining sentences in the paragraph reemphasize reader benefit.

Asking for Action

The action close in sales letters is the same as in other types of communications: Specify the action, preferably in terms of reader interest; make action easy; and, if appropriate, motivate prompt action.

A weakness that still occurs in the action section of sales letters is a pushy and demanding attitude, often displayed by the trite phrases mentioned in the book on business correspondence published in 1919. Even if the reader is prepared to buy, a phrase such as *run down to your nearest drugstore right now!* is enough to send the letter to the nearest wastebasket right now.

Be sure that the reader understands exactly what the necessary action is and how accomplished. Make this action easy. Don't ask for a letter in return, only a pencil check on a postage-paid card, or perhaps a signature. If you want the reader to telephone, give the telephone number. If you want the reader to come into a store, give the location of the store and the hours it is open.

The paragraph shown below is from a publishing house to a high school teacher:

> Just return the enclosed card and we will have our salesman, Andy Brown, call on you. He will bring a free copy of *Practical English for Tomorrow's Leaders* and discuss with you the benefits of using this book in your classroom.

The following paragraph is from a hotel promoting a bridal suite to a bridegroom-to-be:

> Simply fill out the enclosed reservation card, mail it to us, and we will have this beautiful suite waiting for you and your bride—along with fresh flowers and a chilled bottle of champagne.

The following paragraph is from a letter promoting package delivery by a taxicab company:

> Give me the opportunity to prove that Yellow Shuttle and Yellow Rush are everything I've said. Paste the enclosed stickers near your telephones and call 536-0000 for your next package delivery.

The men's clothing store, after devoting a full page to their quality clothing that "tends to wrinkle," used as an action close only the name of the store, OAK HALL, with the phrase "since 1859" and the address of their store locations. If they had been selling by mail, they would have ended with specific instructions on how to order or would have referred the reader to attachments that included exact instructions.

A sales letter in response to a request for information is shown in Figure 10–3. This letter meets the description of "favorable information" discussed in Chapter 8, but because of more detailed information is similar to an unsolicited message.

Planning and Writing Persuasive Requests

Persuasive requests differ from routine requests (discussed in Chapter 8) in that they do not ordinarily open with the request itself. They are a variation of the indirect letter (discussed in Chapter 9) but are most like regular sales letters discussed previously in this chapter. In effect, the arrangement of persuasive letters, using the time-honored *attention, interest, desire, action* sections, differs little from the indirect order of arrangement used for bad-news messages.

At times you may not be sure whether a particular request should be treated as one that the reader will be happy to grant or one that will require persuasion. *If you are not sure, it is better to treat the message as a routine one and to open with the request itself or state it early in the letter.* As with communications of other kinds, use the direct order unless you see a definite reason to use another arrangement. In some instances, requests that require a great deal of explanation and a sales approach can be effectively arranged in the direct order. Opening with the request and following with convincing, you-approach details is far more effective than an arrangement that causes the reader to wonder through several paragraphs what the letter is all about.

In usual practice, however, do not open a persuasive request with a statement of the request itself. Use an attention-getting section, as in sales letters, that states or implies reader benefit. If there is little reader benefit possible, open with convincing and interesting details about the product or service.

A sales-oriented persuasive request is illustrated in Figure 10–4. The first paragraph attracts attention and leads to discussion of the idea. The middle

Communication Brief

Persuasion and Ethics. Does the mere ability to persuade entitle a man to the uninhibited use of the power that persuasion gives? This question, which is a fundamental one, appears as early as Plato's attack on the school of Sophists, in Athens, who were concerned with persuasion purely as a technique without reference to the ends to which it might be applied. The question is very much alive today. To take a few examples from among many possible ones: Has a politician running for office the right to inflame prejudice and passion on the matter of race? Has the manufacturer of cigarettes, which are presumably harmful, the right to persuade the public to smoke?

Cleanth Brooks and Robert Penn Warren, *Modern Rhetoric*, 3d ed. (New York: Harcourt, Brace & World, 1970), 264.

paragraphs build interest and conviction, as does the next-to-last paragraph. The last paragraph includes an action close. This letter, like many sales letters, is friendly and informal, a natural approach to a friend. As with all communications, adaptation according to the reader and to the purpose of the message is desirable and necessary.

In persuasive requests, as in sales writing, make the major portion of the letter convincing by describing the suggested action in vivid, specific, positive words that show reader benefit. By presenting features of the product or facets of the idea in terms of reader interest, you convince the reader to buy or to accede to your request or proposal. In order to convince the reader, avoid phrasing or exaggeration that would cause disbelief. Use specific language and vivid description to present favorable aspects.

The Collection Series

Collection messages are classified here as being in the early, middle, or late stages in the collection series. The early stage consists of reminder messages in the form of notes, obvious form letters, or stamped reminders on duplicate bills.

Middle-stage messages are more individualized. They are individually written and dictated or planned to give the appearance of personally directed letters. Middle-stage collection letters are longer than either the early or late messages because they must develop an appeal. Late-stage letters are shorter and more direct. They speak firmly of the urgency of the situation and of the importance of immediate payment.

The collection series differs from organization to organization in the number of messages in each stage. It also differs in the length of time from the beginning of the series until the end. It may differ according to the particular group of customers of the same organization.

As a general rule, the total time of the collection series is longer for good credit risks than for poor ones. More mailings are included, and more time is allowed to elapse between mailings. A typical series may consist of two to four reminders (the early stage of the series), two or three inquiries and appeals (the middle stage), and two or three urgency letters, the final one of which is an ultimatum.

Greentrees Civic Association

6780 MESSICK ROAD MEMPHIS TENNESSEE 38138

June 23, 19--

Mr. and Mrs. Joseph E. Langley
8504 Black Oak Cove
Memphis, Tennessee 38138

Dear Mr. and Mrs. Langley:

Attention

Are you aware that there is an organization in your new neighborhood that is dedicated to protecting and possibly enhancing the investment value of your new home? This organization is the Greentrees Civic Association, an organization of homeowners in the Greentrees Subdivision led by nine elected Officers and Directors.

Interest and desire

These officials, aided by various committees, maintain a watchful eye for developments that could breach the guarantee that the neighborhood continue in the same high or higher standard of existence. By having quarterly meetings of the general membership, the Association provides a forum for residents to exchange common ideas and interests. Many times, professionals in such fields as insurance, energy conservation, electrical contracting, law enforcement, security patrols and the like are invited to speak.

Civic Association officials represent the subdivision as a unified body before the various commissions, councils, and boards of local government. The membership is kept informed by a bimonthly newsletter that is mailed to the members' homes.

The social event of the year is the annual dinner dance held in early November of each year. Members and their friends have dined sumptuously and danced to the music of Tony Barrasso in such places as the Skyway of the Peabody Hotel, the Memphis Hunt and Polo Club, the Memphis Racquet Club, and the Grand Ballroom of the Ridgeway Hyatt Regency.

Action

Can you guess how much the annual membership dues are? Did you say $10? If so, you were correct. Membership is as easy as putting pen to paper. Put your pen to your check. Make the check payable to Greentrees Civic Association and send it to the address on the letterhead. Your membership acknowledgment card will be on the way to you by return mail. Begin immediately to support your Civic Association and help your concerned neighbors as they work to improve and protect the quality of life and investment in the neighborhood.

Sincerely,

O. Norris Avey, Jr.
O. Norris Avey, Jr.

FIGURE 10–4
Persuasive request

Intervals between mailings vary from ten to thirty days, with longer intervals at the beginning of the series and shorter ones toward the end.

The series may be lengthened or shortened. It is shortened when readers are considered to be poor credit risks or when conditions indicate that the collection process should be accelerated.

The number of mailings may be reduced and the intervals between the mailings shortened, or some of the steps in the usual series may be omitted altogether. Perhaps there will be no reminders, one appeal, and then an urgency letter, followed by an ultimatum.

Regardless of the length of the series, the tone of the message changes from the beginning to the end.

All collection messages should include a statement of the amount due and the due date.

Early-Stage Collection Messages

The first step in the collection series is the statement, usually a monthly statement, of the amount due.

Reminders may be additional statements with a stamped notation that the bill is past due. Instead of a second or a third statement, the reminder or reminders may be short, simple requests presented as form letters, printed notes, or, occasionally, greeting cards.

Letters, if used in the early part of the collection series, are quite obviously form letters and are based on the assumption that the obligation has been overlooked. These form letters, as well as any other follow-up reminder messages, are purposely impersonal and routine. This approach is the opposite of what is considered the best approach in many other forms of communications. Used in the early stages of collection, they imply something to this effect:

> Look, we realize that you have merely overlooked this obligation, as you have been prompt in making past payments. But you understand that of course we must remind you, as we do all other customers, when your check does not arrive on time. Your notice that comes in this form letter (or greeting card, stamped message, note, etc.) is the same one that we send to everyone. We still like you.

Yes, it is quite a feat to imply all the ideas and attitudes in the preceding paragraph with only the words "just a gentle reminder" or "did you forget?" But, in effect, that is what you are doing in a well-planned reminder message early in the collection series.

In reminder messages we may use humor if we do so with discretion. As in all communication, we must be extremely careful when using a humorous approach because it can very easily appear to be sarcasm.

Resale and *sales promotion* are also used in reminder messages. You have previously learned that resale and sales promotion can be used to soften a message, as in refusal letters. You are using these passages for the same purpose early in the collection series, as well as for the obvious purpose of promoting sales.

Because of the softening effect, however, we most certainly would not use resale, sales promotion, humor, or any similar approach in the late stage of the collection series. At that time we don't want to soften the approach. We want to emphasize the urgency of the situation and insist that the bill be paid immediately.

A reminder to a customer with a good credit rating, owing a relatively small amount, is shown in Figure 10–5.

Middle-Stage Collection Messages

The use of humor, resale, and sales promotion may or may not be appropriate for the middle stages of the collection series, depending on the type of merchandise sold, the customer, the particular credit policies of the company, and other considerations.

These approaches soften the urgency of the message. Whether or not they should be included depends on what tone is most appropriate and effective. If you use several messages in the middle stage of the collection series, humor, resale, and sales promotion are more appropriate for the first letters than for later ones.

Be careful with the use of humor in all collection messages. Although we are not always required to be deadly serious, a light touch indicates that the writer is not really concerned—so why should the debtor be concerned?

In the middle stage, we may begin with an inquiry directed toward the applicant (although the letter may not be individually written or dictated), followed by a letter or letters built around an appeal of some kind. In these letters we bring into use a central theme similar to the central selling theme of sales letters. Figure 10–6 illustrates a theme: a good credit rating. Figure 10–7 implies a possible loss of customers.

Messages throughout the series should become increasingly forceful, but "forceful" does not mean that the letters should be rude, sarcastic, demanding, or impolite. We should always refrain from using this tone, regardless of the length of the series. Choose a courteous approach not only from the standpoint of consideration for the reader but also because this approach is more likely to be effective in collecting.

Remember the two main purposes of collection letters: *to get the money and to maintain goodwill.* In addition to maintaining goodwill, a courteous tone is also more likely to result in the collection of the overdue amount. In middle-stage messages, the assumption is no longer that of the reminder stage, that is, that the account has merely been overlooked.

An inquiry attempts to obtain a response from the reader. Perhaps the customer is dissatisfied with the merchandise, or perhaps because of unexpected financial difficulties the person cannot pay. We should not, however, state these things in our letter to customers or make excuses for the readers.

Late-Stage Collection Messages

Late-stage collection efforts are often in the form of telephone calls, telegrams, or even personal visits. They may also consist of letters.

Regardless of the collection methods, attempts at collecting long-overdue accounts state specifically when the amount must be paid and what action will be taken if it is not paid. The writer should not mention a lawsuit if there is actually no possibility of a suit. A late-stage message is illustrated in Figure 10–8.

NEWBURG HOSPITAL
Coastal Highway
Newburg, SC 29209

November 17, 19--

Mrs. Robert Shaw   Account: # 0000000
1223 Plantation Estates   Patient Name: Saundra
Newburg, SC 29207   Date of Service: 8/17/--
                                    Guest Balance Due: $85

Dear Mrs. Shaw:

Thank you for the opportunity to serve you as a patient. We
appreciate the confidence you have shown in us by choosing
Newburg Hospital.

While reviewing our accounts, we found that the account referred
to above remains unpaid. As this may be an oversight on your
part, we have mailed this reminder.

Please send your payment for the amount shown as GUEST
BALANCE DUE within the next ten days. If paying by mail, please
write your Guest Account Number on your check or money order.
If you prefer, you may pay by credit card by supplying your
credit card number and expiration date on the attached form.
Please indicate the type of card you are using. We accept
MasterCard, VISA, American Express, and Healthline.

If payment has been made since the date of this reminder, please
accept our thanks.

Sincerely yours,

Laura Winfrey

Your Guest Representative

FIGURE 10–5
Reminder (longer than usual reminders; courteous and sales oriented)

December 7, 19--

Mr. Donald Morgan, C.P.A.
1359 Second Street
Philadelphia, PA 19104

Dear Mr. Morgan:

Attention, reader interest

When you started your business, a good credit rating made it possible for you to benefit from credit purchases.

I'm sure you want to protect your good credit rating so that you can continue to receive equipment and supplies by the convenient credit plans you have enjoyed in the past.

Conviction

Quality Office Products has continued to honor this privilege because you have always settled your accounts satisfactorily. At the present time, however, your account is five months past due. Invoice #97231, which covers a shipment of five calculators for a total of $813.75, remains unpaid.

Action

To preserve your good credit rating, send your check for $813.75. A stamped, addressed envelope is enclosed for your convenience in making immediate payment.

Sincerely,

Margaret Rose

Margaret Rose
Credit Manager

pw
enclosure

Quality Office Products

4646 Poplar Avenue   Philadelphia, PA 19043   215 243-5123

FIGURE 10–6
A letter of appeal for payment, based on retaining credit rating

September 20, 19--

Mr. John Johnson
Johnson's Steak House
5555 Poplar
Memphis, TN 38111

Dear. Mr. Johnson:

This copy of the "Kiss Me Kate" program includes your attractive, full-page advertisement on page 3. The program has been passed out to 5,600 theater-goers in the first two weeks of our production. Seven more performances are scheduled.

Attention

Many of our members have commented favorably on your new "after-the-theater dinner" promoted in the program copy you furnished us. Your location near the theater makes our audience a select group of prospective customers for your restaurant.

The programs for our next show are being prepared for the printer, and we're sure you will want your advertisement in them and in all programs for our current productions, as we agreed in your contract last June.

Conviction

Just send your check for the $200 balance due in the enclosed, addressed envelope, or drop the payment by the theater, and your program copy will be in for the entire season.

Action

Sincerely,

THEATRE MEMPHIS

Karen J. English

Karen J. English
Advertising Chairman

FIGURE 10–7
A letter of appeal. The central theme is the possible loss of customers.

June 13, 19--

Mr. Jonathan Wiley, Owner
Wiley Wholesale Foods
3211 Liberty Avenue
Franklin, PA 19019

IMMEDIATE PAYMENT REQUIRED

Your account of $4,012 is long overdue. Your office furniture was
purchased on November 19 of last year.

Please telephone me immediately at 000-0000 in order to arrange
payment and thus protect your credit rating.

This is your last notice from this office.

Harold Bowman

Harold Bowman
Credit Manager

━━━━━ **Quality Office Products** ━━━━━

4646 Poplar Avenue   Philadelphia, PA 19043   215 243-5123

FIGURE 10–8
Late-stage collection
letter

Summary

Effective sales messages convince the reader or listener that the suggested purchase will meet the particular need of a specific individual and that the purchase
will be more valuable than the necessary cost or effort to acquire the product
or service.

The customer must be convinced to believe that the companies manufacturing and selling the product are trustworthy and reliable. The customer must
also believe in the salesperson or salespersons who present the product, service,
or idea.

A well-chosen mailing list can make selling by mail a specialized and economical approach, as messages should be sent only to persons who are likely
to have an interest in the offered product or service.

Often the most economical way to obtain a mailing list is to purchase it
from an organization that specializes in preparing and selling mailing lists, or
in leasing these lists.

The feature most likely to convince the prospective buyer that the product
or service best meets the individual's particular needs is called *the central selling point*.

In order to determine the most effective central selling point, the seller must analyze the product or service and the possible needs of the prospective buyer. Once the central selling point is chosen, the sales letter is built around a theme that presents the central selling point.

Special characteristics of most sales letters are these:

1. An overall informal approach.
2. Special emphasis on descriptive, vivid, forceful words and phrases.
3. Special emphasis on the you-approach, especially from the standpoint of presenting the prospective purchase in terms of reader benefit.
4. Increased use of the mechanical means of emphasis.

A pattern of arrangement long used in planning sales letters is that of attention, interest, desire, and action.

The writer must present detailed, specific, convincing evidence in terms of the reader's interests.

Solicited sales messages are planned and written in much the same way as unsolicited ones, except that less emphasis is given to obtaining the attention of the reader. The reader is already interested in the product or service, as shown by the preceding inquiry.

Persuasive requests are treated basically as sales letters.

Granting and using credit is a necessary and valuable business activity. Credit is beneficial to both the lender and the debtor, but it must be used wisely. Well-planned and well-administered credit policies and procedures are an important aspect of profitable business management.

Letters about credit—credit inquiries and replies, credit approvals with specific information, and necessary credit refusals—decrease the number of collection letters.

Collection messages can be divided into those that come in the early, middle, or late stages of the collection series. Although the tone of the message becomes more forceful from the beginning of the series to the end, the writer should never resort to threats, rudeness, or sarcasm.

Test Yourself: Chapter Review

1–2. Name one advantage and one disadvantage of buying by mail.

3. What is meant by a *central selling point?*

4–5. What is an advantage of a central selling point? A possible disadvantage?

6–7. What are two important steps that come before the choice of a central selling point?

8–11. What are four characteristics that distinguish many sales letters from other kinds of business letters?

12–15. What are the four steps of the long-used "pattern" for a sales letter?

Which of each pair is the better choice for a sales letter?

16. (Paragraph fairly near the end of a sales letter)
   a. The cost is $250, which is not expensive for this quality product that saves electricity.
   b. For $250, a one-time expense, you will reduce electricity costs for as long as you own your house.

17. (Letter to sell a magazine about to be published)
    a. If you want to subscribe to this magazine, just drop us a note.
    b. To reserve your premier issue of *Southpoint,* just place the token into the slot in the red card and mail it in the postcard reply envelope.

18. (Opening paragraph of a letter that accompanies a catalog that specializes in "down home" products)
    a. We are proud of our new catalog of old-timey products; we look forward to your order.
    b. How long has it been since you've seen a cigar-store Indian, a surrey with a fringe on top, or a hitching post on Main Street?

19. (From a catalog description of a printed velvet jacket)
    a. This velvet jacket is lovely because of the many jewel-like colors and its soft texture.
    b. Where there is music in the air and the anticipation of a happy evening, wear seven sparkling jewel colors in this luscious velvet jacket.

20. a. This desk is 60 inches long and 40 inches wide.
    b. This spacious desk, 60 inches long and 40 inches wide, provides plenty of room for you to spread out your work.

21. a. This car is economical to operate.
    b. According to tests conducted by *Consumer Reports,* this particular model averages 24 miles to the gallon in city driving. How will you use the extra time and money you save?

22. a. This investment plan is profitable and safe.
    b. You will earn 9.5% interest, compounded quarterly, by investing in these bonds. The principal and interest are insured until maturity.

23. a. Do you want the grass to be greener on your side of the fence?
    b. Are you ashamed that your neighbor's yard always looks better than yours?

24. (From a television commercial for a furniture store)
    a. Hurry, hurry, hurry down to the Smith Store, save hundreds, thousands, in our going-out-of-business sale! (The same kind of sale the store held last year.)
    b. The fine traditional furniture you have admired all year is now waiting for you—at savings up to 40 percent during our August sale.

Test Yourself: Correct Usage

(Related to material in Chapter 10 and principles of correct usage). Insert necessary punctuation, including quotation marks, hyphens, and apostrophes, and remove punctuation that has been inserted incorrectly. Choose correct word or sentence from each pair or group. Make any other necessary changes.

1. You do not convince a reader to buy with vague generalities. But with specific facts presented in terms of reader interest.

2. Sales letters have many advantages, for example you can present your product to a specific group of potential customers.

3. Having several disadvantages, one of which is that people call them "junk mail.

4. Because you can mail sales letters to specific groups of potential customers provided you have accurate mailing lists you can vary the central selling point for each different group.

5. Some sales letters use low price as the central selling point in such letters the price is emphasized not subordinated.

6. A central selling point is the (principal, principle) feature of a product that is most likely to appeal to the greatest number of buyers.

7. We must give specific objective details about the product we are attempting to sell.

8. Be sure that the reader or readers' (understand, understands) the necessary action and how it is to be accomplished.

9. If an individuals name is inserted into a previously prepared letter the name should be shown in the same type as the letter itself.

10. Buying by mail has several advantages one of which is (convenience, convenince).

Cases

1. a. Choose a product, real or imaginary, that you believe could be sold successfully by direct mail. Briefly describe this product.

   b. Briefly describe your mailing list.

   c. What will you use as your central selling point? Why? (Do not use price as the central selling point in this problem.)

   d. Write an attention-getting beginning for your letter. This beginning should be related to your central selling point.

   e. Write a sentence or longer passage that illustrates the use of *psychological description* as the term is used in this chapter. This portion of a sales letter, which describes concretely some feature of the product and also shows the reader benefiting from this feature, may or may not be related to your central selling point. (Almost all products or services have features in addition to the central selling point that should be described.)

   f. Write a sentence or longer passage that subordinates the stated price.

   g. Write an action close that refers in some way to the central selling point.

2. Look at several advertisements of approximate full-page length in magazines and newspapers. Analyze these advertisements according to these points:

   a. Is the advertisement built around a central selling point? If so, what is it? Is this theme carried from the beginning of the advertisement to the end? Do you feel that the feature chosen as the central selling point is an appropriate one? Why or why not? Can you think of another feature of the product or service that could be used as a central selling point? Is it also stressed in the advertisement?

   b. Is the product or service described in terms of actual reader benefit? Give examples.

   c. Is humor used in the advertisement?

   d. Would this advertisement make you buy the product, provided it is something you need, want, and can afford?

3. Analyze a number of sales letters as you did the advertisements in the preceding problem. In addition to the factors considered for the advertisement, evaluate the letters from these standpoints:

   a. Did the writer make effective use of the mechanical means of emphasis, such as special arrangements, color, unusual spacing, all capitals, or underlining?

   b. Is the attention-getting beginning effective? Does it illustrate one of the characteristics of securing attention illustrated in this chapter? Is a theme built around a central selling point used in the attention-getting section of the letter?

   c. Does the action close specify action in terms of reader benefit, make action easy, and motivate prompt action? Does the action close include a reference to the central selling point?

   d. Does the letter answer all questions that might logically occur to the reader?

   e. Would this letter sell the product or service to you? Why or why not?

4. Using the information given in one of the advertisements you analyzed, or in a similar advertisement, construct a direct-sales letter. Choose your advertisement with care; make sure that your product is one that could effectively be sold by mail. If the advertisement does not include all the information that your reader will need, assume reasonable details.

5. Using the information given in an advertisement, construct a sales letter to be sent to retailers. Assume names, addresses, and any needed explanation or details.

6. Look at the advertisements for this year's new cars. Pick the ones you would most like to buy. Assume that you are selling this car. Write a sales letter to persons who are likely to be good prospects. Ask them to come to the showroom for a demonstration. You will need to know a great deal about the automobile in order to make your letter convincing. It should do a great deal more than ask the potential customers to come in to look. You must offer proof

in your letter that the automobile is the one they should buy.

7. Follow the instructions given in the preceding problem except that you will choose some product other than an automobile—for example, a motorcycle, camera, sailboat, or any other item you would like to buy. Investigate the features of this product, as well as the features of competing products. Write a sales letter to persons who seem to be good prospects. (You may use a direct-sales letter or a sales promotion letter of some kind, depending on your chosen product.)

8. Write a direct-sales letter, to persons similar to yourself, about one of your favorite possessions that sells for no more than $50. Choose an object that could be effectively sold by mail. Consider the reasons you particularly like this product; its weakness, if any; and the approach that is most likely to sell the same product to other people.

9. You own a taxicab company in your city. You have begun a desk-to-desk scheduled package delivery shuttle between three leading business centers—the airport, downtown, and Easthaven (or use the names of three actual business districts in your city). Your shuttle includes these features:

- Customer can telephone before 9:30 A.M. for delivery to one or both of the other centers by noon. If customer calls by 2:30 P.M., delivery can be made by 5:00 P.M.
- Rates are $6 for total deliveries to the same address and up to 25 pounds. For customers who sign up for everyday service, the rate is reduced by 20 percent. (This regular service is known as the "Yellow Shuttle.")
- The *Yellow Rush* service, with higher rates, will deliver to any point within the city in no more than an hour, except for unforeseen emergencies.

  You ask the reader to telephone you or, if someone else in the company is in charge of package deliveries, to pass the letter along.

10. You are the general manager of an old hotel, the Arlington, in Hot Springs, Arkansas. Hot Springs is a popular resort town known for its scenery, pottery shops, spas, art galleries, and horse racing. The hotel has been completely refurbished.

    You read announcements of engagements in newspapers of cities in Arkansas and surrounding states. You are to prepare a letter to be sent to each bride and bridegroom asking them to spend their honeymoon in the Arlington. (How will you address the letter?) Write the contents of the letter, which will be duplicated for each individual couple by

a microcomputer equipped with word processing software.

Some of the features of the hotel are shown in the following list:

Spacious honeymoon suites (two) with a magnificent view

Lovely dining room, two à la carte menus. Magnificent breakfast buffet and Sunday brunch

Lounge located on the rooftop

Fresh flowers and a bottle of chilled champagne for the honeymoon couple

Lovely pool

Horseback riding

Beautiful landscaped grounds

Horse-drawn surrey available for a romantic ride through the winding streets of historic Hot Springs

Rates for honeymoon suites $100 to $175 a day

Other rooms from $60 to $80 a day

11. You are the manager of a tax consulting firm in your city. (Give it a name.) Realizing that the recent changes in the tax laws will cause many individual taxpayers who fill out their own returns to make costly mistakes, you write a sales letter to increase your clients in the middle-income group.

    The basic philosophy of your tax consulting service is client satisfaction through able assistance by capable, honest, and courteous tax consultants. By knowing the new tax laws and how they affect your clients, you can save them both time and money. You provide the clients with economical help in the preparation of their income tax returns, confidentiality, year-round income tax service, and audit assistance. Fees are based solely on the complexity of the return. The average fee last year was $100 for each tax return. Your fee entitles the client to assistance with tax estimates, audits, and tax questions. Write the letter.

12. Bring a product to class. Give a three-minute sales presentation about this product. As your instructor directs, record this message.

13. Write a 30-second television or radio commercial for any product or service, real or imaginary. Do not modify existing commercials unless your modification is truly original. If you have access to a tape recorder, record your message. (If you prefer, write a one-minute commercial.)

14. Form into committees of five or six. Elect a sales manager for each group. Think of a new product or service to be put on the market. Analyze your product or service as to its strengths and weaknesses, especially as to how it compares with similar products or services. Is your product or service one that can be

effectively sold or promoted by mail? Should you use direct-sales messages, or should the product be sold through retail outlets? Who will be your most likely prospects? How will you determine your mailing list? What will be the central theme of your message? As your instructor directs, hold sales meetings to answer the preceding questions and others that occur to you.

15. Write an appropriate sales message for the product or service studied in the preceding problem.

16. You are an associate and the director of marketing for Magic Mountain, Inc., a recently created ski resort in the Swiss Alps.

   People come from three nearby cities on weekends the year round, but particularly during the ski season. Magic Mountain has attracted tourists from France and Germany; occasionally, people come from England and Italy. But it is only during the Christmas holiday and February ski vacation that the village becomes international.

   The summer is slower, but still profitable. The Olympic-sized swimming pool and the tennis courts offer a good alternative for people tired of the crowded beaches on the French Riviera.

   However, can Magic Mountain break even with only six profitable months out of twelve? Most businesses close for the spring and fall. Business owners know that the season lasts only six months, and they expect to generate as much profit in those six months as a normal operation would in a year.

   Part A. You are thinking of developing vacation packages to be sold by travel agencies and tour companies in the United States, offering special rates in your hotels, one-half of winter rates. Compose a letter to be duplicated and sent to organizations in the United States and elsewhere; these organizations will in turn sell Magic Mountain. What will you say in your letter? What is the status of the U.S. dollar at this time, compared to currency in Switzerland? Why would you want to go to a luxurious resort in the Swiss Alps in the spring or fall? Complete any necessary research.

   Part B. Assume that your plan is accepted, and that you are asked to write sales letters to be sent to prospective visitors. Consider the groups to whom you will address the letters; perhaps a different message should be sent to each group; for example, retirees, students, teachers, yuppies, members of professional groups.

17. You are the owner of a small security systems company. You decide to write to recent victims of burglaries that are reported in the newspapers. Members of the police department have issued a public statement that homes that have been burglarized once are more likely to be burglarized again than are other homes.

   You are to prepare a sales letter to be mailed to these prospects. Your system includes the following features:

   Heat-detection feature that contacts the fire department when a certain level of heat is detected

   Forced-entry detection that contacts the police department

   All windows and doors protected

   Medical-alert button that calls ambulance with directions to your residence

   Low installation fee that varies with size of home protected but averages about $300. This fee may be paid on an installment plan.

   Maintenance fee of $35 monthly

   Meets all requirements of insurance companies that allow a reduced rate for protected homes

Persuasive Requests

18. As Dean of the College of Business Administration (your college), you are interested in persuading several of the leading businessmen and businesswomen in your city to give informal speeches at the university. One man in particular, Mr. Sam Smith, Jr., is president of one of the largest cotton brokerage firms in the United States.

   You know that Mr. Smith graduated from your college. You also know that he is an extremely busy man. His contribution as an entrepreneur would be especially valuable to the students, as the college presently does not offer courses in the commodities exchange market. You will not be able to pay him for his time. You want him to share his experiences, problems, and rewards in building his own business. Ask him to speak to your school. Any week night during the month of March will be satisfactory.

19. Write a fund-raising letter for your church or for your civic or professional organization.

20. You have been appointed chairperson of a local "Stop Smoking" committee. Write a letter to be published as an advertisement in the local newspaper.

21. Write a letter to secure new members for the Society for the Advancement of Management, or for a similar professional organization. Obtain the information you will need in order to write a convincing letter.

22. You are the assistant director of Elite Agency, a firm that specializes in providing assertiveness training for organizations, as well as teaching organizational interpersonal communication skills and effective public speaking.

   Several months ago Gregory Lane, director of Elite,

asked you to speak at the annual banquet of "Up and Coming," a nonprofit organization that provides job training services and seminars on interview techniques and resume writing to underprivileged adults. Ann Prescott, director of "Up and Coming," specifically requested you to speak. You feel that the publicity from the event will help Elite because some graduates of "Up and Coming" later go to work for your company's clients. Even more important, you believe that the organization contributes worthwhile service to the community.

Part A. Now Mr. Lane insists that you go to an out-of-town conference instead. The conference, which would cost Elite more than $900 for your expenses, is quite similar to one you attended last year; you feel that the "Up and Coming" banquet is more important. How will you convince Mr. Lane that you should speak at the "Up and Coming" banquet instead of attending the conference? Make notes about what you will say.

Part B. Assume that Mr. Lane asks you to put your remarks into a memorandum to him (he has made such requests before) so that he can evaluate your request. Write the memorandum.

Part C. Assume that Mr. Lane still insists that you attend the conference. Write a letter to Ann Prescott offering to prepare a videocassette (of yourself speaking) to be shown as part of the banquet program. You will prepare the cassette in the length she prefers.

Collection Messages

23. The Raleigh office of Tax Consultants, Inc., has been unable to collect from Mr. Fred Dangerfeld. He operates a hammer-handle manufacturing business in his garage. Every year for the past ten years Tax Consultants, Inc., has prepared the income tax return for his small business. This year his return was prepared in January. Since his return was more complex than in prior years, Tax Consultants, Inc., billed Mr. Dangerfeld $285 for tax consulting services. Thirty days later you (the manager) sent a duplicate of the original bill with a reminder.

Since your reminder failed to bring in the money, after another thirty days you sent your first collection letter to him. Mr. Dangerfeld has always paid promptly in the past; you are surprised that your reminder letter did not convince him to pay his bill. Now, thirty days later, you will write a second letter. What should be your approach? Write a convincing letter.

24. Thirty additional days have elapsed, and still no answer from Mr. Dangerfeld. You try to telephone but cannot get an answer. Write a letter. What will you say?

25. Thirty more days go by. You have telephoned twice, and someone has said that he was unable to come to the phone. Write a letter.

26. You are the credit manager for an appliance store. Mrs. Felix Jones has always been a good customer of yours. She has bought several major appliances from you, as well as small ones occasionally. This is the first time that you have had any difficulty collecting from her. You have already written her once when she missed her first payment because you were sure it was just an oversight on her part. This brought no response. She has missed another payment. You feel you must remind her again and insist on payment. You do not want to lose the goodwill that has built up, but you feel that something is wrong when she misses two payments in succession. Write her a letter attempting to work something out with her and request payment.

27. You are the credit manager of an agricultural chemical company. John Travis, a plantation owner, bought fertilizer for $10,084 in March. He has been buying on open account for more than twenty years. He has always paid in full, but only after one or two collection letters.

At the end of March you mailed him a regular monthly statement but received no reply. At the end of April, you mailed another statement with a past-due notation. At the end of May, you wrote a letter asking for the full amount due; you did not receive an answer. You wrote a stronger letter at the end of June but received no reply. You send a representative to the plantation to see him. The representative is told by the farm manager that Mr. Travis has been in Europe but is expected to return on July 15.

It is now July 20. Write to Mr. Travis. What should be your approach at this time?

28. You are the owner-manager of a local dance studio. The three daughters of Dr. and Mrs. Frank Williams have been taking dancing lessons for three years. Write a collection letter to Mrs. Williams, who has always paid for the children's lessons promptly. Now the bill is three months past due. Lessons for the girls cost $240 a month. You are on friendly terms with Mrs. Williams. The girls are excellent students, and you don't want to lose them. A reminder note and a note of inquiry have already gone unheeded. The annual dance recital is coming up next month, with extra expense for yourself and the parents of the young dancers. A newsletter was sent to Mrs. Williams at the beginning of the year explaining that the tuition payments are due at the beginning of each month. You have tried to telephone but receive only recorded messages; your calls have not been returned. The girls still come to lessons regularly, delivered and picked

up by Mrs. Williams' household helper. You last talked with Mrs. Williams in December, more than four months ago, at a meeting of all parents to discuss the annual recital. If this letter obtains no response, what will you do?

Write Your Own Assignments and Solutions

29. Write your OWN problem with a solution, for a direct mail sales letter or a persuasive request, as directed for the kinds of communications described in Chapters 6, 8, and 9. Give all the information that another writer would need to write a letter, memorandum, or other material as a solution to your problem. As with previous assignments for Chapters 6, 8, and 9, this approach provides practice in describing a situation and giving instructions as well as in writing sales material and persuasive requests.

Evaluation Sheet: Sales Letters and Persuasive Requests

	Yes	No	Not Sure
1. Does the letter open with an effective attention-getting paragraph or section?	___	___	___
2. Is the letter built around an appropriate central selling point?	___	___	___
3. Is the you-approach used throughout?	___	___	___
4. Is the positive approach used throughout?	___	___	___
5. Is the product or service presented in terms of reader benefit?	___	___	___
6. Is the product or service presented specifically, vividly, and correctly?	___	___	___
7. Is format used to aid readability and attract and hold attention?	___	___	___
8. Is all necessary information presented in an easy-to-read form?	___	___	___
9. Is the letter convincing?	___	___	___
10. Is the letter interesting?	___	___	___
11. Is the price subordinated and presented along with reader benefit? (It should not be subordinated if price is central selling point, but ordinarily it won't be.)	___	___	___
12. Does the action close specify action, make action easy, and, if appropriate, motivate prompt action?	___	___	___
13. Does the letter omit such trite phrases as "Act now" and "Don't delay"?	___	___	___
14. Is the letter sincere?	___	___	___
15. Is the letter completely free of misrepresentation?	___	___	___
16. Is the letter correct in every way?	___	___	___

CHAPTER 11

Planning the Search
for Career Employment

Chapters 11 and 12 are planned to help you communicate effectively in order to secure employment. Chapter 11 emphasizes the research phase of the job-seeking process and the preparation of a resume. (An alternate spelling is résumé.) Chapter 12 presents the application letter and other letters about employment, plus a discussion of the employment interview.

An outstanding letter of application, submitted with a well-organized, attractive, and convincing resume, can be the deciding factor in securing the kind of employment you are seeking. Although no written presentation alone will get a job for you, it can provide an interview, at which time you continue the process of convincing the interviewer that you are the best possible choice for the position.

What matters most in the search for employment is the ability to handle the job. The most creative, attractive, and appropriate letter and resume will not substitute for a lack of skill or experience, just as a cleverly worded sales letter will not create sales on a continuing basis unless a truly good product backs up the letter.

The terms resume *and* data sheet *are usually used interchangeably. The word* resume, *which is used in these chapters, means the same as the term* data sheet *that you may have seen or heard elsewhere.*

Regardless of your outstanding qualifications or of a favorable job market, you should take the initiative in your job search instead of waiting for an employer to offer a position or to advertise one. *Taking the initiative has several advantages.*

You become aware of differing opportunities and are able to compare prospective employers and employment opportunities. You are more likely to find a better job when you actively seek one because you learn about more openings. You are better able to consider your particular strengths in relation to the needs of differing employing organizations.

Another obvious advantage is that your initiative and dedication in looking for a job tell the employer a great deal about you, including the fact that you have enough energy and ambition to plan and conduct a thorough, organized campaign to place yourself. The quality of your work after being hired, with resulting opportunities for advancement to a higher position, is likely to be similar to your efforts in finding and obtaining the job.

In addition, as you survey employing organizations, you will no doubt find one or more in which you are especially interested. Your special interest in a particular organization, which will be apparent in your written application and interview, elicits a positive response from the employer. An applicant who very much wants a job with a particular organization has a definite advantage over an equally qualified applicant who just wants a job—anywhere.

Solicited Application Letters and Resumes

A solicited application is written in reply to advertisements, announcements, or other requests for applicants. Ordinarily, you should use the two-part application, a letter and a resume, for both solicited and unsolicited applications.

You may find advertisements in your local newspaper for career employment in your chosen field. Another place to find announcements of openings in a specialized field is professional journals, although these openings may require moving to another part of the country. Many advertisements, particularly for executives and engineers, appear in *The Wall Street Journal* and the *National Business Employment Weekly*.

Writing a solicited application letter differs little from writing a solicited sales letter—that is, an answer to a request for information about a product or service. You must convince the reader that the product you are selling—yourself—is the one that should be selected. As in your sales messages, you convince your reader by specific evidence, not by a high-pressure approach.

Build the opening section and all remaining sections of the application letter and resume around a central selling point. The central theme, based on the central selling point, tells how your most important qualification, or perhaps a group of related qualifications, can benefit the particular employing organization. *Emphasize the strength or strengths that you believe will be more applicable to the position for which you are applying, and include other positive points as well. The employer looks at your entire background, personality, ability, attitude, and potential value to the organization.*

Unsolicited Application Letters and Resumes

Unsolicited applications can be considered a form of direct-mail advertising, similar to messages planned for direct-mail campaigns to sell a product or service.

Prepare a mailing list of organizations for which you would like to work. This list should consist of names of organizations along with names, titles, and addresses of people responsible for receiving and reviewing applications. Instead of sending your application to a personnel department, try to find the name of the individual, such as a department head or the manager of an office or division, who would be responsible for hiring you.

Make absolutely certain that the addressee's name is spelled correctly and that his or her title is correct. A telephone call to the organization will provide this information. Preparing your mailing list will require that you do a great deal of research in order to select the organizations and individuals to receive your application.

You are not likely to receive favorable replies from all the applications you mail. Depending on current employment conditions in your area of specialization and on your background and qualifications, you may receive a request for an interview or for further information from only a small percentage of your total list.

Ordinarily, you should send the two-part application, consisting of a letter and resume, as a unit. Some applicants, however, send only a letter and offer to send a complete resume on request. If you decide to use only the letter,

A personnel manager reads stacks of application letters and resumes. Numerous applications are received for advertised positions, a reason that unsolicited applications may be a better approach.

include enough convincing, specific details to make the reader want to know more about you. All resumes shown in this chapter are intended to be sent with the application letters illustrated in Chapter 12.

Each letter you send should be individually typewritten or prepared on a word processor. To do otherwise is to suggest that the letter is only one of many, that you are looking only for a job, any job, and that you are not especially interested in the organization to which the letter is addressed.

Resumes are often printed or reproduced by some process, such as photocopying, that results in attractive copies difficult to distinguish from individually typewritten or word-processed material.

Analyzing Your Qualifications

When you plan a sales campaign, one of your first steps is to make a product analysis. You look at the product, test it, and compare it with competing brands. You then decide on your central theme, or the most important selling feature, also called *the central selling point.*

As you plan a job-seeking campaign, you make this same analysis about yourself. You analyze the "product," compare it with competing ones, and note how the product fits the market for which you are preparing your application. Although this analysis is for your use only, it will be far more beneficial and complete if it is in written form.

You will have several features to stress, but the main theme of your presentation will depend on the kind of work for which you are applying, as well as on the type of organization. Because the emphasis will differ according to these considerations, an individually tailored application letter, as well as an individually planned resume, is more likely to be effective than the same two-part application sent to organizations with varying needs.

Because you will not always be sure of the varying needs of each organiza-

*Communication
Brief*

If one were to take a closer look at what an accountant does for a living, one would find that an effective CPA spends a considerable amount of time using effective communication skills. Not only does a CPA need to develop suitable interpersonal skills in order to work effectively with co-workers and clients, but a CPA must have sufficient written communication skills as well in order, among other things, to complete reports, letters and memoranda, to interpret rules and regulations and to select appropriate titles for accounts so that similarities and differences are apparent for accounting systems users and auditors.

George Costouros and James B. Stull, "Oxen, Tallies, Whips, and Daggers: Why Accountants Invented the Alphabet," in *Proceedings, 51st ABC International Convention* (Los Angeles: Association for Business Communication, 1986), 194.

tion, you will not always be correct in your choice of the central selling point. Usually the central selling feature will be either your education or your experience. *For most persons completing a college degree, especially young college graduates with limited experience, the central selling point is some facet of the educational background, ordinarily the major field.*

After you have been out of school for several years, your experience is likely to become the most important selling feature if it is similar to the kind of work for which you are making application. If you have diversified experience, emphasize successful experience in a job similar to the one being sought.

In certain instances, extracurricular work or an avocation will be the most convincing central theme. For example, a football star may be hired as a sporting goods salesman; in this case, the football experience is of more value than is the student's major in, for example, journalism. If the same student were applying for a job as a newspaper reporter, the application should be built around the academic major. The football experience should be mentioned but given only limited coverage.

As when selling a product, do not stress the central selling point so much that you omit or overly subordinate your other selling features. You cannot be completely sure that you are choosing the most logical central selling point. In addition, you are likely to be hired on the basis of overall qualifications, consisting of education, experience, personality, attitude toward work, and the ability to grow and develop in usefulness to the employing organization.

As you analyze yourself, you will no doubt find that you have weak and strong points. As you present yourself to prospective employers, stress strong points; subordinate or leave unmentioned those that you consider to be weaknesses. *Never misrepresent in any way.* The positive approach, as in other communications situations, "accentuates the positive and eliminates the negative." You can often present in positive terms what you consider to be a weakness. For example, instead of saying, "I have no experience except for part-time work in a grocery," say

My four years of experience as a checker and office employee with A&P Grocery Company were valuable because they gave me experience in working harmoniously with other employees and in courteously serving the customers. I worked an average of twenty-five hours a week during the entire four years of attending college, yet maintained a grade point average of 3.2, a score that qualified me each semester for the Dean's list.

Other examples of points to emphasize and subordinate will be given later in this chapter as you learn to prepare the application letter and resume.

Education

If you are completing college, education to be considered in your self-analysis consists especially of work leading toward a degree. Other educational preparation consists of high school subjects, technical or business courses, and other specialized schooling, as well as educational experience obtained in military service. Consider courses that apply to the job you are seeking, including those within your major field and any others that especially relate.

Consider your scholastic standing overall and in your major field. Whether or not you mention your scholastic standing depends on what it is. According to the principle of the positive approach, you are not obligated to emphasize a negative aspect. If your average is just enough to obtain a degree or very slightly above, emphasize the degree and omit the actual grade-point average.

The degree is a real accomplishment, even if other persons have surpassed you in A's and B's. But if you are asked for your exact standing, be truthful. By being truthful, according to an old adage, you are not forced to remember what you said. *Some organizations immediately disqualify any applicant who is discovered to have misrepresented even the slightest bit of information.*

You may wish to give your grade point average only in your major field, not the overall average, as the standing in your major field is likely to be higher. This performance in your major field should be of most concern to the employer. In some resumes you should mention research projects or papers that are particularly relevant. After you have completed graduate work, mention of a thesis or dissertation is considered an essential part of your application.

Include specific skills and abilities developed in your education program, such as ability to work with computers or other office equipment, especially if you are likely to use this equipment in your future work. If you have used these machines in previous employment, mention this ability in the section on experience. If you have not actually used them but have had training in their use, mention your ability in the educational section of your resume.

As you complete the analysis of your educational preparation, you will probably find that it should be your central selling feature. From the standpoint of emphasis, as you have already learned, this preparation, in terms of how it will benefit the reader, should be described in more detail than other features, and it should be presented before less important information.

Work Experience

Work experience is ordinarily one of the two most important elements of career preparation, although some college students complete degrees with no work experience whatsoever. If you have no work experience, you should particularly stress your educational preparation. You should also show how participation in professional and social organizations gave you experience in leadership positions and in working with other people.

Some applicants have the idea that only related work experience should be mentioned in the application letter or on the resume. This approach is unwise. Work experience of any kind, including volunteer work, as long as it is legal and honorable, is better than no experience at all. Any work, even the most menial, indicates that you have the energy and initiative to seek and hold a job.

Remember to include experience acquired in military service, which could be your most important and relevant experience and the central theme of your entire application. As you continue with your self-analysis, make a note of all special accomplishments, such as exceeding a sales quota, earning a promotion, or receiving certificates of recognition for unusual achievement.

Activities, Achievements, and Personal Characteristics

In this portion of your analysis, list extracurricular activities; social and professional organizations, including membership and offices held; and any other meaningful activity or accomplishment. Include honors, awards, publications, and other recognitions. (Scholastic awards are usually mentioned with your other educational achievements.) Foreign language abilities, hobbies, personal business ventures, and many other facets of your total experience may have a bearing on your ability to fit into the particular organization to which you are applying.

Check yourself in these and similar areas:

Ability and willingness to assume responsibility

Ability to adapt to changing situations

Ability to communicate in oral and written form

Leadership

Judgment

Self-confidence and poise

Appearance

Sense of humor

Neatness

Ability to make decisions

Ability to persevere

Ability to think logically and creatively

Ability and desire to work with other people

Ability to work alone

Courtesy and diplomacy

Emotional and physical health

Maturity

Dependability

Promptness

Ambition and enthusiasm

Most important, ask yourself if the field of work being considered is in line with your real interest and ability. What do you want from your career?

When you attempt to emphasize a great many things, you succeed in emphasizing nothing. On the other hand, you are not presenting the best possible picture of yourself if you omit favorable data that may show your ability to be a good employee.

After you have made a complete and objective self-analysis, you should have a realistic appraisal of yourself for the job-seeking process. You still have the task of choosing the best method of presenting qualifications and determining which points to stress and which to subordinate. In order to answer these questions, you need to know something of your prospective employer.

Analyzing the Employment Market

A market analysis is the next step in your job-seeking process. You must know your employer and the job requirements in order to show that your qualifications meet the employer's needs. Although many items of information cannot be obtained until the interview, or perhaps not until you actually begin work or have worked for a considerable time, much information will be available if you diligently look for it.

What information will you need? You will need enough to ascertain that the organization will offer you sufficient opportunity, provided you are hired, to justify your accepting this employment. Although this statement may seem obvious, it is the most important answer you are seeking. As you make this investigation, you will also gain enough information for intelligently planning your presentation to the specific organization.

You should not take the attitude that you must accept a job that offers little opportunity for growth or for the kind of work you prefer. You may be forced to accept an offer that is less than ideal, but at least you should aim high. On the other hand, remember that you are not stuck forever in any position or company. Although frequent changes do not look good on your record, many, if not most, persons change jobs several times during their lifetime. Usually it is easier to find work if you already have a job than if you do not.

Although you may not stay with your first full-time job, you should choose it with care. In one way or another, it will affect your entire career. In addition, the employing organization will spend time and money in hiring and training you—perhaps a great deal of time and money. If you do not enter into an employment contract with the sincere desire to succeed and to remain with the organization, you are not being completely fair to the employer or to yourself.

Another purpose of research into potential employing organizations is to obtain information about how to sell yourself intelligently. If you can determine your possible duties, you will have a better idea of which qualifications to emphasize in order to show how your abilities will be of the most possible benefit to the employer.

Another advantage (as well as an obvious necessity) of doing research into the job market is to know which organizations have openings for persons like yourself. You can assume that many large organizations will periodically employ persons with widely used specializations, such as engineering, accounting, or sales. For positions such as these, unsolicited letters of application are appropriate and useful. You can, in fact, use unsolicited letters for all possible openings, but you will not always receive a favorable reply.

Even if an unplanned "hit-or-miss" approach seems to succeed, it is still far from being the best method. You are not able in this way to fit your qualifications to the particular employer. You are also likely not to find the organizations for which you would most like to work.

Where will you find all this information? Printed sources will provide some of the information you seek. Annual reports of the firms in which you are interested include far more information than the financial statement does. They also tell something of the product or services, as well as the location of the home office or branch offices. They may give information about management policies.

The *College Placement Annual* is especially applicable to persons graduating from college. A copy of this book is often available through the college placement office. Employing organizations are listed alphabetically and also by occupational specialties and geographic locations. Other information includes brief notations as to the kinds of openings, the educational background of the applicants being sought, and the proper person to contact in the organization.

A similar book is *Career: The Annual Guide to Business Opportunities.*

Moody's Manuals of Investments, although intended primarily for potential investors, also provides information essential to the potential employee. Information included in these manuals consists of a summary of the history of each organization, method of operation, location, products or services, and the financial structure. These books are available in most libraries.

Standard and Poor's Manuals are also planned primarily for investors. They contain information similar to that contained in *Moody's Manuals.* Another publication of this corporation is *Poor's Register of Directors and Executives, United States and Canada.* The directory may be useful for finding the name and title of the person to whom you should send your application for employment.

The *Business Periodicals Index, The Wall Street Journal Index*, and other indexes are useful in locating magazine articles that have been written about particular business organizations in which you are interested. Annual reports are likely to be available in libraries.

Many government and professional organizations issue publications describing employment opportunities and the necessary qualifications for employees. Much of this literature is available through college placement offices and public and school libraries. You can also learn about job openings from professional journals in your field.

Perhaps the best way of all to learn about prospective employers is to ask employees who are doing work similar to the kind you would be doing. As in any other survey, the more people you ask, the more valid your data are likely to be.

Advantages of the Two-Part Application

A two-part application enables you to use the letter to present highlights of the detailed information included on the resume. These important features are presented from the standpoint of what they will do for the reader. As in other sales messages, the letter is more coherent and emphatic when it is built around a central theme.

Prepare the resume; then choose from it important elements to be included in the letter. The letter interprets your most important qualifications (from all those shown on the resume) in terms of reader interest—much as you present important elements of a product when writing a sales letter to be sent with leaflets and brochures. Prepare both parts of the two-part application after you have made a detailed analysis of your qualifications and have researched the companies that interest you.

The Resume: A Report on Yourself

The right kind of resume will obtain the interviewer's attention. It will also continue the sales presentation throughout the interview and the negotiation process.

A well-prepared resume should be a truly superior expression of your talents and

Question: What are frequent weaknesses in resumes?

Answer: The most important weakness, however it occurs, is a resume that does not present the applicant in the most favorable way for the particular position sought. Although many factors prevent a resume from being completely effective, some of the more common weaknesses are listed below:

Believing that a resume must be no longer than one page. A resume must be concise, but keeping it to one page is not as important as presenting yourself in the most convincing way possible. For most young applicants with little experience, a one-page resume is likely to be sufficient.

Omitting positive, specific details about work experience and education. Job titles and length of experience are not enough.

Submitting an application (letter and resume) that is less than absolutely perfect in appearance.

Copying a textbook or other example exactly. You are different in some or many ways from the person described in an example of a resume. Individualize your own resume to present your own particular qualifications.

Crowding information together so that it is hard to read.

Emphasizing (by choice of format, spacing, content, wording, other methods) unimportant information and omitting emphasis on your most valuable education, experience, or activities.

Errors in spelling, capitalization, and word usage.

Using a mixture of styles; for example, mixing sentence fragments, which are preferred in resume format, with complete sentences.

---

background. It should be a credit to your creativity and to your ability to put ideas and information into convincing words. The most effective resumes sell ability, talent, and potential as well as education and past experience.

A resume, unlike most kinds of business writing, is appropriately written in less than complete sentences. Specifically worded phrases, as illustrated in all resume examples in this chapter, have several advantages: They eliminate the need for the pronoun *I*, they save words and space, and they place emphasis on important, positive qualifications.

Although you must not misrepresent in any way, you should not understate your qualifications. Two or three hundred applicants may also want the job for which you are applying; now is no time to be modest.

Be sure that your resume, like the letter that accompanies it, is absolutely perfect in appearance, including quality and color of paper, arrangement on sheet without crowding, and clear type. If you do not use printed resumes (which may have more disadvantages than advantages because of impersonality), try to prepare your resume using a word processor and a laser or daisy wheel printer. Do not use a dot matrix printer.

Use bond paper of at least 20-pound weight and 25 percent cotton content (also described as "rag" content). Paper may be white, ivory (off-white), cream, buff, light gray, or similar neutral colors.

In addition to weight, cotton content, and color, paper also has differing textures; for example, smooth, linen, and pebble. A recent study by Krajewski and Wood,[1] in which respondents were given samples of stationery from which to choose their favorite colors and textures, resulted in the following stated preferences:

Color		Texture	
Ivory	33 percent	Linen	48 percent
Cream	27 percent	Pebble	28 percent
White	20 percent	Smooth	22 percent
Gray	20 percent		

A study by Nelson and Smith,[2] based on replies from 120 respondents, resulted in these findings:

Color	
Important or Noted	33 percent
Not Important or Noted	64 percent
No response	3 percent

Based on the 33 percent of the total respondents who stated that color is important or noted, those respondents stated the following preferences:

White	29 percent
Off-white	27 percent
No preference	43 percent
No answer	1 percent

Based on these two studies and others, you will always be safe to use off-white (ivory) or white paper. In the Nelson and Smith study, some respondents mentioned that any color except white or off-white is unacceptable. Pink, green, yellow, blue, "pastels" and "loud and bright" colors were considered unacceptable.[3] (No doubt the 64 percent of the original group of respondents who replied that color is not important or noted would "note" a resume printed on such colors as purple or bright red.)

Resumes described as being in the *reverse chronological* order present both education and work experience in reverse chronological order. *Functional resumes* are built around qualifications and abilities rather than on time periods of education or years of work experience. *Combination resumes* combine portions of both the reverse chronological and functional arrangements.

Basic parts of resumes arranged in the chronological order are these: the employment objective, which may be included in the heading; education; work experience; skills, publications, activities, and other relevant data; and references, or a statement that references will be furnished on request. A summary sometimes follows or replaces the objective.

Examine the resumes shown in Figures 11–1 through 11–10 as you consider

[1]Lorraine A. Krajewski and Susan A. Wood, "Employer Preferences for Resume Format." Paper presented at 17th Annual Meeting, Southwestern Federation of Administrative Disciplines, March 1, 1990.

[2]Sandra J. Nelson and Douglas C. Smith, "Employment Interviews and Instruments: Critical Information for Students." *1989 Proceedings, International Conference*, Association for Business Communication, 59–68.

[3]Ibid., 62.

Juan Gomez

107 Butler Street, Seattle, WA 98504
Telephone: 206-000-0000

Objective

To begin work as heavy equipment sales representative, with an opportunity to progress to sales management or company management.

Education

Bachelor of Business Administration degree, double major in marketing and engineering technology, Washington State University, Pullman, Washington, May, 1990.

—Special emphasis in computer science and business management.
  Grade point average, 3.43 on scale of 4.0.

Work Experience

Inspector/Surveyor, Washington State Department of Transportation, Pasco, Washington, June, 1989 through August, 1989.

> Supervised multimillion-dollar asphalt surfacing project
> Trained new employees
> Watched over contractors' activities
> Kept precise records of daily activities
> Managed survey crew of five persons

Inspector, Washington State Department of Transportation, Pasco, Washington, June, 1988 through August, 1988.

> Inspected $230 million concrete paving project
> Performed concrete tests and analyses
> Ran computerized slope indicator on high risk landslide zones
> Trained and supervised seven new employees
> Inspected latex bridge overlays

Technician, Washington State Department of Transportation, Pasco, Washington, May, 1987 through August, 1987.

> Performed general ledger work for project engineer
> Calculated estimates for upcoming construction season
> Dispatched asphalt to construction sites
> Surveyed highway at progressing points of operation

Marketing Agent, Paramount Management Associates, Inc., Richland, Washington, February, 1984 through August, 1986.

> Successfully implemented own marketing strategy for area

Other Information

Served four years in United States Air Force, 1980-1984.
Willing to relocate and travel.
Can provide excellent references from employers and professors.

FIGURE 11–1 Resume of a graduating senior with responsible summer employment

TIMOTHY ADAMS

393 Buntyn
Memphis, TN 38111
Telephone: 901-323-0000

Objective

Accounting position with opportunities to build strong professional career. Intend to continue education as a candidate for MBA.

Education

—Attended Memphis State University Memphis, Tennessee, from the fall of 1985 through the summer of 1990 in the Fogelman College of Business and Economics. Graduated cum laude, 1990. Received B.B.A. with major in accounting. Maintained 3.88 average in courses within the business college while working full time.
—Attended Memphis State as a music education major from fall 1978 to spring 1980.

Work Experience

—Employed by the Memphis Grain and Hay Association, 160 South Front, Memphis, from the spring of 1980 to the present. Worked way up from technician to licensed grain inspector. Duties include:
  —Grading grain sampled from barges, railcars, and trucks;
  —Taking grain futures quotations from the Chicago Board of Trade and relaying them to members of the Memphis Board of Trade;
  —Coordinating job assignments and supervising work crews;
  —Training new employees.

Achievements

—Acknowledged for editorial contributions and several speeches included in the textbook *Speaking in Public*, written by Dr. Michael Osborn of Memphis State.
—Wrote and participated in address by Memphis Grain and Hay Association to Seminar at the Food Sanitation Institute in Nashville, Tennessee.
—Selected as team captain in accounting system class. Led project for the Small Business Institute at Memphis State to document and suggest improvements in the accounting system of Cetacea Sound, Inc., a company installing communication equipment for Federal Express.

FIGURE 11–2 Accounting graduate. Excellent educational qualifications. Good experience, but in different field. Strong "Achievements" section.

CAROL CHEN
5012 Jennings Way
Sacramento, CA 95608
Telephone: 916-000-0000

Objective: Secretarial position with opportunity for additional responsibility.

Special Skills and Abilities: Typewriting speed: 90 words a minute, 99 percent accuracy. Shorthand, 100 words a minute. Experienced in use of photocopy equipment, transcribing equipment, computer terminals and microcomputers. Ability in creative writing, as evidenced by two awards in high school; all A's in English, high school and college; three published essays, two poems, and one short story, state and regional publications.

Education: Associate degree, 1990, Humbolt State University, Arcata, California. Secretarial and office management concentration. Instruction included practice on word processors and microcomputers. Grade point average, 3.2 on scale of 4.

Diploma, Arcata High School, Arcata, California, 1986.
Member of Honor Society.

Related Experience: July, 1990–Present. Secretary, State of California, Sacramento. Work in State Office Building as general secretary in Vocational Rehabilitation Department.

Responsible to three counselors. Schedule appointments, handle other telephone calls. Greet visitors. Take dictation in shorthand from three counselors and from other workers in Vocational Rehabilitation Department. Transcribe on text-editing typewriter. Prepare reports. Use computer terminal. Occasionally help with counseling. Transcribe from recorded cassettes notes dictated by counselors.

Other Experience: June, 1986–May, 1990. Summer and part-time work. (Earned all of college expenses, including living costs.)
Waitress, Holiday Inn, Arcata. Lifeguard, Fountain Valley Country Club, Fountain Valley, California. Aide, Childcare Nursery School, Arcata.

References: On request, references will be furnished by present supervisors, including three counselors; professors at Humbolt State University; high school teachers; and employers and supervisors of part-time and summer work.

FIGURE 11–3 Applicant who seems to be very well qualified for secretarial position. She considers the "Special Skills and Abilities" section important as indicated by its placement before "Education" and "Experience," one of which usually follows "Objective."

the usual parts of a resume. Although the following discussion applies primarily to reverse chronological resumes, the kind most frequently used, all resumes require a heading. Most require an objective unless the objective is clear from either the heading or the summary. All report education and work experience, although functional resumes do not report details of experience and education according to exact time periods.

Heading

The heading should include your name, address, and telephone number. Sometimes these items of information are used alone to make up the entire heading

ROBERT R. ARNOLD
2461 North Crestview
Provo, UT 84604
801-000-0000

CAREER OBJECTIVE	System analysis and design in field of office automation and information processing.
EDUCATION	Bachelor of Science Degree, Information Management. Brigham Young University, Provo, Utah, August, 1990. Grade point average, 3.0 on 4-point scale; 3.82 in major. Work included these courses, among others:

System Analysis and Design   Business Management
Advanced Programming Logic   Financial Analysis
Business Communication   Marketing

EXPERIENCE AND ABILITIES	Programming. Skilled in computer programming using knowledge of Lotus 1-2-3 and WordPerfect software.
	Analysis. Completed a system analysis and design project for a video rental franchise. Analyzed and developed the changeover for a video rental system from manual to computerized, including writing software using a database management system. Sounds Easy Video, St. George, Utah, 1989–1990.
	Accounting. Responsible for daily bookkeeping of a national restaurant franchise, Po-Folks, 1986–87. Assisted with weekly money management and financial records for a church, 1988.
	Communications. Gave several presentations on systems and procedures in office automation and other related fields. Brigham Young University, 1987–1990.
	Leadership. Shift supervisor in charge of operations and personnel while on job (Po-Folks), 1986–1987. Successfully completed Air Force ROTC officer training camp, 1988. Voluntary representative and district area supervisor for church.
OTHER INTERESTS	Songwriting and performing. Have recorded six songs.
REFERENCES	References from professors, employers, and community leaders will be furnished upon request.

FIGURE 11–4 Combination resume. Applicant chooses not to use reverse chronological order for experience.

without some kind of descriptive title as *Resume, Data Sheet, Vita,* or *Qualifications of.* Your *objective* may be included in the heading instead of being listed in the first section of the resume; for example, *Sherry Clara Aldridge's Qualifications for Accounting Work with Arthur Andersen and Company.* Another method of showing the objective in the heading is to follow your name with a description of your occupation, provided you are applying for similar work; for example, *Joe Lee Cole, Industrial Psychologist.*

To list "accounting work" in the heading or in the separate section of the resume entitled *Objective* is too vague and general if you are aware of a particular opening that can be described in more specific terms. Avoid being overly specific when you are not exactly sure of the kind of work available to you; on the

---

ABIGAIL C. DUPRE

8476 Rothschild   Metairie, LA 70005   Telephone: 504-000-0000

EMPLOYMENT OBJECTIVE:

To sell commercial real estate with progressive company and to use education, ambition, and energy to increase company's sales.

SUMMARY OF QUALIFICATIONS:

University education with strong major in real estate. Experience in real estate office and sales experience in another field. Have lived in Metairie and New Orleans since childhood; many business acquaintances.

PROFESSIONAL EDUCATION:

Completing Bachelor of Business Administration degree with major in real estate at the University of New Orleans. Degree to be received in May, 1990. Have worked throughout college years and paid all expenses.

"A's" and "B's" in following real estate courses:

Real Estate Principles   Housing Determinants
Real Estate Appraisal   Real Estate Finance
Real Estate Law   Commercial Developments

Now enrolled in these courses: Internship for Real Estate
                               Sales Management

Completed a real estate appraisal using a regression analysis on a Univac Computer.

Attended four seminars at New Orleans Board of Realtors.

WORK EXPERIENCE:

Have worked part-time in family firm, Dupre-Fisher Real Estate, New Orleans, since sophomore year in high school. General clerical work, bookkeeping, correspondence, communication with clients and potential buyers. This company specializes in residential property.

Sales representative, summers, 1988 and 1989, Shopper's News, Nantucket, Massachusetts.

OTHER ACTIVITIES:

Enjoy horseback riding, fishing, reading. Active in Neighborhood Association. Friends of the Library volunteer.

REFERENCES: References will be furnished upon request.

FIGURE 11–5 Resume of student whose central selling point is education, combined with experience in family business.

WILLIAM THOMAS KING'S QUALIFICATIONS
FOR AIRFRAME AND POWERPLANT MECHANIC

Home Address

3931 Meadow Lane
Olive Branch, MS 38654
601-000-0000

School Address

Memphis Area Vocational-
Technical School
Aviation Complex
2752 Winchester Road
Memphis, TN 38116
901-685-0000

Available to begin work on July 1, 1987

Education

Diploma, Airframe and Powerplant License, Memphis Area Vocational-
Technical School, Aviation Complex, 2752 Winchester Road, Memphis, TN
38116 (September 1989–June 1991)

Diploma, Aviation Structural Mechanic H, Hydraulic A, Marine Aviation
Training Support Group-90, Naval Air Technical Training Center, NAS,
Millington, TN 38054 (December 1985–March 1986)

Diploma, Hillcrest High School, 4184 Graceland Drive, Memphis, TN 38116
(June 1985)

Work Experience

Attendant/Mechanic, Roy's Chevron, 7144 Old Highway 78, Olive Branch,
MS 38654 (Part-time) Supervisor: Roy Collier (January 1990–Present)

Aircraft Hydraulic/Pneumatic Mechanic, United States Marines, VMAT-102
MCAS, Yuma, AZ 85369 Supervisor: GynSgt. H. A. Omach (August 1984–
August 1988). Honorably discharged as E-5 Sergeant. Major duties included
inspecting, repairing, and performing preventive maintenance on the Douglas A-4M/TA-4F hydraulic and pneumatic systems and components and
wheel braking assemblies.

Maintained power control packages, used specifications, blueprints, and
necessary tools and test equipment. Requisitioned supplies, equipment, and
special tools required in missions. Performed and supervised technical training of personnel, maintained records and reports, inspected shop maintenance as a Collateral Duty Inspector for Quality Assurance.

Attendant, Guidry's Texaco, 1315 Winchester Road, Memphis, TN 38116
Supervisor: Joe Guidry (August 1982–May 1984)

FIGURE 11–6
Graduate
of vocational-
technical school

William Thomas King   page 2

Organizations and Licenses

Aviation Maintenance Foundation, Inc. From 1983 to Present

Airframes License December 4, 1990

Powerplants License to be completed on July 1, 1991

Qualified to Operate the Following Equipment

AHT-63/64 Hydraulic Test Stand	MMG-1a/2MG-2 Electric Power Unit
TA/JG-75 Aircraft Tow Tractor	NAN-1/1a/2/3 Nitrogen Servicing Unit
Cornice Brake	Microfiche Maintenance/Parts Reader
Oxyacetylene Welding Equipment	Retrieval System Machine (MIARS)
Maintenance Info. Automated	

Own a complete set of hand tools for airframe and powerplant maintenance

References

Mr. John Litterer	Mr. Jack Doty
Machinist	Instructor
4601 Gwyck	Memphis Area Vocational-
Olive Branch, MS 38654	Technical School
601-895-3325	2752 Winchester Road
	Memphis, TN 38116
	901-354-1955
SSgt. Earl Combes, USMC	Mr. Roy Collier, Owner
Instructor, F-18 Program	Roy's Chevron
860 E. Grangeville	7144 Old Highway 78
Apartment #68	Olive Branch, MS 38654
Handord, CA 93230	601-895-6676
209-584-9436	

FIGURE 11–6
(continued)

other hand, don't be so general that you say nothing at all. ("I'll do anything, and I can do everything" is not usually a good approach when seeking career employment, although being a generalist is often more advantageous than being able to work only in a narrow specialization.) You are likely to have much competition. Don't eliminate possible opportunities by a too specific description of the job you seek.

Perhaps you should give two addresses and telephone numbers in the heading of the resume, especially if you expect to change your address soon. Students often give their school address and their home or permanent address.

Employment Objective

If you do not state the employment objective in the heading of the resume, you should state it in the first section of the resume. Although the objective is sometimes omitted, the resume is much less readable without it. The reader

---

ALISON TUCKER GREEN
218 South Harwood
Anderson, IN 46001

Telephone: 317-000-0000

EMPLOYMENT
OBJECTIVE:

High school teacher of business subjects, Indianapolis area.

SUMMARY:

Recent undergraduate and graduate degrees, Ball State University, Muncie, Indiana. Graduate assistant, two years, including office work and classroom teaching. Spent twenty-two years in various parts of world as Navy wife. One year's experience as secretary and bookkeeper. Twenty-five years' experience as household executive, mother, hostess, financial planner.

EDUCATION:

Master of Education degree from Ball State University in August, 1989, with a 3.5 grade point average based on a 4-point scale. Graduate work included internship in teaching and a comprehensive thesis. Title of thesis: "Improving Instruction in Word Processing at the Secondary Level."

Bachelor of Business Administration degree, Ball State University, August, 1986. Major in accounting, minor in management information systems. Several other upper-division courses in business management. Grade point average of 3.68 in major.

WORK
EXPERIENCE:

Library Assistant, Ball State University, October, 1989–present. General library duties. Now working at Circulation Desk.

Experience in various areas of unpaid employment while husband served as Naval officer, 1960–1982. More than half the time was spent outside the United States. These experiences abroad will be beneficial in teaching because numerous students now in high school will work outside the United States or with people from other countries.

Secretary-bookkeeper, Best Insurance Agency, Norfolk, Virginia, 1959–1960.

OTHER
INTERESTS:

Church and community responsibilities; reading; creative writing; music.

REFERENCES:

Eight persons who have offered to provide recommendations are listed on the attached sheet, with their positions, addresses, and telephone numbers. This list includes undergraduate and graduate professors, a member of the City Council, a librarian, and two other professional people.

FIGURE 11–7 Resume for a woman who has been away from the job market because of husband's career. She could also have chosen the functional format.

must look through other sections or at the accompanying letter in order to determine your employment goals. This alone could result in your application being discarded when many other more complete and readable resumes are on the reader's desk.

As a truly qualified candidate, you will be able to handle a variety of responsibilities related to your educational background and past experience. Even if you begin in a specialized area, you must be able to assume additional

---

1982 Punahou Street   Telephone:
Honolulu, HI 96822   808-000-0000

WALTER R. WILLIAMS
STATEMENT OF EMPLOYMENT ASSETS
FOR A CAREER IN PUBLIC ACCOUNTING

OBJECTIVE: To become associated with a progressive accounting firm, initially as a staff accountant, with the goal of advancement to partner.

DEGREE: Bachelor of Science in Accounting, major in public accounting, minors in data processing and management, University of Hawaii, 1990.

Technical Accounting: Advanced Accounting, Cost Accounting, Tax Accounting, Auditing Methods, Managerial Accounting, Financial Accounting, Cases in Federal Income Tax, Governmental Accounting

Computer Systems: Electronic Data Processing Systems and Methods, Information Systems, Computer Program Languages, Decision Mathematics

Communication: Business Communication; fifteen hours of English and journalism; conducted regular meetings of the University of Hawaii Accounting Club; kept minutes of Data Processing Management Association meetings; prepared various reports on financial conditions of seven companies for accounting courses.

Business: Business Environment, Theory of the Firm, Business Law, Finance, subscribe to *Business Week* and *The Wall Street Journal*

Management and Leadership: Office Management; Behavioral Management; Personnel Management; Marketing Management; Secretary of Data Processing Management Association, one year; Vice President of University of Hawaii Accounting Club, one year

Ability to Work with People: Student tutor in accounting, one year, fifteen hours a week
Active member of Society for Advancement of Management, two years
Active member of Accounting Club, three years
Active member of Data Processing Management Association, two years
Active member of Tennis Club, four years
Sold advertising space to businesses for Student Directory

REFERENCES: On request, references will be furnished from professors and business people.

FIGURE 11–8 Functional resume of accounting major with little work experience

duties to be truly valuable to the employing organization. Few organizations want an applicant who will be content to remain at an entry-level position. Thus your objective may indicate, without appearing presumptuous or obvious, that you are looking for employment with opportunities for growth. For example:

Objective: Beginning accounting and auditing work with eventual
managerial responsibilities.

Even if the heading of your resume refers to your employment objective, you may include an employment objective section as long as you avoid repeating the objective verbatim. Such an arrangement emphasizes the objective.

REBECCA S. ROSENBERG
1472 Tutwiler Avenue
Cincinnati, OH 45208
Telephone: 513-000-0000

Objective

To obtain a position in Sales Training/Development in a business setting, preferably with Electronic Data Systems Corporation, and use ability to help others increase sales effectiveness through positive personal relationships.

Work Experience

October, 1983—Present. Sales Representative, Checks, Inc., 417 Constitution Square, Cincinnati, OH 45230

Responsible for establishing and increasing sales through direct personal contact at approximately 200 banks in northern Kentucky.

Conducted and aided cross-selling and security training programs for bank personnel in more than 30 banks. Now writing training programs for all branches of Checks, Inc.

Perform cost analyses of banks' operating procedures. Develop and implement cost-saving programs tailored to meet the particular needs of each bank.

Have maintained healthy growth in sales each quarter, often reaching highest sales per quarter in company.

November, 1981—October, 1983. Customer Service Representative, Checks, Inc., Cincinnati, Ohio.

Responsible for phoned-in questions or problems from bank customers.

Promoted and established goodwill through written and telephone communications.

Served as support representative between salespersons and production.

June, 1981—November, 1981. Sales clerk, Gold's Appliances, 412 Maple, Cincinnati, OH 45208. Supervisor, Harris Gold.

September, 1980—June, 1981 (Part-time). Seating hostess, cocktail hostess, bartender, Steak & Ale Restaurants, Cincinnati.

FIGURE 11–9 Example of resume emphasizing work experience, with secondary emphasis on education. Although many resumes do not exceed one page, a two-page (or even longer) resume is permissible.

Introductory Summary

The objective may be included in a section of the resume referred to as an *introductory summary, summary, overview,* or a similar term. The summary includes an abstract of overall capabilities. Such a summary is especially beneficial in a long resume, one of several pages, but it may be used in one of regular length.

An introductory summary of a resume serves the same function as the *synopsis* or *executive summary* of a report. The most important and relevant ele-

Rebecca S. Rosenberg   page 2

Education

Completing Bachelor of Business Administration degree at the University of Cincinnati at end of Spring semester, 1990. Completing entire college program while attending classes at night and working full time.

Major in marketing. Grade point average in major, 3.1 on a 4-point scale.

Completed Motivation Sales workshops by Zig Ziglar (1988) and Don Hudson (1986).

Completed Dale Carnegie courses in Human Relations and Sales (1984–85).

Other Facts

Enjoy sailing, backpacking, jogging, reading, gardening, and the challenge of helping people learn to increase their sales ability.

References

Professor T. C. Fung
Department of Marketing
Cincinnati Technical College
Cincinnati, OH 45209
513-532-0000

Lucille Garcia, Branch Manager
Eastgate, Covington National Bank
Covington, KY 41015
606-258-0000

Don Hudson, Instructor
Motivational Sales Workshops
2809 International Lane
Madison, WI 53704
608-767-0000

FIGURE 11–9 (continued) Notice that a heading is required on the second page of a two-page resume.

ments are given first, in a very much condensed form, followed by supporting details. As with a synopsis of a report, the reader knows immediately what the entire resume is about and the outstanding qualifications of the applicant. A resume long enough to require an introductory summary is more likely to be one of a person with considerable work experience, not a person with little experience who is about to finish college, although such a summary aids readability in any resume.

The introductory summary may be used in addition to, and immediately following, the *objective* section. Often the two sections may be combined to make the resume more concise.

CHRISTINA C. MONTAVELLI
3617 Boston Road
Senatobia, MS 38668

Telephone: 601-000-0000

OBJECTIVE:	To work as a Contract Coordinator with Business Service Centers, Federal Express Corporation.
EXPERIENCE:	**Technical Assistant,** Aircraft Support Shops, Federal Express Corporation, December 1984–Present.
	Responsible for requisition and follow-up of materials for six shop areas and management personnel. Compile bid packages for submission to vendors for purchase of automatic test equipment. Coordinate technical support with approximately fifty vendors. Initiate all facilities management. Maintain automated payroll.
	Clerk, Federal Express Corporation. October, 1982–December, 1984.
	Received cash bags from Eastern Division centers. Reconciled daily transactions. Researched invoice discrepancies. Communicated with customers by telephone.
	Administrative Assistant, AAA Finance, Como, Ohio, May, 1981–June, 1982.
	Computed, assembled, and closed loan packages. Collected by letters and telephone. Maintained all bookkeeping records.
EDUCATION:	Presently enrolled in evening classes at Northwest Mississippi Junior College, Sophomore majoring in business management. Current academic status, with 3.13 grade point average on scale of 4.0. Have completed college work while working full time.
	Have completed following seminars and workshops, plus others:
	"Making Unions Unnecessary," The Center for Values Research Group, Dallas, Texas, 1989.
	"Problem-Solving and Decision-Making," Organizational Training, Federal Express Corporation, 1988.
	"Human Relations," Federal Express Corporation, 1987.
	"Communication in Business," Federal Express Corporation, 1986.
OTHER FACTS:	Girl Scout leader. Active in civic and neighborhood work.
REFERENCES:	References from present or past supervisors, co-workers, or professors will be furnished upon request.

FIGURE 11–10 Employee applying for higher position in present company

Education

An important section of most resumes is entitled *Education, Professional Training and Education, Professional Education, Academic Experiences,* or some similar wording. Choose the most appropriate simple heading that best describes your educational experiences. The section on education often should come after the *objective* section or after the *summary,* if included. Place first the section you want to emphasize, which will most likely be either *education* or *experience.*

If you are a young graduate with little work experience, education is probably what you should emphasize most; it is your central selling point. If you have had extensive work experience, even if you are just now completing college, related work experience is likely to be as important or more important than your degree. After you have been out of school for a few years, work experience is almost surely the major qualification for work in the same field, although education remains important. In any event, give sufficient attention to both education and experience to convince the reader of your qualifications.

Use care in the wording of the education section of the resume. Ordinarily, if you mean *education,* say *Education.* When you word headings, use the same simple, direct, straightforward, specific approach that is best for all business and professional communication. *You need not, and should not, work for a cute or clever approach.* If you are qualified for the opening, say so in simple, concrete language. If you are not qualified, fancy headings will not do any good, although they may brighten your readers' day by giving them a good laugh.

The content of the section on educational experience is discussed earlier in this chapter under "Analyzing Your Qualifications."

To repeat and emphasize: give specific, concrete details (which are of necessity incomplete), interpreted in the light of how your particular educational experiences have prepared you for the job for which you are applying.

Work Experience

Your present or most recent experience is ordinarily the experience most relevant to your application. From the standpoint of a potential employer, what you are doing now is of far more concern than what you did five years ago.

At times, however, a period of employment other than your present or most recent becomes the period you should emphasize. For example, if you worked for seven years in sales, decided to try teaching, then gave up teaching to apply for another sales job, you should stress your sales experience even though it is not the most recent. There are situations, however, in which the teaching experience could be the most important part of your overall experience and the major field to be emphasized. For example, if you are now applying for a job with a publisher that distributes high school textbooks, your high school teaching experience is likely to be far more valuable than your previous experience in selling real estate.

Present your qualifications from the standpoint of how the employer will benefit from hiring you. To do so, emphasize your experiences that seem to be the most advantageous to the successful handling of the job. This orientation in a resume is another application of the you-attitude.

When using the reverse chronological order, account for all periods of time since you began work. Or, if you have many years of experience, account only for the past ten years if you prefer. When you have had many short-time or part-time jobs, it is not essential to give exact dates of employment, with names and addresses of all employing organizations. You can summarize some work experience; for example, 1982–1983, part-time jobs at service stations, grocery stores, and drugstores while attending college full-time.

A *functional* resume groups items around four or more key job functions. This arrangement is beneficial to people with wide experience and to those with little experience (see Figure 11–8). A functional resume is particularly appropriate for a "job-hopper" whose frequent changes would receive unwanted emphasis if presented in detail in the usual reverse chronological order. The functional resume emphasizes important and impressive capabilities and accomplishments, not years of experience. You can use it to avoid mention of dates, names, and places that might be considered undesirable but would be necessary when using the reverse chronological arrangement, in which you should account for all time periods.

A possible disadvantage of the functional resume is that it is unfamiliar to some employers; it is used far less often than reverse chronological resumes. Because of its difference, some readers may be annoyed not to find expected information in expected places. They may also believe that you have used the functional resume in order to deceive or to be evasive.

Other Appropriate Sections of a Resume

You are free to choose headings to best describe your qualifications, accomplishments, and abilities that do not fit under headings of experience or education. Some examples of often-used sections are *Professional Affiliations, Publications, Activities, Community Work,* and *Additional Information.*

A section described by such a heading as *Personal Data,* which includes age, height, weight, marital status, and other such bits of information is no longer included in most resumes. Now this information is more likely to be omitted because personal characteristics are not relevant to successful performance in most jobs. Employers cannot legally hire applicants on the basis of information that has nothing to do with the ability to succeed in the particular job for which the applicant is being considered.

The question of whether to include age and other personal data with your application is still debatable. Most people who work in placement or personnel departments agree that you are free to omit completely all such information if you choose to do so. On the other hand, there is nothing to prevent you from giving information that you feel will be to your advantage, although you should not imply that you feel you will be hired because of any personal factors.

Some items of personal data should almost always be omitted, including race, religion, and political party. Even these kinds of sensitive information, however, may belong on some resumes. For example, if you wish to be an assistant to a congresswoman who is a Democrat, you should mention your activities in the Democratic party. (If you worked for her election and don't mention that fact, you don't deserve the job.)

In some such instances, experiences in church work, religious organizations on campus, or political organizations may be important to an unrelated job for which you are applying. Such work may show leadership ability and assumption of responsibility. If you have spent a great deal of time in these activities, perhaps you have few other outside interests to report. You must use your own judgment whether to show these items in your employment application. Usually you should omit them.

References

References are not always listed on a resume. In the reference position, which is ordinarily the last one, you may include a statement such as "References will be furnished on request," or you may omit the statement entirely.

Whether or not to include specific references is another debatable question.

If you are applying to only a few employers and you have been given permission to use as references people whose names will favorably impress the employers, then list these names. Some employers still expect references, or the mention of references, as an essential part of all resumes. Do not list people as references until you have their permission to do so.

When you are mailing a great many unsolicited applications, you are wise to omit the names of people who will recommend you. Offer to send further information and names of references later. Although potential employers are unlikely to contact the persons you name until after an employment interview, they could do so. You then run the risk of having the persons who have agreed to recommend you bothered unnecessarily by inquiries.

If you do include references, always state the individual's full name, business organization or occupation, address, and telephone number. Provide a copy of your resume to each person who has agreed to act as a reference.

Some employers prefer listed references. According to a recent research study, 71.2 percent prefer references on a resume.[4]

Illustrations of Resumes

Various types of resumes are shown in Figures 11–1 to 11–10. Letters to accompany these resumes are shown in Chapter 12, Figures 12–1 through 12–10.

Summary

When looking for employees, most organizations consider these factors: job-related experience, job-related education, dependability, the ability to cooperate with others, and a willingness to work.

When looking for employment, you can use an unsolicited application letter and resume to advantage. This approach shows that you have a special interest in a particular organization and that you have the initiative and ambition to research employing organizations in order to make an intelligent effort to place yourself. Another advantage is that you are more likely to find the kind of work for which you are best suited and that offers the opportunity you are seeking.

In order to plan an effective search for employment, analyze your qualifications and the employment market. After your analyses are completed, plan and write the letter and resume to show how your qualifications meet the needs of the employer.

The application letter is a kind of sales message. The accompanying resume is a report on yourself and is also a form of sales presentation. Like other sales messages, these materials are more effective when they are built around a central selling theme.

For most young college students, education is the most appropriate central selling point. Other central selling themes are work experience and, in special circumstances, extracurricular activities, hobbies, or special interests.

Like other business messages, the two-part application should make the most effective use of the you-attitude and the positive approach.

[4]Glynna Morse, "A Study of the Preferences of Executives for the Style, Format, and Content of Resumes." *1987 Proceedings, International Conference,* Association for Business Communication, 100.

1. What is meant by a central selling point as it is applied to resumes?

2. Name one advantage of using a central selling point in preparing a resume.

3–4. One of two factors is usually the central selling point. What are the two?

5. What should be *your* central selling point? Why?

6–7. What are two steps that you should take before preparing a resume?

8. What is meant by the two-part application?

9. What is meant by the term *solicited* application?

10. What is an advantage of submitting an *unsolicited* application?

11–12. Name two published sources that are useful for obtaining information about prospective employers.

13–14. What is an advantage of including an "objec-tive" section at the beginning of a resume? What is a possible disadvantage?

15. What is the purpose of the introductory summary?

16–17. What is an advantage of a functional resume? What is a possible disadvantage?

18–19. What is an advantage of a resume arranged in the reverse chronological order? What is a possible disadvantage?

20. Name one kind of personal information that should ordinarily be omitted from a resume.

Note: Cases for both Chapter 11 and Chapter 12 are given at the end of Chapter 12. Because both chapters are about seeking employment, assignments are interrelated. Additional cases that apply to these chapters are included in the Cases section following Chapter 16.

(Related to material in Chapter 11 and principles of correct usage.) Insert necessary punctuation, including quotation marks, hyphens, and apostrophes, and remove punctuation that has been inserted incorrectly. Choose correct word or sentence from each pair or group. Make any other necessary changes.

Improve the following passages from resumes.

1. Designed window displays, wrote advertising copy, and advertising copy was written by me and my assistant.

2. Completed courses in English, Accounting, and History.

3. Starting in high school, you will note that I worked in several responsible jobs.

4. One years sales experience in a womens clothing store.

5. Scholarship recepient.

6. Responsible to three (counselors, councilors).

7. (Principle, Principal) responsibilities were financial ones.

8. Planned (capital, capitol) expenditures.

9. Earned (90 percent, ninety percent, 90%) of college costs.

10. Sold advertising space to business's.

11. Member of Methodist church.

12. Majored in phys ed, Eng., and minored in math.

Evaluation Sheet: Employment Resumes

	Yes	No	Not Sure
1. Is the resume presented throughout from the reader's standpoint?	___	___	___
2. Is the resume built around a central selling point?	___	___	___
3. Is the factor considered to be the central selling point (usually education or experience) placed before less important information?	___	___	___
4. Is more space given to the central selling point than to less important factors?	___	___	___
5. Is the resume worded throughout in phrases with no first- or second-person pronouns?	___	___	___
6. Is sufficient emphasis given throughout to favorable details, with less favorable details subordinated or omitted?	___	___	___
7. Is the resume completely factual and truthful?	___	___	___
8. If arranged in the reverse chronological format, are *both* education and experience presented in the reverse chronological order?	___	___	___
9. Is the resume absolutely perfect in appearance?	___	___	___
10. Is the resume absolutely perfect in spelling, word usage, and all other elements of grammatical correctness?	___	___	___
11. Are enough positive details given about both education and experience to present yourself in a favorable way?	___	___	___
12. Does the heading include your name, address, and telephone number?	___	___	___
13. Does the resume contain an appropriately worded employment objective?	___	___	___

CHAPTER 12

Completing the
Job-Finding Process

After you have analyzed your qualifications and the job market and have completed your resume, you are ready to write the application letter.

This chapter includes discussion about application letters, the employment interview, and other letters about employment. Illustrations of application letters accompany the ten resumes shown in Chapter 11. Also illustrated are a thank-you letter, a follow-up letter, a letter of acceptance, a letter of refusal, and a letter of resignation.

The Letter of Application

As you plan your letter of application to accompany a resume, keep in mind the following guides:

1. Use the positive approach. Emphasize strengths and subordinate weaknesses, but do not misrepresent.

2. Use the you-attitude in that you stress benefits for the reader. Do not use a "hard-sell" method, but state your work experience and educational background in specific and positive terms, *especially as they relate to the work for which you are applying.*

3. Show that you are definitely interested in the position and the employing company, but don't sound as if this is your last chance.

4. *Don't copy a letter written by some other person—or one from this book or any other book.* This warning applies to all letters and written material of any kind. Besides the unethical nature of using someone else's work, such copying, even with changed details and paraphrasing, is almost certain to result in stilted, unnatural wording. No one else can express your ideas and your personality as well as you can. In addition, sometimes personnel managers (as well as teachers) know exactly the book in which the letter originally appeared.

5. Use the words *I, me,* and *my* as natural and necessary, but do not use them to excess. Avoid beginning several sentences with *I.*

6. Don't ask for sympathy. This is not the you-approach or the positive approach. You will not be hired because your baby needs shoes but because you can do a good job and earn more for the employer than you are paid. (You must earn more, or you are not a profitable investment.) If a job should be filled because of sympathy, the applicant begins work at a disadvantage and not on a businesslike basis.

7. Don't be unduly humble, and don't apologize for taking the reader's time. Remember that the employer is not doing you a favor by hiring you. If you are qualified and a hard worker, the employing organization will benefit from the employment.

8. Don't complain about past or present employers. Even if you have real grievances, discussing these almost always sounds as if you are to blame. If you find it necessary to explain why you are leaving and this explanation is because of a real dissatisfaction that must be stated, do not mention it in the letter or resume. Save this discussion for the interview.

9. Don't boast or sound overly aggressive or presumptuous—although it is just as important not to sound unsure of your abilities. A straightforward businesslike approach will let you take the middle road between egotism and a doubtful, overly humble tone. Give concrete examples to prove your abilities; do not merely state that you have these abilities.

10. Don't lecture or waste time stating the obvious.

11. Don't mention salary, fringe benefits, or working conditions in the application. To do so will emphasize the I-approach, not the you-approach.

Question: How should I address a letter of application?

Answer: Address the letter to an individual, *not* to an organization. Use a conventional letter arrangement that includes an inside address and a salutation.

Try to find the name of the person who is likely to interview you and address your letter to this person. (You may have been told in an advertisement or position announcement the person to address. If this is the case, follow the instructions exactly, although determining the correct courtesy title helps to personalize your letter.)

Make sure you know the addressee's position in the organization, sex, and, if possible, how the person prefers to be addressed—for example, *Dr., Mrs., Ms., Mr., Professor.*

Be absolutely sure that you spell the addressee's name correctly.

Always use a courtesy title in *both* the inside address and the salutation. This advice applies to all business letters except those that omit completely the salutation and the complimentary close—styles that should not be used in application letters unless you find it is absolutely impossible to obtain an individual's name.

When addressing a letter to a box number, as often requested in advertisements, use a letter style that omits the salutation and the complimentary close. When writing to a box number, you have no appropriate word to use in a salutation; thus you should omit it. Do not—repeat, *do not*—use *Gentlemen, Dear Sirs,* or *To Whom It May Concern.*

Such information will be given to you during the interview. If it should not be, ask at that time for information you must have before making a decision.

12. Don't try to be overly clever, at least for most jobs. If you are being considered as an advertising copywriter or for similar work, your application letter and resume may be in a more original or unconventional form. Whatever the position, you do have the problem of making your letter stand out from all the others, but you could work so hard for attention that you receive the wrong kind, even to the extent of being eliminated from consideration.

13. Work for original phrasing and eliminate trite, unnecessary, stereotyped wording. Avoid such phrases as these: "May I present my qualifications?" "This is my application. . . ." An aptly worded letter will make this fact clear without stating it obviously.

14. Word the first paragraph so that the reader clearly understands that you are applying for a particular kind of job.

Examples of Letters of Application

Application letters shown in Figures 12–1 through 12–10 accompany the resumes shown in Figures 11–1 through 11–10 in Chapter 11. These examples, like all others throughout the text, are not given as exact patterns; they are *not*

107 Butler Street
Seattle, WA 98504
June 15, 19--

Mr. H. B. McDowell, President
Northwest Heavy Equipment Company
1880 SW Broadway
Portland, OR 97201

Dear Mr. McDowell:

May I work for you and increase your heavy equipment sales in the
state of Washington?

Mrs. Anita Klein, who works for the Washington State Department
of Transportation, told me that you will soon have a sales
representative to retire. I am acquainted with your representative,
Mr. Goodman. I met him several times during the summers of 1988
and 1989 when I worked on Washington highways. He can tell you
of my successful work during those summers, often spending 70 or
more hours a week on the job.

I observed much of your equipment in operation during these
summers. I am convinced that it is dependable and reasonably
priced. Because you sell quality products and operate your
organization honestly and efficiently, I want to become a part of
your organization.

My college education at Washington State University has prepared
me in two areas that should increase my success as a sales
representative: marketing and engineering technology. In addition, I
worked as a marketing agent for two years before I entered college,
preceded by four years in the United States Air Force. This combined
experience has proved to be far more beneficial than if I had
entered college directly after high school.

Other details of my experience and education are given in the
enclosed resume. May I talk with you at your convenience? I can be
reached at 206-000-0000.

Sincerely,

Juan Gomez

Juan Gomez

FIGURE 12–1
Letter to accompany
resume shown in Fig-
ure 11–1

393 Buntyn
Memphis, TN 38111
August 12, 19--

Mr. James A. Perkins
Senior Vice-President
Federal Express Corporation
P.O. Box 727
Memphis, TN 38194

Dear Mr. Perkins:

As a lifelong Memphian, I have watched with interest and pride the great success of Federal Express. I would like to contribute to your further progress and growth as an accountant with your company. Leadership ability and solid education in accounting should enable me to make that contribution.

A comprehensive course of study in accounting, earning a Bachelor of Business Administration degree with cum laude honors, has prepared me for a challenging and responsible position with your firm. While attending school full time and also working full time, I maintained a 3.88 average in all courses within the business college. This is the same dedication I would bring to Federal Express.

The ten years with the Memphis Grain and Hay Association developed leadership ability. In addition to duties as a grain inspector, I have been appointed both supervision officer and training officer. I work closely with customers and with officials of the United States Department of Agriculture and maintain daily contact with members of the Memphis Board of Trade. Through these duties, I have learned the value of good interpersonal communication skills.

The enclosed resume contains more information about my background and experience. Should you need any further details, I will be happy to furnish them.

Please write or telephone to let me know when I may talk with you about working for Federal Express. I can be reached in the evening at 323-0000 or at the address shown above.

Sincerely,

Timothy Adams

Timothy Adams

Enclosure

FIGURE 12–2
Letter to accompany resume shown in Figure 11–2

5012 Jennings Way
Sacramento, CA 95608
July 24, 19--

Dr. Wanda Rider, President
The National League of American Pen Women
The Pen-Arts Building
1300-17th Street, N.W.
Washington, DC 20036

Dear Dr. Rider:

Secretarial skills, an ability in creative writing, and a willingness to assume responsibility qualify me for work as your executive secretary. Because of an interest in writing, I am especially eager to work for the National League of American Pen Women.

Dr. Elaine Thompson, Professor of English, Humbolt State University, Arcata, California, told me that you are thinking of adding this position. She has also graciously agreed to serve as a personal reference.

Present responsibilities with the Vocational Rehabilitation Department, the State of California, have prepared me to assume similar responsibilities for you and to work at a higher level. I can handle your correspondence quickly and accurately; keep records and make reports; travel to all meetings; and communicate with members located throughout the world. I can edit and write.

A number of people, including present and past employers, will tell you that I am dependable and energetic. My present employers know of this application.

During the last two weeks of August, I plan to be in the Washington area. Will you write me at the address shown above, or telephone 916-000-0000 to arrange an interview? Please call after six any evening. If you plan to be in your home in Memphis during this two-week period, I can stop in Memphis on my way to Washington, about August 16.

Sincerely,

Carol Chen

Carol Chen

Enclosure

FIGURE 12–3
Letter to accompany resume shown in Figure 11–3. Applicant wants to move from California to Washington, D.C.

2461 North Crestview
Provo, UT 84604
August 7, 19--

Box 3313
c/o Nevada Business Journal
2375 East Tropicana
Las Vegas, NV 89109

SUBJECT: Employment in Information Systems Management

Your entry-level position in information systems management, as
advertised in the August issue of Nevada Business Journal, is one
that I can fill successfully because of my specialized education and
work experience.

Your organization can benefit from my knowledge, dedication, and
hard work. I can quickly learn your policies and the unique
responsibilities that are part of every job. You will find that I am
dependable, as shown by near-perfect attendance; I missed four days
during four years of college classes.

As shown on the enclosed resume, my course work at Brigham
Young University prepared me for all the responsibilities you
describe. In addition, I have on-the-job experience in system analysis
and design and in writing software.

I am willing to relocate to Las Vegas or elsewhere in order to build
a worthwhile, challenging career. One week from today, after
commencement on August 14, I will be free to talk with you about
your organization and what I can offer.

Will you write me at the address shown above or telephone me at
801-000-0000? You can ordinarily reach me after 6 p.m.

I am looking forward to talking with you.

Robert R. Arnold

Robert R. Arnold

FIGURE 12–4
Letter to accompany
resume shown in Fig-
ure 11–4. Application
was sent in answer to
advertisement; writer
does not know name
of company or individ-
ual. The functional ar-
rangement is a good
choice in this kind of
situation.

8476 Rothschild
Metairie, LA 70005
December 10, 19--

Ms. Elaine Schmitz
Vice President, Real Estate Sales
Schmitz Enterprises
5118 Park Avenue
New Orleans, LA 70105

Dear Ms. Schmitz:

Because of a college major in real estate and work experience in a real estate office, I can do a good job for Schmitz Enterprises as a sales representative.

My entire college career has been aimed toward a career in commercial real estate. Years of part-time work in my family's firm, Dupre-Fisher Real Estate, have prepared me for work with your organization. I wish to sell commercial and investment property, not residential. In addition, I plan to leave Dupre-Fisher to prove that I can succeed on my own merits, not because my father is president of the firm.

I have thoroughly researched your organization. Of the many companies I studied in order to determine where to build a career, yours seems to be the one that offers the greatest challenges. You are rebuilding New Orleans. This is the kind of opportunity I am seeking—for the benefit of my employer as well as myself.

The enclosed resume provides further information about my abilities, background, and interests. Please write me at the address shown above or telephone me at 504-000-0000.

Sincerely,

Abigail C. Dupre

Abigail C. Dupre

FIGURE 12–5
Letter to accompany resume shown in Figure 11–5

to be used by substituting personal details, as mentioned above. Tailor your own letter and resume to best display your particular abilities, using your own judgment and creativity.

The Employment Interview

When your resume and application letter accomplish their purpose, you will be asked to come for an interview. As you no doubt realize, a successful interview is crucial to obtaining the employment you wish.

3931 Meadow Lane
Olive Branch, MS 38654
April 30, 19--

Mr. Thurston Drew
Maintenance and Engineering Department
Federal Express Corporation
P.O. Box 727
Memphis, TN 38194

Dear Mr. Drew:

Mr. Jack Doty suggested I write you about your opening for an aviation mechanic in your Memphis Maintenance and Engineering Department. Mr. Doty is an instructor at Memphis Area Vocational-Technical School, where I will soon complete a 22-month training program in aviation mechanics.

Military training, as described on the enclosed resume, provided actual experience in performing preventive maintenance inspections and repairs on aircraft hydraulic and pneumatic systems. While supervising the training of technical personnel, I coordinated maintenance records and allocated tools and materials.

In December 1988, I received an Airframes License and will receive a Powerplants License in July of this year. I have the tools necessary for airframe and powerplant maintenance and am willing to travel or relocate.

You can reach me by telephone (601-000-0000) most evenings after seven. Will you please call to arrange a time when we can talk about putting my maintenance and repair skills to work for Federal Express? I look forward to talking with you.

Sincerely,

William Thomas King

William Thomas King

Enclosure

FIGURE 12–6
Letter to accompany resume shown in Figure 11–6

Only under unusual circumstances is only one person interviewed for a single opening. This necessary and desirable competition requires that the successful applicant continue the sales presentation throughout the interview, presenting superior qualifications and potential for services and development.

Preparing for the Interview

You have spent much of your life preparing to interview for employment in which you are interested and for which you are qualified, although you may

218 South Harwood
Anderson, IN 46001
February 10, 19--

Dr. Emma Chang
Director of Personnel
Indianapolis Public Schools
79 East Washington Street
Indianapolis, IN 46024

Dear Dr. Chang:

As a high school teacher in Indianapolis, I can offer maturity,
ability to work harmoniously with all age groups, energy, and
qualifying degrees.

As shown on the enclosed resume and transcript of undergraduate
and graduate work, I am prepared to teach most business courses
taught in Indianapolis high schools. My particular areas of
specialization are accounting and management information systems.
My teaching internship consisted of classes in personal finance,
bookkeeping, and word processing.

The people listed as references on the attached sheet will speak
highly of my ability and dedication. They will also tell you that I am
dependable, energetic, and sincerely interested in entering and
remaining in the teaching profession.

I have reared five children, seeing them through school from
kindergarten to college. Now it is my turn to teach the children of
other people.

My experience elsewhere than in the classroom has prepared me for
success, I believe, more than a comparable time spent in teaching
would have done. I now bring the enthusiasm of a young beginner
and the knowledge and maturity gained from travel and various life
experiences, in addition to recent undergraduate and graduate
degrees. I have nothing to unlearn.

Please write or telephone me at 317-000-0000. I will come for an
interview at your convenience.

Sincerely,

Allison Tucker Green

Alison Tucker Green

FIGURE 12–7
Letter to accompany
resume shown in Fig-
ure 11–7

1982 Punahou Street
Honolulu, HI 96822
June 1, 19--

Mr. John G. Springer, Partner
Pannell Kerr Forster, CPA's
1714 Makaha Towers
Honolulu, HI 96816

Dear Mr. Springer:

A comprehensive educational program in accounting at the University of Hawaii, leading to a Bachelor of Science in Accounting degree, is an important qualification for beginning work with your firm. In addition, I offer competence, dedication, and ambition.

For the sake of my future employer and for my own benefit, I wish to begin and remain with a progressive accounting firm where I can grow professionally. I realize that years of hard work and outstanding ability are necessary in order to reach the level of partner. I have the necessary ability, stamina, and determination.

Will you write me at the address shown above or telephone me at 808-000-0000 to arrange an interview?

Sincerely,

Walter R. Williams

Walter R. Williams

Enclosure

FIGURE 12–8
Letter to accompany functional resume shown in Figure 11–8

not have been consciously making this preparation. Your educational background, your avocations, your work experience—all these have made you ready for the work for which you are now applying, as well as for a favorable presentation of your qualifications during the interview.

The research that led you to apply to the organization will also enable you to participate in a pleasant and successful employment interview. Your knowledge of the organization, as well as your interest in it, can favorably impress the person or persons with whom you talk. This knowledge will be even more beneficial in that it adds to your self-confidence and enables you to ask necessary and intelligent questions.

If you have made your detailed self-analysis and have studied the particular organization to which you are applying, as well as related organizations, you have accomplished a major portion of your preparation for a successful interview. Review your self-analysis and a copy of the letter of application and

1472 Tutwiler Avenue
Cincinnati, OH 45208
April 22, 19--

Mr. Ray Fleming, Director
Sales Training and Development
Electronic Data Systems Corporation
7171 Forrest Hill Lane
Dallas, TX 75230

Dear Mr. Fleming:

Please consider me for the position in your Sales Training and Development Department, as advertised in *The Wall Street Journal*. I offer nine years' experience in sales and sales training, plus a college degree in marketing.

As sales representative for a bank supplier, Checks, Inc., I conduct training classes in cross-selling and security for bank employees. The ability to work with others, as well as to lead, is established by the success of these programs.

My education has been directed toward sales and training. While working full time and going to college at night, I have also completed several Motivation/Sales seminars. I have extensive training and experience in customer service.

My present employers will substantiate the information in my application. After I have talked with you and am being seriously considered for employment, you may get in touch with officials at Checks, Inc. They will provide recommendations, in addition to those shown on the enclosed resume.

Please write to the address shown above—or telephone 513-000-0000—to arrange a time to discuss my career with your firm.

Sincerely,

Rebecca S. Rosenberg

Rebecca S. Rosenberg

Enclosure

FIGURE 12–9
Application letter to accompany resume shown in Figure 11–1

3617 Boston Road
Senatobia, MS 38668
December 7, 19--

Mr. Don Colvin, Senior Manager
Business Service Centers
Federal Express Corporation
Box 727, Department 3731
Memphis, TN 38194

Dear Mr. Colvin:

Nine years in the Aircraft Support Shops of Federal Express and five additional years of financial experience, two at Federal Express, qualify me for the position of Contract Coordinator, Business Service Centers.

As Technical Assistant, Aircraft Support Shops, I have gained valuable knowledge of Federal Express's operating procedures. I have had the opportunity to interact with many departments while accomplishing varied assignments. This experience has provided insight into the company's internal operations and has increased my ability to communicate effectively with others. I have used this communication ability almost continuously while dealing with other Federal Express employees and with outside contacts.

Prior to employment with Federal Express, I served as an administrative assistant for a small loan company. Responsibilities grew from receptionist-secretary to loan agent. Through this growth, I became familiar with contractual agreements and the legal requirements of each.

My education at Northwest Mississippi Junior College, completed on a part-time basis, has added to my ability to analyze and solve business problems and to plan and supervise. In addition to formal classwork, I have attended numerous workshops and seminars, some of which are listed on the enclosed resume.

Having worked in aircraft maintenance almost from its inception, I know how exciting and challenging a new division can be. I request the opportunity to be a part of such a division with the Federal Express family.

Please telephone me at 601-000-0000 (office) or 601-000-0000 (home) to arrange an interview. My supervisor knows about my application and has offered to recommend me.

Sincerely,

Christina C. Montavelli

Christina C. Montavelli

FIGURE 12–10
Letter to accompany resume shown in Figure 11–10

An appropriately dressed applicant on his way to an employment interview

the resume before you go for the interview. Make sure that the details are firmly in your mind. Giving conflicting information will cast doubt either on your integrity or on your memory.

Take with you to the interview two copies of your resume, even if you have previously submitted one to the employing organization. The interviewer is not certain to have a copy, although he or she should have recently reviewed both your letter and resume. In some cases you will go for an interview with organizations to which you have not submitted a resume, especially when the interview has been arranged through college placement offices. For such interviews, bringing along two copies of the resume can save a great deal of time that would otherwise be spent in giving information that can be concisely stated in a well-organized resume. Also take with you a list of references if such a list was not included in your resume.

Careful attention to your appearance, including neat and appropriate clothing, favorably impresses most interviewers and adds to your self-confidence. Male applicants should wear a dark business suit with a white shirt, a good-quality tie, dark socks, and black leather shoes.

Women applicants should prefer a two-piece suit, with the jacket matching the skirt. Although they should look businesslike, their appearance need not be severe and masculine. An appropriate blouse can soften the suit and still retain a conservative image. Jewelry and makeup should be inconspicuous.

Care with your appearance shows that you have a sincere interest in both the job and the organization; it implies that you will fit in with other employees and project a professional impression that will benefit your organization as well as yourself.

Good clothing is not inexpensive, but your education and other preparation for career employment have not been inexpensive. Invest in suitable attire that will be good for months or years on the job.

Before the day of the interview, try to learn the name of the person who will interview you, with the correct spelling and pronunciation. In many instances you will be interviewed by more than one person; the more you can learn about these people, the better prepared you will be.

Learn the exact location of the interview, including the street address, building, and room number. Determine the route to this location and how long the trip will take. The day of the interview is no time to become lost.

Take with you a notebook and pen. A good-quality, fairly small briefcase is convenient and impressive for both men and women applicants.

You cannot completely prepare for all aspects of the interview. As in all other communication situations, the outcome will be affected by the personalities of both the applicant and the interviewer and by the circumstances of the environment. If you are truly qualified for the position, however, and if you have learned to communicate effectively in other interpersonal encounters, you are likely to be successful in the employment interview.

Arriving for the Interview

Plan to arrive a few minutes early so that you are not rushed. Be relaxed and poised, not out of breath and nervous.

When you arrive at the office, identify yourself to the receptionist. When you are called into the office, greet the interviewer by name. Shake hands firmly. Be confident. Wait for an invitation before seating yourself. Do not smoke.

The first few minutes, probably the first few seconds, are crucial. Fairly or unfairly, decisions are often made based on first impressions.

Proceeding with the Interview

Allow the interviewer to open the conversation. The interviewer may begin with casual conversation to put you at ease, such as remarks about your trip, your school, or the weather. Or the interviewer may begin by asking direct questions or giving you background information about the organization or about the particular job for which you are applying.

The interviewer perhaps will ask you to expand on the information in the resume, which is of necessity condensed. You may be asked, for example, to give more details about your work experience.

You may be asked to explain why you left a position or positions, to describe the type of work that you liked best and least, to state what you feel you accomplished on each job, and to express your opinions as to whether your supervisor and co-workers were capable and cooperative. Be careful when commenting on this topic; your interviewer is not really asking about your co-workers and supervisors but about yourself. But, as in all other situations, do not be untruthful. Remember, though, that your own competence and spirit of helpfulness and dedication will usually result in your finding the same qualities in other persons.

Principles of communication you have studied previously apply to your

An employment interview. From the interviewer's face, can you determine whether the applicant is being favorably considered?

attitude toward the interviewer and your conduct in conversation. You have learned, as in written communication, to approach all business interpersonal situations on a straightforward basis of equality. Although you may have much to gain or lose in your search for employment on the outcome of an interview, the representative of the employing organization also has a purpose essential to the welfare of the organization—that of finding the best person for the job.

If you sincerely believe that you are this person and can convince the interviewer of this fact without building resentment because of your egotism or an overly aggressive approach, both you and the employing organization will have benefited from the relatively short time spent in talking about your professional future.

What questions will you ask? Don't be in a hurry to shower the interviewer with questions, many of which will be answered in the course of the conversation. On the other hand, don't merely sit and wait for information to come your way, and do not answer in monosyllables. Although you should not try to take charge of the interview, seize the opportunity to present yourself in the most favorable light. If you cannot communicate well enough to do so, you may leave the impression—probably an accurate one—that your communication skills will be less than ideal for your career. (Perhaps you will wish to ask a friend to help you practice for the interview.)

If you have done adequate research into this organization, along with other organizations, you already know something about the company, including its offices and branches, products, and services. You can also find its recent growth and earnings. By reading company brochures, you will know a great deal about training programs and employee benefits.

The interview is two-sided. The company interviews you and you interview the company. One area of vital concern will be your opportunities for growth and responsibility. Are you likely to become "locked in" regardless of your hard work and ability? You will need to know the company policy on promotions, whether higher positions are filled from the inside or whether you will need to count on moving within a few years to an organization that offers greater opportunity.

Most of all, you will want to know whether the work is the kind for which you are especially well prepared. Is it the kind in which you can excel and maintain a sincere interest? Is this an organization in which you can feel that your work matters and of which you can be proud, not only for the benefit of the employing organization but also for yourself and your family? Without sincere pride in the employing organization, an idealistic person will not be satisfied with a good salary alone. On the other hand, a good income is essential for most persons as a symbol of competence and accomplishment—to say nothing of its being necessary for comfort and security.

If you are not fitted for the job for which you are being considered, or if it is not a job in which you can be content to spend a portion of your life, the real benefit that you derive from an interview is determining unsuitability.

Responding to Questions

Besides being asked questions about your previous education and work experience, you may also receive surprising questions that are planned to test your ability to think quickly and to react positively and confidently under stress. The following list contains some of the most frequently asked questions, but no list can include all that you may receive. A knowledge of yourself and of the employing company, however, will help you to respond well to any kind of question. Be prepared.

1. *Tell me about yourself.* This is your opportunity to continue the sales presentation that you began with your application letter and resume. Present your qualifications in relation to how they will benefit the company.

2. *Why do you want this job?* Show that you have researched the company and know its overall purpose and opportunities. Continue to stress benefits that you can offer to the company.

3. *Why have you chosen the field of (accounting, sales, management, and so on)?* This is an opportunity to impress the interviewer, without seeming to be egotistical, with your strengths in your particular field and your interest in professional growth. Do not talk about salary or leisure time. Emphasize your knowledge of, and liking for, the work itself.

4. *Why should we hire you?* Be prepared to convince, continuing with your central selling point.

5. *What salary would you expect?* Try to let the interviewer state the salary, which you may negotiate later. Prefer to leave discussion of salary until you have convinced the interviewer that you are the best person for the job.

6. *Why do you want to (did you) leave your job?* Be as positive as possible by stressing benefits of relocating without dwelling on negative aspects of your present or former job.

7. *What are your long-range goals? (Where do you expect to be ten years from now?)*

8. *What are your greatest strengths?* State qualities you possess that will be helpful in the job for which you are applying. Prove that you have these qualities by giving concrete evidence of past accomplishments.

9. *What are your weaknesses?* Be extremely careful as you respond to this question. Do not volunteer anything negative unless you can turn the negative into an asset; for example, "I tend to become impatient when I do not meet my goals"; "I tend to become overly involved and committed, but with time management skills and delegation skills I am able to meet my goals"; or "Perhaps I am a workaholic at times." Another possibility is to mention a relatively unimportant area that is not related to the job, or to mention a minor job-related area and show how you are working to improve your ability.

10. *How do others describe you?* Show that you work well with other people.

11. *Can you work well under pressure?* Give concrete examples.

12. *Can you work without close supervision?* Give concrete examples.

13. *Do you have plans for continued education and study?* Show that you expect to keep learning all your life. Be specific about any plans for continued formal education.

14. *What subjects did you like best in school?* Do not be untruthful, but do not mention your love for ancient history or poetry if you are applying, as an example, for a position in accounting or management.

Other questions that may be asked are these:

15. *What do you do in your spare time?*

16. *Are you willing to relocate?*

17. *Are you willing to travel?*

18. *What is the one most important factor you are looking for in a job?*

19. *What extracurricular activities did you participate in when you were in school?*

20. *Do you belong to professional organizations? Which ones?*

21. *Were you in military service?*

22. *Do you have any impairments, physical, mental, or medical, that would interfere with your ability to do the job for which you have applied?*

23. *How long have you been a resident of this city?*

Certain questions should not be asked in an employment interview. For example, women are asked questions that would not be asked of male applicants, such as "Who takes care of your children while you work?" or "Do you think your career will interfere with your marriage?" You are not obliged to answer these questions; some applicants state that they prefer not to do so. You are usually wiser to try to determine the intent of the question. For example, if

A physically handicapped person is entitled to equal opportunities for employment.

a job requires travel and you are able and willing to do so, assure the interviewer of your understanding that travel is a component of the position and of your willingness to meet your responsibilities and obligations.

Ending the Interview

You can usually ascertain by the interviewer's remarks and nonverbal signals when the interview is coming to a close. Use these last few minutes to summarize a few important qualifications and to express your continued interest in working for the company. Express appreciation for an informative and interesting interview.

The interviewer will probably tell you when you will be notified or what is the next step in the employment procedure. Offer to supply any additional information or to provide references. Do not linger once it is clear that the interview is over.

Following Through in the Employment Search

Your efforts should not end after completing the interview. Continue to indicate your interest in the position and appreciation for the interview, but do not annoy the interviewer or demand an early decision.

```
                                              24815 Wyandotte Avenue
                                              Mentone, CA 92359
                                              January 11, 19--

Mr. Robert J. Samuels
Sales Manager
Yohanak Corporation
2091 Risser Road South
Madison, WI 53507

Dear Mr. Samuels:

Thank you for a most pleasant and informative interview. I am very much
interested in working for the Yohanak Corporation.

The opportunity that you mentioned for possible work outside the United
States in a few years appeals to me. As shown on my resume, I speak and
write French and Spanish, in addition to English.

I will be glad to supply any more information you may need.

                                              Sincerely,

                                              Carlos Rodriguez
                                              Carlos Rodriguez
```

FIGURE 12–11
Example of a thank-you letter

Thank-You Letters

Within a day or two after your employment interview, mail a thank-you letter. This letter is a matter of courtesy; you should send it whether or not you feel that you are being favorably considered. The thank-you letter is ordinarily short because you have little to say. It is a goodwill message. Sincerity and a natural, conversational tone are the major requirements. A thank-you letter is illustrated in Figure 12–11.

Many applicants do not send thank-you letters after an interview, perhaps because of a mistaken idea that to do so is "pushy," or, more likely, because of simple procrastination or lack of effort. That few persons send these letters is a point in your favor to make you stand out from other applicants. The letter serves as a reminder of who you are. Even more important, it shows continued interest and initiative.

At times you will have additional information to convey in the thank-you letter. For example, perhaps you have been asked whether you would move to another city and you have requested time to think it over. If you have made up your mind in the day or two before the thank-you letter should be mailed, you may state your decision in the letter. Or perhaps you have read the brochures provided for you or you have been asked to submit the names of persons to recommend you if these names were not included on the resume.

Additional information is not a requirement. Send a thank-you letter even if you have no new information to convey.

```
        1982 Punahou Street
        Honolulu, HI 96822
        July 7, 19--


        Mr. John G. Springer, Partner
        Pannell Kerr Forster, CPA's
        1714 Makaha Towers
        Honolulu, HI 96816

        Dear Mr. Springer:

        As a follow-up to my application letter and resume mailed to you on
        June 1, I wish to emphasize to you my continued interest in
        employment with Pannell Kerr Forster.

        Will you please arrange an interview? I can be reached by telephone
        (808-000-0000) mornings before ten and evenings after six. Or, if
        you prefer, write me at the address shown above.

        I am eager to contribute my energy and ability to the future
        progress of your accounting firm.

        Sincerely,

        Walter R. Williams

        Walter R. Williams
```

FIGURE 12–12
A follow-up letter

Follow-Up Letters

Follow-up letters may be helpful when you have not heard from the employing organization within a reasonable time after the interview. The exact time varies; some college seniors are interviewed near the beginning of their senior year and notified within a month or two of graduation. Usually, however, the applicant is notified within a few weeks or even within a few days.

You may also write a follow-up letter after submitting an application letter and resume if too much time seems to elapse before you are called for an interview.

Provided they are well written and used at the proper time, follow-up letters accomplish several purposes. They show that you are still interested in the organization and that you are diligent in your efforts to obtain employment. These letters may also report additional information not included in the application letter and resume or reported in interviews—for example, the completion of related courses, additional work experience, or special scholastic honors or other accomplishments.

Avoid a demanding or hurt tone, and don't indicate surprise that you have not been asked for an interview. But don't apologize for writing.

A follow-up letter is shown in Figure 12–12.

24815 Wyandotte Avenue
Mentone, CA 92359
February 9, 19--

Mr. Robert J. Samuels
Sales Manager
Yohanak Corporation
2091 Risser Road South
Madison, WI 53507

Dear Mr. Samuels:

Yes, I accept your offer of a position as a sales representative for northern California. I look forward to working with you and the other people at Yohanak.

Your letter with the attached handbook is helpful and descriptive. The conditions you mention are satisfactory: a salary of $19,000 a year, plus 10 percent commission over quota; a company car; all expenses; and full employment benefits.

As you requested, I will begin work on March 1 by reporting to your Madison office for orientation. I will be there at 9 a.m.

Please let me know if there is anything else I should do between now and March 1.

Sincerely,

Carlos Rodriguez

Carlos Rodriguez

FIGURE 12–13
Letter of acceptance

Job-Acceptance and Job-Refusal Letters

Job-acceptance letters, like other good-news and routine informational letters, are usually best arranged in the direct order, with the acceptance in the first sentence, as in Figure 12–13. Your job-acceptance letter should include any additional information that the employing organization may need and any questions of your own.

In job-refusal letters, remember to express appreciation for the employment offer. As in other negative messages, your letter will be more psychologically convincing and acceptable if reasons are given before the refusal, as in Figure 12–14.

Do everything you can to keep the goodwill of the reader and of the organization.

5012 Jennings Way
Sacramento, CA 95608
September 25, 19--

Dr. Wanda Rider, President
The National League of American Pen Women
The Pen-Arts Building
1300-17th Street, N.W.
Washington, DC 20036

Dear Dr. Rider:

Thank you for offering me the position as your executive secretary.

After meeting with you in August, I was even more impressed with the importance of the work you are doing with the American Pen Women. And, as expressed in earlier letters and in the interview, I am very much interested in your organization.

Since I talked with you on August 18, however, changes have occurred. Because of a legacy from my grandmother, I have decided to continue my education, working toward a four-year degree in creative writing and television production at the University of Southern California.

Dr. Rider, I regret that timing is such that someone else must be your next executive secretary. Best wishes as you continue your work.

Sincerely,

Carol Chen

Carol Chen

FIGURE 12–14
A letter of refusal

Other Communications about Employment

After you are employed, your communication ability will be valuable as you learn the responsibilities of your particular position and the policies and procedures of the organization. You will read and write materials of various kinds, many of which have been discussed in preceding chapters.

Communications Used in the Hiring and Training Process

Additional letters and memorandums about employment include inquiries about prospective employees, replies to such requests, good-news and bad-news letters about jobs, and instructions to new employees. The communications and principles that apply are discussed and illustrated in Chapters 6, 7, 8, and 9.

COUNTRYWIDE COMPANY INSURANCE

Home office: New York City
420 Madison, 10577

October 15, 19--

Mr. Martin O'Conner
Communications Supervisor
Countrywide Insurance Company
420 Madison Avenue
New York, NY 10577

Dear Mr. O'Conner:

Working at Countrywide has meant a great deal to me. Thank you,
Mr. O'Conner, for hiring me and for being helpful and considerate
throughout the fifteen months of employment.

The association with you and the other fine people at Countrywide
has taught me many things that will continue to be of benefit. You
helped me succeed in my first job and in making the adjustment
from my small home town to New York City. You have my deepest
appreciation.

In spite of my gratitude and high regard for Countrywide Insurance
Company, I plan to leave on November 1 to begin work with
Horizon Press here in New York. I have been offered a job as
editorial assistant with the possibility of becoming an editor.
Because this is the kind of work I have always wanted to do, this
letter is my official letter of resignation.

People at Horizon Press have agreed for me to stay a week or two
beyond November 1 if you need me to train a replacement, which I
will be glad to do.

Best wishes to you and to my other co-workers at Countrywide. You
will have my enduring friendship and respect.

Sincerely,

Sally Ann Benson

Sally Ann Benson
Secretary

FIGURE 12–15
Letter of resignation

Letters of Resignation

Even though you are leaving your present position, your letter of resignation can be important to your future career. It may influence recommendations from your present employer. In addition, you could possibly wish to return to your present organization.

A written resignation is often required. It becomes part of your personnel file. The letter should be written at least two weeks before you plan to leave—except in rare and justified circumstances. You should discuss your plans with your immediate supervisor before you prepare the written resignation.

Do everything you can to maintain friendly, pleasant relationships, as shown in Figure 12–15. Apart from the fact that you owe your employer for what you have gained from your work—and you have almost certainly gained something in addition to your paycheck—leaving a negative impression with your present employer is a poor start for your new job.

Summary

The application letter, sent with a resume, forms a two-part application package. In addition, the letter is a sales message, arranged similarly to a sales letter for a product or service.

You should build your letter around your most outstanding qualification in relation to the position sought. Your central selling point will probably be either education or experience.

The purpose of the application letter and the resume is to obtain an interview. The tone should be straightforward and businesslike; you must show confidence in your ability but refrain from appearing egotistical or overly aggressive. Substantiate positive qualities by concrete evidence of past experiences and accomplishments.

Preparing for the employment interview is necessary for its success. Learn as much as possible about the organization and the interviewer. Wear conservative, attractive, and businesslike clothing and arrive on time.

Questions asked by the interviewer seek knowledge about your background, poise, communication ability, and potential.

Send a thank-you letter after every interview. A letter of resignation should be sent two weeks before the effective date.

Test Yourself: Chapter Review

1–7. Name seven "don'ts" that apply to letters of application.

8. Briefly describe the first paragraph of an application letter.

9. Briefly describe the ending paragraph of an application letter.

10. Why is it not advisable to begin several paragraphs with *I*?

11. Why should you ordinarily not mention salary?

12–16. Give five suggestions for preparing for an interview.

17–19. Name three things that you should take to an interview.

20–26. Name seven questions that an interviewer is likely to ask.

27–28. What are two purposes of a thank-you letter?

29–30. What are two purposes of a follow-up letter?

Note: Cases for both Chapters 11 and 12 follow the next section. Because the two chapters are interrelated, the cases, which are planned for written assignments and for discussion, apply to both chapters. Several cases in the Cases section following Chapter 16 also apply.

Test Yourself: Correct Usage

(Related to material in Chapter 12 and principles of correct usage.) Insert necessary punctuation, including quotation marks, hyphens, and apostrophes, and remove punctuation that has been inserted incorrectly. Choose correct word or sentence from each pair or group. Make any other necessary changes.

1. The application letter should be on good quality bond paper. Letter perfect.
2. An application letter should make a good impression, it should convince the prospective employer to interview you.

Improve the following passages from application letters.

3. Enclosed herewith you will find my resume.
4. Thanking you in advance, I am respectfully yours,
5. I want to be interviewed on Tuesday, September 11th, some time in the afternoon.
6. During the passed month I have studied English.
7. It is alright to contact my employer.
8. All my past employers except 2 will reccommend me.
9. I can begin work on Monday November 6 1990 in your Los Angeles office.
10. My College degree should increase my success as a sells representative in two areas. Marketing and engineering technology.

Evaluation Sheet: Application Letters

	Yes	No	Not Sure
1. Is the letter presented throughout in terms of reader benefit?			
2. Is the positive approach used throughout—a tone of quiet confidence, without egotism or presumption?			
3. Does the first paragraph make clear that the applicant is applying for a particular job?			
4. Does the letter omit stereotyped expressions?			
5. Is the letter written in the words of the applicant, not paraphrased or lifted from examples in textbooks?			
6. Does the letter omit references to salary or benefits?			
7. Does the letter omit obvious statements?			

	Yes	No	Not Sure
8. Does the letter include specific and positive details to convince the reader of the applicant's ability and suitability for the opening?	___	___	___
9. Are *I*'s, *me*'s, and other first-person pronouns used naturally and as necessary, but not to excess? Do most paragraphs begin with some other word?	___	___	___
10. Does the writer specifically request an interview?	___	___	___
11. Does the letter indicate that the applicant is familiar with the employing organization because of previous research?	___	___	___
12. Is the letter absolutely perfect in appearance and correctness?	___	___	___

Cases for Chapters 11 and 12

1. Prepare a self-analysis similar to that discussed in Chapter 11. Include your education, experience, hobbies, personal characteristics, likes and dislikes, ambitions, and anything else that will affect your success in obtaining employment.

   Make this study complete. Ordinarily it will be more detailed than your resume, but by making a thorough self-analysis you will be better able to decide which items to include and which to emphasize. This analysis is for your use only.

2. Make a list of the kinds of employment for which you are qualified and in which you are interested, based on your self-study. Approach this study from one of two ways:

   a. Assume that you are near graduation and that you are looking for full-time career employment. This assumption is the more valuable one if you expect to graduate within a year or two or if you now have in mind definite career objectives.

   b. Prepare the list of various kinds of work in relation to part-time or summer jobs. Include only the kinds of work that really interest you and that offer opportunities for career employment after graduation.

3. Make a study of employing organizations that seem to offer the opportunities you are seeking. Use the sources described in Chapter 11 and any other useful ones. Write a memorandum to your instructor about how you proceeded in the investigation. List the three organizations toward which you plan to direct your efforts and the reasons for these choices. Give your first choice, with reasons.

4. Prepare a resume from the detailed studies you have made so far. You are to send the letter and a resume to each of the three organizations you have chosen. Depending on the kinds of organizations to which you are submitting your resume, you may be able to use copies of one resume for the three companies.

5. Write a letter of application to accompany the resumes you prepared for Case 4. These letters should be individually composed and typewritten for each of the three companies.

6. Mail the letters and resumes you have prepared, or if you are not interested in obtaining or changing employment at this time, save the letters and resumes to be used or modified later. Be sure that the envelopes you use are of good quality and of standard business length so that the letter can be folded in approximate thirds. The envelope should match the paper in weight and quality.

7. Follow through with interviews, thank-you letters, and, if necessary, follow-up letters. (If you did not actually mail the applications, assume that you did so and that three weeks have elapsed. Write a follow-up letter showing your continued interest and asking for an interview.)

8. Assume that you are interviewed by representatives of each of the organizations. Write one or more thank-you letters, as directed by your instructor.

9. Assume that three weeks have elapsed since your interview with each of the organizations. Write one or more follow-up letters, as directed by your instructor.

10. Assume that you are offered the position. Write a letter of acceptance. Assume reasonable details about dates of employment, location, or other necessary material to include in your letter.

11. Assume that you are also offered a position from the organization that was your second choice. Write a letter refusing the position.

12. Assume that it is now two years later. You have decided that you would now like to work with the organization that was originally your second choice. Write

a letter of inquiry, reminding them that you were offered a job two years ago. Offer to send a current resume. (In actual use, perhaps you would be wiser to send a current resume *with* the present letter.)

13. Assume that you are successful in obtaining employment with the organization to which you wrote in Case 12. Write a letter of resignation to your present employer.

14. Analyze the following application letter, an actual one, which, with a resume, was sent to a small publishing company. You can find many needed improvements, but can you find anything about the letter that is *right?* What?

Dear Sir:

I am writing you this letter because I have a full time job in which my time is limited and because so many establishments are not even accepting applications. So, in order to save both your time and mine, I thought I would send you a brief resume so that, if you have any openings, you can call me for an interview at your convenience. If you have no openings, possibly you could file this until such time that you have.

I have heard that you employ a good many proofreaders. This is something I feel I could do well. I have not done this for another before (I do a little freelancing in my spare time.), but I have a feel for the English language that many seemingly do not. I am willing to take whatever tests might be necessary to establish my ability.

My work record follows, along with a couple of references. Although I prefer that my present employer not be contacted—I might be fired on the spot for considering another job—the one prior to that can vouch for my reliability. I have missed no days in the past two years of 55 to 60 hours of work a week and before that, including a 3 day absence for a bout with pneumonia, I missed a total of 5 days at my previous job in the three years I worked there. Also, I am habitually early.

I would appreciate it enormously if you would consider my application. Thank you for your time.

CHAPTER **13**

An Overview of Reports: Writing Proposals and Report Plans

Your ability to excel in reporting knowledge and techniques can be an outstanding asset to your career in business. Reports of many kinds are vital in the everyday operation of modern business activity. Your ability to gather, organize, analyze, and present needed information may be the determining factor in your success, and the lack of such an ability can keep you in a lower-level position.

The Nature and Purpose of Reports

A report is a written or oral message planned to convey information or to present a solution. Under this broad and simple definition, many letters, memorandums, telephone calls, and personal conversations are forms of reports. A report may also be a formal written one of hundreds of pages, on which many persons have worked for months or years.

Reports may consist of written and spoken words, columns of figures, charts, computer printouts, or a combination of all these and other forms. Although any kind of report conveying business information is a business report, the definition must be narrowed as it pertains to the study and discussion of reports prepared for business purposes.

In a definition that follows, the word *effective* has been inserted to describe what reports should be, not necessarily what they are. Because even a poor report is called a report, the wording of the exact definition of the term is complicated. Thus:

> An effective business report is an orderly, objective presentation of factual information with or without analysis, interpretation, and recommendations, which is planned to serve some business purpose, usually that of making a decision.

Other descriptions of a report are that it

- is a management tool;
- may vary according to purpose, format, time prepared, subject matter, scope, length, readership, and other factors;
- may vary widely in form, length, and content;
- may merely report information, without analysis, or may report information and, in addition, analyze the information and include recommendations;
- may be planned only to analyze existing information;
- is usually written for one reader or for a small group of readers;
- usually moves up the chain of command;
- tends to be written in a style more formal than that used for other types of business communication;
- ordinarily is assigned;
- may be prepared at specified, regular intervals or only for a special need;
- requires careful planning and organization;
- answers a question or solves a problem.

When planning reports, we must give special attention to organization and to an objective, nonbiased approach. Because reports are often longer than letters or memorandums, they must be especially planned for readability and an orderly progression of thought.

All over the globe every moment of the day, someone is being asked to make a search and write a report on some state of fact, or else to read and analyze one, so that action may be taken.

Among the many useful documents that may strictly or loosely be classed as reports there is no essential difference of outlook or method. The student writing a book report for a Freshman English course is doing on a small scale and with a single source the same thing as the president of a corporation who prepares his annual report to the stockholders, or as the President of the United States when, with the aid of all his departments, he reports to the people on the state of the Union.

Jacques Barzun and Henry F. Graff, *The Modern Researcher*, rev. ed. (New York: Harcourt, Brace & World, 1970), 4.

Communication Brief

Informational and Analytical (Problem-Solving) Reports

Informational reports simply present information, with no attempt to analyze or interpret the meaning of the data or to make recommendations for action.

Analytical reports also provide information and in addition include analysis and interpretation. Those that include recommendations are also referred to as *recommendation* or *problem-solving reports*.

Informational reports tend to be shorter than analytical ones, but this distinction is not applicable to all. Informational reports can be of any length, depending on the amount of information to convey. Conversely, an analytical report can be short. (*Long* and *short* are relative terms, in reports as well as in everything else.) We do, however, often hear the term *long analytical report* or *complete analytical report*. *Complete* may mean that the report contains various preliminary and supplementary parts, as discussed and illustrated in Chapter 16. The word may also be used to signify that the report and the investigation that precede the report are broad in scope.

The distinction between informational and analytical reports will be important as you consider a proposed project. One of your first steps, especially if you are a new employee, will be to find out exactly what is expected in a report.

Formal and Informal Reports

Purpose and readership determine the degree of formality. As when used elsewhere, the words *formal* and *informal* are relative as they describe reports; there is no exact and distinct dividing line. Reports that are not definitely and conclusively formal are best described as informal, a description that fits most business and professional writing and speech. In written messages, the words *formal* and *informal* are used to describe format, writing style, or both.

*Improve
Your Writing*

Question: Please list words and phrases that are frequently misused.

Answer: Of the many, here are a few:

All right consists of two separate words. Although *alright* is often used, this spelling has not received general acceptance.

Bad and *badly* are not interchangeable in use and meaning. *Bad* is an adjective; *badly* is an adverb. You would feel bad if you caused your friend to be badly hurt.

Party should not be used, except in legal papers, to mean *person.*

Imply and *infer* are often confused. *Imply* means to suggest or to indicate. *Infer* means to assume. A speaker or writer implies. A reader or listener infers.

The reason is because is not considered correct, at least in writing. Prefer *the reason is that* . . . .

Plus should not be used as a conjunction to mean *and.*

Media (channels of communication) is a plural word. *Medium* is the singular.

Criteria is a plural noun; *criterion* is singular.

Try and is colloquial usage. Prefer *try to.*

Comprise means to include or to consist of. *Compose* means to make up. The parts compose (make up) the whole; the whole comprises (includes) the parts.

A pronoun used as an object is in the objective case: *for him* and *me* . . . (object of preposition *for*); *gave my mother and me* . . . (object of verb *gave*); *gave the other students and me a holiday* . . . (indirect object).

Format

A completely formal written report includes preliminary and supplementary parts omitted from more informal arrangements, as shown in Chapter 16. Such a report is also described as a *complete report.* Some of these preliminary parts are *letter of transmittal, letter of acceptance, table of contents, list of tables,* and *synopsis.* Supplementary parts include a *bibliography, appendix sections,* and perhaps an *index.*

Informal reports may be presented in letter or memorandum format or in various other short-form arrangements. In addition, informal reports are prepared on preprinted forms in order to simplify preparation and to aid reader comprehension.

A long report is likely to be arranged in the formal (or complete) format, and a short report is likely to be presented as a memorandum or in some other informal report arrangement. This distinction, however, does not always apply. A fairly short report—six or seven pages, for example—may appropriately include preliminary and supplementary parts if these parts are necessary or helpful to the reader.

Wording

Formal writing includes no contractions, expressions that could be considered slang, or abbreviated sentences or sentence fragments. An informal writing style may include contractions and casual, conversational phrases or modes of expression. Most reports are written more formally than routine memorandums, but all business and professional writing should be interesting, natural, and easy to read.

Formal and informal writing styles are discussed in Chapter 3.

Writing Styles

A report that is formal in format and wording is likely to be written in the *impersonal writing style,* which is also called the *third-person objective style* or the *impersonal tone.* An informal report is more likely to be written in the *personal writing style.*

The difference between the two styles is this: The impersonal style includes no first- or second-person pronouns; for example, *I, we, us, you,* or *your.* In addition, the impersonal style includes no implied *you's* or the contraction *let's* (*let us*).

The personal and impersonal writing styles are discussed in Chapter 3.

Reports in the Direct (Deductive) and Indirect (Inductive) Arrangements

Like all other forms of written communication, reports can be arranged in the direct (deductive) order or in the indirect (inductive) order, as described in Chapter 5. In addition, they can be arranged in chronological order, but this arrangement usually does not give proper emphasis to whatever should be emphasized.

The indirect arrangement (as applied to reports) begins with an introduction, presents findings and their interpretation, and ends with conclusions and recommendations. This arrangement is also described as the *logical* order—an inexact and nondescriptive term in that a well-organized report arranged in the direct order is also logical if it makes sense.

Many analytical reports, especially short ones, present conclusions as the first section of the report. (Conclusions may be only recommendations, or they may present the writer's most important interpretations and also include recommendations, either stated or implied.) This "gist of the message" is followed by purpose, methods, or other necessary explanatory material, followed by supporting facts and interpretations on which the conclusions and recommendations are based.

Compare the direct and the indirect arrangements:

Indirect arrangement	Direct arrangement
Purpose, methods, other introductory material	Conclusions (includes recommendations, either stated or implied)
Findings	Purpose, methods, other necessary explanatory material
Conclusions (includes recommendations, either stated or implied)	Findings

Even if a report is presented in the inductive (indirect) order, the use of a synopsis combines the features of both the direct and indirect arrangements in the overall report "package," which consists of the preliminaries, the report itself, and the supplementary parts. (See Chapter 16.)

The synopsis (also called an abstract) is a greatly condensed version of the complete report and includes summations of the introduction, findings, conclusions, and recommendations. Because of the placement of the synopsis before the actual report, the report package is arranged in the direct order because the gist of the entire report is presented before supporting details and information.

A Problem-Solving Situation

Research, like the even broader term *communication,* applies to almost everything we do. As we attempt to solve ever-occurring problems, large and small, we engage in a form of research, although much of it is far from being objective and scientific. Suppose, for example, that when driving to work you find a severe traffic jam on the street you usually travel. Under ordinary conditions this street is the most direct route to your office. You have an important appointment at 9:15, and it is now 8:15. If normal traffic conditions prevailed, you could reach your office in half an hour.

Your problem is—what to do? Should you wait here and hope that the stalled automobiles will move on, or should you detour, provided you can work yourself onto a side street? (A comparable business problem would be to decide whether an organization should continue with the present and heretofore successful method of operation or, because of unexpected difficulties, change the method of operation.) Will the more indirect route, which is ordinarily slower because of school zones, residential areas, and stop lights, provide a quicker method of reaching the office?

You obviously do not put this statement into written form, but, on a simple level, this situation is like a problem you face when you undertake a business research project: You state the problem, choose a method or methods of finding information, collect and organize data, evaluate and interpret their meaning, and arrive at a solution to the problem, whether or not your particular solution is the best possible one.

Using this example of traffic congestion, you would probably undertake the action and arrive at a solution at the same time—that is, you would embark on the assumed solution and collect and organize the data in your mind as you move along. Then your report would be presented orally to your employer and associates when you finally arrive at the office. As you meander through the side streets or wait in your automobile in the traffic jam, you are collecting data as you keep track of the time. This may be unfavorable data, but you made your choice, right or wrong, when you turned off the main thoroughfare or decided to wait.

Some business, professional, and government organizations seem to make their decisions in just this way; they go ahead and turn or remain immobile on a jammed street and figure out as time passes whether or not they made the right decision. Research could lead to a wise plan of action.

What kind of research could you do to determine the best route to your office? You could study the maps and determine the mileage by both routes. You could turn your automobile radio to the station that reports traffic conditions; perhaps you can learn the extent of the traffic blockage and when the street can be expected to be back to normal. The radio voice might also tell you something of the traffic conditions on the side streets you are considering. If you have telephone or radio contact with your office, you could find out how important it is that you arrive at the regular time, for perhaps the important appointment you are hurrying to has been cancelled for some reason, or perhaps it could be delayed.

This question, however, is not relevant to your subquestion of which route will provide the quickest trip to the office; it does apply to the question that you started with: what to do. These questions should not be analyzed together, but ones such as these tend to become jumbled as we find ourselves entangled in a problem or, especially, when putting the report into written form.

In the problem-solving situation, you would collect all this information, analyze it for its validity and applicability, and arrive at a conclusion on which you would make your recommendation of the better choice of the two courses of action.

Your conclusion has been based partly on assumptions, or *inferences*. If the radio voice has told you of a three-car accident that is blocking all lanes of traffic, you infer that it will be some time before your regular route is ready for travel. Your calculations of the mileage by both routes can be considered a fact if you are sure that the mapmakers were accurate—but then this assumption is also an inference. (*Even though we can never be completely sure of most things, we must treat some inferences as if they were facts, at least until we have time to investigate them further.*)

Reasonable inferences supported by sufficient facts may serve as a basis for recommendations, although at times these recommendations will be incorrect. Your value judgments, unsupported by facts, should not be used as a basis for recommendations. From a practical business standpoint, the fact that the side streets making up the indirect route are more picturesque is not relevant to your question of which way to drive to the office. Your appreciation of flowering trees and clumps of daffodils is a value judgment, even though many people would agree with you.

Another method of research would be to call to a person in the next car: "Sir, have you ever driven down Flamingo Street to Cherry, then to Rhodes and Barron, and then on Lamar to downtown?" If he has driven this route recently, his advice would compare to what you might find in a business journal of how another business organization solved a problem similar to the one you are now trying to solve. In addition, his reply to you is *primary* research, based on your brief interview with him.

As you may have realized, much of successful business research and report writing is the application of mere common sense. But then common sense cannot be exactly described as "mere."

Determining and Defining the Purpose of the Report

Determining that a problem exists is not difficult from the standpoint of knowing that something is wrong or needs improvement. Stating in specific terms exactly what you wish to determine in order to solve the problem is more difficult.

If the research project has been assigned to you, as ordinarily it will be, make sure that you and the person who authorized the report are in complete agreement about the purpose of the report, including limitations and boundaries of the study; *you need to know exactly what you are and are not attempting to find out.* You also need to discuss cost considerations.

The first and most important step in the report process is specifically stating your purpose.

Limiting the Problem

The boundaries of a research problem are referred to as the *scope. Delimitations* is a term used instead of *scope* to describe specifically excluded parts that might have been expected in the report. The term *limitations* means situations or handicaps, such as lack of time or money, that prevented a complete research study or a thorough presentation.

In this book, the term *scope* is used to indicate boundaries; *limitations* are limiting or detrimental factors.

However you use these terms as headings of a report, you must limit the scope of a report problem by exact and definite boundaries. You consider the scope in order to state the problem in definite and specific wording, as well as to plan research procedures.

A Tentative Report Plan

Before beginning research to find the answer to a business problem, consider preparing a report plan, even though it must be a tentative one. Such an outline of procedure, although it may change during the research process, is a more efficient approach than no plan at all.

An example of a report plan is shown in Figure 13–1.

A Tentative Table of Contents

A tentative table of contents is shown in Figure 13–2. If you prefer, refer to such an outline *as* an outline, as you have done when planning papers for other purposes. Whether you describe it as an outline or a table of contents, such a written plan for the material to be included and the order of presentation will aid you throughout the research, interpretation, and writing processes.

A Proposal

As previously mentioned in this chapter, *report plans*, such as the one illustrated in Figure 13–1, are proposals for research projects. The terms *proposal, research proposal,* and *proposal report,* however, are used to denote a longer and more

TENTATIVE TABLE OF CONTENTS

FIGURE 13–2
Example of tentative table of contents based on research on topic different from that shown on report plan in Figure 13–1

Solicited and Unsolicited Proposals

Proposals are *solicited* or *unsolicited*. Solicited proposals are submitted in response to requests for such proposals, which are often in the form of printed announcements. *Unsolicited proposals* are originated by the person or persons who submit them.

Requests for proposals come from government agencies, educational institutions, foundations, business and professional organizations, and many other groups and individuals. Announcements that request proposals may include detailed, specific instructions as to how the proposals are to be submitted, arranged, and written. These instructions should be followed exactly.

Unsolicited proposals differ little from solicited ones, although they may be more difficult to prepare because of the lack of guidelines. If no information is provided, the proposal should be prepared in the most easily read format and in the one that seems most likely to obtain the desired results because of the proper use of emphasis.

All the attributes of effective writing apply to the preparation of proposals of any kind. Organization, conciseness, and readability are of particular importance. As in all communication, your ideas are most likely to be accepted if your readers are convinced that what you propose will meet their needs and desires.

Suggested Contents of a Research Proposal

The sequence of information shown in Figure 13–1 can be adapted and expanded to serve as a research proposal. Such a proposal might contain the following areas of content:

1. A cover sheet showing the title of the proposal; the name of the person, with position and organization, to whom the proposal is submitted; any necessary identifying numbers or phrasing to show that the proposal is in response to a particular announcement or set of specifications; the name, position, employing organization, address, and telephone number of the person or persons submitting the proposal; and the date the report is submitted.

2. An abstract that summarizes the entire proposal.

3. A table of contents if the proposal is long enough for a table of contents to be helpful.

4. An introductory or background section, provided such information is necessary before going directly to the statement of purpose.

5. A specifically worded statement of purpose with necessary subcategories.

6. A summary of related research.

7. Procedures, which may be described as *methodology* or *sources of data*.

8. Personnel to be involved in the project, with a summary of their background and qualifications.

9. Facilities and equipment to be used in the project.

10. Cost estimate, which may necessitate a long, detailed budget and a firm contractual maximum.

11. Provision for reporting results.

12. Provision for evaluation of research.

13. Provision for putting results into effect.

14. Suggestions for probable further research.

DIAMOND RESEARCH ASSOCIATES

1917 Catbird Court
Memphis, TN 38119

September 20, 19--

Mrs. Helen Rockwell, Owner
Rockwell Bookstore
397 Grove Park
Memphis, TN 38117

Dear Mrs. Rockwell:

This is the written proposal you requested in our conversation on September 16.

The Problem and Purpose

Before you can safely invest time and money in an additional bookstore, you must have objective evidence about the probability of success. The purpose of this research study is to determine whether the Kirby-Keswich community, Memphis, Tennessee, is likely to be a profitable location and whether a bookstore should be established in this community at the present time.

Methods of Research

I plan to study the community and to make recommendations based on published information, primarily the latest available Census data; personal and telephone interviews with people experienced in the retail book industry; and my own observations, experience, and analysis.

This gathered information will be compared to similar information about the location of your presently owned bookstore at 397 Grove Park. Recommendations will then be made based on all this gathered data.

I understand that I will not consider the feasibility of locations in any other area of the city or the possibility of expanding your present bookstore.

The Final Report

Results of the research study, with detailed recommendations, will be presented in a formal report arrangement, as you requested, suitable for presentation to bankers, investment counselors, accountants, or other financial analysts. The report will be neatly and accurately prepared using word processing equipment and the best quality bond paper.

FIGURE 13–3
Example of a proposal
in letter format

Mrs. Helen Rockwell   2   September 20, 19--

My Qualifications

My educational background consists of a Bachelor of Business Administration degree from New Orleans University, with majors in finance and real estate, and a Master of Business Administration degree from Columbia University, with specializations in finance and investments.

I was employed for seven years as an officer in a bank in St. Louis. For the past five years I have been self-employed, working as a business consultant and financial counselor, in addition to handling my own investments. A list of individuals and corporations for whom I have prepared studies similar to your proposed one will be furnished upon request.

Cost

Your cost will be based upon my actual time spent, with an upper limit of eighty hours. The charge is $65 an hour, plus expenses. I estimate that the study can be completed in no more than forty hours. No extra charge will be made for typewriting or for five complete copies of the report. Additional copies may be obtained for only the cost of photocopying.

Time of Completion

The research and the final report can be completed within two months from the date of our agreement.

Mrs. Rockwell, I believe this proposal answers all your previous questions. If you have additional ones, telephone me at 685-0000.

The attached form, which will remain with this proposal, serves as our contract. I am enclosing an additional copy of this proposal, also with an attached sheet. I have already signed both copies. Please sign one of the copies and return to me. I will begin work on your project immediately.

Sincerely,

Blair Diamond

Ms. Blair Diamond, Consultant

Enclosures

FIGURE 13–3
(continued)

Proposals are arranged in various formats, including letters and memorandums, which are appropriate for short, simple proposals. A proposal in letter format is illustrated in Figure 13–3.

A report is a written or oral message planned to convey information or to present a solution. Although the basic qualities of effective reports are the same, for the most part, as those of all effective communication, in report writing we must give special attention to planned organization for coherence and readability and to an objective tone and nonbiased approach.

Summary

The following classifications of reports are often used together:

- Formal format and writing style; impersonal tone; inductive (indirect, logical) arrangement
- Informal in format; formal or informal writing style; personal tone; direct or indirect arrangement, depending upon type of information

The basis of a report is a problem. The first and most important step in the report process is determining what the problem is and stating it exactly, with necessary and helpful subcategories.

The report writer should think through the complete problem-solving process before beginning the research project, even though the plans will be somewhat tentative. As a guide to further steps, a written report plan saves time and keeps the researcher on track.

A proposal is similar to a report plan, although often longer and more detailed. Some proposals must be long and detailed in order to present all necessary information. Others are shorter and are often presented as letters or memorandums.

Test Yourself: Chapter Review

1–2. Briefly describe the difference between *informational* and *analytical* reports.

3–4. Briefly describe the difference between the *personal* and *impersonal* (*third-person objective*) writing styles.

5–6. Write sentences to illustrate the personal and the impersonal writing styles.

7–8. Briefly describe the difference between *direct* and *indirect* report arrangements as the terms apply to reports.

9. What is the first and most important step in the report process?

10–14. Name five items that may be included in a proposal.

15–17. Name three formats in which proposals may be arranged.

18. What is an advantage of using the impersonal (third-person objective) writing style in reports?

19–20. Distinguish between *formal* and *informal* as the terms apply to report formats.

Test Yourself:
Correct Usage

(Related to material in Chapter 13 and principles of correct usage.) Insert necessary punctuation, including quotation marks, hyphens, and apostrophes, and remove punctuation that has been inserted incorrectly. Choose correct word or sentence from each pair or group. Make any other necessary changes.

1. You are likely to write more informational reports than analytical ones, being factual only.

2. One of your first steps will be to find out what is wanted. Especially if you are a new employee.

3. The impersonal writing style only contains third person pronouns.

4. Many reports present recommendations as the first section, especially short reports.

5. Employers want people to write and speak well and who can also think read and listen.

6. Preparing reports, presenting them, and to keep accurate records are all important employment responsibilities.

7. Doing research is more enjoyable to some people than to write a report.

8. Reports should be objective, clear, and they should be well organized.

9. Keep sentences relatively short, and they should be concise.

10. The charts are introduced and the report writer points out the highlights.

11. It is dangerous to generalize from insufficient information, we are all guilty of this occasionally.

12. Some recommendations must be based on inferences we sometimes cannot have all necessary facts.

Problems

1. Determine which classifications (informational or analytical; formal or informal format; formal or informal writing style; personal or impersonal tone; direct or indirect arrangement) are likely to apply to the following reports:

   a. A teacher reports students' absences to the Veterans Administration by circling the names of students with poor attendance. He prepares a memorandum about unusual situations.

   b. An engineering consulting firm studies the buildings on a college campus and makes recommendations about the conservation of energy. The report is eighty pages long and includes various preliminary and supplementary parts. The last section of the report includes recommendations.

   c. A vice president of a business organization interviews applicants for the position of sales manager and chooses the three who seem to be best qualified. She describes the three applicants in a memorandum to the president of the organization, with her recommendation.

   d. At the end of each month, the manager of an apartment complex submits a letter that includes information about expenditures and occurrences throughout the month and a short analysis of the progress and profitability of the complex. The monthly reports are prepared from daily listings of expenditures and activities. These listings, along with the monthly report, are submitted to the owner of the complex.

2. For each of the following problem situations, state the problem (purpose) either in the form of a question or as an infinitive phrase. For example, a report planned to study the advisability of providing career apparel can be stated as:

   Should the Countrywide Insurance Company provide career apparel for its women employees? (*Question*)

   Purpose: To determine whether the Countrywide Insurance Company should provide career apparel for its women employees. (*Infinitive phrase*)

   Be specific, but omit subcategories of the problem.

Assume necessary and reasonable details, including names.

a. A restaurant manager wants to know how to improve crowded conditions at the midday meal.

b. A restaurant manager wants to know how to increase profits on the midday meal.

c. A restaurant manager wants to know the choices most often made from the luncheon menu.

d. A college professor is trying to decide whether to authorize monthly deductions from her paycheck for deposit in a tax-sheltered annuity fund.

e. The professor had decided to invest in a tax-sheltered annuity fund, but she does not know which one to choose. She has narrowed her choices to three.

f. An office manager must choose a copying machine.

g. A business education teacher must choose typewriters for a classroom to be used for beginning typists.

h. A Chamber of Commerce wants to know what local citizens think of the chamber's services and purposes.

i. A dean of a college of business administration wants to determine the business course or courses that former students believe to have been most beneficial to them.

j. A discount department store wants to know something of its "image."

k. A large construction company is considering adopting a pension plan.

l. The Park Commission is thinking of installing Muzak in all offices.

m. A manufacturer needs to know how to market a new product, a compact refrigerator-icemaker.

3. Choose a question that you wish to investigate in order to report the results in a formal business report. Prepare a tentative report plan, as shown in this chapter. Include a tentative title, statement of purpose, scope (or scope and limitations), readers, and sources and methods of collecting data.

4. Prepare a tentative table of contents for the research you planned in Problem 3.

5. Assume that each of the following paragraphs is the first one of a report planned to determine which magazines, if any, should be added to those now available in the teachers' reading room. Consider all examples to be taken from the first part of the report body, not from the preliminary or supplementary parts.

Example A: The purpose of this study is to determine which magazine subscriptions, if any, should be added to the present collection available in the teachers' reading room.

Example B: With the assistance of the members of the Library Committee, I have completed a study of the magazines in the teachers' reading room. Although deciding whether or not we need any more—and which ones—was quite a hassle, you'll find our recommendations at the end of this report.

Example C: Subscriptions to the *Journal of Business Education, Business Education Forum,* and *The Secretary* should be added to the collection currently available in the teachers' reading room.

Example D: I recommend that subscriptions to the *Journal of Business Education, Business Education Forum,* and *The Secretary* be added to the collection currently available in the teachers' reading room.

(1) Which example(s) indicate(s) that the report is arranged in the direct order? The indirect order?

(2) Which example(s) indicate(s) that the report is written in the personal tone? In the impersonal (third-person objective) tone?

(3) Which example(s) indicate(s) that the report is written in the informal writing style?

(4) Which example(s) is (are) most likely to be taken from a complete and formal analytical report?

(5) Each of the four examples was taken from an analytical report. How can you tell?

6. Assume that each of the following paragraphs is the first paragraph of a report planned to determine a suitable location for an addition to a chain of restaurants named Country Vittles. Consider all examples to be taken from the first paragraph of the report body, not from the preliminary or supplementary parts.

Example A: A Country Vittles restaurant should be built on Highway 20 West in Galena, Illinois.

Example B: I recommend that a Country Vittles restaurant be built on Highway 20 West in Galena, Illinois.

Example C: The purpose of this study is to determine possible locations for a Country Vittles restaurant and to determine which site should be chosen for the next addition to the Country Vittles chain.

Example D: I've completed the study of possible locations for Country Vittles. Because everybody likes country cooking, I'm convinced that we need to build restaurants all over the world. But because we don't have the bread (cornbread or otherwise) for all these, I've picked out the best bet for our next restaurant. You'll find my recommendation at the end of this report. Everybody is going to be surprised.

(1) Which example(s) indicate(s) that the report is arranged in direct order? Indirect order?

(2) Which example(s) indicate(s) that the report is written in the personal tone? In the impersonal (third-person objective) tone?

(3) Which example(s) indicate(s) that the report is written in the informal writing style?

(4) Which example(s) is (are) most likely to be taken from a complete and formal analytical report?

(5) Each of the four examples was taken from an analytical report. How can you tell?

(6) Of the four passages, Example D is likely to be the most undesirable. Why?

CHAPTER 14

Gathering Information
for Reports

The preceding chapter emphasized the first steps of the report process: determining the problem, defining it in specific terms, and deciding on the methods of finding a solution to the problem. This chapter moves to what is ordinarily the next step in the report process: gathering information on which a decision can be based.

Sources of Information

Sources of data are described as *secondary* or *primary*. The word *secondary* is used to mean that data have already been gathered and recorded by someone else. *Primary* describes data that have not already been gathered and recorded by someone else. Primary data are obtained through observation, experimentation, and surveys. Surveys use questionnaires and formal or informal interviews. Interviewing is done in person or by telephone. *Primary data is your original research.* Any data gathered in *any way* by someone else is *secondary* data.

Secondary research should ordinarily be the starting point in the data-gathering process. Whatever problem you are trying to solve, similar ones are likely to have occurred in other organizations or with other individuals. The solutions to these problems may be reported in business periodicals or elsewhere. Although these problems will be at least slightly different from your own, your knowledge of what other individuals and organizations have concluded in similar situations can help to answer your own questions.

Basic Sources of Secondary Information

In addition to the general guides to information described in the following sections, many other reference sources that are not listed here because of limited space may be helpful to you in your particular research project. Most libraries provide brochures and other printed material to guide you to reference sources on their own shelves and in other libraries.

The Card Catalog or Computer-Accessed Information

During past years (and at the present time in some libraries) the card catalog provided the only guide to books available in a particular library. Now some large libraries have fully automated systems. Information that formerly was shown on cards is now displayed on the screens of computer terminals. In addition, some books are listed and described in microformat, such as microfilm or microfiche.

Card catalogs or lists of books displayed by computers provide, in effect, bibliographies of material on almost any topic you might choose to research; numerous titles are likely to be available.

For many research projects, needed data will appear in journal articles, pamphlets, newspapers, or government documents, all of which are indexed elsewhere than in a card catalog or comparable computer files. Books, however, still provide information that cannot be found elsewhere, in a convenient, inexpensive, and readily available form—at least in large, comprehensive libraries. Books, like all other sources, must be chosen with care.

Computer terminals, which are replacing or supplementing card catalogs in many libraries, provide information that is not found in typical card catalogs. For example, the "complete record," which is obtained by keying in a code number for each book as shown on a shorter record, indicates whether or not a book is "on the shelf" and ready for checkout. If the book has already been checked out, the complete record gives the date when the book is due.

As with all computer usage, directions for use must be followed exactly. When using a card catalog, you may be able to find a desired book even if you are unsure of the exact spelling of an author's name. A computer is less accommodating. Specific instructions are usually posted by each terminal.

Computer files, like card catalogs, may be accessed by author, title, and subject. The guide, *Library of Congress Subject Headings,* is useful in narrowing your topic to be researched; this two-volume guide is likely to be placed in your library near the computer terminals.

Guides to Books

A major guide to books, whether or not they are in your particular library, is *Cumulative Book Index: A World List of Books in the English Language,* New York: H. W. Wilson, 1928–present. The *Cumulative Book Index* includes books published in the English language all over the world, recorded by author, title, and subject.

Other guides to books on a particular topic are *Books in Print* and *Subject Guide to Books in Print,* New York: Bowker, 1957–present. They include books "in print" and currently available for purchase in the United States. *Canadian Books in Print* lists books available from Canadian publishers.

Encyclopedias and Dictionaries

Comprehensive encyclopedias are useful in all types of research, especially as a starting place and for general background information. They may also include a list of supplementary reading materials for your particular topic.

In addition to general encyclopedias, a number of specialized ones are available for coverage of specialized areas of knowledge. Some of these are the *Encyclopedia of Social Science, Exporter's Encyclopedia, Accountant's Encyclopedia,* and *Encyclopedia of Banking and Finance.*

Dictionaries remain an important library source. In addition to general dictionaries, there are many specialized ones, just as there are specialized encyclopedias. In fact, the terms are overlapping; one book described as an encyclopedia may be similar to another described as a specialized dictionary. Some books use both terms in their titles, as in the *Encyclopedic Dictionary of Business,* published by Prentice-Hall.

Handbooks and Manuals

Handbooks are similar to specialized encyclopedias and dictionaries. They tend to be more complete, usually more so than a book described as a dictionary. A business handbook presents a condensed picture of an entire field of business.

These handbooks, which are frequently revised in order to include only accurate and relevant information, include the *Handbook of Auditing Methods, Industrial Accountant's Handbook, Handbook of Business Administration, Handbook of Insurance, Management Handbook, Marketing Handbook, Sales Executives' Handbook,* and *Real Estate Handbook.* Many other manuals and handbooks are also available, such as the *United States Postal Manual* and the *United States Government Organizations Manual.*

Yearbooks and Almanacs

Yearbooks, in addition to those that supplement encyclopedias, include publications of various countries, trades, and professions, as well as the *Statistical Abstract of the United States.*

Almanacs, such as the widely available *World Almanac* and *Book of Facts,* contain a wealth of information on many and varied subjects. Similar information, particularly about Canadian topics, is given in *Canada Yearbook* and *Corpus Almanac of Canada.*

Biographical Directories

Biographical directories provide information about leaders or well-known persons, living or dead. The best known is *Who's Who in America,* which summarizes the lives of living Americans who have achieved prominence in any field. A similar reference is *Canadian Who's Who.* Specialized directories include *Who's Who in Insurance, Who's Who in Education,* and *American Men and Women of Science,* as well as many other occupational fields. In addition to those that are specialized according to profession, directories are also specialized according to geographic regions, as *Who's Who in the South and Southwest.*

Who's Who in Finance and Industry is a directory of prominent business people. Another directory is *Who's Who in Finance and Industry* (Canada). *Poor's Register of Corporations, Directors and Executives* is a similar publication but more exclusive. The *Biography Index,* published quarterly, is a guide to biographical material in books and magazines.

Business Services

Business services provide business information of many kinds. Some of these publications and service organizations are listed and described below.

Moody's Manuals summarize data for all major companies. They are issued annually in bound volumes. They include the history of each company, a description of products or services, locations of home office and most important plants, a list of officers and directors, and financial data.

Corporation Records, a loose-leaf publication of financial information and other facts about the corporations described, is published by Standard and Poor's Corporation.

Another well-known service organization is Predicasts, Inc., which provides various services in addition to forecasts and market data classified by company, product, and service.

Guides to Periodicals and Pamphlets

Periodicals, that is, magazines, journals, or serials, are often more helpful than books for use in business research. Various indexes serve as a guide to the contents of general and specialized periodicals. Some of these indexes are listed and described below.

The *Readers' Guide to Periodical Literature* is a guide to articles in about 160 general-interest magazines, such as *Reader's Digest, Good Housekeeping, Time, Newsweek, Business Week, Fortune, Atlantic Monthly, Harper's,* and others.

The *Business Periodicals Index* and the *Canadian Business Periodicals Index* are guides to articles in business, industrial, and trade magazines.

The *Applied Science and Technology Index* is a guide to articles in about 200 English language publications on scientific and technological subjects.

The *Public Affairs Information Service Bulletin*, referred to as *PAIS*, classifies periodicals, government publications, and pamphlets by subject, especially in the areas of economics and social conditions, public administration, and international affairs.

The *F & S Index of Corporations and Industries* (Predicasts, 1962 to date) covers company, product, and industry information from more than 750 financial publications, business-oriented newspapers, trade magazines, and special reports. The *F & S International Index* includes information about Canada and the rest of the world outside the United States, including operations abroad of U.S. companies.

Other indexes are the *Engineering Index, Education Index, Business Education Index, Biological and Agriculture Index, New York Times Index, Wall Street Journal Index,* and the index to *Fortune*. In addition, many large newspapers are indexed in guides available in local and regional libraries.

Computer Databases

Thousands of computerized databases provide a comprehensive, time-saving method of research. Many of the sources described in this chapter are now available in both printed and database form.

Computerized databases can be accessed through the use of telephone lines and modem-equipped computers. A more recent development is the storing of databases on compact laser discs, thus eliminating the cost of using telephone lines to access databases stored in distant places. These discs, which

A Merrill-Lynch representative at work. Computer databases provide instant access to current detailed information.

FIGURE 14–1
Manual versus computer searching of indexes and abstracts. (Concept by Ann Denton, illustration by Barbara Forte)

are frequently updated in order to contain the most recent reference sources, are stored in libraries where they are immediately available through the use of computers.

An illustration of a computerized library search using telephone lines, as opposed to using printed sources, is shown in Figure 14–1. Costs of such a search are based on time and whether the results of the search are transmitted immediately over telephone lines, transmitted later at night rates, or mailed from the reporting location.

Comprehensive database services that provide numerous databases are DIALOG Information and Bibliographic Retrieval Services (BRS). The Dow Jones News Retrieval Service provides full text news from *The Wall Street Journal* and other Dow Jones sources. Databases that pertain particularly to business are ABI/Inform, which offers information similar to but more comprehensive than in the *Business Periodical Index;* Predicasts Terminal System; and Accountants' Index.

Methods of Primary Research

Primary research goes beyond secondary research. In turn, primary research by one individual (or a group) becomes secondary research for future researchers. The term *primary research* describes collection of data by all methods except reading the words of other writers. Usual methods of primary research are *observation, experimentation,* and *surveys* of various kinds. Primary research (in a well-worn phrase) expands the frontiers of knowledge. Both secondary and primary research are useful in *analytical* (problem solving) reports as well as in informational ones. Many reports, however, should not be based *only* on secondary data.

Observation

Observation, as the term describes a method of research, means the examination of phenomena under real, presently existing conditions. Observation under controlled or manipulated conditions is referred to as *experimentation.* Observation as a method of research is often casual and informal; it may also be carefully planned, with observed actions or occurrences recorded and tabulated. The term may also be used to describe a search through company records. Many accounting and auditing reports are based on an examination and analysis of financial records. Hence, the method of data collection is observation, although such reports are not usually described as such.

Experimentation

Scientific experimentation is reliable and accurate, more so than any other research method. But even experimentation is subject to error. In addition, many business problems are not of the type that lend themselves to experimental research.

In business, as in other areas, the purpose of experimental research is to determine the effect of change under a given set of conditions. The conditions must be carefully constructed so that only one variable is tested at a time. For example, an experiment to determine the effect of career apparel upon employee morale would be difficult to conduct in a completely scientific manner because of the element of human behavior.

Surveys

Surveys are widely used in obtaining business information. They are conducted through personal and telephone interviews and through questionnaires, often sent through the mails.

The survey is open to criticism because it depends completely on verbal responses, and words are inexact. (All other methods of research also have weaknesses.) When filling out a questionnaire or talking with a researcher in a personal interview or on the telephone, the respondent is likely to provide untrue, incomplete, or inaccurate and misleading information. Even when respondents wish to provide complete and accurate answers, they often do not do so because of inaccurate memories, lack of knowledge and detailed information, a tendency to give the expected response, and any number of other reasons.

Influences of all kinds enter into results of interviews and questionnaires, as into all other areas of oral and written communication. People who answer an interviewer's question are affected by their perceptions of the interviewer, of the situation, and of themselves. Their mood of the moment influences their responses and whether a questionnaire sent through the mail is returned.

Regardless of the interviewer, questionnaire, or topic being investigated, respondents tend to exaggerate income, education, social status, and other important aspects of their experiences. Respondents tend to minimize unfavorable aspects. These inaccuracies occur even when there is no possibility that questionnaires can be identified.

Another weakness of the survey method is that questionnaire design, which is extremely important in achieving accurate information, is often approached casually and haphazardly. A poor questionnaire or poorly structured interview is almost certain to result in incomplete or incorrect data. Questionnaire construction requires much thought and time. Ideally, a questionnaire is tested with a small group before it is used on a large scale.

Questionnaires and interviews are so widely used, often with poorly designed survey instruments, that respondents do not consider their answers important or do not answer at all. Another weakness is that the researcher has no way of being sure that respondents who return questionnaires are representative of the entire population being surveyed. For example, if a member of Congress asks his or her constituents whether or not to introduce a bill, respondents will most likely be those who will benefit from the proposed law or those who have some special reason for not wanting it. Many people without special interests, who are more likely to make a wise decision, do not take the time to return questionnaires.

If you survey alumni of a school and ask questions about jobs and salaries, those who feel successful are much more likely to return questionnaires, even if their names are not used, than those who feel otherwise. The researcher who attempts to obtain the mean or median salary of such a group would report an average salary higher than the typical salary of all class members.

Even with its many weaknesses and disadvantages, the survey method is the only practical way to obtain many kinds of information. It is difficult to determine what people think, know, or believe without asking them. We cannot know their likes and dislikes, their desires, or their intended actions. We cannot gain the benefit of their recommendations without asking for them. In addition, events that have already occurred evidently cannot be observed. They must be described by others in written or spoken words.

Constructing Questionnaires

When you plan a questionnaire, your goals are to secure a satisfactory rate of return and complete, objective answers. Another consideration is the ease and accuracy with which results can be tabulated and analyzed.

With the questionnaire, include a convincing explanatory letter, usually on a separate sheet but sometimes at the top of the printed questionnaire. The most effective way to convince readers to respond is to show them benefits to themselves. Even if there is no immediate benefit, many people will cooperate if you carefully and convincingly explain the purpose of the study and why you need their opinions. To increase returns, do everything possible to make response easy; for example, make the questionnaire as short as possible, ask for check marks instead of long written replies, and enclose a stamped, addressed envelope.

Write and Arrange Questions Carefully

How you construct the questionnaire, including its physical appearance, will influence the percentage of returns and the value of the answers. Specific principles of questionnaire construction are listed below.

1. Make the questions easy to understand and concerned with one topic only. Avoid ambiguous wording. For example, the question "Why did you buy your last car?" could lead to the response of liking the color, the price, or the design. Another respondent might answer that he bought the car because he had wrecked his older one, or because his wife wouldn't let him buy a motorcycle. Avoid broad, relative terms such as *often, a long time,* and *seldom,* unless these terms are specifically defined.

2. Make the questionnaire easy to answer. Providing blanks to be checked facilitates response as well as the researcher's tabulation of the answers.

3. Provide for all likely answers. Although some questions can be answered by a *yes* or a *no,* many are somewhere in between. Provide for categories such as *I don't know,* or *no opinion, disagree,* or *strongly disagree.* Allowing for shadings of opinions is much more descriptive and accurate than mere *agree* or *disagree* responses.

4. Ask only for information that the respondent is likely to remember.

5. Keep the questionnaire as short as possible by asking only for needed information.

6. Avoid questions that touch on pride or personal bias, or those that give the effect of prying. Such areas include age, income, morals, and personal habits. A question about education may have an alienating effect with persons of limited educational background. Information about age, income status, or education may be necessary in order to accomplish the particular purpose of the report. Even if you need this information, however, you will ordinarily not need the exact age, the exact income, or the exact number of years the person has been in school.

To encourage response, as well as to facilitate evaluation of the answers, provide ranges from which the respondent may choose to show age and income. For example, you can show age brackets *under 21, 21 to 25,* and set up income brackets in the same way. Age and income brackets can be an important consideration in marketing research when planning products to manufacture or outlets for distribution.

7. Arrange questions in a logical order.

8. If the questionnaire is mailed, enclose a stamped and addressed envelope.

Question: I am never sure exactly how to use a colon. Please explain.

Answer: Within a sentence, use a colon only after a complete thought.

CORRECT: The shipment consists of four categories of equipment: computers, printers, monitors, and modems.

INCORRECT: The shipment consists of: computers, printers, monitors, and modems.

INCORRECT: The kinds of equipment are: computers, printers, monitors, and modems.

Colons are used before a tabulation.

CORRECT: The kinds of equipment needed are these:

computers

printers

monitors

modems

Colons are used before long quotations and after the salutation in a business letter.

A use of the colon is explained and illustrated in the following passage from *Fowler's Modern English Usage,* 2nd ed. (Oxford University Press, 1965), 589.

> . . . *but has acquired a special function: that of delivering the goods that have been invoiced in the preceding words.*

9. Avoid leading questions—those that by their wording suggest an answer.

10. Provide for the respondent's additional comments, if any, by using open-ended questions that allow for comments in the respondent's own words. Although these answers are more difficult to tabulate than those that are shown by check mark, the comments may be the most helpful answers of all. In addition, open-ended questions may encourage respondents to speak freely.

Besides mailing questionnaires, you may do a survey by personal interviews, either face-to-face or by telephone.

When you conduct a survey through face-to-face or telephone interviews, you should draw up a form of questionnaire as a guide. Present questions to all respondents in a uniform way, and, as in written questionnaires, make your wording objective and specific. Include necessary information about why you are questioning the reader and how the answers will be used. If you can find a reasonable reader benefit, subtly point it out. And, as in other request letters, stating when the completed questionnaire is needed will help to prevent procrastination and a delayed or forgotten return.

Figure 14–2 is a questionnaire planned to determine the opinions of residents of an apartment building for people of retirement age.

The following questionnaire is part of a study being conducted by a graduate student at Central College. The questions are designed to reflect your opinions on a number of factors in your living environment at Retirement Towers.

PLEASE DO NOT PUT YOUR NAME OR ANY OTHER IDENTIFYING REMARKS ON YOUR ANSWER SHEET. We wish the responses to be totally anonymous. After you have finished answering the items, put your answer sheet in the accompanying envelope, seal it, and return it to the desk. The management of this development WILL NOT have access to your responses.

TO ANSWER THE QUESTIONS, put a check mark in the space above the response that most closely matches how you feel about each particular question.

1. How long would you like to live here?

As Long as Possible	Doesn't Matter	No Longer than Have to

2. Would you recommend this place to friends or relatives if they were looking for a place to live?

Definitely Would	Probably Would	Don't Know	Probably Not	Definitely Not

3. If you were to move again, would you like to live in another place like this?

Definitely Would	Probably Would	Don't Know	Probably Not	Definitely Not

4. What educational level did you reach?

Elementary School	High School	College	Trade or Vocational School	Graduate School

5. Do you have any physical impairments or medical problems that require special care?

		please specify:
No	Yes	

FIGURE 14–2 Questionnaire to determine opinions of residents of a retirement development

FOR THE FOLLOWING QUESTIONS, please check the boxes that represent how important each factor is to the satisfaction or dissatisfaction you feel about Retirement Towers as a place to live.

1	2	3	4	5
Essential	Very Important	Moderately Important	Not Important	Definitely Unimportant

	Essential	Very Important	Moderately Important	Not Important	Definitely Unimportant
6. Closeness to shopping and church	1	2	3	4	5
7. Size of units	1	2	3	4	5
8. Available recreational activities	1	2	3	4	5
9. Appearance of apartment and building	1	2	3	4	5
10. Response of management to requests for repairs or maintenance	1	2	3	4	5
11. Security of building and surrounding neighborhood	1	2	3	4	5
12. Other residents with lifestyles and background similar to mine	1	2	3	4	5
13. Privacy	1	2	3	4	5
14. Availability of medical services	1	2	3	4	5
15. Building features designed for special problems (grab bars, ramps, etc.)	1	2	3	4	5

FIGURE 14–2 (continued)

Arrange Questions in an Appropriate Sequence

The sequence of questions can influence cooperation, interest, and the final results of a questionnaire. Use special care with beginning questions. As in other forms of communication, opening statements are emphatic by virtue of their position. If personal questions even slightly threatening to the ego must be included in the survey instrument, they should not be asked first. And, as in instructional material, questions should move from the simple to the complex. (As much as possible, keep all questions simple.)

Early questions should build reader interest and provide motivation for completing the questionnaire. In some survey situations, questions should proceed from the general to the specific.

Interviewing in Person and by Telephone

Personal interviewing must be limited to a relatively small geographical area unless cost is of no consideration, an unlikely occurrence. Telephone interviewing, although it has other disadvantages, is less expensive and time consuming. All types of interviewing must be carefully planned and conducted, and responses must be recorded carefully and completely.

Personal Interviews

Personal interviewing has the following advantages of oral communication over written communication: immediate feedback, nonverbal communication, and the ability of the communicator to explain further when the respondent doesn't understand the question. Human errors enter into the interview process, however, through all the many ways that communication goes astray. In addition, the respondent may consider the questions an invasion of privacy. The reaction of the respondent to the interviewer is reflected in the information being supplied. Also, because the interviewer interprets responses, these interpretations may be less than completely exact.

Interviews, especially when they are given to many respondents, are ordinarily limited to eliciting specific, factual data that the respondent is likely to remember. All interviews should be given according to the same plan of procedure. Questions should be asked in the same sequence and in exactly the same words to all respondents, explanations should be given in the same way, and the other details of all the interviews should be the same. Because of the varying reactions of the persons being interviewed, procedures cannot be exactly planned in advance, but an effort should be made for all interviews to proceed in the same way.

In addition to interviews limited to factual information, there are *depth* interviews that are unstructured and informal conversations. These interviews must be done by competent, highly skilled researchers. Psychologists often use this type of approach.

Telephone Interviews

Interviewing by telephone is quicker and less expensive than interviewing in person. Random sampling can be used in selecting respondents to be called, provided the population is limited to individuals with listed telephone numbers. Because of the number of people with no available numbers and because some listed numbers are never reached, the selection is not truly random.

Some people consider all telephone calls (except for reasons that are of some benefit to themselves) as an intrusion on their time and an invasion of their privacy. Because of these attitudes, they refuse to cooperate, or, if they do so, are likely to give inaccurate or incomplete answers.

Telephone interviewing, in spite of its weaknesses, may be desirable in some instances. If so, the interviewer should use the same care and courtesy as in personal interviewing. As in all surveys, explanation of the purpose and benefits of the survey will help to obtain respondent cooperation.

Summary

Methods of obtaining information include primary and secondary research. *Secondary research* involves obtaining information that has already been gathered and recorded by someone else. *Primary research* involves finding original data that have not been found and recorded by someone other than yourself.

The *Business Periodicals Index* is a basic guide to articles that have appeared in specialized business magazines. Various other indexes serve as guides to specialized and general-interest periodicals.

Methods of primary research are observation, experimentation, and surveys.

Experimentation, scientifically and objectively done, is reliable and accurate, but even experimentation is subject to human error.

Surveys employ the use of mailed questionnaires and formal and informal interviews. Some interviews are conducted by the use of written questionnaires or a preplanned series of questions asked by the researcher. Surveys also are conducted by telephone and person to person. Surveys are widely used in research of many kinds. Their frequent use results in a disadvantage because many respondents are tired of completing questionnaires or do not believe that they are important.

Questionnaires must be constructed with care in order to encourage response, to obtain the needed information, and to facilitate tabulation of results.

All methods of research are subject to the many kinds of human error that are inevitable in communication.

Test Yourself: Chapter Review

1–2. Describe the difference between primary and secondary data.

3. Name one guide to books.

4. What is the best-known biographical directory?

5–6. Name two kinds of information that can be found in *Moody's Manuals*.

7. What is the name of the best-known guide to articles in general-interest magazines?

8. What is the name of a well-known guide to articles in business, industrial, and trade magazines?

9. What kind of information is found in the *F & S Index of Corporations and Industries?*

10–12. Name three methods of primary research.

13–14. What are two weaknesses of surveys?

15–19. Give five suggestions for questionnaire construction.

(Related to material in Chapter 14 and principles of correct usage.) The content of the following sentences is correct, but ONE in each pair is incorrect in some way. Look for errors in punctuation, including use of the hyphen and the apostrophe; spelling; sentence structure; grammar; and word usage.

1. a. Statistical data and other information obtained from surveys is often presented in tables and charts.
   b. From gathered data a reporter draws conclusions upon which to make recommendations.
2. a. Many surveys consist of questionaires sent by mail.
   b. Researching topics in books, newspapers, magazines, journals, government documents, and reference works can result in a comprehensive and accurate presentation.
3. a. Because much information in published form is available in libraries secondary research is sometimes referred to as library research.
   b. Not all secondary research, however, is obtained from published sources in libraries.
4. a. We must build on the experience of other people because there is no time to do otherwise.
   b. Secondary research should ordinarily be the starting point in the data gathering process.
5. a. What are the leading professional journals in your field of study?

b. Does your library have open stacks, if not how are books examined?
6. a. Information of many kinds, especially statistical information is collected and published by the federal government.
   b. The first Census of Population was taken in 1790, and it has been repeated at ten-year intervals since that time.
7. a. Not all research ends with definate results.
   b. At times, specific recommendations are undesirable.
8. a. A research assignment should be regarded as a priviledge that could lead to increased responsibility.
   b. Many reports are similar in arrangement and approach.
9. a. Some research is planned for the purpose of determining whether a planned course of action is feasable.
   b. Libraries can be both fascinating and frustrating.
10. a. The survey method of research has many weaknesses, but a careful researcher can decrease these weaknesses.
    b. A competent researcher must be familar with library sources.
11. a. After a proposal is accepted, the researcher is free to procede with his research.
    b. Research can be extremely time-consuming work.

1. Prepare a tentative bibliography of at least five recent sources that seem to apply to the problem for which you prepared a report plan. Use the bibliographic form shown in Appendix C.
2. Prepare an annotated bibliography (see Appendix C) of five or more recent journal articles on one of these topics:
   a. Communication as applied to one of these fields:
      - accounting
      - business education
      - management of a small business
      - personnel management

   - marketing
   - office management
   - your major field of study, if not listed above

   b. New developments in one of these fields:
      - accounting
      - business education
      - management of a small business
      - personnel management
      - marketing
      - office management
      - your major field of study, if not listed above

3. Prepare a list of periodicals that apply especially to your major field of study.

4. Does your school classify books according to the Dewey Decimal system, the Library of Congress system, or both? How does the public library system in your city or town classify books? Write a short memorandum report to your instructor in which you describe the methods of classification.

5. Use *Moody's Manuals* or Standard and Poor's *Corporation Records* to find information about a large national corporation. Write a short memorandum to your instructor in which you describe the kinds of information available in the reference source.

6. Can you think of a question that should be answered in your employing organization or in your school or university? Which method or methods of research should be used in finding the answer to this question? Explain.

7. Explain how the following questions (not from the same questionnaire) violate the principles of effective questionnaire construction.

   a. Don't you feel that you earn more interest at United Bank?

   b. Do you bathe daily?

   c. How much do you earn each month?

   d. How much have your grocery bills increased since 1976?

   e. How do you manage when your weekly check won't cover your expenses?

   f. Do you approve of Bill Number 213 now being considered in the Senate? Yes _____ No _____

   g. Do you leave work early?
      Always _____ Occasionally _____ Sometimes _____ Never _____

8. Find a questionnaire that was sent through the mail or administered during an interview. Analyze this questionnaire according to the ten suggestions included in the section of this chapter entitled "Write Questions Carefully." As your instructor directs, present your analysis in a memorandum addressed to your instructor, or be prepared to show the questionnaire to the class and to comment on its construction.

9. You are the administrative assistant to the president of M & D Builders. With the addition of the Quick & Hot Cafe, next door to your office, many employees are completing their lunch in thirty minutes instead of the hour now allotted for lunch. Three women have requested a thirty-minute lunch break with a half hour later arrival time, 8:30 instead of 8:00. Then they could take their children to school.

   Other workers would like to continue to arrive at 8:00 and leave at 4:00 instead of 4:30. A few mentioned that they prefer present hours, 8:00 to 4:30, with an hour for lunch.

   Although it would be more convenient for you and the office manager if everyone came and left at the same time, with staggered lunch breaks, you want to do all you can to provide convenient schedules for everyone.

   The president, Harriett Glover, asked you to write a memorandum for her signature. Ask employees to state their preference according to the alternatives listed above. Ms. Glover and the office manager, Bert Lance, will make the final determination after evaluating their responses. Design a simple questionnaire for employees to complete.

CHAPTER 15

Interpreting with Graphic Aids

Graphic aids are helpful in both written and oral reports to emphasize and interpret written material. They are also used to convey supplementary information not included in the written report. Graphic aids should be considered as supplements to words, not as substitutes for them. They are especially helpful when used to emphasize important points and to show trends and relationships.

The terms chart *and* graph *are often used interchangeably. In this chapter, chart refers to any form of graphic illustration other than a table.*

Graphic aids, if wisely planned and attractively presented, bring out relationships that could be easily overlooked. A well-planned chart can present and analyze important points that would require many pages to explain and discuss.

Some reports consist mostly of tables, charts, and other graphic aids, with supporting text to explain and comment on the graphics. For business reports prepared to serve as a basis for decision making, a complete form is preferred, with supporting evidence to justify conclusions and recommendations. In some situations, the same report may be prepared in summary form and in complete form.

Tables, not charts, should be chosen for the presentation of numerous figures, particularly if the reader is interested in exact amounts. Approximations, trends, and relationships are best shown on a chart of some kind. A chart can be considered a pictorial representation of data.

Some kinds of information should be shown in more than one way in the same report. For example, the reader may need exact numbers shown in a table in addition to approximate figures used to show trends on accompanying charts. A detailed table can serve as the basis for many charts, which are used to illustrate, interpret, and emphasize various aspects of information shown in the table.

Placement of Graphic Aids

Ordinarily, you should place a chart, table, or other graphic aid within the text of a report as near as possible to the portion of text that it is used to illustrate or explain. If the graphic aid is not closely related to the material being discussed, place it in an appendix. Tables and charts, like other supplementary material, should go into an appendix if they cannot be considered an essential part of the report itself.

Extremely long tables or other kinds of material should be placed as appendices even if they cannot be considered supplemental. Your reader is referred to these appendices as relevant material is discussed.

Long tables placed in appendices may have short summary tables placed within the text of the report. They are woven into the discussion, as illustrated in the following list:

> During 1990 the following increases and decreases, shown in percentages of dollar sales for 1989, occurred for each of the three products in each of the three districts:
>
> Eastern: Product A, +12; Product B, +5; Product C, −10
>
> Western: Product A, −20; Product B, −10; Product C, +15
>
> Southern: Product A, +15; Product B, −25; Product C, +40

This simple arrangement, like a listing of other kinds of information or questions, adds emphasis and aids immediate comprehension of the displayed data. This table is in effect part of the discussion. Tables as short and simple as the one shown need not be labeled and numbered unless the omission would result in confusion or inconsistency with other illustrations throughout the report.

Short summary tables may be used even when other tables and charts are also included in the text of the report.

Although often longer and more formal than the preceding table, all graphic aids should be part of the discussion in that they directly relate to the point being discussed. Anything that stops the reader's flow of thought, such as an unrelated illustration or inconvenient placement, is distracting and undesirable.

At times the discussion of a chart or other graphic aid may extend through several pages. When this occurs, the illustration should appear near the beginning of the discussion.

Discussion of Graphic Aids within Text of Report

Introduce a graphic aid before presenting it, and, preferably, follow it with a few lines of discussion. In introductory remarks to the graphic aid, point out highlights of its information. By identifying items of major importance as shown on the table or chart, you are able to refer subordinately to the illustration, as:

Question: Which pairs of words are most frequently confused or misused?   *Improve*
Answer: Affect and *effect* are the clear winners.   *Your Writing*

Affect is a verb that means "to have an influence on"; for example, "Will
the change in billing procedure affect costs?" *Affect* also means "to assume," as
in "She affected a Southern accent." The psychological term *affect* refers to a
feeling, emotion, or mood, but *affect* used in this way is seldom encountered
outside the field of psychology.

Used as a verb, *effect* means "to bring about"; for example, "to effect a
change." Used as a noun, *effect* means a result or the power to produce results;
for example, "The effect of the change in our billing procedure is a 22 percent
savings." Another example of *effect* used as a noun is "When can the change
be put into effect?"

The greatest increase in sales occurred in District 1 (72 percent) and the smallest
in District 7 (17 percent), as shown in Table 3.

Although you should refer to the table, do not build introductory sentences
around the fact that certain tables or charts follow and that the reader should
look at them. Instead, emphasize important elements of information that are
shown in following tables or charts, which are referred to subordinately.

Identification of Graphic Aids within Text of Report

Use identifying titles and numbers on all illustrations throughout the report
with the exception of minor tables or listings that can be considered a part of
the text itself.

Labeling and Numbering

Traditionally, tables are not grouped with other forms of illustrations but are
numbered separately throughout the report. This traditional method of numbering is being replaced by some writers and organizations with the word *Figure*,
which may be used to refer to all kinds of illustrations, numbered consecutively
throughout the report.

Writing Appropriate Titles

Like subheadings in a report and titles of all works, titles of tables and other
graphic aids should concisely but accurately describe the data presented in the
illustration. Titles of tables are usually placed above the table, in larger type
than material in the table itself. In typewritten work, use solid capitals with no
underscore. Titles of charts or figures are usually placed at the bottom of the
illustration, shown in regular type. Titles of charts and other illustrations may
also be placed at the top.

*Improve
Your Writing*

Question: Which comes first, a punctuation mark (comma, period, question, exclamation mark, colon, semicolon) or a quotation mark? I have seen periods inside quotation marks when such a usage seems to make no sense at all. An example is this:

"Amazing Grace," a well-known hymn, is one of the most requested in the South and probably in the entire nation.

Surely this placement is not correct. The quotation marks apply to the song title, not to the rest of the sentence.

Answer: Your example is indeed correct, although you are right in your opinion that the arrangement doesn't make a great deal of sense. On the other hand, you as a writer are saved a great deal of time by the constant rule that, regardless of use or meaning, the comma is always placed in this position.

- The period and the comma are *always* placed *inside* quotation marks.
- The colon and the semicolon are *always* placed *outside* quotation marks.
- The question mark and the exclamation mark are placed either *inside* or *outside* quotation marks, depending on the meaning of the sentence. If the question mark or the exclamation mark applies to the quoted matter, it is placed *inside* the quotation marks; if it applies to the sentence as a whole, it is placed *outside*.

This usage is confusing to many writers, but it is especially confusing to those who have lived in English-speaking countries outside the United States where the usage is likely to be different—and perhaps more logical.

Citing the Source

If tables, charts, or other illustrations are prepared by the report writer, they are considered primary. This fact may be shown thus: *Source: Primary.* It is also acceptable, and more usual, simply to omit the source note for primary data. Credit must be given for material taken from another source; for example,

Source: *U.S. News and World Report,* May 15, 1990, p. 34.

These source notes are usually placed one double space below a chart or table, but at times they may be placed underneath the title.

Format of Tables

Tables are necessary for presentation of exact, detailed information. They often serve as a basis for additional visual aids, often charts of various kinds that illustrate specific groups of data that are part of the total data in the table.

The format of a simple table is shown in Figure 15–1. Figure 15–2 shows an example of a ruled table. Notice that Figure 15–1 could be varied by listing the Fabrics at the left, with the three remaining columns headed by Eastern District, Western District, and Southern District.

```
                              Table 1

NEWBURG FABRICS, TOTAL SALES BY DISTRICTS AND PRODUCTS, 19--
             (shown in millions of dollars, rounded)

                                    Synthetic
District          Cotton           or Blends          Wool

Eastern            200                100              50
Western            400                200              150
Southern           300                400              20
```

FIGURE 15–1
Example of unruled table

Format of Charts

A basic consideration in the construction of charts of all kinds is that they be kept simple. Charts that are complexly designed in an attempt to convey many kinds of information are counterproductive because they are harder to understand than carefully chosen words. Several simple charts that clearly show limited quantities of data are preferable to one complicated, hard-to-read visual aid.

The types of charts most frequently used are the *bar, line,* and *pie* graphs, with numerous variations of the bar and line. Vertical bar charts are also referred to as *column charts,* or *column graphs,* and pie charts are also referred to as *circle,* or *segment,* charts or graphs.

In line graphs, the independent variable (time, cause) is *always* shown at

```
                   Table 2
     LANGUAGES USED BY AMERICAN FIRMS
          IN FOREIGN CORRESPONDENCE
```

Language	Number	Percent
English	66	100
Spanish	15	23
French	11	17
German	2	3
Portuguese	2	3
Chinese	1	2

FIGURE 15–2
Example of ruled table. (The numbers and percentages shown refer to the respondents of a survey form.)
(Source: Retha H. Kilpatrick, "International Business Communication Practices," *The Journal of Business Communication,* Fall 1984, 37. Used by permission.)

Using Lotus 1-2-3 to produce a bar chart

the bottom (the x-axis), and the dependent variable (effect) is shown on the vertical axis (the y-axis). This guide also applies to vertical bar charts, although the factor that is considered to be the independent variable may vary according to the relationships to be compared.

Bar Charts

Bar charts, both horizontal and vertical, compare quantities. The length or height of the bars indicates quantity. All bars should be the same width.

A horizontal bar chart is shown in Figure 15–3. A vertical bar chart is shown in Figure 15–4.

Bilateral Bar Charts

A bilateral bar chart shows increases and decreases from a central point of reference. Bilateral bar charts may be used for any series of data containing negative quantities. They are often used to show changes in percentages.

The bilateral bar chart shown in Figure 15–5 is based on the amounts shown in the table in Figure 15–1 and the percentages shown in the short, unlabeled table under the section of this chapter entitled "Placement of Graphic Aids."

Multiple Bar and Subdivided Bar Charts

Variations of the simple bar chart, in addition to bilateral bar charts, include multiple bar and subdivided bar charts, with variations and combinations of each.

A subdivided bar chart is shown in Figure 15–6. Percentages shown on bars are not usually included, but they provide more specific information. A multiple bar chart (without subdivided bars) is shown in Figure 15–7. Figures

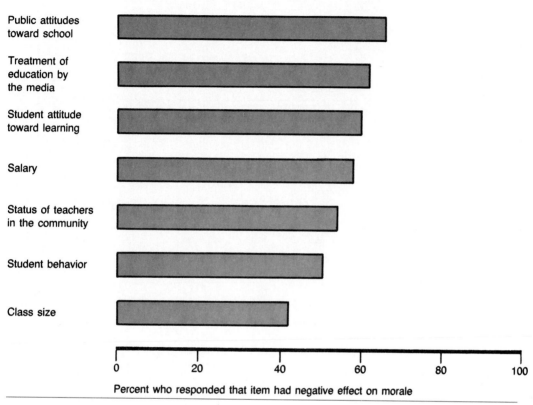

FIGURE 15–3 Horizontal bar chart. (Source: U.S. Department of Education.)

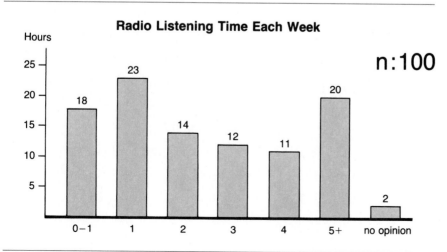

FIGURE 15–4
Vertical bar chart

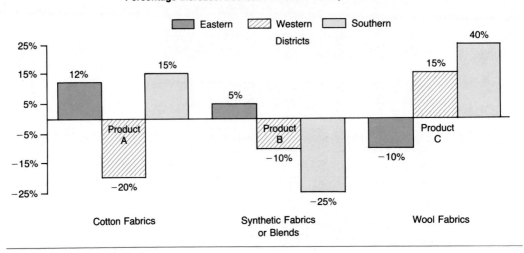

FIGURE 15–5 Bilateral bar chart

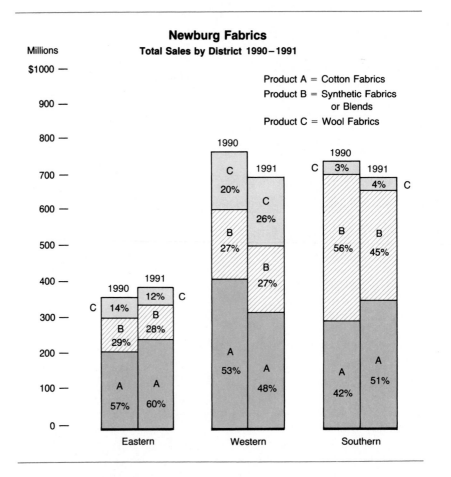

FIGURE 15–6
Subdivided bar chart

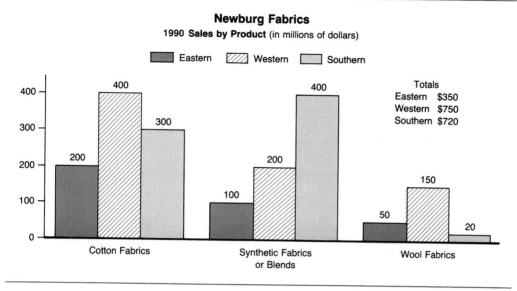

FIGURE 15–7 Multiple bar chart

are based on Table 1 in Figure 15–1 and the short table under the heading "Placement of Graphic Aids."

Charts of all kinds, but particularly bar charts, can be varied in numerous ways. In designing them, choose the arrangement that will vividly, yet simply, compare the relationships you wish to emphasize.

Another kind of bar chart is the 100 percent subdivided bar. *These charts may consist of either vertical or horizontal bars.* They differ from ordinary bar charts, in that all bars are the same length or height, with each bar representing 100 percent. These 100 percent bar charts serve the same purpose as pie charts (discussed later in this chapter) because they show divisions of the whole; they are far more useful than pie charts when a number of 100 percent items are to be compared, as seven years are compared in Figure 15–8.

Line Charts

A line chart is used to show changes over a period of time, as illustrated in Figure 15–9. A line chart is often used to show rises and falls of the stock market, as well as for many other purposes.

A cumulative line chart, as shown in Figure 15–10, is also referred to as a component-part line chart or as a belt chart. The top line represents the total. Color or crosshatching distinguishes the component parts.

Pie Charts

A pie chart, also described as a circle chart (or pie graph or circle graph) shows the component parts of a whole and serves the same function as a 100 percent subdivided bar. Exact quantities or percentages should be shown; frequently, *both* quantities and percentages are shown. A pie chart is illustrated in Figure 15–11.

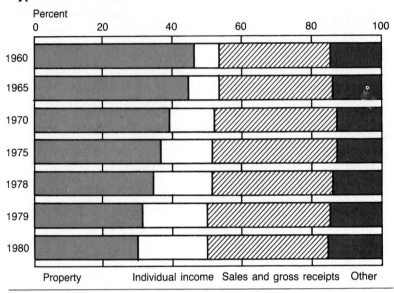

State and Local Government Taxes—Percent Distribution, by Type: 1960 to 1980

FIGURE 15–8
100 percent subdivided bar chart, horizontal bars. (Source: U.S. Bureau of the Census.)

Pictographs, Maps, Drawings, and Flow Charts

As mentioned previously, charts can be varied and combined in numerous ways. In your choice of illustration, aim for accurate and vivid representation and simplicity. Maps are also useful to show geographical differences.

Data shown in the pictorial chart in Figure 15–12—the divided dollar bills—could have been depicted in pie charts or in 100 percent subdivided bars.

Drawings are frequently used in many reports and other kinds of writing,

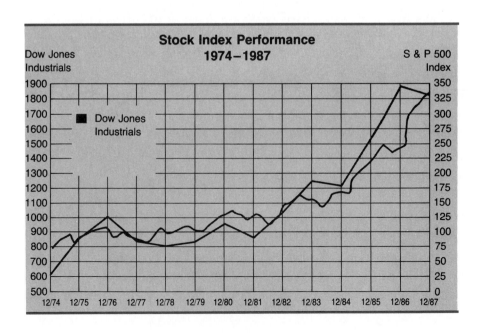

FIGURE 15–9
Multiple line chart

Outlays for Transportation

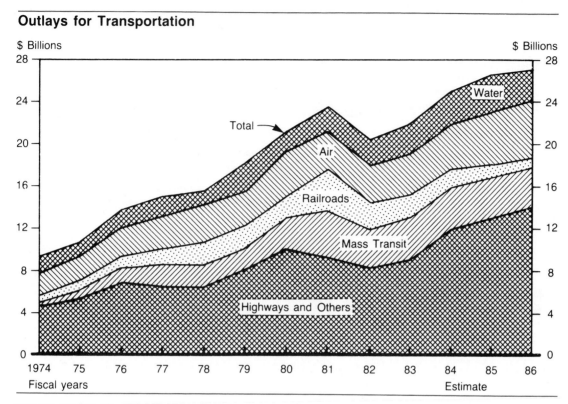

FIGURE 15–10 Cumulative line chart. (Source: Executive Office of the President, Office of Management and Budget.)

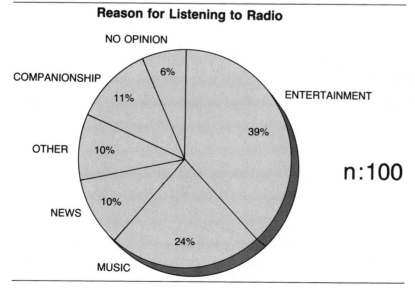

FIGURE 15–11
Pie chart

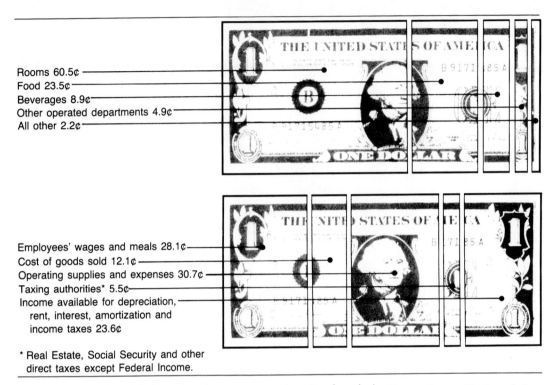

Rooms 60.5¢
Food 23.5¢
Beverages 8.9¢
Other operated departments 4.9¢
All other 2.2¢

Employees' wages and meals 28.1¢
Cost of goods sold 12.1¢
Operating supplies and expenses 30.7¢
Taxing authorities* 5.5¢
Income available for depreciation, rent, interest, amortization and income taxes 23.6¢

* Real Estate, Social Security and other direct taxes except Federal Income.

FIGURE 15–12 Pictorial chart showing component parts of a whole. (Source: Prepared by Pannell, Kerr, Forster.)

particularly technical material. Many times, a drawing can save an extraordinary amount of words. Drawings are necessary to depict mechanical processes and equipment.

An example of a flow chart is shown in Figure 15–13.

Accurate and Honest Presentation of Data

The purpose of graphic aids is to show trends and relationships quickly, clearly, and accurately. Poorly constructed graphics do the opposite. Some of the ways these distortions of quantities, trends, and relationships occur have already been mentioned as the various types of graphic aids were discussed. In summary, distortions are likely to be caused by one or more of the following:

1. An inappropriately chosen grid. (A grid is the network of horizontal and vertical lines on which the chart is plotted.)

2. Inappropriate plotting on the grid; for example, not keeping the time schedule uniform.

3. Beginning the quantitative axis somewhere other than zero without making the omission immediately clear to the reader. This omission results in cutting off the bottom of a line or bar chart. Use all such charts with extreme caution. Even when readers are warned by boken lines that the scale has been broken, they are more likely to notice the overall effect of the chart than the broken lines.

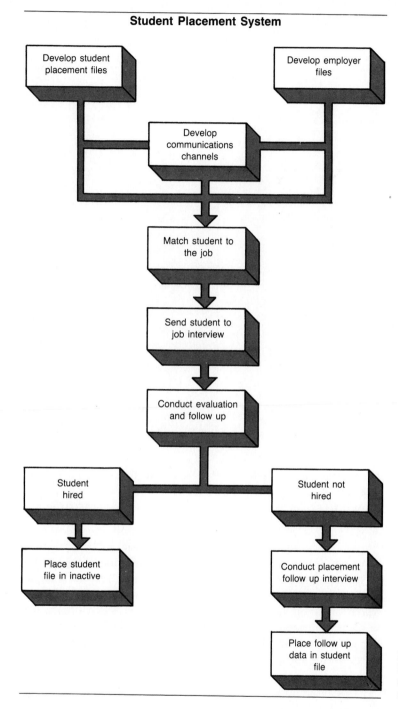

Student Placement System

FIGURE 15–13
Flow chart. (Source: *Occupational Outlook Quarterly*, Spring 1982, 37.)

Notice the effect of cutting off the bottom of the vertical bar graph shown in Figure 15–14. If the columns begin at the horizontal line (which has been added to the original chart), the differences between the amounts shown in the three columns would seem to be drastically increased.

At times, because of lack of space, a scale must be broken so that it does not begin at zero. In Figure 15–15 (a chart planned to be shown on a projector

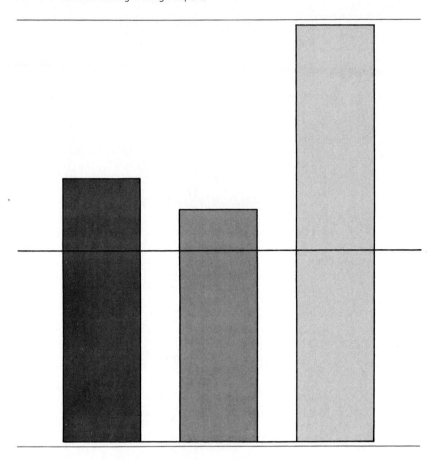

FIGURE 15–14
Illustration of how a vertical bar chart can be distorted by starting at some point other than zero

to illustrate an oral report), the "jog" on the vertical axis indicates to the viewer that the entire chart is not shown. If the chart had started at zero and was drawn to scale, it could not have fitted on a transparency in such a readable form.

4. Varying more than one dimension in bar charts or pictograms. For example, if you are comparing hog production, use three hogs of identical size to indicate that three million were raised in 1990 as compared to 1980, when one million were raised, shown by one hog of identical size. Do *not* attempt to make one hog three times larger to show the increase in number for 1989. (Unless you need something to do, forget about drawing hogs and use a simple bar graph or table. If your data are no more extensive than the numbers given here, forget about a chart.)

In order to prevent misinterpretation, in addition to distortion caused by the design of the graphic aid, observe the following guidelines:

1. Interpret the information shown in the chart to the extent that you are sure your reader will understand its meaning. (*The charts shown in this chapter are used to illustrate the different kinds of graphic aids, not to present the information itself. Thus, discussion of the information presented on the charts is less than would be required if the charts were used in a business or technical report.*)

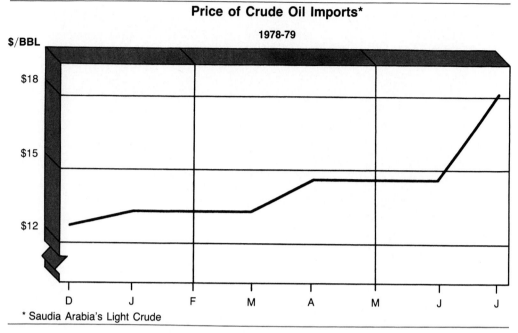

FIGURE 15–15 Illustration of chart with a scale break

2. Give credit where credit is due, as when using verbal passages other than your own.

3. Make sure that titles, legends, and explanatory notes adequately describe the purpose and content of each chart.

Graphic Aids Constructed by Computers

If you were to attempt to draw each of the graphic aids shown in this chapter, you would find that such a project would require a great deal of time and artistic ability. A few years ago you would have constructed any necessary graphic aids by using pens, pencils, compasses, protractors, and rulers. For important material, you would perhaps have sent your suggested drawings to a professional artist within or outside your organization.

Now almost all graphic aids can be quickly and easily constructed by computers, which can convert raw data into tables, charts, and designs of many kinds. Such presentation is possible through the use of mainframe computer terminals or microcomputers. You are likely to have a terminal or a microcomputer at your desk.

If you have the proper equipment and software, you can select the kind of design you wish and, by a simple procedure, instruct the computer to show your selected display on the screen. Then, when your design meets your specifications, it can be printed in various ways. Some equipment will transfer graphic aids onto color prints, transparencies, and 35-millimeter slides.

Although the actual construction of graphic aids is far easier than it was in past years, you still have the responsibility of choosing the most appropriate

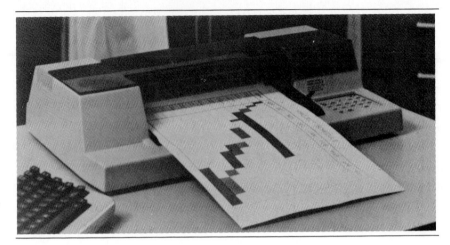

FIGURE 15–16
The computer is an excellent tool for constructing graphic aids

chart to display your particular data. In some instances, you will need several different charts in order to present varying aspects of your data. All the principles of graphic presentation discussed in this chapter apply, whether or not they are constructed by a computer. As construction becomes easier and quicker, you will find that you increase your use of graphic aids.

Computer-made graphics are illustrated in Figures 15–16 and 15–17.

As with other improvements and innovations that speed routine work, computers do not decrease the importance of your knowledge, judgment, and careful thought. Instead, you will find it even more essential to know the basic underlying principles of communication tasks that can now be handled automatically, once you have made correct choices and given appropriate, exact instructions.

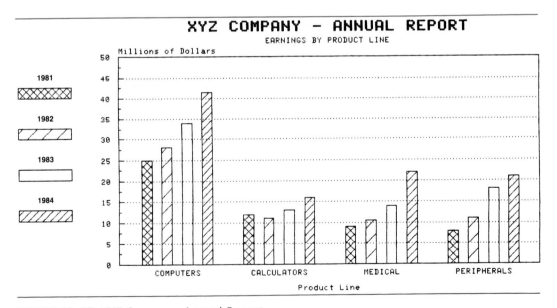

FIGURE 15–17 XYZ Company, Annual Report

Summary

Use charts, tables, and other illustrations to express meaning quickly and clearly, but do not use them solely to impress.

Choose the appropriate type of chart, table, or other graphic aid to best convey the desired meaning or comparison. Some information should be shown in more than one way in the same report. For example, the reader may need exact figures instead of trends and relationships; if so, present these figures in tabular form.

Place a graphic aid within the text of the report, as near as possible to the portion of the text that is used to illustrate or explain. If it is not closely related to the material being discussed, it should be either omitted or placed in the appendix of the report. Tables and charts, like other information, belong in the appendix if they can be considered supplementary to the report itself.

Introduce the graphic device before presenting it and, preferably, include a few words of discussion after the device has been presented. Point out the highlights of the graphic aid.

Make sure that graphic aids are constructed so that relationships are not distorted. Use reasonable proportion. Start at zero or show by broken lines that, because of space limitations, it was impractical to start at zero.

Carefully label each graphic device. Provide a descriptive key (also called a legend) if it will be helpful to the reader.

Keep all tables and charts simple. Do not try to show too much information on one chart.

Test Yourself: Chapter Review

1. Unless tables and charts are clearly supplemental, where should they ordinarily be placed?

2–3. In addition to bar charts, what are the two most frequently used charts?

4. What is another name for a bar chart?

5. What is a bilateral bar chart?

6. What is an advantage of a 100 percent bar chart?

7. What kind of information is displayed on a line chart?

8. What is a flow chart?

9–10. Name two ways in which charts are sometimes distorted so that misrepresentation occurs.

Test Yourself: Correct Usage

(Related to material in Chapter 15 and principles of correct usage.) Insert necessary punctuation, including quotation marks, hyphens, and apostrophes, and remove punctuation that has been inserted incorrectly. Choose correct word or sentence from each pair or group. Make any other necessary changes.

1. Tables not charts should be chosen for the presentation of numerous figures.

2. If you have the proper equipment and software you can construct various kinds of charts by using a personal computer.

3. Constructing charts with computers or other electronic equipment is faster than to draw them with a pen.

4. Construct charts so that relationships are not distorted, data should not be misrepresented.

5. Carefully label each chart, a descriptive key (called a legend) should be provided.

6. Applying all the techniques of effective graphics, they will (affect, effect) the finished report.

7. Bilateral bar charts are described by another name; they are also called positive and negative bar charts.

8. He said, "Between you and (I, me), some charts are harder to understand than ordinary tables would be."

9. The supervisor said, "You have done a good job for your company and (I, me), especially in graphic presentation."

10. He asked, "Is the decision to change our reporting (procedures, proceedures) (definite, definate)?

Problems

1. Which chart would you construct to illustrate the following types of information? As your instructor directs, construct these recommended charts using assumed quantities. If you can think of more than one kind of chart for one or more of the sets of data, describe the trends or relationships that each kind best conveys.

   a. The Dow-Jones average, by year, for the past twenty years.

   b. Comparison of sales of the Local Corporation by product line (four major classifications of products):

      for the past year

      for the past five years

      for the past twenty-five years

   c. Comparison (by either percentage or number) of white collar, blue collar, service, and farm workers in the U.S. labor force for each year ending in five or zero from 1955 to the present.

   d. Breakdown, in percentages, of how the federal government budget was spent last year.

   e. Breakdown, in percentages, of how the federal government budget was spent each year for the past five years.

   f. Comparison of ten major companies to show increases and decreases in net profits from 1985 to 1986.

   g. Total production of automobiles in the U.S. by years, from 1974 through 1986, and production by General Motors, Ford, Chrysler, and "other" manufacturers.

2. Bring to class a photocopy of a graphic presentation in a magazine, newspaper, or textbook. Be prepared to show this graphic aid on an opaque projector (or make a transparency). Is the chart the most appropriate one for the particular data and the desired comparison of relationships? Is the chart correctly and accurately made?

3. Present the information requested in Problem 2 in a memorandum attached to the illustrated chart or other graphic aid.

4. This problem is based on Table 1 (shown in Figure 15–1) and Figures 15–5 (which is based on information shown in the section entitled "Placement of Graphic Aids"), 15–6, and 15–7.

   a. Write an introductory paragraph or paragraphs for Table 1 and Figures 15–5, 15–6, and 15–7.

   b. Construct a table to show total sales, by product and district, for 1988. You can find amounts for 1988 by converting percentages shown in Figure 15–6 to dollar amounts, rounded as in Figure 15–6.

   c. In 1989 and 1990, Newburg Fabrics sold fabrics to markets abroad, as well as in the United States. Percentages sold to foreign markets are shown below:

      1989: Cotton, 37%; Synthetic or blends, 62%; Wool, 12%

      1990: Cotton, 41%; Synthetic or blends, 58%; Wool, 27%

   How many kinds of charts or tables could be effectively used to depict this information? Construct one or more, preceded by an introductory paragraph or paragraphs.

5. Can you think of other kinds of graphic aids in addition to those shown in this chapter? If so, describe them to the class.

6. Look at one issue each of *Fortune, The Wall Street Journal, USA Today,* and *U.S. News and World Report.* Write a memorandum to your classmates describing your findings, including a photocopy of one or more charts. Include in or with the memorandum at least one graphic aid of your own to convey in easy-to-read format your findings about the number and kinds of graphic aids you found in the four publications.

CHAPTER 16

Analyzing and Organizing Data: Writing and Formatting the Report

After you have collected the data, you evaluate them and organize them for presentation in the most appropriate form. A systematic method of collecting and recording information simplifies the remaining steps of the research process.

At some point you will stop formally adding to the collection of data and finish the research process. If additional information or opinions come to light, however, you cannot afford to ignore them merely to end the search, although at times you may be tempted to do so.

Conclusions, Based on Findings; Recommendations, Based on Conclusions

Valid conclusions are based on complete and relevant data interpreted objectively in the light of the problem to be solved. Recommendations are based on conclusions about what the data mean.

Ordinarily, the conclusions and recommendation section is the last section of a formal, analytical report arranged in the inductive order. Conclusions and recommendations are sometimes presented in two separate sections. In some long and comprehensive reports, each major section is treated as a separate report; the writer arrives at conclusions based on findings presented in each section. The entire report concludes with a summarizing section.

To repeat and emphasize: *Report evidence, interpret this evidence, and make recommendations. Your conclusions, usually in a report section with recommendations, are based on clearly stated evidence.*

Interpreting with Statistics

Simple statistical terms include the following:

- *Mean:* The arithmetic average obtained by totaling the figures and dividing by the number of cases.
- *Median:* The midpoint, or middle value, in a series of values arranged in the order of magnitude.
- *Mode:* The most frequently occurring value. (The mean, median, and mode are all measures of a central tendency.)
- *Range:* The spread between the lowest and the highest values in a series.
- *Standard deviation:* A measure of dispersion in a frequency distribution —that is, a measure of the spread of the normal distribution.

This book cannot cover the study of statistics in detail. You need a basic knowledge of statistics, however, for analyzing and interpreting your research findings.

The term *average* can mean almost anything or nothing, depending on how it is used. In other words, the *mean* may be meaningless. For example, a statement can be literally true that the average income of a college graduating class of a particular year is $97,000 a year, but it is very unlikely that this figure is

Communication Brief	As a cub reporter, Mark Twain was told never to state as fact anything that he could not personally verify. Following this instruction to the letter, he wrote the following account of a gala social event: "A woman giving the name of Mrs. James Jones, who is reported to be one of the society leaders of the city, is said to have given what purported to be a party yesterday to a number of alleged ladies. The hostess claims to be the wife of a reputed attorney.
	Clifton Fadiman, ed., *The Little, Brown Book of Anecdotes* (Boston: Little, Brown, 1985), 554.

> Averages and relationships and trends and graphs are not always what they seem. There may be more in them than meets the eye, and there may be a good deal less.
>
> The secret language of statistics, so appealing in a fact-minded culture, is employed to sensationalize, inflate, confuse, and oversimplify. Statistical methods and statistical terms are necessary in reporting the mass data of social and economic trends, business conditions, "opinion" polls, the census. But without writers who use the words with honesty and understanding and readers who know what they mean, the result can only be semantic nonsense.
>
> Darrell Huff, *How to Lie with Statistics* (New York: W. W. Norton, 1954), 8.

Communication Brief

the typical income. A few extremely high figures distort the mean. Suppose that the graduating class consisted of only ten members. Each of nine of these persons is now earning about $15,000 annually, and the tenth one earns $835,000, making the arithmetic mean $97,000. If this figure is used to mean that each of the members is a potential customer for a yacht, you have misinterpreted the data.

Organizing the Data

Like evaluation, organization of the data should not be left for a certain time period in the research and reporting process. Keep organization of data in mind throughout the study, as you decide what to present where. In addition, a tentative table of contents or outline that you prepared at the beginning of the study helps you in the final process of arranging ideas and prevents the investigation from going astray. As you put the report into written form, you are likely to see needed changes in the preliminary plan. After the first draft of the manuscript, you are likely to make further changes.

Note cards are useful for organizing material. Write on separate cards the headings of the report that seem to describe major divisions. Include headings from the tentative table of contents, as well as additional ones that now occur to you.

After you have noted on the cards the possible divisions, arrange them in the order that seems to be natural, whether or not this sequence agrees with the original outline. As you study and sort the cards, you often find a new arrangement that will best express your ideas.

> To be worth much, a report based on sampling must be a representative sample, which is one from which every source of bias has been removed. . . . A psychiatrist reported once that practically everybody is neurotic. Aside from the fact that such use destroys any meaning of the word "neurotic," take a look at the sample. That is, whom has the psychiatrist been observing? It turns out that he has reached this edifying conclusion from studying his patients, who are a long, long way from being a sample of the population. If a man were normal, our psychiatrist would never meet him.
>
> Darrell Huff, *How to Lie with Statistics* (New York: W. W. Norton, 1954), 18–19.

Communication Brief

This method of organization also helps you to see weaknesses and omissions in the presentation, as well as redundancies. A logical sequence of topics for the complete report is essential whether the plan of arrangement is the direct (deductive) or the indirect (inductive) order. *If you are using the traditional and formal report arrangement presented in the inductive order, you begin with the introduction, follow with findings and analyses, and end with conclusions and recommendations.*

Even though you already have this arrangement in mind, you must decide on the arrangement of topics in the middle section of the report, as well as on the arrangement of information in the introductory and concluding sections. The content of the various preliminary and supplementary portions of the formal report, such as the synopsis, offers few problems in organization. You can safely leave the exact planning of these sections until the report itself is completed. (See Figure 16–4.)

Planning reports to be arranged in the direct order requires the same careful attention to an orderly sequence of ideas. *In the direct order, as you remember, you place recommendations at the beginning of the report, as well as any necessary explanatory conclusions, and follow with supporting information.*

Format of Headings

The format and arrangement of headings will depend on the complexity of the material and the need for breakdown into various divisions. For example, if a report outline includes headings to correspond to I, II, III, IV, and V (main headings); A, B, C, and D; 1, 2, 3, and 4; and a, b, c, and d, the text of the report must include four levels of headings in addition to the title. With one level of division, only one form of heading is necessary in addition to the title. Unless you are following a specified format or are directed otherwise by a required guidebook, any form of heading—for example, sideheads in all capitals or centered headings, either in all capitals or in capitals and lower case—may be used. *Headings should be consistent and indicate the order of importance or "weight," of each section.* Placement and capitalization indicate the relationship of each heading to all the rest.

The traditional outline arrangement has headings preceded by roman and arabic numerals and by letters in capitals and lowercase, as shown below.

FIRST-DEGREE HEADING (TITLE)

   I. Second-Degree Heading

      A. Third-Degree Heading

      B. Third-Degree Heading

         1. Fourth-Degree Heading

         2. Fourth-Degree Heading

            a. Fifth-Degree Heading

            b. Fifth-Degree Heading

   II. Second-Degree Heading

The divisions of the report outline, which are also shown on the table of contents, may be used in a report according to the following method.

FIRST-DEGREE HEADING

The first-degree heading (title) is centered and typed in all capitals. When the title consists of more than one line, usually these lines are double spaced; the first line is longer than the second, and the second is longer than the third. (Titles should be as short as possible, but they should also be exact and descriptive.)

Second-Degree Headings

Second-degree headings, using the arrangement shown here, are centered and underlined. They describe the major sections of the report and correspond to the headings preceded by roman numerals, as shown in the report outline.

Third-Degree Headings

Third-degree headings correspond to A, B, C, and following letters, as shown in the report outline. In this plan of arrangement, they are placed at the left margin, typed in capitals and lowercase, and underscored.

Fourth-degree headings—Placement at the paragraph indention on the same line with the text distinguishes fourth-degree headings from third-degree ones. The underscore and the dash separate the heading from the remainder of the paragraph.

Fifth-degree headings are placed at the paragraph indention, on the same line as the text. These headings, however, are integral parts of beginning sentences.

Use no single subheadings. For example, instead of using an "A" heading, with no "B," omit the "A" heading.

The alternate plan described below, as well as other variations, may be used for headings within the text of a report.

Type the title as a spread heading, like this

TITLE OF REPORT

One space is left between each two letters, and three spaces are left between words. Thus the first-degree heading is a spread heading. Second-degree headings are centered in all-capitals, and third-degree headings are centered and underscored, as illustrated below.

SECOND-DEGREE HEADING

The main heading, or second-degree heading, is centered. Before the advent of word processing, which with some systems has made line spacing more difficult to vary than with typewriters, a triple space was left before the main heading and a double space afterward (when manuscript itself was double spaced). Now a more usual way is to leave two or three blank spaces before or after the main heading. (As with all work, check a specified handbook or determine which arrangement is preferred.)

Third-Degree Heading

At least a triple space usually precedes a third-degree heading, although some writers leave only a double space.

Fourth-degree heading.—This heading is set in on the first line of the paragraph, with no extra space preceding it in addition to the usual space left before the beginning of all paragraphs, whether using single or double spacing.

Fifth-degree headings, which are also underlined, are the beginning words of the first sentence of the paragraph.

Letter Reports

The term *letter report,* as used in this discussion, refers only to a report presented in a usual business letter arrangement. (Using a broad definition of reports, many of the millions of business letters written every day can be described as reports because they convey information.)

Figure 16–1 illustrates a report presented in letter form. This letter is an *analytical* report because the writer analyzes the reported information and makes a recommendation. It is also an *authorized* report, as indicated by the opening words *You requested.* The overall writing style, as well as the format, is *informal.* It is written in the *personal tone* as indicated by the words *you, your,* and *I.* Because the recommendation comes at the end of the report, the message is in the *indirect (inductive)* order. The letter could have been arranged in the *direct* order. Because the recommendation is qualified, however, preceding explanations aid understanding.

The information shown in Figure 16–1 could have been presented in various other ways. In this particular instance, a letter seems to be the best choice because it is more personal, friendly, and informal. Similar findings presented to another person within the writer's organization would ordinarily be given in memorandum format. The material could have been presented to Mr. and Mrs. Hobbs in a short report in manuscript style, accompanied by an individual letter transmitting the report, although such formality is not necessary in this instance.

7900 Creek Bend
Houston, TX 77071
October 14, 19--

Mr. and Mrs. Melvin Hobbs
2157 Rolling Water Cove
Houston, TX 77069

Dear Mr. and Mrs. Hobbs:

As you requested, I have made a study of the advisability of trading your fully paid-for residence on Voss Road for the equity in Dungreen Townhouses. I was happy to make this study for you. Detailed specifications are given on attached sheets.

Favorable factors are these:

* By trading the fully paid-for house for the equity in the eight-unit townhouse complex, you will not be required to pay capital gains tax on the house. Both the house and townhouses are investment property.

* Because of the greater overall value, the townhouse complex will appreciate more, in dollar value, than the single-family house.

* Attractive, well-located rental property is becoming scarce.

* The price of the townhouses is less than replacement costs.

* The non-escalating interest rate of 8¼ percent is extremely low.

* Finally, and most important, these townhouses will shelter some of your high taxable income. Although tax advantages decreased, beginning in 1987, because of changes in tax laws, some advantages remain.

Another factor, less advantageous, is the amount of time that must be devoted to management. In addition, the complex could be hard to sell quickly should you need to do so. You could be forced to sell at a loss.

The real estate exchange is a sound financial decision if you are sure you want a long-term investment. Personal considerations must be left up to you, but I believe that part-time management services would be economical and convenient.

Sincerely,

Robert Hutchinson

Robert Hutchinson, CPA

wht
Attachments

FIGURE 16–1
A letter report

Progress Reports

Progress reports, as the term indicates, relate progress on a project of some kind, including research studies.

The term *progress reports* refers to subject matter, not to format or special arrangement. You may arrange such reports in any of the formats used for other reports in this chapter or in other arrangements not shown here.

Figure 16–2 illustrates a progress report in the form of a memorandum.

Other Informal Reports

Reports can be presented in various forms other than letters and memorandums. An example of a report arranged as a manuscript is shown in Figure 16–3. This report could have been presented as a memorandum similar to the one illustrated in Figure 16–2.

Whatever the chosen format, length, and formality of a report, its readers are influenced by neatness and an attractive appearance. Keep in mind that formal reports are sometimes expected to be arranged in a conventional, expected format, perhaps in exact conformance with a particular style manual.

The report illustrated in Figure 16–3 could have been presented in various other formats. *For example, the recommendations section now shown at the beginning is often placed at the end, following the reported findings. If the report were arranged in this way, it would be similar to a shortened version of the formal analytical report, Figure 16–4, except for the omission of the various preliminary and supplementary parts.*

Formal Reports

The basic principles of report writing apply to all kinds of reports, whether of a minor, limited nature or of extensive coverage.

The researcher must understand the problem and be able to state it exactly. The next steps are to find the necessary information, to evaluate and interpret this information, and to organize it in the most readable and appropriate form. This procedure remains the same although the finished report may be presented in one of several forms: the complete, formal arrangement, a more informal report arrangement (in that some or all of the preliminary and supplementary parts are omitted), a letter, or a memorandum.

Comparing Formal Reports with Informal Reports

For reports arranged as manuscripts, such as Figure 16–3, there is no exact dividing line between "formal" and "informal" format, as discussed in Chapter 13. The overall length and the inclusion of preliminary and supplementary parts are the most obvious differences.

Some similarities of formal and informal reports are these:

1. The purpose of the report and the method of investigation should be clearly stated in both formal and informal reports.

DATE: June 20, 19--

TO: Board of Directors, Playhouse on the Square

FROM: Karen Robins, Manager   *Karen Robins*

SUBJECT: PROGRESS OF STUDY TO DETERMINE NEEDED
IMPROVEMENTS IN SOUND-SYSTEM EQUIPMENT

Since you authorized my research study on May 7, I have taken the following steps:

1. Interviewed all the permanent and visiting staff of Playhouse on the Square in order to determine their opinions about needed improvements in our sound-system equipment. These people are quite knowledgeable on the subject because of their experience in other theatres in the city and elsewhere.

2. Talked with the architect, J. B. Herring, who designed our new building. He suggested possible changes in our present sound system.

3. Searched all local libraries for published information pertaining to sound systems for theatres similar to Playhouse on the Square.

4. Discussed our needs with two representatives of Audio Communications Consultants, the firm that installed our present system.

The following actions will be completed within the next six weeks:

1. Visit theatres similar to the Playhouse in St. Louis, Louisville, Dallas, and San Diego, as authorized at our last meeting.

2. Talk with all possible suppliers of sound equipment, some of whom are in the cities mentioned in Item 1.

3. Organize and evaluate all gathered information and prepare report in written form for presentation at September meeting of Board of Directors.

I will send you additional progress reports as I move toward a solution to improving our sound equipment. Thank you for authorizing me to research this problem.

FIGURE 16–2
A progress report

RECOMMENDATIONS FOR REPLACING PRESENTLY OWNED
TYPEWRITERS WITH PERSONAL COMPUTERS, WORD PROCESSING
SOFTWARE, AND PRINTERS

Prepared for

James T. Buchanahan
Administrative Director

Countrywide Insurance Company

by

Mary Duncan
Office Manager

Chickasaw Branch Office

August 20, 19--

FIGURE 16–3
Short recommendation report to be submitted with attachments containing supporting information. (Attachments are not included in this illustration.)

2. Objectivity and a nonbiased approach are essential, regardless of the format and arrangement of the finished report.

3. Conclusions and recommendations, if included, must be clearly based on reported findings.

4. Footnotes or another method of documentation must be used as needed to establish credibility and to give credit where credit is due.

The most important consideration in choosing format and arrangement is the nature and purpose of the report, along with the needs and expectations of the readers.

RECOMMENDATIONS FOR REPLACING PRESENTLY OWNED
TYPEWRITERS WITH PERSONAL COMPUTERS, WORD PROCESSING
SOFTWARE, AND PRINTERS

Purpose and Scope of Study

The purpose of this study is to determine whether the
typewriters owned by Countrywide Insurance Company should be
replaced by personal computers equipped with word processing
software and letter-quality printers. Factors considered are cost of
the equipment and all supporting materials, time and money to be
saved after installation, and typists' efficiency and morale.

Not considered in this study are Countrywide offices outside the
United States and Canada or possible changes in word processing
centers now in use in the home office and in seventeen major cities.
Research following the present study will determine the particular
choice of computer, software, and printer most desirable for
Countrywide offices. Still further research will indicate the cost and
time necessary to provide training for the users of the new
equipment.

Findings

1. Except for twenty-four IBM personal computers used in
    executive offices in the home office, all secretaries and typists
    throughout the Countrywide organization use electric
    typewriters. (Centralized word processing centers in the home
    office and seventeen other major cities are not considered here.
    Even in these offices, however, numerous typewriters are in
    use.)
2. According to Inventory Control, Countrywide Insurance Company
    owns 4,420 electric typewriters, 3,220 of which are self-
    correcting with memory capacity and 1,200 are self-correcting
    without memory capacity. For the past twenty years,
    Countrywide has routinely replaced typewriters after five
    years. Attachment A is a list of typewriters of each kind, with
    the purchase price and date of purchase.
3. An experiment conducted by Ms. Rita Richards, secretary in the
    Chickasaw Branch Office, indicated that letters and other
    materials are more attractive when prepared using word
    processing and a letter-quality printer. Examples of letters
    prepared on typewriters in use in the Chickasaw office are

FIGURE 16–3
(continued)

> shown in Attachment B, with other letters prepared with a demonstration Zenith computer.
>
> 4. According to Ms. Richards' experiment, one-fifth to one-fourth of a typist's time is saved by the use of word processing. In addition, the secretary who participated in the experiment had only three weeks' experience with the Zenith computer and the software package. As typists become thoroughly familiar with word processing, even more time will be saved. One of the most important advantages of word processing is that corrections of all kinds can be made without retyping the entire page. (See Attachment C, which gives results of time studies.)
>
> 5. According to estimates reported by three sales representatives and two journal articles (see Bibliography), within five years 90 percent of all offices will be equipped with some kind of word processor.
>
> 6. Another important advantage of word processing, among others, is that material can be stored on disks, rather than in file cabinets. This time-saving feature also saves office space and makes material easier to find.
>
> Recommendations
>
> I recommend that personal computers, with word processing software and letter-quality printers, be purchased to replace typewriters in all Countrywide Insurance Company offices.

FIGURE 16–3
(continued)

The Report Package

Complete formal reports are comprised of three major divisions: preliminaries, the report body (or report proper), and supplementary parts. These three major divisions make up the *report package*.

The following list of report parts is not intended to be used for all formal reports. Few reports need all the preliminaries, and preliminary parts not shown in this list are desirable for some reports.

The preliminary and supplementary parts preceded by a check are the ones most often used. The others may be included or omitted depending on the particular report situation. An index is likely to be omitted from all kinds of business reports. A well-made table of contents makes an index unnecessary and even undesirable, except in book-length manuscripts. In addition, an index is difficult to construct. (See examples in Figure 16–4.)

Preliminaries

√ Cover

  Title fly

√ Title page

Letter of authorization

Letter of acceptance

√ Letter of transmittal

√ Table of contents

List of charts and tables

√ Synopsis

Body of the report

Introduction (may be divided into sections; see Figure 13–1, Chapter 13)

Text of the report, usually divided into several major sections

Conclusions and recommendations, which are often combined into one section, or summary, if report is merely informational

Supplements

√ Appendix (or appendices)

√ Bibliography (may also be called "References")

Index

(The bibliography may precede other supplements.)

An Example of a Formal Report

A formal report is shown in Figure 16–4, using the "References Cited" method of documentation, which is similar to the APA (American Psychological Association) method and the latest MLA (Modern Language Association) method, discussed in Appendix C. (The appendices referred to on the table of contents are not included in this textbook.)

Summary

A short, informal report, as considered in this chapter, is any reporting or analysis or information *not* presented in the complete, formal arrangement that includes preliminary and supplementary parts. A report decreases in formality as preliminary and supplementary parts are omitted. Except for length, format, and formality, all effective reports are similar. Informal reports, whatever their format, are often presented in the direct order, but the choice of arrangement depends more on the content of material than on the degree of formality desired.

Reports differ in many ways among organizations. No particular format is suitable for every purpose or for every organization, and sometimes no particular format is specified but the choice is left to the judgment of the report writer.

You may be free to use the format of your choice, although you are more likely to use a form and arrangement already established for previous reports prepared by other writers in your organization. If this is the situation, conform exactly to the stipulated format. To do otherwise results in distraction for the reader, who expects to find certain kinds of information in a certain place in the report.

ANALYSIS OF RADIO AUDIENCE PREFERENCES
IN AMERICAN FORK, UTAH

Prepared for
Dr. Larry Hartman
Interwest Broadcasting Group

by

John Munoa
Research Coordinator

April 5, 19--

FIGURE 16–4
Example of a formal
report

April 5, 19--

Dr. Larry Hartman
Interwest Broadcasting Group
Triad Center, Suite 5884
Salt Lake City, UT 84337

Dear Dr. Hartman:

Here is the report you requested about radio audience preferences in
American Fork, Utah. A reference booklet about the area is included
as an appendix, along with information about researchers and
complete results of the telephone survey.

The research went very well. We believe the findings will assist you
in setting up KFRK-FM.

If you need information about format specialists or advertising
agencies in the Salt Lake area, I can make recommendations. If you
would like to discuss the findings or recommendations of this
report, please telephone me at 619-000-0000.

Sincerely,

John Munoa
Research Coordinator

mt

ii

FIGURE 16–4
(continued)

CONTENTS

iii

FIGURE 16–4
(continued)

SYNOPSIS

Choosing the proper program format and target audience are vital aspects of operating a radio station. The purpose of this report is to determine the most appropriate target market and format, including musical selections and news coverage, for KFRK-FM, a new radio station in American Fork, Utah. Breaking into a saturated radio market can be successfully accomplished if the right format and audience strategy are used.

Recommendations are that KFRK-FM adopt a hybrid format, blending Soft Rock and Easy Listening music. The station should also develop an aggressive in-house news team, providing short newsbreaks once an hour. National news and local news should be included. KFRK-FM has the opportunity to become the number one FM news source in American Fork.

KFRK-FM's target audience would be 51 percent of the total radio audience in American Fork.

iv

FIGURE 16–4
(continued)

AN ANALYSIS OF RADIO AUDIENCE PREFERENCES

IN AMERICAN FORK, UTAH

INTRODUCTION

The purpose of this report is to determine the most appropriate target market and format, including musical selections and news coverage, for KFRK-FM, a new radio station in American Fork, Utah. This study is necessary in order to help the owners, Interwest Broadcasting Group, establish the station as a leader in the area, which already includes many other AM and FM stations.

This report is based on a study conducted by Group Five Research Team, four researchers working under the direction of Dr. Owen Rich, of Brigham Young University. Dr. Rich's colleagues recognize him as an expert in the field of broadcast research.

Group Five collected data by means of a telephone survey conducted in American Fork, Utah, during the first two weeks of March, 1988. They made calls using a random sample of telephone numbers drawn from the current American Fork telephone directory.

1

FIGURE 16–4
(continued)

2

The sample size for the survey was 100 people. This gives the survey a confidence level of 95, with a sampling error of .10. These levels are considered acceptable for a pilot study (1:47).

PRESENT AND POTENTIAL RADIO COVERAGE

IN THE AMERICAN FORK AREA

American Fork is part of the Salt Lake radio market, which is one of the most saturated markets in the United States. More than 35 stations broadcast in an area that should realistically have about 20 (4).

The reason for the great number of stations is that when the FCC granted licenses in the Wasatch Front area, each community was thought of as a separate market. However, as time passed, the stations from Ogden to Payson have gradually fused into one huge market. American Fork, 30 minutes from Salt Lake City and 20 minutes from Provo, receives radio broadcasts from both cities as well as from other surrounding areas.

The population of American Fork doubled over the past census period and is expected to do so again. A 5,500 exclusive home development is planned for the area between American Fork and

FIGURE 16–4
(continued)

3

Alpine. Other planned developments indicate that the area will be one of the fastest growing in the United States during the next decade. Thus, radio listeners will increase in number, along with consumers of all other services.

NECESSARY DECISIONS ABOUT KFRK-FM

Because of high saturation in the American Fork listening area, trying to break into the market with a new station is a gamble, but it can be a successful one if the owners choose the exactly right format and properly promote this unique format.

Targeting an Audience

One key aspect of finding the perfect format is choosing the correct target audience, which is a demographic segment of the total population toward which a station's programming is aimed. Awareness of the target audience is essential to effective and appropriate programming.

In small towns like American Fork, stations usually choose the entire population as the target audience. By trying to provide "a little something for everyone," they hope to capture all demographic

FIGURE 16–4
(continued)

4

groups (3:136). For example, a station in Vernal, Utah, has a schedule in which it plays a Country selection, followed by a Hard Rock Selection, followed by an Easy Listening selection.

In larger radio markets, stations target demographic groups by choosing formats that appeal to those groups. The stations also gear their news coverage advertisements to the tastes and needs of the target audiences (2:77).

Developing a Format

Some of today's standard formats, based on kinds of music, are listed and briefly described below. These classifications, with artists mentioned as examples, were used in the telephone survey to encourage understanding and consistency in responses.

1. ROCK   (Bon Jovi, INXS, Aerosmith, U2)

2. SOFT ROCK   (Miami Sound Machine, Sade, Air Supply)

3. COUNTRY   (Willie Nelson, The Judds, Ricky Scaggs)

4. EASY LISTENING   (Tony Bennett, Frank Sinatra, Johnny Mathis)

5. BEAUTIFUL MUSIC   (Ray Coniff, Henry Mancini, Percy Faith)

6. CLASSICAL   (composed by Mozart, Chopin, Stravinsky)

7. BIG BAND   (Glen Miller, Duke Ellington, Tommy Dorsey)

FIGURE 16–4
(continued)

5

8. TOP 40 (Madonna, Wang Chung, Whitney Houston, Janet Jackson)

9. JAZZ (Kenny G, Lee Ritenour, Dave Grusin, Jean Luc Ponty)

10. OTHER

In most major markets, stations usually stay within the boundaries of their chosen formats. Recently, however, more and more hybrid formats are appearing. These hybrid formats are chosen in an effort to reach certain demographic groups in creative new ways.

In Orem, Utah, a new station targeting the "Baby Boomers" has chosen to mix the mellow songs of the Sixties and Seventies with contemporary hits. They hope to appeal to nostalgia with the old songs while still projecting a "hip" image by playing contemporary selections.

Covering the News

Another prime consideration essential in establishing the overall image of a radio station is news coverage. How often should the news air? How long should the news last? What should the focus of the news be? The answers to these questions depend upon the

FIGURE 16–4
(continued)

6

particular target audience. The news on an Album Oriented Rock station, with the 17 to 24 age group as the target audience, will be different from the newscast on a Beautiful Music station with a target audience of listeners in the 35 or older age group.

THE AMERICAN FORK AUDIENCE

Preferences of the 100 respondents are consistent with those expected of the reported age groups. These groups are not expected to change substantially because people who are moving into the American Fork area are younger than the average of the national population.

Age of Respondents

As shown in Figure 1, 51 percent fall between the ages of 25 and 44. Only 26 percent are 45 or older. The largest segment is the 35-44 age group, 28 percent.

Determined from previous studies, Soft Rock and Easy Listening are the two kinds of music most preferred by the age groups 25 to 44 (5).

FIGURE 16—4
(continued)

7

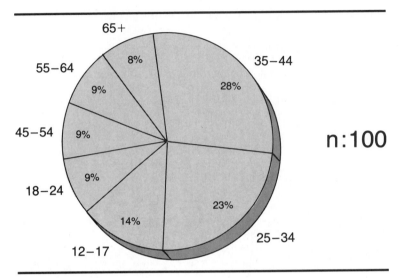

Figure 1. Age of Respondents

<u>Sex of Respondents</u>

Of the 100 respondents, 66 percent are women, as shown in Figure 2.

According to previous studies, Soft Rock and Easy Listening are the two kinds of music most preferred by women (5).

<u>Occupation and Income of Respondents</u>

The largest number of respondents, 32 percent, consider their occupation as professional, as shown in Figure 3. The largest number, 47 percent, preferred not to discuss their income; 15

FIGURE 16–4
(continued)

8

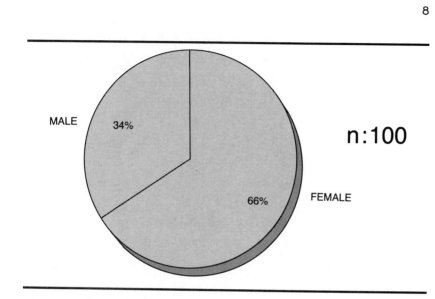

Figure 2.   Sex of Respondents

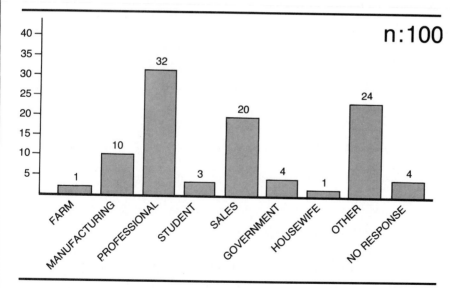

Figure 3.   Occupation of Respondents, Shown in Percentages, Rounded

FIGURE 16–4
(continued)

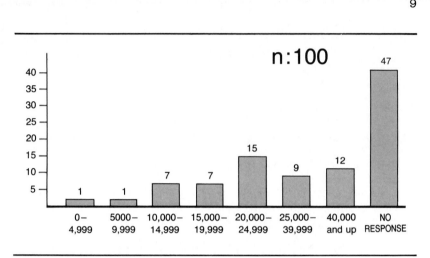

9

Figure 4.   Income of Respondents

percent earn from $20,000 to $24,999, and 12 percent earn $40,000

or more, as shown in Figure 4.

Music Preferences of Respondents

   Of the 100 people surveyed, 21 percent prefer Country, 19 percent

prefer Soft Rock, 18 percent prefer Easy Listening, and 12 percent

prefer Rock. The remainder are divided among other formats in

groupings of 10 percent or less, as shown in Figure 5.

Newscast Preferences of Respondents

   When questioned about news frequency, 53 percent stated that

they would like to hear news reports once every hour. As to the

FIGURE 16–4
(continued)

10

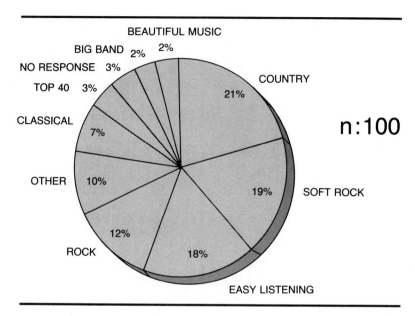

Figure 5.   Music Preferences of Respondents

focus of the news, 60 percent prefer an equal mixture of national,

regional, and local news, while 22 percent prefer only local news.

The favorite radio station at this time, as far as newscasts are

concerned, is KSL-AM; 60 percent of the respondents said that if an

important news event happened, they would turn to KSL-AM. No

other station comes close to KSL-AM.

FIGURE 16–4
(continued)

11

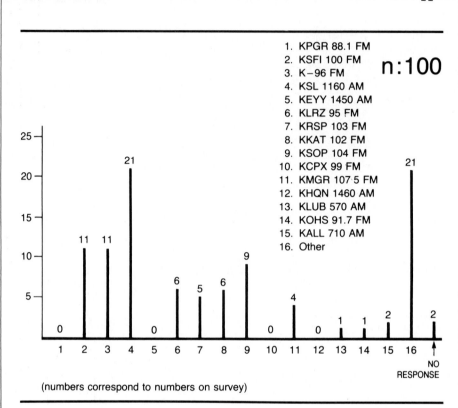

1. KPGR 88.1 FM
2. KSFI 100 FM
3. K–96 FM
4. KSL 1160 AM
5. KEYY 1450 AM
6. KLRZ 95 FM
7. KRSP 103 FM
8. KKAT 102 FM
9. KSOP 104 FM
10. KCPX 99 FM
11. KMGR 107.5 FM
12. KHQN 1460 AM
13. KLUB 570 AM
14. KOHS 91.7 FM
15. KALL 710 AM
16. Other

n:100

(numbers correspond to numbers on survey)

Figure 6.   Favorite AM and FM Stations of Respondents

Favorite AM and FM Stations of Respondents

KSL-AM is the overall choice of respondents, not only for

newscasts; 21 percent claim it as their favorite, as shown in Figure

6.

The favorite stations shown in Figure 6 do not specialize in the

kinds of music, Soft Rock and Easy Listening, chosen as the

FIGURE 16–4
(continued)

12

preferences of 37 percent of the respondents. No Soft Rock or Easy Listening station is shown to be a leading station.

CONCLUSIONS AND RECOMMENDATIONS

KFRK-FM should combine Soft Rock and Easy Listening formats and develop an aggressive, in-house news team.

The hybrid music format is logical not only because of reported music preferences but because of the age and sex of American Fork listeners. The age groups of 25 to 44, which make up 51 percent of respondents, have been shown by previous studies to prefer Soft Rock and Easy Listening. Another result of previous studies is that these two formats are preferred by women. Of the 100 respondents, 66 percent are women.

Newscasts should be three to five minutes in length, presented hourly. The news should generally be of broad focus, but it should have a local flavor. KFRK-FM has the opportunity to establish itself as the number one news source on the FM dial.

Now is an optimal time to put the station on the air. The September 1 target date is a realistic one.

FIGURE 16–4
(continued)

REFERENCES CITED

1. Dominck, Joseph, and Wimmer, Roger D. Mass Media Research.
    Belmont, California: Wadsworth, 1983.

2. Fletcher, James E., ed. Handbook of Radio and TV Broadcasting.
    New York: Van Nostrand Reinhold, 1981.

3. Hybels, Saundra, and Ulloth, Dana. Broadcasting: An Introduction
    to Radio and Television. New York: D. Van Nostrand, 1978.

4. Kampmeyer, Chris. Lecture. Brigham Young University, Provo,
    Utah, March 3, 1988.

5. Rich, Owen. Lectures. Brigham Young University, Provo, Utah,
    March, 1988.

13

FIGURE 16–4
(continued)

Test Yourself: Chapter Review

1. What is your understanding of a "short, informal report"?
2. What is a letter report?
3. What is an analytical report? (This term was also discussed in previous chapters.)
4. When a report is presented in a formal format, is the personal or impersonal tone (writing style) more likely to be used?
5. In a letter report, which writing style, personal or impersonal, is more appropriate?
6. For a report presented as a memorandum, is the personal or impersonal tone (writing style) more likely to be used?
7. For a report presented as a memorandum, is a direct or indirect order of arrangement more likely to be used, provided the report is primarily informational?

Test Yourself: Correct Usage

(Related to material in Chapter 16 and principles of correct usage.) Insert necessary punctuation, including quotation marks, hyphens, and apostrophes, and remove punctuation that has been inserted incorrectly. Choose correct word or sentence from each pair or group. Make any other necessary changes.

1. At some point you will stop (formally, formerly) adding to the collection of data and continue with the report process.
2. At times the collected data will not fall into (discrete, discreet) divisions.
3. The choice of divisions of reports (is, are) very important, therefore spend all the time necessary to achieve the best possible arrangement.
4. (Rewrite sentence 3 so that it is a complex sentence with an introductory subordinate clause.)
5. Avoid an excessive number of "I's." Even if you are appropriately writing in the personal tone.
6. Avoid starting numerous paragraphs with "I" or "we," which gives too much emphasis to the words. (Hint: Notice the weak use of "which," without a specific antecedent.)
7. Various methods can be used for organizing data, for example some people use note cards.
8. The mean median and mode are 3 measures of central tendency.
9. Carefully analyzing the data takes time and effort but they are necessary for objective reports.
10. Headings show organization and flow of thought is emphasized.

Problems

1. More than one overall plan of organization is possible and acceptable for most reports. As discussed in this chapter, a study of three possible sites for a new factory could be presented with major report divisions about each site or by the arrangement (often preferable) of major criteria by which the sites are judged. In the following report situations, you have no way of knowing the best possible arrangement because of limited information. By assuming reasonable details, however, you can list major categories into which findings could be organized. Describe these categories in the form of major headings of the report.

a. You have interviewed a representative group of citizens about their opinions of the overall quality of your city government.

b. You have obtained the opinions of personnel managers about the preparation of effective employment resumes.

c. You have interviewed office managers about the importance of attractively arranged and typewritten business letters and how these letters can be prepared.

d. You have compared two possible employers in order to determine where you want to apply for a job.

e. You compare two competing brands of equipment with which you are familiar.

f. You report on the fringe benefits offered by your employing organization or another organization with which you are familiar.

g. You question recent graduates of the educational institution that you attended in order to find their opinions of improvements that should be made in the educational program. Assume that this study is limited to students in your major field.

h. You try to determine how a small real estate company can increase profits.

2. As you did in Problem 1, determine major report divisions of problems listed in Problem 1, Chapter 13.

3. If you prepared a tentative table of contents for a major report, as directed in Problem 4, Chapter 13, recheck your table of contents at this time. Make any necessary changes.

4. From the following examination scores of twenty-one students, compute the mean, median, and mode. What is the range?

   99, 98, 97, 96, 96, 96, 92, 90, 87, 83, 80, 79, 79, 79, 79, 75, 71, 69, 68, 61, 59

5. Improve the following sentences, taken from reports, from the standpoint of objective, specific wording. For example, instead of saying that costs have increased by the enormous figure of 45.2 percent, say that they have increased 45.2 percent and be specific about particular costs and time periods.

   a. The XYZ equipment is shamefully overpriced. In comparison, competing models sell at bargain-basement prices. (Assume amounts.)

   b. The tremendous increase in stupid paperwork in our oddball office proves that it is foolish to tolerate the old copier another day.

   c. The oppressive income tax awards sluggards and incompetents and penalizes those who are competent and hardworking.

   d. I can't believe that we have fallen so disgracefully behind last year's quota. (Assume amounts.)

e. This amazing increase in profits—72 percent—is unquestionably due to the superb and creative leadership of our outstanding management team.

f. Enormous difficulties in production contributed to a startling date of completion, which was extremely late.

g. The unbelievable increase in defects—27 percent—is undoubtedly the result of lax supervision.

6. **Questionable research findings.** Assume that you are the Director of the Bureau of Educational Research at Central College. You have been away from your office for two months because of illness, but you are now assuming full responsibility again.

   You find that during your absence your assistant, Elbert Siskin, has completed the following research studies:

   a. He has surveyed the alumni of the college class with which you graduated. He received a 30-percent response to his mailed questionnaire. He found that the mean and median earnings of the class far exceed the national average of college graduates of the same year. He has written a news release about his findings in which he strongly indicates that graduates of this particular college are better prepared to move ahead because they receive better instruction, as proved by the survey. You have told him that the news release is not to be published.

   b. He has studied the drop policy of the same college by checking student grade records before and after the policy was liberalized to the extent that students can now drop a course at any time before final examinations. After the change in policy, the grade point average increased. He believes that the results of his study show that the increase can be attributed to the fact that because students now have a less stressful semester, they are able to relax and make better grades.

   c. While completing the previous survey, he also learned that more freshmen than seniors drop out of college. He concludes that freshmen courses are more difficult than senior courses.

He has written an article for a prestigious journal explaining the results of studies b and c. He wants to list you as the co-author because of your recognized name. You would not dream of having your name appear on the article, even though you are sure it would not be accepted.

You have talked with Elbert and tried to point out, as tactfully as possible, the weaknesses of his research. He insists that you put it all in writing. He says that he wants a copy to be put into his personnel file because his work during your absence has not been appropriately recognized. He asks that a copy be sent to *your* supervisor. You *do* want to keep Elbert as your assistant, at least for a time. He works extremely hard and writes fluently and convincingly—if logic is not considered. In addition, because of the backup of your work, you currently have no time to look for another assistant.

Write a memorandum to Elbert. A copy is to go to your supervisor, Kay Roland, Academic Vice President, who works at some distance from your office and knows nothing of the situation. [Perhaps you should telephone Kay first?]

Another important consideration is that Elbert had no legal right to look at the students' grades because of privacy laws. Evidently the University official who gave him permission to examine the records made a serious error.

Decide upon what should be included in the memo. Write it clearly but diplomatically. Include a notation that a copy is to go to Kay Roland.

Evaluation Sheet: Contents and Writing Style, Formal and Informal Reports

	Yes	No	Not Sure
1. Is the title completely, specifically, and clearly worded?	___	___	___
2. Do major headings adequately describe and include the minor headings placed under them?	___	___	___
3. Do major headings adequately describe the contents of the report as stated in the title?	___	___	___
4. Are headings of each group parallel in wording and form?	___	___	___
5. If the report is expected to be in the third-person writing style (impersonal tone), is this style maintained consistently throughout the report, including the concluding section? (This style also omits all implied "you's.")	___	___	___
6. Does the introduction (often described by some other name) include a specifically worded statement of purpose?	___	___	___
7. Does the introduction include the scope (if not exactly stated in the purpose) and the methods of research?	___	___	___
8. Are all unusual technical words or other unfamiliar terms defined as they are used, in the introduction, or in a separate glossary?	___	___	___
9. If necessary for understanding, does the introduction include a brief description of the historical background of the problem? (If this section is long, it should be placed in a separate section of the report.)	___	___	___
10. Is the entire report written in an interesting style, with most verbs in the active voice and few expletives ("It is," "There are," and so on)?	___	___	___
11. Are sentences fairly short, although varied in length and type?	___	___	___
12. Does thought flow logically from the beginning of the report until the end?	___	___	___
13. Is the report written throughout in an objective style, with no personal opinions or judgmental words?	___	___	___
14. Does the report present both sides of the question being investigated?	___	___	___
15. Are all major points substantiated with concrete, convincing evidence?	___	___	___

	Yes	No	Not Sure
16. Is the present tense used in all instances where it makes sense?			
17. Although subheadings are used, as they should be, does the text read coherently without the headings?			
18. Is the report easily readable throughout?			
19. Are techniques used to display with proper emphasis the points that should be emphasized?			
20. Are all paragraphs fairly short?			
21. Are topic sentences used to make paragraphs clear?			
22. Are words simple, but exact?			
23. Is the report concise?			

Evaluation Sheet: Format for Formal Analytical Reports

	Yes	No	Not Sure
1. Does the report include a cover?			
2. If a cover is used, are the title and the author's name shown on the cover or through a "window"? (Other information may also be visible.)			
3. Does the title sheet contain at least the title, name of the reader, name of the writer, and the date?			
4. Is the information on the title sheet attractively arranged?			
5. Does the report contain a letter of transmittal?			
6. If the report contains a letter of transmittal, is it presented in a complete letter arrangement?			
7. Does the report include a table of contents?			
8. Do all headings on the table of contents match exactly the headings in the report itself?			
9. Does the report include a synopsis?			
10. If a synopsis is included, does it summarize the *complete* report, including purpose and other introductory material, findings, and conclusions and recommendations?			
11. Is the synopsis no longer than two single-spaced pages? (Synopsis can also be double spaced.)			
12. Is the report double spaced? (Some manuscript reports are correctly single spaced.)			
13. Are subheadings arranged in order to indicate immediately the importance of each section?			
14. Are paragraphs divided between pages so that at least two lines of a paragraph are left at the bottom of the page and two lines are carried to the top of the next page? (Two- and three-line paragraphs cannot be divided.)			
15. Are all paragraphs relatively short?			

	Yes	No	Not Sure
16. Are at least two lines (preferably more) left after subheadings near the bottom of a page?			
17. Are pages numbered properly? (Ordinarily, the first page is not numbered, or, if so, the number is centered about one inch from the bottom of the page. Numbers for following pages are placed at the margin point in the upper right corner, about one inch from the top of the page?)			
18. Overall, does the report have an attractive appearance—open and not crowded?			
19. Is at least one inch left for all margins—top, bottom, and sides?			
20. Are corrections made neatly?			
21. Are sources of information completely documented in a consistent, widely used arrangement?			
22. Are graphic aids used as necessary or desirable?			
23. Are graphic aids placed as close as possible to the material they illustrate?			
24. Are graphic aids properly labeled and numbered?			
25. Are graphic aids constructed in a form that does not misrepresent?			
26. Are graphic aids introduced by written material before they are presented?			
27. Are appendices numbered and labeled?			
28. Is the bibliography consistently worded in an arrangement recommended by a leading style manual?			
29. Is the report typewritten on good quality bond paper?			
30. Are you proud of your report?			

Cases for Chapters 13 through 16

Instructions

In the following cases, much of the necessary information is given, although in some instances additional research is required. You are free to make reasonable assumptions and to add minor details. Retain the overall content and meaning of the problem to be solved, and do not change facts and instructions given with each case.

The names of individuals and organizations are fictitious. Addresses given are not actual ones. If real names of individuals or organizations are used, the use is completely coincidental.

Do not lift phrases, sentences, or paragraphs from the cases and insert them into your own reports. The wording given is for the most part inappropriate for use in your "solutions" to the cases.

Unless you are given specific instructions in the case itself, use the format and arrangement you consider best for the particular information and situation. For all cases, more than one format and order of arrangement is acceptable and appropriate. As in all writing, work for simplicity, clarity, and reader interest.

CASES THAT REQUIRE NO FURTHER RESEARCH

1. The Company Store

You are an accountant with Paule Company, a division of the conglomerate Worldwide Corporation. Paule employs 520 people, and manufactures sprinkler systems. Other divisions of Worldwide manufacture a wide range of products, including small appliances, candy, barbecue grills, household items, books, cameras, lights, and many more. Several employees have inquired about the possibility of purchasing, at below retail cost, products produced by other divisions of Worldwide.

An inquiry was made to other divisions about purchasing their products. They offered to sell their products to Paule at cost, plus freight and handling expenses. Even with these added costs, the price to employees would be less than could be found at discount stores.

Because management officials want to give employees every possible benefit, they opened a company store to sell products at the same price it costs Paule to obtain them, with no added charges for selling expense or providing the space for the store. These costs are to be considered additional employee benefits.

A vacant room was converted into the company store, which is open two hours a day, two days a week. Employees come into the store during their coffee breaks or at lunch time. They have the option of paying cash for their purchases or paying through payroll deductions. Repayment through payroll deductions can be spread over one, two, three, or four pay periods.

Employees seem to be delighted with the store. Reaction has been extremely favorable.

It is now the time of year when the annual cost-of-living increase is announced to employees, along with a statement and breakdown of additional benefits they are receiving. The benefits are quoted on a dollar-per-hour basis. You have been asked to determine how much the company store benefits the employees in the form of a dollar amount per hour, per employee. This determination is necessary in order to establish whether the amount should be included in the annual statement to employees. (For morale purposes, you want to include the amount if it "looks good." If it is extremely small, just let the employees know the store is there, even though most of them have already used it.)

You cannot determine in this calculation the exact benefit to employees of being able to buy merchandise at less-than-retail prices. Although this benefit is important, it cannot be included in the hourly figure because savings differ, depending on the type of merchandise and the varying prices at department and discount stores.

Data for cost breakdown are these:

- Depreciation of the 15-foot by 20-foot room is to be considered over a period of 15 years, or at the rate of $30 a month.

- A one-time expenditure for equipment for the store (sign and lock for door, shelving, telephone, cash register, and showcases) is $700.

Two employees work in the store. One is a middle-management employee who earns $12 an hour. Another is a clerical employee who earns $6 an hour. Each works in the store two hours a day, two days a week. In addition, the middle-management employee spends approximately eight hours per month in placing orders, verifying shipping dates, receiving merchandise, handling returns, and other miscellaneous duties. You should consider that, in addition to these two employees, other personnel expenses should be charged to the store, including a receiving department clerk, an accounting clerk who handles the banking function for the store, and a payroll clerk who handles payroll deductions. Since you have no way of knowing exactly how much of their time should be charged to the store, you decide to estimate these costs at $100 a month.

You know that the regular hourly wage is not all that each employee earns, so you add a benefit factor of 25 percent to the personnel costs of the two employees assigned to the store. You decide to leave the miscellaneous cost at $100, an estimate that you believe to be high enough to include added benefits.

The average monthly inventory of the store is $5,000. The cost of money, at the present time, is 14 percent. The average monthly receivable balance of the store is $2,000. (As an accountant, you know you must include interest costs.)

Telephone expense allotted to the store is $5 a month.

Find the hourly benefit to each employee. Report this to President Susan Bradley. She has had no part in the store development and may not be familiar with why it was organized, how it works, and how much it costs. She does take responsibility each year for writing the message to the employees, as she wants them to be happy.

2. Macon Industries*

As director of the Transportation Department of Macon Industries, a large corporation with a fleet of 5,000 vehicles, you have been asked to look into what the president feels is an excessive number of accidents involving company vehicles.

From your records you find there were 2,319 accidents during the past 24 months. The causes of 1,725 of these accidents were charged to the employee operating the vehicle. Of these accidents, 401 involved 157 employees who had had two or more accidents in the 24-month period, but 53 of these 157 have left the company.

The remaining 104 employees were given a series of tests:

---

*Used by permission of Dr. Ruth C. Batchelor, Associate Professor Emeritus of Business Communication, New York University.

a. Eye test by company doctors to check vision

b. The standardized Porter Reaction Test

c. Road test (in a vehicle similar to the one(s) in which the accident(s) had occurred) to determine driver habits, driver attitudes, operating proficiency, and knowledge of vehicular equipment. The road tests were conducted by driver-training experts supplied by the National Safety Council.

The results of these tests, along with other employee information (age, sex, date of initial employment with company, previous job, position or positions held in company, accident record, etc.), were placed in individual employee portfolios.

An examination of the 104 portfolios reveals that of these 104 accident repeaters:

98 are in 19–27 age group

63 have eye deficiencies

89 have bad driving habits

94 have fewer than 5 years with the company

all 104 are male

88 are on their first job

21 have very poor reaction time

91 do not have adequate knowledge of equipment

61 have received no formal company training

72 have poor driving attitudes.

Write a memorandum report to the president clearly defining the problem, presenting your data, interpreting the data, and making suitable recommendations.

3. Hudson Textiles, Inc.*

Hudson Textiles, Inc., a large manufacturing company with twelve plants throughout the nation and with their head office in New York, will pay a full tuition refund to those New York office employees who have completed one year's service and who matriculate in a degree-granting institution. Originally designed to combine business experience with formal education for the benefit of the company that pays the bills, the plan is generally regarded as a fringe benefit and as an incentive to ambitious employees to go to college. At the present time, 44 of the 200 eligible employees in the New York office take advantage of this benefit.

A recent survey showed that over the past four years, an average of 75 percent of those obtaining a college degree at company expense quit Hudson within one year and 12 percent quit before obtaining a degree. The company is expanding each year and needs college-trained personnel for middle-management positions not only in the New York office but also in various plants throughout

*Used by permission of Dr. Ruth C. Batchelor, Associate Professor Emeritus of Business Communication, New York University.

the country. Thus, Hudson pays college tuition for lost employees and is forced to hire college-trained personnel from the outside at substantial wages for middle-management positions and to train these employees who have had no company experience. More than three-quarters of the existing middle-management positions are filled with employees having fewer than four years with Hudson.

You have been asked by Mr. Thomas J. Robertson, President of Hudson Textiles, to make some recommendations to ease this situation.

As a beginning, assume you review written exit interviews of lost employees for the past four years and find that 92 percent of 125 ex-employees who received their college degrees at Hudson expense gave as their reason for leaving Hudson the fact that they had received no recognition in the form of promotion after their graduation. Further, 84 percent added that they felt "mere payment" of tuition had not been sufficient reward for their six to eight years of attending evening classes for a degree. Over half of these ex-employees (67) expressed a feeling of bitterness toward Hudson because "outsiders" with college degrees held management positions.

Assume also that you collect data by conducting a series of individual interviews with a sample of 100 employees (44 student-employees, 50 nonstudent-employees eligible for college entrance, and 6 recent college graduates, graduated at Hudson expense) in the New York office.

Of the 44 student-employees, 5 frankly state they intend to clear out of Hudson for better jobs as soon as they complete their degrees; 10 hint at the same by saying they will "probably" look around after graduating; and the remaining 29 say they have no plans. None indicates any definite plans to stay with Hudson.

Of the six graduates, two were promoted to middle-management positions after receiving their degrees; but only one of these seems happy with his promotion, which included a raise as well as a title. The remaining four are frankly looking around for jobs with other companies. One of these four summed up the feelings of the others when she said: "No one in management or in personnel ever asked me how I was getting along (in college) nor congratulated me when my name was on the Dean's List for five successive semesters. I thought surely when I graduated, Mr. Robertson would write me a letter. If Dean Crosby had not sent me carbons of the letters he sent on six separate occasions to Mr. Robertson regarding the honor I had received, I would have believed no one at Hudson knew I was attending college. . . . Of course, I'm grateful to Hudson for paying my tuition; but I represented Hudson at the University and I can honestly say I was a good representative . . . . [F]rankly, I expected a promotion and a raise."

You select the 50 nonstudent-employees out of the

total of 156 of those eligible on the basis of their indicated interest in obtaining a college education, although they are not currently participating in Hudson's tuition refund plan. Forty-eight of these 50 expressed their belief that it is company policy to fill middle-management positions from the outside; 27 of these 48 feel the extra work involved in getting a degree would not pay since the degree apparently would not lead to a promotion. Two of these 50 employees are not in the plan because they are momentarily expecting transfer to a Western branch. Both express the hope that Hudson will extend the benefit to employees in other cities where colleges offer evening degree programs.

All of the student-employees and the six graduates indicate that there is no periodic review made of their academic progress or achievements, that no recognition is given in the form of raises or promotions based on academic achievement, and that some supervisors are seemingly not aware of the act that an employee in their charge is attending school. Ten of 44 student-employees feel that their supervisors are holding them back from promotion because they are attending college. Thirty of the student-employees and only one of the college graduates indicate they think it is Hudson's policy to recruit outsiders for middle-management positions.

Write a report to Mr. Robertson, clearly defining the problem and its implications to the company, using the information given to you but presenting it logically and in your own words. Before you present your data, tell how you secured it and why you chose this particular way of collecting data. Why was it necessary to interview the non-student-employees? State specifically the questions you asked each group of employees. Present the data clearly, draw your conclusions from the data, and state your recommendation to Mr. Robertson.

4. Survey of Residents of Retirement Building

Refer to Figure 14–2 in Chapter 14. The following data are the assumed results of the questionnaire. Assume that you have surveyed the 242 residents of the apartment building, Retirement Towers. (You might also think of a more enticing name for the building.) You received 180 responses. (Husbands and wives completed individual questionnaires.) Report the results of your study in an appropriate and readable arrangement.

Question 1. As long as possible, 102; Doesn't matter, 58; No longer than have to, 20. Question 2. Definitely would, 40; Probably would, 71; Don't know, 10; Probably not, 39; Definitely not, 20. Question 3. Definitely would, 37; Probably would, 62; Don't know, 22; Probably not, 37; Definitely not, 22. Question 4. Elementary school, 6; High school, 94; College, 49; Trade or vocational school, 19; Graduate school, 12. Question 5. No, 122; Yes, 58; Can't climb stairs, 51; Wheelchair, 5; Special diet, 2.

Question	Essential	Very Important	Moderately Important	Not Important	Definitely Unimportant
6	41	80	52	2	5
7	86	39	45	10	0
8	92	45	9	14	20
9	102	38	35	5	0
10	127	32	21	0	0
11	142	22	16	0	0
12	71	32	25	42	10
13	123	47	10	0	0
14	67	62	45	6	0
15	65	66	31	18	0

5. Recommended Content of Resumes

Part A This assignment is based on a study completed in 1986 by Dr. Glynna Morse, Memphis State University, and used here with the permission of Dr. Morse. A questionnaire was sent to 120 executives randomly selected from a directory of firms within a 75-mile radius of Memphis, Tennessee; 73 executives responded. Results of a portion of the study are shown in Tables I through VI.

TABLE I
Number of Employees in Firms of Executives in Survey

Number of Employees	Number of Respondents	Percentage of Respondents
20–39	24	32.9
40–79	20	27.4
80–199	15	20.5
200–499	6	8.2
500 or more	8	11.0
Total	73	100.0

TABLE II
Executive Preferences of Resume Styles

Style of Resume	Number of Respondents	Percentage of Respondents
Chronological	41	56.2
Combination	23	31.5
Functional	6	8.2
No preference	3	4.1
Total	73	100.0

TABLE III
Executive Preferences for Category Formats

Category Format	Number of Respondents	Percentage of Respondents
Two-column arrangement	35	47.9
Underlined side headings	25	34.2
Centered headings	6	8.2
No preference	7	9.6
Total	73	99.9*

*Percentages may be more or less than 100 percent because of rounding.

TABLE IV
Executive Preferences for Main Heading Formats

Heading Format	Number of Respondents	Percentage of Respondents
All lines centered	48	65.7
All lines blocked at left	13	17.8
Name centered with address and phone number on one line	4	5.5
Name blocked at left, address and phone number at right	4	5.5
Other	1	1.4
No preference	3	4.1
Total	73	100.0

TABLE V
Executive Preferences for Job Objectives

Job Objective	Number of Respondents	Percentage of Respondents
Job objective with additional description	35	47.9
General job area	22	30.1
Specific job title	9	12.3
No objective on resume; state in application letter	7	9.6
Total	73	99.9*

*Percentages may be more or less than 100 percent because of rounding.

TABLE VI
Executive Preferences for References

Use of References	Number of Respondents	Percentage of Respondents
References listed	52	71.2
References will be furnished	18	24.7
No mention of references required on resume; to be furnished when requested	3	4.1
Total	73	100.0

a. Assume that you are Dr. Morse. Write a synopsis of approximately one single-spaced page summarizing the results of your study.

b. Write an introductory passage to precede each of the six tables.

c. Write a recommendations section of a report based on the data shown in Tables II through VI.

Part B Compare the results of the Morse study with data published in books or periodicals in the past two years. Write a memorandum (or other form of report requested by your instructor) about the similarities and differences of all these sources.

CASES THAT REQUIRE FURTHER RESEARCH

6. Your Own Subject, Your Own Report

Ideally, this problem is an actual one you have encountered in your business or profession. You can solve a real problem and complete a class assignment at the same time. With your instructor's approval, prepare a report based on real problems or questions in your business or profession.

7. Recommending Equipment

Assume that your office has need for one of the following items:

a. an electric typewriter

b. a desk calculator

c. a photocopier

d. a voice-writing and transcribing machine (or machines) for use in a private office

e. a microcomputer

f. a similar item of equipment or office furniture

Investigate the brands available and recommend your choice, considering the particular needs for your organization.

8. Combining Your Efforts

With your instructor's permission and assistance, investigate some problem in your school or community. This research can be planned as a class project with individual class members investigating some phase of the problem and preparing individual reports. The total findings can then be combined for an overall report on the situation. Or the class can be divided into committees, with each to assume special responsibilities in researching and reporting a portion of the situation. If your topic has been investigated previously, try to obtain the results of these investigations. Test these results, or use the information to form the basis for further investigation of the problem. Present the results of your study in the form suggested by your instructor.

9. Career Apparel

Your study should determine whether career apparel should be provided by an organization with which you are familiar or one that you can study. (This is the same problem posed in earlier chapters in relation to the hypothetical Countrywide Insurance Company.) Include information based on library research, the opinions of persons to wear the apparel, possible suppliers, and costs.

10. A Report of Three Cities

Your company is preparing for labor negotiations. The manager of industrial relations wants figures to compare living costs in Houston, where the company has headquarters, with two other cities in which branches are located, Seattle and New York. Find the latest figures published by the U.S. Bureau of Labor Statistics or find the figures in another recent and reputable source. Write a report to Miss Roberta Hardin, manager of industrial relations. You are her assistant.

11. Three More Cities

Follow the instructions given in Case 10, but compare your city with two others in which you think you would like to live.

12. Happy Inns

You work for Happy Inns. You have been asked to investigate three companies that are possible considerations for acquisition. (For the purposes of this assignment, choose the three companies or study those suggested by your instructor.) No negotiations have yet been made with any of these companies, and you do not want your research publicized. You cannot go to these companies for information but must confine your investigation to their annual reports and other published sources. Find all the published information you can about these companies. Present a summary of your findings in a report to the president of Happy Inns of America. Include possible problems and advantages likely to occur with the acquisition of each company.

Modify this problem as your instructor directs. Perhaps you will wish to consider only one company or to prepare the report for your own organization. You have not been asked to make specific recommendations about any of the companies because much further research would be necessary.

13. Determining Employment Opportunities in Your Career Field*

Examine the classified advertising section of five consecutive Sunday editions of your local newspaper. (If you do not live in a large city, examine issues of the Sunday newspaper from a nearby city.) Try to determine employment opportunities for people like yourself.

For example, if you are a beginning accountant, look for openings that you feel capable of filling. The advertisements may include such terms as *staff accountant, entry-level accountant,* or *recent graduate.* If you are an experienced accountant, look for openings at a higher level. Examine advertisements carefully. Some do not have descriptive titles, yet offer employment opportunities in your field.

As other examples, if you are seeking a job as an executive secretary, look for this job description or such terms as *administrative secretary* or *secretary to top executive.* You can perhaps be even more specific and investigate, for example, opportunities for mechanical engineers in manufacturing or in whatever area you are experienced or interested. State exactly the purpose and scope of your research.

Determine from the advertisements answers to these questions: Which qualifications are most often listed? What is the average salary? How are you asked to apply? Do advertisements indicate opportunities for promotion? Is travel or relocation necessary?

Present the answer to these questions, plus others that you believe to be important, in appropriate report form. Charts or tables will be helpful for presenting your findings in the most readable style.

14. Investigating Employment Opportunities

Investigate two organizations for which you would like to work. Study their annual reports, recruiting brochures, and other secondary sources published by some individual or organization other than the organizations you are investigating. Talk with at least one present employee of each

*This problem is adapted from one written by Dr. Ed Goodin, Associate Professor of Management, University of Nevada, Las Vegas. It is used here with Dr. Goodin's permission.

company. Also try to find past employees, who may be able to tell you more than present employees. Try to find people who are or were in jobs similar to the one you seek.

Consider all aspects that are important to you on the job, including whether or not relocation is likely and whether there are opportunities for promotion. In the concluding section, summarize the reasons you have chosen one company over the other.

15. The Concerned Citizen

Look into legislation that you consider unfair to you or to some segment of the population. Write a report about this law, or these laws, and make recommendations for change, with reasons. Remember that you are most convincing when you give specific, definite evidence. Although your mind is made up before you start (you could decide that you are wrong), use an objective approach and wording. Be considerate of your reader. Make photocopies of your report and send it to your senators and representatives.

16. Sales and Marketing

Assume that you are the new sales manager of a company that sells a product that you know well or one about which you can find complete information. Compare this product with its leading competitors. Write a report in which you compare your product with the others. Include strengths and weaknesses. Summarize with recommendations for features to be stressed in sales campaigns. Also include recommendations for improvement of your product.

17. You have decided to open a small retail business in your town or city. For the purpose of this research, assume you have the necessary capital. Decide on the kind of business according to your real interests and present knowledge. For example, if you like to play tennis, investigate the possibility of starting a tennis shop. If you love books, consider a bookstore, and so on.

The purpose of this report is to determine the location in your town or city to establish your store. Use information from the Bureau of the Census about particular areas in your city. Also consider the location of competing businesses.

A variation of this report is to assume that you are a consultant preparing this preliminary study for some other person.

Prepare the report in the form and arrangement recommended by your instructor.

18. Your aunt, age 72, has asked you to investigate the most recent models of automobiles and to recommend one that she should buy. She wants the least expensive car available, provided it has the following features, ranked in importance in the order listed: safety, ease of handling, comfort, durability, economical fuel consumption, and sporty apearance. She wants a four-door model with room enough for herself and at least three friends.

What is your recommendation? Write a letter to your aunt, carefully explaining the basis for your choice. Perhaps you should attach brochures describing the automobile chosen and two or three leading contenders. Do not rely on brochures alone; use other sources to determine the attributes of the automobiles.

19. What are the leading professional journals in your major field? For example, if you are majoring in accounting, what are the leading accounting journals? Examine at least three recent issues of two of the leading journals; recommend one of the two for other people in your career field. To support your recommendation, include this information:

Kinds of articles

Extent and kinds of advertising

Photographs

Frequency of publication

Cost

Sponsorship (For example, some journals are published by professional organizations.)

You will need to give information about both journals and show clearly the basis of your preference.

20. Examine five recent issues (Monday–Friday) of *The Wall Street Journal*.

Write a memorandum report to your instructor about the number and kinds of graphic aids you found in the five issues. If you find instances in which graphic aids do not conform to the principles given in this textbook, mention these discrepancies in your report. Copies of some or all of the graphic aids will be helpful to your discussion.

21. This case also is based on examining five recent issues of *The Wall Street Journal* (Monday–Friday). Analyze the advertisements, considering only large advertisements and not the classified sections or advertisements of only a few lines. You are likely to find that a great number of these advertisements are for computers or investments of different kinds. What are other leading categories? Use tables with your written discussion to analyze the advertisements in the five issues.

22. Compare five annual reports. Choose the most recent ones available. Annual reports are ordinarily available in the Reference Room of your library.

a. What are the similarities and differences? Overall, which of the five annual reports do you believe is the most effective? The least effective?

b. Assume that you are a consultant asked to recommend improvements for the report that you consider the least effective. Write a preliminary recommendation of one or two pages to the communication supervisor of the company involved. (Use an assumed name for the supervisor.)

23. Fashion Merchandising

Assume that you have been hired as a buyer or manager for a chain of small stores specializing in misses or junior fashions. Study fashion publications in the field and make recommendations to your supervisor about purchases for the next season. Give special attention to presently fashionable items or styles that should be increased, decreased, or dropped entirely. Present this information as simply as you can, but give sources of your information and the basis for your recommendation.

24. Investment Counseling

Assume that you are an investment counselor. Your friend, Ann Moore, asks your advice about what to do with $75,000 cash that she inherited. She is 42, single, with no dependents. She owns a large townhouse that she bought for $40,000 fifteen years ago. She earns $27,000 a year and has no debts except for mortgage payments of $260 a month. She is happy with her residence and does not plan to move. She has been employed by the federal government for seventeen years.

She is interested in investing the $75,000 for long-term growth. What do you recommend? She must be given specific reasons supported by adequate background information. Present your findings in a letter to Ann.

25. Write a report on one of the following subjects. The use of secondary sources is likely to form an important part of your investigation. According to the directions of your instructor, you may wish to add primary sources by interviewing people who, because of their background, education, or work experience, have first-hand knowledge of the subject you are investigating.

a. What a business executive should know in order to communicate effectively with business people in Japan. (Or choose Saudi Arabia, Russia, Mexico, or any other country or part of the world with culture and customs different from those in the United States and Canada.)

b. How _____ (name of real or imaginary product) should be promoted in _____ (name of country or part of the world in which culture and customs differ from those in the United States and Canada).

c. Communicating through the use of color.

d. The use and misuse of statistics.

e. The changing English language.

f. Laws that apply to honest advertising.

g. Careers in the field of business communication.

h. How an understanding of kinesics (body language) relates to effective communication for business and the professions.

i. How an understanding of proxemics (communication through the use of personal space) relates to effective communication for business and the professions.

j. Planning meetings and conferences.

k. Effective listening.

l. Increased job satisfaction through communication.

m. The open office.

n. Interviewing (to obtain a job).

o. Interviewing (to select employees).

p. Parliamentary procedure.

q. Quality circles.

r. Teleconferencing and videoconferencing.

s. Special telephone services.

t. Electronic mail.

u. Overcoming job-related stress.

v. Writing sales messages.

w. How to dress for success (men) or how to dress for success (women). (Don't depend only on Molloy's famous books by the same title; use additional sources, preferably more recent ones.)

x. Using a computer to construct charts and graphs.

y. Using a computer for letter writing and other short communications (a form of word processing).

z. An overview of software packages for word processing.

aa. An overview of software packages for financial analysis.

bb. Differences in word usage and spelling: England and the United States.

cc. Techniques for effective television appearances.

dd. Regional language and usage (expressions peculiar to one or more sections of the United States).

ee. Designing questionnaires.

ff. Positive versus negative words. (Include examples, and add other elements of persuasive and diplomatic words and phrases.)

gg. Optical scanning methods of computer input.

hh. Voice recognition as a method of computer input.

ii. Legal considerations that affect written and oral communication within and from a business organization.

26. Combine three or more related topics listed in Case 25. For example, parts e, bb, dd, and ff are concerned with language usage. You could combine these related topics into one report. Other similar groups can be chosen, or you can combine similar topics of your own with one or more of those shown.

27. Report Assignment on Intercultural Communication

Note: Students should read Chapters 18 and 19 before beginning Case 27 or the following variations of Case 27.

This assignment is partially a group report and partially an individual report. It provides experience and knowledge in these important areas of communication: primary research, secondary research, report writing, evaluating and editing the written work of other students, oral presentations, interpersonal communication, communication within groups, supervision (by chairperson of each group), and intercultural communication.

Much time will be saved in gathering material because members of each group share information. Furthermore, in organizations several people are likely to work together on long reports.

Because of varying class sizes and other factors, *specific directions for this case must be provided by your instructor.* Depending upon the approval of your instructor and any necessary modifications, follow the suggestions given below:

a. Fill out a questionnaire (to be prepared by the class members or by the instructor) to determine the country or area of the world in which each student is most interested. The questionnaire should also request information about the reason for each student's choice of country or group of countries; for example, some students are particularly interested in Germany or another country because their parents, grandparents, or other ancestors came from there. As another example, some students will want to study Japan because they now work or hope to work for a Japanese firm in the United States. In addition, the questionnaire should be designed to determine whether students have visited their chosen countries or worked with persons from these countries.

b. Divide into groups of four to six. As much as possible, groups should be formed to allow students to study the country of their choice.

c. Elect (or ask the instructor to appoint) a chairperson for each group.

d. Decide upon the particular topic of intercultural communication each group member is to research. As an example, a group studying Japan (or any other country) might divide research and writing responsibilities into these areas, some of which may overlap:

1. Government and economic conditions

2. Probable attitudes toward people from the United States (or toward people from Canada or your particular native country)

3. Social and religious customs and holidays

4. Nonverbal communication, particularly the use of space and time

5. Business etiquette

6. Cost of living, methods of travel, housing, other necessary information for a person planning to make a business trip to Japan.

e. Write, as a group, an introduction that will be used for the combined report.

f. Cooperate with other group members by giving and receiving information applicable to particular subtopics. For example, if you are preparing a section of the combined report that relates to nonverbal communication, share with the student preparing a section on government and economic conditions any important information about his or her topic that you find in your own research.

g. Write your section of the report after completing the methods and extent of research specified by your instructor.

h. Supply every other member of your group with a photocopy of your section of the completed report.

i. Decide, as a group, the order in which the various report sections should be arranged. Write a table of contents for the entire report. (This table of contents is to be used by all group members.)

j. Edit, in a group meeting, the report sections previously prepared by all group members.

k. Write, as a group, a concluding section that includes recommendations.

l. Write a letter of transmittal to your instructor (individually or as a group). Along with other information, specify the author of each section of the report. (Your instructor will perhaps base much of your individual grade on the portion of the report for which you were directly responsible.)

m. Write, as a group, a synopsis of the entire report. Photocopy this synopsis for the entire class.

n. Prepare and deliver oral presentations to the entire group. These presentations may be done individually or as a panel, but all reports on each country should be given on the same day.

o. Distribute your synopses to all class members after you have given your oral report.

p. Plan a visit to the country on which you are now an expert.

28. Report Assignment on Nonverbal Communication and Intercultural Communication (a Variation of Case 27)

Follow the instructions given in Case 27 with the following modifications:

a. The overall topic of your report is nonverbal communication, with an emphasis on nonverbal communication in various cultures.

b. Each group studies nonverbal communication in a particular country or area; for example, Saudi Arabia, Japan, China, England, Germany, U.S.S.R., France, Australia.

c. Individuals in each group choose or are assigned some particular element of nonverbal communication; for example, kinesics; proxemics; use of and attitudes toward time; business dress and appearance; attitudes toward women in business and the professions. Thus, as in Case 27, each student reports on an individual topic; for example, how people in Saudi Arabia use personal space (proxemics).

29. Report Assignment on Written and Oral Communication in Various Countries

Modify the instructions in Cases 27 and 28. For example, each group is assigned a particular country. Subcategories might include the use of the telephone or face-to-face communication versus written communication; style and formality of letters; words usage (especially applicable to the study of England); meetings and conferences; courtesy; formality.

30. Report Assignment on Nonverbal and Intercultural Communication (Variation of Case 27)

Each group is assigned a certain aspect of communication to be investigated; for example, nonverbal communication (which can be divided into separate factors), business etiquette, living conditions, social customs and taboos, written and oral communication. As with Cases 27, 28, and 29, each student in the class has an individual topic, although it is related to all other topics and closely related to the topics of class members in the same group. Students in each group research a particular area of communication as it applies to a particular country. Thus, the subject of one student's investigation might be nonverbal communication in Japan. Another student, a member of another group, might investigate living conditions in Japan or in any other chosen country.

CHAPTER **17**

Speaking to Groups

*Public speaking, like other methods of communication, is influenced by the entire person-
ality of the sender of the message, the particular situation, and the receivers of the
message. The ability to be a capable and convincing speaker is important to your success
and to your professional growth.*

*This chapter is only a beginning guide toward your goal of effectively presenting
yourself and your ideas from a public platform. Even an entire book or an entire course
would be only a beginning; the perfection of your speaking ability is up to you. Instructions in this chapter, however, contain the basic information you will need as you begin
or continue your study and practice of becoming an outstanding speaker.*

Compare Oral Presentations with Written Communication

The principles of effective communication through written letters, memorandums, and reports discussed in preceding chapters also apply, for the most part, to effective oral presentations. Precise use of language, clarity, empathy, knowledge of subject matter, appropriate emphasis and organization—all these qualities are necessary for the successful transmission of a message in either written or oral form.

Both written and oral reports begin with careful and thorough research and an objective analysis of data. As in other forms of communication, you consider the probable reactions of the audience to ideas and recommendations. The same principles that apply to objective interpretation and presentation of data in written reports apply to oral presentations. Emphasis must be on data and what they indicate, not on the writer's or speaker's beliefs and desires.

Like written messages, oral presentations can be presented in the direct or the indirect order. When presented in the direct order, however, an oral report should have a specific, emphatic ending, often in the form of a short summary.

Many people find speaking much easier than writing. For others, facing an audience is terrifying. The best way to build confidence in yourself—and to make your speech convincing and informative—is to know your subject thor-

This speaker appears confident, sincere, well-prepared, and successful. The clip-on microphone allows freedom of movement and provides consistent, noise-free amplification.

oughly and to understand that your purpose is to inform and to convince, and perhaps to entertain, but not to impress the audience with your cleverness and knowledge.

If you are completely familiar with all portions of the subject (even though you don't know *all* the answers) and if you sincerely want to pass this knowledge on to your listeners, you are likely to express your ideas clearly and convincingly.

An advantage of oral communication over written communication is that you have instant feedback. Another advantage is that your facial expressions, tone of voice, and gestures help to make spoken words clear, convincing, and effective.

Graphic illustrations are used in oral reports and other presentations, just as they are in written communications. They can be used effectively, or, as in written reports, they can be misleading, distracting, and unnecessary. The principles of graphic illustration discussed in this chapter apply to both written and oral reports. Moreover, when you use illustrations in an oral presentation, remember that every member of the audience must be able to see the entire illustration easily. And, as in written reports, the illustration should not be expected to convey the most important elements of the presentation, but to supplement the information presented through words.

A difference between written and oral presentations is the extreme importance of nonverbal messages in oral communication of all kinds. Although nonverbal elements exist also in written material, nonverbal communication is more obvious and important in oral interaction.

Analyze your Subject to Decide What to Include

Expressing your central idea in a few words enables you to see the subject in its entirety and to understand the relationship of each part of the report to the central idea. Only when you look at your topic in this way can you decide on the best way to present it.

If a report is to help your listeners make a decision, consider carefully the issues involved. Does the recommended action provide a solution to an existing problem? What benefits will accrue from your suggested solution? Are your recommendations practical and realistic? Is the topic a controversial one about which you are not likely to obtain agreement? Will your recommendation, al-

---

Never forget that no matter how brilliant and well constructed your formal address is, even the most attentive listener is not going to absorb your entire message. This is a tragedy, but like all tragedies it must be faced, not denied.

Our concentrated attention wanders, literally every few seconds, even when we are attempting to overcome such a natural failing. You can prove this very simply by saying a sentence equivalent in length to two or three lines of printed type, then asking your listener to repeat what has just been said. Not once in a hundred times will you hear the sentence repeated exactly as you spoke it.

Steve Allen, *How to Make a Speech* (New York: McGraw-Hill, 1986), 39.

Communication Brief

though beneficial overall, result in undesirable side effects? Most important of all, does your report supply sufficient evidence, provided by objective and reliable methods of research, to convince your listeners of its credibility?

Decide on the essential information and explanation to be included; then resolve how to present it in the available time. Always work for simplicity. Be interesting and clear. At times you must also be convincing. A multitude of details is not simple, interesting, clear, or convincing.

Write a specific statement of purpose for your presentation. (What do you hope to accomplish?)

Write an Outline of Key Ideas in Their Order of Presentation

After you have stated specifically the purpose you hope to accomplish through your oral report and your central idea, estimated your listeners' reactions, considered the occasion and the environment, and analyzed the subject in terms of what must be included, you are ready to prepare an outline of how you will express and expand on the central idea. This planning process is similar to preparing a tentative table of contents for a written report.

The skeleton of your entire speech, an outline contains your main ideas in the sequence you will present them. Other helpful, interesting, or perhaps amusing details will be added as you progress in the planning of your talk.

Even though you are giving an oral presentation based on a previously prepared written report, do not assume that your oral report should follow the same outline. For one reason, you are not likely to have enough time to discuss each subdivision in the same order and detail as in a complete written report. In addition, in order to facilitate understanding, you may need to include some background information not in the report itself. And, from the standpoint of emphasis and interest, you may wish to spend more time on conclusions and recommended actions than on detailed findings, as you often do when preparing a written synopsis.

Consider Time Limitations

It is absolutely essential to plan oral presentations to fit the material into the allotted time. The best way to plan your time exactly is to practice your speech with the aid of a tape recorder. Even this timing will not be exact, except in the case of a speech that you read word for word, because of unintentional departures from the planned sequence of topics and unforeseen interruptions.

Do not read an oral presentation from a written text unless it is to be recorded or published in your exact spoken words. In most business and professional presentations, reading the report is much less desirable than the more casual and usual method of "telling" or "talking" the report.

Even without a tape recorder, you can estimate time fairly well by estimating the number of words in a planned talk. Although speaking rates vary somewhat, the average rate is 110 to 150 words a minute. If you do not have interruptions because of questions or periods of presenting graphic aids, your average

Question: Please list some words that are frequently mispronounced.

Improve Your Speech

Answer: Many words are pronounced differently, by many people, from the sounds indicated by dictionary markings.

Listeners from Boston or other northern cities are likely to believe that southerners mispronounce all words, and southerners may have the same opinion about people from Boston and other localities. This difference, however, is a matter of regional accents, not real mispronunciation of words. Other extreme differences, caused only or mostly by places where we happen to live, occur between British speech and American speech. Although speech is becoming more standardized because of television and increased interaction between people from everywhere, many regional and national differences remain.

In addition, some words can be correctly pronounced more than one way; take your choice. "You like to-*may*-toes, I like to-*mah*-toes; you like *e*-ther, I like *i*-ther."

Your question is a valid one, however, because some particular pronunciations, for no discernible reason, seem to differ greatly from the pronunciations shown in dictionaries and usually considered correct.

For example, a syllable is often omitted from *incidentally*, resulting in *incidently*.

The word *sales* is sometimes pronounced *sells*, even though the meaning is clear in the speaker's mind. *Sales* is a plural noun. *Sells* is a verb.

In parts of the South and perhaps elsewhere, *ask* is sometimes pronounced *ax*.

An additional syllable is added to *regardless*, resulting in *irregardless*, which is not a recognized word.

To list all words that are mispronounced would require a book of dictionary length. Such books have already been written.

---

speaking rate can be used to determine how many words you can speak in, for example, a 25-minute period.

You should work to make the report or other oral communication no longer than it needs to be to convey the desired information and to achieve the desired results. As with written communication, however, too much concern with brevity may result in your audience's lack of understanding, acceptance, and conviction.

Even more important than length is quality, although from the standpoint of courtesy and consideration speakers should stay within their specified time periods. It is extremely inconsiderate to run on into the allotted time for a following speaker. You are also being inconsiderate of your audience when you are unnecessarily slow and repetitious. Such an approach is not likely to build favorable listener response.

Estimate Listeners' Reactions

As with all communication, predicting the probable responses of your listeners will enable you to express your ideas more persuasively and diplomatically. If your listeners are likely to be pleased with your findings and eager to follow your suggestions and recommendations, your presentation will be far easier and more enjoyable than if you expect opposite reactions.

Estimate the knowledge and background of your listeners about the subject of the report. Your listeners' interpretation of everything you say will be influenced by their past experience, especially as these experiences pertain to the content and approach of the report.

Consider your audience as a group, as well as a collection of individuals who make up that group. What characteristics do your listeners have in common? Do the members of your audience think of themselves as part of the group, subject to group values, goals, and standards of behavior? Do the members of the group have a common motive or goal? Do they like and accept one another?

Some groups contain individuals whom other members recognize, sometimes unconsciously or informally, as leaders. If you can identify these leaders, perhaps you should direct a portion of your message directly to them, although this approach must be used with extreme caution and should not be noticeable to the rest of the audience.

Understand the Occasion and the Environment

Communication of all kinds is affected by the environment in which it occurs. As a speaker you can do much to control that environment or to adapt the presentation to the setting and the situation. The acceptance of your remarks, of your ideas, and of yourself will be influenced by the setting in which they are presented. As you plan your report or other oral presentation, be sure that you have the answer to these questions:

1. Why is the meeting being held? Is it a regularly scheduled meeting or one called for a special purpose?
2. What is the relationship of your report to the presentation of other speakers?
3. What is the sequence of oral presentations?
4. How will listeners be affected by the time your report is presented?
5. How much time do you have available for your presentation, and can you expect to have your listeners' undivided attention for this period of time?
6. Where is the meeting to be held?
7. Is the room small or large, and will listeners be crowded together or scattered over a too-large area?
8. Will you need and have available a public-address system?
9. Is a speaker's stand available?
10. Is equipment available for the use of transparencies or other graphic aids?
11. Will there be enough light for you to read your notes without hesitation?

12. Will the room be heated or cooled to a comfortable temperature?

13. Will the room be free from outside noises?

14. Will your listeners be comfortable in all other respects of environment?

15. Is the room of a size and arrangement that all members of the audience can hear your words and look at you? Can you see all members of the audience?

If possible, examine the room and equipment well in advance of your talk. If that is not possible, at least arrive early on the day of your presentation and consider the environment in relation to your talk. An early examination of the setting may result in a modification of your planned presentation; for example, if you have planned to use transparencies and find that they cannot be easily seen by every person in the room, you are wise to omit them altogether or to enlarge them.

Even the most thorough preparation and planning cannot prevent all distractions or disturbing elements. Although you should do everything possible to arrange for the environment most conducive to the acceptance of your talk, an outstanding, interesting, convincing presentation will do much to atone for unfavorable aspects of the setting. And the most pleasant room and conditions will not compensate for a mediocre presentation.

Consider the Use of Graphic Aids and Other Illustrations

Graphic aids can add to the clarity and interest of an oral presentation. They can also weaken the oral presentation by detracting from the spoken words. Use illustrations only if they are needed to supplement your talk. Do not assume that your most important goal is to comment on the information presented by graphic aids but that the illustrated material supplements your spoken words.

Graphic illustrations such as bar or line charts express relationships much more quickly and accurately than spoken words do. The same advantages that graphics bring to written reports are brought to oral reports; in many instances, graphic aids are even more necessary for oral reports.

An overhead projector can be used to project written or pictorial material. Many photocopy machines can make a transparency from the original copy in a few minutes.

Duplicated handouts also serve as a visual aid. Some speakers believe, though, that the use of such material distracts from the immediate proceedings. Avoid distributing several pages at one time, some of which do not apply to what is being discussed at the moment. Members of the audience, instead of looking at the speaker or participating in discussion, may spend their time reading the handouts.

Also consider the use of slides and videocassettes.

Graphic aids and other illustrations, wisely planned and used, are helpful in presenting an interesting informative oral report. To be effective, however, they require the same careful planning and organization as the remainder of the report. Your talk should be far more than commenting on your illustrations and other aids.

Flip charts and other visual aids can strengthen oral presentations.

Be careful not to become so involved in presenting the illustrations that you lose your audience. Talk with the audience, not to the illustrations. The illustrations are not telling the story; you are.

Build Self-Confidence

Remember that you will naturally feel somewhat nervous before you are to make an important oral presentation, or maybe an unimportant one, if you are inexperienced in public speaking. Some speakers of long experience state that they continue to have stage fright before they actually begin speaking but that it disappears as they address the audience. Some people believe that this stage fright is beneficial as long as it is not so severe as to be paralyzing. They say that when they are not nervous at all they know that they are too complacent—and consequently will not give an enthusiastic presentation.

Your nervousness should not be so extreme as to result in shaking hands or a trembling voice, embarrassing not only to yourself but also to your listeners. Take comfort in the fact that most of your terror will not be apparent to the audience. A slight touch of shyness is more appealing to some people than the

Communication
Brief

> The brain starts working the moment you are born and never stops until you stand up to speak in public.
>
> Anonymous

opposite demeanor of extreme confidence and aggressiveness. On the other hand, being ill at ease indicates that you are more interested in making a good impression than in bringing a message to your audience or in talking with them.

Suggestions for building confidence are these:

1. Try not to be afraid in advance. Worrying or being afraid won't change anything for the better, but only make matters worse. Use the time you would spend in being afraid in preparing your talk.

2. Be completely and thoroughly prepared. After all that preparation, you'll be an expert on the subject. And why should an expert be nervous?

3. Unless you are positive that your listeners are actually hostile (an unlikely situation), assume that they are friendly and supportive. This assumption is likely to be correct whether they are friends, acquaintances, or strangers.

4. The audience is made up of *people*. Don't think of your audience as a mass of faces. Speak to your audience as you would to one friend or a small group of friends.

5. Look at people and notice their reactions. As you see your audience accept and respond to your words and actions, your confidence will increase.

6. You are likely to make a few mistakes. So do all the other experts.

Look at People as You Talk with Them

You talk with *people,* not with a vague, collective mass. You are communicating with *individuals,* with people like yourself.

When you talk with people, *look at them.* In a pause just before you begin speaking, look out over the room and focus on one person—then look at the other people. Let your eyes meet theirs, briefly. Make sure that you include members of the audience at far edges of the group. This action is a form of greeting, perhaps even more important than your spoken words of greeting. This pause also prepares your audience for your opening remarks by getting their attention. Otherwise, if you rush too quickly into your spoken greeting, some of your words will be lost to some of your listeners. By your glances, you invite your audience to enter into a conversation with you.

The audience's part of the conversation, when you are speaking without verbal responses from your listeners, is communicated through facial expressions, nods or frowns, posture, and actions. As will be discussed further in regard to nonverbal communication, your listeners provide vivid, instant feed-back without saying a word.

An opening scan of the audience (do not extend it too long) relaxes you because it takes your mind away from yourself, so that you can concentrate on your audience. When you think of your audience instead of yourself, your stage fright will decrease.

After you have prepared your listeners and yourself, start talking with them. Speak rather slowly at first until your listeners have had time to become accustomed to your voice. Every person has unique voice qualities and speaking characteristics. After a few sentences, speak at your natural rate, making sure that each word is distinct. (If you have not listened to your recorded voice, preferably as a rehearsal of the particular talk you are preparing, you are not yet ready to give that talk.)

As in the initial eye-contact with your audience, continue to include your listeners in all parts of the room. Avoid directing your attention to one part of the room or to only a few individuals. Do not look very long at any one person.

Make sure that everyone in the room can hear you. If you are not sure, ask. If necessary, adjust the public address system or project your voice.

Speak conversationally with a relaxed voice. If you shout or strain, or assume the pose and gestures of an orator, you are not being conversational.

As mentioned earlier, using a tape recorder is immensely helpful in im-proving your tone of voice and gaining a conversational approach as well as in checking on pronunciation, logic, appropriate use of emphasis, conciseness, timing, and all other qualities of effective speech. A tape recorder is almost as essential as a pen or typewriter in preparing yourself to give an outstanding oral presentation. Video equipment that records both sight and sound is even better but is more expensive and less convenient to use.

Understand the Importance of Nonverbal Communication

Nonverbal communication occurs constantly, whether in speaking to groups or conversing. It is impossible not to communicate with other people around you, even when you do not speak.

Nonverbal communication includes gestures and other bodily movements, facial expressions, posture, clothing, and overall appearance, use of time and space, and various other methods of expressing meaning. You communicate by tone of voice, rate of speech, the "oh's" and "ah's" that you insert into speech, pauses, hesitations, and silence. You also communicate through what you omit from your spoken words.

Like all other forms of communication, nonverbal messages should be sincere. Planned gestures and body movements usually appear to be just that—faked. Use gestures naturally to reinforce the meaning you are expressing through words. Too much hand movement is distracting and annoying.

Videotape equipment is helpful in determining whether your gestures and other forms of nonverbal communication are appropriate and effective. If such equipment is not available, ask friends to evaluate your speech from all aspects, especially the use of gestures, posture, and overall movement. It may be danger-ous to try to "spice up" your talk by adding gestures, even if you are now using

Communication Brief

The major differences in American and English pronunciation are intonation and voice timbre. . . . Our voice timbre seems harsh or tinny to the English, theirs gurgling or throaty to us. English conclusion: Americans speak shrilly, monotonously, and like a schoolboy reciting. American conclusion: the English speak too low, theatrically, and swallow their syllables.

Stuart Berg Fletcher, *Listening to America* (New York: Simon & Schuster, 1982), 210–11.

none. In case you are using too many hand movements, make an effort to avoid these distracting movements.

Following the advice given in preceding sections of this chapter will take care of many problems of nonverbal communication. For example, if you are sincere, enthusiastic, and knowledgeable and have a well-planned presentation, your sincerity, enthusiasm, knowledge, ability, and consideration of your audience will be apparent to your listeners. You will exhibit confidence and develop belief and trust by the overall excellence of your presentation.

Enthusiasm is contagious. If you are not enthusiastic about your subject, you cannot expect your listeners to be.

You communicate more through your nonverbal messages than with words. Much of nonverbal communication is unplanned; thus, it is a sincere form of communication. Your nonverbal messages are influenced by your feelings about your listeners, your subject, and yourself. Nevertheless, some nonverbal communication is unlike your real feelings. For example, if you frown because you are nervous or afraid, you will not be understood or accepted; the frown may be mistaken for dislike of your listeners. Even if the frown is correctly interpreted, it results in a negative impression and is a form of distraction.

Suggestions for effective nonverbal communication are these:

1. Sincerely like your audience.
2. Know your subject thoroughly in order to appear confident.
3. Be well dressed, but not overdressed.
4. Look your listeners in the eye (but not too long at any one person) and talk with them.
5. Avoid excessive, meaningless gestures and nervous movements.
6. Keep calm.
7. Remain objective. Do not let your anger show, no matter what the provocation.
8. Speak clearly and pleasantly. Make sure that you can be easily heard throughout the room, but don't shout.
9. Smile, but not continuously.
10. *Relax.* (You can't if you're unsure of yourself. That's why the nine preceding suggestions are important.)

Use your knowledge of nonverbal communication to analyze the feedback you receive from your audience. Nothing is more satisfying to a speaker than

Notice the various kinds of feedback to the speaker.

to notice a look of intense interest on the faces of the listening audience. After a few speaking engagements you will soon learn to recognize sincere approval and agreement. If your listeners are only pretending to be interested in your remarks, you will learn to recognize simulated approval and agreement. If your listeners are sitting straight in their chairs and looking you in the eyes, steadily and directly, beware. This is a pose of faked attention. Watch for listeners leaning toward you, even when you are sure they are having no difficulty in hearing. This attitude is a sign of sincere attention.

Notice such telltale signs of boredom as fidgeting, random glances around the room, and looking at watches. (If they are pretending to be interested in your remarks, they will not look at their watches. Frequent checkers of time are honestly telling you to move on.)

You can tell by facial expressions, to a great extent, whether or not your audience agrees with you. You can tell when they do not understand or when they are disappointed or annoyed. You can always tell when your audience is pleasantly surprised (perhaps astonished) that you are doing such a good job.

Nonverbal communication, in addition to listening, is discussed in more detail in the following chapter.

Avoid Distractions

Besides the distractions previously discussed, various other actions and mannerisms hinder the understanding and acceptance of your intended message.

Although you cannot eliminate all distractions, careful planning will do much to prevent them.

Avoid the annoying time-consuming practice of shuffling sheets of paper that contain your notes, particularly if you are using a public address system. The sound may be greatly amplified.

Also avoid moving the microphone unless it is necessary to achieve a desired volume of sound. Many speakers move the microphone unnecessarily, resulting in distracting noise.

Use note cards, approximately 5-by-8 inches, rather than sheets of paper. They are easier to handle without shuffling and noise, and you can turn them less obviously. Put the cards into a notebook designed especially for the size of card you are using.

Make sure your notes are large enough for you to see as the notebook lies on the speaker's stand so that you will not be forced to lower your head or hold the notebook in your hands. If you have thoroughly prepared yourself for the presentation, you will have no need for constant use of your notes, but having them available will add to your poise and confidence. Do not write your notes in great detail; they will be harder to refer to and will require more cards and thus more turning of cards than if only major ideas are listed. Do not take the risk, however, of omitting important information from your talk because you do not have it in your notes.

Another distraction is frequent glances at your watch or at a clock in the room. Although you must keep close track of time, you should do it inconspicuously. A solution that you may find helpful is to tape a wristwatch with an easy-to-read dial to the inside cover of the notebook containing your note cards. If you are standing with the notebook placed on a speaker's stand, you can look at the watch so unobtrusively that your viewers will never guess it is there.

In addition to taking your listeners' attention away from your spoken words, distracting actions and mannerisms indicate a lack of confidence. They result in a rather negative approach, not a cheerful, positive one.

Take Credit

After the presentation, when you are complimented, say "Thank you," "I'm glad you liked it," or something else that indicates you also think you did a good job. Never say "Oh, that was terrible," "I forgot and left out some of it," or "I was absolutely scared to death." Your excellent presentation will remain an enjoyable memory.

Summary

Principles of effective communication to be used in written messages also apply to effective oral presentations.

Predicting the probable response of your listeners will enable you to communicate more persuasively and diplomatically. The environment, as well as the speaker and other members of a group, influences listener response.

Careful planning of all phases of an oral presentation is necessary for success. It involves analyzing which items of information must be included, how to present the pertinent information in a specified time, the sequence of presentation, and control of the environment.

Test Yourself: Chapter Review

1–2. What are two advantages of outlining a presentation?

3. What is an advantage of oral communication over written communication?

4–6. Give three suggestions for estimating audience reactions.

7–11. Name five questions about the physical environment of your oral presentations that you should try to determine in advance.

12–20. Given nine suggestions for effective nonverbal communication as you make an oral presentation.

Test Yourself: Correct Usage

(Related to material in Chapter 17 and principles of correct usage.) Insert necessary punctuation, including quotation marks, hyphens, and apostrophes, and remove punctuation that has been inserted incorrectly. Choose correct word or sentence from each pair or group. Make any other necessary changes.

1. (50, Fifty) people came to hear the famous speaker.

2. He spoke at (1, one) p.m. on Monday, (July 9, July 9th).

3. The admission fee was ($15, $15.00, fifteen dollars).

4. He stated that he had graduated from college only (7, seven) years ago.

5. He said that he would conclude his talk before (2, two) o'clock.

6. He stated that he believes that about (4, four) (%, percent) of the student body came to hear him.

7. The auditorium (accommodates, acommodates, accomodates) about 1,500 people.

8. Overall, his visit was a delightful (occasion, occassion), for he made the audience feel at ease.

9. In order for listeners to have confidence in a speaker the speaker must have self-confidence.

10. The speaker was complementary about our beautiful tree shaded campus.

11. In passed years much of the campus was bare now it looks like a park.

12. The speaker unlike previous ones who came to our school did not use visual aids.

13. Other speakers brought poorly made slides and hard to read transparencies.

14. The speaker asked the President of the Student (Council, Counsel) and (I, me) to sit on the stage; I was highly (complemented, complimented) by this honor.

15. President Brown (who, whom) we thought would be away returned in time to introduce the speaker.

Problems

1. Give an oral report to the class based on a written report you have prepared earlier in the course. Adhere strictly to your allotted time as assigned by your instructor or as agreed on by you and your classmates. If audiovisual aids are appropriate and practical, use them to illustrate and emphasize. Allow time for questions from your audience.

2. Prepare an outline of a speech on a subject with which you are thoroughly familiar.

3. Prepare a short talk to present to your classmates. Plan the time according to your instructor's specifications of the amount of time available. Choose some subject related to communication but preferably one that is not discussed at length in this book. For example, dis-

cuss the use of visual aids in oral presentations, perhaps limiting your talk to the use of one particular kind of visual aid. Other possible suggestions include recent developments in technology that speed the process of transcription; the choice of a voice-writing machine; differences between language usage in Great Britain and America; regional differences in pronunciation or word usage.

All these topics are broad enough for long presentations. If you attempt to cover them in a short talk, you will of necessity be giving only a broad overview. Or perhaps you can limit your topic to some particular aspect of these subjects; for example, a few examples of extraordinary word usage in the Ozarks, or from any other section of the country that you know well. In addition to these suggested topics in communications, many more will occur to you.

The suggested list of topics for written reports given in Case 25 in "Cases for Chapters 13 through 16" (following Chapter 16) can be used for oral presentations.

4. Tape-record a speaker on television or on the radio. Evaluate the performance according to principles presented in this chapter.

5. Members of the class are to form into four- to six-person groups. Assume that the members make up a panel on a convention program. Each group is to select a topic similar to the one described in Problem 3. One member of the panel is to act as both chairperson and master of ceremonies. On the day of the class presentation, each member is to be allowed a specified time, according to the total time available, in which to present a report on one aspect of the overall subject. The chairperson is to introduce the panel members to the class before they make their presentations. After all presentations have been made, allow time for the audience to ask questions, which may be directed to any member of the panel.

6. Use the evaluation sheet on oral presentations as your instructor directs. Perhaps you may wish to ask your classmates to evaluate your presentation according to the statements on the sheet.

Evaluation Sheet: Oral Presentations

	Strongly Disagree	Disagree	Not Sure	Agree	Strongly Agree
1. The speaker has an accurate and comprehensive knowledge of the subject.	___	___	___	___	___
2. The speaker was poised and confident.	___	___	___	___	___
3. The speaker was sincere and friendly.	___	___	___	___	___
4. The speaker was dressed appropriately; overall appearance helped presentation.	___	___	___	___	___
5. The speaker's voice—tone, pitch, speed, enunciation, other—helped presentation.	___	___	___	___	___
6. The speaker opened and closed the presentation effectively.	___	___	___	___	___
7. The speaker held the attention of the audience.	___	___	___	___	___
8. The speaker gained the confidence of the audience.	___	___	___	___	___
9. The speaker used visual aids wisely and effectively or as desirable and necessary.*	___	___	___	___	___
10. The speaker spoke in a conversational tone, as if talking with the audience, not lecturing.	___	___	___	___	___
11. The speaker maintained appropriate eye contact with the audience, without too much reliance on notes.	___	___	___	___	___

*Check "Agree" or "Strongly Agree" if speaker used no visual aids and you also believe they should not have been used.

	Strongly Disagree	Disagree	Not Sure	Agree	Strongly Agree
12. If the speaker referred to notes at all, such use was not obvious or distracting.	_____	_____	_____	_____	_____
13. With the exception of necessary excerpts to illustrate a portion of the talk, the speaker did not *read* the speech.	_____	_____	_____	_____	_____
14. The speaker responded well to questions.	_____	_____	_____	_____	_____

CHAPTER 18

The Importance of Listening and Nonverbal Messages in Interpersonal Communication

Communication is a complex process. We cannot describe the characteristics of oral communication as completely distinguishable from those of written communication, for many of the principles are the same. For example, in all kinds of communication we are concerned with understanding and acceptance. To achieve these goals, we must have a proficiency in language and an empathy with the receiver of the message, plus knowledge of the subject matter. In written communication we are concerned with such things as spelling and punctuation. The comparable factors in oral communication are pronunciation and tone of voice, although tone of voice can be much more expressive of emotions than spelling or punctuation can ever be.

In oral communication we can make far more effective use of feedback than in written communication. We can immediately judge our listeners' reactions, at least to a certain extent, especially when we are conversing with only one individual. If we become aware of misunderstanding, we can repeat our ideas in different words or ask for questions. The immediate feedback in oral communication is one of its most important advantages. A disadvantage is that we do not have an opportunity to revise our remarks before *they reach the receiver of the message, as we can do when our words are written.*

Like reading, listening involves receiving the verbal messages of other persons. While listening, we also continuously receive nonverbal messages along with spoken ones, another major advantage of oral communications over written ones. Effective listening consists of more than hearing and comprehending spoken words. We must also be aware of nonverbal messages. We should keep in mind, however, that we will never be able to interpret nonverbal communication exactly, and to attempt to do so can result in further miscommunication and incorrect interpretation. As the word is used in this chapter, listening *consists of more than the words that we hear; it also includes an awareness of the many messages sent without words.*

Self-Acceptance and a Respect for the Listener

For successful interpersonal communication, the individual must have a positive self-concept and a sincere respect for the other participant or participants in the shared communication process. For understanding and acceptance, there must be no attitude of inferiority or superiority, no expression or implication of undue humility or condescension.

This assumption of *I-acceptance, you-acceptance* is crucial to effective interpersonal relationships. Some persons, after reading about and considering the *you-attitude,* which has been emphasized in business communication, may feel that this *I-you approach* is in conflict. It is not. We cannot truly value another person without also respecting ourselves. In addition, as mentioned in the discussion of the you-attitude in Chapter 5, the consideration of the reader or listener does not preclude the concern for our own welfare or for that of our employing organization. To think otherwise is to be disloyal to our employing organization as well as to ourselves.

Interpersonal communication depends not only on words, nonverbal signals, and the environment but also on relationships. What we say to an old friend will be different from what we say to someone we have just met, even if the words are the same. Some long-married couples seem to know what the other is about to say before the words are uttered. This is a form of sharing, so that past experiences, including frequently used words, carry over to all our present relationships.

Such a mutual understanding may be less than a real understanding, however, in that one or both of the partners assume too much and no longer listen to the other person as of *now,* but to the person remembered. This is a way of taking the other person for granted. Such relationships can also occur between business and professional associates.

Communication must be two-way, but we still tend to think too much in terms of ourself, the sender. When we give most of the attention to ourself, we concentrate on the means of transmitting ideas, not on the back-and-forth exchange that is most conducive to frank and sincere understanding and expression. We try to impress our audiences with our own importance, our knowledge, or our authority.

When we cut off the opportunity for feedback, we not only fail to receive ideas and information from other persons, but also we are not sure that the listener completely understands our message. Even if the hearer receives the message clearly, being shut out from participation in the oral interchange is certainly not conducive to accepting ideas or instructions. Ask for the other person's opinions. They may be valuable to you, even if you think you don't need them. You do need their opinions.

Many people hesitate to say "I don't know" because they feel that it shows a weakness. Many times there will be instances when you don't or can't know—and you will be wise, usually, to say so, immediately and frankly. Being a "know-it-all" is attempting to put yourself on a higher plane than your listeners, even if you are thoroughly informed on the subject.

You can go too far the other way—toward an attitude of timidity and lack of self-confidence that will get you nowhere, unless it is to an employment agency to look for another job. But being an expert on every subject, especially an unqualified expert, can be just as damaging. Harry Truman commented

Do you think that these executives—on a street in a financial district—could be gossiping? Are they enjoying their conversation?

during his presidency on what he considered to be the attitude of many college graduates of the time. He said, "I always try to tell them that it's what you learn after you know it all that counts."

Exchange of ideas is as vital to one's business or professional career as it is to one's personal life. Many business conversations take place as they are described in the following sections ("Conversation," "Dialogue," and "Silence"). Unfortunately, all communication is not of the urbane, democratic nature advocated in these passages, which were taken from an aritcle entitled "Time to Talk Things Over" which appeared in *The Communication of Ideas*, a small book published by the Royal Bank of Canada in 1950.[1] "Time to Talk Things Over" will be as appropriate many years from now as it was in 1950. Universal, timeless observations do not change in value.

Conversation

It is important for most people to talk and to be heard, to voice their problems, to get things off their minds. A really satisfying talk is one of the greatest pleasures there is.

Conversation has four main purposes: to give information, to get information, to persuade, and to show a human interest in other human beings. . . .

Conversation is the simplest form of dialogue. It was conversation, in this form, in the age of Socrates, an age without pocket books or their latter-day substitutes, which laid the foundation of the civilization we enjoy. It was conversation of which the New Testament was composed. It was conversation among scholars in a bookless world which revived learning at the end of the dark ages.

[1]The material in the following sections is reprinted from *The Communication of Ideas* (Montreal: The Royal Bank of Canada, 1950), 129–141. With permission of The Royal Bank of Canada. (No author or editor given.)

Good conversation stretches your mind. Even if no usable conclusions are reached through a conversation, there is profit in the exercise, for we have churned up our minds so as to see new views. But to make the best of it, people must realize conversation as a mental occupation, and not merely a dribbling into words of casual thoughts.

Conversation consists of both transmission and reception. One man put it neatly when he said: "I like so much to talk that I am willing to pay my audience by listening in my turn." To speak and to listen brings into the midst of the group masses of experience, anecdotes, cross-lights, quotations, historical incidents, the whole range of minds centred upon the topic from all points of the compass.

There can be a lively diversity of views expressed without appeal to any book of rules of order. You do not need an elaboration of formality, just ordinary politeness. For example, a brilliant conversationalist is not one who holds a group spellbound, but one who draws everyone else in.

Intelligent conversation is fit only for intelligent society. It is downright abhorrent to narrow-minded people who are fixed on a plane of the commonplace and dull. Nothing can be more deadly boring than this: two persons saying words about something in which neither is interested. Ragbag conversation about threadbare things is unprofitable, depressing and futile. You would die of shame if you heard it played back on a tape recorder.

The mistake that many earnest and persistent talkers make is to suppose that to be engrossed in a subject is the same thing as being engrossing. The self-centred person talks without reference to his listeners' interests. If he has been reading about dinosaurs or water pollution or the state of unrest in mid-Africa, he brings out all that is in his mind on the topic.

Story-telling is not conversation, but parlour entertaining. The person is a bore who, on the sidewalk or in a café, on the train or in an office, buttonholes you to listen to anecdotes and jokes pulled out of the air. As Ernest Dimnet wrote in *What We Live By:* "Stories are the stupid man's wit."

Dialogue

Dialogue is conversation with a purpose. It is reason's only weapon. It is a civilized operation, democratic and constructive, and those who refuse dialogue are playing a game with some serious overtones. . . .

Democratic institutions and political freedom cannot survive without discussion, criticism, and deliberation. Are we too busy enjoying life to engage in a dialogue designed to make possible the continuation of life? Or too ignorant? Or too lethargic? Or too parasitical? All these entered into the decline of the Roman Empire.

To take useful part in reaching decisions is to seek understanding through consideration of alternatives. In this debate, traditions and dogmas rub each other down. We attain insight and understanding.

A dialogue is not a bargain-basement transaction with haggling and bickering, a low form of negotiation. Neither is it a situation in which A confronts B in a contest, but a conversation in which each presents facts and each considers the other's facts. It is a reasonable exchange of ideas, bringing into being a new body of knowledge. It takes you out of the doldrums of fiddling with good intentions into the region where you act with knowledge and understanding.

Monopoly of the conversation has no place in dialogue. The ball must be thrown back and forth. There is give and take. Participants expect to find things out by examining ideas and facts from several points of view.

. . .

Question: Is it true that the use of language is becoming more casual and informal? What are authorities doing to stop the erosion of the English language? Why don't people try to use proper and formal language?

Answer: Yes, language in the United States is less formal than it was one hundred years ago or earlier. So is almost everything else.

"Authorities" do not regulate the use of language. They could not do so if they tried. Compilers of dictionaries and writers of English handbooks merely reflect what is considered correct and effective language usage of the time. Makers of dictionaries look for word usage in recent books from respected, scholarly authors.

Some communication situations are more formal than others. Your conversation with friends is likely to be worded in less formal language than your remarks in an employment interview. Your written language differs according to the message being conveyed, your readers, and the purpose of your communication.

The English language, like all others, has always been in a process of change. It will continue to change. What some people now consider erosion of the language will someday be accepted as standard usage.

The previous remarks, however, do not mean that you should be unconcerned with language. Many people write too informally in situations that require more formality. Correct, clear, coherent, diplomatic writing, adapted to the individual reader and purpose, is likely to attain the appropriate level of formality.

Be especially careful with the use of slang in all written work. Not only is it too informal, but it is likely to be misunderstood.

Impartiality in listening to points of view is a great aid to the making of good judgments about what is being discussed, and this requires that we try honestly to see things through the other person's eyes.

Many irritations in society are due to the fact that some people do not recognize problems that others think are important. Two cultures may have institutions that look very much alike to the outside observer, and words in their languages which are so alike as to suggest the same meanings, but the realities are different.

When we go abroad we are accustomed to accommodating ourselves to evident differences, such as those of dress, language, and architecture. Where we run into trouble is in the little differences: the taste of coffee in England, the siesta hour in Italy, the sounds in the narrow streets of Paris, the rosary of devotion formed by the 24,000 bell-ringing shrines in Benares. These things, nevertheless, are an essential part of the everyday life of people living in those places.

This is not to say that we must be pleased by all sights and sounds. It is quite possible to form and hold a strong opinion of our own and yet to realize that it is after all only one point of view.

Silence

Sometimes it is well to converse mostly in pauses. Mozart is quoted as saying: "My rests are more important than my notes."

There are, of course, modes of silence: that of listless ignorance and that of intelligent attention. To ask oneself what can be left unsaid is a golden attribute in diplomacy, and it plays a big part in that everyday tact that helps people to get along better with one another.

Sometimes it is well, during a dialogue, to remain silent even though it makes you appear eccentric. One man, popular on committees, carried a little card which he set up on the table before him. On it he had written: "Keep quiet." James Simpson, the clerk who became chairman of Marshall Field and Company, smoked cigars so as to be sure he would keep his mouth shut in conferences. Perhaps he was copying the geese migrating over the mountain Taurus, which is full of eagles. These geese took up stones in their bills to restrain their gaggling, thus passing over the eagles without being heard.

Silence is not to be confused with listening. Every participant in a dialogue has the duty to listen. Listening intently and asking pertinent questions provide you with the needed information for orderly mental processing.

. . .

When you listen attentively you may learn about options that are not at once visible. You listen to the facts, but you concentrate on finding what they all add up to. If you are too busy thinking of what you are going to say next, you miss the points and end up in the confusion of a completely unrelated line of talk.

Effective and Efficient Listening

Listening, like reading, involves receiving the verbal messages of other persons. However excellent the spoken or written message sent to us, we cannot rely solely on the knowledge and skills of the speaker or the writer. We must exert an active effort to receive these messages.

The Importance of Listening

Various studies have indicated that most businesspersons spend from 40 to 60 percent of their working day in listening. The business manager usually spends even more. A manager is paid to listen, even though he or she does not charge by the hour, as does a psychoanalyst. Management is basically decision making, and decisions are based on information about problems and possible solutions. Much of this information is presented orally. In order to make intelligent decisions, the manager must listen—completely, exactly, and critically.

In addition to the obvious purpose of receiving information, our listening is essential to the persons we supervise. "Oh, if someone would only listen!" is a cry heard on occasion in occupations of all kinds, a cry that sometimes disappears in despair because individuals have given up the hope that anyone will ever listen. Employees want to feel that they count, that they are a part of the organization, that their words are worth hearing or reading. This is a universal human desire, and being promoted to management status does not change this feeling, for none of us is ever completely secure in our relationship with others. We all want to be heard, but not enough of us want to listen.

Managers and company presidents often proclaim their open-door policies and go so far as to admit everyone who comes in the office. Then they interrupt by anticipating the speaker's words, looking at the clock, or indicating that they are impatient in some way. They are likely to do too much of the talking themselves.

A warm-up period of small talk between strangers gives each time to make those mysterious little adaptations that result in what we then call being on the same wave length.

There is a psychologist at York University in Toronto, Dr. Vello Sermat, who spent four years developing a test to help explain how people become friends. He's applying it now in his research center and estimates that he'll have the answer in about ten or fifteen years. While we wait, I only know that strangers have to get used to one another for a few minutes before anything can begin, and small talk is more socially acceptable than feeling and sniffing.

The next point is Look. Give the person you're with the flattery of your total attention. Don't let your eyes stray to see who has just come in or what's happening across the room. The most charming people I know give the impression that they've waited all day to speak to me alone.

Barbara Walters, *How to Talk with Practically Anybody about Practically Anything* (New York: Doubleday, 1970), 117.

Communication Brief

Listening, like all other communication, must be sincere to be effective. It must be sincere to be real.

Information received from oral words is likely to be far less permanent in the mind of the receiver than are written words. Studies show that people usually forget from one-third to one-half of what they hear within eight hours after hearing it.

When considering the trend to decrease the number of memorandums and other written messages (a suggestion appearing frequently in business articles and textbooks), keep in mind that part of the meaning is lost in oral communication. This loss will always occur to some extent, regardless of improvements in listening ability.

Make notes about oral instructions as an aid to remembering. If done wisely, this notetaking can improve listening; but if done unwisely and to excess, it will hinder. You can become so involved in getting everything down that you fail to listen for the most important points. When oral exchange of ideas and information is convenient for the speaker and listener, your notes as a listener can be effective for later use as a memo would be. An added advantage of oral communication, compared to written messages, is the back-and-forth flow of ideas and reactions, and the necessity of writing a memorandum is eliminated. But it is absolutely essential that good listening techniques be applied.

Barriers to Listening

Why do we not listen? Think of the reasons you have not listened to others. Why have you not received these messages? Why do persons not listen to you as you engage in conversation or speak to groups? Or why do they not understand you or remember what you said?

Check your listening habits. Could the quality of your listening have any relationship to:

1. Your actual physical ability to hear?
2. Attention to the speaker's voice, appearance, pronunciation, accent,

use of grammar, or mannerisms—to the exclusion of what the speaker is trying to say to you?

3. Discounting and disregarding what the speaker is saying because you do not like his or her physical appearance, voice, pronunciation, accent, use of grammar, or mannerisms?

4. Listening to words only, not to the underlying feeling behind the words, much of which is communicated by nonverbal methods?

5. Listening for details to the exclusion of the overall meaning, or to the exclusion of the ideas and principles on which the details are based?

6. Allowing preconceived beliefs about the particular subject being discussed to prevent you from receiving the speaker's ideas?

7. Allowing emotional feelings about the subject to "turn you off," especially if the speaker uses emotional words?

8. Concentrating on notetaking to the extent that you lost the train of thought?

9. Interrupting?

10. Being sure that you already know all there is to know about the subject?

11. Inattention because you do not like to consider unpleasant, complicated, or difficult subjects?

12. Inattention because you are tired, sleepy, hungry, and want to go home?

13. Inattention because you know that whatever is said, you could say it better?

14. Inattention because you have more important things to think about?

15. Boredom because you have already heard too many speeches, lectures, discussions, conversations, and people "talking at you"?

16. Inability to keep your mind on the subject?

17. Inattention to the speaker's words because you are trying to think of a reply, or of a question to ask during the discussion period?

18. Confusion because you don't have the faintest idea of what the speaker is talking about and have never heard the words before?

19. Lack of understanding because you do not look at the speaker to grasp the full effect of what is being said, as well as to notice gestures, facial expressions, and other nonverbal signals?

20. Lack of concentration because your mind moves faster than the speaker's voice and wanders into side paths so that you lose the train of thought?

What other considerations enter into your reception of spoken words? Barriers, or noise as applied to communication, have already been discussed in Chapter 1. As listeners we cannot control all the sources of noise that prevent our receiving the message exactly as the sender intended. We cannot control the actual physical noise in the room, nor can we control miscommunication caused by the speaker, such as using inexact or incorrect words. By our careful attention and thought, however, we can recognize these inconsistencies and adjust our thinking to them.

Perception affects our reception of the message in any form of communication, especially in the listening process. We cannot immediately remove all the barriers to the accurate and complete perception of the intended message. For example, we cannot simply resolve that we will dispense with all our own preconceived notions and prejudices (we all have them) and find them gone. But our recognition of these particular biases, probably even our acceptance of them (if it is reasonable to accept a prejudice), can serve as a warning that they interfere with our reception of the spoken message as well as of the written one.

Look back at the twenty reasons as to why you may not be receiving communications sent orally to you. How many of these have to do with perception? Perhaps it would be quicker to list those that do not relate to perception.

Listening, like reading, requires attention and energy. The better you listen, however, the less demanding it seems to be. Six bad habits that prevent effective listening, as stated by Nichols and Stevens, are listed below. These comments are concerned mostly with listening to a lecturer or a discussion leader, but they also appear to direct, face-to-face discussion.

1. *Faking attention.* You are deceiving only yourself, for you will not deceive other persons for very long. Besides, you are cheating yourself out of the opportunity to learn whatever it is that is being said.

2. *"I get the facts" listening.* Although Nichols does not say that facts are unimportant, he says that memorizing facts is not the way to listen. When persons talk with you, they usually want you to understand their ideas. We should remember facts only long enough to understand the ideas that are built from these facts. Then the understanding of the ideas will help the listener to remember the supporting facts more effectively than does focusing on facts alone.

3. *Avoiding difficult listening.* Concentration is necessary in order to understand a lecture or a discussion. We should be willing to devote the effort needed to grasp the meaning. If we are affected with this listening habit, we should make a planned and periodic effort to listen to difficult material, lectures, and discussion topics that require mental effort, such as radio commentaries, panel discussions, and lectures.

Communication Brief

Franklin Delano Roosevelt, 32d president of the United States, found the polite small talk of social functions at the White House somewhat tedious. He maintained that those present on such occasions rarely paid much attention to what was said to them. To illustrate the point, he would sometimes amuse himself by greeting guests with the words, "I murdered my grandmother this morning." The response was invariably one of polite approval. On one occasion, however, the president happened upon an attentive listener. On hearing Roosevelt's outrageous remark, the guest replied diplomatically, "I'm sure she had it coming to her."

Clifton Fadiman, ed., *The Little, Brown Book of Anecdotes* (Boston: Little, Brown, 1985), 475–76.

4. *Premature dismissal of a subject as uninteresting.* G. K. Chesterton once said that there is no such thing as an uninteresting subject; there are only uninterested people.

5. *Criticizing delivery and physical appearance.* The content of the message is always more important than the form of the delivery.

6. *Yielding easily to distractions.*[2]

Another reason we have difficulty in listening is that our thought processes move much faster than the speed of the spoken word. The average lecturer speaks at about the rate of 125 words a minute. The minds, even on a slow day, move several times faster. Because of this difference, our minds wander, and we anticipate what is coming next, which may or may not be what actually does come next. Or we mentally take a little rest because we think we know what the speaker is going to say. If our thought processes were slower than the spoken word, we would be even worse listeners. We would not have time to notice the speaker's nonverbal clues, to determine the feeling behind the words, or to notice the speaker's particular use of words and word meanings.

All these functions enter into effective listening, as well as actually hearing the words themselves. But as we do all these things, we should not fail to concentrate on what the speaker is saying at the moment—and often this is exactly what happens. We get so tangled up in our own thoughts, which have perhaps started in relation to something the speaker has said, that we lose the train of thought or miss a great deal of what has been said. This is especially true when we are listening to lectures, but it can be true when we are in a group or listening to one individual.

You can become a better listener if you actually try to do so. Good listening not only benefits you from the standpoint of knowledge and information, it is also a matter of courtesy toward the speaker—and just plain good manners.

Sympathetic versus Critical Listening

You engage in sympathetic listening when you observe the twenty considerations previously mentioned—for example, listening mainly for content and not to the speaker's accent, pronunciation, or grammar; recognizing your own particular bias; and giving the speaker your undivided, conscientious attention.

Sympathetic factors that make for good listening include all the aspects of actively being willing to receive the message, insofar as it agrees with your own intelligent observation. Critical listening involves evaluation. Listen critically, for you cannot and should not accept completely everything you hear, just as you cannot accept or believe everything you read.

The world is full of propaganda, high-pressure advertising, and public relations experts and speech writers who distort facts to suit their own particular purposes. Even if the message is not planned to be deceitful, the speaker may be misinformed. Individuals may be absolutely and completely sincere and also absolutely and completely mistaken.

Just as you evaluate what you read, you must evaluate what you hear; but

[2]Ralph G. Nichols and Leonard A. Stevens, *Are You Listening?* (New York: McGraw-Hill Book Company, 1957), 104–111.

do not evaluate too soon, before giving the lecturer or the conversationalist an opportunity to present the complete story or to express opinions. Avoid interrupting the flow of thought directed toward your mind (either interrupting with your own thoughts or interrupting with spoken words). No one can honestly and completely evaluate another's words until actually listening to those words.

Consider the reliability of the speaker's words. Are they based on facts or on inferences or value judgments? Also ask yourself:

- Is the speaker up to date? Has the speaker taken into consideration that what was true yesterday is not necessarily true today?
- Is the speaker competent, as well as nonbiased? Even well-meaning, sincere persons can be misinformed.
- Is the speaker giving complete information? Although "the statement is never the whole story," has the speaker abstracted the most important information?
- If points are omitted, do you believe that these omissions were intentional?
- Does the speaker express ideas in abstractions and generalities instead of using specific, concrete language?
- Does the speaker attempt to persuade by relying on emotional words and phrases instead of on rational, objective language?

Nonverbal Communication

Nonverbal communication permeates all speech and much, if not all, of written communication. Estimates from authorities in the field indicate that nonverbal messages make up as much as 70 to 90 percent of the transfer of meaning and emotion in face-to-face interaction.

You have been sending and receiving wordless messages all your life. It is impossible not to communicate, even when you remain completely silent and motionless.

A business letter communicates nonverbally by its attractive appearance, or lack of it, as well as by the time it is sent. The choice of letter styles also sends messages about the writer and the company from which the letter comes.

Your written application letter and resume are judged by their appearance and correctness, perhaps beyond your other qualifications for employment. Your appearance and actions during an employment interview are likely to be far more important than your words.

Because much nonverbal communication is unconscious, it is likely to be sincere. You can improve interpersonal relationships by learning to receive the unspoken and often unplanned messages of other people and by becoming aware of your own unspoken language.

It is important to remember, however, that the methods of nonverbal communication should not be considered as tools for manipulation of other people, for looking into their minds and determining their innermost thoughts. You could not do so even if you wanted to, regardless of how much you know about nonverbal communication. Psychologists and others who study nonverbal communication base their decisions about individuals on long-term study,

What does this man's office communicate about his position in an organization?

and even then some of their judgments are incorrect. Isolated movements, postures, actions, facial expressions, and other bits of nonverbal communication should not be considered alone. Like words, sentences, and paragraphs, nonverbal communication should not be taken out of its context. It should be interpreted according to the environment, the particular situation or circumstances, and previously established personal relationships.

Nonverbal communication is inseparable from the total communication process. Ray Birdwhistell, a pioneer in the field of *kinesics* (popularly referred to as *body language*), remarked that studying communication apart from its nonverbal aspects is similar to studying noncardiac physiology.

Kinds of Nonverbal Communication

Human nonverbal communication takes the form of sign language, action language, or object language, according to Ruesch and Kees, researchers and writers in the field. They state:

> In broad terms, nonverbal forms of codification fall into three distinct categories:
> —*Sign language* includes all those forms of codification in which words, numbers, and punctuation signs have been supplanted by gestures; these vary from the "monosyllabic" gesture of the hitchhiker to such complete systems as the language of the deaf.
> —*Action language* embraces all movements that are not used exclusively as signals. Such acts as walking and drinking, for example, have a dual function: on one hand they serve personal needs, and on the other they constitute statements to those who may perceive them.
> —*Object language* comprises all intentional and non-intentional display of material things, such as implements, machines, art objects, architectural structures, and—last but not least—the human body and whatever clothes or covers it. The

embodiment of letters as they occur in books and on signs has a material substance, and this aspect of words also has to be considered as object language.[3]

Others describe the kinds of nonverbal communication differently, but, given a broad interpretation, their descriptions fit into one of the three categories listed by Ruesch and Kees. *Proxemics* (discussed below) means communication through personal space, but the use of space involves *actions*, particularly actions that place us in relation to other persons. Proxemics also includes the use of object language, as, for example, in the placement of office furniture.

Kinesics for the most part is action language, but it also includes the use of objects.

Paralanguage can be considered as a kind of action language. This term is applied to tone of voice, hesitations or speed of speech, and to other variations of language other than the actual words.

Metacommunication is implied meaning, which may be intentional or unintentional. For example, the often-used phrase, "Good luck!" may imply that the listener must have luck to succeed. To say: "You are dressed like a young executive today" could imply that the listener, on other days, looks like an impoverished college student. Metacommunication is closely related to the connotative meaning of words, discussed in Chapters 1 and 3.

We communicate much through personal appearance, which is achieved through both action language, including posture and movements, and object language, as expressed by clothing, jewelry, handbags, and makeup.

Eye contact, facial expressions, actions and gestures in response to our companions, and everything else we do, in addition to the use of words, express meaning. The adage "actions speak louder than words" was used long before there was an abundance of popular books on nonverbal communication.

Your study of nonverbal communication will be of interest and benefit you. A few of the many books on the subject are listed in the bibliography at the end of this book.

Communication by Time and Space

The use of time and space communicates nonverbally by action language, object language, or both. As with all other forms of nonverbal communication, the use of time and space often occurs in conjunction with spoken words.

Edward T. Hall says:

> Time talks. It speaks more plainly than words. The message it conveys comes through loud and clear. Because it is manipulated less consciously it is subject to less distortion than the spoken language. It can shout the truth where words lie.[4]

Hall is well known for his theories about time and space as elements of nonverbal communication. A professor of anthropology, Dr. Hall is especially concerned with the ways in which persons of different cultures respond to nonverbal communication. For example, he found that people from Arab and Latin

---

[3]Jurgen Ruesch and Weldon Kees, *Nonverbal Communication* (Berkeley: University of California Press, 1970), 189.

[4]Edward T. Hall, *The Silent Language* (Garden City, N.Y.: Doubleday, 1959), 23.

American countries stand closer to other persons when they are conversing than we do in America, and that persons of some other cultures are much more casual than Americans about the use of time.

Hall uses the word *proxemics* to describe his theories and observations about zones of territory and how they are used and defended by persons of different cultures. According to Hall, there are four kinds of interpersonal distance: intimate distance, personal distance, social distance, and public distance.

The intimate distance, close phase, is the distance of lovemaking and wrestling; the intimate distance, far phase, is six to eighteen inches. The personal distance, close phase, is one and a half to two and a half feet; far phase, two and a half to four feet. The social distance, close phase, is four to seven feet, and the far phase is seven to twelve feet. The public distance is twelve to twenty-five feet or more.

Impersonal business occurs at the close social distance, which is also a very common distance for persons at a casual social gathering. Desks in the offices of some people, especially executives, are large enough to hold visitors at the far phase of social distance. Some executives come from behind their desks and sit closer to the person being interviewed, or about the same distance away but without the desk to act as a barrier. Hall says:

> The ability to recognize these various zones of involvement and the activities, relationships and emotions associated with each has now become extremely important. The world's populations are crowding into cities, and builders and speculators are packing people into vertical filing boxes—both offices and dwellings. If one looks at human beings in the way that the early slave traders did, conceiving of their space requirements simply in terms of the limits of the body, one pays very little attention to the effects of crowding. If, however, one sees man surrounded by a series of invisible bubbles which have measurable dimensions, architecture can be seen in a new light. It is then possible to conceive that people can be cramped by the spaces in which they have to live and work. They may even find themselves forced into behavior, relationships, or emotional outlets that are overly stressful. When stress increases, sensitivity to crowding rises—people get more on edge—so that more and more space is required as less and less is available.[5]

You may have noticed that students often sit in the same place in a classroom day after day, even when seats are not assigned. They also tend to sit in the same general location in all classrooms. Some people sit in the same pew in church for a lifetime, except when strangers unintentionally take their place. Then the owners of the territory look annoyed and uncomfortable. In *The Territorial Imperative* Ardrey discusses human tendencies to identify with an area over time and to defend it against aggressors.[6] We have favorite chairs or favorite spots in a house that we think of as our own. We sometimes resent the intrusion of others.

We carry with us at all times a kind of invisible bubble that we consider to be our own space, wherever we are. We may become uncomfortable when someone intrudes on this space.

Height adds status. One businessman put his desk and chair on a raised

---

[5]Edward T. Hall, *The Hidden Dimension* (Garden City, N.Y.: Doubleday, 1966), 23.
[6]R. Ardrey, *The Territorial Imperative* (New York: Atheneum, 1966).

A nursing supervisor communicates through her facial expressions and with her body that she is alarmed about an emergency. Notice the tense, rigid position of her hand and finger on the notebook.

platform to increase his feeling of authority. Another not only used an elevated chair but also fastened the visitor's chair to the floor so that the visitor could not move the chair toward the desk, thus intruding on the businessman's space. (No doubt these two men are less than perfectly happy in their jobs.)

We communicate through space by the arrangement of our offices. If you interview persons or frequently talk with visitors, your desk becomes a barrier. The desk is less a barrier if the visitors can sit beside you. If the visitor is sitting directly in front of you, the wider the desk, the wider the barrier.

Although certain business relationships call for a degree of separation and formality, we are often too much concerned with separation, importance, and dignity, and not enough with real communication. A living-room setting in your office, if you are fortunate enough to have this arrangement, can aid conversation and open communication. Such a setting can also send other messages with object language, or, more bluntly, act as a status symbol.

Kinesics

The field of *kinesics,* or body language, is still inexact and nonscientific compared to many other areas of knowledge. For example, our judgments of the psychological meaning of the way a person sits in a chair or how one's hands touch the face, hair, or other parts of the body cannot be viewed as an exact interpretation or, in some cases, even an approximation of the meaning. Even researchers experienced in the field realize this fact and emphasize it, but many people

*Many people wave
their eyeglasses
around, point with
them, put them on and
take them off, contin-
ually push them up,
and chew on the ear
pieces. (This kind of
nonverbal communica-
tion is more difficult
with contact lenses.)*

continue to regard body language as an exact one, if only they could learn to read it. Birdwhistell's comments about the tendency to consider kinesics as an exact language are presented below.

> Almost as soon as the linguist or the kinesicist meets someone he is asked, "What can you tell me from my speech or my body motion?" More fearful or more coquett-ish respondents manifest considerable anxiety that their behavior is going to reveal their deepest secrets to the expert. . . . However, the specialist cannot determine how distinctively individual any particular performance is before he knows his structure and individual range of behavior for a particular behavioral area . . . the scientific study of expressional behavior must await extensive experimentation before we can test productive value and reliability of clinical judgments.[7]

This discussion should not be interpreted to mean that body motions are unimportant in nonverbal communication. It is an overstatement, however, to describe body motions as a "language." Avoid hasty inferences and generaliza-tions in your receiving of nonverbal communication; these assumptions are dangerous in all forms of communication. If you had never heard the terms *body language, kinesics,* or *nonverbal communication,* you would interpret, often correctly, the emotions of other persons according to their body movements. You are more likely to be able to analyze the movements of persons you know well.

You can recognize in yourself the effect of your emotions on your body. The expression "walking on air" would certainly not apply to your steps when you are discouraged and depressed. You do not clench your fists when you are

[7]Ray Birdwhistell, *Kinesics and Context* (Philadelphia: University of Pennsylvania Press, 1970), 33.

happy and relaxed. Your hands sometimes shake a little when you are anxious or suffering from stage fright. You may put your hands on your hips when you are "laying down the law."

Even without books or research studies, we would all realize the importance of kinesics to the transmission of ideas and emotions. You can tell a great deal about the feeling of other persons, particularly those you know well, before they say a word. You learned to do so when you were very young.

To reemphasize: do not interpret posture and gestures out of context and base conclusions on isolated events. For example, the arms-across-the-chest position, which is said to indicate resistance or to be a defensive posture, may mean only that one is cold. If your listeners, however, continually face you with folded arms, they are not receiving with great joy your information or instructions. If you are standing with your hands on your hips while you talk with them, no wonder you are meeting resistance with such a dictatorial pose. Also notice your own emotions and feelings in relation to these well-known poses and to several others. When you assume these poses, you are likely to be conveying messages to others about your emotions. For example, when you feel insecure you may give yourself a sense of protection by crossing your arms. You may find that you assume the same position when you resist the suggestions of others. You are not likely to do so when you are relaxed, confident, and in agreement with other people.

Throwing up the hands indicates resignation. Both hands behind one's back indicates deep thought. Drumming of fingers indicates boredom. We scratch our heads when we are puzzled. This gesture is so well known, or at least so widely accepted, that the term "scratching our heads" indicates bewilderment and has become a cliché. Humans, as well as animals, tilt their heads slightly whenever they see or hear something that interests them.

Shaking a fist indicates anger in our culture. Natives of New Guinea pretend to shoot a bow and arrow when they are angry. This action makes sense to them, for they use bows and arrows to kill.

For men, the gesture of unbuttoning the coat is a sign of openness, of frankness, of acceptance. A coat can be used in various ways to communicate nonverbally. Men running for political office are often photographed with their coats slung over their shoulders to picture a boyish, hardworking, honest approach. The hero of the play "How to Succeed in Business Without Really Trying" made it a point to be in the process of putting on his coat as he entered his boss's office. This action indicated that he had been working hard and had removed the coat, but that he was now putting it on again to show respect.

There are regional differences, as well as differences between nations, in nonverbal communication. These differences are similar to accents in verbal communication. People in the South are said to smile more than those in Maine or New York. People are said to smile more in Atlanta than in any other city in America. Persons in the South also hug one another more often than those in the North, or so it has been reported. This display of affection has been described as hypocrisy, but it is not hypocrisy if it is based on sincere emotions. Sincerity is the most important element of all communication.

At times nonverbal communication differs from messages conveyed verbally; that is, our words say one thing and our bodies say another. The nonverbal message is likely to be the correct one, and it is likely to be interpreted as the correct one.

Summary

For successful interpersonal communication, you must have a positive self-concept and a sincere respect for the other participant or participants in the sharing of the communication process. There must be no attitude of inferiority or superiority.

Interpersonal communication depends not only on words, nonverbal signals, and the environment but also on past relationships.

Businesspersons spend from 40 to 60 percent of their working day listening. Listening requires attention, energy, sincerity, and empathy. Listen both sympathetically and critically.

Various barriers prevent effective listening. Many of these barriers are related to perception, attitudes, and opinions. By recognizing these barriers, you can minimize their effect.

To be a better listener:

- Concentrate. Remain alert.
- Listen sympathetically but also critically.
- Listen for general meaning and for ideas.
- Take notes as necessary and appropriate, but do not let notetaking interfere with the reception of a message.
- Notice the speaker's nonverbal communication.

Three elements of nonverbal communication are sign language, action language, and object language. Space and time are also used as methods of communication. *Proxemics* refers to the use of personal space. Americans do not view time and space, in relation to communication, in the same way as people in some other countries do.

Kinesics means "body language." Like all areas of nonverbal communication, this field of study is far from an exact science, although many patterns of action have been observed by research studies.

Many factors enter into nonverbal communication: dress and appearance; use of time; facial expressions; posture; eye contact; tone of voice; choice of possessions; arrangement of homes and offices; gestures; and actions of all kinds.

It is important not to interpret nonverbal messages out of context and not to attach a great deal of importance to one or a few occurrences. You can never know exactly what is in the minds of other people.

Test Yourself: Chapter Review

1. According to your text, what is the approximate percentage of time that businesspeople spend in listening?

2–3. What is meant by sympathetic listening? By critical listening?

4–6. Name three questions that should be considered when judging the words of a speaker.

7. According to your text, what percentage of the transfer of meaning is accomplished by nonverbal communication?

8–10. Give examples of sign language, action language, and object language.

11–12. What is meant by the terms *proxemics* and *kinesics*?

13–14. What is meant by paralanguage? By metacommunication?

15–20. Name six barriers to effective listening; these barriers may include poor listening habits.

Test Yourself: Correct Usage

(Related to material i_____ ___ and principles of correct usage.) Insert _____ includ-ing quotation mark_____ and remove punct_____ correctly. Choose c_____ each pair or grou_____ changes.

1. An individual_____ pretation of _____ affect on o_____

2. The (above_____ also apply_____

3. Each of th_____ have exc_____

> **Library of Congress Classification System**
>
> A   General Works
>
> B   Philosophy. Psychology Religion
>
> C   Auxiliary Sciences of History
>
> D   History: General and Old World
>
> E-F   History: Western Hemisphere
>
> G   Geography. Anthropology. Recreation
>
> H   Social Sciences
>
> J   Political Sciences
>
> K   Law
>
> L   Education
>
> M   Music
>
> N   Fine Arts
>
> P   Language and Literature
>
> Q   Science
>
> R   Medicine Agriculture
>
> T   Technology
>
> U   Military Science
>
> V   Naval Science
>
> Z   Bibliography: Library Science

4. Listen critically, for you should not except everything that you see or read.

5. Almost everyone, who has visited Mexico, is aware of the residents casual attitude toward time.

6. One reason that people don't listen, is that they are too busy thinking of a reply.

7. Listening is extremely important, many managers and teachers do not listen well, for they are accustomed to talking.

8. An expert lecturer, is not always a good listener.

9. A good listener however is likely to be a good conversationalist.

10. One reason that we find it hard to listen, is that we are constantly bombarded with words.

Problems

1. How c_____ ____rrier to effecti_____

2. Think _____ __nication durin_____ give special _____ ication at you_____ munication aff_____ s, your attitu_____ ur state of m_____

3. /_____ _o eight mem-_____ low or choose _____ ertains to com-_____ ese discussions. _____ r conclusions to _____ y of the methods

c. Intelligent TV commercials

d. Some aspect of nonverbal communication

e. Barriers to listening

f. Some particular problem of your college or university

4. "Comments and Bits of Information" assignment, as described in Question 4 at the end of Chapter 1: find a comment or bit of information that applies to topics discussed in this chapter. As your instructor directs, prepare this in written form and/or present it to the class.

5. To illustrate communication through tone of voice, see how many messages you can communicate with the word "oh." Or two students can illustrate different meanings by the use of each other's name. (John-Marcia, Marcia-John, etc.) Or use a nonsense phrase, such as "kiss a checkered cat," to express fear, security, anger, approval, joy, self-confidence, depression, and other emotions.

6. What kinds of information do you communicate non-verbally to your instructor? To your classmates? To your employer?

7. How can a business letter communicate nonverbally?

8. How can the arrangement of a business office communicate nonverbally?

9. How do business managers communicate nonverbally to employees?

10. Ride a bus, stand at a street corner, or sit on a park bench. Observe the appearance and actions of other persons around you. Without speaking, what are they communicating to you? Whatever your answer, it is only a guess or an inference. What is your guess based on? Consider how you could be wrong. Suppose that a stranger has the same assignment and is observing you. What might this stranger assume about you—and would this assumption be correct?

11. What are some of the meanings that silence can communicate? Discuss and illustrate.

12. Tape-record a story, one that is about five minutes long. Prepare a short test based on the story. Play the story for your classmates and check to see how many questions they have answered correctly. Within two weeks, play the tape again and note improvements. (This project is also a test of how well you have organized and told the story and of how clearly you have pronounced the words.)

Note: Topics suitable for oral or written reports applicable to this chapter are 25 c, h, i, w, and cc in "Cases for Chapters 13 through 16" following Chapter 16.

Intercultural Communication

The term intercultural communication *is used in this chapter to mean the process of interchanging thoughts and meanings with people from other cultures, particularly people from countries other than our own.*

An Overview of Intercultural Communication

The study of intercultural communication has received much interest and attention during the past decade, although intercultural communication itself is as old as civilization. In recent years the ease of travel, the development of multinational organizations, and international tensions have made us realize that we must communicate and cooperate with people unlike ourselves in order to succeed or even to survive.

As with any other area of knowledge or interest, several descriptive terms have come into use. Other designations for intercultural communication include *cross-cultural communication*, *trans-cultural communication*, *interethnic communication*, and *international communication*. (The term *international communication* is also used to describe communication between governments, a usage that is not considered here.)

The word *culture* means the total system of values, beliefs, customs, religions, art, education, and manners. To a certain extent the background and experiences, and thus the culture, of every individual differs from that of every other individual. Families who live on the same block are often very different from one another, even when all are of the same nationality. People who grew up and have remained in the same neighborhood, however, are likely to have values, beliefs, customs, religions, and manners more like those of their neighbors than those of people who live in another part of the nation. Their culture is even less likely to be similar to that of people who have spent their lives in other countries or have been influenced by family and friends of other nationalities.

Barriers to intercultural communication include the inability to speak and write the same language, but using a common language is no guarantee of complete understanding between people of different cultural backgrounds. Important differences arise and remain because of ways of thinking and value systems.

In the words of Peter S. Adler:

> Nation, culture, and society exert tremendous influence on each of our lives, structuring our values, engineering our view of the world, and patterning our responses to experience. No human being can hold himself apart from some form of cultural influence. No one is culture free. Yet, the conditions of contemporary history are such that we may now be on the threshold of a new kind of person, a person who is socially and psychologically a product of the interweaving of cultures in the twentieth century.[1]

The Increasing Frequency and Importance of Intercultural Communication

The number of Americans working abroad is fast increasing. As reported by the President's Commission on Foreign Language and International Studies in 1979, 20,000 American organizations export goods or services to foreign mar-

[1]Peter S. Adler, "Beyond Cultural Identity: Reflections on Cultural and Multicultural Man," in *Intercultural Communication: A Reader*, 2d ed., ed. Larry A. Samovar and Richard E. Porter (Belmont, Calif.: Wadsworth, 1976), 362.

> One way to understand the cultural foundations of managers is, obviously, to conduct an in-depth study of each culture represented by the various managers in the organization. This, however, would be a very time-consuming and expensive task.
>
> A frugal, yet just as enlightening, way to learn the basic values of a culture is to study the traditional forms of cultural expression: art, music, or language. An analysis of cultural expressions can lead to an understanding of the culture as a whole.
>
> Language, like art, is an expression of culture. More specifically, language can be thought of as a direct expression of the thought patterns common to a group of people.
>
> Linda McCallister and Constance S. Bates, "Language as a Proxy for the Study of Culturally Based Managerial Values: An Analysis of German and American Expressions," in *Proceedings, 51st ABC International Convention* (Los Angeles: Association for Business Communication, 1986), 68.

Communication Brief

kets, and 6,000 American companies have overseas operations.[2] Since 1979, the increase has been more rapid than ever; these figures have by now drastically increased. Countless companies that originated in the United States are now multinational with subsidiaries all over the world. The budgets of some multinational companies are larger than the budgets of some nations.

In addition, many Americans work in the United States or abroad for foreign employers, and many people from all over the world live and work in the United States. People from the United States establish businesses in South America and elsewhere. Professional people from practically every field spend or have spent years abroad. Overall, the need to communicate on an international level is becoming more important each year.

Individuals of all nationalities come to the United States and Canada for employment and for many other reasons. Businesspeople come to learn about technology or management methods, and American businesspeople go to foreign countries for the same reason. Foreign firms establish American branches. Some foreign firms join with American firms (for example, Toyota and General Motors). Students from all over the world come to America to study.

Students come to the United States from all over the world. Japan sends students more to learn our way of thinking and doing than to learn class material.

Even if you should never leave your home country, an unlikely occurrence, you will almost surely work with men and women from foreign countries. No doubt you now share classrooms with students from nations other than your own—or you may *be* a foreign student studying in America. In any event, like all people, you will benefit by cross-cultural associations and experiences as you learn to communicate.

Understanding and Accepting Customs Other Than Our Own

The word *ethnocentrism* describes the tendency to view all other people, at times unconsciously, by using our own culture as a guide to interpret their actions,

---

[2]*Strength Through Wisdom: A Critique of Capability/A Report to the President,* from the President's Commission on Foreign Language and International Studies (Washington, D.C.: Government Printing Office, 1979), 125.

*Improve
Your Writing*

Question: When I move from one section of the country to another, or from the United States to Canada, should I make a conscious effort to learn the particular regional expressions of the locality and to use them in my writing and speech?

Answer: No. You may be suspected of insincerity or even of making fun of expressions that have not previously been your own.

After you remain in a region for months or years, you are likely to use many of the expressions native to the region even if you do not consciously try to do so. In the same way and for the same reason—the environment—you will change your accent and method of speaking, at least somewhat. When you return to your home environment, you will eventually return to the language you hear there.

Overall, however, regional differences cause few problems. Language differs everywhere, to a certain extent, not only in varying parts of the country but from one part of a city to another, from one occupation to another. What is usually described as "standard usage" is appropriate and clear anywhere.

Regional words and phrases are more common in oral communication than in written messages.

The word *regional*, as it describes language, does not mean the same as *colloquial*, although the words are often confused. *Regional* describes the usage of people in a geographic location. *Colloquial* means informal, or the language that is often used in conversation but should not be used in informal writing. *Regional* words and phrases can also be described as *colloquial*, but *colloquial* language is not necessarily *regional*.

---

customs, values, religions, and manners. Richard E. Porter describes ethnocentrism in this way:

> We place ourselves, our racial, ethnic, or social group, at the center of the universe and rate all others accordingly. The greater their similarity to us, the nearer to us we place them; the greater the dissimilarity, the farther away they are. We place one group above another, one segment of society above another, one nation-state above another. We tend to see our own groups, our own country, our own culture as the best, the most moral. This view also demands our first loyalty and, carried to extremes, produces a "my country first—right or wrong" attitude. . . .
>
> The way we view our world is a function of our culture, and it affects our social perception. . . . As we encounter people with differing world views, our communicative behavior is hampered because we view events differently; we use frames of reference that may seem vague or obscure to others, just as theirs may seem to us. Our perceptions become clouded and our attitudes interfere with our ability to share perceptions with others.[3]

Porter is not advocating that we change our own customs and system of values to agree with those of people from other cultures with whom we try to

[3]Richard E. Porter, "An Overview of Intercultural Communication," in *Intercultural Communication: A Reader*, 2d ed., ed. Larry A. Samovar and Richard E. Porter (Belmont, Calif.: Wadsworth, 1976), 6–7.

American businessman exchanges business cards with business-man from China. Exchanging business cards is considered essential in China, Japan, and many other countries.

build harmonious relationships; to do so is neither necessary nor desirable. Neither should we try to change the personal outlook of those with whom we communicate.

Stereotyping is a communication error likely to occur as we consider people from other cultures, who in turn see and communicate with us in light of their stereotyped impressions. We are forced to generalize somewhat as we study the usual customs and thought patterns of the country that we are to visit (as much as can be learned from books and other sources), but we should continue to consider individual differences. Just as no two people in Gary, Indiana, are identical, no two people from Saudi Arabia, France, or Japan are identical.

As a rule, educated people in countries other than the United States know more about our nation than people in the United States know about other countries. *Reader's Digest* has a foreign readership of more than 100 million in thirteen language editions. Motion pictures and radio and television programs are distributed throughout the world. American products are advertised and sold throughout the world.

Sometimes, however, the views of people from other countries are distorted by the same sources from which they receive their information. No doubt some television viewers believe that everyone in Dallas is as wealthy as the Ewing family in the popular television series. Because of television and other media, the United States is perceived as an extremely affluent and wasteful society. Visitors to the United States comment on the numerous automobiles discarded in junk yards. Most of the world has reason to envy the American standard of living, even in recession years.

People outside the United States have developed stereotypes about Americans (used here to describe people from the United States), just as Americans have done concerning people from other countries. They often do not consider differences among individuals, which occur not only from nationality to nationality, but also from family to family in the same small town and from individual to individual within each family. Americans may be judged as inaccurately and as unfairly as they have at times judged others. (Even stereotypes, however, are likely to be at least partially true—or to have been true in the past as they apply to certain people or groups.)

The following list of characteristics, not necessarily shown in order of frequency or importance, may indicate how people from other countries *expect* Americans to be and to act. This image is reinforced by each American who behaves in one or more of these ways. Notice, however, that some of these characteristics are positive, not negative, and are no doubt regarded as positive by non-Americans. Other characteristics seem worthy to Americans but not so much so to other nationalities; an example, as compared to Latin America and Eastern cultures, is our preoccupation with time and our efforts to "improve each shining hour."

ambitious	violent
impatient	generous
rich	hurried
extravagant	money-hungry
wasteful	racist
arrogant	self-confident
boastful	outgoing
loud	intelligent
blunt	stupid
rude	ignorant of other cultures
immature	feel superior to other cultures
disrespectful	little regard for the past
direct	rough
own too many guns	little regard for art or music
hardworking	no class consciousness
former neighbors of Elvis Presley	honest (for the most part)
country music stars	sincere, but naive
sloppy (tourists)	will not learn other languages
no concern for family or ancestors	poorly educated in liberal arts
aggressive	abusers of English language

Fortunately, few Americans can be accurately described by *all* the preceding terms. Neither can all Asian, African, European, Australian, or Latin American people be accurately described by all our stereotypes of them.

Nevertheless, actual differences do exist among different cultures. Eastern values differ from Western values. As could be expected, the majority of people who now live in the United States are far more like Europeans than they are like people from India or China (but, as always, there are exceptions). The United States is made up of immigrants from other countries and of their descendants; for many years, these immigrants were mostly from European countries, in addition to the black people who were brought from Africa. Although American Indians are considered to be the only native Americans, their ancestors are believed to have come from Asia sometime in the distant past.

The culture of the United States differs little from that of most of Canada, although again there are exceptions, particularly in the provinces where the French language predominates. Just as parts of Canada differ from parts of the United States, however, so do areas of the United States differ widely from each other. Stereotyping and other weaknesses in intercultural communication occur not only among people of different nationalities at home or abroad, but also among people from different regions of the United States. Southerners stereotype people from the North in various flattering and unflattering ways, and the opposite is also true. In addition, ethnocentrism applies to residents of the United States as they compare themselves to residents of other parts of the country.

L. Robert Kohls, in *Survival Kit for Overseas Living*, describes ethnocentrism in these words:

> An equally key point is that every group of people, every culture, is, and has always been ethnocentric; that is, it thinks its own solutions are superior and would be recognized as superior by any right-thinking, intelligent, logical human being. It is significant that to each group, their own view of the world appears to be the "common sense" or "natural" view.
>
> Let's take a brief look, by way of example, at Americans and the cultural characteristics of cleanliness. We generally consider ourselves among the cleanest people in the world. We're quick to criticize many other countries and cultures as being "dirty." Yet consider for a moment the following:
>
> - When Americans bathe, they soak, wash, and rinse their bodies in the same water—though they would never wash their clothes and dishes that way. The Japanese, who use different water for each of these steps, find the American way of bathing hard to understand, even dirty.
> - An orthodox Hindu from India considers it "dirty" to eat with knives, forks, and spoons instead of his own clean fingers.[4]

Successful communication with people from other countries results not only from acceptance and objectivity, but also from a number of other factors. Probably the most important are patience and a sense of humor.

Another problem is that societies are constantly changing, sometimes rather rapidly. If you do not believe that the ideas and perceptions of many people in the United States have changed, talk with someone who remembers the years before World War II or look at a number of old movies. It is true that change is ordinarily more rapid in the United States than it is in countries with extremely old cultures, such as China and India, but change occurs everywhere all the time. Consider the rapid progress and "modernization" that have occurred during the past few decades in Japan, which is also an old, traditional society. Because change is so constant and often rapid, research about countries we plan to visit must be based on recent sources, or at least supplemented by recent sources.

---

[4]L. Robert Kohls, *Survival Kit for Overseas Living* (Chicago: Intercultural Press, 1979), 19–20.

Communication Brief	*Deru kugi wa utareru* ("the nail that sticks up is hit") is a well-known saying in Japan. Japanese children hear it continually from parents and teachers. It reflects an important cultural attitude. Japanese are fond of the saying because it suggests their abhorrence of egocentricity and their wish to avoid being singled out for praise or blame. More importantly, this saying reminds them of the pain experienced when one fails to blend harmoniously into a group. It is this desire to lose oneself within the confines of a group that is most characteristic of the Japanese.
	Delores Cathcart and Robert Cathcart, "Japanese Social Experience and Concept of Groups" in *Intercultural Communication: A Reader,* 2nd ed., edited by Larry A. Samovar and Richard E. Porter (Belmont, Calif.: Wadsworth, 1976), 58.

Nonverbal Messages in Intercultural Communication

As discussed in Chapter 18, nonverbal communication, a constant process, is extremely important in oral messages of all kinds, more so than verbal communication. It is also present in written messages. Nonverbal communication is even more important in intercultural communication because of language barriers and differing background and perceptions.

The Use of Time

Americans live by schedules, appointments, and alarm clocks. We value promptness and deplore the waste and passing of time. Natives of some other countries exemplify the idea heard but not usually practiced in the United States, "Take time to smell the roses."

Americans do not like to be kept waiting, although most do not object to a five-minute delay. A comparable time to be late for an appointment in Latin America is likely to be forty-five minutes or so. Even then, the appointment may not be with one individual alone, as several appointments are scheduled at the same time.

Even after obtaining an appointment, the American who wants to get down to business immediately is likely to be disappointed. In the American culture, discussion is a means to an end: the deal. The goal is to get to the point quickly, efficiently, and neatly; this is not the expected procedure in Latin America, the Middle East, or elsewhere in the world, where discussion is considered part of the spice of life. What we consider as strictly business becomes a social affair.

Edward T. Hall and William Foote Whythe explain our attitude in this way:

> The American desire to get down to business and on with other things works to our disadvantage. . . . The head of a large, successful Japanese firm commented: "You Americans have a terrible weakness. We Japanese know about it and exploit it every chance we get. You are impatient. We have learned that if we just make you wait long enough, you'll agree to anything."

Whether or not this is literally true, the Japanese executive singled out a trait

*Communication
Brief*

The Japanese dislike having to negotiate with young people. They feel that a person must have 15 to 20 years' seniority with a firm in order to negotiate business. They find it hard to believe a young executive has real power and consider dealing with him a waste of time as well as an insult to their dignity. . . . The Japanese males are extremely chauvinistic, and sending a female executive would be worse than sending a young executive.

Mark Zimmerman, *How to Do Business with the Japanese* (New York: Random House, 1985), 99.

of American culture which most of us share and which, one may assume from the newspapers, the Russians have not overlooked, either.[5]

To Arabs, work is a curse. "In the Middle East, from pre-Biblical times down to the present, the ideal has always been to escape the curse of work, to earn, or rather acquire, riches through a stroke of luck, by finding a treasure, by finding favor in the eyes of a king, and so on."[6]

Americans have found that business dealings with the Middle East are frustratingly slow. The director of corporate planning for W. R. Grace and Company made fifteen trips to the Middle East in three years and still had no business to show for it. It took Steelcase, Inc., one and one-half years to get into the market, but this is considered a remarkably rapid time.[7]

Although people throughout the world are becoming more Westernized than they were formerly, vast differences still exist in their outlook toward time.

The Use of Space (Proxemics)

Americans feel uncomfortable when crowded together and require their own personal space, as do the British and northern Europeans. People around the Mediterranean, including France, seem to enjoy closer personal contact, as can be observed in the crowded homes, trains, buses, and sidewalk cafes. (Such crowding is perhaps not always a matter of choice.) People in Latin America, the Middle East, and some other countries also crowd together. In Saudi Arabia and other countries, pushing and shoving in a public place is not considered impolite.

In our culture, physical contact is reserved for intimate moments. Such reservations do not exist in a number of other cultures.

Americans, like people in Britain and northern Europe, want their own "bubble of space" and feel violated when others intrude without a special invitation. We also maintain greater personal distances, particularly in business and formal situations.

Because people from countries such as Saudi Arabia stand and sit closer together than we do, to Americans they seem to be crowding in and being pushy and demanding. Americans, in turn, may seem cold and distant to Arabs.

[5]Edward T. Hall and William Foote Whythe, "Intercultural Communication: A Guide to Men of Action," in *Communication and Culture,* ed. Alfred G. Smith (New York: Holt, Rinehart & Winston, 1966), 568.

[6]Raphel Patai, *The Arab Mind* (New York: Charles Scribner's Sons, 1973), 114.

[7]William Miller, "Mideast Is No Easy Mark," *Industry Week,* October 24, 1977, 43.

Other discussion about proxemics, including differences between cultures, is included in Chapter 18.

Other Nonverbal Cultural Differences

Because nonverbal communication is continuous with everyone, multitudes of differences of all kinds exist between people of different cultures. The following examples are only a few of many.

- The Japanese smile is a law of etiquette; the child is taught to smile as a social duty in order to avoid inflicting sorrow on friends.
- Our nods and shaking of the head to indicate yes or no are unknown in some countries, where different movements indicate yes or no.
- The hand symbol used in advertising a well-known beer, touching forefinger and thumb, with the other three fingers extended, is an obscene gesture in parts of Europe.
- In the Middle East, Latin America, and southern European countries, male friends exchange greetings with hugs and kisses on the cheek. In these countries, there is also more touching while carrying on casual conversations and more hand gestures and "body language."
- Arabs disapprove of using the left hand to take food from a serving dish; to do so is considered unclean.
- Colors have various meanings in different cultures.
- Eye contact differs according to the particular culture. People from some cultures maintain eye contact to the extent that Americans become uncomfortable. People from some other cultures are taught to avoid direct eye contact in order to show respect.

Language Differences and Difficulties in Intercultural Communication

English is the principal language of international business. English is taught in elementary schools, high schools, and colleges (or their equivalents) throughout the world. The study of English receives far more attention abroad than the study of other languages receives in the United States.

Courses in business communication, taught in English, are common in many countries; they are particularly strong in Japan. These courses are taught under such names as *commercial correspondence, commercial English, business English, business writing, foreign trade practices, business communication,* and *marketing communication.*

English is likely to be spoken wherever one goes, at least by some employees in major hotels. Translators are usually available in the offices of major companies, in the United States and elsewhere. Nevertheless, Americans have a responsibility to learn the language of the people with whom they communicate. Even the best translations are not 100 percent accurate. Some English words have no equivalent in other languages; the opposite is also true.

As you have noted throughout your course in business communication,

Communication Brief

But there are some perils in the avalanche of world English for those countries for whom English is the mother tongue. In the United States, the "tongue-tied American" is giving cause for concern. The English-speaking tourist armed with the motto "Speak slowly and loudly in English" is becoming a prisoner of his or her monolingualism—and something of an oddity in a world that is essentially polyglot. In Africa, as we have seen, most Africans, who are gifted linguists, will know at least three languages. In India, there is a de facto bilingualism. In Europe, English is widely understood—and taught—in all countries, even in France. It appears that the British and Americans, lacking many levels of language competence, are exceptional—and exceptionally handicapped, perhaps.

Robert McCrum, William Cran, and Robert MacNeil, *The Story of English* (New York: Viking, 1986), 350.

language difficulties occur even between persons whose native language is the same. Words have varying connotations, nonverbal communication intrudes into verbal messages, the language itself is not exact, and speakers and writers do not always choose words to express their intended meaning. Listeners do not listen, and readers do not or cannot read well. Even greater difficulties occur between people of different cultures.

In addition, although people from other countries may have studied English throughout their school years, textbook English is not complete preparation for conversing with Americans or putting their thoughts into natural-sounding sentences and compositions. These people are not prepared for numerous idioms and slang expressions that we take for granted. For example, how would you explain to someone who had never heard the terms "You're pulling my leg" or "wild-goose chase"? And how would you explain that relief is not really spelled R-o-l-a-i-d-s?

On the other hand, foreign students may have a greater knowledge of "formal" English than American students, including the rules of sentence structure, parts of speech, and punctuation.

How, then, do all these considerations affect the way we should speak and write to someone from another culture? First, we must be absolutely correct in our use of the English language (assuming, as is usually the case, that we are using English), avoiding colloquial expressions, regional expressions, and slang. Even disorganized conversation and poor writing usually can be understood by other Americans, at least after questioning the speaker or rereading the written material. Such communications will remain incomprehensible to foreign-born readers and listeners.

All the features that increase readability are doubly important in intercultural communication. Use simple language and short sentences and paragraphs. Be particularly careful of connotative meanings. As much as possible, use the denotative, or "dictionary," meaning of the word. Do not be overly informal. Avoid exaggerated expressions like "This coat weighs a ton" and "I'm so hungry I could eat a horse." Such expressions, weak in any communication except in the most informal conversation, seem absurd to listeners or readers who never heard them before.

If you have learned to be a good communicator in the many ways stressed throughout your course in business communication, you will be far better pre-

Communication Brief

It's easy and fun to point out the differences between the American and the English vocabulary: the differences seem quaint and there are comparatively so few that we can easily spot them. Many of the differences are merely a matter of preference: we prefer *railroad* and *store* while the English prefer the synonyms *railway* and *shop*, but all four words are used in both England and America. In addition, we know or can easily guess what *braces*, *fishmonger's*, or *pram* means, just as the English know or can figure out what *innerspring mattress*, *jump rope*, and *ice water* mean.

Finally many of the words that once separated American English from English English no longer do: our *cocktail* (1906), *skyscraper* (1833), and *supermarket* (1920's) are now heard around the world, and the English increasingly use *radio*, *run* (in a stocking), and *Santa Claus* instead of *wireless*, *ladder*, and *Father Christmas*.

Stuart Berg Flexner, *Listening to America* (New York: Simon & Schuster, 1982), 203.

pared to communicate with persons everywhere than you would be otherwise. Even then, work for empathy and sensitivity, using the same consideration that you expect from your reader or listener. To a person from another country, you are the "foreigner."

Differences in Written Business Communication

Business letters reflect the culture of the country from which they come. Letters from Americans, like face-to-face interchange, are likely to seem blunt and impolite to Japanese readers and perhaps even to people in England, who are nearest to America in cultural patterns except for people in Canada. A letter that we consider to be diplomatic—as well as clear, concise, direct, and businesslike—may convey an impression of abruptness and lack of courtesy to some foreign readers.

A study completed by Retha H. Kilpatrick in 1984 reports the opinions of representatives from sixty-six American and foreign companies who carry on international correspondence. According to her study, English, Spanish, and French-speaking countries dominate the list of countries with which American firms correspond. The vast majority of American letters sent to other countries are written in English. Foreign languages used most often in correspondence to American firms are Spanish, French, and German. An analysis of letters collected during the research study showed that American letters are more personal, informal, and less "flowery." Letters from other countries tend to be less personal, more formal, more courteous, and more flattering.[8]

In Japan, many business letters are still written by hand or with extremely slow typewriters. (Typewriters are slow because of the more than 2,000 necessary characters. Word processing is now coming into use.) Telex is the primary method of communication for foreign communication. For domestic business, telephone and personal calls are used more than business letters are.[9]

---

[8]Retha H. Kilpatrick, "International Business Communication Practices," *Journal of Business Communication* 21, no. 4 (Fall 1984): 33–44.

[9]Saburo Haneda and Hirosuke Shima, "Japanese Communication Behavior as Reflected in Letter Writing," *Journal of Business Communication* 19, no. 1 (Winter 1982): 23.

Question: How can I continue to develop my ability to write well?

Answer: Continue to write. Continue to read.

Study books and articles about writing. Enroll in continuing education classes or regular college courses. Develop a real interest in the fascinating world of language.

Think about words as you use them. Keep an unabridged dictionary in a convenient location. Refer to it often.

The study of language is unending. No one ever attains a complete mastery of the English language; even if it were possible to do so, it would be impossible to keep up with the constant changes that occur.

Experiment with different kinds of writing, including poetry, essays, short stories, or even novels. Write to the "Letters to the Editor" column; your opinion needs to be read.

If you are able to do so, buy a personal computer, word processing software, and a printer. Because you are able to compose directly at the keyboard and to revise without retyping, writing will be fun, not work.

Most important of all, enjoy your creative ability as it is expressed in writing.

A letter written in Japan, as quoted by Jean Johnston, begins this way:

> Now we are in the splendid autumn season. I hope that you are enjoying the best of health and that things are going very well with you and with your association. I want to offer sincere congratulations to you.

A paragraph within the letter is this: "Although I myself am a man of little ability . . . ."[10]

Japanese people, throughout their letters and in their conversation, assume an attitude that to Western minds seems to be entirely too apologetic, servile, and overly humble.

Jean Johnston lists other appropriate phrases for opening letters, all relating to the seasons. These phrases are used whether or not the writer knows the reader, much as we use "Sincerely" or other words as complimentary closes. One of the opening phrases recommended for January is "In this fierce coldness . . . ." A recommended opening for May is "In this season of fresh greenery . . . ."[11]

(Japanese people are very mindful of the seasons; for example, the traditional Japanese haiku, a poem of seventeen syllables, must include a reference to a season.)

Haneda and Shima describe Japanese letters in this way:

> As long as you observe the rules, you are always on safe ground. No matter how difficult the situation may be, you can begin a letter with stereotyped greetings which serve as a buffer to bad news or refusal.

[10]Jean Johnston, "Business Communication in Japan," *Journal of Business Communication* 17, no. 2 (Spring 1980): 66.

[11]Ibid.

An example of a salutation is this: "Allow us to open with all reverence to you." The closing sentence of the same letter is "We solicit your favor."[12]

"Sorry" and "regret" are two words often used by the Japanese. Other people well experienced in overseas life say that you should not use these words unless you are prepared to admit your mistake and pay for it. But when a Japanese writes "We are sorry" in reply to a complaint or claim, he does not necessarily mean that he would take legal responsibility but that he sympathizes with the customer who is not satisfied, whether the customer is right or wrong. So the eventual refusal is not inconsistent with apologies at the beginning in Japanese.[13]

Letters from England seem to be like the letters written in the United States fifty to one hundred years ago. They contain phrases that we consider old-fashioned and wordy. (Letters from England, like those written in America and everywhere else, with the possible exception of Japan, vary widely. The differences reported here should be considered as general trends.)

Much of the world has been influenced by England. Although English and business communication are taught in many parts of the world, instruction and textbooks are likely to be more British than American. Thus, letters coming from Hong Kong, Australia, India, and many other countries resemble those from England. As a general rule, they all tend to be more formal than the average letter written in America, more impersonal, and, compared to American letters, more "old-fashioned" and stereotyped.

When we write to people in other countries, we should not try to conform to their styles, although we should be careful of our own wording and approach. To open letters with phrases like "Now the rustling winds of autumn" would sound insincere coming from a Chicago or Los Angeles office. When we write, however, we should especially careful not to be overly informal, an approach that is usually unwise even when writing to Americans. We should use a polite, diplomatic approach and clear, correct, precise English that is not likely to be misunderstood or misinterpreted.

Overall, the principles of effective communication that you have learned throughout the course apply in relationships with anyone, although your messages should be adapted to your reader's culture and nationality. This adaptation is only another instance of consideration for the reader, or the you-approach.

Preparation for an Overseas Assignment

As in all other circumstances requiring new knowledge and responsibilities, the answer is research. Find out as much as you can about the country to which you are going. Even more important, make sure that you know exactly why you are being sent there and what your responsibilities are to be, particularly your communication responsibilities. (This step is the same as the first one in the research process when beginning a project that will result in a written report.)

[12]Haneda and Shima, 24, 27.
[13]Ibid., 25.

Careful and comprehensive research should precede an overseas assignment. Preparation is especially important for women travelers because of varying attitudes toward women in business.

Learn the language if at all possible. Short intensive courses are highly successful in giving even a beginner enough language ability to survive.

Other questions to be considered are the cost of living, schools, and recreational facilities. Learn about the history, government, and financial condition of the country. Determine its relationship to the United States.

You can find much of this suggested information from published sources. Talk with people who have been there. Build friendships with natives of the country and learn from them much that you will need to know.

Another bit of preparation that must not be overlooked is to make sure that you have an adequate supply of business cards. Although business cards are routinely used in America, most people do not doubt your credibility or professionalism if you do not present them. This is not true in many other countries of the world; you *must* have them. Ideally, these cards are printed on one side in English; on the other side they are printed in the language of the people who are to receive them.

Many other areas of information apply: various kinds of nonverbal communication, response to invitations, gifts, introductions, views about religion, socializing, work habits, management styles, etiquette, ethics, and many, many more.

Summary

Culture means the total system of values, beliefs, customs, religions, and manners. Although cultural differences exist everywhere to a certain extent, they are more extreme between people from greatly differing countries.

The number of Americans working abroad is increasing, as is the number of people from other countries who now visit or live in the United States and Canada.

We tend to view all other people by using our own particular culture as a guide. Stereotyping is a frequent communication error as we consider people from other countries.

People from some other cultures, particularly Latin America and the Middle East, are much more casual about the exact use of time than are persons in the United States. Cultures also differ in their use of personal space and in various other methods of nonverbal communication.

Most international business is transacted in the English language. Even a common language, however, does not eliminate differences and difficulties in the use of language.

Business letters written in America tend to be more informal and personal than letters written in many other countries. Because Americans wish to be concise and direct, their letters may seem blunt in comparison to those from other countries.

For an overseas assignment, you should attempt to learn the language and to find out as much about the country as possible. Even more important, work for adaptability and sensitivity.

Test Yourself: Chapter Review

1. What is your understanding of the meaning of the term *intercultural communication?*
2–4. Name three other terms that mean approximately the same as *intercultural communication.*
5. What is your understanding of the word *culture?*
6. What is the meaning of the word *ethnocentrism?*
7. Summarize the differences in the use of time in the United States and Latin America.
8. Summarize major differences in the use of personal space in the United States and some other countries of the world.
9. What is the primary language used in international business?
10. Briefly describe the differences between business letters in the United States and Japan.

Test Yourself: Correct Usage

(Related to material in Chapter 19 and principles of correct usage.) Insert necessary punctuation, including quotation marks, hyphens, and apostrophes. Remove punctuation that has been inserted incorrectly. Choose correct word from each group. Make any other necessary changes.

1. The way we view the world is affected by our entire background it is called perception. (Rewrite this sentence.)
2. Our culture exerts a tremendous influence on our lives structuring our values engineering our view of the world and patterning our responses to experiences.
3. No 2 people in Sacramento California are identical and no 2 people from Egypt Japan or Brazil are identical.
4. Some of the stereotypes by which americans are judged are positive not negative.
5. The nail that sticks up is hit is a well known saying in Japan.

6. If (management, managment) (personal, personnel, personel) are to succeed in a (foreign, foriegn) country they must understand (it's, its) culture.

7. Intercultural communication is not new it is as old as humanity.

8. The Japanese see decisions as a product of the (consensus, concensus) of the group not of an individual.

9. You may put your hands on your hips when "laying down the law."

10. Cultural identity is a aspect of a persons (existence, existance).

Problems

1. Report problems about intercultural communication are included in Case 25 in the cases following Chapter 16. They are also referred to after Chapter 17 as topics for oral presentations. These assignments can be used in various ways, either here or with the preceding chapters, or with all three chapters.

2. Ask one or more persons from other countries to visit your class and to comment on one or more of the areas of information presented in this chapter. (Possibly members of your class are from a country other than your own. If so, they should be considered the "experts" for this particular chapter.)

3. Suppose that someone who had never been to the United States asks you to describe what the people are like. What would you say? Put your remarks into a written reply of no more than one page. (This is indeed an abbreviated assignment. Libraries are filled with books about the people of the United States.)

4. Suppose this person has asked you to describe the culture of the city or town in which you live. Follow the same instructions as for Problem 3.

5. Describe the characteristics of a foreign country you have visited or one that you have read about.

6. Do you think that the actions of people in the United States are similar to their letters—as much as actions and letters can be similar? Explain.

7. Why is translation not 100 percent accurate?

8. From your reading or from your classes in management, marketing, or other areas, give examples of how advertising policies, product names, or slogans used in the United States have been ineffective elsewhere.

9. Which features of letters widely used in the United States (and discussed in this book) serve approximately the same purpose as phrases in Japanese letters?

Note: Cases that pertain to intercultural communication are included in Problem 25 in the section following Chapter 16. An additional exercise is shown in Appendix D, Exercise 11.

APPENDIX A

Effective and
Efficient Dictation

Pointers for Effective Dictation

1. Plan the content of each letter or other bit of writing to be dictated. In preceding chapters you learned to make a brief outline of each message to be written or dictated. A brief outline of each letter may consist of only a few words; perhaps on the letter itself you may make a note of the contents of each paragraph. Less detailed planning will suffice after you have obtained considerable experience in writing and in dictating, but some planning will always be essential.

2. Speak clearly at a fairly even pace. If you are dictating to a machine, make sure that it is adjusted properly and that you speak directly into the telephone or microphone. Be sure that no distracting noises detract from the clarity of your voice.

3. Give special instructions before you begin dictating the material to be transcribed. For example, specify the number of copies, unless you want only the usual file copy, and the persons to whom the copies are to be sent. If a particular letter is to be transcribed first, say so at the beginning of the dictation, especially if you are using a machine. Give special mailing instructions.

Perhaps for a long, complicated letter or manuscript the first copy should be in the form of a rough draft for you to revise before the final copy is typewritten. If so, give this instruction at the beginning of the dictation.

4. (For dictating to a secretary) Set aside a certain time of the day. A morning hour is best. The secretary then has the rest of the day to complete the transcription process, return the letters for your signature, and put them in the mail. Do not dictate late in the day and ask that the work be completed before the secretary goes home unless the message is unexpected and urgent.

5. Be sure that a dictionary and other reference materials are available for the secretary or other person who transcribes the work.

6. Dictate paragraph endings. If you are an expert writer, you know more about where the paragraphs should begin and end than does the transcriber. In addition, as you have learned in preceding chapters, paragraph construction is really a part of the composition; you can change emphasis and meaning by rearranging paragraphs.

7. Dictate unusual punctuation. Punctuation is also a part of the composition itself; and, as in the construction of paragraphs, punctuation conveys a portion of the meaning. If you are sure that the transcriber knows the rules for the ordinary and expected use of punctuation, to dictate each comma may indicate that you do not trust the ability of the transcriber.

On the other hand, some persons prefer that all punctuation be dictated. This approach has an advantage in that your meaning as it comes through spoken words is more immediately clear, just as meaning through the written word is made more immediately clear through punctuation. Dictating all punctuation speeds up the transcription process. If you follow this procedure, however, make sure that you are completely sure of the best punctuation for your work.

8. When dictating directly to a secretary, ask that the material be read back when desirable or necessary. This reading-back process is one of the advantages of having an individual take your message in shorthand instead of using a voice-writing machine.

9. Provide the transcriber with the letter to be answered or any other related materials that will assist in the transcription process.

10. Spell out all proper names if they are not available in the letter being answered or in related materials. Spell out all unusual terms.

11. Even though errors that occur in the transcription process are not your own, you are responsible for them. You are responsible for all facets of your written communication, including the work of the person who transcribes your words and the person to whom you delegate writing assignments. Check all work carefully and thoroughly until you are sure that the transcriber or writer is conscientious and accurate. Even if you are confident of your assistant's ability and dedication, your checking of the copy is an extra safeguard.

Undetected errors can be costly and embarrassing. If you feel that a transcript should be redone, ask the person who transcribed it to retype the material, but make sure that your instructions are clear and that your reasons are justified. Time and money are wasted if the dictator of the message requires work to be done when it is only slightly less than perfect.

Some persons read their finished letters and notice that the phrasing, although correct and clear, could be improved from the standpoint of graceful wording—and the letters are redictated and/or retyped. Almost all written work could be improved by rewriting and rewriting again, but in the usual business office there is no time to construct literary masterpieces. The efficient business writer is able to dictate good letters on the first trial, in most instances, although they may not be as good as they could be with endless time to revise them.

Under the best of circumstances, however, some letters and other communications must be dictated and transcribed more than once. As mentioned earlier, a rough draft of complicated material may save time in the overall process, but excessive duplication of effort is an expensive procedure.

12. Add handwritten notes for a personal touch, but use judgment and discretion. Some organizations frown on this practice. If they are overused, or used inappropriately, they appear as an inconsiderate shortcut.

13. Play back your voice occasionally when dictating to a machine. You may be surprised!

14. Choose a letter arrangement that is easy to type, without unnecessary indentions or centering. A standard line length for all letters is most efficient, as it is almost impossible for either the dictator or the typist to estimate at the beginning of some letters whether they will be long, medium, or short. The long line (70 spaces, elite; 60 spaces, pica) can be used for all letters, with adjustments for very short letters made by leaving extra vertical spaces before the inside address.

An Example of a Dictated Letter

The following letter is an example of how dictation might sound if it were to be transcribed by a secretary in a word processing center or by any secretary transcribing from recorded dictation. The words and phrases in italics are your instructions, as the originator of the letter, to the person transcribing the letter. Portions in regular type make up the content of the letter.

Operator, this is (your name) of (your department), Telephone 2782. I have a letter with the usual file copy. Address the letter to Ms. Wendy *W-e-n-d-y* Ritger *R-i-t-g-e-r*, Developmental Editor, Allyn and Bacon. *That's A-l-l-y-n and B-a-c-o-n*—160 Gould *G-o-u-l-d* Street, Needham *N-e-e-d-h-a-m*, Massachusetts 02194.

Dear Ms. Ritger: As you requested, I have reviewed the three chapters from Jeane—*J-e-a-n-e*—Brown's proposed textbook on international marketing. My detailed comments are shown on the enclosed evaluation sheets. *Paragraph.* Chapter 2—*Use the numeral 2*—is excellent *comma*—in my opinion—*comma*—except that it is unusually—*underline unusually*—long. Perhaps it should be divided into two chapters—*comma*—with the addition of some of the material from the present Chapter 3. *Paragraph.* I am not completely satisfied with the present table of contents. *Do not capitalize.* Perhaps as Professor Brown completes the textbook the overall organization can be improved. I have noted on the table of contents what I believe to be needed changes. With this exception I have not written on the manuscript itself—*comma*—but only on the evaluation sheets. *Paragraph.* All of Professor Brown's material seems to be accurate and up to date. In addition, she writes well. *Paragraph.* Thank you for asking me to review this material. If you would like for me to look at following chapters, I can do so after I return from Japan late in August. Sincerely, (your name), Vice President, International Marketing Department.

Enclosures—*colon*—Evaluation sheets, manuscript. *Operator, I have the enclosures in my office. I will put them into a large envelope, along with the letter. You need not address an envelope. Thank you.*

Problems

1. Use one of more of the letter examples shown in previous chapters as a basis for dictation; this beginning assignment will allow you to test your recording equipment, your voice and enunciation of words, and your instructions. After you dictate the letter, play it back. Could someone who had never heard your voice clearly understand every word? Were instructions clearly given? Continue dictation practice with letter examples until you are completely satisfied with your dictation.

2. Dictate the letter or letters used as a basis for Problem 1, but this time do not refer to the letter as you dictate. Listen to your recording. Did you include all details? Did you indicate paragraphs and punctuation? Did you spell out all names and other words that may be unfamiliar to the transcriber? (Letters need not be exactly like the original ones, but they should convey the same information and be correct and courteous.) Play back your dictation. Did you forget to include necessary details?

3. Repeat the dictation of letters dictated in Problem 2, but this time precede your dictation with brief notes about what each letter is to contain. Play back your dictation. If possible, have it transcribed.

4. If you have kept copies of letters you wrote as assignments for previous chapters, use one or more of these letters as a basis for dictation. Do not dictate directly from the completed letters; instead, write a few notes to remind you of what you intend to include in each paragraph. Dictate the letters and play them back. Have them transcribed if possible.

5. Use one or more cases from chapters about writing letters and memorandums as a basis for your dictation. Choose at least one case that you have not previously written. Make notes about what to include in each paragraph. Dictate all letters. Play them back. Have them transcribed if possible.

Evaluation Sheet: Dictated Messages

	Yes	No
1. If people other than yourself dictate recorded messages, did you identify yourself by name and department?		
2. Did you indicate the kind of document being transcribed? (letter, memorandum, report, other)		
3. If you need the finished copy of one or more documents by a certain time, did you so indicate at the beginning of the dictation?		
4. If you want carbon copies or photocopies, did you so indicate?		
5. If you wish to see a rough draft before the final copy is typewritten, did you so indicate?		
6. Did you give format guides if the desired format is different from the one ordinarily used?		
7. Did you give names and addresses, spelling out if there is a possibility that they could be misunderstood?		
8. Did you spell out all names and other words throughout each message if there is a possibility that they could be misunderstood?		
9. Did you dictate punctuation—unless you are sure that the transcriptionist will insert punctuation exactly as you would have done?		
10. Did you dictate paragraph endings?		
11. Did you indicate enclosures?		
12. Did you speak clearly and distinctly throughout the entire dictation period?		

APPENDIX B

The Appearance and Format of Business Letters

The overall appearance and format of a letter, memorandum, or report affect the reception of the intended message. If a reader's attention is drawn to obvious erasures, poor centering, or an unusual arrangement rather than to the words themselves, the intended meaning is delayed or perhaps incomplete.

An even greater disadvantage of an unattractive letter, memorandum, or report is that of discourtesy to the reader, as if the writer does not care enough to make sure that the message is sent out in perfectly typewritten, well-arranged form.

Choosing the Most Appropriate and Efficient Letter Style

The choice of a letter style is important from the standpoints of appearance and efficiency. Letter styles convey different impressions of the company.

For example, the simplified letter (Figure B–4) is considered to be progressive and modern, although the style itself is far from new. A new style is the one described in this book as the functional (Figure B–5). Neither of these styles is widely used in comparison to the full-block, modified-block, and semiblock styles (Figures B–3, B–2, and B–1), which are considered more conservative than the simplified or the functional. In addition, the modified block and the semiblock are considered more conservative than the full-block style.

The Semiblock and the Modified-Block Letter Arrangements

The semiblock style (Figure B–1) is considered somewhat conservative; it is used much less than it was a number of years ago. In the semiblock style, as in the modified-block (Figure B–2), the date may be backspaced from the right margin point to align at the right margin; it may be centered, or it may begin at the center. The most time-saving method is to begin the date and closing lines at center. The most attractive placement of the date, however, may depend on the letterhead design. The date should *not* be placed at the left margin when using the semiblock or the modified block arrangements.

Although not shown in Figures B–1 (semiblock) and B–2 (modified block), various special parts, such as the attention line, subject line, and enclosure notation, can be added, as with any other letter style. (The subject line is an expected part of the simplified letter, Figure B–4, but it can be included on any other letter arrangement.)

The use and placement of special parts are explained later in this appendix under the heading "Arranging the Usual and Special Parts of the Letter."

The modified-block style (Figure B–2) is exactly like the semiblock style (Figure B–1) except that the paragraphs are not indented.

The Full-Block Letter Arrangement

The full-block style shown in Figure B–3 is a continuation of the trend toward simplicity and ease of use. All lines, including the date and closing lines, begin at the left margin. Paragraphs are always blocked.

This letter arrangement is more efficient than the semiblock or the modified-block because no extra time is required for paragraph indentions or placement of the date and closing lines. In addition, many writers believe that the full-block arrangement provides an attractive, businesslike appearance.

The Simplified Letter Arrangement

The simplified style shown in Figure B–4 omits the customary salutation and complimentary close. As in the full-block arrangement, all lines begin at the left margin. The simplified letter always includes a subject line typewritten in all capitals. An extra line space (a triple space) precedes and follows the subject line.

The simplified letter has certain disadvantages, at least in the opinion of some office managers and business writers. They do not wish to give up the usual conventional salutation and complimentary close. They say that because these letter parts have been used so routinely for many years, readers expect them; even if the reader does not consider the omission of his or her name as being unfriendly, the omission may be distracting.

MEMPHIS STATE UNIVERSITY
THE FOGELMAN COLLEGE OF BUSINESS AND ECONOMICS
Memphis, Tennessee 38152

Office Administration Department

December 18, 19--

Mr. Joe Galloway, Office Manager
Countrywide Insurance Company
5983 Maplewood Cove
Memphis, TN 38117

Dear Mr. Galloway:

As you requested, I am sending you a group of letters that illustrate various letter styles. I am glad to help you in this way in the preparation of your new correspondence handbook. You are wise to pick one particular arrangement to be used by all offices and departments.

This letter illustrates the semiblock style. This arrangement is also called the modified block with indented paragraphs.

When referring to letter styles, remember that terminology differs widely. The basic formats, however, are standard.

This old and rather conservative arrangement would be appropriate for use at your insurance company, but I do not enthusiastically recommend it. Although the paragraph indentions effectively separate the paragraphs, they are not really necessary, for there is always a blank line space between paragraphs. This letter is less efficient than one with no indentions.

Sincerely,

Binford H. Peeples

Binford H. Peeples, Professor

sn

FIGURE B–1
The semiblock style
(also described as the
modified block with
indented paragraphs)

MEMPHIS STATE UNIVERSITY
THE FOGELMAN COLLEGE OF BUSINESS AND ECONOMICS
Memphis, Tennessee 38152

Office Administration Department

December 18, 19--

Mr. Joe Galloway
Office Manager
Countrywide Insurance Company
5983 Maplewood Cove
Memphis, TN 38117

Dear Mr. Galloway:

This letter illustrates the modified-block letter, which is also
described as the modified-block with blocked paragraphs. In addition,
it is described simply as the block, or the blocked.

If you should decide to adopt this style, or the semiblock shown in
the preceding letter, I believe that you should recommend that the
date and the closing lines begin at center—that they <u>not</u> be
backspaced from the margin point. Although they often are placed
by the backspace method, beginning them at the center or near the
center is quicker and just as correct and attractive.

In all the letters shown so far, "standard" punctuation has been
used. This term refers only to the colon after the salutation and the
comma after the complimentary close. The "open" style will be
shown in the next letter, the full-block. In open punctuation the
colon and the comma are omitted. Either style of punctuation can be
correctly used with any letter style.

As you may have decided by now, there is no exact answer as to the
best letter style for every office and every situation.

Sincerely,

Binford H. Peeples

Binford H. Peeples
Professor

shn

FIGURE B–2
Modified-block style

MEMPHIS STATE UNIVERSITY
THE FOGELMAN COLLEGE OF BUSINESS AND ECONOMICS
Memphis, Tennessee 38152

Office Administration Department

December 18, 19--

Mr. Joe Galloway
Office Manager
Countrywide Insurance Company
5983 Maplewood Cove
Memphis, TN 38117

Dear Mr. Galloway:

This letter illustrates the use of the full-block style.

Because of the efficiency with which this letter can be typewritten,
its use is growing in popularity.

Some persons object to this arrangement because everything is at
the left; they believe that the date and the closing lines should be
centered or backspaced from the right margin in order to give
balance to the letter. Other persons prefer the crisp, businesslike
appearance of the full-block style.

Notice that the open style of punctuation is used in this letter.
Although open punctuation is not an essential characteristic of the
full-block arrangement, the two styles are often used together.

You will notice that the simplified letter, shown next in this series,
is a modification of the full-block style.

Sincerely,

Binford H. Peeples

Binford H. Peeples, Professor

sn

FIGURE B–3
The full-block style

MEMPHIS STATE UNIVERSITY
THE FOGELMAN COLLEGE OF BUSINESS AND ECONOMICS
Memphis, Tennessee 38152

Office Administration Department

December 18, 19--

Mr. Joe Galloway
Office Manager
Countrywide Insurance Company
5983 Maplewood Cove
Memphis, TN 38117

THE SIMPLIFIED LETTER

Mr. Galloway, do you like this letter style? It has several advantages, but possibly some disadvantages, too.

It is the easiest letter of all to set up and type. In addition, it has a businesslike, no-nonsense look about it. A subject line, which can be used in any letter style, is always included in the simplified style.

Some persons feel that this letter arrangement is unfriendly and impersonal because the customary salutation and complimentary close are omitted. These lines are unnecessary, though, for if the letter is written as it should be, the reader will believe and understand that it is "sincere," "cordial," and "very truly yours." Besides, all the persons we address as "dear" are not really dear to us, using the ordinary meaning of the word.

Perhaps you will choose this letter to be the standard one for your office. If not, I think full-block would be a good choice. Either the semiblock or the modified block could be your standard arrangement, if you prefer their appearance—but your typist will lose some time in setting them up.

Binford H. Peeples

BINFORD H. PEEPLES, PROFESSOR

sn

FIGURE B–4
Simplified style

The Functional Letter Arrangement

Figure B–5 is described here as the *functional* letter style to connote practical simplicity. At the present time, this letter format has no official name in widespread use.

The functional arrangement is in several ways more desirable than the simplified style illustrated in Figure B–4, at least in the opinion of many writers. Not all letters require or benefit from the use of a subject line, which is a required part of the simplified style.

For example, a subject line is not necessary for the letter shown in Figure B–5 and would result in a more impersonal approach. In addition, the writer's name and title are shown in capitals and lowercase in the functional arrangement instead of in the all-capitals usually used in the simplified style. The writer's name in all-capitals, with the reader's name shown in smaller letters, implies a writer-approach, not a reader-approach.

The functional arrangement is a variation of the simplified style. It could be described as a simplified version of the simplified letter style. This functional arrangement is not widely used for the same reasons that the simplified arrangement is not widely used: it is considered "different" and impersonal. The use of the functional style is increasing, however, because of its simplicity and efficiency.

The simplified and the functional styles have advantages in certain correspondence situations. For example, in letters to an organization, not to an individual, the customary salutation for many years has been "Gentlemen." This form of salutation is now considered discriminatory language, as discussed in Chapter 3. By using letter styles that require no salutation, such as the simplified and the functional, you can omit the salutation entirely.

Sometimes you cannot determine whether the reader is masculine or feminine because of names that can be either. Spellings are different for some names, such as "Marion" and "Marian," but not for all, such as "Leslie." Although women whose names can be either feminine or masculine show as a "Ms." or "Mrs." before their typewritten name, they do not always do so. When using the simplified or functional style, the writer can address a letter, for example, to Leslie Brown and omit the salutation entirely, as the salutation is not included in these styles. Another choice is "Dear M. Brown" to denote either sex.

Unless you cannot determine whether the reader is masculine or feminine, *always* include a courtesy title in *both* the inside address and salutation. (See examples in Figures B–1, B–2, and B–3.)

Personal Business Letters

Personal business letters are letters from an individual about personal business matters, *not* letters from a representative of an organization. Personal business letters are written on personal stationery or plain paper.

Never write personal business letters on printed letterhead stationery of the employing organization. Doing so implies that you represent the organization by whatever you say in the letter.

The application letters and other letters about employment illustrated in Chapter 12 are examples of personal business letters. Personal business letters are also written on many other subjects to other individuals or to organizations.

The University of Mississippi
School of Business Administration
University, Mississippi 38677

Department of Management and Marketing   (601)000-0000

June 4, 19--

Franklin Heating and Cooling
Highway 41 Plaza
Lake City, FL 32055

Your comments regarding a recent article of mine are very much appreciated. I believe, though, that by reading the complete report of my research into the causes and effects of bankruptcy you will see that there is redress available to those who feel that provisions of the Bankruptcy Reform Act favor the debtor to the detriment of the creditor.

A provision in the Bankruptcy Act allows any state to pass legislation prohibiting its residents from selecting the federal exemptions. This would force them to take the state exemptions, which, in most cases, are not as lenient. So, it is up to each state's legislature to decide whether to allow the federal exemptions to be used.

After reading the enclosed report, and discussing it with your board of directors, you may want your firm to take a position on this controversial issue. Your state legislative delegation would probably welcome your comments and your support.

Please write again after reading the enclosed report and let me know if you feel further research is warranted.

Vanessa Dean Arnold

Vanessa Dean Arnold
Associate Professor

bd

Enclosure

FIGURE B–5
Functional letter style, with omitted saluta-tion and complimen-tary close

Letters from an individual may be arranged in any of the letter arrangements illustrated in Figures B–1 through B–5, except that the return address, if not printed on the sheet, is typewritten immediately above the data. A return address for a personal business letter is illustrated below.

```
5290 Sonata Court
Oklahoma City, OK 73130
June 27, 1991
```

Arranging the Usual and Special Parts of the Letter

With the exception of the *simplified* style and the *functional* style, business letters will almost always contain (besides the body of the letter) the following parts:

- letterhead
- date
- inside address
- salutation
- complimentary closing
- signer's name and title
- typist's initials, referred to as reference initials

Other lines used on many letters, as desirable or required, are the following:

- attention line
- subject line
- typewritten company name preceding name of writer
- enclosure notation
- copy notation, formerly referred to as the carbon copy notation
- postscript

The *simplified* and *functional* styles omit the salutation and complimentary close, as illustrated in Figures B–4 and B–5.

Letterhead

Letters coming from a business office, written by a company representative about matters concerning the company, should be typewritten on printed letterhead stationery.

The choice of letterhead is important to the overall appearance of company correspondence. It should include all needed information, including the company name, address, and telephone number. If the company name does not specifically indicate the type of business, this information should be made clear by additional descriptive lines.

The complete letterhead should fit within the top two inches (twelve vertical spaces) of the sheet. A deeper letterhead will leave too little space for the letter itself, causing a crowded appearance for long letters or increasing the number of two-page letters.

Ordinarily the left side of letterhead stationery should be left blank. Like a too-deep letterhead, printing at the side decreases the amount of space available for letters and may result in unattractive centering.

Date

The date is ordinarily set up in this way: November 18, 1990. Do *not* abbreviate the month. Do *not* use an abbreviated form, such as 11-18-1990. Another form that is increasing in use is this: 18 November 1990. All letters, like all other written messages, should be dated. The date is ordinarily placed on about line 14 or 15 from the top, a position that is about two spaces below a two-inch letterhead.

Inside Address

The name, title, and complete mailing address make up the part of the letter described as the inside address. The individual's name should be preceded by a courtesy title except in the rare instances when the writer cannot determine whether the addressee is masculine or feminine, as previously discussed.

Examples of inside addresses are shown below:

Mrs. Ruth Billings
Apartment 17-B
1187 Mockingbird Lane
Yonkers, NY 10028

Mr. Bill Bond, Manager
ABC Appliances, Inc.
95 State Street
Camden, NJ 08108

Dr. Laura McCormick
4646 Poplar
Austin, TX 76105

Ms. Wendy Ritger
Developmental Editor
Allyn and Bacon, Inc.
160 Gould Street
Needham, MA 02194

Inside addresses should be single spaced, like the rest of the letter.

Salutation

Salutations for the preceding inside addresses are these:

Dear Mrs. Billings:

Dear Dr. McCormick: (or Dear Doctor McCormick:)

Dear Mr. Bond:

Dear Ms. Ritger: (or Dear Editor Ritger:)

If you use the reader's first name in conversation, your salutation should also do so, as shown below:

Dear Ruth:

Dear Laura:

Dear Bill:

Dear Wendy:

Be extremely cautious with the use of the reader's first name. Do *not* use it to address a person you do not know or one who could possibly be offended by such familiarity. Readers in Europe, more so than in the United States, are likely to be offended. The salutation is followed by a colon, *not* a comma. Omit the colon only if you also omit the comma after the complimentary close. This style is referred to as *open punctuation;* its use is infrequent.

Complimentary Closing (or Complimentary Close)

Always use a complimentary closing when you use a salutation; omit it when you omit a salutation, as illustrated in Figures B–4 and B–5.

Frequently used complimentary closings are these:

Sincerely,

Sincerely yours,

Cordially,

Cordially yours,

Less frequently used closings are these:

Yours truly,

Very truly yours,   *Often considered "old-fashioned"*

Yours very truly,

Respectfully,   *Reserve for formal letters, often to a person in a high position*

The "truly" closings are considered more formal than the more frequently used closings, and some writers consider them old-fashioned. (Other writers consider *all* complimentary closings and salutations old-fashioned.) The closing "Respectfully" should be used rarely, if at all; it is not appropriate for routine business letters but is sometimes used in letters addressed to people in high positions, particularly in government; for example, to a United States senator. Even for such addresses, however, the more frequently used complimentary closes are appropriate.

Do not use a formal closing as *Very truly yours* with an informal salutation such as *Dear Wendy,* and do not use *Cordially,* an informal and personal closing, when writing to an organization or to a person with whom you are not acquainted.

Signer's Name and Title

The typewritten name and title may be placed on the same line or on separate lines. For example:

Mary Holt, President or Mary Holt
                    President

or

Henry Wade, Director
Department of Employee Benefits

A man should *never* use the courtesy title of "Mr." with his typewritten name or with his signature. A woman, however, may precede her type-written name (*not* her signature) with a courtesy title in order to let the reader know how to address her in a responding letter. (In a letter addressed to a woman, use *Ms.* as the courtesy title if you do not know the preferred courtesy title.)

Typist's Initials (Reference Initials)

The reference initials are usually placed at the left margin two lines (a double space) below the last line of the signature block. If the person who signs the letter has dictated it, only the initials of the typist are necessary. An illustration:

Cordially yours,

Wayne Johnson, President

en

Enclosure Notation

The enclosed notation is used on each letter with which something is enclosed. Sometimes the word "attachment" is used instead to indicate an attachment, not an enclosure. The enclosure notation is placed one or two spaces below the reference initials.

Copy Notation

The copy notation is placed a double space below the enclosure notation unless the letter is running low on the sheet; if this is the case, the copy notation may be placed a single space below.

The copy notation may be arranged in one of the following ways or in other variations. The "cc" denotes carbon copies, which are now usually replaced by photocopies. The "cc" is also interpreted as "computer copy."

Copy to Mrs. Harriet Jenkins

Copies to Jenkins and Harris

cc: Harriet Jenkins and Walter Harris

Postscript

If you use a postscript, it should be the last item on the letter. The purpose of the postscript is to emphasize, not to include material that has been mistakenly omitted from the letter.

Typewritten Company Name Preceding Name of Writer

The company name, if used in signature block, appears like this:

> Sincerely yours,
>
> SMITH MANUFACTURING COMPANY
>
>
> Mary Duncan, Treasurer

Many organizations do not use the company name in the signature block; they consider it unnecessary because the name is shown in the letterhead. If the company name is included in the signature block, it should be typewritten in all-capitals.

At least three blank lines should be left for the penwritten signature, as when the company name is omitted.

Attention Line

The attention line, when used, is usually placed a double space after the last line of the inside address and a double space before the salutation. It may also follow the company name.

Smith Manufacturing Company
2081 Hickory Ridge Road   or
Macon, GA 30567

Attention Sales Manager

Ladies and Gentlemen:

Smith Manufacturing Company
Attention Sales Manager
2081 Hickory Ridge Road
Macon, GA 30567

Ladies and Gentlemen:

This use of the attention line is less desirable than addressing a letter to the Sales Manager, by name, if the name can be determined, as shown below:

Ms. Ann Barnes, Sales Manager
Smith Manufacturing Company
2081 Hickory Ridge Road
Macon, GA 30567

Dear Ms. Barnes:

When addressing a letter to an organization, as in the first example above, you may omit the "Ladies and Gentlemen" or other salutation, along with the complimentary close, resulting in the functional letter style if all lines begin at the left margin.

Subject Line

The subject line, an expected part of the *simplified* letter style and all memorandums, may also be used in any other letter arrangement. Word a subject line with care so that it will describe specifically the most important contents of the letter. A subject line is not always desirable, especially when the letter involves bad news or another unpleasant subject.

The subject line is usually placed a double space below the salutation. If no salutation is used, the subject line is spaced a triple space below the last line of the inside address. Illustrations are shown below:

Ms. Ann Barnes, Sales Manager
Smith Manufacturing Company
2081 Hickory Ridge Road
Macon, GA 30567

Dear Ms. Barnes:

SUBJECT: REQUEST FOR ADJUSTMENT, INVOICE NO. 1239

{First line of paragraph}

Smith Manufacturing Company
2081 Hickory Ridge Road
Macon, GA 30567

REQUEST FOR ADJUSTMENT, INVOICE NO. 1239

{First line of paragraph}

The word "Subject" may be included or omitted at the beginning of the subject line, as illustrated above.

Heading of a Multiple-Page Letter

The heading of the second and following pages of a letter includes the first line of the inside address, the page number, and the date. The heading may be set up in one of three ways:

Mr. John D. Richardson   2   February 18, 1990

Mr. John D. Richardson
February 18, 1990
page 2

Mr. John D. Richardson, February 18, 1990, page 2

Illustration of Placement of Parts of a Letter

Figure B–6 illustrates the placement of the usual and special parts of a letter discussed above. In actual use, few letters would need all the special parts.

Horizontal Centering

Margins at sides and bottoms should be at least one inch wide. When using elite type, set margins for one of the following line lengths:

LETTERHEAD
{The letterhead should require no more than two inches, or twelve vertical spaces.}

April 11, 19-- {date on line 14 or 15 from top of sheet}

Smith Manufacturing Company {three to eight lines below date}
2081 Hickory Ridge Road
Macon, GA 30567

ATTENTION SALES MANAGER

Ladies and Gentlemen:

SUBJECT: REQUEST FOR ADJUSTMENT, INVOICE NO. 1239

{First line of first paragraph. All paragraphs are single spaced, with a double space between paragraphs.}

{Second paragraph}

{Third paragraph}

{Last paragraph. No rule can be given for the number of paragraphs a letter should contain. Paragraphs should be fairly short for easy reading.}

Sincerely yours, {a double space below last paragraph}

THE NOBLE CORPORATION {company name in all capitals}
            {Three or more lines for signature}

Vicki Woo, President {could also be on two lines}

rt

Enclosures: Check and contract {not always specified}

Copy to Robert Wilson, CPA, Wilson Associates

P.S. The enclosed brochure contains a special offer that will increase your equipment sales.

FIGURE B–6
Vertical placement of letter

70-space line, margins at 15 and 90. (Use for long letters, those that require a full page and two-page letters.)

60-space line, margins at 20 and 85. (Use for medium-length letters.)

50-space line, margins at 25 and 80. (Use for very short letters.)

Many typists use a long line for all length letters and adjust vertical spacing accordingly.

Corresponding settings for pica type, using 40 as center, are 10 and 75 (long); 15 and 70 (medium); and 20 and 65 (short).

When you use the usual and special parts of the business letter in the expected and conventional arrangement, you add to the readability of the letter. All parts serve a useful purpose (with the possible exception of the salutation and complimentary close) in that they present needed information in an easy-to-find and understandable form.

TWO-LETTER ABBREVIATIONS FOR STATES
(and Guam, Puerto Rico, U.S. Virgin Islands, and District of Columbia)

Alabama	AL	Montana	MT
Alaska	AK	Nebraska	NE
Arizona	AZ	Nevada	NV
Arkansas	AR	New Hampshire	NH
California	CA	New Jersey	NJ
Colorado	CO	New Mexico	NM
Connecticut	CT	New York	NY
		North Carolina	NC
Delaware	DE	North Dakota	ND
District of Columbia	DC		
		Ohio	OH
Florida	FL	Oklahoma	OK
		Oregon	OR
Georgia	GA		
Guam	GU	Pennsylvania	PA
		Puerto Rico	PR
Hawaii	HI		
		Rhode Island	RI
Idaho	ID		
Illinois	IL	South Carolina	SC
Indiana	IN	South Dakota	SD
Iowa	IA		
		Tennessee	TN
Kansas	KS	Texas	TX
Kentucky	KY		
		Utah	UT
Louisiana	LA		
		Vermont	VT
Maine	ME	Virginia	VA
Maryland	MD	Virgin Islands	VI
Massachusetts	MA		
Michigan	MI	Washington	WA
Minnesota	MN	West Virginia	WV
Mississippi	MS	Wisconsin	WI
Missouri	MO	Wyoming	WY

TWO-LETTER ABBREVIATIONS FOR CANADIAN PROVINCES

Alberta	AB	Nova Scotia	NS
British Columbia	BC	Ontario	ON
Manitoba	MB	Prince Edward Island	PE
New Brunswick	NB	Quebec	PQ
Newfoundland	NF	Yukon Territory	YT
Northwest Territory	NT		

Evaluation Sheet: Letter Format

	Yes	No	Not Sure
1. Is the letter attractively centered on the sheet, with the date on approximately line 15 or two spaces below the letterhead?	___	___	___
2. Is the date shown in full, NOT abbreviated?	___	___	___
3. Is a courtesy title (Mr., Mrs., Ms., Miss, Dr., and so on) shown on BOTH the inside address and the salutation?	___	___	___
4. Is the letter single spaced, with an extra space left between paragraphs?	___	___	___
5. Are all abbreviations omitted everywhere; except in courtesy titles or for a few other words, such as *incorporated,* that are routinely abbreviated?	___	___	___
6. Do most of the paragraphs start with some word other than *I* or *we?*	___	___	___
7. Is the letter arranged in one of the widely used letter styles, not in a mixture of styles?	___	___	___
8. Is the two-letter state abbreviation used in the inside address? Is this abbreviation followed by one space and the zip code?	___	___	___
9. Are all paragraphs fairly short?	___	___	___
10. Is the first paragraph no more than five lines? (Even a shorter one is better.)	___	___	___

APPENDIX **C**

Documentation: The Appearance of Reports

Placement of Footnotes and Other Reference Notes

If footnotes are placed at the bottom of the page, they are separated from the text by a solid line (the underscore) one and one-half inches long, beginning at the left margin.

A disadvantage of bottom-of-page footnotes is that they make a manuscript more difficult to type. An advantage is that the reader can more easily see the footnotes than if they are placed on a page at the end of the manuscript. Another consideration is that an arrangement other than the traditional bottom-of-page placement seems to some readers to be less formal and professional. When using bottom-of-page footnotes, shorten subsequent ones, whether or not you are using a bibliography. Shortened forms are illustrated later in this appendix.

Here is an example of "References Cited" notes: (4:51) refers to the fourth item in the bibliography (which may also be called "References," "References Cited," or "Sources of Data"), page 51. A reference without a page number, such as (7) refers to the complete item 7, regardless of what it is—book, article, interview, or government document. All items in the bibliography are arranged alphabetically, *but all must also be numbered.*

Numerous footnotes or parenthetical citations are distracting no matter where placed, but they must be used when they are necessary for proper credit to the original author. If you find that you are using an excessive number, to the extent that much of your report consists of bits and pieces of others' works, perhaps you are doing too much citing and not enough analysis and interpretation of your own.

Shortened Footnotes or Endnotes

Shortened forms of footnotes or endnotes are used for subsequent references. A simplified note consisting of the author's name, with page numbers, is usually preferable to the older, hard-to-remember Latin forms, although at times the term *Ibid.* may save unnecessary repetition of long titles, such as government publications with no author shown. Use of standard reference forms, including *Ibid.*, is explained below. *Unless you see a real need to use Latin abbreviations, however, prefer the simpler, modern arrangement.*

For example, in a subsequent reference to a book by Edward T. Hall, you may use this footnote:

Hall, 217.

If you refer in the same paper to two or more works by the same author, the title must be included in all footnotes:

Hall, *The Silent Language*, 217.

If you use materials written, for example, by both Jane Hall and Edward T. Hall, complete names must be included in all footnotes. Assume that you use two books by Edward T. Hall and one by Jane Hall. The shortest form of the footnote would be as follows:

Edward T. Hall, *The Silent Language*, 217.

Examples of shortened footnotes are shown in Figure C–1.

Environmental Services, Inc. currently employs 10 generalist secretaries to support 33 principals. The functions now being performed by the secretaries are decentralized. One secretary works in each department.

---

[7]Kleinschrod, 11.

[8]Jeffrey D. O'Neal, "We Increased Typing Productivity 340%," *The Office*, January 1988, 95.

[9]Kleinschrod, 3.

[10]Anderson and Trotter, 11-12.

FIGURE C–1
Example of shortened footnotes. Because the complete form is used the first time a reference is cited, this method of footnoting may be used with or without a bibliography.

Latin abbreviations have long been used as subsequent footnote references. The most commonly used ones are these:

Ibid. (ibidem). This term means "in the same place." It is used to refer to the immediately preceding footnote: Ibid., 12.

Op. cit. (opere citato). This term means "in the work cited." It refers to a previous footnote, but not the one directly preceding: Brown, op. cit., 14.

Loc. cit. (loco citato). This term means "in the place cited." It refers to a preceding entry but not the one directly preceding. This abbreviation is used only when the page number for the second reference is the same as the first.

The following series of footnotes or endnotes illustrates the use of *ibid., op. cit.,* and *loc. cit.*

1. Joanna Brown, *Reflections* (Boston: Allyn and Bacon, 1981), 8.

2. Ibid., 142. [Brown's work, but another page]

3. Ruth Kemp, "Tomorrow," *Reader's Digest,* March 1982, 14.

4. Brown, op. cit., 147. [Brown's book, different page]

5. Kemp, loc. cit. [same article, same page as footnote 3]

If your report or other written work includes a bibliography, the footnote form, including the first time a reference is cited, may be shortened. It is also correct, and often considered preferable in formal reports, to show complete information in the first footnote reference to a work, even when a bibliography is included. To do so is essential if no bibliography is included. (See Figure C–1, note 8.)

Reference Citations in Text of Report

Shortened footnotes may be inserted into the text of a report that includes a bibliography, as discussed under "Placement of Footnotes and Other Reference Notes." To summarize:

Author-date system: (Johnson, 1984).

Number System: (2:25) (The first number refers to item 2 in the bibliography; 25 is the page number.)

An illustration of a passage from a report (using the number system) that refers to two interviews is shown in Figure C–2. This passage refers to the bibliography (references) shown in Figure C–4. A passage that refers to a published source is shown in Figure C–3. Notice that (6:28) refers to page 28 of the sixth item in the bibliography.

Age groups influence book sales. A great number of avid readers in the United States are within two age groups, according to managers and owners of Memphis bookstores (9, 10). These two groups are people of college age, or near college age, and retired individuals, or those nearing retirement age.

FIGURE C–2
Passage from report that refers to items 9 and 10 in the bibliography shown in Figure C-4

Of the 1,594 employed persons age 16 and over, 636, or 39.9 percent, are employed in professional and managerial positions; 632, or 41 percent, are in technical, sales, and administrative support positions (6:28).

FIGURE C–3
A passage that refers to item 6, a published source, in the bibliography shown in Figure C-4

Bibliographies

The bibliography is considered as a supplement to a formal report. It may come before or after appendices, depending upon the material included as appendices. Page numbering is often simplified by placing the bibliography first. The Arabic numerals used in the report proper continue in sequence throughout the supplementary parts.

An annotated bibliography briefly describes each listed reference, as in these examples:

Gunning, Robert. *New Guides to More Effective Writing in Business and Industry.* Boston: Industrial Education Institute, 1964.
   Gunning, best known for the development of a readability formula, offers help to the business and technical writer toward the clear expression of ideas. The theme is that clear expression is based upon exact thinking and understanding.

Dohan, Mary Helen. *Our Own Words.* New York: Alfred A. Knopf, 1974.
   The story of the making of the American language, from its Anglo-Saxon roots and its beginnings among the earliest settlers and pioneers, through its development during periods of immigration and social change. The book includes an introduction by Alistair Cooke.

REFERENCES

Published Sources

1. "Book People." The Bookdealer's Profile, January 1989, 15-16.

2. "Book Publishers Turn to a Happier Chapter." U.S. News and World Report, 18 June 1984, 64.

3. "Book Publishing." Standard and Poor's Industry Survey, January 1989, 74 (C).

4. Hirsch, E. D., Jr. Cultural Literacy. Boston: Houghton Mifflin, 1987.

5. "Neighborly Memphians Put into Statistical Focus." The (Memphis) Commercial Appeal, 30 January 1984, 4-5 (A).

6. U.S. Bureau of the Census. Twentieth Census of the United States, 1980: Neighborhood Statistics Program. Washington, D.C., 1984.

7. U.S. Bureau of Industrial Economics. U.S. Industrial Outlook. Washington, D.C., 1984, 23.

8. Williams, Becky Hall, ed. 1988 Writer's Market. Cincinnati: Writer's Digest Books, 1988.

Other Sources

9. Donnelly, Mary, Owner, Midtown Bookstore, 918 Union Avenue, Memphis, Tennessee 38111. Personal interview, November 21, 1988.

10. Harrison, Jason, Assistant Manager, Rockwell Bookstore, 397 Grove Park Road, Memphis, Tennessee 38117. Telephone interviews November 2, 4, and 14, 1988.

11. James, Mary, Consultant, 319 Copley Square, Boston, Massachusetts 02111. Letter, October 16, 1988.

12. Johnson, Robert, Professor, Georgia State University, Atlanta. Lecture, September 12, 1987.

FIGURE C–4
Bibliography. Also described as *References, Works Cited,* or similar terms.

Footnotes (or Endnotes) with Corresponding Bibliographic Entries

The examples of footnotes or endnotes and bibliographic entries that follow are in the format shown by *MLA Handbook for Writers of Research Papers*, 2nd ed., Modern Language Association, 1984. Actual footnote entries used throughout this book are based on *The Chicago Manual of Style*, 13th ed., 1982, the guide used for Allyn and Bacon books and the books of many other publishers.

The format shown by the *MLA Handbook* and *The Chicago Manual of Style* are very similar; in many cases they are identical. For example, in the first illustration (Arn Tibbetts) the formats are identical in both style manuals for footnotes and bibliographic entries. All following entries are also identical, with a few minor exceptions. A difference that existed before the latest edition of *The Chicago Manual of Style* is the presentation of multiple authors in bibliographic entries. Before the latest edition the names of all authors were reversed; now the name of only the first author listed in the entry is reversed.

In the following examples, *F* indicates footnote (or endnote) and *B* indicates an entry in a bibliography.

For a book with one author:

F   [1]Arn Tibbetts, *Practical Business Writing* (Boston: Little, Brown & Co., 1987), 225.

B   Tibbetts, Arn. *Practical Business Writing*. Boston: Little, Brown & Co., 1987.

For a book with two authors:

F   [2]Eugene Ehrlich and Gorton Carruth, *The Oxford Illustrated Literary Guide to the United States* (New York: Oxford University Press), 441.

B   Ehrlich, Eugene, and Gorton Carruth. *The Oxford Illustrated Literary Guide to the United States*. New York: Oxford University Press, 1982.

For a book with three authors:

F   [3]Robert McCrum, William Cran, and Robert MacNeil, *The Story of English*. (New York: Elisabeth Sifton Books. Viking, 1986), 349.

B   McCrum, Robert; William Cran; and Robert MacNeil. *The Story of English*. New York: Elisabeth Sifton Books. Viking, 1986.

For a book with more than three authors:

F   [4]Robert J. Kibler et al., *Objectives for Instruction and Evaluation* (Boston: Allyn and Bacon, 1974), 153.

B   Kibler, Robert J.; Donald J. Cegala; David T. Miles; and Larry L. Barker. *Objectives for Instruction and Evaluation*. Boston: Allyn and Bacon, 1974.

For an edited book:

F   [5]David Rattray, ed. *Success with Words* (Pleasantville, N.Y.: Reader's Digest Association, 1983), 120–126.

B   Rattray, David, ed. *Success with Words*. Pleasantville, N.Y.: Reader's Digest Association, 1983.

For a book revised by a person other than the original author:

F   [6]H. W. Fowler, *A Dictionary of Modern English Usage*, 2d ed., rev. Sir Ernest Gowers (Oxford: Oxford University Press, 1965), 157.

B   Fowler, H. W. *A Dictionary of Modern English Usage.* 2nd ed. Revised by Sir Ernest Gowers. Oxford: Oxford University Press, 1965.

For a book with no author given:

F   [7]*The Chicago Manual of Style,* 13th ed. rev. (Chicago: University of Chicago Press, 1982), 42–44.

B   *The Chicago Manual of Style,* 13th ed. rev. Chicago: University of Chicago Press, 1982.

For a chapter of a collective work:

F   [8]Merwyn A. Hayes, "Nonverbal Communication: Expression Without Words," in *Readings in Interpersonal and Organizational Communication,* 3d ed., edited by Richard C. Huseman, Cal M. Logue, and Dwight L. Freshley (Boston: Holbrook Press, 1977), 55–68.

B   Hayes, Merwyn A. "Nonverbal Communication: Expression Without Words." *Readings in Interpersonal and Organizational Communication,* 3d ed., edited by Richard C. Huseman, Cal M. Logue, and Dwight L. Freshley, 55–68. Boston: Holbrook Press, 1977.

For a book in a series:

F   [9]James A. Smith, *Creative Teaching of the Language Arts in the Elementary School,* Allyn and Bacon Series in Creative Teaching, vol. 2 (Boston: 1967), 30.

B   Smith, James A. *Creative Teaching of the Language Arts in the Elementary School.* Allyn and Bacon Series in Creative Teaching, vol. 2. Boston: 1967.

For an unpublished work:

F   [10]Myrena Sue Jennings, "A Comparison of Middle Managerial Written Business Communication Practices and Problems and Collegiate Written Business Communications Instruction" (Doctoral dissertation, Georgia State University, 1974), 271.

B   Jennings, Myrena Sue. "A Comparison of Middle Managerial Written Business Communications Practices and Problems and Collegiate Written Business Communications Instructions." Doctoral dissertation, Georgia State University, 1974.

For an article in a journal:

F   [11]Robert Gunning, "The Fog Index after Twenty Years," *Journal of Business Communication* 6 (Winter 1968): 3.

B   Gunning, Robert. "The Fog Index after Twenty Years." *Journal of Business Communication* 6 (Winter 1968): 3.

For an article in a general magazine:

F   [12]Robert Kuttner, "The Poverty of Economics," *The Atlantic,* February 1985:78.

B   Kuttner, Robert. "The Poverty of Economics." *The Atlantic,* February 1985, 74–84.

For an article in a well-known reference book:

F   [13]*Encyclopaedia Britannica,* 1977, s.v. "Printing."

B   *Encyclopaedia Britannica.* 1977, s.v. "Printing."

F   [14]*The Concise Oxford Dictionary of Current English,* 5th ed. s.v. "Communication."

B   *The Concise Oxford Dictionary of Current English.* 5th ed., s.v. "Communication."

For a newspaper article:

F   [15]*Boston Globe,* 18 January 1982, 1.

B   *Boston Globe,* 18 January 1982: 1.

For government publications:

F   [16]U.S. Congress, House Committee on Business, *Operating Small Businesses,* 79th Cong., 2d sess., 1946, H. Rep. 1888, 63.

B   U.S. Congress, House Committee on Business. *Operating Small Businesses.* 79th Cong., 2d sess., 1946. H. Rep. 1888.

F   [17]Social Science Research Council, *Labor Force Definition and Measurement,* Bulletin 56 (Washington, D.C., 1947), 10–11.

B   Social Science Research Council. *Labor Force Definition and Measurement.* Bulletin 56. Washington, D.C., 1947.

F   [18]U.S. Bureau of the Census, *Twentieth Century of the United States, 1980: Population,* 2: 98.

B   U.S. Bureau of the Census. *Twentieth Census of the United States, 1980: Population,* vol. 2.

F   [19]U.S. *Constitution,* Art. I, sec. 4.

B   U.S. *Constitution.* Art. I. sec. 4.

For interviews:

F   [20]Personal interview with James X. Tennyson, Manager, Conrally Company, Midland, Texas, 19 November 1988.

B   Tennyson, James X., Manager, Conrally Company, Midland, Texas. Personal interview, 19 November 1988.

F   [21]Telephone interview with Mary Key, Supervisor, Raven Corporation, Dayton, Ohio, 19 November 1988.

B   Key, Mary, Supervisor, Raven Corporation, Dayton, Ohio. Telephone interview, 19 November 1988.

For letters or memorandums:

F   [22]Letter from Marjorie Jacobs, President, X-View, Incorporated, to Richard Rayner, 19 November 1988.

B   Jacobs, Marjorie, President, X-View, Incorporated. Letter to Richard Rayner, 19 November 1988.

Footnote (or endnote) and bibliography formats of materials not illustrated in the list above, such as leaflets, brochures, manuals, speeches, minutes of meetings, or radio or television programs, should be arranged similarly to one of the examples shown. A titled brochure or leaflet with no author given is arranged similarly to a magazine article with no author given. *A speech is presented similarly to an interview or a letter.*

If you cannot find examples or instructions for primary or secondary data that you wish to document, simply give all necessary information in a logical, readable order, as much as possible like the arrangement of other footnotes or bibliographic entries. It is better to give too much information than too little. If expected information is not available—for example, date of a publication—show in footnotes and bibliographic entries that the data was omitted in the source you are quoting.

Consult a complete style manual for more detailed information about documentation. Choose any one of the leading ones or follow the instructions of your teacher or supervisor.

The Physical Appearance of a Report

Work for an attractive appearance. Your readers are favorably or unfavorably impressed by the overall appearance of the report.

Margins

If the manuscript is to remain unbound, use a six-inch line, which provides slightly more than one-inch side margins. For manuscripts to be bound, move side margins an additional one-half inch to the right.

On the first page of a report manuscript, leave a two-inch top margin. On the following pages, leave a top margin of approximately one inch. On all pages, leave a bottom margin of one to one and one-half inches.

Spacing

Formal reports are traditionally double spaced, but many organizations are now preparing all typewritten work in single-spaced form to economize. Your choice will depend on organizational policy, purpose, readership of the report, and cost considerations.

Headings

Be consistent in the use of headings. (See Chapter 16.) Use the same format for headings of the same weight. *Use no single subheadings.*

Pagination

The first page of the report itself (the "report proper") is considered as page 1. This page number is centered about one inch from the bottom of the page or omitted. Page numbers of following pages are placed in the upper right-hand corner, on line 5 to 7 from the top. Thus the "approximately one-inch" top margin refers to the "white space" above the page number. Triple space after the page number before beginning the first line of text.

Additional Guides to Report Appearance

1. Use sturdy, good-quality paper, preferably 20-pound weight.

2. Use standard-size paper, $8\frac{1}{2}$ by 11 inches.

3. Use a self-correcting typewriter or word processing equipment if possible.

4. Make corrections neatly. If a self-correcting typewriter or word process-

ing equipment is not available, use an eraser, correction tape, or correction liquid. (Correction liquid is useful only for material that is to be photocopied.)

5. Be sure that typewriter keys are clean and that the typewriter or computer printer ribbon is clear.

6. Leave at least two lines of a paragraph at the bottom of each page and carry over at least two lines of a paragraph to the next page. Thus, three-line paragraphs cannot be divided.

7. Follow a subheading (caption) near the bottom of a page with at least two lines of type, preferably more. A wider-than-average bottom margin is preferable to a subheading with insufficient following material.

8. Indent paragraphs in all double-spaced material. Paragraphs are usually indented five spaces, but they may be indented eight to ten spaces. Paragraphs of single-spaced material may be indented or blocked. Leave a blank space between all paragraphs.

A Brief Guide
to English Usage

Punctuation as an Aid to Readability
  The Apostrophe
  The Comma
  The Semicolon
  The Colon
  The Dash
  The Hyphen

  Parentheses
  Quotation Marks
Capitalization
Writing Numbers
Frequently Misspelled Words
Exercises

This appendix section is of necessity an incomplete guide to the use of the English language. Many comprehensive handbooks on English usage, some of them excellent, are available for your use through school and public libraries. Every writer should own one or more reliable handbooks, as well as a large, up-to-date dictionary.

See Chapter 4 for instructions about sentence construction, frequently confused or misused words, and frequently occurring grammatical errors.

Punctuation as an Aid to Readability

The Apostrophe

1. Use an apostrophe in contractions.

- won't
- it's (it is)
- couldn't
- you're (you are)

Avoid contractions in formal writing.

2. Use an apostrophe to indicate the possessive case of nouns and indefinite pronouns.

- Mary's cat
- anybody's guess
- a stone's throw

- a year's experience
- two years' experience
- women's shoes
- children's books
- the student's paper (one student)
- the students' paper (more than one student)
- Mr. Ross's automobile
- The Rosses' automobile (an automobile owned by more than one person named Ross)
- Jefferson Davis's home or Dr. Jennings' office (see note)
- Bob and Mary's house (joint ownership)
- Bob's and Mary's shoes (individual ownership)

Note: If a singular noun ends in *s*, the apostrophe and *s* are usually added; but if the second *s* causes difficulty of punctuation, the apostrophe alone may be added.

3. Use an apostrophe in plurals of lowercase letters and abbreviations followed by periods and (preferred) in plurals of capital letters, figures, abbreviations not followed by periods, and words referred to as words.

- c's
- Ph.D's
- B's or Bs
- CPA's or CPAs
- 8's or 8s
- the 1940's or 1940s
- and's or ands
- %'s or %s

Be consistent in your use of the apostrophe. For example, use *and's* or *ands*, but do not use both in the same paper. According to some English handbooks, *and's* is preferred.

Note: The use of the apostrophe is sometimes described as being an aspect of spelling, not of punctuation.

The Comma

1. Use a comma to set off an introductory subordinate clause from an independent statement.

- If Johnny can't write, one of the reasons may be a conditioning based on speed rather than on respect for the creative process.
- If you don't like the weather in New England, wait a few minutes.
- Although the ability to type is a requisite to many jobs, it should no more be considered purely vocational than the ability to read or write the English language.
- When in doubt, tell the truth.—Mark Twain (Introductory element with "you are" understood.)

2. Use a comma after introductory participial phrases.

- Dreading the long, boring task, he left it until the afternoon.
- Having received the notice of cancellation, we tried to stop shipment.
- Elated over the news of his promotion, he kissed everyone on the third floor.

Distinguish between a participle, which is a verb form used as an adjective, and a gerund, which is a verb form used as a noun. A gerund is also referred to as a verbal noun. In the following sentences the gerund acts as the subject; it should not be followed by a comma:

- Seeing is believing.
- Driving along the Natchez Trace is a memorable experience.

3. Use a comma after introductory infinitive phrases.

- To enter the stacks, go to the admission desk and present your identification card.

An infinitive, like a gerund, is *not* followed by a comma when it is used as the subject. In the following sentence, both clauses of the compound sentence contain an infinitive used as the subject:

- To err is human; to blame it on someone else is even more human.

4. Use a comma after an introductory sentence element consisting of a long prepositional phrase or of two or more phrases.

- In addition to the many books in the general library, many others are shelved in specialized collections.

5. Use a comma after introductory words and phrases.

- Confidentially, this policy is to be changed.
- Nevertheless, we must continue the usual procedure throughout this month.

6. Use a comma to separate words, phrases, or clauses in a series.

- He visited Spain, Italy, and France.
- His morning consists of eating breakfast, reading the newspaper, and sitting in the sunshine.
- Go to the end of the hall, turn left, and follow the arrows on the wall.

7. Use a comma to separate coordinate clauses joined by and, but, for, or, nor, yet.

- All would live long, but none would be old.—Benjamin Franklin
- To be good is noble, but to teach others how to be good is nobler—and less trouble.—Mark Twain
- The show had no chronological order, nor did it have an intelligent narration.
- Short words are best, and the old ones when short are best of all.—Winston Churchill

In short sentences the comma is sometimes omitted, as in:

- I came late and you left early.

8. Use a comma to set off nonrestrictive (nonessential) clauses; do not set off restrictive clauses that come within or at the end of a sentence.

- Our salespeople, who are paid a salary plus commissions, earn from from $1,500 to $3,000 a month. (nonrestrictive)
- Salespeople who attended the national meeting met our new president. (restrictive)

9. Use a comma to set off parenthetical (nonrestrictive, nonessential) or appositive words or phrases.

- He said that, in the first place, he was not interested in our product.
- The sales manager, Harvey L. Wells, is a friend of the customer's sister.
- The store first opened its doors on Monday, May 13, 1904, in St. Louis, Missouri, on the bank of the Mississippi River.
- The statement is true, perhaps, that our prices could be reduced.

Words that are at times used parenthetically are at other times used adverbially. If a word or phrase can be considered supplemental, interrupting, or explanatory, precede and follow the word or phrase with commas. In the following sentences, *perhaps, however,* and *also* are used as adverbs and, because of their placement in the sentence, should not be set off by commas:

- It is perhaps true that our prices could be reduced.
- However it happened, it was not according to customary office procedures.
- The second statement is also false.

10. Use a comma to separate adjectives of equal rank if the conjunction is omitted.

- She is an efficient, considerate sales representative.

Do not use commas between adjectives of unequal rank, as in:

- The cold late autumn days are here again.

To check whether a comma is needed, try inserting the word *and.* If the expression now makes sense, use a comma.

11. Use a comma to set off contrasting expressions.

- The world is becoming warmer, not colder.

The Semicolon

1. Use a semicolon between main clauses that are not joined by one of the coordinate conjunctions (and, but, for, or, nor, yet).

- Punctuation is more than little marks to be sprinkled like salt and pepper through written words; punctuation determines emphasis and meaning.

2. Use a semicolon between main clauses joined with a conjunctive adverb.

- A readable writing style is simple and direct; consequently, it requires less punctuation than a more formal, complicated style.

- Semicolons are useful for clarifying meaning through punctuation; nevertheless, a great many long compound sentences such as this one, with the main clauses joined by a semicolon and a conjunctive adverb [*nevertheless*], tend to suggest a rather heavy and formal writing style.

Important Note: Substituting a comma for a semicolon to separate main clauses, as in sentences constructed like the preceding ones that contain no coordinating conjunction, is considered a serious error in punctuation and sentence construction.

3. Use a semicolon to separate items in a series if they are parallel subordinate clauses, or if they are long or contain internal punctuation.

- Those attending included Susan Smith, a college professor; Mark David, a field engineer; Diana Watson, an executive secretary; and Leonard Watson, a credit manager.
- We use language to talk about language; we make statements about statements; and we sing songs about songs.

4. Use a semicolon to separate complete clauses joined by a coordinate conjunction if the semicolon will increase readability when clauses are long or contain internal punctuation.

- The semicolon, which is sometimes overused, indicates a stronger break in thought than that indicated by a comma; but it is not as strong as that indicated by a period and somewhat different in usage from a colon.

The Colon

1. Use a colon to introduce a series of items.

- The points to be considered are these: cost, speed, and simplicity.
- Three possible areas of operation could be the source of the loss: shipping, advertising, and collections.

2. Use a colon to introduce long quotations or descriptions.

3. Use a colon after such words as "the following" or "as follows."

The Dash

Use a dash to show a sudden change in the structure of a sentence or to indicate emphasis.

- Indeed, it was a long leap from the jungle home of the chimpanzee to our modern civilization—and apparently we didn't quite make it.[1]
- Several items—a stapler, two calendars, and three or more chairs—were lost by the movers.

Do not overuse the dash, especially in formal writing, as it may give a "scatter-brained" appearance.

---

[1]Wendall Johnson, *People in Quandaries* (New York: Harper & Bros., 1946), 268.

The Hyphen

1. Use a hyphen to join a compound expression used as a single modifier before a noun.

- Is this an interest-bearing note?
- We need up-to-date equipment.

Omit the hyphen when the first word of the compound is an adverb ending in *ly*. Omit the hyphen when the modifier comes *after* the noun:

- Is this note interest bearing?

2. Use a hyphen in some compound words in which the hyphen is considered part of the accepted spelling, such as "self-control" and "sister-in-law."

Consult a dictionary to determine hyphenation of compound words.

3. Use a hyphen to divide words at the end of a line.

Do not divide words unnecessarily, as many lines ending with hyphens can be distracting. When you must divide to avoid extreme unevenness of typewritten lines, follow these guides:

- Divide only between syllables.
- Do not divide a word with fewer than seven letters.
- Do not separate the following syllables from the remainder of the word:
  a syllable that does not contain a vowel (could*n't*)
  a first syllable of only one letter (*e*cology)
  a last syllable of one or two letters (extreme*ly*)
- Do not divide hyphenated words at any place other than at the hyphen. (well-being)
- Divide after a one-letter syllable within a word unless the word contains successive single-letter syllables. (congratu-lations)
- Try to avoid dividing proper names and numbers.
- Do not divide the last word of a paragraph or the last word on a page.

Parentheses

1. Use parentheses to set off explanatory or nonessential material.

- A choice of commas, dashes, or parentheses (used in pairs) can be used to set off parenthetical material.

You can change the meaning slightly according to your choice of punctuation. Dashes are more emphatic than commas. Parentheses indicate a more definite separation in meaning from the rest of the sentence than commas imply.

Quotation Marks

1. Use quotation marks to enclose the exact words of a writer or speaker.

2. Use quotation marks to enclose titles of songs, magazine and newspaper articles, poems, reports, and other short written works.

3. Use quotation marks to enclose slang expressions.

4. Use quotation marks to enclose words used in an unusual way.

Note: Quotation marks are placed with other marks of punctuation in this way:

- Place commas and periods inside quotation marks.
- Place colons and semicolons outside quotation marks.
- Place question and exclamation marks inside the quotation marks when they refer to the quoted material, outside when they refer to the sentence as a whole.

Capitalization

Do not capitalize unless there is a definite reason to do so. Some writers capitalize unnecessarily.

Capitalize	**Do not capitalize**
Cost Accounting II (name of specific course)	major in accounting (general subject field)
I am taking a course in French. (proper adjective)	I am taking a course in history. (general subject field, not a proper adjective)
President Carpenter (title used as part of name)	He is president of his fraternity.
The President (of the United States)	Our company has a new president.
West Coast (section of country)	He rode west into the sunset. (direction)
Mother is late. (used as name)	My mother is late.
Mississippi River (*River* is part of name)	Mississippi and Tennessee rivers
He said, "We shall proceed." (direct quotation)	He said that we would proceed. (indirect quotation)
Summer Series of Lectures (part of title)	This summer is unusually cool. (season shown in usual way, not poetically or as a personification)

Writing Numbers

1. Spell out numbers one through ten if no large number appears in the same sentence.

Another rule for spelling out numbers is to write in words any number that can be expressed in no more than two words—which is, in effect, numbers one through one hundred. In business writing, however, the "through ten" rule is more readable and saves time.

2. Spell out numbers that represent time when they are used with "o'clock." Use figures with A.M. *and* P.M.

3. Spell out the smaller number when two numbers come together.

- We ordered sixteen 24-inch mirrors.

4. Spell amounts of money shown in legal documents; follow with the amount shown in figures.

Do not use this method of expressing numbers in ordinary business writing.

5. Use figures, regardless of the expressed quantity, to state:

- *dates:* April 15, 1990—*not* April 15th
- *money:* $5, $17.20, 5 cents
- *percentages:* 5 percent
- *page numbers:* page 7

6. Spell out numbers at the beginning of sentences.

Frequently Misspelled Words

accommodate	competent	February
accompanying	congratulations	forcible
acknowledging	controlled	guaranteed
acknowledgment	convenience	handling
across	deficiency	incidentally
advisable	definite	indispensable
all right	desirable	interfered
attorneys	discrepancy	introducing
bargain	efficient	journeys
beginning	embarrassing	legible
believe	enclosed	leisure
beneficial	equipped	management
benefited	exceed	noticeable
bulletin	excellent	occasion
business	existence	occurred
calendar	familiar	occurrence
chargeable	feasible	pamphlet

parallel	procedure	separate
permanent	proceed	similar
personnel	quantity	sincerely
precede	questionnaire	surprise
preceding	receive	transferring
preferred	recipient	traveling
prevalent	referred	truly
privilege		

Exercises

Exercise 1: Sentence Structure

State whether each of the following sentences is simple, complex, compound, or compound-complex.

1. The Atlanta hotel industry fared well in 1989.
2. Although improvement is forecast in two or three years, several unexpected events put the hotel industry to the test.
3. Because the districts are made up of two or three counties each, some farmers believe that the districts should be divided.
4. One-half of the faculty members expect to use the computer from six to ten hours a month.
5. Of the total number of respondents, 70 percent listed letters of recommendation; 63 percent listed manuscripts; and 51 percent mentioned grant applications.
6. Fifty respondents state that they will use the word processing center at least once a week.
7. Demand is off in all segments, and a number of hotel managers are reevaluating their market strategies.
8. Although human beings have a wide range of acceptable working conditions, they will not work efficiently outside these limits of human tolerance.
9. In order to decrease error, we should duplicate these forms.
10. The clerk who will duplicate the forms is away from the office.

Exercise 2

The ten sentences in Exercise 1 are correctly punctuated according to guides given in Appendix D. State the reason for each mark of punctuation in the ten sentences in Exercise 1.

Exercise 3: Sentence Structure

Improve each sentence and state its weakness.

1. This statement is only one illustration of the ways in which words can have several meanings. As I shall discuss later.
2. I shall also speak of barriers to communication many of these barriers are of our own making.
3. Even secretarial work was not acceptable for many years, women were said to be too weak, physically, for office work.
4. Knowing that words have differing meanings to various individuals, the word "tree" may remind you of a magnolia, an oak, or a pine.
5. Meaning is in the mind therefore all communication is imperfect.
6. The expression "walking on air" would not apply either when you are tired or depressed.
7. Verbal communication only transfers about 25 percent of our meaning.
8. Believing the subject to be important, the lecture was detailed.
9. Typists can make corrections, move words and paragraphs around, and additions and deletions can be done automatically.
10. I shall relate their discussion of communication to management. Especially toward management by women in the clothing industry.
11. Women typists were known as "typewriters" in the early years of office work, in addition, they "manned" the heavy machines.
12. The woman at the computer smoking a cigarette is breaking office rules.
13. Playing is better than to work, at least at times.
14. To understand this essential tool of good management.
15. Open communication within an organization saves time, reduces frustration, and much expense is saved because of increased cooperation.

Exercise 4: The Apostrophe

Circle the correct word.

1. (That's, Thats)
2. (someone else's, some elses) problem.
3. (You're, Your) not going alone, are you?
4. (Your, You're) sister knows my brother.
5. (John's, Johns) car is now paid for.
6. Mr. Jones has one (year's, years', years) experience.
7. Miss Black has three (year's, years', years) experience.
8. This (mans, man's) overcoat is to be returned to him.
9. These (boy's, boys') bikes are here.
10. Mr. (Johnson's, Johnsons') house is on the corner.
11. Mr. (Ross', Ross's, Rosses') store has been there for seventeen years.
12. The (Davises', Davis's, Davises) automobile, which belongs to the entire family of nine persons, is quite battered by now.
13. (Jim's and Mary's, Jim and Mary's) family consists of three boys.
14. (Jim's and Mary's, Jim and Mary's) personalities are completely different.
15. A cat indicates contentment and affection by (its, it's) purring.
16. (Its, It's) fortunate
17. that two (companies, company's, companys, companies') are
18. building (their, they're) plants in our city,
19. especially since our own (company's, companys, companies, companies') earnings are decreasing.
20. An optional spelling of *employee* is *employe;* perhaps there is a shortage of (e's, es).

Exercise 5: Commas, Semicolons, and Colons

Insert necessary commas, semicolons, and colons. Some sentences need more than one mark of punctuation, and some are correct as given. Do not use additional periods. If you believe a sentence needs no further punctuation, write ''correct'' by the sentence.

1. Nonverbal communication includes all messages except written and spoken ones.
2. Nonverbal communication which consists of many forms permeates all speech and much of written communication.
3. We can never learn to read a person like a book fortunately for we are all too complicated for that.
4. Many people take an overly simplified view of the subject.
5. As we all know perfect communication cannot be achieved by reading a book.
6. Ruesch and Kees classify human nonverbal communication in three broad categories sign language object language and action language.
7. We also communicate by tone of voice which differs according to our mood and the person with whom we are talking.
8. Much of nonverbal communication is not silent however regardless of Hall's title *The Silent Language.*
9. The slamming of a door is not silent and it is most expressive.
10. Some communication is silent nevertheless it is at times most expressive.
11. We all want to express ourselves and to receive the messages of others.
12. We communicate nonverbally to machines and they communicate nonverbally to us.
13. We push a button to receive black coffee the machine responds by supplying the coffee.
14. *Verbal* describes both written and oral messages.
15. In the United States and the Western European countries personal distance zones are greater than in Arab countries.
16. Believing that height adds status a businessman put his desk and chair on a raised platform.
17. We carry with us a kind of invisible bubble that we consider to be our own space.
18. As you interview persons or talk with visitors your desk becomes a barrier between you.
19. Crossing your arms denotes resistance.
20. The pupils of our eyes enlarge when we are looking at something that pleases us they contract when we are displeased.
21. There are regional differences as well as national differences in nonverbal communication and people in the South especially in Georgia smile more often than those in Maine or New York.
22. Because nonverbal communication is mostly unplanned it is one of the most sincere forms of communication.
23. The four zones of personal distance are these intimate personal social and public.
24. All communication is imperfect not entirely accurate or complete.
25. We can improve our communication by becoming aware of what other people are trying to tell us through nonverbal communication.
26. Nonverbal communication should not be taken out of context the spoken message the environment and previously established relationships.
27. Authors in the field include Edward T. Hall who wrote

The Silent Language and *The Hidden Dimension* Ray Birdwhistell author of *Kinesics and Context* and Flora Davis who wrote *Inside Intuition*.

28. Perhaps communication can bring us all closer together and actually make possible the often meaningless ''Have a nice day.''

Exercise 6: Hyphens and Quotation Marks

Use hyphens and quotation marks as needed in the following sentences. All other marks of punctuation are used correctly.

1. A well written refusal letter does not present the refusal in the last sentence.
2. Is this letter well written?
3. Preparations are now being made is an example of the use of the passive voice.
4. The blocked arrangement is one of the most widely used letter styles.
5. The time saving factor must be kept in mind when choosing a letter style.
6. The new production manager displayed admirable self control when he was referred to as old fashioned.
7. The expression buzz off was not understood by the teacher.
8. He said, we will survive.
9. The best sales messages do not use high pressure techniques.
10. Have you read the poem The Road Not Taken?
11. Other poems by the same author include A Mending Wall.
12. The student said, I do not understand.
13. Phrases such as Act today! and Hurry! are not usually effective in the action section of a sales letter.
14. The term resale is not an exact synonym for the term sales promotion.
15. He used this cliché: out of the clear blue sky.
16. The teacher made this statement: Personalize the favorable and impersonalize the unfavorable is good letter writing advice.
17. Show where each of the following words can be correctly divided at the end of a typewritten line. Some cannot be correctly divided.

compound	no-hitter
alone	shouldn't
elopement	drollery
stopping	pizzazz
stopped	plight

Exercise 7: Writing Numbers

Circle the correct word.

1. The graduation was (two, 2) weeks ago on
2. (May 8, May 8th) 1985.
3. (Seventeen, 17) books are now overdue.
4. The cost is only ($5, five dollars, 5 dollars, $5.00).
5. The wedding is to be at (5, five) o'clock.
6. The wedding is to be at (5, five) P.M.
7–8. Place an order for (11, eleven) (25-, twenty-five) pound bags of flour.
9–10. The interest rate of (7, seven) percent is stated on page (4, four) of the sales contract.
11–12. We brought (thirteen, 13) suitcases, (5, five) garment bags, and 172 boxes of books.
13–14. The hall is (19, nineteen) feet, (2, two) inches wide.
15. The copies cost (5¢, 5 cents, five cents) each.

Exercise 8: Spelling

Check *a, b, c,* or *d* to indicate a misspelled word. If all four words are correct, check *e*. No group has more than one misspelled word.

1. ___ a. accommodate
   ___ b. truely
   ___ c. occurred
   ___ d. discrepancy
   ___ e. all are correct
2. ___ a. accompanying
   ___ b. traveling
   ___ c. occasion
   ___ d. desirable
   ___ e. all are correct
3. ___ a. definate
   ___ b. acknowledgment
   ___ c. traveling
   ___ d. noticeable
   ___ e. all are correct
4. ___ a. sincerely
   ___ b. accross
   ___ c. management
   ___ d. leisure
   ___ e. all are correct
5. ___ a. similar
   ___ b. efficient
   ___ c. embarrassing
   ___ d. questionnaire
   ___ e. all are correct
6. ___ a. seperate
   ___ b. deficiency

___ c. convenience
___ d. introducing
___ e. all are correct

7. ___ a. controlled
___ b. congradulations
___ c. interfered
___ d. recipient
___ e. all are correct

8. ___ a. quantity
___ b. procede
___ c. procedure
___ d. precede
___ e. all are correct

9. ___ a. advisable
___ b. bargain
___ c. all right
___ d. attorneys
___ e. all are correct

10. ___ a. believe
___ b. beginning
___ c. February
___ d. recieve
___ e. all are correct

11. ___ a. guaranteed
___ b. handling
___ c. incidentally
___ d. feasable
___ e. all are correct

12. ___ a. priviledge
___ b. journeys
___ c. companies
___ d. existence
___ e. all are correct

13. ___ a. efficient
___ b. bulletin
___ c. handling
___ d. guaranteed
___ e. all are correct

14. ___ a. excellent
___ b. equipped
___ c. exceed
___ d. personel
___ e. all are correct

15. ___ a. pamphlet
___ b. familiar

___ c. excellent
___ d. enclosed
___ e. all are correct

16. ___ a. benefical
___ b. preferred
___ c. parallel
___ d. occurrence
___ e. all are correct

17. ___ a. chargeable
___ b. acknowledging
___ c. benefited
___ d. bulletin
___ e. all are correct

18. ___ a. permanent
___ b. surprise
___ c. calender
___ d. competent
___ e. all are correct

19. ___ a. discrepancy
___ b. desirable
___ c. indispensible
___ d. referred
___ e. all are correct

20. ___ a. legible
___ b. deficiency
___ c. preferred
___ d. similiar
___ e. all are correct

Exercise 9: Word Choice

Circle the correct word.

1–2. All the sales people (except, accept) Mr. Barnes voted to (except, accept) the proposed schedule changes.

3. Can we (adapt, adopt) the suggested course outline for

4. use with the newly (adopted, adapted, adept) textbook?

5. Free (advice, advise) is said to be worth as much as it costs.

6. What do you (advice, advise) me to do about the situation?

7. What do you believe will be the (affect, effect) of the tax increase on inflation?

8. To (effect, affect) improvements in employee morale, we should communicate more openly and completely.

9. Our emotions are often (affected, effected) adversely by physical or mental fatigue.

10. That statement is not (all together, altogether) correct.

11. The family will be (all together, altogether) for Christmas.

12. We have (already, all ready) made plans for our vacation.

13. On Friday, June 1, we will be (already, all ready) to leave for Spain.

14. She had the diamond (appraised, apprised).

15. I was not (apprised, appraised) of the transfer of the manager.

16. Do not dress (formally, formerly) for the party.

17–18. My ring is too (lose, loose); I fear I shall (lose, loose) it.

19. Communication systems that conform to (moral, morale)

20. (principles, principals) increase employee

21. (moral, morale).

22. In (passed, past) years, the test was

23. (passed, past) by a higher percentage of high school graduates.

24. The (personal, personnel) manager does not discuss her

25. family or any other aspect of her (personal, personnel) life.

26. The speaker was asked to (precede, proceed) with his

27. presentation without delay, as the (preceding, proceeding) speaker had exceeded the time limit.

28. (Sometime, Some time) in the future, I hope to spend

29. (sometime, some time) in Australia.

30. The (stationary, stationery) is weighted

31. down with a brick. It is now (stationary, stationery).

32. (Who's, Whose) the new man in the group?

33. (Who's, Whose) yellow sports car is in my parking space?

34–35. (Your, You're) too unsure of (your, you're) ability.

36. "With our (compliments, complements)" means that whatever is offered is free.

37. The artist was most (complimentary, complementary)

38. about our use of (complimentary, complementary) colors.

39. The (continual, continuous) interruptions seemed to annoy the speaker.

40. After working (continually, continuously) throughout the morning, we spent two hours at lunch.

41. The Student (Council, Counsel) includes a few representatives from the Graduate School.

42. Faculty (councilors, counselors) advise students about the preparation of class schedules.

43. A bit of rather cynical (council, counsel) is "If you've

44. got it, (flaunt, flout) it."

45. (Formerly, Formally), the ceremony was conducted quite

46. (formerly, formally); it is now much more casual.

47. (Its, It's) a lovely day.

48. You can't judge a book by (its, it's) cover.

Exercise 10: Word Choice

Circle the correct word.

1–2. Various estimates from recognized authorities (indicate, indicates) that forms of nonverbal communication (make, makes) up as much as 75 percent of the transfer of meaning and emotion in face-to-face interaction.

3. A business letter or a report (communicate, communicates) through appearance.

4. Nonverbal communication, as well as written or spoken words, (is, are) sometimes misinterpreted.

5. Care and judgment in classifying and assigning types of letters (is, are) highly desirable.

6. A cleverly phrased sentence or vivid, descriptive words (is, are) of little value if the message is not based on accurate knowledge.

7. The invitation was sent to my husband and (I, me).

8. Three members arrived early—Mr. Hames, Mr. Baker, and (I, me).

9. It was John and (I, me) who presented the skit.

10. (Who, Whom) is the new salesperson?

11. (Who, Whom) telephoned about the contract?

12. (Who, Whom) did you say called?

13. Miss Brown, (who, whom) you met in St. Louis, is the new sales representative in Maine.

14. Mr. Wilson, (who, whom) I thought would go to Maine, has left our organization.

15. Miss Jones taught my sister and (I, me) when we were in the first grade.

Exercise 11: All Marks of Punctuation, Including Apostrophes, Hyphens, and Quotation Marks

Insert necessary punctuation and remove punctuation that has been inserted incorrectly. (The topic discussed in the sentence examples is intercultural communication.)

1. In recent years the ease of travel the development of multinational organizations and international tensions have made us realize, that we must communicate with people unlike ourselves.

2. In order to succeed or even to survive we must learn to communicate, and cooperate.

3. The word culture means the total system of values beliefs customs religions, and manners.

4. Families, who live on the same block, are often different from one another.

5. Even if you never leave the United States you will almost surely work with people from other countries.

6. Many American countries export goods to foreign markets and many American countries have overseas operations.

7. Although Americans do not like to be kept waiting most do not object to a five minute delay.

8. Even after obtaining an appointment Americans are not always allowed to transact business without further preliminaries.

9. Arabs disapprove of using the left hand to take food from serving dishes to do so is considered unclean.

10. Courses in business communication are taught in many countries they are especially strong in Japan.

11. Language difficulties occur even between persons who's native language is the same.

12. Although your guests from some other country may have studied English in school textbook and classroom instruction does not completely prepare them for conversation with Americans.

13. Letters from American writers like face to face communication are likely to seem blunt to some Japanese readers.

14. People from some other parts of the world especially Latin America and the Middle East are more casual about time, than are most people in the United States.

15. Even a common language however does not eliminate differences and difficulties in communication.

16. When you talk with people from other countries avoid slang expressions like cool and gross.

17. One student from Syria did not know the meaning of the expression Youre pulling my leg.

18. To a person from another country you are the "foreigner.

19. A paragraph from a Japanese letter begins this way. Now we are in the splendid autumn season.

20. Japanese people are very mindful of the seasons for example the traditional Japanese haiku a poem of seventeen syllables must include a reference to a season.

Exercise 12

In the following groups of sentences, one of the four is incorrectly punctuated. Choose the one that is definitely incorrect. (Hyphens and apostrophes are considered marks of punctuation.)

1. ___ a. By any and all standards, English is a remarkable language.

___ b. It is, to begin with, the native tongue of about 300,000,000 people.

___ c. Estimates of the number of English words range from 500,000 to one million.

___ d. Of course, bigger isn't necessarily better, often it is a good deal worse.

2. ___ a. The biggest French dictionaries contain only about 150,000 words, and the biggest Russian dictionaries are limited to about 130,000.

___ b. Syntax—the rules for putting words and other linguistic elements together to make meaningful statements—is the most complicated part of linguistics.

___ c. Latin nouns were ordinarily inflected in five different "cases".

___ d. Our syntax, although relatively simple, is not as simple as it looks.

3. ___ a. The first inhabitants of the British Isles, who left any linguistic traces, were the Iberians.

___ b. Some words have changed completely in meaning during the past few centuries, and meanings will continue to change.

___ c. By far the most interesting surnames are those identifying people by what they did for a living.

___ d. During the early Middle Ages, rural communities were largely self-sufficient.

4. ___ a. Timber, another major English resource, was seldom shipped overseas, it was too valuable as construction material.

___ b. Some of the commonest Welsh names, however, were originally English.

___ c. Within a century after the first printing press, the old, expensive handwritten book had vanished.

___ d. Writing is the quickest method yet devised of transferring information from one human brain to another; most of us can absorb information from a printed page in less than a third the time we would need to hear it by ear.

5. ___ a. Unlike many other languages, English does not have grammatical gender.

___ b. It has been said that a dictionary is not a law book, but a history book.

___ c. In recounting the stories of great events, movements, and leaders, an ordinary history book can slight the day to day life of the people.

___ d. The English language owes a continuing debt to the Holy Bible, above all to the King James Version of 1611.

6. ___ a. In many languages, including Shakespeares English, two negatives can reinforce each other rather than cancel each other out.

___ b. In standard usage at the present time, however, two negatives do make a positive.

___ c. Well-placed intervals of summary, description, or weak action can thus be welcome relief.

___ d. Someone once said that poetry is best appreciated by children, barbarians, and the very old.

7. ___ a. At it's best, poetry is the highest, most intense use that we can make of language.

___ b. Language, the essential human medium of communication, is only a set of symbols.

___ c. Writing poetry can be the most daring enterprise of language, and like every other venture into the unknown, cursed with a high failure rate.

___ d. One often-heard objection to poetry is that it is too abstract.

APPENDIX E

Legal and Ethical Considerations That Apply to Written and Oral Communications

Defamation (An Attack on One's Reputation)
Invasion of Privacy
Laws Pertaining to Employment
Laws Pertaining to Credit and Collections

Laws Pertaining to Sales
Copyright Laws
Social Responsibilities of Business Organizations

Business communication, written and oral, is concerned with almost every conceivable topic and situation. Many and various laws apply, as they do to all other business activities. Basic legal considerations most relevant to frequently occurring communication situations are summarized below. This summary is of necessity incomplete. A complete discussion of applicable legislation and legal precedents would fill numerous thick law books.

Ethical approaches to communication, as to other business activities, ordinarily prevent serious legal problems. Your knowledge of applicable laws, however, can save embarrassing and costly mistakes. If you are ever in doubt about legal matters affecting your communication efforts, do not proceed without investigating further. Many companies have their own legal departments; most organizations provide legal counsel in doubtful situations.

As stated by Lee et al., in Business Communication,

The written record that you produce when you write a business communication is, in essence, a legal contract. The partners in this contract are you and your business as the "makers" and your communication partner and the business he or she represents as the "receivers." When you write business messages, consider the following factors:

1. *A written communication is acceptable as legal evidence in a court of law. You and your company may be forced to carry out your promises, or you and your company could be sued for breach of contract.*

2. *Your signature on a letter indicates that you agree with and approve of its contents.*

3. *You cannot legally change your mind once your written communication reaches the receiver unless you can prove that circumstances have changed enough to legally release you from your previous commitments.*

4. *If your written statements indicate that a person is unfit to perform his or her job or that a company is unfit to carry on its business, you and your company may be sued for libel.*[1]

Defamation (An Attack on One's Reputation)

Written defamation is known as *libel;* oral defamation is known as *slander.*

A true defamation must be communicated, or "published" (made known to others); it must be based on a malicious intent; and damages must result. Damages are assumed to result from written statements that ridicule others and hold them up for public contempt. If the statements are true and are needed to convey necessary information to the public, libel or slander will not ordinarily be upheld.

Nevertheless, "truth" is often difficult to prove. Even if a court case is won, communicators and their employing organizations are far wiser to avoid the litigation, which is expensive and often damaging to public relations and company goodwill, regardless of who is to blame and the outcome of the case.

Writers of letters about past or present employees and credit applicants must be especially careful to avoid remarks that could be interpreted as libel. Because of such danger, some organizations refuse to release any information about employees other than dates of employment or the title of the employee's position. Writers who provide credit information make sure that the applicant has given the organization as a reference, thus implying that information can be released. All applicants must be made aware that credit information is being requested. Letters or other communications that report an applicant's credit history should include the statement that the information being released is to be considered confidential and is to be used only for the specified purpose for which it is requested.

Writers of collection letters, as well as people who collect in person and by telephone, must be especially careful not to damage the debtor's reputation. Even a letter individually addressed to the debtor can be interpreted as being "published" if the letter is intercepted and read by another person, provided the writer can be assumed to know that such interception was likely to occur. Collection letters should be mailed in sealed envelopes and marked *Personal and Confidential.*

A legal right to communicate defamatory information to certain persons is known as *privilege.* For example, dictation to a secretary, testimony in court, and consultation with a lawyer are ordinarily considered privileged information, as is information about past employees if provided at their request. Neverthe-

---

[1]LaJuana W. Lee, Sallye S. Benoit, Wilma C. Moore, and Celeste Stanfield Powers, *Business Communication* (Chicago: Rand McNally, 1980), 395–396.

less, as mentioned earlier, many organizations prefer not to take a chance that a libel suit will result; thus, they release only limited information.

Similar to privileged information is "fair comment," the right to comment fairly about persons in public life, one of the attributes of free speech. The comments must not overreach fairness or be directed toward an individual's personal life.

Words themselves may be considered libelous. (As you already know and as this textbook has emphasized, negative words should be avoided even if there is not the slightest possibility of a libel suit. They are not conducive to effective and harmonious communication of any kind.) Some of the many words that may be considered libelous are these:

lazy	drug addict	alcoholic	loafer
worthless	inferior	thief	freeloader
inefficient	insolvent	crazy	shiftless
crook	kickbacks	psychotic	deadbeat
dishonest	misconduct	corrupt	fraud
incompetent	quack	incapable	swindle
drunk	bum	bankrupt	racketeer

When you must report negative information in *any* communication (and make sure that such reporting actually is necessary), do so in specific, neutral words. Report events with dates and objective details. Negative, "name-calling" words are dangerous and usually unfair. They reflect adversely on your own communication abilities. In addition, they may result in a libel accusation.

Invasion of Privacy

The right of privacy is more likely than libel to be the basis for litigation, although libel and the invasion of privacy often overlap. The right of privacy prevents the use of an individual's name, picture, or likeness without the individual's written consent. Other invasions of privacy, similar to libel, include placing a person in a false light and publishing embarrassing private information.

The contents of a letter belong to the writer, not to the receiver. A letter should not be publicized without the writer's permission. To do so results in an invasion of privacy.

Privacy is violated when letters, reports, memorandums, records, and other written materials are read by people not entitled to examine them. Technology has provided various methods of invasion of privacy, including the illegal use of recording equipment. Powerful binoculars and telephoto cameras can be used to look through windows at papers left face-up on desks. Methods exist for photocopying material through a sealed envelope or for reading it without opening the envelope. All such methods are unethical and illegal.

You as a writer should take necessary precautions to guard against confidential materials being read by others. Keep such materials in a secure place, never left lying face-up on your desk. Increase the privacy of mailed letters by using envelopes with a random-pattern lining or by inserting an opaque sheet around the letter.

The Privacy Act of 1974 was enacted to prevent the misuse of personal information gathered by the federal government. It gives individuals access to their personal files and enables them to learn how the information is to be used.

The Family Educational Rights and Privacy Act of 1974 gives parents and students age 18 and older the right to examine their files in public schools and colleges unless the students waive these rights. (Students sometimes waive their rights to establish credibility of references who add information to the files.)

Laws Pertaining to Employment

The Civil Rights Act of 1964 (Title VII), with amendments in 1972 and 1978, prohibits employment discrimination based on race, color, religion, sex, or national origin. Certain exceptions to the antidiscrimination provisions permit the requirement of a person of a particular sex or religion by an educational or religious institution; the exclusion of a member of the Communist party; discrimination justified for national security; and employment preference provided to veterans and American Indians.

Additional laws forbid discrimination because of age, marital status, number of children, or any other factor not directly related to the ability to perform the duties of the particular position for which applicants are sought. Interviewers for employing organizations should confine their questions to activities and abilities that are specifically job-related. Although applicable laws apply only to discrimination, not to asking certain questions, these questions may indicate discrimination and may result in discrimination. (Further discussion of employment interviewing is included in Chapter 12, "Completing the Job-Finding Process.")

Laws Pertaining to Credit and Collections

Some laws that pertain to credit and collections also relate to libel or slander and to the invasion of privacy, discussed earlier. Other laws about credit forbid discrimination and are similar to laws that apply to fair employment practices.

The Truth in Lending Act (1968) requires that credit terms be clearly stated in writing. This provision permits consumers to compare credit costs from different lending institutions.

The Federal Wage Garnishment Law (1968) limits the amount (percentage) of a debtor's earnings that can be garnished in one week. The law also protects the debtor from discharge because of garnishment for any one indebtedness.

The Fair Credit Reporting Act (1970) regulates credit bureaus, credit reporting companies, collection agencies, detective agencies, and the use of computerized information about debtors. The act was passed for the purpose of increasing confidentiality, accuracy, and relevancy of information about credit applicants. A person who is refused credit has the right, under certain circumstances, to be informed of the nature and source of the information on which the credit refusal was based.

The Equal Credit Opportunity Act (1974) forbids discrimination because of sex or marital status. Subsequent amendments apply to discrimination because of race, color, religion, national origin, or age. These laws, however, do not prevent lenders from making necessary inquiries and making lending decisions on credit worthiness based on the ability to pay and past credit history.

The Fair Credit Billing Act (1974) was passed to protect consumers against inaccurate and unfair credit card practices. A creditor must acknowledge a written complaint about a bill within thirty days and investigate and resolve the problem within ninety days. Other stipulations prohibit charging interest, closing the account, reporting the debtor to a credit-rating organization, or pushing collection procedures until ten days after the creditor has answered the inquiry. The act also requires creditors to inform debtors about who has received reports of delinquency.

The Fair Debt Collection Practices Act (1978) prohibits collection efforts that result in oppression, harassment, abuse, or mental distress. Collectors are not permitted to use abusive language, anonymous telephone calls, telephone calls before 8:00 A.M. and after 9:00 P.M., or collection letters that resemble those from credit bureaus, courts, or government agencies. A collector is forbidden to continue to contact debtors (after one legal information call) after being requested in writing to stop.

The New Bankruptcy Act (effective in 1979) establishes a list of federal exemptions from bankruptcy and enables each bankrupt debtor to choose between applicable state exemptions and federal exemptions. (Bankruptcy laws differ from state to state.) Overall, recent federal legislation has made it easier for individuals and small businesses to declare bankruptcy and has extended debtors' rights.

Laws Pertaining to Sales

Consumers are protected by law from deceptive sales and advertising practices.

The law of contracts binds both the buyer and the seller to the terms of the contract. "Fine print in a contract may be construed under certain circumstances as an intent to conceal."[2] Technical terms unlikely to be understood by the average consumer may also be interpreted as an attempt to conceal. "Plain language" laws passed by various states provide for writing that is likely to be understood by the "average" reader.

Fraud, according to law, is a deliberate misrepresentation of facts in order to deceive. Such misrepresentation need not consist of written or spoken words but may consist of omission or concealment. (Reasonable and ethical decisions concerning the content of advertising, sales letters, and other sales materials are discussed in Chapter 10, "Writing Persuasive Messages.")

Copyright Laws

Copyright laws, which were strengthened with the passage of the U.S. Copyright Law that went into effect on January 1, 1978, do not permit the copying of copyrighted material without permission from the copyright owner, except

[2]Martin J. Ross and Jeffrey Steven Ross, *Handbook of Everyday Law* (New York: Harper & Row, 1981), 314.

for certain "fair use" privileges as specified in the law. Copyright laws apply not only to printed materials but also to sound recordings and computer software.

Social Responsibilities of Business Organizations

What responsibilities do business organizations have to the neighborhood, city, and society in which they exist? Do they have further obligations than to pay taxes, abide by all laws, pay and treat employees fairly, and make a reasonable profit for shareholders?

Some officials do not believe in charity for charity's sake, but only in contributions that will have a beneficial effect on their company in one way or another, including building a positive company image. Although such officials are likely to encourage civic activities of their employees and to make cash or other contributions to recognized fund-raising campaigns, they admit that the well-being of their own companies is uppermost in their minds.

Although corporations, like employees, must continue to be concerned with the welfare of their own establishments, they are in effect citizens, and often wealthy ones, of their environment. Like individual citizens, they have the responsibility to improve the neighborhood and the society in which they live. Although they make a major—sometimes a vital—contribution by providing employment and paying taxes, such benefits are not necessarily the extent of their responsibilities.

As you move into responsible positions in your organization, some of the decisions about company involvement will be yours. The same basic principles that apply to communication between individuals, especially sincerity, apply to communication from organizations to the public.

Although business efforts toward social responsibility have increased during the past decade, the public's opinion of business organizations has dropped. Increased media coverage of corporate disasters and instances of fraud or misconduct have created an image in the mind of the public that is hard to overcome.[3]

Corporations have realized the importance of their public image, and they are trying to improve their position. Gone is the "public be damned" attitude that was once held by some companies.[4] New social responsibility programs have been established by many large corporations.

For business organizations, communication is the most important aspect of being socially responsible. If the goal of business charity is not only to help the community but also to create a more positive image, the public must know of their contributions. Apart from the fact that responsible officials sincerely want to improve the society that sustains the organization, social responsibility and public relations can be considered as a long-term investment. In order for

[3]Jarol Manheim and Cornelius Pratt, "Communicating Corporate Responsibility," *Public Relations Review*, Summer 1986, 13.

[4]Terry Anderson, "Social Responsibility and the Corporation," *Business Horizons*, July-August 1986, 22.

companies to survive and remain competitive, particularly in this era of fierce competition from other countries, they must be able to communicate successfully to the public that they maintain high-quality standards and are concerned about the welfare of the consumer.

Index

Professional Graphics

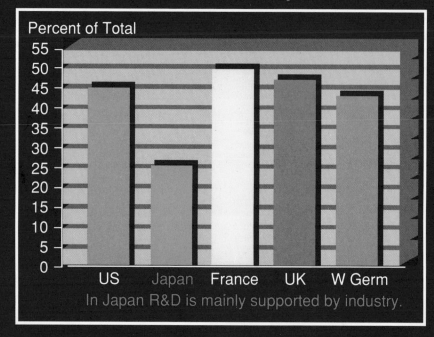

Percent of Total

US	Japan	France	UK	W Germ

In Japan R&D is mainly supported by industry.

Bar charts are the easiest graphic images to understand and are preferred for illustrating multiple comparisons and complex relationships. These figures demonstrate how simple comparisons can be enhanced by using shaded backgrounds and outlined text. Note the ease of interpreting and understanding the relationships among the data in these figures.

Business & Industry
Total Audio Visual Spending

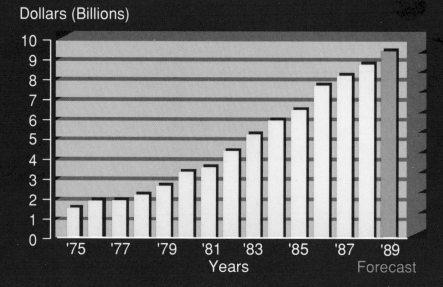

Dollars (Billions)

'75 '77 '79 '81 '83 '85 '87 '89

Years

Forecast

Direct Imports

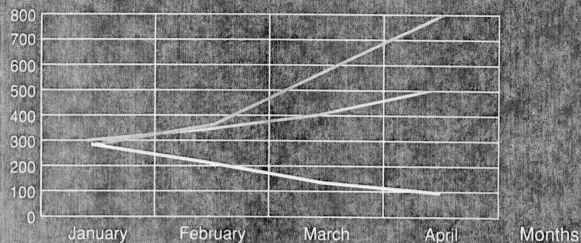

Dollars (Thousands)

Months

A line chart is an effective method of displaying relationships among data and trends over time. Notice how the horizontal and vertical grid lines aid understanding of the chart by providing additional reference points for the reader.

California Orange Production

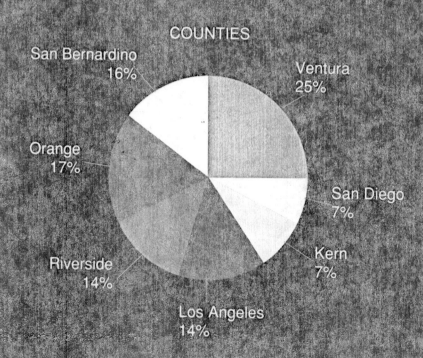

COUNTIES

San Bernardino 16%

Ventura 25%

Orange 17%

San Diego 7%

Kern 7%

Riverside 14%

Los Angeles 14%

Pie charts are used to show the size or value of individual segments in relation to the whole. This chart, for example, indicates the contribution of each county to California's orange production as a whole. Readability and understanding are enhanced by adding titles and respective percentages to the chart.